P9-BZK-728

WEST GA REG LIB SYS
Neva Lomason
Memorial Library

THE BLAIR YEARS

THE
BLAIR
YEARS

EXTRACTS FROM

THE ALASTAIR
CAMPBELL DIARIES

ALFRED A. KNOPF · NEW YORK
2007

This Is a Borzoi Book
Published by Alfred A. Knopf

Copyright © 2007 by Alastair Campbell

All rights reserved. Published in the United States by Alfred A. Knopf,
a division of Random House, Inc., New York.

www.aaknopf.com

Originally published in Great Britain by Hutchinson,
an imprint of the Random House Group Limited, London, in 2007.

Knopf, Borzoi Books, and the colophon are registered trademarks of
Random House, Inc.

ISBN 978-0-307-26831-0

Manufactured in the United States of America
First United States Edition

Contents

For Fiona

Our children, Rory, Calum and Grace

And our parents, Donald and Betty Campbell,
Bob and Audrey Millar

Introduction

On May 12, 1994, Labour leader John Smith suffered a heart attack. I heard the news from Hilary Coffman, John's press officer, as I was on my way to work at the *Today* newspaper, where I was assistant editor. I could tell from the tone of Hilary's voice that he was in all probability dying, if not already dead. I diverted to the House of Commons, where the news was confirmed to me by a tearful Jack Cunningham, John's close friend and colleague. Amid the sadness I felt during a long day spent writing and recording tributes, I had two other very powerful instincts. One, that Tony Blair would be the next Labour leader. And two, though Blair and I had never discussed the possibility, that I would work for him.

Even the day before John's death, a straw poll of opinion formers might well have put Gordon Brown ahead of Blair as most likely leader. But polls are inevitably based upon the question 'what if?' Nobody was expecting John Smith to die that May morning. We were expecting him to lead Labour into the next general election against John Major's governing Tory Party. When a 'what if?' suddenly becomes directly relevant, moods can change and strange things happen. What many people had largely taken for granted – that Brown would follow Smith – was now being questioned, and the qualities Labour most needed to reverse a series of electoral failures were suddenly, and widely, thought to be best embodied in Blair.

Through that day, as I scuttled back and forth between my office in the Commons and 4 Millbank, where the TV and radio stations covering Parliament are based, I carefully avoided questions of succession. But when, on BBC's *Newsnight* programme, I was asked direct who I thought would take over, I said what I thought: Tony Blair.

I do not have a great memory – one of the reasons I keep a diary. But I do have a vivid recollection of my first meeting with Blair. He had just been elected to Parliament in 1983 and my partner's brother, a lawyer, had told me to keep an eye out for the new member for Sedgefield. He is bright, I was told. Very funny, engaging. He is not your average or typical Labour MP. So when I saw him entering the members' lobby in the House of Commons, where I was then working for the *Mirror*, I went over to introduce myself. He was wearing a badly fitting beige suit. He had an enormous smile, which would one day become famous the world over. After a little bit of small talk about family and mutual friends, we were onto a subject both of us spent a lot of time thinking about – what more did Labour need to do to win power?

In the ensuing years, I would have numerous such conversations with him, Gordon Brown, Peter Mandelson, Philip Gould, and many others. I worked closely with all four, me as a political journalist who never hid his colours, Gould as a dedicated and obsessive pollster and strategist, Mandelson as first the party's campaigns director and then as an MP, Brown and Blair as the two glittering Labour talents of their generation.

They had flourished under Neil Kinnock's leadership. Under John Smith, Brown and Blair were seen as the youth to complement the older man's experience, but they were often impatient at the pace of change. They did not believe that governments lost elections – though John Major's faltering and divided post-Thatcherite administration might help in that process. They thought Oppositions had to win them, and worked tirelessly and restlessly on the policy and strategic decisions they believed essential if Labour were to get back into government.

Brown was always seen as the senior figure, not least by Blair, and the reversal of that position in the wake of John Smith's death would be the source of some considerable tension, creative and not so creative, during the days that followed, and then on and off during the entirety of Blair's 13-year leadership.

Blair came to national prominence on the back of two issues in particular – the trade unions and crime. On the first, as employment spokesman, his deft changing of Labour's policy on the closed shop established his modernising credentials and, just as importantly, showed he was not scared of a fight. On the second, particularly in the wake of the killing of James Bulger, a Liverpool toddler tortured and murdered by two youngsters, he showed his ability to articulate issues of social concern in a way that others on the left and right of politics struggled to. 'Tough on crime, tough on the causes of crime', a line hammered out with Brown, was one of his most enduring sound bites when he became Shadow Home Secretary.

But there has always been a lot more to Blair than style and sound bite, good communicator though he is. He joined the Labour Party because it is the party that best captured his own beliefs and values, developed in a comfortable and caring middle-class upbringing, reinforced by a Christian faith that runs deep. But he feared that unless the party adapted to the modern post-Cold War, post-Thatcherite world, it would ossify and die. He was always pushing at the outer edge of modernisation. That modernising zeal was what ultimately made the offer to work for him irresistible. I took some time to think about it. I had a nice life, a young family, a good salary and a growing broadcasting portfolio, so it was not a straightforward decision. I had a reputation for picking fights. I have never been good at hiding what I feel. I have a temper. I admitted to him at the time I was worried about the idea of subsuming my whole ego and persona in someone else's ambition. I had also had a serious psychotic breakdown in 1986 and was concerned that the pressures of the job he was offering might lead me once more down some very dark and dangerous alleyways.

He knew all that. 'I'm not worried if you're not worried,' he said. I said what if I am worried? 'I'm still not worried,' he said.

I had my partner Fiona, my parents and many friends, Neil Kinnock among them, pleading with me not to do it. They feared it would take over my life, that I would end up loathing the media and getting angry at the share of the load I might have to carry for politicians, who can be a difficult breed. They were right; right too that at times it put an almost intolerable strain on relationships at home. Yet for all that, even with all the Tory and media bile that came my way, I am glad I did it, and grateful for the opportunity he gave me to make a difference in turning Labour from a losing to a winning party, and one comfortable using power to make change.

It was his boldness that finally won me over. On a walk in France in the summer of 1994, he confided that in his first conference speech as leader he intended to launch a review of the old Clause 4 at the heart of the party's constitution, which committed Labour to economic policies it no longer believed in let alone pursued. That boldness shows itself again and again through these pages – in his determination to ensure that modernisation of the party cut so deep, across virtually every major area of policy, that the public could not fail to notice it; in the new 'fairness not favours' relationship he forged with the trade unions, which he felt had not fully understood or faced up to change; in his constant driving for an agreed economic approach that set the context for virtually all of the major domestic changes that would follow. It shows itself too in his campaigning skills. On the road, he could be a nightmare to be with, fussing and fretting, engaging in endless circular conversations that seemed to be going nowhere. But then he would decide a course of action, settle himself in his own mind, and reveal himself as a formidable campaigner.

Once in power, he was clear about the initial priorities, and again boldness and leadership were called for – in establishing Labour's competence on the economy; in showing that modernising public services did not just mean pouring in money, but forcing them too to face up to difficult reform.

From his first visit there in opposition, he could not be shaken from a belief that peace in Northern Ireland was possible, and there too he showed bold leadership and infinite patience. These pages show boldness in his approach to modernising Britain's constitution, where he studied the failed attempts of the past before devising his own, at the time unpopular, strategy for making devolution something that happened, rather than something that was talked about and never delivered. We see it again in his determination to make a difference in the Balkans, notably over Kosovo, in Africa, in the Middle East, his reaction to the atrocities of September 11, his handling of crises, and yes, in Iraq, a policy he pursued without any doubt about the unpopularity of the path he was treading, but convinced that the threat from Saddam Hussein and weapons of mass destruction was real.

Yet if he could be bold with the big decisions, sometimes he could be overly dismissive of small issues and small decisions with the capacity to do disproportionate damage. Conversely, at other times he could be overly concerned about things that ultimately don't matter a great deal, how he was seen by this person or that; minor personnel issues that should not have detained him too long. Today, he has a thick skin, hardened by experience. It was not always so.

It nonetheless says something about the thicker-skinned Blair that when I saw him last year to say I intended to publish extracts from my diaries, with a particular focus on him, around the time of his leaving office, his first reaction was not that of the paranoid politician desperate to know what negative stories the harshness of 24-hour observation by an intimate might reveal. Instead, he said: 'I hope it comes over that, despite everything, we were always able to have a good laugh.' Perhaps because it is often my mood in the driving seat, rather than his, I am not sure it does, at least not in the way we often did at the time, but I think it does come through that Blair's optimism and resilience saw him through many difficult moments.

What I hope this book does is help to paint a rounded picture of a man of enormous drive and vision, who was determined to use his time in power to make a difference and brought about a lot of change for the better. But it is a diary, not a paean of praise. It records without hindsight what I saw, said, heard, thought, felt and did during many of the key moments of his leadership. It records good days and bad days. The pressures. Things going wrong as well as things going right. Moments of disagreement as well as moments of harmony and accord. The good moods and the bad moods, usually his the former and mine the latter.

My first recollection of writing a diary was as a young child growing up in Yorkshire when my father Donald, a vet, was hospitalised after an accident involving a sow that escaped its pen as he was injecting her piglets. As he recovered in the hospital near our home in Keighley, I wrote him daily digests, a mix of my own mundane life – what I ate, what I did at school – combined with reports cribbed from the sports pages. At various points in my life since, I have kept a diary. But in working for Blair an occasional habit became a conscious decision to record events as closely as I could. I kept a diary every day I was there, usually, though not always, recorded on the same day, never more than a day or two behind. Tony was aware that I was doing so, aware too that at some stage I would probably publish it, and never objected.

In part there was an element of therapy about it for me, and even in these extracts, a fraction of the total diary, some of the intense anger and frustration I felt from time to time comes through. I also found it helpful as a discipline, a way of keeping on top of things, and giving some kind of order to often chaotic and confusing events around me. There were periods when I wondered how I found time. But I did. In total, from the summer of 1994, when Tony Blair first asked me to work for him, to the autumn of 2003, when I resigned from Downing Street, I wrote well over 2 million words. I cannot be sure exactly how many words I wrote because I have not yet fully transcribed the whole diary. The extracts here amount to around 350,000 words. So about a sixth.

I do intend to publish them in full, some years down the track, chronologically, probably in four volumes covering two years each: volume 1, the Opposition years; volumes 2 and 3, our first term in power; volume 4, 2001 to 2003, dominated by September 11, Iraq and the government's dispute with the BBC, still ongoing when I left. I have also kept a diary since leaving, which includes the clearing of the government by the Hutton Inquiry into the death of government scientist David Kelly, and the subsequent resignations of the chairman and director general of the BBC. It covers also the period when I went back to help on the campaign to secure our third election victory, but offers a slightly different perspective, from a position at one remove from the centre. That too can wait till another day.

The focus here is very much on Blair himself, and some of the key issues and events during his 13 years as Labour leader. I said after I resigned in 2003 that I would not make life difficult for him. Even though I believe the overall picture of him is favourable, in something as intense and personal as a daily diary there is likely to be material his enemies could seek to use against him. But at least any attacks will be less potent, politically, as his premiership becomes the stuff of history rather than daily political action, analysed to the nth degree by a media which seems to me to have lost any sense of perspective about people in power, or sense of responsibility about how politics and politicians are seen, and the impact on our democratic health. There is another reason why I wanted to publish something, focused on him, close to the time of his departure. Namely that I always intended, on my terms, to be part of the mix that starts to shape the first draft of historical judgement around him. This is my first contribution to that, and the large number of writers and film-makers who wanted me to cooperate with their projects on Blair's legacy now know why I have resisted their efforts. I prefer to do my own.

As Blair leaves, the focus has shifted to Gordon Brown, and I have applied something of the same rule to him. I worked very hard to help get Labour back as a party of government, after seeing them for most of my adult life in opposition, Margaret Thatcher winning her first general election as I completed my university education. I have seen close up how hard the job of Prime Minister is, and I have no desire to make it harder for anyone, let alone Gordon, who has been central to New Labour winning power, and staying in power. This book, as the title makes clear, is about Blair not Brown.

I hope it conveys something about the man and the times, from someone who for the years covered here probably spent more time with him than anyone apart from his wife. Indeed, fairly regularly Cherie pointed out that I certainly spent more waking hours with him than she did.

Because it was well known that I was keeping a diary, at the Hutton Inquiry in 2003 I had to hand over extracts relevant to the events being examined. I freely admit that the letter I received by fax while on holiday in France, asking to see these extracts was like a body blow. As is clear from pages 741ff, the Prime Minister at times seemed even more worried than I was about what my pen may have recorded. We were at the height of one of the most intensely difficult periods for the government, for the Prime Minister, and for me personally. To decide which extracts should be sent to Lord Hutton, I had to sit down with a QC, Jonathan Sumption, and go through my diaries for that period line by line. It was a draining, emotional process which on one occasion reduced me to tears. At the end of it, I asked Sumption what he thought. A medieval historian in his spare time, he said his first, rather selfish thought was the wish that there had been people like me keeping diaries like mine in the Middle Ages.

I have no idea what people will make of this book. I am probably too close to it all, both the events and the process of publishing. I know some newspapers and commentators will come to it with minds made up, and look to find those parts that help confirm their prejudices. It is what is wrong with some of them in the first place, and why I have next to no respect for them, and no real interest in their views. Amid the enormous cuts I have made are many which relate to my dealings with a 24-hour media that has in my view changed for the worse not only political debate but politics itself, as the politicians have to devote so much time and energy to dealing with people who believe their role is not to impart information and fuel healthy debate, but to undermine where possible the actions, decisions and motives of politicians. It is a sad irony that we have more media coverage than ever, but less understanding or real debate.

But I hope genuinely interested, open-minded readers will both enjoy and learn from the diaries. Though these are extracts, I hope they give some sense of what modern politics is like on the inside. I hope they reveal things about Blair, about leadership, about the events and characters under examination, that add to people's understanding of some of the challenges Britain and its politics are facing.

I was in a very privileged position and have remained conscious of that in deciding what to include in this book. There are some conversations so private they will never see the light of day. There are others that are perhaps borderline, including some of the conversations I witnessed between Tony Blair and other world leaders. As we are talking about historical figures addressing issues of real significance, I hope that one day these can go into the historical mix in their entirety. But in some instances, where I have felt myself crossing the line, relaying details of conversations the participants would have assumed to be confidential for some time to come, I have veered towards exclusion. I have relied on my own judgement in most cases, sought the advice of others in some. I have tried to balance various demands – fairness to the people involved, the national interest, the demands of history, the desire to give a full and compelling account of a fascinating period.

It is also the case that as a former government employee I was duty-bound to submit the manuscript to the Cabinet Office for vetting. The opinions of a number of different parts of government were fed into this process.

Where former colleagues, policy experts or intelligence officials felt there was a risk to Britain's national interest from publication or that I risked breaching the Official Secrets Act, I made deletions.

I am nonetheless confident in the integrity of what is published here, and hope that some of the material considered inappropriate for publication now will be available in the future.

Even with the cuts I have made, there will be people who feel it is wrong in principle to publish a book like this. On that, we just have to disagree. There will be many accounts of the Blair years as history makes its judgement. Having recorded events as closely as I did, immediate and raw, it seems to me perverse not to put some of that account into the public domain. Once this and future volumes are published, I intend to donate the transcripts to a UK university as the basis of an academic project which I believe can be a resource for students of politics, of Europe, of Ireland, of our relations with the US, and many other issues studied in universities and addressed to greater or lesser degrees in my diaries.

I hope too that it can provide a valuable study of life at the sharp end of politics in the spotlight of a relentless 24-hour media, and that from what we did right in dealing with it, and what we did wrong, political and other decision makers may gain from that study.

I wrote these diaries either in an A4 diary, or in notebooks, occasionally on looseleaf. I have rewritten only where the original made no sense or lacked any context, or where avoidable legal complications presented themselves, or where the publishers and editor felt explanation was required for a lay reader. Where I have made changes for legal reasons, or as part of the vetting process, I have sought to ensure both meaning and emotions are unchanged. What I have not done is put in thoughts of today on events of yesterday. I have not looked over any other records, newspapers or research material. It is a record of events as I saw them unfold.

There is no 'line to take', something of a challenge for a control freak like me. Dip into one page, and you could find evidence of me feeling very down on TB, as you must come to know him. Look in on another, and I stand in admiration of his leadership skills. Similarly, on one page TB may be positive about a colleague or a fellow world leader, while elsewhere, in different circumstances, a different view is expressed. Views on different policy areas evolve and change. So there are times when I and others express views which may contradict views expressed elsewhere, or felt today. That is not just the nature of a diary, but the reality of the lives we lead, whether in politics or not. Recorded here, for example, are fairly regular spats between me and Peter Mandelson. Yet I still view Peter not just as a vital part of the New Labour story, but as a good friend.

As for TB, it is fair to say we too have had our moments, and some of these are recounted. But overall, I can honestly say I like and respect him more at the end of his leadership, having seen the qualities he brought to it, than I did at the start. I believe Britain is a better country as a result of the economic, social and political changes made since 1997, and a lot of the difficult change in particular was driven by Blair. A lot of the change to get us into power in the first place was driven by him too, and his record of three successive general election victories, unprecedented for a Labour leader, says something about a relationship with the British public that I do not believe our media has ever really understood.

Progress in Northern Ireland alone should stand as a historic testimony, and these pages make clear how much of that was down to his refusal to accept that part of the country he led should simply have to accept living in conditions closer to war than peace. But there are many others – an independent Bank of England, a Scottish Parliament and Welsh Assembly, elected mayors, a reformed House of Lords, regenerated cities, something close to full employment, a minimum wage, improved investment in reformed schools and hospitals, student numbers rising, particularly among people from poorer areas, spending per school pupil doubled, health spending trebled, the biggest hospital-building programme since the NHS was founded, crime down substantially, new rights for gays which the Tories now feel they have to support, the fall of Milosevic, London 2012, progress in Africa, Britain stronger in Europe if not, as he would have wished when we started out, in the euro. As for Iraq, I hope the pages that follow will add to a debate that will take years, decades, to settle.

I hope too that people will read this and understand that for all its faults, our political process is a good one, and the means by which much meaningful change is made. That is not a very fashionable view to hold, but as someone who has operated at senior levels in journalism and politics, around a decade in each, it is my respect for the media that has shrunk, and my respect for politics that has grown.

A lot of the change under Blair has been for the better, at home and abroad. He had a clear objective the whole time – the modernisation of Labour leading to the modernisation of Britain – and by and large stayed focused upon it. But along the way, there was a lot of paddling under the water, there were a lot of unexpected events, a myriad interesting and complex personalities and relationships in Britain and all around the world. These extracts give a taste of them. No one pen can ever record the full story of a leadership as long and varied as Blair's. But this is my first chapter.

Acknowledgements

I chose to publish with Random House because of a long-standing friendship with chief executive Gail Rebuck and her husband Philip Gould, who have lived with the preparation of this book for almost as long as I have. Many people at Random House and Hutchinson have been involved along the way, and I would like to thank in particular Gail, Susan Sandon, Caroline Gascoigne, Rowena Skelton-Wallace, Caroline Knight, Charlotte Bush, Sally Barrass, Helen Judd, Anna Simpson, Eric Hibberd, Mark Handsley, Myra Jones, Katherine Fry and Vicki Robinson. Thanks also to lawyer Martin Soames. I am also grateful to the audiobook team, Zoe Howes, Alexa Moore and Katy Brier who made three days locked in a soundproof booth more pleasant than I anticipated it would be.

Richard Stott has been a terrific editor to work with, as I knew he would be from my days working for him in journalism. He and I are hugely indebted to Mark Bennett who helped me transcribe the diaries and has worked tirelessly on the various edits since. Thanks to literary agent Ed Victor for his support and wise counsel, and for his past and future support of Leukaemia Research. Thanks also to his PA Linda Van.

I would like to thank the people who are in the book, the characters who made my time with Tony Blair so fascinating. I owe thanks to him for the opportunity he gave me to witness the events I witnessed. And I want to thank all those who worked with me in opposition and in Downing Street. There are dozens I could mention, but if I could pick out one, it is my former PA, Alison Blackshaw.

Above all I want to thank my family: Fiona and our children, Rory, Calum and Grace, my mother Betty, my brothers Donald and Graeme, my sister Liz, and Fiona's mother Audrey. It is a source of great sadness to us all that my father, Donald, and Fiona's father, Bob, are no longer with us. I owe them enormous thanks too, and I like to think they would have enjoyed this book.

Acknowledgements

The Diaries

BOOK ONE

Preparing for Power

July 1994–May 1997

Who's Who
July 1994–May 1997

Shadow Cabinet

Tony Blair — Leader of the Opposition (referred to throughout as TB or Tony)

John Prescott — Shadow Deputy Leader (JP, John P)

Gordon Brown — Shadow Chancellor of the Exchequer (GB)

Robin Cook — Foreign Affairs (RC, Robin C)

Margaret Beckett — Health 1994–95, Trade and Industry 1995–97 (MB, Margaret B)

Donald Dewar — Social Security 1994–95, Labour Chief Whip 1995–97 (DD, Donald D)

Jack Straw — Home Affairs (Jack S, JS)

David Blunkett — Education (DB, David B)

Harriet Harman — Employment 1994–95, Health 1995–96, Social Security 1996–97

Andrew Smith — Shadow Chief Secretary to the Treasury 1994–96, Transport 1996–97

Frank Dobson — Environment 1994–95, Environment and London 1995–97 (FD, Dobbo)

George Robertson — Scotland (George R, GR)

Mo Mowlam — Northern Ireland (Mo)

Chris Smith — National Heritage 1994–95, Social Security 1995–96, Health 1996–97

Jack Cunningham — Trade and Industry 1994–95, National Heritage 1996–97

Michael Meacher — Transport 1994–95, Employment 1995–96, Environmental Protection 1996–97 (MM)

Ron Davies — Wales

David Clark — Defence

Joan Lestor — Overseas Development 1994–96

3

Gavin Strang	Agriculture
Ann Taylor	Shadow Chancellor of the Duchy of Lancaster 1994–95, Shadow Leader of the Commons 1994–97
Derek Foster	Labour Chief Whip 1994–95, Shadow Chancellor of the Duchy of Lancaster 1995–97
Lord (Ivor) Richard	Shadow Leader of the Lords
Lord (Derry) Irvine	Shadow Lord Chancellor

Leader's Office

Tim Allan	Press officer
Alastair Campbell	Press Secretary (AC)
Hilary Coffman	Press officer
Jon Cruddas	Trade union liaison
Kate Garvey	Personal assistant to TB
Bruce Grocott MP	TB's Parliamentary Private Secretary
Anji Hunter	Head of Office (AH)
Peter Hyman	Speechwriter, policy adviser
Sue Jackson	Head of Support Services
Liz Lloyd	Policy adviser
Pat McFadden	Policy adviser
David Miliband	Head of Policy (DM, David M)
Sally Morgan	Political secretary (SM, Sally M)
Geoffrey Norris	Policy adviser
Jonathan Powell	Chief of Staff
Terry Rayner	Driver

Key advisers outside the Leader's Office

Peter Mandelson	Labour MP for Hartlepool (PM, Peter M)
Philip Gould	Political pollster and strategist (PG, Philip G)
Charlie Falconer	Barrister, close friend of TB (Charlie F)

And Others

Paddy Ashdown	Liberal Democrat leader 1988–99
Ed Balls	Adviser to GB

Martin Bell	Journalist and independent parliamentary candidate
Cherie Blair	Wife of TB (CB)
Carole Caplin	Friend and adviser to CB
Alan Clark	Conservative politician, friend of AC
Murray Elder	Former Chief of Staff to Labour leader John Smith
Alex Ferguson	Manager, Manchester United, friend of AC (Alex F)
David Frost	Broadcaster
Neil Hamilton	MP for Tatton
Michael Heseltine	Deputy Prime Minister
Anna Healy	Labour Party press officer
David Hill	Chief Spokesman for the Labour Party
Alan Howarth MP	Conservative, crossed the floor to Labour
Fraser Kemp	Labour Party election coordinator
Glenys Kinnock	MEP, friend of AC family
Neil Kinnock	Former Labour leader, friend of AC family (Neil, NK)
Michael Levy	Businessman, Labour Party fund-raiser
Jack McConnell	General Secretary, Scottish Labour Party
Margaret McDonagh	Labour's Senior Campaign Organiser (MMcD, Margaret McD)
John Major	Conservative prime minister to 1997 (JM)
Fiona Millar	AC's partner, latterly assistant to CB (FM)
Rupert Murdoch	Chairman, News Corporation
Roz Preston	Assistant to CB
Tom Sawyer	General Secretary, Labour Party 1994–98
Margaret Thatcher	Former prime minister
Charlie Whelan	GB's press spokesman (Charlie W)
Rosie Winterton	JP's office (RW)

Wednesday, July 27, 1994

TB called me and asked me to go and see him in the Shadow Cabinet room. I arrived at 1.30 and into the kind of turmoil you normally associate with moving house. Boxes and crates of John Smith's papers and possessions on the way out, TB's on the way in, and nobody quite sure where everything should go, and all looking a bit stressed at the scale of the task. Anji Hunter and Murray Elder were in the outer office, and I got the usual greeting from both, Anji all over-the-top kisses and hugs, Murray a rather distant and wary smile. He said Tony was running a bit late. He went in to tell him I was here. A couple of minutes later John Edmonds [General Secretary of the GMB (General and Municipal Boilermakers) union] came out, and looked a bit miffed to see me. Tony's own office was in even greater chaos than the outer office so he was working out of the Shadow Cabinet room. He turned on the full Bunsen burner smile, thanked me for all the help I'd given on his leadership acceptance speech, and then, still standing, perched his foot on a packing case and got to the point, rather more quickly than I'd anticipated. He was going on holiday the next day, and he still had a few key jobs to sort out. He was determined to get the best if he could. He needed a really good press secretary. He wanted someone who understood politics and understood the media, including the mass-market media. They don't grow on trees. He said it had to be somebody tough, and confident, someone who could make decisions and stick to them. Historically the Labour Party has not been blessed with really talented people in this area of politics and political strategy but I think we can be different. Gordon is exceptional, so is Peter, so are you, and I really want you to do the job. It's called press secretary but it's much more than that. He'd assumed I didn't want to do it because I was doing so much media now, and really branching out into broadcasting. He'd sounded out Andy Grice at the S Times, who had said no. But really, he said, I would like to get the best I can and that has to be you. I know you've got reservations but I just ask you to think about it over the holiday. Even though I expected it, and had thought about it, I didn't quite know how to react. I'd gone in there with a list of names to suggest, and a raft of arguments against the idea. I said I'm not sure I'm suited to it. I've got a big ego of my own and a ferocious temper. I can't stand fools and I don't suffer them. I'm hopeless at biting my tongue. He said I've thought about that, but I still think you're right for it. I said money might be a problem. I would be earning way into six figures this year, and it's not easy to take a big cut. Also, I could do lots for you from the outside, like I did on your leadership speech. It's not the same, he said. I agreed to think about it. Even as I left the office, though I'd raised all the reasons against, I had a feeling I would end up saying yes. I bumped into David Hill as I left who was none too happy because he reckoned Tony would move to get rid of Hilary [Coffman, his partner]. I told him I would put a word in, and I did.

Glenys Kinnock [married to Neil, Euro MP for South Wales East from 1994] phoned to say that Neil [Kinnock, Labour leader 1983–92] had got the Brussels job (as European Commissioner) and did we want to go round for dinner? Fiona and I were both thrilled. Neil had done so much, and taken so much, and was desperate for a real job that could make a difference. He was up in Salford doing an interview with Ryan Giggs [footballer], who was a lovely bloke, but it sort of summed up the drift in Neil's life since he gave up the leadership. We all went round to Ealing to celebrate after Neil had taken the call from John Major. I told Neil about my chat with Tony, and he said I'd be absolutely mad. You've got a great number at the moment. You're in total control of your own position, you can make it big in broadcasting if you want, and you'll be giving it up for one of the shittiest jobs known to man.

Saturday, July 30 (holiday, France)
The day before we left to go on holiday, I told Richard Stott [editor of Today]. He had been so good to me when I went bonkers (in 1986), and when I was pushed out of the Mirror, that I felt bad at the thought of leaving him just when it looked like Today was on the move a bit. He said he hoped I didn't go, but I could tell from the tone of his voice – the usual jocularity was gone – and the look in his eye that he reckoned I had probably written my last piece for him.

8

Thursday, August 4

I phoned Tony as planned, and said I still had a lot of misgivings and intended to take the whole month to think about it. He said we should meet up. He was down near Toulouse, which was a good four or five hours from Flassan. I mentioned that Neil and Glenys were coming over next week, and I could sense he was worried. 'Neil will be opposed to you doing this, and for genuine reasons of friendship, because he knows how tough it will be. But it will be different. I promise you. If I can get the best people around me, it will be different.'

Tuesday, August 9

Cherie called to say they were on their way. Tony felt it was important we thrashed it all out and tried to reach a decision. Some holiday this was turning out to be. Neil and Glenys were arriving in a couple of days, and I'd have Neil and Fiona in one room trying to talk me out of it and Tony and Cherie in the other trying to talk me into it. And God knows where everyone was going to stay. I had to drive down to Avignon to meet them, and pack them and all their bags into the Espace while they dumped their battered old Citroën. Their ability to withstand chaos had already made an impression on me when I'd been helping Tony with his leadership leaflet and speeches, but this was something else. They were travelling with a few battered old cases and a black bin liner into which Cherie had thrown the last-minute stuff, including, Fiona noticed, some old carrots. We got home at 1.30.

Wednesday, August 10

The kids were getting on fine, and Tony, Cherie, Fiona and I sat down in the sitting room, with the overhead fan forcing us to speak up, to go over the pros and cons. Tony said that in opposition, what you said, how you said it, and how it was reported, was a large part of your armoury. Governments can do things. They can set the agenda with their actions. Our words are going to be vital, and I want your help in that. He said tactical minds are two a penny, but strategic minds are hard to come by and you've got a strategic mind. You will be a key adviser, answerable only to me, part of the inner team with JP, GB and Robin C. We discussed his conference speech. I said he had to make clear he was of the centre left, but where he could make progress for Labour in a way nobody else could was through emphasis on centre, not left. He started to lay the themes out: said he wasn't impressed with the way Jack Straw kept bashing the Lib Dems, they could be useful both tactically in hitting the Tories, and also strategically in trying to forge a progressive alliance. Said he liked to think Owen, Jenkins, Williams[1] could support most of what we do. Went over thoughts on a reshuffle, RC to the Foreign Office, Jack Cunningham to DTI, maybe Mo for education, but she'd done some silly piece of nonsense in the *Mail on Sunday* about privatising Buckingham Palace so there was still some growing up to do around the place. We stopped after lunch and went to play football with the kids at Bedoin. Then back to it, more on the Libs, more on the strategy for the Tories, and also started to discuss salary. He reckoned he could push it to £75,000, which he'd defend on the basis he wanted the best, but it was still a big drop. We went for a long walk up through the hills behind the village and he ran through his view of the main papers and the main opinion formers. He wanted to know whether I was capable of building bridges with Montgomery.[2] I reminded him that the day I got the heave from Montgomery's *Mirror*, Neil and Roy Hattersley [deputy leader of the Labour Party, 1983–92, peer 1997] led a major parliamentary attack on MGN, and he (TB) did a piece for the *Mirror*. I said that was when I first realised there was a bit of steel behind the smile. I said I wasn't good at grovelling. The *Mirror* needed Labour more than Labour needed the *Mirror*. Mmmm, he said. Not so sure. He said he was hoping to recruit Tom Sawyer. He told me GB thought I was hostile to him. I said he shouldn't. I used to work very closely with him, and I think he thinks that when I went on *Newsnight* the day that John died, and said you'd be leader, that was some thought-through strategy to get a head of steam up. It wasn't. I'd actually said to *Newsnight* I just wanted to do a tribute but they threw me the question at the end, who'd be next leader, and I said you. It was pretty obvious by then. Tony said he still believed GB was in many ways a superior politician. We had dinner at the restaurant down the hill, and while the kids played football Tony regaled us with stories of him and JP getting sworn in as Privy Councillors, JP agitating at the flunkies telling him what to do.

Thursday, August 11
Neil and Glenys arrived. Glenys was in a different place to Neil on whether I should do it. She said Neil was totally opposed but she felt

[1] David Owen, Roy Jenkins and Shirley Williams, former Labour Cabinet ministers who, with Bill Rodgers, defected to form the breakaway Social Democratic Party, in 1981.
[2] David Montgomery, chief executive of Mirror Group Newspapers, 1992–97. Campbell departed acrimoniously as political editor, 1993.

that I was dedicated to the Labour cause, we'd got a new leader, he'd asked me to do the job, he was obviously determined that I should do it, and it was hard to say no. Neil kept saying things like – why live your life at the beck and call of a bunch of shits (the press) when you could be the new [Brian] Walden [former Labour MP and TV presenter], the next Jeremy Paxman [TV political journalist], the next Michael Parkinson [chat-show host], whatever you want? Cherie's mum was due to leave and I had to drive her to Marseille airport. TB came along and again we chatted over the issues. Gale was clearly worried about the whole thing. She'd told me a while back she was scared for Cherie and the children. It was just such a big thing, one step from being Prime Minister, and then the family might as well say goodbye to normality. On the way back, I told Tony in graphic detail about my breakdown. I said I thought it was important he knew, because I had to assume that ultimately I had cracked because of pressure, and the pressure was as nothing compared to what we would face if I did the job. I said I was sure I was a stronger person than ever, but he needed to know there was a risk. He said he was happy to take it. By now, he had also let me know, and sworn me to secrecy, that he was minded to have a review of the constitution and scrap Clause 4. I have never felt any great ideological attachment to Clause 4 one way or the other.[1] If it made people happy, fine, but it didn't actually set out what the party was about today. It wasn't the politics or the ideology that appealed. It was the boldness. People had talked about it for years. Here was a new leader telling me that he was thinking about doing it in his first conference speech as leader. Bold. I said I hope you do, because it's bold. I will, he said. And he had a real glint in his eye. He knew that in terms of the political substance, it didn't actually mean that much. But as a symbol, as a vehicle to communicate change, and his determination to modernise the party, it was brilliant. He'd first mentioned it in our walk up the hill yesterday.

[1] This was in essence a rerun of the argument after the 1959 defeat, when the then leader Hugh Gaitskell proposed amending Clause 4 of the Party's 1918 constitution. The Clause, close enough to Labour's heart and history to be reprinted on membership cards, proclaimed the aim of 'Common ownership of the means of production, distribution and exchange'. Wholesale nationalisation in other words. Gaitskell lost out because questioning Clause 4 was, in the words of one Labour historian, like trying to 'persuade Christian fundamentalists that they need not believe in God'. Gaitskell's attempt at modernisation not only failed, but deepened the divisions in the Party. To Blair, such a high-risk, resonant symbol was the example he needed. Clause 4 had to go to show a new Labour Party was being forged and it meant business.

On the drive back from Marseille, a hint became an intention, and he asked me to start thinking about how best to express it, and how best to plan the huge political and communications exercise that would follow. Whether it was deliberate or not, I don't know, but he had found the way to persuade me, and I told him that I would do the job.

I phoned Peter M in the US. It was obvious that Peter's judgement was largely trusted by Tony and indeed it had been Peter who first sounded me out on his behalf, when he came round for dinner, spent a couple of hours skirting round the issue, finally blurted it out and I said no way. I told him Tony had talked me into it. He said he was pleased. It was the right thing for the party, and he was sure it was the right thing for me. He said I hope we don't fall out, which I thought was a very odd thing to say, but on reflection maybe not. I suppose people working closely together often do end up falling out and there was bound to be tension from time to time in that we would often be advising Tony from different perspectives on the same issues. He said I should consider him as an extra mind I could call on whenever I wanted, but equally I could always tell him to get lost. Later, he spoke to Tony and said he wasn't sure about keeping on Hilary Coffman. I told Tony that I was sure she had to stay, and it was important that I could decide, provided he was happy, who worked for me.

Friday, August 12

As part of the Blairs' chaotic travel plans, we had to set off at 4am so that I could get them to Marseille railway station. Fiona and I, and Neil and Glenys, couldn't believe the way they went from place to place on holiday. Why can't they settle in one place? We arrived at the station at 5.35 and the train wasn't due to leave, so we thought, till 6.15, so I started to get the half-asleep kids and the assortment of bags sorted while Tony went to check where the train was going from. With Euan still asleep and refusing to wake up, Tony came charging out, said they'd got the times wrong, it was about to go. He looked very odd in a pair of holiday shorts and what looked like a suit jacket. He picked up Euan and as many bags as he could carry. I did the same with Kathryn and Cherie hustled Nicky along and we just made it as the platform attendant started to blow his whistle. It turned out it wasn't their train at all, but an earlier one which had been delayed but they decided to stay on board and hope they could find seats. Then just before the doors closed, Tony and I had one of those leaving-train conversations loved by film directors in need of a device. I said

August '94: Building the case for a new constitution

I still had huge misgivings but I would do it, and I would never give him and the party anything less than 100 per cent. He said I was right to feel nervous, but together we could change the face of British politics for a generation, and change the world while we're at it. At which point, as he was right in the middle of this momentous statement, the door shut automatically, angrily, forcing our dear leader to jump back. All of a sudden he looked bewildered. He gave me a little wave, the big smile, and off he went. I drove back to Flassan, wondering what on earth I was letting myself in for. Got home as everyone was getting up and over breakfast agreed we could not cope with chaos like Cherie seems able to. Neil asked me outright if I was going to do the job. I said yes. He said it's good for Tony, bad for you and the family, and I'm totally opposed. You'll hate the crap, the detail, the wankers you have to be nice to. Glenys said Neil, don't do this, he's made up his mind and we should support him. I said I've told him I'll do it, Neil. 'Have you shaken on it?' 'No.' 'Well, don't.' I said he was really serious about winning, but he would need help and I felt I had to help when he asked me like that. Neil even asked if I wanted to be his chef de cabinet but I said no, I'd made my mind up.

Tuesday, August 16
Spoke to TB in Italy. Said he was furious that Neil was trying to talk me out of it. I said it was for good reasons. Neil is a real friend, and he loves my kids like his own. He's worried for us.

Sunday, September 11
I'd been pre-booked to do the papers on *Frost*[1] with Bernard Ingham[2]. Over breakfast, with Frost, de la Billière,[3] Mo, Hanley[4] et al, Barney Jones[5] said to Bernard: 'What would you advise Alastair to do with Mandelson?' Bernard stopped stuffing his face for a moment and said 'Slit his throat.'

Tuesday, September 13
TB was meeting Rupert Murdoch [chairman of News Corp.]. He phoned me from the car as he was heading home. Said he didn't feel it went terribly well.

[1] *Breakfast with Frost*; David Frost, TV journalist and presenter.
[2] Former press secretary to Prime Minister Margaret Thatcher.
[3] General Sir Peter de la Billière, Commander, British forces in the Middle East during the first Gulf War.
[4] Jeremy Hanley, Conservative MP and chairman of the party, 1994–95.
[5] Editor, *Breakfast with Frost*.

Wednesday, September 14

Gus Fischer[1] called. Murdoch had been hugely impressed by Blair. Gus said he could easily see Murdoch backing him. Gave nothing away but made a really strong impression. Meeting at 3.45 with Peter M, Philip [Gould], Pat [McFadden], Anji and [David] Miliband to go over conference problems. The planned slogan was Labour's New Approach, which was fine as far as it went, and it was a good enough umbrella but it didn't really do the business as far as I was concerned. I said we're looking for something bigger and bolder. We were talking about New Labour, and the clearer we were about that, in strategic terms, the better. I knew there would be opposition because it was so bold. But if he was going to dump Clause 4, we had better make the most of it. And New Labour was a big, bold message that would give us real direction and momentum.

Thursday, September 15

Shadow Cabinet meeting, Brunswick Square. TB certainly delivered on his no complacency message. He told me later he'd sounded out JP for the first time on the constitution. He didn't explode. Said he would think about it. I'd been scribbling some thoughts on a slogan for conference. New Labour, New Britain was the best. It was bold, it was clear and it would give us momentum. And if he did Clause 4, it would really drive through. TB expressed some of the nervousness the others had. The problem was that New had an opposite, and you couldn't guarantee there wouldn't be a lot of hostility.

Monday, September 19

Met JP and tried out New Labour on him. Not overwhelmed. But not totally hostile. I didn't know how far TB had gone re his discussion on Clause 4, and I sensed JP didn't know everything, so we didn't really get to the point. But I was relieved he didn't just say no. He agreed that TB had a short window during which he could really make the kind of impact that would basically set us up for the election. But everyone else was wobbling on New Labour, New Britain. Pat and Jon Cruddas both said it could really backfire. Peter M and Philip were really worried about it. The speech was really coming on. We already had the basic argument and some great passages, and if he did Clause 4, it could be sensational. I can't believe we're having a great argument about whether we can stick NEW Labour on a backdrop. New Labour, New Britain. We're changing the party to show

[1] Chief executive of Rupert Murdoch's News International, 1994–95.

we're fit to be trusted to change the country. It's obvious, but I was worried even PM and PG were baulking at it.

Tuesday, September 20

More trouble re the slogan. JP had been on to Anji and he was not happy either with mine, or with Labour's New Approach. He thought there was a danger they looked presidential. I called him, and said I was convinced we should go for New Labour, New Britain, but it wouldn't work if he felt he couldn't sign up to it. He said he was worried we were saying to the party, you've always failed and we're only going to succeed if we change everything. What's new? The leader. But are we saying more than that? I said we were making clear the party had changed, and it was going to carry on changing as it became fit for power. I said it's not different to his traditional values in a modern setting, but it brings it home more clearly to the non-political audience. He said he didn't want the party thinking we were saying they were failures. They had to know this related to what they believe in. 'This kid has got some agenda and it's exciting and all the rest but maybe my role will be to be the cautious one saying are we sure? Like his Clause 4 plan, how do you know it won't cause a two-year riot in the Party? Is it worth it? Now I know why he wants to do it but we have to think it through. Last year we rowed about one member, one vote, now Clause 4.'

Thursday, September 22

TB asked me if JP was really hostile on the constitutional change plan. He says he's not totally opposed but thinks you must be off your head. OMOV [one member, one vote] last year, Clause 4 this, when are we going to get on to things people care about? TB said he needed something big and symbolic that people would notice, then they would hear us on the other policy areas too. This was the route to doing what John wanted. The public had to know we were serious about change. He signed up finally to New Labour, New Britain, and gave me the go-ahead to get it signed off.

Friday, September 23

Office meeting, Pat taking us through some of the difficult outstanding issues. He was worried Tony had said drop the red flag. He said even Fraser Kemp thought we might be going too fast for our own good. I said by the way, the slogan is agreed. TB and JP are both up for it, so it's New Labour, New Britain. Pat did his best Private Fraser from *Dad's Army*, we're all doomed. Cherie's 40th birthday party at

Frederick's. Odd kind of do. Didn't feel right being photographed going in, by Alan Davidson [celebrity photographer] of all people, and I couldn't quite work out the guest mix. Family, a bit of politics, law, and friends that didn't always seem like Tony's kind of people. Maybe he is a lot more eclectic than we are. Cherie had certainly been given a makeover. She looked great, but it was an odd do.

Tuesday, September 27

Conference meeting with TB and JP. JP not great about the brochure we were doing. Said he was getting worried about new, new, new. Agreed he would do the New Labour, New Britain speech but just wanted to urge a bit of caution. As things stood, he was against doing Clause 4 in Tony's speech. He thought Tony had all the momentum he needed, and it was OTT. TB said once we do this, people will wonder what the fuss is all about. I said all people like JP are saying is be careful – to some people this is like going into church and taking down the cross. Oh for heaven's sake, he said, people believe in God, and they believe in Christ. Name me a single person who actually believes in what Clause 4 says.

Wednesday, September 28

Everyone talking about GB's 'gobbledegook'.[1] JP in to see TB and this time we could hear the raised voices. That was not always a bad sign with John. Sometimes meant he was getting something off his chest before coming round. Or it meant he was negotiating.

Friday, September 30

Went through the Clause 4 section of the speech, and it didn't work. He said what do you think? Is this madness we're even considering it? I said no, definitely worth doing, but we've got to get it right. He said there has to be a signal to the outside world that we're serious about change, and this is it. Peter Hyman suddenly chipped in: did you know there are more Indian waiters in Britain than there are coal miners? Blank faces all round. Tony was beginning to look exasperated. His hair was wild, two big prongs of it heading off towards the ceiling. He folded his arms across his chest, put his head down, and groaned. 'I cannot believe this is so difficult. It's ridiculous.'

Saturday, October 1

Felt bad leaving home because Rory had been sick during the night.

[1] Brown had spoken about 'post-neoclassical endogenous growth theory'.

Up to Tony's and chaotic scenes. Photographers gathering outside. TB had added a whole lot more to the speech overnight. We worked in separate rooms on separate drafts and then met to compare notes. Derry called and said he'd read the latest draft and there was an awful lot of verbiage in it. TB locked himself away in his little study, his desk a mass of papers, earlier discarded drafts, papers with his own handwriting, lines straight through it, rejected even before it became a draft. He had a new A4 pad, a red pen, and off he went, with a Do Not Disturb sign etched on his face. I left him and went downstairs to make a cup of tea. Carole [Caplin, friend of Cherie Blair] was there. She had made a strong impression on me when I first met her a couple of days earlier, and had been troubling me. She was pretty and odd in equal measure. I'd asked her where she fitted into the whole Blair scene, and she'd said she was just an old friend that Cherie had called on to give her a hand. I took from that she was a lifelong friend, so I said I was surprised I'd never met her before. In fact she'd known CB before but then went to the US and came back just after John Smith died. She said she was into holistic healing, and I confessed I didn't know what that was. You could tell in one look that she was big into health and fitness. She looked great. She made lunch, which was a great mix of different salads. Cherie said Carole would be going with them in the car and on the plane and I said the press would be straight on, asking who this strange woman was. Carole said she didn't want any attention, but my instinct said otherwise. It was hard to dislike her, but she made me feel very uneasy. Anji told me Carole had introduced herself as TB and CB's guru. Weird.

Sunday, October 2

Although we'd had our differences when I was a journalist, I'd always got on OK with JP and TB had asked me to make sure he was kept in the loop and onside re the speech on Tuesday. It wasn't easy. John instinctively knew what the plan was, but he had to be persuaded bit by bit. I think if we'd have said from the day Tony became leader: by the way, John, he's going to stand up and scrap Clause 4 in his first conference speech, we might have ended up with a disaster. But the thing about JP is that he is open to persuasion if the argument is strong and this argument was strong. We had a decent draft by now, with or without the Clause 4 change, but TB was still not sure. I was telling him that we had to keep Carole C out of the public eye.

Monday, October 3

Woke up at 5, nervous and tired. Got the papers and read them in the bath. JP stuff pretty bad. I went to see him before he did *GMTV* and then in to see TB, who was pretty fed up. I said this stuff is all froth and it'll get blown away if you do a decent speech tomorrow. I had another session with JP to go through the draft again, then wandered over to the Winter Gardens. We had a good speech but now Derry had thrown in a spanner. Derry is not your obvious natural politician but he has a big brain and, more important in this context, Tony thinks Derry has a brain the size of a melon. So when Derry gets on to him and says he doesn't think it's a good speech – no, worse, he thinks it's a BAD speech – Tony listens and there's a danger we're going back to square one. I was really pissed off with Derry. We had less than a day to go and he's saying go back to scratch. We asked him for detailed comments and when they came through, they were fairly marginal so Tony realised he'd been exaggerating. It wasn't that bad. It just wasn't brilliant, but we had a bit of time left yet. At lunch JP came up and read the speech, said it was fine, have a debate, blah blah blah, and TB said let's be clear what I'm saying: Clause 4 is not an adequate expression of what we stand for, and I'm saying this debate is about what goes in its place, something around which we can all unite. I said, right, John, we're doing an interview tomorrow night and I'm asking you: so Mr Prescott, this new statement Tony Blair talks about, could that go in the party's constitution? And JP doesn't look wild about it, but he says yes, if it's agreed by the party, it could. But as we leave, he says I'm not sure this is what we need right now, a bloody great row through the party, but let's see. I showed the first 20 pages of the speech to Neil, who liked it. I then did a briefing of the political editors, which was weird, me still a working journalist spelling out the purpose of the speech they'd be covering tomorrow. Nobody had a whisper of the Clause 4 plan. So far so good. Tom Sawyer was in the loop and seemed pretty relaxed, said he thought he could get some union guys out in favour tomorrow, and was confident we could carry the party OK.

Back at the hotel, Tony met Neil and set out what he intended to say in detail. Bloody great, said Neil, right thing to do. The last time the three of us had talked together, we were in France, TB and NK on different sides of the argument. I felt a real sense of privilege, in terms of witnessing history, to be in the room with one leader of the Labour Party explaining to another why and how he was changing the Party's constitution as a means of giving real power and symbolism to the modernisation process the older man had started. Neil said: I

October '94: Kinnock backs Blair over Clause 4

never had a conference speech as good as this the night before I made it. Don't mess around with it too much. TB to NK: I knew you said these speeches were a nightmare, but I didn't realise how big. NK to TB: you'll feel great tomorrow night, I promise you. That is a helluva speech. Neil left and then TB asked me to rewrite the economic and investment sections while he worked on the middle. I gave him Neil's changes, which he liked. He gave me Derry's, which I didn't like. TB had to go out to Scots night and Peter M came up to see me. He said it was strong but it lacked clarity. It would be bad if he said something, the meaning of which we all knew, but which had to be explained in a TV studio afterwards. I agreed, always best to call a spade a spade. But if he stands up and says I'm scrapping Clause 4, you cannot guarantee the right reaction. If he makes a passionate but rounded argument about New Labour, what we stand for in the modern world, and then says let's argue and agree a new definition of what we stand for, you can win the whole hall round. One slow handclap halfway through this and we're over before we begin. TB came back and had another mini-explosion about the state of the ending of the speech. He asked why I wasn't working on it. I said because I'm in here listening to you complaining about it. Can I go now please? And I went. Back to the word processor in the little room down the corridor, where the pile of uncleared-away room-service trays was growing.

Time to widen the loop. We had a meeting in my room with Peter M, David Hill, Hilary C, Peter Hyman, Anji, Tim [Allan], Murray, Philip G. Some of them knew the full story. Others had picked up the vibes. I told them straight out that the headline from the speech would be Blair scraps Clause 4. I thought Hilary's eyes were going to fall out. David gulped and then whistled. Murray looked ill. I read them the current draft re the constitution, and I said very few people knew what was going on, but I said JP was one of them and he was basically on board. Murray pressed me repeatedly what basically on board meant. I said he was on board. He would be fine, and supportive, and would say that Clause 4 was too narrow a definition of modern socialism. Saw TB later and said the only way to do it is to put the word 'constitution' in there. So we're not just talking about a debate about what we stand for, but we're clear that we're going to debate a new constitution. That is enough. David M and I rewrote that section and I took it to JP. Before I showed him the text, he said 'If you're talking about a new constitution, you've got to say so.' I couldn't believe it. He'd got there at exactly the same point as the rest of us did. I showed him the words. He tested the arguments to destruction and the arguments held up. He said he could live with it. I said great, but could you go 10 rounds in the TV studio defending it? Course I can. He wasn't exactly delirious but, like me, he liked the boldness and he liked Tony's style.

Tuesday, October 4

About an hour and a half's sleep. Peter M came round about seven and said he was really nervous. There is a small chance Tony will end up dead in the water as a result of this. Tony asked me what the chances were that he'd be out of the job if he went through with it. I said about 10 per cent. JP remained the key to this. I went to see him again. Pauline [John's wife] was in bed still. I said can we be clear that you will put your name to a new statement of objectives and that you're happy for TB to use the word constitution in that part of the speech? He said I'm not pretending I'm totally comfortable with it but he's the leader and I'm the deputy and I can see why he wants to do it. I can see the ups as well as the downs on this and I'll support him on it. I borrowed his red pen and he and I went through another round of it, and got a final agreed version which I took to TB. Later he came up to see TB and said you've got your agenda and I'll back you on it, but there are things I want us to do as well, and I want your backing for them. JP was a very canny operator and was likely to be using this to press for his own position in a future government. Tony now had to get on with telling other key Shadow Cabinet people. Robin Cook came in, sat down in the chair by the fireplace. They spent a couple of minutes on small talk before Tony got to the point. Robin deflated visibly, paused, then said: Tony, you're making a terrible mistake. 'Why?' Because it is divisive, people will not want this debate, it will cause you nothing but problems. 'Are you telling me people will fight to save a piece of language that no longer represents what any of us stand for?' Yes. 'Who?' Dennis Skinner [Labour MP for Bolsover]. In any event, it's an emblem. You don't need to change it. 'Well, you may think me crazy but I intend to do it. It is my strong instinct that it's the right thing to do.' You may well win but by the time the blood is cleared from the carpet, I doubt you will think it was a fight worth having. 'Nobody, if they are presented with a better alternative, should feel the old Clause 4 is worth spilling blood for.' TB said JP and GB were on board and it was obviously important RC supported it too. Robin started from a very negative position but TB said he hoped he could win him around. RC went straight to see JP.

I was confident it would go well now. I had a last run through

October '94: The great Clause 4 gamble

the whole text with TB and then the disk was taken through for autocue rehearsal. Even though he did it in a very soft whisper, stopping only to check points or correct literals, by the time he got to the bit that mattered, even in that room, with the half a dozen or so people in there, you could feel hairs standing on necks. Anji said it was the first time she'd seen the whole speech and it was brilliant. As first leaders' speeches went, this would be unforgettable. We were driven over. I was clutching the original, driven by Neil's old driver, Mike Joy. Caution won't win elections. Courage will. Any doubt I had that it was the right thing to do finally went.

TB had spoken to a few more people, Margaret B,[1] [John] Edmonds, [Bill] Morris [general secretary of the TGWU (Transport and General Workers' Union)], and still not a whisper. I walked up with him to the point where he was being held before going on. 'Oh well, here goes,' he said, smiled and walked on. There was a ballsiness to his enthusiasm which I liked. I wandered round the side to watch and there was a real buzz of excitement. There was a real warmth towards him. I was standing next to Tim Allan and when they laughed really loud at one of the jokes we'd not been sure about, I said to Tim: this is going to be fine. When it came to the moment, George Robertson summed it up brilliantly later when he said that as the applause died, you could hear the sound of pennies dropping all around the hall. It had worked. The hall was electrified, and so were the media. David English [Associated Newspapers' chairman] was in raptures. We regrouped briefly in the little office behind the stage, to go through the joint press conference. Neil came in, really enthusiastic, told Tony it was brilliant, loved it. NK and JP never the best of friends, and JP cooled a bit, but was still on for what was to follow. We'd arranged for TB/JP to do a joint briefing in the press room. I told them to follow the cops. We went through but some fucker had moved the lectern and the police just marched on. Ended up doing it on the top of the stairs, all a bit messy but the content was fine.

Wednesday, October 5

Up early and skimmed through the papers. Took them through to TB and said you might as well have a read of them because you will never get a better press than this for a speech. I know, he said. There was a terrific atmosphere around the place. I also had my first public media spat. Anna Healy told me Nick Jones [political correspondent,

[1] Margaret Beckett, former deputy and acting leader of the Labour Party, was defeated as leadership candidate by Tony Blair.

BBC radio] was reporting that JP had been unhappy and that he had not been kept in the loop throughout. It was an obvious story to go for, but it misrepresented the situation. I bawled him out publicly, and said I wanted it corrected on air. He did. I went early to the *Mirror* lunch, another weird experience. It's fair to say these people had effectively given me the boot, and I felt they were taking the political heart out of the paper, but I stayed pretty shtumm, TB did the talking and he was on form.

George Pascoe-Watson [deputy political editor of the *Sun*] came up to me, and said they had some topless pictures of Carole Caplin. He said they'd got a reporter up to the hotel-room door and Carole had said she was a personal secretary. They were asking what her role was. I got Anji to get a message to TB and filled him in when he came off the platform. I said it was probably handleable but if she was a gold digger, or a media plant, heaven knows where this could lead. She and Cherie were obviously friendly and presumably she'd confided all sorts of things. TB didn't exactly look happy but he said he did not believe this would be being done with Carole's knowledge. I spoke to Carole, who at first denied doing topless pictures but then said maybe topless, nothing else, a long time ago. I said she might as well tell me the truth because we would have to deal with it. These papers would be into her big time and we needed to know what they would find. We prepared a statement for me to give to the *Sun*, which distanced Tony from the whole thing, and I spoke to Stuart Higgins [editor], who said they were not doing it as a big deal, and agreed he would keep it distant from Tony. When I'd said earlier she hadn't done topless, he said 'Why am I staring at her tits then?' I didn't think Carole had been candid and told her so, and I said it would be better for everyone if she left Blackpool. Once the *Sun* appeared there was a mini-frenzy. Peter M and I tried to play it light, chucking out the *Sun* vendor in the foyer, overlooking the irony that Murdoch was still paying my wages. Pauline Prescott was worried for Cherie, said you just never know where people are coming from, and whether there is some other motive there. It may be innocent but you just don't know.

Friday, October 7
The Carole problem was worrying me. Said to TB that I understood why CB felt angry that we were trying to say who her friends ought to be, but it was important she got from the outset that the honeymoon wouldn't last for ever, and the press would be after her if they could, and Carole had the potential to be a real problem for all of us.

It may be fair or unfair but there we are. He said he knew that Cherie had been incredibly warm up to now but it all changed. I spoke to CB, said I was sorry I'd had to be so direct but this had the potential to do real damage. I may be overreacting but I may not be.

Saturday, October 8

Robin C more on board. Took the boys to play football with Neil. Back to find Fiona and Glenys talking about how much the *Sun/News of the World* would pay for Carole's story if she was as close as she was saying. I suppose what was happening was that Cherie could see Tony having to become more and more absorbed with the job, the absolute determination to win, and there would be less space for her and the family, and she was looking around for support. Glenys said the same as Derry had, that she'd had a rough childhood and because we saw her as a sophisticated lawyer, maybe she found it all a lot harder than we thought. I remembered what Joe Haines[1] said when I called to ask whether he thought I should do the job. He said make sure you think about Fiona. It is very hard to be married to these all-consuming jobs.

Monday, October 10

Hilary felt I had been over-brutal re Carole, and I said maybe, but we shouldn't underestimate the potential damage to Tony. It was important everyone got the message we were in a different league. I could tell TB was wondering if I'd overreacted too and it's true I was probably thinking worst-case scenario, so maybe going over the top. I said he and Cherie were big figures, and there were various types of people: people they could trust, who were likely to be people they had known for some time; people they would have to get on with, because it went with the job; people who would want to know them because of who they were; and among them would be people on the make, for money, for association, for the kick of saying they were close. You're far more trusting, and you have a much sunnier disposition than I do, but I think you have to be ultra careful about new people coming in. TB said that he felt Carole was probably more sinned against than sinning, and that she had been a great help to Cherie, who suddenly found everyone writing about her, scrutinising her and what have you. TB was seeing Jonathan Powell at 11 and I had a brief chat with him afterwards. Really bright, and eager, and

[1] Joe Haines, former press secretary to Harold Wilson [Labour Prime Minister, 1964–70 and 1974–76] and Mirror Group political editor until 1990.

struck me as someone who wouldn't easily get fazed. Meeting with JP to go over strategy for the Tory conference. Had to push them to the right. TB keen that we build up Michael Portillo [Conservative employment secretary].

Thursday, October 13

TB told me Cherie had taken a knock re Carole. I had to understand this was all new and difficult for her, she was actually quite shy, and to find that even your friends are being approached and written about, it takes a bit of getting used to. He said again he thought I'd been harsh, but JP agreed with me that you were unlikely to make new friends once you got into a job like his.

Meeting with Peter M, Peter Hyman, Miliband and Pat Hewitt who is chairing the Social Justice Commission. Main focus child benefit, welfare to work, higher education. Pat said real difficulties. We were talking about targeting. I said you could easily mount the argument that it was socialism, helping most those who need it most. But Peter M was worried whether the sums we were talking about – £300m – justified the political price of breaking universality. David M was nervous about it. Pat H wanted to go further, said this should only be the start of the process. Felt it crazy that the rich parent got the same child benefit as the poor parent. I'd only ever known Pat as Neil's press person, which was never her real thing. But she was really impressive on policy and on policy detail. The commission could be a big thing for us. There was a lot of talk about Shadow Cabinet shake-up. Robin's people were putting it round that he would be the best Shadow Chancellor, lot of interest in Margaret B. Drove back to Bournemouth and went to the BBC party. Lots of whingeing about the way we treated them last week. Dinner with John Monks [TUC (Trades Union Congress) general secretary] at a Law Society bash. He reckoned my problems were 1. Mandelson 2. Unions/Edmonds 3. Shadow Cabinet 4. JP. He said if you can keep all of them basically in line, you've cracked it.

Saturday, October 15

TB called asking why *Indy*, *Guardian* and others had given Major a good press. Probably sympathy, I said. I really wouldn't worry. That was a speech that will be forgotten by Monday. We talked over the article I'd drafted for the *News of the World*. He was keen on emphasising that Major was unable to hold firm in the centre ground, partly because of his record, partly because his party won't let him. He was in no doubt Major being pushed to the right was in our interests, and the conference had clearly helped on that. It was a huge strategic error because the issues that mattered were on the centre ground – economy, health, education. I had another go at dissuading him from sending the boys to the Oratory.[1] I said that line in Major's speech about people doing the best for their own children was laying down a line of attack. What did he gain from going to the Oratory? You get all the grief politically, Euan will get attention he won't want or need, and is it really that much better than the school down the road? Discussed Shadow Cabinet. He was moving towards Jack Straw to Home Office.

Monday, October 17
Finally started full-time. Fiona drove me in, and I said TB's a lovely bloke, but he is so relentlessly modernising I feel myself getting more traditional by the day. I didn't feel at all like I was going in for the first day at a new job. Jonathan Powell's appointment confirmed. Fiona angry that CB was still so hostile to me over Carole. Can't she see you're just doing your job and trying to protect TB?

Thursday, October 20
I'd only ever seen reshuffles from the media side of the fence, and could never understand why they always took so long. Surely the PM or Leader of the Opposition just did his list and told people what was what. Er no. First he had to decide what HE wanted. Then he had to find out whether that is what THEY would be prepared to do. And he had to get buy-in from the other big beasts, and if anyone said no to something, or started to negotiate, it was back to the drawing board. Plus there was all the planning going on on the junior jobs, which the Shadow Cabinet people themselves may not want. It was like a big jigsaw puzzle, but the shape of the puzzle kept changing. Margaret B felt that she ought really to be one of the big four jobs, having stood in as leader following John's death. And Mo was really not keen on N Ireland. I couldn't understand why anyone would not jump at NI. It had the potential to be about as interesting, and as important, as any other job. But I think she thought she was in for one of the big domestic jobs. MB eventually agreed to health, which in Labour terms was a big job, but she was clearly disappointed not to be in one of the top four. Robin making clear not happy. PMQs [Prime Minister's Questions]. I saw something of the actor in TB, the careful preparation, the rehearsal,

[1] The London Oratory school, a Roman Catholic grant-maintained school in west London.

the need for time to compose himself, the need for assurance and reassurance. But it paid off. He looked and sounded the part, and the Tories were troubled by him.

My farewell do at the Reform. Mum couldn't believe there were so many Labour leaders there – Tony, Neil, Jim [Callaghan, Prime Minister 1976–79]. Richard [Stott] made a hilarious speech, his basic theme that it was noble of TB to give up everything to be my press officer. Said the real reason Fiona had never married me was that like so many other women, she was waiting to see if Peter M changes his mind.

Sunday, October 23

TB sounded very chirpy, said he'd really enjoyed being able to work on his own for a few hours. I said I was a bit worried about him saying he was already feeling he needed space. What did he think it would be like being PM? You'd get no space at all. You can't even go out for a walk without a great palaver. He said maybe that's why I want to hang on to more space now.

Monday, October 24

Surprised to find Peter M at Tony's. Cherie very chilly. Went over the basic message for today, and made some last-minute changes to the Social Justice Commission speech. TB not sure whether this was going to be seen as too radical or not radical enough. Got to the Connaught Rooms and could see TB was distracted. 'I hate it when the press get into the family.' I said that's why they do it. Speech went well, but in the car on the way back, he looked fed up. People were staring at him through the window and he was smiling, but his face wasn't happy. 'Do you like it when strangers come up to you like that?' Sometimes I do, sometimes I hate it, he said. But I know there's no way back from it now. I just console myself with the thought that one day it will be someone else, but hopefully I'll have done a fair bit with the time I get. He asked if I was glad I'd done the job. I said up to a point. It was hard work, harder even than I thought it would be. He said he was worried I worked too hard, and I needed to relax whenever I could. Called CB who could barely bring herself to speak to me or Anji at the moment. It struck me as odd that the press weren't asking if CB was still going to Carole C exercise class. Seemed obvious question. Perhaps they just assumed CB had dropped her because of the fuss in Blackpool. Anji and I could scarcely conceal our exasperation that the basic posture was still to defend Carole. Spoke to Derry, who agreed it might be better if Carole was out of their lives, but it may be better to leave things until the story had calmed down. Also, he said, I know you have a job to do, but there have to be areas of their lives that Tony and Cherie are allowed to treat as totally private.

Tuesday, October 25

Didn't sleep well. The Cherie situation was a problem. I thought about writing to her, to point out that she more than anyone but Tony had fought for me to do the job, and I was only doing what I thought was best for them. Decided against. Major called TB and said he would be making a statement and setting up an inquiry into the conduct of public life. TB didn't like the sleaze issues. Said reality was our politics was probably least corrupt of anywhere in the world, and while the party advantage was there, the trouble was it ended up tarring all politics. He was excellent in the Chamber and the Tories seemed bewildered. TB spoke to Jim Callaghan who we originally thought might sit on the committee, but eventually settled on Peter Shore [Cabinet minister in Wilson and Callaghan governments]. TB there till midnight working out the last bits of the reshuffle. Ann Clwyd being very difficult. Felt very sad watching Peter Pike [formerly front-bench spokesman on housing] leave after TB had asked him to leave the job.

Wednesday, October 26

TB said hated the reshuffle. Peter H said his friends had said TB far too soft yesterday. TB to Walworth Road for renaming as John Smith House. Tories started trying to put round one or two sleaze stories re Tony, e.g. whether all his media payments declared. Didn't fly though. I just don't think people felt he was in it for money. Threatened the Guardian with a writ if they hinted at wrongdoing. TB said this was why he hated the focus on sleaze. Once that became the currency of politics, the media would love it, and if you try hard enough, you can make Mother Teresa look sleazy, if you manage to establish there is something wrong in the motives of the people who want to help her. Observer offered 1500 words for TB. Got Tim [Allan] to start drafting and went to meet Jane Proctor of the Tatler. She said Tatler readers were flocking over to Labour so she would like to do something with us. Anna [Healy] and Hilary [Coffman] said that there was a buzz Peter M was to be a whip, and TB said if he was the story, rather than women into big jobs, he'd be livid. Went to the gallery to try to explain names being touted as whips were absurd.

Friday, October 28

TB constantly reanalysing his approach yesterday, which meant he wasn't happy about it. I said even the *Mail* were going at Major, and the news for him yesterday was bad. I just hate all this, he said. It is not what politics should be about. And I think the public just end up thinking all politics is bad. He was also worried that Cherie was now being targeted as a way of getting at him. She is as tough as old boots, he said, but it does unnerve me. Derek Foster told me he was having a real problem with Don Dixon over Peter M. The demonology went deep, beyond reason, considering the role he'd played in getting us to where we were. JP came in a bit worried because he'd been late declaring a Concorde trip. Sundays chasing all manner of stories re Tony's campaign funds and Register of Members' Interests. We had to emphasise the word actionable to a number of them.

Monday, October 31

I alerted Derry to the [Oratory] school problem. He said, again, that you had to be careful about crossing the line on what were in the end personal decisions. I said sure, but where there were political implications, it was as well to be open about them. TB called re today's debate on privileges committee, and agreed to meet to get line right for JP. Both not happy that all politics focusing on this at the moment, and keen to get on to Post Office privatisation tomorrow. JP asked me to work on a flourish at the end which would be what was used on TV, but we toned it down after hearing the Speaker was going to criticise the *Guardian*. Chat with TB re Cherie. He said he thought we should get it written about that she was being targeted by the Tories, which was fair enough. I used it to raise again my view that he was leading with his chin in sending Euan to the Oratory. I couldn't see the point of generating all the fuss it would cause. He said they'd decided it was the right school for Euan and that was that. I felt it would give him a political problem, and put Euan in the spotlight in a way I thought they wanted to avoid. The press would say it made the kids fair game. He was adamant that grant-maintained or not, it was the right school for him, and he was going, and he felt the public would understand he wanted the best for his kids. 'I am not going to sacrifice my kids' education for political correctness. It is not as if it is a private school, for heaven's sake. It is a state comprehensive.' Up to a point, I said. I asked him to imagine the Heseltine speech [Conservative Deputy Prime Minister ('Hezza')] on the Labour leader who expected ordinary kids to go to the local sink school but shipped his own kids across London to a GM school the likes of which his party opposed. He said Tories sent their kids to private schools. I said they believe in private education, we don't. I asked if the local schools were really that bad, and he said all he knew was the Oratory was the best school for Euan. I said imagine the boost to the morale of the local school if you did send your kids there. He said that was the first persuasive argument I had put, but he was still not budging. Their minds were made up.

Monday, November 7

Meeting with TB, Geoff Norris, Miliband and Pat McFadden re Scotland. West Lothian Question[1] and how best to answer. He did an interview with the *Daily Record* and Pat identified three problems. 1. Did not push Scottish Parliament as first Queen's Speech priority. 2. Compared devolution politics with N Ireland. 3. Didn't go as far as George Robertson re sacking quango bosses. Didn't seem disastrous to me but you could never tell with the Scottish press. TB said he really wanted me to make efforts to get on with GB and Peter M. Said you three are the key to a real strategic capability and you have to work together. You are the least prima donnaish and you tend not to have your own angle. But I really want you all working together.

Tuesday, November 8

Peter M still expressing ignorance at why he was currently so unpopular. He said he'd stopped talking to journalists. Agreed that was sensible, and key to him being 'normalised'. Peter operating hidden was not sensible and wouldn't be effective. I said everyone had to understand how draining it was the time and energy we spent dealing with the issue, working round it, persuading people Peter was not as bad as his enemies said. Meanwhile we were trying to make sense of GB's tax reform press release. TB had one of his 'would Robin be better?' moments, but it passed quickly. He said the election would be fought largely on tax, trust, the economy, and for all that he could be difficult to work with, GB had a great mind and operated at a far more strategic level than anyone else in the Shadow Cabinet.

Thursday, November 10

TB raised GB again. Said it was difficult because he obviously felt

[1] See note on page 105.

old allies were against him and yet if only he could be fully harnessed, he is brilliant. We are going to have to sort it out. Also emphasising the need for us to be the party of living standards. I heard from Philip that Peter had spent four hours with JP the night before, went to see JP. I asked how it went. He was in total grump mode. He said the jigsaw was falling into place and it was obvious Gordon was carving him out of the election because he wanted to be in charge of strategy. So I've given up a front-bench portfolio but now I don't do the big election job. I said I didn't think it was all finalised. He said Harriet Harman had told Ian McCartney [Labour front-bencher] that Ed Miliband [policy official, later special adviser to GB and younger brother of David] was leaving her to work on GB's election strategy team, and GB's off to the States etc etc, it all fits. I said he knew he was essential to everything we did, and he said he was tired of being told nothing could happen without him. He looked crestfallen, said he was disappointed. He had a relationship of trust and he valued that. I said I would report back he was not happy. Re Peter, JP said he could work with him OK, but he sometimes felt Peter almost enjoyed being unpopular and he certainly enjoyed everyone thinking he was all-powerful.

Friday, November 11
TB said JP had not wanted the strategy job when they discussed this before. That's why he felt he should take a portfolio. GB was the best strategic mind we had. He said I can't be doing with all this, the time and energy I have to use on psychology.

Monday, November 14
Tony sitting on his own on the sofa in the office, working in the near dark. 'Put some bloody lights on and stop looking so depressed,' I said. He said I don't know what's wrong with me. I said you're tired, you're fed up with some of the problems you're dealing with, if you're like me you're feeling guilty about not seeing your kids enough and it's cold and miserable outside.

Tuesday, November 15
Met JP with Philip Gould. JP in jocular form: 'Advance, friend or foe, whichever thou art.' He was finally signed up to the idea that maybe we could learn something from focus groups. It was odd how polls were accepted as part of the political scene but there was something somehow wrong about actually sitting with a small group of individuals and trying to find out in depth what they really thought about

November '94: Prescott fears being frozen out

politics. JP said he had mistrusted polling before because he felt at the last election it had been tailored to a pre-planned strategy. He was obviously pleased at his own position, which was strong. He connected with people in a way that most politicians didn't. PG tried to emphasise the nature of the real change that was taking place. People were coming over because they sensed we had changed. JP said in the end though it's about policy. Fair wages, of course they like that message. But what matters is whether we do the minimum wage, and how much it is. He said I know your first loyalty is to Tony, that it was difficult for me with GB, and I had to play a deep game re Peter M, but he hoped I could be straight with him and he was worried that last week I was holding something back. I said he had to see it from TB's perspective. He knew the people he rated and trusted and he just wanted to get them working together properly.

Wednesday, November 16

Queen's Speech. Up at crack of dawn and in with TB to go through the speech line by line. John Pienaar [BBC political journalist] called to say Number 10 were saying Major would threaten a general election if the EU Contributions Bill was defeated. TB went off for the Lords procession and when he came back was worried about it. He had really prepared but found it tough. If there is a worse nightmare than this, I've never had it, he said. He started nervously, but warmed up after taking a few interventions.

Monday, November 21

The *FT* 'Tory yobboes' story[1] was brilliant, running pretty well on the news and I spent most of the day trying to fuel it. TB was keen we push two lines: 1. it shows how desperate they are 2. that on the strategic questions they are getting it wrong and we are getting it right. TB doing *Standard* drama awards at the Savoy and we organised a doorstep on the Maples memo[2] which was even better in full than David Hill's edited highlights last night. In the car TB said what it exposed was the total lack of a political strategy at Central Office. He did a word-perfect clip on the way in. TB and Richard Wilson [actor] had a chat about what it was like dealing with sudden fame. Joan Collins

[1] The Speaker, Betty Boothroyd, promised to take action against Tory 'yobboes' who were being incited by John Maples, the Conservative Party's deputy chairman, to disrupt speeches by Tony Blair.
[2] Maples wrote a memo saying that the Tories should not discuss the NHS as it was a discussion they could never win.

made a beeline for TB but he was taken through to have his picture taken with Maggie Smith, who was pretty offhand, and Tom Courtenay [actors] who was really nice. Said his dad would be really proud of him meeting TB. At the lunch I was sitting with David Hare[1] and his wife and told him I would never have let him have the access he did for *Absence of War* and I didn't think he used it well. Also suggested to Stephen Glover [media commentator] that he return to his planet and find the other three beings who thought Major was wittier than TB during the Queen's Speech debate. What a deeply unpleasant man. I had a really nice chat with John Oates, vicar of St Bride's, who said he often talked about the address I did at John's memorial service.[2]

Tuesday, November 22

Meeting with Philip and Peter M in which PG started re his strategy paper. I said before that we needed to sort out exactly who was doing what and how it all fitted into the structures TB wanted. PG knew what I was talking about, PM feigned ignorance. I said he should not be briefing the press on anything to do with TB or strategy. He said he was not at all sure TB would agree with that. I said I spent a good deal of my time defending him to his colleagues on the basis that he was no longer all over the press, but it was hard to keep doing that. It was always difficult having these conversations because he tended to deny outright that he was briefing the press, as with the Grice story. Also, he was so witty with it that we usually ended up having a great shouting match and then the meeting would end perfectly amicably. As we walked through Westminster Hall, and I headed off back to the office, he startled onlookers by suddenly yelling out, in the campest voice he could muster: 'Love you lots.' It is impossible not to like him, but I told TB that if Peter wasn't reined in and just part of the team, it would be a problem not just for me but for him as well. Anji was totally with me that it was intolerable if Peter was briefing. I said I'd never done a job I didn't enjoy and I could easily walk away from this, and I would if it was not possible to do on my terms. She spoke to TB who then spoke again to Peter. Anji called later to say that TB had said he wanted both of us working for him, but if he was forced to choose, he would keep me. Got home, Fiona said TB had called and

[1] Playwright. In the run-up to the 1992 election Neil Kinnock had allowed Hare close access for the writing of his play about a fictionalised Labour leader.
[2] John Merritt, *Daily Mirror* and *Observer* journalist. Campbell's closest friend from their days on the *Mirror* Training Scheme together. Died from leukaemia at the age of 35 in August 1992.

that I was upset re Peter. I said I wasn't upset, I was just determined to get everything sorted out and running properly.

Thursday, November 24

Picked up by Terry,[1] to TB's. He was still in his pyjamas getting Nicky his breakfast. Radio blaring out the Tory revolt. On the way in, going over PMQs, he wanted to do a specific question on the EU Budget, one on why he wasn't doing the debate, and a wrap on the various disasters – hitting them as an ill-disciplined rabble.

Sunday, November 27

A quiet day enlivened by some very Robinesque shenanigans over a Grice story saying there had been a TB/RC rift over Robin's non appointment to the Economic Policy Commission. TB asked me to convey to Robin that he was not very happy at what his 'friends', who were widely assumed to be Robin, were saying to the press. I loved these chats with Robin, because he managed to combine innocence, wit and political dexterity. First he professed total ignorance about the story. Not seen it. Not heard about it. I read it to him. 'It's garbage,' he said. 'I AM on the commission.' Oh, said I, knowing – or certainly assuming – he was not. He called me back within an hour to say he'd opened his NEC [National Executive Committee] papers and it did indeed appear that it was not intended he was on it. Given the news management problem we now had, he said, and the suggestion of a rift with Tony, which none of us want, might it not be sensible if we said that he was, as chair of the National Policy Forum, entitled to attend the Economic Policy Commission? I ran it by TB, who was fine. Spoke to Charlie Whelan, who said GB would not be happy with that. TB said he was fed up having to sort out egos. Robin claimed GB had specifically asked him to be on the commission. TB said he was sure GB always intended he shouldn't be on it. 'I'm perfectly relaxed,' said RC, sounding anything but, 'but I think my formula helps us out of the problem.'

Tuesday, November 29

TB read through his Budget speech again. He said again if there was anything more nightmarish than these big parliamentary set pieces, he didn't know what it was. Said we had no idea how nerve-racking it was.

---

[1] Terry Rayner, driver from the Government Car Service, later one of Blair's drivers at Downing Street.

Wednesday, November 30

The *Mail* had been on about Euan going to the Oratory. They had it as a fact and wanted our comment. We put together a short statement on the train and got it to David Hughes at the *Mail* via Hilary [Coffman]. Then heard it was the splash, which seemed to surprise TB, for all the discussion we'd had. Got to Dudley, fish and chips in the car, then the bleeps started coming through re the Oratory. I called Cherie to warn her and said it was important the kids didn't get too caught up in it. 'I didn't know you cared about these things,' she said, not without sarcasm. I said you'd be surprised. I said it was always bound to come out, it did not surprise me it was the *Mail*, they and the Tories would play it for all it was worth, and I'm simply alerting you. I had to phone Robin to get a line on what was going on re Bosnia. He said my advice is to look serious and sober, look straight ahead and say something unutterably pompous. He did make me laugh, sometimes intentionally.

Thursday, December 1

Up just after 6, Oratory story going big. Agreed with *Breakfast News* they could do one question on it but otherwise we'd stick to what we discussed yesterday. I went in to see TB, who was standing stark naked reading the *Mail*. He said they hadn't carried our side of the story. There's a surprise. No, come on, he said, I know what you think but it's a Catholic comprehensive school and Euan's primary school is a feeder school. I said they're not interested in facts. They're interested in inflicting political and personal damage and this is the first thing they've got. He said his real concern was the effect on Euan but he was also asking what the effect on the public would be. I said it would be a lot worse in the party. Lots of people would support the idea you put your kids before politics, but if the Tories can make the hypocrite charge stick, and the party helps them just by keeping it as a running sore, it could be bad. It was also the case that the press were bored with kicking Major and praising you and this would let them get stuck into you a bit more. The Tories were going mainly on the fact it was a GM school. If I was them, I'd go more on Mr Community shipping his kids across London because the Labour community schools weren't good enough for them. He and I had been over the same argument so many times but now it was here and we were having to deal with it so we just had the arguments again. I tried my best to help, got a script done to make the best of the facts, and suggest he urge the Tories not to turn his children into a political football. He worked out what he was going to say on the school,

34   *December '94: Row over the Oratory*

said it, nothing more, nothing less, and moved on. On the way into the press gallery, Jonathan Haslam [Major's press secretary] said 'For once you've got the pads on.' I can't say I felt much like defending the whole thing. Jacques Arnold [Conservative MP for Gravesham] asked JM the question that let him off the leash and they were really going for it. It was a blessed relief afterwards when the press surrounded David [Hill] rather than me, because he'd been more on top of the detail. I went downstairs and found TB with Hilary, GB, Peter M, Bruce [Grocott], and all pretty down. There had been a thought TB should put out a statement, which I thought was too defensive and better Blunkett do it. DB was up for being supportive. We had to cancel yet another meeting with Philip [Gould]. He said the worry was if this became a defining moment. TB asked again what was the public reaction. I said again, mixed. Some would support you. Others will say hypocrite. The damage comes if the party really helps the Tories keep it going, and you have hypocrisy and division rolled into one, and it all gets to you more than the usual because the family is involved. Not that I told you so. DB did an excellent interview but the news was awful. TB said the whole thing was ridiculously overblown, and we should be doing more to push back. This was difficult, because he knew I disapproved and he knew I wasn't very good at doing things if my heart wasn't in it. And we'd been arguing about it for weeks. He went potty when I said he should calm down. Bruce and I were pretty much in despair and feared a read-over into the Clause 4 situation. Pat [McFadden] felt it gave the party the sense he wasn't of them, his strength and his weakness. Fiona and Glenys both livid. I was through the anger on it, now working out how best to contain it. I was amazed the Tories, for all their strong words, hadn't actually got on to the biggest point of vulnerability on it, a Labour leader shipping his kids out of a Labour area because he thought the schools weren't good enough.

Friday, December 2

The office was getting dozens of calls from party members really pissed off, some asking what they were meant to do with their local anti-GM campaigns. TB said up to them. Sue Jackson was virtually in tears. In truth, I told TB, the papers could have been worse, and he thought there would be a difference between the press and the public on this. I said it was the party that was the problem. They felt let down and confused by it. It was a big dent in the halo and the press would now feel they could pile in a lot harder. Plus the community message was blunted. I told him Fiona was barely speaking to me about it, let alone him. He called her and she was reasonably supportive but said she found it very hard to defend. Tim [Allan] was at the other end of the scale, saying TB should do a piece defending his decision as a parent in the *Mail*. I was worried that would just inflame the party further. TB said the problem was that I didn't think his decision was justified. True, but I said I was happy to make the best possible case. Peter M had persuaded him he should do a *Mail* piece, that we had to get his case out, so Peter, Tim and I drafted something. Cherie had phoned and was angry that it was in the papers that she was keener on the Oratory than TB. We chatted for a while and after some polite not really getting to the point, I sensed she was suggesting I had put that out. I said if she really believed that, she ought to have some evidence, and she ought to realise if she was that suspicious it would be quite difficult for me to carry on working for her husband. She said she thought I'd been giving TB too negative a picture of the school because I was personally opposed and it was actually none of my business. I said it was only my business in so far as Tony expected me to deal with the media and political flak, and I felt it was my job to warn him the flak would be considerable, which indeed it was. She said TB was really upset at the coverage. I said I can't be blamed for that. She seemed to think I had some kind of magical powers over the press that I could somehow control what they did report and what they didn't. At one point she appeared to suggest I was personally hostile because she was a Catholic or a barrister. I understood why she was angry and upset but this was ridiculous. We hung up on pretty bad terms. She called back ten minutes later to say sorry. I said I really did understand why this was difficult. She said she felt there was a hostility between us. I suggested the four of us went out and talked it all through. I reminded her that one of the reasons she'd been so keen for me to do the job was that she saw me as someone who would always tell him what I thought. She couldn't just turn because she didn't like what I was saying. She didn't want TB and Fiona involved at this stage. I told TB and he said she was upset but she did not mean to be hostile and she was probably feeling bad about it. It is difficult for Cherie and she doesn't have the same support I have.

Saturday, December 3

Chat with Neil who said 'In his job, you can't divorce the personal choice from the political any more.' Chat to TB and both of us pretty glum. He spoke to Fiona, who as ever was softer on him than she was on me for defending him. She said she could live with his personal choice so long as the policy focused on ensuring kids at the lower end got a decent chance, but if they changed policy to suit his decision, she'd probably leave the party.

Sunday, December 4
I didn't think TB fully grasped the potential damage being caused by the Oratory. He said anyone would think I'd sent him to Eton. I said we had to watch a kind of revenge crossover to Clause 4. At least he could laugh about himself still. 'Not much chance of persuading the country if I can't persuade my press secretary and his missus.' I said I'd had to stop Fiona pinning the *Indy on Sunday* editorial to the front door for Neil and Glenys to read on arrival. We were all going for a party at Helena Kennedy's [QC and campaigner for civil liberties] but Rory, Calum and I left to watch Chester–Burnley on Sky then went back and the whole place was arguing about the bloody Oratory, because the Kennedys were sending their son there too. I left them to it, went upstairs and called JP, who was also getting flak. He said you did all you could but his mind was made up. You warned there would be damage and there is. He said he'd been wary about being too heavy on it because you've got to be careful pushing too hard on family/personal. Watched *Spitting Image*, which had a field day on the Oratory.

Monday, December 5
TB was far more up than at the weekend. I'd noticed that he didn't need that much rest time to get rested. He said he'd recovered his equilibrium and we should never have lost it. On the Oratory we should have been clearer, stronger and had a strategy ready to go. He said I had got very down and hangdog about it, and I was the linchpin of the operation and everyone weakened. Whatever my views, I had to be professional about these things.

Wednesday, December 7
TB said it was important people understand that if we lost a vote on Clause 4, he would have to quit as leader. He also believed that if we lost a vote on Clause 4, we would lose the election because the public would conclude we were not a serious party. 'People need to understand if we lose on this, we might as well pack up.'

Thursday, December 15
TB had had dinner with Roy Jenkins, said he liked his company, and for the first time I can recall he said he had a bit of a hangover. He

said we were working him too hard and yet again he asked Anji to try to get a better grip on the diary. Anji said to him: 'Have you any idea how hard we work for you, and how much we do to keep things out of your diary?' She felt there was nothing there that wasn't either politically essential, or something he'd asked to do, and she asked whether he'd noticed that most days, when he went home to see his kids, she, I and some of the others were still there working for him. I was drafting reactions to the by-election, including a piece for the *Sun* for later editions. When I was going through it with TB he said I should watch my own back with the press; at some point they would turn on me and I should try to avoid giving them the ammunition. I said it was inevitable, but frankly while we were in such a strong position, I was keen to change the terms of the debate, and make them understand that we would decide how we interacted with the media, not them.

Monday, December 19

Late in after taking boys to school. Strategy meeting a bit tired and vague, though Karen Buck [coordinator of campaign strategy] was quite impressive. To Neil's party, which was at a room in the Treasury. Mainly chatting with Charles Clarke[1] and Dick Clements,[2] who felt I was sending off too many letters to the press. Then our office party for the press, with them all swarming round TB. I chatted to Tony Bevins [*Observer* political journalist] then had to deal with a mini-flurry because some of them had gone off with the impression TB had signalled a shift on devolution. These parties are nothing but trouble. Everyone is pretending to be nice to everyone else but basically the politicians loosen up and the journos are just hoovering up stories, some of them even true.

Saturday, December 24

Peter M turned up for dinner unexpectedly, as usual our run-ins ignored and forgotten. We went over all the obvious – Clause 4, TB relations with the Shadow Cabinet, how Jonathan Powell would fit in. He asked if I was enjoying the job and it took me a little aback. I'd been doing it so much I'd stopped thinking about whether I actually enjoyed it. I said there were some great moments. I'd enjoyed conference. I liked the preparation for the big moments and the big

---

[1] Charles Clarke, head of Neil Kinnock's office, 1983–92. Chief Executive of Quality Public Affairs, 1992 to 1997. Labour MP for Norwich South from 1997.
[2] Editor of *Tribune* for 21 years; became senior adviser to Michael Foot [former Labour Party leader] and Neil Kinnock.

December '94: Blair warns Campbell re press

speeches. I liked strategy but I felt we were not at the races yet on that because it was so hard to get buy-in and understanding. We also talked about whether I was too honest and abrasive with TB. I said I felt it was important that I said what I thought and didn't do the sycophantic adviser bit. He said that was fine, but I should not underestimate my ability to faze and unsettle people and it might be better if that particular quality was more directed towards our opponents. It was very Peter. For all that he could be infuriating, at least he was clever and witty.

Saturday, December 31

Train to Preston for the Burnley game. Great game, won 5–1. Nightmare journey back. The train was delayed. Then it stopped at Crewe and after an age they announced it was clapped out and we'd have to wait for another one. And then the calls from the Sundays started, first about some nonsense story in the *Telegraph* that TB wanted to call the head of the Scottish Parliament the 'Premier'. I knocked it down as best I could, bollocked David Wastell (the reporter) but he held his ground. When I spoke to George Robertson I realised why. George said he may have mentioned it as one of the options. Then the Blunkett stuff, *S Times* splashing on Labour plans to tax school fees. I hated doing these calls on the train, with people listening and the signal forever coming and going, but this one had the potential to go neuralgic. TB would go berserk. Which indeed he did when I told him. By now I was at David and Anita Miles's [personal friends] New Year party. 'Are you telling me,' said Tony, 'that one of our own people has done an interview and as a result of it we are going into the New Year with a story about Labour taxing people to educate their children?' I said I am, and the exasperated silence spoke volumes. He went into one of his 'will we ever get serious' tirades. Do we care about what a few activists think, or do we care about what millions of people think? As midnight neared, I was still on the phone to him, and at the stroke of midnight itself was on to David Hill, who had been trying to track down DB. Jo Moore [Labour Party press officer] told me that to make matters worse Bryan Davies, one of DB's team, had told the PA [Press Association] it was being considered. TB said he was sorry I'd had yet another day of my holiday buggered. I said we had to stop all this loose talk all over the place. He'd just got away with an interview with the *Guardian* so why does he need to do one with the *S Times*? It meant we were starting the New Year not on Tory turmoil but on Labour/tax, Labour/chaos, Labour/split, Labour/education mess. I said sorry to go on about the Oratory, but I reckon this one was born of David [Blunkett] feeling the need to protect his left flank because he'd taken a hit in standing up for you over the school. At about 1.20, after our umpteenth call and with us still failing to find DB, we eventually wished each other a Happy New Year. I relayed to him my conversation with Frank Teasdale [Burnley chairman] earlier when he gave us a lift to Preston to get the train back. He said what people found impressive, particularly given Labour's history of division, was that we so obviously had a really tight control over all of the key players in the team. TB said it didn't feel like it tonight.

Sunday, January 1, 1995

Woke up early anxious about the Blunkett situation. TB asked me to persuade the BBC it wasn't a story. I said it's hard to maintain that when your education spokesman has said on the record that he is thinking about it. Short of him going out and denouncing himself, we can't pretend it didn't happen. He said it is so unnecessary and it's so damaging. I said I know it is, but we don't get very far just because you keep telling me that. We have to decide what to do. He said I can't believe this is New Year's Day and I am having to spend the day dealing with a total own goal. 'And you are,' he added, as something of an afterthought. GB also went berserk, saying DB should not be opining about taxation at all. Eventually I spoke to DB and said we'd spent the whole of last night and today picking up the pieces, that TB had gone ballistic, that we had to knock VAT on the head, and stay only with the review of charitable status. I got TB to call him to emphasise the point and clearly he did because when DB called me he said that when he said Happy New Year, TB just about grunted the reply. At TB's behest, David Hill called the BBC explicitly to disown the VAT policy just before the news. DB said to me later he was 'flabbergasted' when he heard it. Nick Jones said TB and GB had forced DB to backtrack against his will. I was feeding Grace at the time and dropped the spoon. TB said he'd be shocked if DB was still defending the policy. As well as this, we also had Martin O'Neill on *The World This Weekend* effectively rewriting energy policy. TB was now on overdrive. 'This just isn't a serious party. Until we face up to the scale of change needed to make it serious, we might as well not bother. We're finished.' I then had a rash of calls from press keen to follow up the backtrack line and I didn't disabuse them. GB called and said he was 'very, very angry'. He was fed up being portrayed as the cautious conservative one getting in the way of the great radicals Blunkett and Cook. 'Here we are, we've just won a great VAT campaign , we've got VAT likely to be an issue at the election, food and books and the rest, and thanks to Blunkett the issue is now LABOUR and VAT. It is a disaster.' I've rarely heard him as angry as he was today. 1. He should not be getting into tax at all. 2. This is just playing to the party. He said you have to put the fear of God into these people, or they will do it again and again. The story was raging until news that Fred West[1] was found dead in his cell. I called DB to warn him the papers would be grim, without confessing I had been responsible for some of the grimness. He said he was prepared to accept he made a mistake and we should learn from it and now get on with the job of sorting the policy.

Tuesday, January 3

First day back in office having had no rest at all. Jonathan Powell's first day so went to see him downstairs in the basement to give him my take on the various challenge areas: Clause 4, sorting education policy, the Big Guns [TB, JP, GB, RC] relationships, TB's informal style, short-termism, the relative inexperience of the office. Powell struck me as professional but I wondered if he quite knew what he was in for re the ways of the party. Jonathan was flabbergasted when Anji said TB still more or less defended Carole Caplin.

Wednesday, January 18

Big Guns at 4 and we tried out the idea of TB doing overarching campaign, Reaching out to Britain, with the three strands out to the other three – JP (attack plus party), GB (fairness/campaigns) and Robin (Clause 4). I could sense JP's antennae twitching straight away, particularly re RC doing the Clause 4 campaign strand. RC, so on board at the moment that it was hard to fathom, said it was important TB's campaigning was not restricted to Clause 4 and that he was happy to 'provide cover'. GB said repeatedly that he felt there was a danger in wrapping all the campaigns together, that it would all be seen in the Clause 4 context and we would lose out on the anti-government front. RC gave total support, JP was a bit narky, whereas GB fought hard to maintain an independent campaigns function. TB said he would think on. As they went into Shadow Cabinet, RC took me aside and said had I noticed how GB was distancing himself from TB, and

[1] Fred West, a builder, and his wife had been charged with multiple murders after the discovery of bodies at their home in Cromwell Street, Gloucester. West hanged himself in jail as he awaited trial.

dropped not very subtle hints about his self-belief regarding the Shadow Chancellor's job.

Thursday, January 19

A bit sparky between JP and Peter M, which started with JP complaining about documents not being properly circulated and ended with him accusing PM of being there virtually as GB's representative, which given PM and GB were barely speaking was a bit implausible. JP not happy the fairness campaign was being run as a separate entity, but it was clear GB wanted to keep it that way. Peter said there can be different tramways in a structured campaign and JP said 'Yes, and this is a different tram.' TB looked strained at the whole thing. Jonathan Powell was looking on pretty aghast. I felt I'd tried pretty much everything to work out a structure that could bind people in, but it was going to be a hard slog. Peter M mentioned that the *Sunday Times* were doing some big piece on the battle of the spin doctors which was going to compare me doing badly with Howell James [Major's political secretary; friend of Mandelson] doing well. I said don't look so pleased about it, and we both laughed.

Friday, January 20

Feeling knackered and pissed off. TB called me, Tim [Allan] and Peter H into his office and said we were going through a difficult phase, but what was clear was that when we cut through to the public it was as New Labour, and there could be no going back on modernisation. He said he was going to have to bite the bullet with JP and make clear GB would be in charge of election strategy. I sensed real trouble but he said people had to play to their strengths and GB was the best person for it, and JP should concentrate on membership, political education, motivating the party.

Sunday, January 22

TB still in his pyjamas. On good form though, and we all agreed had to push on social justice and upping the stakes re Clause 4/modernisation. Bill Morris went into overdrive on *Frost*, saying there was creeping intolerance in the party. Going through questions in the car on the way in I gave him some more difficult questions. 'Are you by instinct a tax cutter?' Mmm, what's the best way to answer that? He called GB, who said it's not a question of instincts. The Tories are by instincts tax cutters and they've raised them by 7p in the pound. Top answer. In the Green Room, I tapped him on the shoulder and said 'Are you really Labour?' And he said 'What are you asking me that for?' before realising I was back in prep mode. In fact both questions, or variants, came up. John Humphrys [broadcaster] and the editor came in and Humphrys made some crack about me being the real leader of the party. TB didn't seem too bothered, and did a brilliant interview. I was watching with some of the *On the Record* team. 'Vintage,' said John Rentoul [journalist]. 'He's a different class,' said one of the knob twiddlers. TB not that happy with his own performance but he was not always the best judge and was often too hard on himself when he was good, and not hard enough when he wasn't.

Thursday, February 2

In to finish work on the NI broadcast responding to Major. It seemed the only thing TB could usefully do was be supportive, look good and sound good and he did all that. He wrote in a section I didn't like about peace being a tender plant we had to cherish and the demons must not blight it. His big worry on N Ireland was that JM hadn't really put the argument, and he thought he should, like he was Major's pressman or something. Clause 4 discussion, with Pat [McFadden] and Jon [Cruddas] feeling we would probably just about win the Young Labour vote, so I started to build the press up to it, with hopefully TB swinging some votes on Friday, and JP doing the same on Saturday. So I started to build it as the first electoral test on Clause 4. Rosie [Winterton][1] told me JP not happy with that so I went to see him. He said it was a strategic decision and he should be involved in that, not just asked to turn out as a fucking performing seal at the weekend.

Friday, February 3

TB said he reckoned that in our own very different ways, GB, Peter M and I were geniuses, the best in our fields at what we did, and the key to his strategy. But it drove him mad that we couldn't get on. I said I can get on with anyone but it has to be based on an understanding of what we're all doing. He accepted of the three of us, I was trying hardest to make it work. But he said when GB was motivated, he had a superb strategic mind and he would be brilliant come the election. Peter was brilliant at developing medium-term media strategy, and spotting trends and analysing how to react, and you are second to none at shaping message and driving it through the media. Fine, I said, but we are all flawed in our own way. He said when he

[1] Rosie Winterton, adviser to John Prescott, latterly an MP.

was on the way up, the three of them could not have been closer. GB was strategy, he gave it intellectual context, PM was delivery. They were brilliant together. I said it doesn't mean you can recapture it now.

Saturday, February 4

Spent most of the day locked in the Bedford on the seafront in Brighton working on TB's speech. GB came on and said he felt we should put something on Europe in it, and not say Major was facing both ways but that he was becoming more anti-European to appease that faction. TB agreed but wanted to repeat that the rebels were in charge of the policy over Europe. We were busy trying to build up the importance of the vote and present that and the conference itself as evidence of the changing face of Labour. Anji and Peter came to my room in the hotel while I was working on the speech. I hate noise when I'm trying to write but PM was talking away, who is talking to the Sundays, have we got pictures sorted with the delegates? I was very short with him. He rightly said we should have cameras in for the Young Labour meeting and I said TB and JP decided yesterday not to and there was no point reopening it. He said we should not take decisions like that. I said well, often we do, and sometimes it's because you've been bending Tony's ear. He waltzed out.

I carried on working on the speech, and was doing good stuff once everyone had left. I was interrupted by a call from Tom Watson, Young Labour organiser, who said the Clause 4 vote was 4–1 in our favour. Amazing. I went through to tell TB, who was pleased. We agreed he should do a doorstep with some Young Labour activists at 2.30 but he wanted to speak to Peter before we did it. We called him up and immediately had an argument about clothes. I was strongly of the view he should wear a shirt and tie, if not a suit. PM thought he should wear cords and an open-necked shirt and TB and he were continuing this conversation as we were trying to finish the wretched speech. Even if TB had been the one wanting his advice, I felt it was another instance of Peter winding TB up over total trivia. The speech was a priority. His shirt wasn't. I could feel myself losing it, said he could not just swan in, upset what we were doing, then waltz out again. TB was like a dad trying to shush two squabbling brothers. 'Cut it out, you two, for heaven's sake.' Then we moved through to my room and PM was on the edge and eventually tipped over. He said I'm sick of being rubbished and undermined, I hate it and I want out. 'Get out then and we can finish the speech.' 'That's what you want, isn't it, me out of the whole operation.' I said I just wanted to be able to do a job. He started to leave then came back over, pushed at me, then threw a punch, then another. I grabbed his lapels to disable his arms and TB was by now moving in to separate us and PM just lunged at him, then looked back at me and shouted: 'I hate this. I'm going back to London.' He went off and he was still shouting at me from the corridor, saying I was undermining him and Tony and I'm thinking who the hell might be out there hearing or watching all this. We sent Anji to go and reason with him. I looked out of the window at the group of photographers waiting for our doorstep, and mused on what they'd just missed. TB clearly felt I'd been too heavy and had provoked him, and perhaps he had a point. He said I had to get along with him. Anji said she felt she had been too hard on him recently. I said she shouldn't give an inch. This thing had to be put on a proper professional footing in which we all knew what everyone else was doing.

We did the doorstep, which was fine, then TB saw Peter and said they were going to go for a walk. It was like a classic family explosion, grim and upsetting at the time, but afterwards leaving the air clearer and people getting on better. I talked to Anji after her session with Peter and she said the truth was we had to accommodate him because TB was clear he needed all the talents of all the people he rated and trusted. I said she should point out to Peter that I spent more time than anyone defending him but I felt that I could get more support in return. TB asked me to speak to him, because he was at the end of his tether. He said you are friends and you shouldn't fall out. I didn't want to fall out but I couldn't be doing with this. But I bleeped Peter and Anji to come up and we had a perfectly nice chat, calm after the storm. I think we both felt a little ashamed we let it get out of hand. Wrote this in the bath. What a bloody day.

Sunday, February 5

Speech went fine, especially good response on Clause 4/social justice. But the best bit was when he totally departed from script and did a big number on why people were in the Labour Party and how we'd only ever done anything worth doing by having the guts to get ourselves in order. What on paper was a good campaigning speech became in delivery a really powerful argument for change. We headed straight back and in the car TB spoke to Henry McLeish [Labour MP for Fife Central], whose wife was in Kirkcaldy hospital dying of cancer, which, as TB said afterwards, puts it all in perspective. We listened to Hezza on the way back, really fighting back for the pro-Europeans. TB was chatting to

Robin C and suggested getting a line running about the Tories' unfitness to govern. I then spoke to Robin, who said I trust you are impressed that I so readily obey the leader. TB also speaking to GB, then Paddy Ashdown [leader of the Lib Dems] about the Europe debate next week. The big story of the day was the Unionists talking about election footing and being nice re Labour. TB spoke to Mo to say we should be very statesmanlike about this, the line should be that peace in Northern Ireland was more important than any desire we might have for a snap election. The *Sunday Times* had a story that the luvvies were deserting us. It didn't strike me as all bad news. Indeed Alan Clark[1] called to say he was going to write a pro-Blair piece on the basis that if he was getting up some of the luvvies' noses he must be good news – what the hell is Emily's List?[2] he said. 'I've come to the view that your boy is a VERY serious figure. I loved his speech.' He said the Tories were sort of getting their act together but Europe was death for them.

Friday, February 10

TB felt the Clarke speech[3] put their divisions beyond repair. TB keen to do an interview. We went through the lines that the gulf was unbridgeable, they could not represent Britain's interests in Europe, and KC was closer to us than majority opinion in his own party. TB was on to me several times from Scotland saying 'defining moment'. Yes, Tony, defining moment. The story was given another lift when Portillo attacked Clarke.

Monday, February 13

At a rail meeting Michael Meacher put on his pained-vicar look. The vicar thing had come to me regularly with Michael ever since TB said he didn't know whether MM was religious or not but he always felt he'd make a better vicar than a politician. Later I bumped into Peter M and greeted him warmly. He said was that a greeting of

---

[1] Conservative MP for Plymouth Sutton, 1972–92; Kensington and Chelsea from 1997 until his death in 1999. Gained notoriety for, among other things, the publication of his diaries in 1993.

[2] A political network whose aim is the election of women members of the Labour party to political office.

[3] Kenneth Clarke's speech to the European Movement had been portrayed as a speech that would glue together the two wings of a divided Conservative Party. It set out new criteria – beyond those in the Maastricht Treaty – which would need to be met before Britain could consider joining a single currency, and consequently provoked outrage from Tory Eurosceptics.

friendship or hostility? I said neither, he should stop reading something into everything. He said he was right to read something into everything I did, that he knew he had to look after himself and he couldn't always rely on the people he thought he could rely on. He clearly had a lot of pent-up anger in there and now, very quietly, both of us anxious that the various people passing by shouldn't hear, it was coming out. He said that since I took the job, I had subjected him to 'unrelenting cruelty', undermining him, persecuting him. I said what on earth is the evidence for that? He said you underestimate the effect you have on people when you speak at meetings, when what you think is a humorous aside is taken by others as undermining. I said it's hardly unrelenting cruelty. He said it is if it happens again and again. I have pushed him over the top, he said. He said he had enough enemies without me joining them. I said do you sometimes think of yourself as your own enemy? He did one of his big 'Aaahs' – 'So that's where Tony gets it from, you're your own worst enemy.' I can hear him saying it. I said Peter, I have tried to involve you in a coherent structured way but I've made clear there cannot be two briefing operations. 'You have NOT tried,' he said, 'you have given me the cold shoulder.' He said he always imagined I would not want him around for the first six months, but the truth was we needed each other and we might as well accept that. I said I was happy to work with anyone but it had to be on a firm basis. I couldn't have him just winding up Tony without me knowing the basis. We should just be open with each other. He said sometimes he wished he wasn't involved at all, and I said it's in your blood, you couldn't live without it. OK, he said, at least I accept I'm schizophrenic about it. I saw TB later and said Peter had been a friend of mine for a long time. I liked him. I defended him when many others attacked him and I valued both his friendship and his advice and professionalism. I wanted to work with him but only if we agreed and knew the rules and all played by them.

Monday, February 20
Jack McConnell called late last night to say the *Mail* were carrying a big blast at TB from Cardinal [Thomas] Winning [RC Archbishop of Glasgow] about the party's refusal to have a pro-life stall at conference. The attack was pretty heavy and TB was livid. He said he couldn't stand it when churchmen played politics like this, especially as TB had been trying to sort this out. His first reaction was to demand a right to reply but he agreed to take soundings – did he really want a Blair v Catholic Church row raging throughout Scotland just as we

were coming up to Scottish Conference. Winning had been written up as a Labour supporter when he became Cardinal and Pat [McFadden] felt from the fact it was the *Mail*, and so heavy and personal, that he was probably reaching out for some right-wing support. Also, Winning probably harboured hopes of becoming the next Pope. Both TB's and my instincts were really to go for him. I called Tom Clarke [Labour MP with strong links to the Catholic Church] and he said while he understood why we were angry, he thought a public response would make matters worse and he would 'have a wee word' with the Cardinal. I was losing my temper at the way everyone had to pander and I said you could tell him he has actually made it harder to sort the issue.

Thursday, February 23

Called TB early on to be regaled with stories of last night's Eddie George [Governor of the Bank of England] dinner. EG had said to TB the City was not worried about a Labour government provided it was TB's government not Old Labour. JP then proceeded to play up to his Old Labour label, e.g. when house prices were being discussed, why do you people talk about housing in terms of house prices not home-lessness? TB said Robin C was not far behind. He laughed and said 'I'm sure I heard Eddie say get me the BA emergency desk as we left.' Pat suggested TB call Winning later, which he did from the car, to say that he would be asking the Scottish Executive to look again at the decision for next year. We ended up discussing what we would do if we lost the election and fell into one of our occasional near hysterical fits when TB and I prophesied how we would tour the world becoming a political freak show as we explained how we turned a 40-point poll lead into a Tory landslide victory.

Thursday, March 2

We spent a lot of the day doing Scottish media, which was always risky because when it came to the Scottish press, TB and I were both hopeless at hiding our irritation at them. There is a 'culture of griev-ance' element to all the media, but the Jocks have it with knobs on. I also think there is something in both me and TB they find irritating in that we are both Scottish in many ways, yet they view us as ultra English. He was born there and his dad is a Scot. My blood is 100 per cent Scots, I play the bagpipes, followed the football team to World Cups, yet to the Scots I was English. Normally TB and I would calm each other down with media irritants but when it comes to the Scots we are our own worst enemy, winding each other up by imitating them, often in their presence. When they came at him over Scotland being more Labour than England, and shouldn't that make him worried about Clause 4, he snapped back: why can't they do better in elections then? Before he did the *Scotsman*, I said he should try to hide his antagonism a bit. GB called and TB said to him he'd had a day full of whingeing Jock journos saying they wanted devolution and they wanted no tax and they wanted Scotland to get more money and they wanted to win the World Cup and why was I stopping them?

Sunday, March 5

Miliband came round to work on the Europe speech before we left for Tony's for a Clause 4 drafting session. We met Peter H on the doorstep at Richmond Crescent, and rang the doorbell to be met shortly afterwards by Cherie standing in the doorway saying it was Kathryn's birthday party. We went to the pub round the corner. It was shut so we wandered back to find TB trying to find us. With the entertainer in full swing, we trooped up to TB/CB's bedroom to work. TB lay on the bed, the rest of us, including Jonathan and Pat who came later, perched on tables or sat on the floor. Derry had done a very good 'rights and responsibilities' passage. I asked TB if he thought Sidney Webb[1] wrote the original lying on a bed with his acolytes on the floor and a racket from a children's party coming through the floor.

Wednesday, March 8

In early to write a new Clause 4 version based on TB's draft. Derry had sent him a new version, with the words FINAL DRAFT rather grandly, and inaccurately, stamped on top. Bruce said he didn't like it, nor the other one. He said show me the words a soft Tory couldn't back. DM said it didn't set out what we stood for. Peter H hated it. I said to TB that he must not fall into the trap of thinking that because something pissed off the party, that would automatically mean it appealed to the public. We could end up where all the public heard was that he had a problem with the party. DM said he couldn't understand why I was so relaxed. I said it was because this was all part of the TB testing to the limit process and I was sure we would get there in the end but it would be fraught and last minute and he would probably write it in the end himself and we would force it through.

---

[1] Socialist activist and author who in 1917–18 helped draft the Labour Party's new constitution, which included Clause 4.

Thursday, March 9

Mega busy. Took the boys to school and started to draw in thoughts from the Clause 4 draft but if anything the mood on it in the office was even more down than yesterday. JP was back and met TB to discuss the draft. We hadn't got the economic balance right, and there was not enough 'music' in it. Derry's draft was too lawyerish. He was also worried it would not get through conference even if it got through the NEC [National Executive Committee]. He suggested we use two full days to get it agreed by the NEC. JP was totally constructive which, given last week, was remarkable. TB spoke to Edmonds [of the GMB] to try to get him to move his members on the Scottish Executive and thankfully he did so. We won 18–12, the news reaching us as we arrived at Heathrow. As we got on the plane, it crossed my mind it was at exactly this time nine years ago that I got on a plane to a Scottish conference and ended the day in a funny farm.[1] I felt a horrible mix of flashback, déjà vu and foreboding. I talked to Pat and Anji about it while TB worked on our draft and Anji asked if I ever worried there was a fundamental flaw in my personality that came out then and could come out again. I said who knows but I don't think so. I think the reason for my current strength and resilience is that whatever is thrown at me, it can't compare with what I felt then, and if I ever got near to it, I'd bugger off.

Friday, March 10

Bad start to the day. Barely slept and room service came charging in at 6.10 with a pot of tea, turning the lights on while I was still asleep. I said what the fuck's going on? He said it was my wake-up call. I said I don't need the lights on. He said he was worried if it was dark he would trip and spill the tea all over the bed. Then he plonked the tea down, opened the curtains and walked out. TB said if we go down today, this is a very, very big blow. 'Ali, why do I do this job? It's bloody agony on days like this.' Even from backstage, without being able to see the audience, you could feel the tension in the hall. He got a fair enough welcome, got into his stride quickly. Brian Wilson's jokes went down a storm and he was away. But as before, the best bits came when he departed from the

---

[1] Nine years earlier, on a reporting assignment for the *Today* newspaper, then owned by Eddy Shah, Campbell had been at the Scottish Labour Party Conference while suffering the beginning of his nervous breakdown.

script, and he was strongest when he was making the link between winning the vote on Clause 4 and winning the trust of the people to win the election. I did the rounds to see what the media were doing with the speech, listened to some of the debate and then started to feel odd and my head was spinning, and I got that awful sense of people crowding in towards me. Déjà vu. A perfectly friendly reporter from Grampian TV asked me a question and I froze, then asked him to go to the press office and I headed in search of fresh air. Thankfully I bumped into David Hill and I felt a sense of reassurance and the moment passed. I went into the hall for the rest of the debate. Helen Liddell, Brian Wilson and John Reid were terrific. [George] Galloway [all four Labour MPs] was exactly what I expected – repulsive. After the debate I went and found a quiet spot in the dark backstage, still feeling anxious and trying to recover myself. Going bonkers at one Scottish Conference, fair enough, but two! I said to David Hill that I was feeling really tired and stressed out and could he take care of the briefing. I confided to TB later that I'd felt close to collapse at one point. 'What, psychologically?' he said. 'More physically but the head was playing tricks.' The pressure had been intense but as nothing to what we'd face in an election campaign. There was still a problem with the computer and we finally got the result as we left for the airport. TB did a pooled doorstep then we headed off, with me still feeling weird. TB was in his usual calm after the storm mode. We listened to the chaotic results announcement on the radio, where Kenny Macintyre [BBC Scotland reporter] said it had been a 'wee stooshie' ['little bit of trouble']. We arrived at the airport, where they had been holding the plane for us, but by the time we got onto the tarmac the doors were closed, and we'd missed it. It meant diverting to Glasgow, which was another blow to the psyche as the airport there played a part in my breakdown.

Sunday, March 12

JP and Rosie came over for a cup of tea at 3.30 and we talked over general principles re Clause 4. JP said he would have to have a clear commitment to full employment and public ownership. Fiona came back and JP was waxing lyrical about her fruit cake. Then, JP having just been raving on about 'the beautiful people', the doorbell rang and it was Tessa [Jowell, Labour MP for Dulwich] coming round with some apples from her garden in Warwickshire. She obviously thought JP was here socially, not realising she'd come in at quite a difficult point in quite an important meeting, when I was trying to persuade JP we didn't need the actual words 'full employment' in the final version, and she was telling us some long complicated story about a meeting with Diane Abbott [Labour MP]. As she left he said: 'Who brings the food parcels tomorrow – Harriet?' To TB's. JP said the whole exercise had done Labour a lot of good. He said let's go through the areas we are likely to agree and leave the economic section to the end. I was pleased that we took out 'any other organisations' in the trade union section and that we injected 'public services essential to the public good', which was better than 'services on which the public depend'. They chatted away for four hours without much real disagreement. TB said you can't believe how hard I've sweated on this, but I could tell he was happy with it at last.

Tuesday, March 14

JP said TB had to know he would never let his ego get in the way of the best interests of the party. He would always argue privately and then get on with the job. But he would not have himself, or the position of deputy leader, undermined. At the moment his authority WAS undermined because Walworth Rd and others were conscious of different power bases. Earlier I'd run into GB in the corridor and he cut me dead, which surprised me. I found out why from TB, who said GB had asked why I was briefing against him. I hadn't, but in his eyes me emphasising that JP's leadership role and Robin C's conversion had been pivotal to winning the vote was tantamount to briefing against him. I was really pissed off he'd gone to Tony like that and accused me of briefing against him. I called him and said 'I hear you think I've been briefing against you. That is completely untrue, and unfair.' 'OK, I accept your denial.' I said 'You have to believe it or we have a problem.' He said he would call me back. Charlie Whelan came over. I said this was a ridiculous situation. If GB had a problem, he should raise it with me himself. I did not brief against him. I wrote GB a note, asking him to accept my assurance and saying that if he ever thought I did that, he should raise it with me direct. He called later and suggested we meet.

Thursday, March 16

I went to GB's office for the meeting I'd been trying to have since he told TB I had been briefing against him. I asked him to accept I didn't brief against him. He said nobody in his office briefed his Inverness speech as wooing the unions, and that even if I didn't brief against him, I didn't brief FOR him and my job was to ensure there was nothing between him and TB. On the current difficulties, he said he had never asked for the campaigns job, he had enough to do trying to sort economic policy, and he had no desire to fight with JP. He was not in the business of divide and rule, as Robin was. He just wanted to get on with the job of winning. He said I know why you have to talk up JP, but it's unfair the way you write me out of the script.

Saturday, March 25

Alan Clark called and when Fiona answered, Alan said 'Fiona, hi, it's Tony, is Ali there?' and for a moment she fell for it. Alan said they were going to go for the 'Tory Tony' tag. I said fine, all your voters will hear out of that is that he must have changed the Labour Party if they're calling him a Tory. It's what we call a strategic conundrum, I said. Mmmm, he said, maybe we're fucked.

Monday, March 27

TB still very 'snappy'. We were still not operating a proper strategy structure, so that strategy was still pretty much TB/AC hand to mouth. Jonathan came to see me to say TB had bawled him out over the lack of good work being done on Europe. Today TB was just raging against one thing after another. I said I think it's his way of getting us to raise our game. Pretty man management it ain't, but he'll be all nice again in a day or two. TB called Peter M from the car and whinged on at him as well. I took the phone and finally got TB to chill out a bit as Peter and I dreamed up the kind of news bulletins that TB might accept as a good job well done: 1. The Queen hails Blair as the best leader in history. 2. Thatcher urges Major to make way for Blair without an election. 3. United Nations pass a resolution saying Blair should be PM now. 4. The BBC can exclusively report another fantastic policy idea from Blair.

Arrived in Glasgow. We drove over to Edinburgh and had dinner with his old school friend Nick Ryden. TB told the hilarious story of when he and GB met in Nick's house for one of the big discussions post John Smith's death. Nick left them to it and they went round and round in circles. TB was clear he should stand because he felt that was the best chance for the party, but GB was not convinced. At one point, GB went to the toilet. Minutes passed and TB was sitting twiddling his thumbs and even wondered if GB had done a runner. Eventually the phone went. TB left it, so then the answering machine kicked in and GB's disembodied voice came on: 'Tony. It's Gordon. I'm locked in the toilet.' They both ended up laughing about it. TB went upstairs and said 'You're staying in there till you agree.'

Tuesday, March 28

Don Macintyre [political journalist and later biographer of Mandelson] said the Tories had decided to make me an issue, as it played into their TB strategy, and I was a 'marked man'. TB said this was about trying to destabilise me, and portray him as my puppet. I wondered whether they thought they had something on me, possibly more stuff about my breakdown, and they were building me up so the papers could then tear me down. It was certainly odd hearing Major talk about me in the Commons on ITN. I remembered what Alan Clark said to me the last time we had lunch: the Tories are 'obsessed' with you, because they think their weakness is they haven't got someone like you. He said it was a way of them avoiding confronting their far deeper problems.

Saturday, April 1

Philip [Gould] and Gail [Rebuck]'s party. CB made a straight beeline for Fiona and complained that I was running their lives, making TB do far too much, and preventing him from being a normal person living a normal life. Fiona, who was due to have lunch with her on Friday anyway, said she stood up for me as best she could but she was pretty heavy. She said TB bothered me far more than I bothered him. Today alone she had been there on five occasions when TB called me, and often it was to have the same conversation we had already had.

Sunday, April 23

TB doing *World This Weekend* so over to Richmond Crescent to prepare for that. I had a perfectly nice and civilised chat with Cherie, in which we both lamented how much of our time we spent having to talk to TB in his underwear.

Tuesday, April 25

TB came back from CB's QC ceremony for PMQs. I had worked out a line of attack which TB improved by watching the news for once and said why aren't the interviewers asking if the Tory rebels have given a guarantee that they will support the government in future votes on Europe. That became the question and then we rehearsed a line to use if Major came back at him with our own divisions – I lead my party, he follows his – which turned out to be the biggest blow TB had yet landed at PMQs, which produced a massive cheer on our side and a look of real pain on theirs. The PMQs hit was gigantic, and with the GMB coming on board re Clause 4, it was a good day.

Wednesday, April 26

TB came back from the NEC in a fairly typical post-NEC mood, and I briefed him on the focus groups. I said there were three main problems: 1. Major still had the potential to become popular again. 2. TB's appeal was not yet clear and too many people saw him as shallow, and 3. There was a sense of the economy improving and we did not have a clear economic message. TB said he was confident his own position would strengthen with exposure, but he was concerned re economic message.

Friday, April 28

A typical day of chaos and over-activity with the Clause 4 vote looming. We went through the usual black humour phase predicting TB's downfall within 24 hours and imagining all the various reshuffle plans of the various contenders. Tom Sawyer called to say there could be a messy start to the Conference tomorrow because [Arthur] Scargill[1] was calling for a court to review whether the Conference was constitutional.

Saturday, April 29

Round to TB's at 8, with Liz [Lloyd] already there. We made relatively few changes, and no major ones. TB hyper again. Got to the office and Jonathan and David M both felt the speech ending didn't work, which had also been worrying TB and me. He asked me to have another go. I said why don't you stand up and say: 'Now, I'd like to turn to the party's name . . .' I meant it as a joke but I could see he was tempted – as a joke. Pat called to say the T & G [TGWU] were joining Unison in opposing us. This produced the inevitable tirade. 'These people are criminally stupid. They simply do not care if we win or lose.' In the short car ride over to the conference (at Methodist Central Hall), TB barely spoke. He had his speech on his lap. He was staring out of the window but taking nothing in, occasionally nodding forward to underline to himself a line from the speech running through his head. This was the moment I knew today would go well. He was withdrawing completely into himself, psyching up to deliver. The speech was good but if he could add 20 per cent in the delivery, we'd have a really good day. We were taken to a little private room, where he was pacing up and down, and nodding to himself every few moments, then firing off questions to me which

---

[1] President of the National Union of Mineworkers from 1982. Founded the Socialist Labour Party in 1996.

April '95: Chaos before Clause 4 vote

didn't really matter, and I'm not sure he even listened to the answers. This was all part of the psyching-up process, running-down time, getting his mind in the zone he wanted it. We made a couple of last-minute changes before checking the script on the autocue. We marked up on his own script the lines that really needed to breathe, then Jackie Stacey [Labour Party staff] led him up to the entrance to the stage. 'Good luck,' I said. 'Go for it.' He smiled and nodded and walked onto the platform. Scargill was hissed as he tried out his legal challenge idea. I watched from the front, sitting next to Bevins, and Skinner who had a new jacket for the day. The plan after the result was for TB to make a short unscheduled speech and he and I went to the toilet at the back to get away from all the fussing and we went over a few lines. We agreed he could get away with the crack about the name of the party. He was quite emotional. He'd always believed that doing this would be an important precondition winning over the kind of people whose support we needed, and the party had responded really well, despite all the dire warnings. He was pumped up and proud, he'd done really well and I said so, and it was bizarre, lots of noise outside, and the two of us hiding away in a grotty undecorated toilet and he says to me: 'I think we're on our way.' Margaret McDonagh got us out to give us the final result and the relief oozed out of him. Some twat with a Trot poster came up to me on the way in and yelled 'Butcher! Traitor!' at me. I stopped and mustered as much visual contempt as I could, then assured him that if we win the general election then don't worry, thanks to wankers like him, there will always be another Tory government along afterwards. These people make me vomit. JP's speech was brilliant, saying how TB's courage and foresight made it possible and it was a great day for the party. Afterwards he took TB to one side, said well done, and now can we have a period of relative calm?

Monday, May 1

Clare Short [Labour frontbencher] called in her usual fount of all wisdom way and said there was a 'malfunction' around TB and the PLP [Parliamentary Labour Party] and the unions were up in arms. She was due to have dinner with TB so I suggested we had lunch and we met at Rodin's. She said she liked TB but trust was running out. People didn't believe he wasn't responsible for a lot of the briefing that went on, there were too many voices around him. She felt Peter M could be an adviser who did not brief the press or he could appear on TV but he couldn't do both. She said there was a feeling that nobody round TB really understood the party, that Jonathan was nice but ineffective. She thought GB was tortured and Robin was a clever egomaniac. I wondered if she ever applied to herself the kind of rigorous analysis she'd subjected others to. Rodney Bickerstaffe [general secretary of Unison] came round for another general whinge. He said TB had to realise he would need the unions at a later stage. I reported back to TB who said they can just fuck off. We will never get elected if every little change produces this kind of nonsense. I said we just had to be careful that division and disarray did not become our main backdrop. He said JP has to understand it could get worse not better but we have set a course and we have to keep our nerve. I bumped into Nick Soames [Conservative MP for Mid-Sussex], who said that his lot had had it. Philip said however bad it felt on the inside, he had watched the news bulletins and from the outside it looked fine.

Wednesday, May 3

Robin C was probing about Peter M and if it was true that 'Bobby' was out of favour. TB put on a big grin and said no. RC looked disappointed. 'I see the *Standard* called him the most hated man in the Labour Party,' said Robin. 'Not by the leader and his staff,' I said, and he smiled. On the unions, TB said if he didn't do anything that someone found difficult, he would end up doing nothing. 'I don't think anyone could accuse you of doing nothing, Tony,' said Robin. 'Though I think we might all benefit from a period of calm.' Despite myself, I couldn't help liking Robin. I liked his speaking style too, his little clipped comments and his perfectly formed sentences that were delivered as if he were in a play, and he was projecting his voice to the back of the theatre. And he was funny and, for the most part, good-humoured, if always with an eye on the main chance.

Thursday, May 4

Local elections. Terry picked me up to go to collect TB/CB to go to Walworth Rd for the results coming in. They were at a dinner in Hyde Park Gardens that had been organised for them to meet Princess Diana. I rang the bell and said could you tell Mr Blair his car is here. I went back to the car and the next thing TB is tapping at the car window and he says: 'Someone wants to meet you.' I get out and she's walking towards me, and she says: 'There he is, can I come over and say hello,' and then she's standing there, absolutely, spellbindingly, drop-dead gorgeous, in a way that the millions of photos didn't quite get it. She said hello, held out her hand and said she was really pleased to meet me, so I mumbled something back about me being more pleased and how I didn't expect when I left the house tonight that I'd end up standing in the middle of the road talking to her. 'It would make a very funny picture if there were any paparazzi in those trees,' she said. TB was standing back and Cherie was looking impatient and I was just enjoying flirting with her. She said she'd told TB she'd wanted to meet the man who protected him because she'd heard so much about me. I asked if he had behaved well and she said yes, very well. I said in that case I think you should come with us to Walworth Road and create an almighty sensation. 'I just might,' she said. There was something about her eyes that went beyond radiance. They locked on to you and were utterly mesmeric. She had perfect skin and her whole face lit up when she spoke and there were moments when I had to fight to hear the words because I'm just lost in the beauty. And I'm thinking how could I have written all those vile things about her. 'Anyway,' she said, 'I mustn't hold you back any longer,' and there's me thinking I would happily be held back for a long time to come. We shook hands again, she said goodbye to Tony and Cherie, we watched her walk back to the house, and off we went. TB groaned loudly and said he couldn't believe it. 'We'd barely started the conversation and she says "What's Alastair Campbell really like?" And she wants to know what you do for me, and how it all works and then she says she'd like to meet you, and how she'd feel a lot happier if she had a press officer as good as you, and all this.' Terry was laughing his head off, I was milking it for all it was worth, and telling TB he really shouldn't feel jealous, she probably quite liked him too, and CB was saying she was probably just being polite. I said I don't think politeness ever extended to feeling she had to walk out in the cold to say goodbye to her guest's staff. I was of course unbearable at Walworth Rd, constantly winding up TB and saying to the rest of the office he was a bit bruised because Diana had just used him as a means of getting to me. Combined with the brilliant results that were coming in, it all made for a pretty extraordinary evening.

Friday, May 5

Up at 6 and round to TB's. Everyone was saying how extraordinary the results were but TB was straight away looking for the downside. Why was turnout so low? What if they dump Major and go for Hezza, would it give them a lift? In the car to the *Today* programme we were regaling each other re Diana. He said he found her extraordinarily political, not in the party sense, but her awareness and her ability to communicate without always being totally clear. I spent much of the day winding him up about her desire to meet me. He said her interest in me was because she was interested in media manipulation. No need to be jealous, I said. His interviews were strong. I bumped into Hanley. 'Still spraying on the image, are you?' he said. 'I think you'll find there's more to him than that,' I said.

Tuesday, May 9
TB, PM, PG, DM, SM, JoP[owell], AH, AC, meeting. The key, we agreed, was an economic message which just wasn't coming together. Also there was a sense in too many of the Shadow ministers almost that policy could wait till closer to the manifesto. But TB was pushing for the policy debate to be quickened. We were at one in saying that it was not enough to say the Tories were useless and that TB was an attractive new leader. There had to be an alternative policy agenda that the public understood and there had to be before anything else an understanding that we would be fine on the economy. JP was doing PMQs so I went up to see him. He was in what I called his short sleeves union rebel shirt, which he always wore when he was just in the office. He was doing health but said 'I can't believe politics is reduced to this, fucking words mumbo-jumbo.' He said he'd been right not to ask a question for 25 years. He went over it again and again, worrying about the emphasis, using his black felt pen to underline where he needed to stress a word. And on it went till he was reasonably happy, then he would go into the little room in the corner, get a long-sleeved shirt and tie and get changed. I'd noticed it was a habit he, TB and I all shared – never bothering who was around when changing clothes.

Friday, May 12
TB and I discussed the need for a proper plan and strategy re the Bank of England. He was sure independence was the answer.

Saturday, May 13
Neil and Glenys, the Stotts and the Braggs were due for dinner, but Neil and Glenys called off in the afternoon. I gave Alan Clark a call on the off chance. The Braggs arrived and Melvyn [writer and broadcaster] was absolutely horrified. He said he loathed Alan C. Alan and Jane arrived in one of his Bentleys, which could barely squeeze through the two lines of parked cars outside. They came to the door, Alan leaving the car parked outside with the engine running and he says: 'Where does a chap park his charabanc round these parts?' He was wearing tight beige trousers the likes of which I don't think the street

had ever seen. I said I wouldn't leave the keys in the car. At one point Fiona mentioned there was a bit of crab in the starter and he went into major melodrama, rushing to the door shouting 'Crab, crab, I can't eat crab,' then throwing up very loudly in the front garden.

Monday, May 15
Meeting on the minimum wage. TB was determined to make the unions understand that he did not operate on the basis of them asking for something and us agreeing to something just short of it. He wanted to have the argument on the basis of it being a real argument about the rights and wrongs.

Wednesday, May 24
Harold Wilson died. I called TB to discuss what to say and who to put up. We agreed he and JP should do the bulk of interviews. I called Joe Haines who was clearly moved and had some good thoughts. He and Harold had never struck me as being close in the later years, obviously in part because of his illness, but even when Joe talked about the worse side of Harold, there was always a fondness and respect there. My last vivid memory was at a service for Sean Hughes [Labour MP for Knowsley South, died 1990] when it was obvious to me that Wilson was moving in and out of coherence. One moment he was saying something nice about Sean, the next he was describing recent meetings with world leaders that you knew hadn't taken place. Physically too he was weakened and now he was dead. During the day TB was developing his argument re Wilson into one about the nature of the party – that Wilson had wanted to do more but had been restricted by the party. It was a way both of playing down the direct comparisons between them but also underlining the nature of change. There is something about the media coverage of deaths now that is upsetting. There may be some sincerity in the attempts to sound upset and moved, but beneath the surface you know they're all just paddling to churn out as much as they can on the latest rolling news sponge. Then life goes on, as it did for us, with the day an odd mix of tributes and focusing on the by-election and women-only short lists. Joe provided an excellent line re Chatham. He said Wilson was once making a speech in the docks there and paid a great tribute to the navy. 'Why do I say that?' he said, at which point someone shouted out 'Because you're in Chatham.' It didn't take long for the black humour to follow. We imagined the kind of obits TB would get if he

ever made it to Number 10. Tim [Allan] suggested we put out words from TB saying 'I saw Harold last week and he seemed fine but then as he knew better than anyone, a week is a long time in politics.'

Thursday, May 25

A whole series of policy meetings which were taking far more of the diary post-Clause 4. On health, Robin agreed that the document was not good enough and was persuaded we should try to get Margaret [Beckett] only to send the executive summary to the National Policy Forum [NPF]. He said it was obsessed with structures not patients, and the overall message wasn't clear. MB came in and was very dogged. She was adamant she wanted to present the whole document and nobody could shift her. She felt we gained nothing from delay. I said I feared it would be seen as old Labour. TB was worried about the trusts not being allowed to own the properties on which they operated. 'At least we would be renationalising the NHS,' she said, referring back to a TB line. There was something very impressive about MB when she was digging in. She was often more than willing to be accommodating and had no hang-ups about 'the Leader's office', like some of them. But when she was settled on something, she listened politely, fiddled with her little bunch of pens that she kept wrapped in a rubber band, and then said no. So she wore us down, which meant we risked presenting a dog's dinner to the NPF. Meacher came in to push for a transport policy document. At the end of the meeting I showed him *Taxi Trade Times*, which had a front-page report slagging us off over his idea that black cabs be treated the same as minicabs. TB said he should review it and err on the side of the black cabs.

Saturday, May 27

Andy Grice called from the *S Times* to say Thatcher had given an interview and said some very flattering things about TB and did I have anything to say? I gave a very anodyne response, which TB wanted me to revise after I spoke to him, and make it less critical of Thatcher. The only scoop of the day was Thatcher praises Blair, which ran on the later broadcasts. Needless to say, he didn't mind that at all.

Tuesday, May 30

TB was really troubled re Bosnia. 'This is the mother of all nightmares. I was reading all the stuff till late and I can't tell you what a nightmare it is.' He called Derry from the car, who urged him not to think that he, as Leader of the Opposition, should have all the answers.

May '95: The impressive Margaret Beckett

All he could do was signal broad support for the government and display his understanding of the issues. Oddly, most of the papers appeared to support withdrawal of UK troops, and Derry agreed we should oppose that strongly. I felt confident he would do well because he was well into his preferred mode of working now. He'd eaten all the facts. He'd analysed the big picture and the politics and now he would sit with a blank piece of paper and hone the argument. As Jonathan [Powell] and I agreed, he could be a total pain when he was doing this, and we were there to have the same conversations with him, again and again until he was happy with the argument. Pain or not, it was the process and provided it led to a good end product, it was worth it.

Sunday, June 4

Really quiet day. Anji called to say that Peter Stothard [editor of *The Times*] had called Jonathan to ask if TB would go to Australia to speak to all the Murdoch editors and hierarchy in mid-July. TB was keen but she and Jonathan thought it might be better to organise around it so that he was visiting other countries too. My immediate reaction was that I liked the boldness of it, which might be diluted if we tried to make out he just happened to be in the region and hey he was popping in to the Murdoch annual bash. There would obviously be a lot of media interest in the Murdoch angle and there would be some rumbling in the party but for all sorts of reasons it was quite an attractive proposition, and I'm not sure it isn't better just to say up-front – Murdoch has asked him to speak to all his editors and top executives and he's accepted, and then turn it into a major speech platform.

Tuesday, June 6

I spoke to TB as he headed for the Scillies for Wilson's funeral with Jim Callaghan and Barbara Castle [former Labour Cabinet minister]. He said they had a wonderful heated argument about devaluation. It was as if they were making the decision today. Bruce [Grocott] came to see me to say he was aghast that TB was thinking of traipsing halfway round the world to speak to Murdoch's lot. He thought the party would absolutely hate it.

Wednesday, June 7

TB was in angry mood because of a letter he had received from Jack Straw written on behalf of JS, Robin C, Frank Dobson and Chris Smith asking to meet him as a group on economic policy. 'This will be Robin's idea and he'll have put Jack up to it and I'm not interested in seeing them as a group.' He said it was like the Wilson era, the belief that all politics was plots and cabals, he just wasn't going to do it. He'd met Lord Tonypandy [former Labour MP and Speaker of the House of Commons, George Thomas] at Harold's funeral and asked if they really were all plotting the whole time as the books suggested. 'All the time.'

Thursday, June 15

Today was the day TB and I both independently reached the settled view that Major was finished. But the rowing with Fiona was getting both of us down and I was trying to work out ways of cutting the workload. But it felt impossible. I had so much on today I couldn't even find time to get up to the gallery and talk to the press. Had a chat with Bruce, who was laying it on thick re TB and the PLP. He said a lot of them didn't like him, and they didn't like a lot that appeared in the papers about him. We had a bit of an up-and-downer. I said they had to be persuaded that one of the main reasons they were likely to keep their jobs, and some of them likely to be government ministers, was because of TB. He agreed but said good times in politics are always followed by bad and when you get the bad times you need friends and TB is not doing enough to make them. I said it was also important that they respected him and they would respect him less if they thought all he was doing was pandering to them. The reason he is where he is and the reason we are doing as well as we are is because he's different, he's not out of the mould, and I think we need to see that as an advantage. TB said we needed to think through how we would deal with Heseltine. He said Hezza would give them energy and purpose and he had 'clanking great balls' that would allow him to impress the public even if they thought he was a bit off the wall. He was in no doubt Hezza would be bad news for us and wanted me to stoke up the leadership row while at the same time giving the sense we wanted Major dumped. BLAIR HAZZA HEZZA SPAZZA, I said, and he laughed, but Heseltine was clearly on his mind more than he'd thus far let on.

Saturday, June 17

Tory turmoil still rampant in the press. I was really depressed, not just fed up, but the full-blown stomach empty but for a knot in the middle, and the mind feeling numb and unable to get out of first gear. I took the boys to football and got through that OK, but I was at a loss how to improve things with Fiona. She said the job had totally taken over our lives and she needed more help in adapting to that. I tried to say I did my best but in truth I'd just taken it for granted. She said I didn't listen to anyone now. I just did what I thought I had to do. I was worried about it all enough to talk to Peter M, who said I should involve her more. Peter said I had to accept that TB relied on me for judgement and for delivery and that dependence would grow as the pressure mounted. It was important Fiona understood that, but for her to do so she had to feel more involved.

Monday, June 19

I had a session with TB to say that I really needed to try to spend less time in the office because things between me and Fiona weren't great at the moment. He said he totally understood – Cherie complained that he only ever came alive when he was talking to me, Peter or GB, that he used up all his emotional energy in the job and she needed support and he was too drained out to give it. He said though he always knew the job would be tough he had never really realised just how totally absorbing it would be, and just how much focus and effort it required the whole time. He said he didn't know what he would do if I wasn't there, and that I had exceeded his wildest imagination about what I would be able to do for him. He felt that PM, Anji and I were the three people he would regard as indispensable but his advice was to try to get home more and involve Fiona more. He wanted to be able to do something for her. But he accepted he was the person who put me under the most pressure – 'apart from yourself,' he added. We discussed the Murdoch trip and agreed it was just about OK though I had slightly shifted to Bruce's view that the party would hate the sight of him traipsing round the world to see Murdoch.

Thursday, June 22

The big excitement after PMQs was that Major was planning to do a press conference in the Number 10 garden. Nobody seemed to know for sure what it was about. He came down and announced he was planning to quit as party leader and call a leadership election. On one level, it was bold. But the fact that he was driven to it just underlined how pathetic he had become and how weakened he now was. It caused a bit of panic at our end. TB was calm and measured and getting irritated at all the chatter. It was a classic time for calm heads. Anji and I managed to ease out everyone apart from JP and GB, who was terrific. He and I sat there rattling out lines at each other and then working out who was best to deploy them. It was basically a desperate move from a weak leader of a disintegrating government.

GB agreed to do the immediate stuff then TB did a round of excellent interviews at Millbank. The media there were in full frenzy mode and we kept reminding ourselves we had to stay calm, measured and talk to the public not the press. There was a sense of real turmoil at Millbank and some of the Tories doing interviews looked close to hyperventilation. Teddy Taylor, Tony Marlow and Teresa Gorman [right-wing, anti-Europe Conservative MPs] were all straight on the case. TB said as we went from one studio to another: 'This is going to unravel for him.' He hammered the main lines of division, lack of direction, the sense of disintegration. Back to the office and GB said we should be saying the challenge for Major is whether he had a radical manifesto for change. TB did that in the next batch of interviews. There was a real sense of excitement around the place but I'm glad to say I felt no sense of the mad adrenalin surge that seemed to be hitting some of the others. I'd been saying to myself for ages that it was important never to lose sight of the real audience, the public, who would not be sharing the sense of mania that was sweeping Westminster. To us, this was just another opportunity to get TB out there showing he was calm, reasonable, moderate and a real alternative to the weak and useless Prime Minister we currently had. 'These are interesting times,' he said. 'This next period will be crucial.' He felt JM might get a short-term lift but that long term he was finished and today was bad for him. He said the ideal for us would now be a contest with bruises which JM survives. He called me again later, said it was a good day for us. I could tell he felt it was bit between teeth time and I felt exactly the same.

Friday, June 23

TB was as ever trying to work out how Major could turn things to his advantage. One minute he was convinced JM was finished, the next that this could be the making of him and the route to recovery. I said I thought there was a real whiff of decay around Major now, and his party just wasn't serious enough. They hated each other more than they hated us, like Labour in the past. Major's focus was now on party not country. We met a rather sheepish and worried-looking Michael Howard [Conservative Home Secretary] on the way into the *Today* studio. Even he was finding it hard to disguise how it felt today. News came through of the T & G leadership result – a win for Bill Morris. The truth was Jack Dromey [TGWU official, and husband of Harriet Harman] just wasn't a high-calibre candidate so another low-calibre candidate got back. I was briefing that our best outcome was JM victorious but bruised, second best was Hezza because the public didn't trust him and he was a divisive figure in the Tory Party, and always would be. On the way down it became obvious Redwood[1] wasn't going to support him. He hasn't planned this, said TB. It is disintegration not strategy.

Saturday, June 24

I watched the first half of the Rugby World Cup Final but then got a call to go to TB's. He was in a state of some agitation. He said he'd barely slept at all and it was the sense of uncertainty and the feeling for the first time since he became leader that someone else had the initiative. He was sure Hezza was on the march and that he would be a more difficult opponent. Equally if Major survived he could remake himself on the back of this, and that would make him a more difficult opponent. I said nobody said it was going to be easy. He said I know but I really want to think through how to deal with this. The picture is changing and we have to change it on our terms. On the way to the airport he got a call from Derry, who was really angry that TB was thinking of cancelling dinner with him, Roy Jenkins, the Master of the Rolls [Sir Thomas Bingham] and the Lord Chancellor's private secretary to attend a conference chaired by 'Mister Rupert Murdoch'. In fact the Murdoch trip was looking iffy again because of the Tory scene.

Sunday, June 25

Summit, Paris. Went for a walk round the back streets with TB. He was in constant fret mode as well as circular conversation at the moment. I suppose the two are linked. 'Can we really beat Hezza?' he asked. 'Of course we can.' 'It'll be difficult.' 'So what?' 'I suppose Major might survive but I think it's wishful thinking really.' 'It is the party that's fucked, and Major is not the great problem.' 'I suppose so.' Then he was back onto what a boost JM could get out of it. He was able to pull himself out of his gloom long enough to do an OK interview with Adam Boulton [Sky News political editor], then we went for another walk and he was back with the same bloody questions again, trying to get the measure of the three names in the frame. I said he was more than a match for any of them and there was a huge gulf between what Westminster thought of Hezza and Portillo, and what the public thought. He said he hated the uncertainty. JP spoke later, and was going hell for leather, causing real problems for the interpreters. At one point you could see half the people in the

---

[1] John Redwood, Conservative MP for Wokingham from 1987; Secretary of State for Wales, 1992–95. Stood against Major for Tory leadership, and lost.

room staring into the interpreters' booths and watching them trying to make sense of it. One of them told us later that she just gave up, it was hopeless. She thought she'd made sense of the first half of a sentence and then he was off into another one. TB said his brother Bill had said he reckoned JM would survive and stay to the election. He'd obviously called Bill over the weekend. He always did when he was worried. He was very lucky to have an older brother who was clever, nice, totally supportive and who had no interest whatever in a public profile and so gave him genuine solid advice and judgement.

Wednesday, June 28

Portillo's treachery was running quite big, with lots of interest in his getting new offices for a campaign HQ. Not much out of PMQs but I scripted a nice line about Redwood's prime ministerial spaceship which would whizz people to Planet Portillo. TB had accepted that Major was the least divisive of the various figures in the frame, that Portillo would split them badly, so would Hezza, but Hezza would cheer them up because he would attack us better than the rest put together.

Thursday, June 29

Complained to Tony Hall [director of BBC News] about the way the BBC were not challenging the false claims the Tories were making about us. My worry was that if this became a real contest, the airwaves would be filled with candidates and their supporters vying with each other to see who could attack us the best, because that is what their party was looking for. They were getting away with murder at the moment and all the BBC can say is why are you complaining, this story is a disaster for them. That is not the point, I told Hall. They cannot just tell lies about us and have nobody challenge it. Meanwhile Redwood was dive-bombing and being exposed as a lightweight. Margaret B and her entourage came over to prepare for her press conference with TB. There was something wonderfully calm and calming about Margaret. TB was moving into his mildly hyper mode that he sometimes gets pre-media events, while she just sat there, took out her compact mirror and touched up her make-up. When she took notes out came the bundle of pens and pencils bound in a rubber band, very schooly but something endearing about it, I don't know what. They ran over the tricky questions, which were all in the area of whether we saw it as Old/New, were we scrapping the market mechanisms, etc. It went fine and they both did well though

I could see TB, like me, could barely take his eyes off a foreign journalist we'd never seen before who parked herself in one of the front rows. 'Did you see that woman?' he said when he came back. 'I can't imagine which one you mean,' I said. As we raved on, he noticed Margaret nearby, listening. 'Oh sorry, Margaret,' he said, with his schoolboy caught by teacher look. 'No, not at all,' she said. 'I quite understand.' We prepared for PMQs out on the terrace, which was searingly hot. TB has a capacity to endure any temperature, loves the sun, held his face up to it almost as if he was in conversation with it, while the rest of us were longing to go inside to cool down. TB was going on Europe/divisions but Major was at his best ever. Really strong. I bumped into Major as he was coming out of the office. There is always a chill. As Tories kept telling me, he loathed me, and could never understand how I had helped build him up when he was advancing through the Cabinet, and then tore into him once he made it to the top. For my part, I couldn't understand why he couldn't understand it, given I never hid my politics. He stopped for a moment, said hello, and I said 'Well done. I don't think there's much doubt about who got the better of today.' 'Thank you.' TB said: 'I don't know what he had for breakfast but I'd like some of it next time.' I bumped into Portillo who had a face like thunder. 'I thought your boss was brilliant today, didn't you?' I said. 'Indeed,' he said and stomped off with that rather painted smile of his.

Home to get Fiona then we went for dinner at TB's, with Pete and Helen [Thompson, personal friends of TB], Charlie and Marianna [Falconer], Ros the nanny and her mum. Charlie is a total star. He is a total mess, with his clothes all over the shop, his shirt covered in ink, spilling and knocking things over, but he is hilariously funny and incredibly nice. He also has a fierce intelligence. He went one by one through the Shadow Cabinet and had us falling off chairs with his analysis. But he also gave TB a real grilling, and just didn't let go, forcing him to define New Labour, and at times I could see TB feeling pressured by it, thinking why am I having to defend all this in the one hour of the day I should be able to relax?

Tuesday, July 4

Tory leadership contest. TB on edge all day. He'd convinced himself again that we were heading towards Hezza, and a real fight because Hezza would do a deal with the right and then just come at us all guns blazing. TB was calling me down every few minutes to have the same conversation again and again. It was a real pain in the arse. 'I hate this,' he said, 'I hate the fact that we just have no control over any of this, that our fate is in the hands of 329 Tory MPs.' I said how do you think John bloody Major feels. Rumours started to circulate that JM had offered Hezza deputy PM and Tory chairman, then that it had all fallen apart. GB and Peter M came over and joined us over orange juice and some very tired sandwiches. Even in their eating styles they were so different, GB a chomper with his jaws pounding back and forth, Peter looking with real disdain at the sandwich and then tearing off little pieces and popping them in his mouth as if they were aspirins. We agreed that whatever the result we would go on the 'two parties' line, that they were divided beyond repair. The result came through and TB leapt to his feet and said 'That's perfect, exactly the result we want.' Norman Fowler [former Conservative Party chairman] said it was a clear win for JM and Robin Oakley [BBC political editor] started to run the Central Office line that it was similar to the scale of TB's leadership election. I paged him to say that was absurd and offensive. To compare a contest caused by the leader's death, and an open field, with a contest caused by the Prime Minister's hopeless leadership of a disintegrating party is ridiculous. GB and I bounced lines off each other and within a few minutes we had an agreed script doing the rounds. The 'two parties' line played strongly, and TB had recovered his confidence. The pain in the arse nagging and endless re-asking of the same questions had been part of the process.

Wednesday, July 5

I got a cab back from David Frost's party with Cherie. It started off OK, but then we turned to the GB/JP/PM scene and I made the observation that a part of all major politicians is deeply egotistical, otherwise they couldn't do the job. She said 'You can talk.' I said what's that supposed to mean? She said you are as complicated and egotistical as any of them. I said some might say I was allowing my ego and my whole life to be subsumed by her husband, so I didn't agree. She said we had to keep Tony calm. Then, as if none of what had gone before meant a thing, we talked about the kids.

Friday, July 7

TB had a really awful meeting with the union general secretaries. He was exasperated afterwards, said they just weren't serious people. Sally [Morgan] said that she always knew when he was losing it with them – he called them 'you guys', then it was 'listen, you guys', then it was 'for heaven's sake, you guys'. Later TB asked me, out of the blue, if I wanted to be an MP. I said why are you asking me now?

He said if I did, and we won, he thought I could become a huge player in the government. I said what, you worried that GB and Peter M won't last the course? He said think about it. I said he had to decide whether I could do more for the cause doing this, and helping him get there, or going into a different mode. I wasn't sure of the answer to that, but my initial instinct said stay with what I'm doing. He'd obviously said something to Peter because he said to me TB thinks you have a future as a key executive player in a top job independent of him.

Saturday, July 8
Paul Keating [Australian Prime Minister] called TB to invite him to stay at his official residence in Sydney when we went to Australia next week. He said he had a few things to teach him about how to deal with Rupert. He said Murdoch is a hard bastard and you need a strategy for dealing with him.

Sunday, July 9
TB called re the T & G speech, saying he was determined to push on the new unions agenda. Lunch at Derry's, which was really nice. We sat out at the back, enjoying the fantastic weather. Derry was on great form, funny as ever, but we also had a really good chat about the whole operation. He and I had very similar views, I think, of the main players and the main relationships. I told Derry what John Smith had once said to me about him – 'Derry is living proof that excessive alcohol consumption does not affect the brain.' 'I'll drink to that,' said Derry. He was worried that TB was 'too messianic', that he felt he could walk on water because he had risen so quickly and done so well since he rose. He also worried that TB did not read widely enough. The T & G in Blackpool put out a six-page document on Labour/union relations which included some very explosive lines in it – there should be no further erosion of the link, a halt to constitutional change. Pain in the arse but I briefed on TB's speech. He'd say an arm's length relationship was better, and also employers would be properly consulted on minimum wage. TB had been out all day so didn't really know the scale of it till he got back. He called after the ITN bulletin at 11. He was almost speechless with rage. 'These people are stupid and they are malevolent. They beg me to go to their conference and then stitch me up, and then they will get all hurt and pathetic when I say what I think. They complain that we want to distance ourselves and then give us all the evidence why we should distance ourselves. I have no option but to go up there and blow them

out of the water. I'm finished with these people,' he said. 'Absolutely finished with them.'

Monday, July 10

Bill Morris all conciliatory on the *Today* programme, and then Robin C on at 8.20, making very pro-union noises, as he said he would, way too conciliatory, virtually congratulating Bill for saying he was prepared to allow an 'equal partnership'. By the time I got round to TB's he was pretty steamed up, but unsure how to deal with it in his speech. Peter M wanted us to go through Morris's statement line by line and take it apart, but I felt that would be too provocative and OTT. TB wrote a very strong section himself, the strongest I'd yet seen, saying we would listen to the unions, but making clear there would be no special relationship and certainly no favours. Very strong stuff in the current atmosphere. He was raging on the train. 'What really gets me is the way they beg me to go to their conference, otherwise nobody will take them seriously, then they go out of their way to embarrass me. It's pathetic. It's just not serious.' He said what he loathed most about it was the sense of it being a ritual – they get him to go, then set him up, then he has to hit back. I called ahead to Bridget Sweeney in the events team to get the speech off the fax before anyone there saw it, and also to organise some autograph hunters and well-wishers so there was a chance of avoiding too many pictures with Bill. Even TB would struggle to hide the contempt today, and it was better he was seen with people. On arrival TB shook Bill briefly by the hand then went straight over to the little crowd that had gathered, signed a few autographs and chatted away for a little while. The atmospherics were very tense and I said to Bill, TB would want to go to a private room and work on the speech so they spent barely a minute together. We had the usual 'any jokes?' chat, and I said – partly as an excuse not to have to think of any – that the message would be even starker if he made no effort to soften them up at the beginning, and if he did the jokes we'd written re Hezza he should do them later in the speech. That is exactly what he did. He went out to polite applause and the first two pages were heard in stony silence as he delivered a very tough message. Then later he departed from the text and did a real tour de force on why he was so passionate about wanting a Labour government, with the subtext that these guys were in danger of stopping one happening. He really worked them over and by the end had most of them up for a standing ovation, which was impressive considering where the atmospherics were during the day. It was probably the toughest message a party leader had given to the unions, and they just about took it.

Thursday, July 13/Friday, July 14
We left for Heathrow at 8pm to set off for the Murdoch event. TB suddenly in a real state re the speech draft, saying it wasn't up to the mark and we had to start all over again on the plane. There was a classic TB moment at the airport, when we were waiting in the Spelthorne Suite, and TB said what do you think about this, and read me a section of a draft. It was pretty good and I said so. 'Lee Kwan Yew[1] sent it to me. Great man. I think we should lift it direct then get the left press to welcome its sentiments, then tell them who wrote it.' We were taken to the plane and as TB and I settled down to start working, a rather unpleasant woman in leather trousers insisted we were in her seat. She was wrong but at least we had our mandatory hate figure for the long flight ahead. We spent the first two hours just talking over what we wanted the speech to do, and then started to write it from scratch. I was working on the New Labour and change passage while TB scribbled manically page after page. At one point, everyone else was asleep as we pressed on. TB was totally lost in concentration and producing good material, which I was honing before Anji typed it up. I was a bit fearful of the potential political downside of appearing to ignore the Murdoch/right-wing agenda so I persuaded him we had to challenge that agenda harder. We landed in Bangkok with something approaching a speech in shape. We managed to get a little sleep on the second leg though not much, but at least the length of the flight had allowed us to get a speech done. My main interest was in ensuring the speech was serious and strong so that we got as much for the message as for the fact that we were delivering it to a Murdoch audience. The party would instinctively not like it, but the response had not been neuralgic and any doubts I had were dispelled by the fact that the person who would be most pissed off that we were doing it was Major.

Saturday, July 15
TB was on the cover of the *Australian* magazine. I really liked the 'nice kind of bastard' headline. It was very Australian but it caught the mix of charm and steel pretty well.

---

[1] Prime Minister of Singapore, 1959–90.

July '95: With Murdoch in Australia

Sunday, July 16

I went out for a swim at 6.45. Absolutely wonderful, literally swimming towards the harbour and the opera house. TB had woken up at 4 and worked on the speech some more, and was now happy with it. I'd arranged for Richard Stott to join us for breakfast and got him to go through the speech from a Murdoch angle. He liked it, thought it had a clear general message and there was enough in it for the News Corp lot, and enough for the anti-Murdoch neuralgics. He suggested we develop the family values section. TB asked what he reckoned Murdoch was thinking. Stott said the thing you have to understand about Murdoch is that he basically hates politicians. He sees them as obstacles to his commercial interests. So I wouldn't worry about his expectations, just say what you think because what you think strikes a chord with most people, whether they're billionaire media moguls or not. There was a bit of criticism of us going still kicking around but TB was confident enough in the speech now not to be bothered. Keating was everything I expected – charming, tough, funny, totally at ease on the surface though probably a real furnace when he got going. On Murdoch he told TB: 'He's a big bad bastard, and the only way you can deal with him is to make sure he thinks you can be a big bad bastard too. You can do deals with him, without ever saying a deal is done. But the only thing he cares about is his business and the only language he respects is strength.' I asked Keating if he could coach TB in how to hate Tories. He said TB was probably right because every time he [Keating] went over the top he went down in the polls. He said one of his favourites was when some guy was laying into him, losing his rag, and he said 'Calm down before you have a heart attack – don't forget I knew you when you had grey hair.' He said to TB: 'I've got some good advice for you about income tax – don't put it up. Ever. Tony, promise me you won't raise income tax. It's death. Labour parties round the world have enough to contend with without hanging that round their necks. It's not worth it.'

On arrival at the island [News Corp took over Hayman Island for the conference] we stepped off the boat to be met by a corporation photographer and cameraman and then Murdoch all smiles and leisure gear and nice to see you. It was an extraordinary place, not exactly my 'tasse de thé' but fascinating nonetheless. The sea was the most exquisite blue, the climate near perfect even for me, and a mix of wild and exotic vegetation alongside very man-made luxury. We were taken first to TB's 'Japanese' suite while PK was taken to the 'Spanish' suite. The bathroom was the size of most rooms, all sunken bath and jacuzzi. A bit tacky but the view was fabulous. We had a valet called Glenn who was clearly thrilled to be looking after TB and would have done anything for us. I got the feeling if TB asked him to jump off the top of the building, he would have. As the barbecue was starting, Keating kept giving me little side of the mouth commentaries. He'd said that Murdoch never really raised issues directly, and sure enough, the conversation kind of meandered around without the nub of issues being really tackled. The reality was the TB/PK world view was very different to the Murdoch view but that just went unsaid. There was an air of fencing to it all. I also got a fascinating glimpse into the way the editors work around him. I said to Murdoch that it was an important speech, that TB had put more of himself into it than any speech outside party conference and I reckoned it would go big, especially now we had fixed for News Corp pictures of the speech to be sent straight away to BBC, ITN, etc. A couple of minutes later, RM spoke across a few people to Stuart Higgins [*Sun*], and later to Peter Stothard [*Times*], and said that it was a big speech TB was delivering tomorrow. Of course, because of the time difference they would be getting it out of London and putting it straight into the paper. Both editors disappeared for a couple of minutes and told me proudly they had ordered London to give it a good show. *The Times* planned to run extracts. I was pleased, but the truth was they had been spun by their boss who had been spun by me. PK chatted up Murdoch for a while and at the end of the evening, Murdoch walking TB back to his suite, I straggled along with Paul. 'He was certainly making all the right noises; said he liked Blair, thought he had guts as well as brains, and he was going to win. The editors were picking up on that, which is why they were behaving the way they were. You have to remember with Rupert that it's all about Rupert. Rupert is Number 1, 2, 3 and 4 as far as Rupert is concerned. Anna and the kids come next and everything else is a long, long way behind.' I took to Keating big time. He told TB, RM was clearly warming to him, which was good up to a point. 'They overestimate the importance of their support for you, but if you can get it, have it. If you are Labour you need all the help you can get to win elections.'

Monday, July 17

Up early after next to no sleep. I went down to the business centre and bumped into Murdoch. I tried to prise him open a bit about what he was thinking but despite the twinkle in his eye, and the general warmth, he was very guarded. Any attempt at big talk was reduced to small talk pretty quickly. I went up to see TB, who was having one last go on his speech. I filled him in on the coverage, which was brilliant. We met up with Keating and then off to hear Murdoch's speech. Fascinating, but a bit chilling, to watch all these grown men, and some women, hanging on every word, and knowing that an inflection here or there would influence them one way or the other. He could hardly have been warmer re TB, real praise, finest young leader in the world kind of thing. He also sent a chill down a few editors' spines when he went on about the failings of some editors, without naming names. TB did a brilliant job. The speech was strong, he delivered it well and as he left the stage you could see the heads nodding and these hard-nosed types all turning to each other and giving little grimaces of approval. TB was not a great one for saying thank you, but he said thanks – the media operation had a touch of genius about it, he said. The whole story could have been the party up in arms about me coming here. Instead we got a message that unites all parts of a new coalition, and coverage that will have made a real impact. Keating's press guy Greg Turnbull said Paul could be a nightmare but he was a great guy to work with, and you couldn't do a job like this unless you felt that commitment. I felt exactly the same re TB. He could be a pain, and way over the top in his demands and expectations, but there was something about him that made you want to give 110 per cent, and of course there was the sense that I was playing a big part in seeing the Tories out of the door, hopefully for some time. Annita [Keating] asked me to look up their son Patrick, who was in London. I asked what he did. She said he was at Saatchi's. 'Enemies of the working people,' I said. 'Like Rupert,' said Greg. Greg reckoned if PK won he would go after a year or so. PK said when he was out of office he planned to have an answering machine with the message: 'You have reached the office of ex-Prime Minister Paul Keating. Now fuck off and leave me alone.'

We said goodbye, boarded the little jet that had been sent down to take us up to Sydney. Onboard was quite the sexiest, most pouting, provocative, overtly sexual air stewardess I have ever seen. I was sitting opposite TB and whenever she served him, she would swivel her near perfect bum towards me, vice versa when she was serving me. Tony and I kept trying to avoid each other's gaze. I was quizzing her on her politics and she was pretty shtumm, TB said please don't talk to her, it only makes it worse. His mind was already turning to things back home, and his desire to get Donald Dewar installed as chief whip. It was an odd choice at first but on reflection he might be made for it. I said it was important we didn't lose him as a media performer. Then TB did his usual thing of getting a new pad and a biro and setting out a few forward challenges on a single sheet of paper. Number 1, I saw, was 'building up GB'. 2. PLP relations. 3. Europe. 4. Economic message. TB obviously felt he would have to do a lot of the economic message work himself. It remained a big problem that we didn't have an economic message easily understood by party and public. After dinner I took a sleeping pill and slept right through, waking up just in time for a quick breakfast before we landed at 6.50. The trip had been a huge success all round.

Written Monday, July 31 (Flassan)

Holiday started with Fiona complaining that she was like a single parent, that three small kids was much harder than my job. We were hanging around on the Sunday when Neil and Glenys called and asked if they could come to stay for a bit. They were there the next evening, entering a bad atmosphere created by the fact Fiona and I had barely spoken on the way down, and rowed most of the time when we did. And I imagined N and G would be pretty offside too. I could sense that Neil was gearing up for one. He did the usual of messing around with the boys in the pool, lots of small talk, very long stories about Brussels, but then easing into UK politics. 'Who'll be chief whip then?' he'd ask, and I'd say probably Donald Dewar, and Neil would make a few disparaging remarks about him. Anything I said about anyone failed to meet with his approval. I'd heard whispers he was a bit disaffected with TB and the whole show, but it came bubbling out all over the place, boiling over on the second evening. All day there was a drip, drip of things – a joke or three about the Oratory, sideswipes about our policy on Europe – 'we don't have one' – endlessly on about JP not being up to it. On their own, there was nothing too serious about any of them but I could tell he was building up for a big old-fashioned NK rage. Indeed, when Glenys called Rachel [their daughter] to find out about her first day at work, I spoke to Rach and said he was really winding up for a big one. It was while Fiona was putting Grace to bed that the next move up the gears came. Neil had done some vegetable kebabs on the barbecue and we were arguing about a French word and I said I wonder if there's a dictionary in the house, at which point he got up, his chair falling over, then he sprinted into the house, saying of course there'd be a fucking dictionary, and Glenys and I looking at each other and just shaking our heads and shrugging. He came back with his cheek muscles flexing like they do when he's close to totally losing it. We were nearing the full explosion, as first he tried to keep his voice under control, but failed every six or seven words; the hand movements getting wilder;

then the heavy sarcasm – 'Oh Margaret Thatcher, not too bad you know, not such a bad person, quite a radical, and of course you had to admire her determination and her leadership – that's what the fucking leader says.' 'Now now,' I said, trying to calm things, but he was in that phase where anything you said just became a spur to further verbal violence. 'Don't "now now" me. I'll fucking tell him too – radical my arse. That woman fucking killed people.' Glenys weighed in now, saying that GB had refused to commit to 0.7 per cent of GDP on overseas aid. 'They haven't got a line on Africa,' she said. 'It's not just Africa,' Neil chipped in, 'they haven't got a line on Asia, Australasia, any continent you mention.' I said that was absurd. 'Prove the contrary then,' he said, and stalked off before I could answer. While he simmered elsewhere, Glenys said in more measured terms the problem was there were parts of the party that felt alienated by TB and the New bit of New Labour. The message was that everything that went before TB was hopeless. I said she and Neil were being too sensitive to that. Tony had been elected to modernise and be the agent of change. But he always stressed Neil's role as having begun all this, and they should not take it personally. She said down in South Wales they thought he only cared about Essex man. I said that was absurd – are you saying we shouldn't try to win back seats we had lost in places like Essex? We should never have lost contact with those people. By now Neil was back and said it was of course impossible for TB to address education policy now because he had chosen to send his own son to the SS Waffen Academy. I said his remark would be funny if it wasn't so ridiculously over the top but I'm afraid his humour had gone now. I said why don't you stop fucking about with the sarcasm and the jibes and say what you're actually thinking – what is the main complaint? Glenys could see it was in danger of boiling over and said she didn't want a big row, but I said no, I want to know what he's saying because my job is to defend Tony and I want to know what the problem is, so he should spit it out. Eventually he spat it out – 'He's sold out before he's even got there.' 'Sold out on what?' 'Everything.' His face was inching ever closer to mine and at one point he picked up a kettle filled with newly boiled water which I feared was heading my way. 'What about a few specifics?' I said. 'Tax, health, education, unions, full employment, race, immigration, everything, he's totally sold out. And for what? What are we FOR? It won't matter if we win, the bankers and the stockbrokers have got us already, by the fucking balls, laughing their heads off. And all that before you go and take your 30 pieces of silver.' 'What's that supposed to mean?' And he spat it out – 'Murdoch.' 'Oh for Christ's sake, is that what this is all about, because we went to see Rupert fucking Murdoch?' 'You imagine what it's like having your head stuck inside a fucking light bulb,' he raged at me, 'then you tell me how I'm supposed to feel when I see you set off halfway round the world to grease him up.' 'We gave him absolutely nothing,' I said. 'You will. And he'll take it. You'll get his support and then you'll get the support of a few racist bastards, and then you'll lose it again the minute you're in trouble.' I pointed out again that if we were going to win, we had to get new support, and he went all patronising and sarcastic again. 'Oh I never knew that, I didn't know you had to get new support. I wish I'd thought of that.' I said we can have a serious conversation if he wants but he shouldn't bother patronising me. More rage. 'Don't you patronise me,' he said. I said re Murdoch, what was the difference, other than in scale, between me working for a Murdoch paper, as I did, and going to his conference. 'The difference is you've got courage and bottle and you'd tell these fuckers what you think. Tony won't do that.' I said that was crap. Glenys said she understood why we went but I had to realise how much it hurt Neil, who felt Murdoch was actually evil. Neil calmed down a bit later and said his 'sell-out' analysis would have carried more conviction if he hadn't sold out once or twice himself.

When we were speaking again, a couple of days later, I said if he attacked Tony, I would defend him because that was my job, and not only did I support the New Labour strategy, in large part I devised it because we have to win new support and that is the key to it: change, compromise with the electorate, call it what you want. I said I believed in what we were doing and one of the greatest difficulties I felt was that people closest to me, including him but most important Fiona, who had basically taken his side in the row, didn't actually support what we were doing at all. I said at least you always had Glenys on side when you were doing the tough stuff. 'There was stuff she didn't believe in too,' he said. There was a chance our friendship would not recover from the venom. The row had taken place at the exact same place where a year ago he had tried to talk me out of working for Tony, which added to the uncomfortable dynamic at work. He said nobody wanted a Labour government more than he did but what was really important was the second term. We had to win at least two terms to make real lasting change. I said one will be a start and I have no doubt we will do things he will be proud of. He then started laying into the Shadow Cabinet, and complained we were woefully thin on talent. I asked if he thought Smith would have won. 'Just.' I said it will be more than 'just' with TB as leader. I said can't you see he makes us much more electable? 'Why do you take NEW Labour so personally? If anything it is your creation, don't knock it.' Finally he started making some constructive suggestions – TB should say in his conference speech that New Labour is Old Labour winning; that 1945 was New Labour, Labour renewing itself to renew Britain, 1964 ditto. After a while the rage subsided and we could have a civilised conversation again, but something had changed. And I was deeply annoyed at the way Fiona had sided against me pretty much through the whole argument. I barely slept the night of the big row, which was hardly a great way to spend a holiday.

The next day the whole thing kicked off again. I said to Fiona that even out of basic solidarity she could have sided with me when I was being assaulted like that, not just verbally but with a bloody kettle thrust into my face. She flew straight off the handle, said I'd totally changed, was completely obsessive, intolerant of any other point of view and she wasn't allowed to say what she thought about anything. I didn't allow any rational argument; everything had to be subsumed to the idea of winning, and it was not a life. I said I'd like to know if she'd be happier if I developed a strategy for losing. This set the scene for another awful day, the only enjoyable parts of which were when I disappeared with the kids. She said she was fed up saying the same things and me taking no notice. I said I was fed up hearing the same things. She said she understood why Cherie was so fed up. There was me, TB, Anji and the office inside a bubble and nobody was allowed in. I was on a gigantic ego trip being lauded to the skies for being brilliant and she was just an appendage. It was really grim. Earlier, when Carolyn Fairbairn [Adviser in Major's Policy Unit and an old friend] came round, we had to go through the pretence that we were having a lovely holiday blah blah. Neil and I were barely speaking other than lobbing in a few sarcastic jibes, e.g. when I said I liked Keating and he'd go off on that, and I'd say at least he wins, and off we'd go again.

Wednesday, August 2

Neil said if ever I wanted his help or advice and support, I had it, and the things he'd said he would say to nobody else. He would be totally loyal and supportive but I had to understand if sometimes things boiled up, especially when he saw us consorting with people he despised. Glenys said friendship like ours was too important to let the job damage it. I said the only way I could do this was 100 per cent to my own satisfaction. Yes, I enjoyed it most of the time, but it was all-consuming, as he knew, which is why he'd advised me against doing it. And I knew there was a price to pay, and it was paid by the family. Neil said he knew how hard it was but you had to work at finding time and space for the family. Beneath it all, Neil was working through real anger at his own position, and the fear that TB and New Labour were about using Neil as a foil, which was nonsense. It's just that TB would push change as hard as it would go, and he was able to do it because he was different. His lack of roots actually in some ways helped politically. He could do things Neil might have wanted to do but would have found more difficult. But it meant it was hard for Neil, and he couldn't yet give Tony credit. He said at one point the Tories are so useless a cheetah could win for us, and Tony is a lot better than a cheetah. I said the second part of the sentence is true; the first is not.

Saturday, August 19

TB was wearing flip-flops, which looked absurd, and I said he should put shoes on as there would probably be press outside the house. Word had got back to Neil that I'd filled in Tony on a toned-down version of our arguments and Neil said the idea that he had lost faith 'defied a response'. That made me think Neil had just wanted to get a lot of stuff off his chest but he was basically there to help me and TB. TB seemed a bit down about things. He then told me, stressing it was in complete confidence and he had not told GB or Peter M, that an intermediary had indicated to him that Alan Howarth[1] was so fed up with the Tories he might consider defecting. It was the best thing I'd heard for weeks but TB said it was by no means in the bag. He wanted me to handle Howarth and make sure we had the conditions right for him if he came over.

Thursday, August 24

Jill Sherman [Times] told me she was a good friend of Sam Hampson [a university friend] and he'd told her what a complete nutcase I was at university. 'Is it true you used to headbutt the cigarette machines until they broke?' 'I'm afraid so.'

Friday, September 1

It was TB's first full day back in the office and we had a session to go over recent weeks, during which we managed fairly quickly to get him into a depressive state. 'So what you're telling me is Gordon

[1] Alan Howarth, Tory MP and former Tory minister.

won't play, John fucked up, the party's Lulus are at it and the press has turned against us?' Pat McFadden said TB underestimated the numbers in the party who didn't really understand what we were about, and we had to answer that. TB was having none of it, and said he needed to go big on the modernisation message. 'This is a classic piece of leftist nonsense – any leader who tries to broaden his party's appeal is then accused of abandoning traditional support. It would be a tremendous mistake for us to respond to that by trimming and cutting back, and I'm not prepared to do it. On the contrary, we have to push on even further and faster.' He was incredibly tanned, which underlined how long a holiday he'd had, and very feisty.

Saturday, September 2

At dinner with Neil, TB said at one point Neil said he couldn't understand why he thought he had a problem with him, to which Tony said 'Come on, Neil, you don't think Alastair wouldn't tell me, do you?' As TB assessed it, Neil's main concerns were education, foreign policy and any sense that New Labour was an attack on him.

Tuesday, September 5

Dublin. Extraordinary start to the day. My bedroom and Mo's were joined by a bathroom so I knocked on the bathroom door before going in. 'Come in,' she shouted cheerily. I pushed open the door and there she was in all her glory, lying in the bath with nothing but a big plastic hat on. I brushed my teeth, trying not to look in the mirror, where I could see Mo splashing around and decided to shave later. She seemed totally unbothered by my seeing her naked in a bath without suds. TB was speaking to Ken Cameron [general secretary of the Fire Brigades' Union] and George Brumwell [general secretary of the Union of Construction, Allied Trades and Technicians] re the minimum wage, confident we could get a figure out but it meant a formula in. I was worried about it but he felt we could brief it as real cooperation, a new mood, actually give the unions a positive briefing for once. Pat [McFadden] and I disappeared to work on the TUC speech. We met up with TB for the meeting with John Bruton [Taoiseach (Prime Minister) of the Republic of Ireland], who seemed in a really bad way. He was twitching, rubbing his eyes, then letting his head fall into his hands. He said the UK government had got themselves caught on the decommissioning hook, it was a mistake, the IRA would never do it and it meant logjam. He didn't doubt Major's good faith but he felt they had handled it badly. TB picked up on the depressive mood. 'God, this is difficult politics,' he said. Bruton, to ease the mood a bit, suggested as a joke that we talk about EMU [Economic and Monetary Union] instead. He said he was absolutely convinced the IRA would not hand over weapons 'as a gesture', that Gerry Adams [president of Sinn Fein and MP for West Belfast] was coming under pressure and that we were heading for deadlock. TB emphasised, rather to their disappointment, that our basic position was one of support for the peace process and that meant support for the government. It became clear the longer we were there that Sinn Fein resented this, that they felt we were doing it for electoral reasons, in that we felt there were 'no votes' in Ireland. Bruton agreed if TB were to split from the government it should be over something big. TB agreed privately the government had made a mistake in getting so firmly onto this hook. As Mark Durkan [chair and later leader of the nationalist SDLP (Social Democratic and Labour Party)] said later, it confirmed nationalist prejudice that all the Brits really thought about or understood was guns. TB was clearly fascinated by the politics of it, and also the scale of the challenge. It was one of those issues where slight nuances could lead to huge progress or massive setback and crisis.

Friday, September 8

Slept badly, probably dreading the dinner tonight. I went home to pick up Fiona then we set off for Richmond Crescent. I was dreading it. The worst-case scenarios were me walking out, or CB refusing to go to conference. Peter M, who was good with Cherie, was already there. TB was going on about the awfulness of his day, hours of JP, Bill Morris and others. Eventually Fiona said we should discuss Cherie, what role and image she was supposed to be developing, what was good for her and for TB, and how we managed conference. Cherie said we had reached the position where she felt unsupported, and she had a poor relationship with the office because she felt we saw her purely as a problem. She said she had a contribution to make beyond being a 'rich lawyer/wife'. I said I accepted there was fault on both sides. Things had got off to a terrible start because of Carole [Caplin] at conference last year. I felt Carole was a problem anyway and they had to understand if she became a story again, I would have nothing to do with it. I was entitled to views and judgements too. I added that I was coming very close to the same position re the Oratory as well. I said that both Anji and I had to take some responsibility for the deterioration in her relationship with the office. That being said, it was obvious she could add a lot. She was a working-class success story; she was a successful professional woman; she held a family together in what were clearly high-profile and therefore often difficult circumstances. If that was what the public knew and saw of her, she would be an asset. But I was convinced that the moment she developed a political profile of her own, somehow independent of Tony, it would be bad for both of them. She said she didn't disagree with that but we had never had a proper discussion about it. TB was getting irritated and ratty. 'This is really quite simple. You have two roles. One is as a supportive wife and mother. The second is as a compassionate, intelligent person who does good things for good causes. There is one danger to avoid: that is the Hillary/Glenys [Clinton/Kinnock] syndrome where you are built up by the media in a way designed to undermine me.' We agreed that Fiona would act as an adviser, paid, that she would work out with Cherie the causes and charities she should become involved with, and take charge of organising her profile. CB would do no interviews but she would do occasional speeches and articles. I asked Cherie what and who she meant by 'the office'. She said me, Anji, Jonathan, Sally [Morgan]. She felt we made decisions for TB without understanding they would have an impact on her and the family. I said I accepted that but they had an impact on our families too. We were all, always, motivated by what we thought he would want, based upon his belief that we should do everything possible to win. I said I'd be more than happy if I spent less time with her husband, and so would Fiona and the kids, but Tony and she had wanted me to do the job, and while I did it, I would do it properly. We then discussed Carole C. I said I felt whilst she was around I would always be worried about her. Cherie said Carole had been a great help. PM and I said we had to find someone CB was comfortable with. My worry was that CB would only be comfortable with someone we were not comfortable with, and that meant Carole. Given how badly it could have gone, the dinner went well. TB was very nice to Fiona, if not so nice to Cherie. Cherie and I were always able to have it out but then get back to being reasonably friendly. She said she often said things she regretted after saying them.

Monday, September 11

Hilary [Coffman] called with a bit of a bombshell. Patrick Wintour had called to say that Seumas Milne [both *Guardian* journalists] had got hold of Philip's 'Unfinished Revolution' memo.[1] It was one of

[1] The *Guardian* had obtained a copy of Philip Gould's memo which not only talked of ending the party's links with the unions but suggested Labour was not yet ready for government. Gould also recommended a command structure where all roads led directly to Blair.

those sinking moments when the words 'Oh fuck' flashed right across the mind. Immediately, I recalled his line about scrapping the union link. But there was more, like him saying we weren't ready for government; the need for a unitary command structure; there was plenty in there and it was all bad, which is of course why it had been given to the *Guardian* by whoever gave it. It was a massive problem. I didn't have a copy at home so I got Patrick to read it to me and I knew from the first two sentences that it was accurate. Jonathan sent me the memo at home and there were actually differences so I was able, honestly, to say to Patrick they'd been given a distorted summary, but what they had was bad enough and of course set up tomorrow's speech to the TUC really badly. I spoke to TB, PG and PM and knocked out a statement for the *Guardian*, making the best of a very bad job. We would have to go on the offensive in the morning though and use it yet again to get over a change and modernisation message. I then sat back and waited for the barrage of calls. TB was plunged into real gloom. 'We are being sabotaged from within,' he said. *Newsnight* flashed up the front page, which had three huge pictures of TB, PM and me, which was a bit of a shock. TB called after his dinner with Murdoch. He said it had been fine, but they were playing both sides against the middle. He said the *Guardian* thing was a blow but 'if you can't stand the heat and all that'. I sensed he was now quite looking forward to tomorrow and using it to hammer a modernisation, no-going-back message. The phones were going mental at home. Fiona said it was appalling to have this happening from within. 'This is the first time I've actually felt sorry for you.' 'Well, thanks.' I finally got to bed at 4 and just after 6 Tony called to say the bulletins had failed to point out the memo was seven months old. At least when the chips were down, I was always able to get up for it, and so was he. I said to TB today could be quite a ride. He laughed.

Tuesday, September 12
Potential disaster turned into something approaching the seizing of an opportunity – namely the chance to set out the modernising agenda once more. The atmosphere changed markedly after the speech. My pager was going endlessly with messages saying he'd done well. He had. Disaster turned to advantage.

Sunday, September 24
TB was working all day on the conference speech at Michael Levy's. He called to say he wanted me to work on the start and on the anti-Tory section. We were now over twice the length and working on two

separate drafts, but we felt we were making progress. TB called later on, to say he'd done some really good work. He also finally managed to track down Alan Howarth, who said he was on for it, and we could decide when he would do it. I said the eve of the Tory Conference was the best time. TB had been worried that Howarth would be lost as a result of some of the madness that happened during the summer. Far from it. He said the Tories had shown themselves to be even more extreme and uncaring. But TB wanted me to think through how we handle it from Howarth's perspective.

Tuesday, September 26

TB and I left in the little car and headed for Totteridge, where we were due to work on the speech at Michael's. TB was determined to break the back of it today. It took ages to get there because of the traffic, but it was during the drive that some of the best thinking on the speech came. TB was firing, and so was I, him rattling out ideas, me rattling out phrases and taking notes as he drove this tiny car with both of us scrunched up in the front. Britain falling apart, only a united Labour Party can unite it. Only a modernised Labour Party can modernise Britain. By the time we got there, we'd virtually rewritten the entire speech and I had a mass of notes to decipher. Michael's place was a bit over the top for my taste, big security gates, white carpets, rolling lawns and all that. But it was a nice place to work, TB in the kitchen, me in the dining room.

Wednesday, September 27

Pre-conference team meeting, to give everyone their orders and make sure they understood that the press would be watching us like hawks. TB cancelled all his meetings, other than those related to the speech. He said the NEC had been pretty grim. Blunkett had voted against rejecting Liz Davies.[1] The highlight of my day, phoning Alan Howarth at home. As so few people knew, I found a very quiet spot at the back of the office, and called him. His first words were 'Do you think I'm mad?' I said far from it. We talked it over, him why he was doing it, his feeling that he was more in tune with us than he was with modern Conservatism, and me trying gently to persuade him that we should do it on that weekend between the conferences. He had a fear that this would be seen as cowardly, but I pointed out that his best hope

[14] Liz Davies, a left-wing barrister and Islington councillor, had been selected by Labour Party members in Leeds North East in 1995 as prospective parliamentary candidate. Labour's NEC vetoed the selection.

September '95: Alan Howarth to defect from Tories

of getting a Labour seat was for the Labour Party to see him as something of a hero, rather than a turncoat, and the key to that was the extent to which his former party reacted. So it was in his interests that we did this with real impact. Obviously he was worried about the reception he was going to get in his new party, but he just had to accept that his former colleagues will be very, very angry with him. But he also had to accept that the best way to the hearts of the Labour Party was to put the Tory Party into a rage. I also had to warn him against the idea of a by-election, because frankly he would not win it for us where he was. He wanted to know how JP would react, and again I said that provided JP felt you were doing this for the right reasons, and provided you accept that the politics of this demanded doing it with a real impact upon the Conservatives, then he would be broadly supportive. He was asking, I suppose, because he knew that deep down tribalists like John, and I felt a little of this myself, think there is something instinctively wrong about switching parties. However, TB had convinced himself, and talking to Alan, so did I, that he was doing it for the right reasons, and what's more, the more I talked to him, the more I felt that this could be one of the really big moments of this parliament, which would help us reshape the landscape in the run-up to the election. He was clearly a decent man. He was worried that the press would get into his family, including his broken marriage. He wondered if him being a Lloyd's name was a problem. He wondered if it would be better to hear both leaders' speeches, before finally announcing his move. I said again I felt strongly that this should be done before their conference. Part of me was worrying that if he got back into his own tribe, he might actually decide to stay there. Eventually he said that he'd made his mind up, and if I thought that was the right time to make the maximum impact, he would go with it. He said the Tories would be absolutely vicious about it, but he was prepared for that. I said you must have tortured yourself about this. Yes, he said, it isn't easy after 20-odd years in the party. But it was definitely going to happen and what with the progress made on the speech today, it had been the best day for some time.

Thursday, September 28

Both Fiona and Rory had been up ill through the night, so I was pretty knackered as I headed off early to meet TB and head once more to Michael's. As the day wore on, he became more and more concerned about the central argument of the conference speech. He put it to one side, wrote the word argument on a single page, then tried to sketch out the absolute core of the argument, time and again, scribble, scribble, scribble, then putting a line through it, then starting again. At one point, with this mass of paper lying around his feet, he thought he'd lost the one that got close to it, and the pair of us were on our hands and knees trying to find the one that he wanted. Liz [Lloyd] was off sick, so Sue Jackson came up to start typing up everything we'd done. It was a bit of a nightmare for her, because the speech was now in bits of paper, so varied in shape and size that we called it the Origami speech. TB and I had lunch and then found a football and went out for a kickabout in Michael's garden. Again, poor Sue was looking at us out of the window as if we were a pair of lost souls, but in fact, the little break did us good, because in the afternoon, we got going again. Michael arrived home, and they played tennis, while Sue and I left for the office. I could feel myself going down with Rory's cold, and also I'd lost my pager. By the time I got to the office, something had happened to TB's mood, because he phoned in a state of near despair. He said he read the draft again from start to finish, and it was hopeless. The argument wasn't clear, the policy sections were dull, and it just would not connect. He said he would have to start all over again. I said, don't be so ridiculous, it's a perfectly good draft and we have three days to work on it.

Friday, September 29
Another day of hell at Totteridge. David M, Peter Hyman and I headed up there through awful traffic and arrived to find TB in a dreadful state. He had a look of near panic in his eyes, which I think alarmed Peter. By now I knew it was essentially part of the creative process that drove him to get the best out of himself, and out of us. Part of him probably believed that the speech was terrible, but what he was doing was forcing himself and the rest of us into a state of worry that would produce better work. I phoned Anji at one point, and told her it was a nightmare, and he was getting on our nerves, pacing around barking out contradictory orders, and we had to get him to calm down. Alan Clark called again and said it was so obvious that we were going to have a good conference, and they were going to have a bad one. He said what would freak out the Tories was if TB really made a pitch for the one nation centre. It was uncanny. There was no way he could have known about Alan Howarth, but what he said confirmed that strategically we were bang on course, which is why Tony's fussing over the speech was so unnecessary. He kept taking out passages which everyone had agreed days ago were among the best in the speech, so then we would rerun arguments that

we thought had been settled before. TB and the speech team went through it line by line, and all of us had the sense that we'd gone backwards again. He was literally pulling at his hair now, saying he was in despair about the speech, and he could not see his way out of it. Somehow, we had lost both the structure and any sense of the forward vision. It was now just a mishmash of different unconnecting passages, and long policy sections that would put the audience to sleep. The coherent theme that we had earlier in the week just wasn't there any more. I went home, pretty depressed about it all, though as Anji pointed out, it always was like this, it was the way he worked on really big speeches. He called in at 8pm and I told him about the conversation with Howarth. Even that didn't cheer him up. He said he was genuinely worried about the speech.

Monday, October 2

When I went up to see TB, he was sitting in his dressing gown, staring into space, just shaking his head and saying it wasn't right. I left him for the office meeting, where I complained about the lack of security concerning the speech, having found two copies of the draft in the corridor outside the office last night. All that mattered in the next 24 hours was getting the speech in shape, though TB was due to do a visit with Kevin Keegan [ex-footballer and manager] and I said we must get an autograph book and a ball. We needed some decent pictures in advance of tomorrow. At a minimum, TB could get Keegan's autograph for the boys, but at best they would do a proper kickabout. He wasn't bad with a ball, and Keegan would in any event know how to make sure he did not end up looking daft. Everyone was horrified at the prospect of TB playing football and being made to look silly but I insisted we get a ball. Keegan was a nice, warm man, and I sensed he was basically onside. There was a huge media turnout. It was a fantastic success and provided the best pictures of the week. I asked Keegan to throw the ball at TB and get him to head it back. Then, they just kept going, I think for 28 consecutive headers. TB said he had never been able to do that, in his entire life, though of course a professional like Keegan can head the ball towards a target in the same way most of us can throw it, so it wasn't that difficult. I said I would tell Tony Bevins about Howarth today. I did so, as the NEC results were being announced, in a little corner by the press tables. I said to him, what is the biggest story that you have ever had literally fall into your lap? The story I did on the IRA, he said. This is bigger, I said. I told him what it was, and I saw tears welling up in his eyes. Are you serious? I said I was. I love you, he said, and I love him. I want to kiss you. We agreed he would not speak to Alan Howarth till Friday, nor to his office, but that he would quietly do some research on past defections. I loved giving a story like this to Bevins. He loathed the Tories, and he loved big stories, and I knew he would do this one properly.

Tuesday, October 3

Brighton is one of the hardest halls going in terms of reaching an audience, as there is something about the acoustics that doesn't quite work, but it was clear from early on that TB was going to go down well. He introduced Mary Wilson [widow of Harold], who was in the hall, and it was clear from the fantastic response she got that there was a warmth in the hall that he would tap into. They wanted him to do well. I was sitting next to Rosie Winterton, who was plying me with Liquorice Allsorts. All the sections that we had really struggled over, and those parts that he asked for me to deliver our best work, what he called the purple patches, really went well, which always made me feel a sense of satisfaction, a job well done. By the time we got back to the hotel, I was totally exhausted. He said he could not have done it without me, and I said next time can we do it without so much emotional grief? We ended up having a huge laugh as we recalled the moment a few days earlier, when we had been leaning on a fence at the back of Michael's garden, looking at sheep, TB saying that at this moment in time, without any speech worth the name, he would rather be that sheep than leader of the Labour Party.

Wednesday, October 4

TB had bumped into Blunkett earlier, who was doing the education debate, which was likely to get focused on the expected Hattersley attack. 'He is a fat, pompous bugger,' TB said. 'You are very wise,' said Blunkett.

Saturday, October 7

They don't invent days like this. I'd gone to bed after speaking one last time to Alan Howarth, talking through the final arrangements, and after weeks of indecision and doubt, he was clearly settled and sounded happy. I still had the feeling, even though I had tried to spell it out, that he didn't realise just how big it was going to be in the short term. I said we would need someone to be with him from the moment the story broke. Fiona and I both woke with a feeling of genuine excitement. I hadn't felt like this since the morning of TB's first conference speech. I could feel everything falling into place. I called Barney Jones at the *Frost* programme, and asked him to discuss this with nobody but Frost himself. I did not give him a name, but said that a Conservative MP would be defecting to us during the course of the day, and we would like his first interview to be on *Frost*. He was gobsmacked. Alan was home now, and sounded more relaxed than ever. He had told his daughter, who was planning to be with him after *Frost* to deal with the hordes. She was obviously a great support, she told him it was the best thing he'd ever done, and she was really proud of him. He said he was incredibly relieved by that. He said he wanted to be in his constituency to take whatever flak came from his local party. Good on him. The more I spoke to him, the more I realised what a basically decent bloke he was. I think the least we owed him was to do what we could to make sure that the reaction in the party worked to his advantage, which is why JP's response was so important. Bevins was calling regularly to keep me up to date with how it was being done at the *Observer*. I tipped off some of the other Sundays, so that they could chase it in their second editions. I said to Bevins it would be better if he tipped off the broadcasters, so that they were ready for later bulletins. Tim [Allan] and Peter H had come round and were playing snooker on the kids' snooker table, while we waited for the story to drop. Tim said this must be how terrorists feel before a bomb goes off. I went back upstairs, and the phones started to go crazy. Everything was working like clockwork. Alan called just before the news came through. He'd had three meetings with his party officials. He said it was really quite moving, as they had in fact been very supportive of him. They have had very amicable conversations. He spoke also to Alastair Goodlad [Conservative chief whip] and he too had not been at all unpleasant. Alan said he was more convinced than ever that he was doing the right thing.

Sunday, October 8

Papers superb. Last night had gone absolutely according to plan, virtually in every detail. It was clear from the interviews with Tory ministers that they were all under orders to mention my alleged bullying of the BBC, and of the press more generally, but it all sounded a bit silly in the context of such a huge story. TB said that the attacks on me were designed to increase my profile and make me less effective. Alan Clark had been on *Frost*, reviewing the papers, and of course he slagged off Howarth in the tribal sort of way you'd expect, but then called me at home and simply said 'Congratters, what a bloody coup, and your fingerprints all over it.' Howarth's interviews were word-perfect. He came over as clear, principled and honest and was being chased around the studios by John Redwood, looking shifty, and Brian Mawhinney [Conservative Party chairman], who looked in a real panic.

Monday, October 9
A sense of real damage to the Tories at the start of their conference. Mawhinney was looking more and more fraught. Alan and I stayed in touch all day, as he was being bombarded with television and radio bids, and must have done 10 or more interviews during the day. The two main lines of attack were why no by-election, which was easy enough to deal with, and why this particular timing? This wasn't so easy, as they were all beginning to say it was vindictive, but Alan's tone was good, and he sounded fine. The Tories' shrill response, against his soft tone, did them no favours.

Monday, October 16
We had another session with GB on the Budget strategy. We had to broaden the debate, make it about quality of life and standard of living, not just about tax cuts. GB was talking about a number of tax reforms that we could put forward. A new approach on tax, and burying the idea of Labour being simply a party of tax and spend, was perhaps the most important plank in the new Labour strategy. There was clearly an argument to be won inside before we took it outside. TB and GB had just about decided that we would not raise the top rate, again despite the inevitable pressures to do so. Again, it was about signalling the scale of change, the acceptance of competitive tax rates in an enterprise economy, and also because we knew that signalling tax rises at that level would simply be used by the Tories as 'evidence' of plans or intentions to raise taxes across the board. GB was still not totally decided but TB was pretty clear. He said the minute we signalled we were raising the top rate, as far as the public is concerned, that was us back to the old ways they rejected.

Wednesday, October 25
At the Big Four meeting, GB laid out the strategy for Robin C and JP, who agreed it made sense, though Robin was being tricky. He said it was a gripping narrative up to the point where we had to decide whether to support tax cuts or not. TB and GB were clear there was no logic in saying you would not support tax cuts, if you then abstained. You might as well vote for them. RC was clearly positioning himself to the left of GB. It was one of the more tense

meetings of the Big Four. TB and GB did a pretty good job of being on the same page, JP had a rather knowing smile on his face most of the time, and Robin did his best to undermine GB's confidence in his own case.

Sunday, October 29

Clare Short was on *Frost*, so needless to say, we had a pretty disastrous start to the day. She was loose on women-only short lists, went off on one about Page Three girls, and then about legalising cannabis. She said it was a personal view, but it was obviously going to run and took over the bulk of TV and radio coverage for the day, thereby blowing out plans to push home on the Tories and the lurch to the right. She was without doubt the most self-indulgent and attention-seeking of all the Shadow Cabinet, and I could not for the life of me understand why TB tolerated her. She went on and on about spin and media manipulation, but it is really all that she ever does herself; look at me, look at me. I didn't bother TB with it, but he called about 3pm, having heard from elsewhere what she'd been up to. 'I'm afraid she's just not serious or professional,' he said. 'Presumably, this has totally screwed up the lurch-to-the-right strategy? It is an entirely self-inflicted wound, born of self-indulgence.' It reached the stage where TB was phoning every 20 minutes to say what a disaster it all was before eventually I said 'Tony, your calls are becoming very repetitive and doing neither of us any good. You and I agree about all of this. We have done all we can for today, let's leave it at that, but please, never tell me again that Clare Short has any redeeming features, because in my view, she has none.'

Tuesday, October 31

TB displayed his continuing almost comic selfishness vis-à-vis my illness [AC had been diagnosed with ulcerative colitis], both in the irritation in his voice when he asked whether I might have to take time off, but also when, as I was leaving early because of the pain in my stomach, he called me back to ask whether we had the right strategy to deal with the right-wing press. I didn't really object, as it happens, because I could see why, in his position, he would want to know he had around him the support he felt he needed, and in any event, he had already asked me how I was. But Anji said at one point to him 'You really are so incredibly selfish. Your only thought in this is the effect on yourself.'

Saturday, November 4

Still not feeling brilliant. I went for a walk with Fiona and the kids, and then Michael Farthing [gastroenterologist and AC's neighbour] came round to talk to me about the disease in general, and the side effects of the drugs. Rabin[1] was shot around eight, and then died about an hour later. I spoke to Robin Cook, and we agreed the statement to put out to PA. TB was genuinely shocked. 'So he's dead then?' He said that several times during a fairly short conversation. I could sense it had maybe brought home to him his own mortality, and that of anyone who puts their head above the parapet in public life. One minute you're the Prime Minister, the next some lulu comes along, and you're dead.

Sunday, November 5

Rabin's death, obviously, was dominating pretty much everything. TB was out in Norfolk with his sister but we were on the phone the whole time, sorting out flights. He called on his way to Northolt to meet Major's plane for the funeral. The CBI [Confederation of British Industry] speech [an important pitch to the business community] was just a week away and I suggested he use the time on the plane to work up a proper draft. He said it might be difficult as he was travelling out with Major, and was due to come back with Prince Charles and Ashdown.

Tuesday, November 7

We went to the Hyde Park Hotel, where TB was making a speech at the *Q* magazine awards, largely as a favour to his old mate Mark Ellen.[2] His little speech was well received, and he posed for pictures with some of the musicians like Eric Clapton, Ronnie Wood and Bob Geldof. He clearly liked mixing with these types, partly because he liked their kind of music, but also in the car back he kept going on about what an extraordinary, fantastic life these people must have, their wealth, adulation from women, and not only are they allowed to be irresponsible, they are meant to be. Of course, if we win, he'll be one of the biggest names in the world, but not with the freedom these guys have.

---

[1] Yitzak Rabin, Israeli Prime Minister, assassinated by a gunman in Tel Aviv because of his determination to broker a peace with Arab nations.
[2] Mark Ellen, editor of *Q* magazine. Oxford contemporary of Tony Blair, bass guitarist with TB's Ugly Rumours band.

November '95: Death of Yitzak Rabin

Wednesday, November 15

I'd worried TB by telling him the *Sun* was doing something on his bald patch. Sometimes these little things got to him more than the big things. He said he wasn't sure the public would want a bald leader, and I fell about.

Saturday, November 18

Tony and I were taking our boys to the Tottenham v Arsenal game, and we went round to pick them up. On the way up, he told me he felt nervous and depressed, and didn't know why. After the game, I was speaking to Bevins, and was told the *Observer* had a full account of Tuesday's Shadow Cabinet meeting. As it was read to me, TB could sense my mood. He said afterwards 'What am I going to do with these people? These are not serious people at all. 'I'll have to tell them that if they cannot be trusted to have serious discussions in the Shadow Cabinet, we won't have them.' I called Charlie Whelan to say I would put out a pre-emptive statement saying there had been a detailed lengthy discussion of our Budget strategy, and there was the widest possible support for GB's approach. TB's immediate suspicion was that it came from Mo. Peter M felt that since she got onto the NEC, she saw herself as the next Edith Summerskill [(1901–1980) doctor, feminist and Labour Cabinet minister].

Sunday, November 19

First call was from Robin Cook. 'It wasn't me,' he said of the *Observer*, adding with his customary wit, 'I think if it was me, I'd have hesitated in describing my own speech as brilliant.' No, I said, but you have plenty of people who would do it for you. He got the point.

Wednesday, November 29

Up at six, ready for the post-Budget interview blitz. President Clinton was in town and unfortunately was going into overdrive in his praise of Major, first at the press conference in Downing Street, then in the address to both Houses, and later at the dinner. He was really pushing out the boat, so much so that only half in jest, I asked his press secretary, Mike McCurry, if he couldn't rein him in a bit. We got the police escort to Wingfield House [residence of the US Ambassador in London]. A minute or two after we arrived, Clinton and Hillary appeared and they had a brief chat in the hall before the two of them went out to do a doorstep. It went OK, but it was not going to penetrate the wall-to-wall Major/Clinton coverage, though whether it mattered much at this stage, I wasn't sure. The meeting itself began with a bit of an embarrassment when TB introduced me to BC as a 'legend in his own lifetime', which must have baffled him a bit. The chairs were laid out as for a formal bilateral meeting, TB and BC facing out to the rest as the two sides lined up opposite each other. He was much bigger than I imagined him to be, both taller and fatter. He had enormous strong hands and size 13 feet that looked even bigger. He said that once he and Boris Yeltsin swapped shoes to see who had the biggest feet, and Clinton did. Clinton had an interesting line about how achievement was less important than definition in the information age. He said there is no point saying what you've done, keep saying what you're going to do, have a clear direction. Reagan and Thatcher did it and didn't have to achieve that much. Like TB, he talked a fair bit about the polls and media, and like TB, he was at his best when talking about how to win support and manage change. He said the Congress having gone against him, and with the press more in conflict mode, he was always striving to get his message over to people direct. He was hugely impressive on strategy, especially considering he had just 45 minutes' sleep on the plane last night. He said it was important to any progressive party of change to have mainstream values, and mainstream economic policies. They got on pretty well, though I thought Jonathan overdid it when he said he could feel a very special chemistry. TB called after the Downing Street dinner, which he said was fine. He said he hated being photographed arriving at the door, because it looked so presumptuous.

Tuesday, December 5

TB and I had a long chat about GB. TB said 'I never actively wanted to be leader and I never expected to be leader. I was always sure, like most other people, that it would be GB. He could still be leader. I would be perfectly happy to be under him. I always felt he would be leader and I would be a reforming Chancellor and then go on to do something in Europe. But when John died, it was not as clear. In fact it was clear to me that I would stand and not Gordon.'

Wednesday, December 6

We discussed TB's 'image problem'. I identified it as an odd mix of being both too aloof and too familiar. We were falling between two stools. People were not sure what he was about. I said we seemed to be too focused on the Tory agenda, and we had to open up a clearer and more definitive left-of-centre agenda that was still New Labour.

Peter Hyman confirmed to me that Harriet was thinking of sending her second son to a grammar school. I exploded and wrote a letter advising her strongly against. I said it would result in political damage to herself; it would be awful for her son, because he would be thrust into the media spotlight; and it would damage the party at a time when the post-Oratory wounds were healing. I expressed myself very forcefully. I showed TB my letter and he said I couldn't send it. I should talk to her instead and say what I thought, but don't send her that letter. Even he was baffled, saying she had just about got over all the fuss about her first one going to the Oratory, and now she decided to go even further. TB and I went over all the old arguments we had been over so many times at the time of the Oratory row. I said this was the issue that most worried our own people. He said whatever you do, make sure Rory and Calum get a good senior school, because if bright kids are not stretched they go off the rails.

Friday, January 5, 1996

Tokyo. We had been advised before coming over to get lots of calling cards and the embassy explained it really was important, not just for us but for TB himself. The Japanese set huge store by calling cards, and the ambassador really felt that we should get some good ones for TB. As the day wore on, and he began to run out of his own cards, and get them mixed up with the cards he had been given, he ended up giving the German Ambassador's card to a businessman from Sony. There was one tricky moment, when TB was introduced to someone and asked who he was, and the ambassador said 'You know, the former prime minister,' and TB said 'Ah yes, I know the face.' There was the odd schoolboy comic moment too, as when a Japanese businessman said 'Ra whole of Japan is rookin fowad to your erection.' I said we are hoping for a big one and TB spluttered while the Jap put his thumbs up and said 'Big one, big one.' The reality was that he was making a big impact though, and the Japanese saw in TB a very new and attractive kind of leader. I wondered if they would have felt the same if they had seen him later, sitting in his bedroom at the residence, wearing nothing but his underpants and an earthquake emergency helmet which we all had in our rooms, pretending to speak Japanese.

Sunday, January 7

Singapore. I had slept for about two hours when I was woken by a very alert cockerel. At breakfast, TB said I had to take more care of myself. 'You'd be useless to me dead,' he said. He said he played tennis, and kept in shape, and he was worried that I worked too hard without doing exercise. We had the makings of a very good speech on the theme of stakeholder economy, and the more I briefed it as our core economic argument, the more confident I became that it was a good description of our economic pitch. Locals from the *Telegraph*, *Guardian* and *FT* were there and I could tell when I started to brief the substance of the speech that they were really up for it. I think it was the *Guardian* guy who first said 'Is this stakeholder economy the big idea?' We were running late, and I went into the church to ask TB if he could leave the service early and he looked at me shocked, and said certainly not. TB felt he was on to something with the stakeholder economy idea. It was a way of conveying the economy is about more than money and jobs, it was also about what sort of country we wanted to be. It worked perfectly in tandem with One Nation. It was also a washing line from which to hang all the different parts of economic policy. David M was ecstatic about the speech, felt finally TB had found a left-of-centre message on the economy. TB said we now needed two things, the sense of the team and main players working in harmony, and the public feeling the Tories were no longer making the economy improve.

Thursday, January 11

The mood in the morning meeting was awful. Here we were, TB just back from a successful trip abroad, his speech setting the agenda, the Tories going through one of their internecine phases, we are way ahead in the polls, but a Martian landing in that meeting would have thought we were on the skids. GB was already moving against the stakeholder economy, suggesting we should broaden it to the stakeholder society. Philip and I argued strongly for sticking with it, saying stakeholder economy had more edge and was less easily dismissed as just warm words. That much was shown by the controversy since he made the speech. I said we finally had a sense of an economic message that set us apart. The trouble was a lack of any real team spirit. A few of us, mainly PG and I, and Donald [Dewar], tried to rub along with everyone, but it was getting more difficult. It was amazing, the way the press thought we ran this well-oiled machine, but inside the machine on days like this, it felt very rickety.

Monday, January 15

It was pretty clear that GB did not believe in the basic stakeholder economy message at all, or if he did, he was determined not to say so. TB was clearly anxious and very twitchy about all manner of things. What is missing most is a strategy that is agreed and understood by everyone. He said 'I'll have to take over strategy myself and run the whole show.'

Thursday, January 18

GB was on the *Today* programme and did OK, but anyone who knew him could tell that he was deliberately emphasising opportunity economy rather than stakeholder economy. Later TB and GB had a private session, GB complaining again that he was never consulted and that we had not thought through the consequences of the speech. He successfully troubled TB, who began to wonder whether we had the right definition of the stakeholder economy.

Friday, January 19

Harriet paged me to say the *Mail on Sunday* had been on to the grammar school that her son was going to. David Hill had advised her to brief the *Independent* and the *Mirror* in the hope the coverage would not be so grisly, and some of the sting taken out, and I said I agreed with that. I told her however she handled it, I thought she was mad to be doing it, and she should fasten her seat belt. TB then claimed we had never had a proper discussion about it and I said that was balls. We had discussed it ad nauseam and I had written her a letter advising against the move which he had refused to allow me to send. 'Do you ever think you would be a better leader than me?' he asked and I said no, because for a start I lacked his patience. He said the MPs wouldn't mind, because I was more in tune with them. Ho ho.

Sunday, January 21

I was playing golf with David Mills [husband of Tessa Jowell] when Tim A paged me to say Clare had attacked Harriet on *GMTV* and it was running big. TB hit the roof when he heard about Clare. 'Anyone would think Harriet had murdered the bloody child,' he said. 'The ability of the party to lose perspective is unbelievable.' I said that on the contrary I felt she got off fairly lightly. But he was absolutely livid about Clare, said he was sick of her self-indulgence. I tried to put personal feelings about both of them to one side. In truth, they were both in the wrong. Harriet should have more regard for JP's point about political consequences from personal actions, while Clare can never resist presenting herself as the conscience of a certain view of the party. But I pointed out to TB that he was in danger of getting damaged himself because he had one rule for some, e.g. Clare being slapped down over drugs when she stepped out of line a tiny bit, and another rule for the Harriets and Peters of this world. He said 'It's a personal decision' is all we need to say. Clare, he said, was simply being unprofessional in doing what she'd done. If you're in a hole, the job of a politician is to think how we get out of it, and help others out of it, not make things worse. I said surely you could see the damage – here we are in the middle of people v privilege, trying to get up equality of opportunity, and she comes and totally fucks it over. It is selfish and stupid, and she needs to understand how we feel.

Tuesday, January 23
PMQs was probably Major's best 15 minutes since TB became leader. He absolutely savaged him over Harriet. TB looked desperate. JP, alongside, was grim-faced, fuelling the accurate speculation that he was deeply pissed off, both with Harriet and the support we were giving her. TB saw JP twice after questions. JP said he could never say he supported what she did, but he would always back TB. I told them that the press really smelled blood now. I had been mobbed after PMQs and the tone of the questions showed they were all convinced she would have to quit. I said she would not be quitting, end of story. That life was likely to get a lot tougher and we had to hold our nerve and not buckle under the pressure. I said the easy thing to do would be to sack her but TB, unlike JM, did not buckle. There was a real intensity to questioning, and an aggression, but I think I did fine. Even though I disliked what she had done, I knew it was now a battle of a different order and we had to win, so it was time to pull out the stops. We were still struggling to get anyone to defend her on TV, but eventually I persuaded Mo to do it, only half jokingly saying that if she didn't I'd reveal her stepchildren were at a public school. Mike Brunson [ITN political editor] called to say the government whips were saying Harriet had private health insurance, which as she didn't gave us the opportunity to say this was now becoming a Tory dirty tricks operation and we could start to turn it. I emphasised that TB would be toughing it out and urging the party to close ranks. It was all a bit depressing though. It's one thing to work round the clock and work your balls off for things and people you believe in. I didn't feel like that about Harriet or her decision.

Wednesday, January 24
We went to see TB, who was very pumped up about the whole thing by now. He said he wanted all hands to the pump. By the end of the day, I do not want anyone to be in any doubt that she is staying, and I want people to be saying we did the right thing in keeping her. There is no alternative to this whatever, he said. If she goes, I honestly believe we become unelectable in the eyes of the public. Not because the issue is so important, but because they would think we were stark

staring mad to allow something like this to become a full-blown crisis. This has got to be seen as a test of our mettle and it is a test that we have to pass. TB went to the PLP and put up a passionate defence of her, and also spelled out the broader political consequences if she went. Peter M and David Hill came back raving, said he had been absolutely brilliant, and turned it. He said she'd done what she'd done, and whatever anyone thought about it, the only people who benefit from continuing division over it are our enemies and it is time to draw a line. He said what matters was the education of all kids, not a row about the education of one. David said you could see them responding and respecting the fact he had balls.

Monday, February 5

TB seemed to have had a bad weekend. He normally came in very bouncy and focused with a list of things for us all to do. But he was very unfocused, distracted. He said he could not see how we could get back on track. Everything we did was seen through the prism of difficulty and fightback, and though he knew that the Tories were posing more of a threat, he felt sure the public did not really want to see him going for the jugular. He felt, however, that they had a story to tell, and we didn't. They were using all their intellectual arguments on rail, economy, health, education. They had simple stories, access to media that would tell them, and it was hurting us. He was in one of his total mithering moods, which was driving me mad, so I left him and said please don't call me back if it is to have the same conversation again. It was striking today how TB was almost deferential to GB. He so much didn't want to upset him or push him offside that he let him make the running. I could sense others noticing it, and TB's authority weakening as a result. I said to him afterwards this was exactly the time when he should be laying down the law, telling not asking, making clear that the speech in Singapore was the core economic message and we all had to push it.

Tuesday, February 6

Philip called after the campaign strategy meeting. He said there had been an extraordinary moment when Chris Powell said to GB they had a script for the next broadcast and GB said 'Show it to Alastair. It's got stakeholding in it.' PG said he made it sound like a disease.

Sunday, February 11

We went to dinner at the Foots, with Salman Rushdie [author, still under the threat of murder]. Jill [Craigie, wife of Michael Foot] was

February '96: TB deferential to GB

terrific company, very funny, and full of terribly bitchy stories about Michael's old colleagues. Michael said TB was a massive asset. He was young, exciting and clever. 'He is a film star,' said Jill, 'a film star.'

Monday, February 19

Bumped into Heseltine. 'Ah,' he said, 'the gloss is coming off. You've had a good run, but now we have the measure of you.' I said that was not how it felt to us, and I would rather be in our shoes than theirs. The Brit awards should have provided some light relief but I hated the whole thing. TB was tense, so was I, Cherie and Fiona were twittering and saying I was being boring and Northern and shouldn't worry so much about things going wrong. TB was at John Preston's [music industry executive, husband of Roz] table and kept looking round to share looks of 'Is this wise?' There was a little flurry of excite-ment earlier when Central Office complained that Virginia Bottomley [Conservative Cabinet minister] should have been given an award to present. They must be mad. Anji came to get us at 9.20 and then we had a long wait hanging around backstage, while TB paced up and down and, when outsiders left us alone, endlessly rehearsing the little speech we'd done about the importance of the music industry. I've rarely seen him so nervous. I suppose it was partly because this was not his usual environment, but also it was such a huge audience, live and on TV, and if something did go wrong, it would be high impact. David Bowie [musician] came in for a chat. They did a lot of small talk, and he gave his views on the various people who had been winning. He said he'd be happy to come out for Labour, but he was worried he would open himself to attacks because he was a tax exile. He didn't exactly help TB's nerves when he said this audience could be hellish and given that some of the musicians from Oasis and Pulp had already misbehaved, anything could happen. After he left, I said 'Oh dearie dearie me' and we went into a little black humour phase, imagining the worst-case scenarios, TB walking onto the stage, and doing a Neil at Sheffield,[1] then getting stormed by some of the druggies and the drunks at the front. After an hour or so, somebody came to take him up to the stage. Even in the time we had been away from the main action, the atmosphere had got a lot worse.

[1] The Labour Party (which was ahead of the Conservatives in opinion polls) held a 'US-style' political rally at the Sheffield Arena on April 1, 1992, a week before the general election. Neil Kinnock's 'triumphalist' display was subse-quently widely criticised.

I didn't like it one bit. As he went on, there were a few cheers, a few boos, but generally, it was just a very pissed, very druggy atmosphere in which he neither looked nor sounded comfortable. Apparently it looked a lot better on TV than in the flesh. Even though it was one of the shortest speeches he had made, it was still fairly long for this kind of event, and maybe a bit too serious. I suppose we just about got away with it but as he came off he said thank God that's done. I had a chat with Mick Hucknall [singer] who said there were going to be a lot of disappointed people if we lost.

Sunday, February 25
JP said he and Pauline had bumped into Major. JM said 'I'll keep the seat warm until you get rid of Blair.' Pauline was seemingly bowled over by how witty and charming he was and said 'He really is as tough as old boots.' Fiona and I went to TB's for dinner. Peter M, who'd done a good interview on *On the Record* today, was there. I said the real bane of TB's life was GB and Peter's inability to get on. Fiona said 'You have to be tough on Gordon and tough on the causes of Gordon.' Peter laughed, and said 'I'm afraid I am the causes of Gordon.'

Monday, March 4
TB said we had to create some sense of excitement and interest in the policy debate. The press did not feel we were telling them an adequate enough story about what a Labour government would be like. He said he was confident in the policy positions but we had to get that debate going in the country. He then moved on to saying he wanted more party reform. 'Why not go to 30% on the block vote?' Sally [Morgan] rolled her eyes and sighed very loudly. 'Please, Tony, let's get through this year's conference on 50–50 first.' Sally, who had been a teacher, could sound and look very teacherish, and that was the manner on this – like a teacher telling a naughty boy not to push his luck. She also had this habit, when she'd made a point, of then looking very closely at her fingernails and stroking them with her other hand, which added to the sense that she had made the only point that mattered, now can we move on. It was all the more effective for being understated. 'Oh all right then,' he said, grumpily, and Sally looked at me and allowed herself a triumphal little wink.

Wednesday, March 6
TB went through what he wanted from Partnership with the People. Tom Sawyer had produced a fascinating diagram analysing our

problem areas. He had written inside a circle 'winning the general election and staying in office'. Orbiting the circle were six boxes. 1. Shadow Cabinet pulling in different directions. 2. PLP not fully on board. 3. Unions preparing to make unreasonable demands. 4. Isolation of party activists. 5. NEC not focused on future. 6. Campaign and media – politicians not in harmony with party machine. It was a good summary. He said 'You don't realise how isolated you are.' And he said JP was a common theme in the six problem areas. We had to address the weakness of the links between the leader's office and the party.

Thursday, March 7

Pat McFadden and I went through the speech for Scotland tomorrow with TB and he suddenly piped up that he had plans for major change to our devolution policy. He wanted to limit the tax-raising powers. He wanted to promise a referendum before the Parliament is established. And he wanted to be explicit that power devolved is power retained at Westminster. That, he said, is the answer to the West Lothian Question.[1] He said it in that way he has of making clear he has thought it through and it will be very hard to dissuade him. I had no problem with any of it, and thought it was both sensible and right. But Scottish politics is a nightmare and Pat rightly said there would be hell to pay in the party, not least from GB, but TB said they'll just have to live with it. He said he had been reading Roy Jenkins' book on Gladstone, and the reason he didn't do home rule was because these same kinds of arguments were being put to him, and they were nonsense. He said he was absolutely clear about this. He intended at some point in the not too distant future to make a big speech on it, then stay for a few days and take all the shit that was flying, and win the argument. 'We would fall 10 points in the polls because of all the noise and then do you know what will happen? The party will breathe a sigh of relief and the public will think we have seen sense and we will finally have a defensible position.' He was terrific when he was like this. I could forgive him all the circular conversations and the weakness with some of his key relationships when he was like this: clear, principled, determined and set to lead from the front. The Scottish media would go into one of their frenzies but he was right – it was

[1] West Lothian Question. First raised in November 1977 by Tam Dalyell, Labour MP for West Lothian, a dilemma raised by Scottish devolution. Dalyell asked how it could be right for Westminster MPs from Scotland to have no power to affect issues of their constituents taken over by the Scottish Parliament, yet be able to have the power to vote on issues affecting England.

the sensible thing to do and only he really had the balls to say and then do it.

Friday, March 8

TB did a new Tory attack section for the Scotland speech and I redid the bit on TB telling the Shadow Cabinet to spell out legislative priorities. It was a perfectly good speech and its New Labour tone all the stronger for the fact he was doing it in Scotland. On the plane to Edinburgh we had the usual last-minute scramble for jokes, which was always a pain because basically he expected me to do them. 'I am not a fucking comedian,' I said. I stopped the air steward and asked if he would ask the pilot to tannoy an appeal for jokes for TB's speech. 'Don't worry,' said TB. 'He's mad.' I came up with a line on Dennis Canavan,[1] who had said TB was autocratic. 'I'm surprised you said I am autocratic, as I expressly told you not to.' TB's speech went down fine and the press all went for the right line – warning on priorities, hard choices, no tax and spend. The Scots media were intrigued by him saying there were 'no plans' to change the number of Scottish Westminster MPs. They were right to be. On the plane down, we discussed Israel. I said he should be careful about Michael Levy. He may be a great fund-raiser and a good bloke, but the press were determined to get their teeth into him big time and even if he has done nothing wrong his whole life, you can see how they'll try to portray him and it could be damaging. TB was sure Michael was straight, and a good thing.

Wednesday, March 13

Clare Short was on the *Today* programme at 7.10 on transport, and was barely comprehensible at points, constantly wittering about the policy being one of 'breathe and move'. Later I played the tape to TB and he sat there, groaning. At the Big Four, JP came bounding in in a great mood for once and boomed out 'Hello, Gordon, how are you?' and GB just stared at his papers and said nothing. JP tried again. How are you, Gordon? And he ignored him. During the meeting, Kate Garvey came in and said there had been a dreadful shooting in Dunblane[2] and a large number of children had been killed. George Robertson was up there, and TB spoke to him. It was one of those events that made everything else stop.

[1] Labour MP for West Stirlingshire/Falkirk West 1984–2000. Independent MSP (member of the Scottish Parliament) 2000–07. Expelled from the Labour Party in 2000.
[2] Thomas Hamilton, a rejected and unbalanced youth worker, massacred 16 children and a teacher in the gym at Dunblane primary school near Stirling.

Thursday, March 14

The media was totally overwhelmed by Dunblane and a real sense of national grief. TB said George had told him there was a strong feeling he ought to go to Dunblane. Major was due to go tomorrow, because he had a fund-raising dinner in Glasgow, and obviously could not go to Scotland without going to Dunblane. TB said if Major asked him to go as an all-party visit he would, but George was very insistent. Back at the House, George came to see TB and said it was his and Michael Forsyth's [Conservative Secretary of State for Scotland] view that both TB and Major should go to Dunblane together. TB said he really did not want to push his way into this, and only wanted to do what was right. George spoke to Forsyth, and they agreed Forsyth should speak to Major and suggest they go together. As we heard nothing, and time was marching on, Anji called Alex Allan [principal private secretary] at Number 10 about 2pm. She said he sounded very nervous and said that the Prime Minister felt it would be tasteless for them to go together. On the contrary, she said, if it was true, as George and Forsyth were saying, that the community wanted TB to go there, the most tasteful thing would be for them to go together. It would be very odd if Major wanted somehow to veto this. TB did not want to be pushy. On the other hand, we did not want to end up in a situation where he was criticised for not going. And Major would surely not want to be criticised for stopping him. I could sense a big row story coming on, which would help nobody. PMQs was of course very subdued and very moving, and during George's statement, which I felt captured the mood best, I found myself with tears rolling down my face. Major said he would be going there tomorrow for the whole House. TB saw him afterwards, just the two of them for part of it, and came back saying 'He really doesn't want me to go, that much is clear.' He said he didn't want to push this, but if GR and Forsyth felt as strongly as they did, they should see Major, which they did. TB said Major had said Thatcher always wanted to do these tragedy visits but he hated it and he felt it would be wrong if there was a big circus there. TB said that was not Forsyth's view, that the community wanted political support. If the community felt they should go together, that will be the best thing to do. Forsyth and George discussed it with Major, and then, with Rachel Reynolds from Number 10, they came through to see TB. Forsyth and I had a perfectly good relationship and as we went in, to lighten the mood, I said 'One day this will all be yours.' It was his view that rather than have two VIP visits, they should do it together. They told Major that the entire community would appreciate it if they both went. He said he had said to Major 'If my judgement is proved wrong, you can sack me,' to which Major had pointed at George and said 'Yes, but I can't sack him.' He finally agreed they should go together. Forsyth said it was very important there was nothing in the press about the discussions about this, and we agreed that he should tell people at his briefing later, that TB was also going with JM. JM, having first been over the top against, now appeared to be over the top for and he asked TB to have dinner with him at the Hilton in Glasgow. TB felt not, not least because we were going to stay at George's. There was an enormous amount of pissing around, before finally getting away in the Number 10 convoy to the airport. On the flight, I had a chat with Jonathan Haslam, but all pretty inconsequential. TB was fretting that they would brief the press that he had barged his way in when in fact he just wanted to do what everyone else thought was right. Major and Norma were chilly with TB, and as for me, I might as well not have existed. It was odd considering we used to be quite friendly but JM, and I suppose she, had never understood that once he became PM, it was a different game. I had built him up in print in part to help undermine Thatcher, but he never saw that. At Glasgow, we split off and headed to Dunblane and George's place. Forsyth was very solicitous and kind. George introduced me to Forsyth's wife, who said she hadn't realised that I was tall and handsome as well as famous! She was very friendly, and I saw a very different side to Forsyth. Later TB started to tell George about his plans on devolution, and I could see George was getting more and more nervous. I watched the Scottish news and it was perfectly obvious that it had been the right thing to do to go together.

Friday, March 15

I called Jonathan Haslam to check whether Major would be wearing a black tie. We had a few hours to spare, and TB used it for a discussion with George about devolution. TB was insistent that our policy was flawed, that the Tories could use the issue both for their tax campaign, and their campaign on the break-up of the UK. He was absolutely sure we would have to pledge a referendum, and make clear that power devolved would be power retained. George feared it would mean tearing up a deal with the Lib Dems, which had given him thus far political cover. Then when George had to go out for a call, TB said I know I am absolutely right on this. This is the reason why every home-rule bid has failed, because they have not had the guts to answer the real questions. He said to George, they would have to make changes in government anyway, to which George said yes, but then we will be in government. What if this stops us getting there, because of the outcry in Scotland? TB said there would be no reason for an outcry. Why shouldn't there be a referendum? If people want it, they should make it clear. Why shouldn't we make clear that power devolved is power retained, because that is the reality? Westminster will always be a superior body.

The Chief Constable and his assistant were both very shaken up. A lot of cigarettes were being smoked. The Prime Minister arrived shortly afterwards, and the Chief Constable gave a presentation of what happened, which was absolutely chilling. He took them through events very factually, very quietly, Hamilton killed them systematically, one by one. It was not clear why he stopped. I felt a bit sorry for Major, who clearly felt he had to respond in some way, but couldn't really find anything to match the enormity of what they'd just heard, and so made an odd-sounding enquiry about whether Hamilton watched videos. 'I know a lot of my colleagues are worried about videos,' he said. The Chief Constable said there was no evidence. TB said very little, simply that the police and the community had the support of everyone. John and Norma totally cut me dead again, which I thought was incredibly petty. Norma had also had a chat with Sandra Robertson [George's wife] who said she found her very cold. The reality was they didn't want us there. We left for the hospital, where there was a huge media scrum. TB first saw a child, then two teachers who were recovering. The hospital was so quiet, very little of the usual hustle and bustle, just very very quiet. TB was as upset as I've seen him. He and Major were then taken into a room filled with groups of doctors, nurses, paramedics, ambulance people, all the different people who had been involved. Again, you were struck by the quiet, the cold sadness that everyone felt, and the trauma those who saw it all were going through. JM was better at this private event than he was speaking publicly. TB and he did a short doorstep, no questions. We headed to the school. This was grim beyond belief. We drove up past an enormous media presence to the school gates. 'Welcome to our school.' Little bags hanging from pegs through the windows. Major, Norma and TB were taken to see a parent who had lost a child. George and Forsyth and their wives were taken through to a room with seven round tables around which parents were being comforted by friends and experts and volunteers. Some were grieving openly, weeping uncontrollably, beyond comfort. There was some trying to raise spirits, but it was impossible. TB came in, and then started to go round table by table. I chatted to the headmaster, Ron Taylor, who told me what it was like going to the gym on Wednesday. There was so little I could do, he said, get the children out, then just plugging wounds with paper towels, anything we could find. TB was taken to see the gym, and there was a large pool of blood where they thought the teacher was trying to shield one of the children. Ron said the man chased them around the room systematically, apparently even following one of them into a cupboard. Ron could not stop talking. His compassion was very powerful and he was clearly a strong character. He said the images just kept coming into his head, he doubted they would ever go away. He said the most chilling moment was when he was stuffing paper towels into a little girl's back wound, and as she rolled over there were two bullet holes in the front too. TB said the woman they had been to see had lost her husband last year and was pregnant. I asked him later what his God thought of all this. How could he see something like this and still believe in some great divine being who offers nothing but good? He said just because the killer is bad, does not mean that God is not good. He and Major then laid a wreath, and did another short doorstep. Though he was as moved as I have ever seen him, part of him was always the professional politician, and he wanted assurance that nobody could say he barged in and that he had handled himself well. Finally, Major spoke to me. 'There are no words for this, are there?' he said. 'Grim,' was all I could mutter. All day, I found it very hard not to cry. You looked at the class pictures and they could have been kids at our school, any school, anywhere. There was a little crowd of local people who TB spoke to, others were watching silently from their homes across the way. It was hard to imagine that this town could ever get back to normal.

In the car to the airport, we were silent. Ron Taylor said he couldn't get the images out of his mind and no wonder. Both George and Forsyth said how plausible many people had found Hamilton. George said that when he took his sons out of Hamilton's boys' club he was attacked by middle-class parents, who defended Hamilton. The whole day was incredibly harrowing and it was wonderful to get home and see the kids. I felt guilty when I watched the news and found myself thinking as the pressmen had done, seeing who came across better, TB or Major. It was TB. Both he and George had handled themselves well. The man who had made the deepest impression was Ron Taylor though. He had a huge task ahead of him and I wanted somehow to help, but knew it was unlikely that I would, or could.

Monday, March 18

Dunblane was still enormous, and the sense of grief around the place, even in London, was palpable. The Queen had gone yesterday and pictures that looked like she had been crying were big everywhere.

The community was now making calls to scale down the coverage and let them grieve in peace. David Mellor [Conservative MP] was doing a big number on gun law. I thought we were terribly weak. I felt we should be calling for a ban on guns. It was the right thing to do anyway but after Dunblane even more so. I was pointing people to George Robertson's remarks at the weekend that it should be necessary to prove the need to own a gun, rather than the police prove unfitness to hold one. Otherwise Mellor was making the running on this.

Wednesday, March 20

TB had agreed with Matthew D'Ancona to do a piece on his religious beliefs for the Easter edition of the *Sunday Telegraph*. People knew he believed in God, if not perhaps how important it all was to him, but I could see nothing but trouble in talking about it. British people are not like Americans, who seem to want their politicians banging the Bible the whole time. They hated it, I was sure of that. The ones who didn't believe didn't want to hear it; and the ones who did felt the politicians who went on about it were doing it for the wrong reasons. We had lunch at the *Sun*, which was pretty tough because by and large this was a group of very right-wing people. In the end, they would do what they were told but TB left in no doubt that if it was up to the people in that room, they would not want the paper to back us. Where they were basically coming from was that the party deep down hadn't changed. Afterwards TB said that was not a good meeting and they are not very nice people, with one or two exceptions. I said did you notice the portrait of Murdoch in the room where we had lunch? It was one of those in which the eyes followed you round the room. Hilarious. But they were all a bit Moonie-fied. As I said to Stuart Higgins afterwards, are you telling me all those people independently came to identical views on Europe?

Thursday, March 21

On the train north, TB was in one of those agonising and demanding moods, complaining that he had to do so much himself to get anything done at all. We had a spat and he just stared out of the window. The journey was one of the worst, because he was fretful, indecisive, and Anji and I were both in foul humour too. At Manchester, I'm afraid my rudeness got the better of me again. During the dinner, a woman came out and said that they bought their tickets a long time before they knew it was going to be hijacked by a politician. I said if you have a problem speak to the organisers. What sort of speech do you expect from a politician but a political one? She said you are just as rude as everyone says you are. I said ruder, because I couldn't stand fools and there were lots of them around. TB said I had to watch my rudeness. He said I know you're in a bad mood but don't take it out on these people. He said I don't mind Anji clearing up afterwards for you but I don't want to have to do it myself as well.

Friday, March 22

There was the usual pandemonium getting ready in the morning, Cherie getting her make-up done; she had lost the boots she wanted for her rather over the top turquoise suit. I was winding TB up all day re the Oratory and the fact that he was getting a bit thinner at the front – 'Chapter 27 – I'm not going bald and it really is a comprehensive.'

Saturday, April 6

The *Sunday Telegraph* was splashing on the row engendered by TB's piece on God. I felt fully vindicated. As I said to TB, 1. Never believe journalists when they say they are doing you a favour or giving you a free hit, 2. Never do an interview without someone else in the room, and 3. Never talk about God. Hilary [Coffman] and David [Hill] felt it wouldn't play too badly but I sensed a mini-disaster, as it was Easter, and they were trying to spin this as Blair allying Labour to God. When you looked at the words, he didn't say that, but he said enough to let them do the story and get Tories piling in saying he was using his faith for politics, and saying you couldn't be a Tory and a Christian. This was the permanent risk with UK politicians talking about God.

Monday, April 8

GB called and we agreed God was a disaster area. TB had called him from Spain because he had not been able to get hold of me. We joked about TB going to Tamworth tomorrow to say he had been resurrected. The papers were pretty mega on TB and God, the splash almost everywhere with several bad editorials saying he was playing politics with God. Fiona and David Hill were still of the view that it was basically OK. When I spoke to TB he admitted it was an own goal, totally unnecessary. 'I should never have agreed to do it and I won't do it again.'

Tuesday, April 9

The US build-up was going well, *People* mag was out, *US News* and *World Report*. Jonathan called to ask what we wanted Mike McCurry

[Clinton's press secretary] to say. I said our media would judge things on the length of the meeting,[1] and the way he was treated, not least the media arrangements. He suggested a joint press call, which might be too optimistic but that was what we should aim for. I said they should also say that TB's stance had been helpful on Ireland. Jonathan called again later to say he had seen Mike and Tony Lake [National Security Adviser], that they said the Tories were pissed off at all the advance hype but they were perfectly happy and would help us all they could. The meeting would certainly overrun, they would do a walk through the garden, and would certainly allow the media in. Also Mike was up for doing a joint briefing with me just for the UK press. They were certainly pulling out a few stops. I had a bet with Bruce that I could get Clinton to say 'Brian Jenkins'[2] in the White House, without just asking him to say it. More good news from Washington, that Colin Powell wanted to come to the dinner at the residence. On the drive back, we got into mildly hysterical mode. We were looking ahead to the US and tomorrow's meeting with Boutros Boutros-Ghali [UN Secretary-General] and I started to imagine what the world would be like if everyone had to have three names, à la Boutros Boutros-Ghali. I said to Fiona Gordon [Labour Party official] that if she married GB, she could call herself Fiona Gordon Brown, which for some reason TB found ludicrously funny, and kept repeating it and laughing.

Thursday, April 11
On arrival, TB disappeared off with the ambassador in the Rolls-Royce to see Alan Greenspan [chairman of the US Federal Reserve], while I left to find the bar where Mike McCurry was coming to meet me and our press. It was a really nice thing for him to do and an excellent meeting. He talked up TB while lowering expectations. He said it had been very odd in the November meeting, because someone in the room had said it was almost as if TB was the senior figure at times. He said Clinton wanted to carry on basically where it left off last time. Mike and I had a chat about how to handle things. He said Clinton wanted to do a walk through the garden, but they were coming

[1] The trip had to be closely choreographed because of the visit made by Neil Kinnock when he was snubbed by Mrs Thatcher's great friend, Ronald Reagan. Kinnock was given less than the half-hour put aside for his interview with Reagan, who had failed to recognise Denis Healey – sent with Kinnock to add weight and experience – referred to the former Chancellor throughout as 'Mr Ambassador'. The snub was rubbed in by a dismissive White House briefing.
[2] Labour candidate, eventual victor in the Tamworth by-election, April 11, 1996.

under pressure from the embassy not do anything that would wind up the story that Major was being punished. Mike and I agreed he would give a very positive readout. They would talk up TB on Northern Ireland, and TB's role in left-of-centre politics. He was clever and funny and had a light touch. He was obviously going to help us make it a success. TB said earlier that we should underline after the by-election that the Tories had no friends at home and no friends abroad. Some of our press assumed the White House was pushing the boat out because of Major's lot helping Bush. TB was really motoring, winning everyone over. I was meanwhile getting the cuttings and speaking to Tamworth. The reception was fine, they had put together a good list of people. I was seated between Tina Brown [editor of the *New Yorker*] and Ben Bradlee's [former editor of the *Washington Post*] wife but I was like a cat on a hot tin roof waiting for the by-election result. I had an interesting chat with Tina and Harry Evans [former editor of *The Times*] about how awful the modern press was. I gave them my usual scenario on how we could lose. It was almost 3am when I finally got the result from Fiona Gordon. 13,700 majority. I felt like bursting into tears. In fact I almost did and later, in the privacy of my room, I did. Fiona G was as cool as a cucumber. I went through to tell TB straight away, and though he knew he shouldn't overreact in public, I could tell he was ecstatic, especially as in the last couple of hours, I'd been winding him up by saying it could be as low as 1,500. I wanted him to be the first on and we had got things lined up so that he could go straight into the [David] Dimbleby programme. We went down to do it and I could only hear TB, not the questions, and I could tell Dimbleby was straight onto tax as his second question. I could see TB was going strong, staying cool and dismissive. The lines on the by-election were easy, fantastic victory for us, humiliation for them, contrast between us with a positive programme for government, them drifting and directionless. I got him to speak to Fiona G and thank her and the team. 'This is unbelievable,' he said. 'They are in real trouble now. I can even see them moving to Heseltine.' No problem, I said.

Friday, April 12

We had breakfast at the *Washington Post* with a very right-wing editorial board who gave him a bit of a kicking but he handled it well. Kay Graham [publisher of the *Washington Post*] was impressive. She showed inordinate interest in his article on God, and wanted a copy faxed to her. We fixed up pictures of TB calling JP and Brian Jenkins, with cameras both ends. TB had spoken earlier to John to say well done.

I'd spoken to him and he said to tell people 'I'm not a class warrior, but a class act.' JP was getting huge coverage by saying he was middle class and prompting lots of coverage about class divides. Then we left for the White House. TB was more nervous than I'd seen in a long time. Several times he took me to the corner of the waiting room to ask about minor details, some not so minor. 'Do I call him Bill or Mr President?' Clinton was waiting just inside the door and greeted everyone individually, then introduced TB to the rest of the US side. There was a fair bit of small talk, Clinton explaining some of the paintings and artefacts, asking about New York, putting people at ease. I was surprised at the level of turnout on their side. Clinton, Warren Christopher [Secretary of State], [Robert] Rubin [Secretary of the Treasury], [Tony] Lake, [Leon] Panetta [Chief of Staff], Nancy Soderberg [US policy official on Ireland], McCurry. The American pool came in and threw one or two domestic questions, and then the next pool, with lots of eager Brits. Peter Riddell from *The Times* broke the silence. 'Do you think you're sitting next to the next Prime Minister?' There was a pause, both smiled and you could feel Clinton's mind whirring, thinking carefully what to say. 'I just hope he's sitting next to the next President,' he said. TB looked nervous, though he got into it. Clinton praised our statesmanlike stance on Ireland, as Mike said he would. The last time I was in this room was as part of the press pool and I can remember thinking how little time you had to ask questions or absorb the atmosphere, and how quickly they bundled you out. It was strange to see them being parcelled out, much the same people I used to be with, and I stayed behind, and then listened to and took part in discussions about the big issues of the day. Clinton surprised me in several regards. His enormous feet were all the more noticeable because his shoes were even shinier than TB's. His suit and tie were immaculate, as was his hair. He had huge hands, long thin fingers, nails clearly manicured and he used his hands a great deal as he spoke, usually to emphasise the point just before he made it. I was also struck at the amount of detail he carried in his head. Like TB, he was good on the big picture, but he backed it up with phenomenal detail. He was a people person, terrific at illustrating policy points by talking about real people, real places. He was also tremendous at working a room. He was more relaxed than at the meeting in London, presumably because this was his territory and he was less tired, but if he made a long intervention, he found a way of addressing part of it to all the different people in the room. It's a great talent in a politician, and in his manner and his speaking style, he engages you, makes you feel warmly disposed towards him. I guess that wasn't a surprise, and it shouldn't have been a surprise that he was so big on detail, but it was. Also like TB, he came alive talking about strategy, campaigns, message. He got it instinctively, more than probably any political leader in the world. There was one revealing moment when Clinton said of our stance on Northern Ireland, 'It's smart,' then a pause, then he added, 'and morally right.' I won my bet with Bruce. The deal was I had to get Clinton to say the words Brian Jenkins, and I couldn't just say 'Say Brian Jenkins.' Knowing as I did how big he was on campaigns and campaign methods, I put a few 'Vote Brian Jenkins' stickers on my notebook and whenever I spoke held it tight against my chest, stickers showing. I could see he was looking at the stickers and after a while he said 'Who's Brian Jenkins?' Our side fell about, and I explained the bet, and he said he was glad to help. TB said straight out: how do you win support for more equity and justice without it meaning more tax? Clinton said the private sector was the key, that we must not be defined simply as a public sector government, but bind in the private sector, emphasise their role in wealth creation. There was a clock just to Clinton's left by the door and after 25 minutes a tall young blonde woman, beautifully dressed all in black, came in, gave him a nod, smiled at the room and then closed the door behind her. It was time to go, but Clinton kept talking, more talking and eventually got up and he carried on talking. Mike and I disappeared into the corner to agree we would say they met for 35 minutes, more than scheduled, very friendly, useful, productive, go over the issues they ranged over. Mike then took us through to the Cabinet room, TB included, and he said he would say it was a 40-minute meeting which covered Bosnia, Ireland, world economy, Europe, mad cow, etc. He had been a terrific help. We then collected our thoughts and went through what TB should say at the stakeout spot. Again, I found myself thinking of previous visits here, on the other side of the fence. In particular when Neil [Kinnock] was stitched up here by a combination of the White House, Number 10 and our disgusting right-wing press. I got a certain satisfaction from seeing them straining to hear his every word, and knowing that this time, because the White House had been so helpful, there was no way they could write this as anything but a success. We then went for a meeting with Al Gore [Vice President], which was fine. I was surprised how heavy he was and how much he relied on cue cards to speak. I was sitting next to someone who was literally ticking off the lines as Gore delivered them.

April '96: And Campbell wins a bet

Sunday, April 14

Charlie Whelan woke me up to say that Clare Short had fucked up on *GMTV* by saying that she thought people like her should pay more tax. She cannot be trusted to behave in a professional or competent way. TB was at Michael [Levy]'s and called several times purely to say how exasperated he was about people like her. It would be so much easier if I did not have the party around my ankles the whole time, he said.

Monday, April 15

I woke to Clare Short all over the papers, being lauded by the Tory press for 'letting the cat out of the bag' on tax, and as if that wasn't bad enough, then she came on the *Today* programme. None of us knew she was going to be on, ostensibly about the Railtrack prospectus being published today. Of course she was asked about tax, and not only defended what she said yesterday, but then launched into an attack on the anonymous sources attacking her. Her language was loose and intellectually lazy as ever, and she made it sound like a principled position when in truth she had simply fucked up. TB and JP both called straight away. TB said the problem was that she was out of her depth. JP said simply 'That woman is fucking mad.'

Tuesday, April 16

Donald [Dewar] and I went to talk it over with TB. He said even though we were all angry, it was important to stay objective about Clare. He said I should remember what Machiavelli said, if you are not going to kill, don't wound. We are not going to kill her, so leave it, he said. I said she was going to continue to build herself up as the great heroine of the left, and it was unacceptable. But TB said there was no real support for her in the party, it was a media thing, which is what made it different from the Harriet situation. There, the party felt I was in the wrong. Here, they think I'm in the right.

Sunday, May 5

I spoke to Michael Levy, who said Cherie had been really low on Friday, and she was convinced I was against her. I said to Michael that I was very sympathetic to her position, but that because she and TB didn't always discuss these things in detail, sometimes we didn't know what line to project and develop. I felt that she believed that when we pointed out what the press might do or say, we were expressing OUR view. For example, when I said she could be portrayed as Glenys or Hillary Clinton, or as a crap mother, or as Islington woman with all the homoeopathy stuff, she felt that was me expressing my view. In truth, that was me trying to explain where I felt our enemies were trying to take her profile. The public saw her as a mother, wife and career woman and because she avoided the overtly political profile, she had a strong image, which could easily be threatened. She said to Michael that she thought I would prefer her to be Norma [Major] Mark 2. I said that was absurd. I just need to know how she and Tony want her to be, in terms of the public image, and we could help get her there. Michael clearly saw himself as a main man. He emphasised again and again how close they were. We are family, he said. He said he could be a conduit with Cherie. I said it was not necessary to complicate things further. Cherie knew what the real problem was between us: I thought Carole [Caplin] was a problem and she didn't.

Monday, May 6

I was woken by GB in a flap because of the papers, which I hadn't seen. 'Child benefit rift' in various forms was leading most of the broadsheets. He clearly felt we hadn't been tough enough in backing him up even though the *Express*, for example, reported that TB had stepped in to back GB. The *Guardian* had another complicating story, namely that we were going to reverse decisions on jobseekers' allowance and unemployment benefit in a victory for the soft left. GB said there had to be tougher briefing on this today, and that we had to get back on track with it. He said he would go on the *World at One*, and we needed a blitz of articles.

Thursday, May 9

The strategy meeting was not just about the speech, but also the campaign on the Lost Generation for next week. A huge amount of work and planning had gone on, at GB's instigation, involving Blunkett, and Jack Straw's people. Peter M therefore got very irritated when Gordon said he didn't think we were ready for it on Monday. Peter and I both sighed volubly, given neither of us had been keen in the first place, but we had actually tried hard to make it happen. Peter got terribly defensive and said Gordon, this was entirely your idea, we have all been trying to make it work without proper direction from you or your office, and now you were rowing back. They started talking very loudly at each other, just a few decibels short of shouting. TB, who for once was sitting in the chair by the TV, rather than at his desk or in his usual place on the sofa, said for heaven's sake keep this under control. Peter then stood up, said no, I won't,

I'm not taking any of this crap any longer, and he stormed out. TB just shook his head, while GB stared at his papers and then started scribbling. Then the meeting resumed as if nothing had happened. I said, looking at Charlie Whelan, that I didn't think it would be helpful if that exchange was in any way communicated to the public. Peter came back later to collect his coat and TB said 'You cannot talk to Gordon like that in a room full of people.' Peter said 'I have had enough. I am not going to put up with it any longer, being undermined and getting no support from here.' He picked up his jacket, walked out again. I looked at TB and he looked at me, and we both stood there shaking heads. TB sat down and said 'What am I supposed to do? It is impossible.' It was so absurd that we ended up laughing, probably because we couldn't think what else to do. To be fair to Peter, he'd endured a fair bit of provocation.

Monday, May 13

TB and I discussed what I should say to Andrew Marr [*Independent* journalist] who was writing about GB/PM. I briefed him and he was clearly very anti Peter and I stressed that the party would be unforgiving on both, but also that anyone who took on the Shadow Chancellor, so close to the leader, could not win. I probably went over the top. I see, I get the message, said Andrew. I stressed that there was no ideological difference, and it was all about personality. I said that they had to get their act together. The fact was the press were onto it and we had to try to shape the coverage. At the weekly strategy meeting, it was comical, the way that Peter was trying too hard being nice to and about GB.

Wednesday, May 15

GB was on *Today* and did pretty well, considering all the crap surrounding it, and managed to get up the Lost Generation. He did a very professional job, though God knows how he felt when he said Peter is brilliant. I arrived at TB's full of anger that this is still going on, but TB said GB did a very good job, and showed why he still has faith in him. But he said he felt his relationship with both of them would never be the same again. I repeated endlessly that I felt there had to be some evidence of them being put in their place to draw a line under this, but he said you could not do that with the Shadow Chancellor. He was livid with JP over his speech yesterday, and called him in once we got to the office. JP said he only ever got listened to when he rocked the boat, and there had to be a real change in procedures and the way things were done. At the Big Four, TB said it had been a dreadful week. Robin said it was important we present whatever way forward we agree not as being about discipline but direction/policy. GB emphasised the need to get back onto the Road to the Manifesto. JP said this forum doesn't work, we don't meet enough, we don't discuss things. This was meant to be a check on policy-making and it hasn't worked. We exist because we do represent different views, and ours are not taken into account. There is no real forum for discussion. TB said if people think it is tough now, they should wait for government. JP asked if the Road to the Manifesto process was going to lead to policy changes and TB said straight out – yes. We went through to the Shadow Cabinet meeting in a really bad atmosphere. Again TB said it had been a dreadful week. There was anger in the party. The obligation on the leadership was to ensure proper consultation and that also meant those consulted had obligations too. He said there would be more involvement of the Shadow Cabinet but nothing justified the lack of discipline. The irony is that there is no great ideological split between us. Far from it. Hostile things make news. Comments about colleagues make news. I promise the broadest possible consultation but there must be reciprocal responsibility and history will pass a very cruel judgement if we fail now. Jack Cunningham was terrific. He said I've been here 26 years and 13 of them at this table in opposition, and that is more than enough. If we cannot have proper discussions in here, then the Shadow Cabinet becomes dysfunctional. He said he had also learned that parties that squabble about power before they get it, do not get it in the end. The public will not vote for divided parties and the Tories must be delighted at the ammunition we had given them. Jack Straw came in, said a lot of this is about political maturity. People are always willing to believe the worst of colleagues and it's bad. We're paying the price for complacency. Ann Taylor said the party was in a state of anxiety, anger and horror. We're beginning to think that we could lose. Earlier TB had said to me I really had to try harder to deal with GB. Your trouble is that you're like me, you cannot understand why people behave like this, but you have to understand we are the exceptions. He felt the Shadow Cabinet had been cathartic and would help us draw a line. The press sensed that TB's leadership could be damaged by this and were going to push it as hard as they could. The inability to keep them in order looked pathetic and unprofessional.

Saturday, May 25 to Saturday, June 1 (holiday in Majorca)
I tried very hard to switch off while we were away. Not easy of course, because Philip [Gould] yaks constantly about the party, and never

tires of discussing the main themes and the main players. He was nagging at me to come up with a fresh slogan for the next stage and into the Road to the Manifesto. We had a couple of brainstorming sessions at one of the little bars on the beach and eventually I came up with New Labour, New Life for Britain. I liked it. It took the basic slogan but gave it a sense of process and energy which would be illustrated by policy rather than strategy.

Friday, June 7

TB was calling so often, and usually about the same thing, that I ended up pretending to be an answering machine – if your call is for Alastair Campbell, and you are his boss, please leave a message after the tone, explaining whether you are saying something you have not already said ten times. At least it was possible to have a laugh with him, and he had no trouble being told when he was being irritating, as now.

Saturday, June 8

Alan Clark called and was in despair. 'I think we're probably fucked,' he said. 'It's like the patient got ill, and the doctor prescribed anti-biotics, but the patient didn't improve, and if anything got worse, so we whacked in a few tons of cortisone but nothing, absolutely nothing, has happened to make things better. So that says to me the patient is enduring a slow and lingering death.' I said you've quite cheered me up, Alan, and he said 'Congratters, I have to say you guys have been playing a blinder, and our people just don't know what to do.' He was in excited, excitable form, emphasising every single word as he spoke – 'AND OUR PEOPLE JUST DON'T KNOW WHAT TO DOOOOO'. I took the kids' football class at school and then to TB's for lunch before heading for Wembley for the England v Switzerland game. I had an unusually pleasant conversation with Cherie. When she wanted to be charming and friendly, that was exactly what she was and it reminded me of the impression she made when we first met. I could never quite fathom why she couldn't maintain that most of the time. The truth was that on most of the occasions we met now, there was usually politeness but not the friendliness there used to be, but today she was full of warmth and good humour, asking after the kids and saying how grateful TB was for everything I did for him etc. The two of them were due to see Robin Butler [Cabinet Secretary] tonight and hope-fully go over some of the questions that I don't think they had really turned their minds to, like where and how they intended to live, and what she intended to do by way of balancing family, career and consort roles. I don't think either of them had really got the measure of the scale of change that was coming if we won. At half-time, Denis Howell [former Labour Minister for Sport] said to me 'If England win, expect a September election.' TB told me about his last dinner with Roy Jenkins at Derry's. He does a good impersonation of Woy. 'I see you, Tony, as someone carrying an exquisite, beautiful, hand-painted vase over a slippery floor and as you proceed across the floor, vase in hand, you can see your destination, and you can see the likes of Harriet Harman and Clare Short lunging towards you, and you don't know whether to run or to tiptoe.'

Saturday, June 15

Manchester bomb. We had to organise TB's reaction on TV. I took the kids' football class and then we set off for Wembley for England v Scotland. We had good seats, but apart from Gazza's goal and Macallister's missed penalty, it was all a bit flat and anticlimactic. However, on the way out, you got a sense of just how much of a feel-good factor you could get going on the back of all this. 'Football's coming home' was being sung everywhere you went, plus the less melodious 'Eng-er-lund.' JP had gone with GB and the two of them were sitting together, and seemed to be getting on, which was progress. I bumped into Nigel Clarke [ex *Mirror* colleague/football reporter] who said he would not be voting Tory for the first time. The Manchester bomb was massive across all the media and yet there was no sense of fear in London, which was odd, and again presumably an effect of the football.

Sunday, June 16

JP called and said he wanted to speak to TB about the labour market paper that was going to the contact group tomorrow. A few weeks ago, that would have spelled disaster but he said he was determined to be onside and he just wanted to know how TB wanted to play it. He said he and GB had a good chat and they had made their peace. He said he had got a bit pissed at Geoffrey Robinson's party but the upside was he bet GB a tenner England would win, and he paid up – 'I must be the only one who's ever got money out of him.'

Monday, June 24

Tony had had dinner with GB last night and tried to get him more focused on economic rebuttal and RTTM [Road to the Manifesto], apparently without much success. TB had done some more work on our reworked RTTM draft and it was excellent. It was clearly written and for once we had a policy-heavy document that was fairly readable. There were still problems ahead though. We didn't have long to go and we still had issues to sort on health, pensions, GB's tax-and-spend argument, and we also had TB's speech on devolution. The morning meeting was fairly straightforward but GB was worrying as ever about the tax-and-spend implications of the welfare paper, and pensions. We were working hard on him re the pledges but as ever with something that wasn't his idea, he was taking a long time to come over. But I think he was moving now. TB had been working on the devolution argument and he said he was adamant he was going to make clear his view there should be no tax rise, there should certainly be a referendum and it should be made clear that Westminster was the ultimate constitutional authority – power devolved is power retained. George Robertson's reaction was not dissimilar to Donald [Dewar]'s, that yet again TB was provoking unnecessary fights, though when you got onto the substance of the arguments, they were not far apart. TB said he could only promise what he intended to deliver, and this was the best way to do it. Referendum; make clear where our instincts on tax lay; and make the big constitutional point. He said every home-rule effort up to now had failed because of over-ambition or overemotionalism. We had to be hard-headed. GR said for some, it would be a political nuclear explosion. TB said I know I am right on this, and I know it has to be done sooner rather than later, as part of the RTTM. GR could see TB was not moving and he said he would have more trouble with the executive, the press, the MPs, and his team. He was sure John McAllion [Labour MP for Dundee East] would resign. He felt you could do the tax and referendum bit, but not the third element. TB said it was a statement of the obvious, power devolved, but power retained.

Wednesday, June 26

There was huge interest in the Scotland stuff now, even with the tabloids, and I spent a lot of time saying it was a mini version of Clause 4 – there was a big argument to be had and we were absolutely confident of winning it. I could tell GR and DD were still suspicious. But they were doing well. It was going so big we agreed GR should go up and do interviews, which he did fine. He was getting flak from the PLP but managing well, as was DD. Brian Wilson said you had to hand it to TB, he liked doing things the ballsy way. But we were not going to get through this without GR and DD. Anji said the news was strong, lots of comparisons with Clause 4, leading from the front, risk, etc. Michael Forsyth looked uncomfortable in the bits I saw.

Major's speech on the constitution was getting a fair bit of play but there was now more interest in us than them on this issue. We got to Wembley for the semi-final with Germany and the atmosphere all the way up towards the ground was extraordinary. I had never really supported England, and for political reasons I found myself rooting privately for Germany, though as I was sitting next to one of JM's bodyguards, even though he was a Scot, I pretended to be backing England. It was one of the most incredible matches I've ever seen and to be fair to England, they could and should have won and there was a part of me willing them on. But by the end I felt relief. 'There goes the feelgood factor,' said Denis Howell. I then felt a total heel when I called home and the boys were crying their eyes out. JM looked a bit ashen. Just as we had been worrying, however irrationally, about the political benefits to him of England winning, so a part of him must have been banking on this. He looked pretty sick and the atmosphere at the back of the royal box was not great. I tried not to let my happiness show as we walked to the car. Once we got in, I said 'Yesss,' and shook my fist. TB said could you save any celebrations until you get home? I said don't pretend you feel any different. When we dropped him off, I said *Gute Nacht, mein Kapitän. Jetzt sind die Tories gefuckt.*

Thursday, June 27
The Scottish press was a disaster area. U-turn. Betrayal etc. Very big and very difficult. Obviously the England defeat was massive down south but there was lots of play for the referendum stuff here too. TB was worried that the whole thing was coming over as an issue purely about Scotland.

Friday, June 28
The papers were grim, even worse in Scotland where it was all a betrayal and sell-out. Here too the headlines were all crisis, backlash, usual stuff. I was still confident it would be OK though George and Jack McConnell said it could be very tricky, and it was very important TB did not fly up and lecture them all. Pat McFadden was working on the speech for Scotland when I arrived at TB's. I had inserted three new passages overnight. One, he will lead the yes campaign and he does not fight campaigns to lose them. Two, nice words about McAllion and George. Three, I do not intend to lead Britain like Major. The Tories' line was to present strength as weakness, saying we were backing down under pressure from [Michael] Forsyth. 'Are we in a mess on this?' TB asked when I got there. There

really was no argument against it. Why shouldn't people have a say in their future? The real problem was that they didn't like the way it was done, they didn't like his style. All the way to the airport, Pat and I were changing the speech and TB was trying to get the Scottish executive on board for the decision this afternoon. TB was in combative form. What do they want these people, another Tory government? Jack McConnell was playing a blinder and was clearly confident. Every time I spoke to him, I felt more confident. We finished the speech on the plane and there was an awful moment when the screen went blank and I feared we had lost the whole thing. TB was now looking forward to this. He was always confident when he felt the argument was right. We were met by George and Jack, who gave me the unbelievably grim Scottish papers. We were organising union leaders and JP to make statements backing him. George said the executive was being very difficult. The real problem was lack of consultation. George was getting hammered in the press and it was largely about the fact they didn't know in advance. I said to Jack McConnell it was amazing how Scottish I felt until I came up to Scotland and heard the Scottish media whingeing. The guy from the *Sun* was a total wanker. Then to see the chair of the Scottish Labour Party [Davie Stark]. TB was appealing for his help and it was clear he would not get it. He said the party felt they were being pushed too far, and this was one step too many. TB said he was happy to apologise for how it all came out, but it was not going to be enough. He felt he was facing a purely emotional response. Also, as TB kept saying, the main objection appeared to be that if you gave people the option, they would not want it. That went for the Parliament, and for the tax powers. We left for the speech venue. The library where it was taking place was absolutely beautiful. TB was OK but at his best when he left the script and got passionate about winning. Bob Thomson of Unison was telling everyone TB was in real trouble, and could be finished on this. TB then did a series of excellent interviews, he was really pumped up and going for it. He wanted me to brief that it was all part of the wider pre-RTTM change. We were late for the Labour executive, which made what was always going to be a hostile atmosphere worse. There was lots of talk of betrayal. One of them said they had been lied to. TB stuck to his guns, made the argument as he had done before and it turned our way when he said you also need the referendum to make sure you have the clear consent of the people which will be needed to get it through the Lords. Bob Thomson said why not just create a thousand new peers? That was what did it for some who came to our side. TB was firm without being rude and gave them a few facts of life. We left for the airport, moderately confident, then Pat called to say we had won 20 to 4 on the new policy, and 16 to 12 on defeating the old one. TB said he never thought we would do as well as that. It was quite a triumph in its own way. On the plane, TB was going through his mail, including a letter from Basil Hume [Cardinal Archbishop of Westminster], saying that he would have to stop taking Communion in a Catholic church.[1] TB wrote back 'I wonder what Our Lord will make of this.'

Tuesday, July 2
NEC. Clare [Short] making endless minor points. She said she objected to the new document describing ourselves as a party of the centre. [Dennis] Skinner, his timing excellent as ever, said 'I'm just relieved it doesn't say we're a party of the right.' Everyone laughed, but she was incapable of recalibrating to circumstances.

Wednesday, July 3
TB was worried about the Catholic Mass story, fearing it was doing us damage, but I honestly felt people would by and large not get the fuss. He was sitting there, in his dressing gown and underpants, his hair all over the place, with a slight look of the mad professor, and I knew it was going to be a long day. We had to have a top line for tomorrow. TB said we had to use tomorrow's 'New Labour, New Life for Britain' launch for another general repositioning of New Labour, the radical centre, all that. I felt there was sufficient build-up. It was about a confident TB marking out the next bold steps.

Thursday, July 4
We got huge and largely positive coverage overnight. Terry [driver] collected me and I was met at TB's by CB saying that the press said TB didn't take his full salary two years ago and she didn't want any more of that populist nonsense this time. TB said he agreed with me that the suggested rises [in MP's pay] were so big that we could wave goodbye to 'many not the few' if we went for it. He was still in his pyjamas, and looked half asleep but he was already honing down the speech I had drafted, and nodding along as he imagined himself saying bits of it. The more aggressively he nodded, the more it meant he could hear himself saying it, and making an impact, and there were more nods

[1] Although an Anglican, Blair often took Communion at a Catholic church in Islington. Hume conceded that it was permissible for him to attend a Catholic church while on holiday in Tuscany.

than usual at this stage, so we were on the right track. He made a few scribbles, asked for the changes to be put in and then went upstairs to get dressed. It was a good strong statement and we had it done by the time we left. I'd arranged for a camera in the car from his place to the House. He was bounding up the stairs when we arrived and was obviously up for it. 'God, nobody can say we have not done a lot in two years,' he said to nobody in particular. He'd agreed GB should chair it with JP away nursing his injured foot. That meant Robin Cook should say something too, so I culled something on RTTM process and called him to say TB would like him to do that part at the launch. For some reason, RC, whose normal complaint would be that he was NOT being used at events like this, went off on one. 'Can we ever plan something and just stick to it? I'm tired of all this last-minute stuff.' I said I'm sure he could handle it and he did one of his long sighs and said 'Well, yes, like a loyal soldier I will but I really must say blah, blah, blah.' In the car to Millbank, TB was getting psyched up, nodding to himself and going over the points he wanted to emphasise. TB did well during the questions though he commented later that GB was trying too hard to look like he was leading rather than chairing the event. *Panorama* were there constantly filming me and Peter M as part of the new obsession they had. TB was pumped up afterwards and we stayed back for a cup of tea with RC, who felt the whole thing went well. The launch was deemed to have gone well upstairs and was still leading the news later on. *Channel 4 News* was awful. They vox-popped people who had no idea what we had announced. Maybe if the fuckers told them rather than playing their silly games.

Thursday, July 11

A truly dreadful day. TB was useless, I was tired and useless and fed up. I was worried it was all about my health, I could not get going. I was having one of my fed up with TB days. He could not make a decision whether to take his pay rise. We were being asked about it all day. I also had a fairly friendly but heavy-edged chat with CB, who of course was concerned that I was trying to persuade him not to take it, which is what he would be telling her. TB was in a real gloom by the time he came back from the Mandela lunch. He said sometimes I think this party doesn't want to be led. To the gala dinner. The Cantona shirt Alex gave us raised £17,500.

Tuesday, July 16

TB and I had another circular conversation on where we were. He still felt the mood had not changed but certainly traditional Tory support was going back and also there was still an air of doubt about us. He said to me and Bruce G – it's really quite simple. If it's New Labour, they'll go for us. If it's not, they won't. Later I ran into Francis Maude [Conservative MP for Warwickshire North]. He usually looked more downcast than probably he was, and he said that the Tory vote was coming back to them, and it was going to be close.

Wednesday, July 24

There was total agreement Clare had to be moved but no agreement as to where. After the Shadow Cabinet results, Anji paged her seven times saying TB wanted to speak to her, and she just ignored it. JP came to see TB and said the TV walkout[1] ought to be the final straw. The woman's a liability, he said, and she doesn't have a leg to stand on. Eventually, well after 10, Sue Jackson found her in a bar and she reluctantly saw TB. He saw her alone and after she left Anji and I went in and he said she had gone completely ballistic, couldn't understand it and she was refusing to move anywhere. I said to TB if she fucked him around too much, he should just kick her out and see if anyone really cared. But even as I said it, I felt it was not sensible politics. That being said, a lot of people were saying to him, politicians and staff alike, that we worried about her far too much. She was not very good and not as popular as she or the press thought. TB said she's crap as a friend but I think she could be even worse as an enemy. These reshuffles were always difficult and he was clearly talking himself into minimal change. I said he would just have to swallow hard, prepare himself for a dreadful day tomorrow and get on with it. It would all be forgotten in days.

Saturday, July 27

TB called from Sedgefield. He said even he could not quite believe the extent to which the left press was falling for the left–right alliance trap on Clare. It is the history of Labour down the years, he said. Inhale the right's propaganda and spew it out in more noxious form. The right say we have ditched our principles, then the left say it with more venom because they talk of hurt and betrayal. He said the key to it all was keeping JP on board.

---

[1] Short had refused to discuss the London Underground strike in a live BBC news interview. She took off her microphone and left.

Tuesday, August 27

I didn't feel very refreshed after the holiday and had mixed feelings about going back to work. Peter M and I went out to see TB at half four at Richmond Crescent. He was wearing shorts and a T-shirt with a big letter Q on it. He was tanned and seemed very chirpy, and moderately sympathetic when I told him we had had something of a holiday from hell, Fiona ill, the house not great. We went through all the various problem areas and he concluded that he needed to get out there more. He realised that he was being seen as all things to all men, a bit managerial even, and it had to be much clearer that he was a conviction politician. The problem was that New Labour was defined by our opponents as an electoral or political device. We had to show that he was New Labour out of conviction. I said the most important challenge of the coming months was for TB to connect with people, and for the party to see that happening, based upon his convictions as a left-of-centre political leader. Peter and I left at seven, having enjoyed a running private joke between us to see how long we would be there before we were offered a cup of tea. We got one just before we left.

Wednesday, August 28

Neil and Glenys came round and we went to the Camden Brasserie. To our and their amazement, Robin and Gaynor [Regan, his secretary] were two tables away. Robin went a weird pink colour, while Gaynor looked sick. RC came over. There was something I needed to fax to him, and could I fax to his office. It was probably a big charade to pretend he was not going to her place.

Tuesday, September 10

Things were hotting up at the TUC in Blackpool. Jon Cruddas called several times to say things were getting a bit hairy. The problem was that Blunkett seemed to be suggesting first compulsory arbitration and then new ballots if a new offer was made to workers. This was taken to mean new legislation on the issue and the unions were up in arms. As ever, the real problem was they didn't know it was coming and felt bounced. John Monks was livid. He later spoke to TB and was only slightly more emollient. Then he spoke to me and said that only TB can kill this. 'You'd better decide if you want it to be razor hot down here, because that's the way you're going on this.' None of us could recall him ever losing his rag like this before and it bode ill. TB spoke to DB and said the worst thing now would be to back down. We got to Blackpool, and on the flight I could tell TB was getting his dander up about the unions and the way they thought they could gang up and dictate policy. We were met by Cruddas and Brendan Barber [TUC deputy general secretary] who wanted TB to rule out legislation, as DB was doing. TB refused and gave every impression that we might do it. There was a very intense and difficult conversation at the airport, where TB said the worst outcome for us was a flip-flop. He made clear he thought if they hadn't overreacted, we could have managed it, but there was no way we could be seen to back down because they had got themselves up in arms. Cruddas and Barber looked really fed up. Brendan just shook his head and said I don't think we're in for a very nice evening. When we got to the hotel, Monks's body language was awful, and the mood was sour. TB did a doorstep where he did not say what they wanted him to, and the mood got even worse. I had these wankers from *Panorama* following me around, and they said TB was resiling from stories planted by spin doctors. I engaged a bit but I'd decided the best approach was to get heavy if they talked real bollocks, but basically take the mick out of their sad little obsession. The line I pushed with the industrial hacks was that there were no plans for legislation but it had not been ruled out. TB was locked away with Monks for 20 minutes before the dinner. Monks looked crestfallen. He had one of those faces that tended to show sadness and vulnerability anyway, accentuated by his walk, which was slow and a bit unconfident, but tonight he looked really fed up. Pat [McFadden]'s view was that they all wound each other up, egged on by the labour correspondents, and they were prone to headless chickenry. I tried to explain this was cock-up not conspiracy. I warned TB the media would be full of chaos, confusion, etc, and he said that is better than backdown. I don't want any sense of backdown. 'Nil panicandum,' he said. Brendan and others clearly thought TB was behind all this. They were going on strike again and he said it gave us the chance to say there should be a ballot and these people were showing why there needed to be new ways of looking at this. He said to me and Jon C 'We have to look in control even when we clearly aren't. What matters here is people realise we are serious about New Labour.' He was politely received at the dinner, but I was in and out most of the time trying to get the press in a better place. *Panorama* around again, and I accused them of lying in front of other journalists. TB had a drink late on with Monks, Barber, John Healey [TUC campaigns director] and Jon C and the mood was a bit better but not much.

Tuesday, September 17

I called TB and he said he was writing an article in response to a cartoon in the *Guardian*. I said you're doing what? Have you gone mad? He said that a lot of the critiques against us started in this way and we had to challenge them. Tony, I said, please don't write an article in response to a cartoon. People will think you are bonkers.

Wednesday, September 18

Major was on *Today* and I thought was particularly poor. His new buzzword was the 'morality' of a low tax, small state. As Andy Marr said, it was a bog standard economic speech with the word morality in it. It was clearly a response to the idea of TB being a Christian Socialist, but it was not at all clear to me what he was talking about. Peter M persuaded TB to do the *World at One* to respond and engage in the debate. I was reluctant at first, but was won over and TB was really on form again. Everyone upstairs was commenting on how good he was at the moment. I called him and asked to be put through to the New Labour Cartoon Rebuttal Unit. He laughed but said we did have to tackle the underlying arguments because they were bollocks. The left was always a whisker away from making the charge of betrayal, which would then be used against us by the right.

Thursday, September 19

TB was doing an interview with Mary Riddell [journalist] and we discussed beforehand how he should try to open up a bit more on the personal front. People wanted to know more about what he was, where he came from as a person, who and what shaped him. He said I hate doing all that stuff, people hanging their lives out for others to stare at. I said it was important because some people out there would only connect with us through him and his personality, and until they had got that they would not even get near the whole policy area. He did his usual policy stuff with Mary, and was on good form and when she started to push him on the personal front, he started hesitantly on the kids. Then she asked him if he ever felt stalked by tragedy – dad's stroke, mother's death, John Smith's death, and he went through each of them and how he felt and when he talked about his mum he really opened up, and I found it quite moving. I had never really heard him talk about his mother in such detail before and there was a real naturalness and warmth in his words, and a look in his eyes that was half fond, half sad, and when he had finished talking about her, he just did a little nod and a sigh and then looked out of the window. I said to him afterwards I'd never realised he was so close to his mum because he had never really opened up like that before, even in private. He said she was a wonderful woman and he still felt guided by her. What would she make of where you are now? I asked. Heaven knows, he said. I think she would be anxious for me, but proud. Dad is always saying I wish she was here to see this, she would be so proud. He said he hated talking about this kind of thing in interviews, because there were things he felt should stay personal. He said the thing that his mother's death had given him above all was a sense of urgency, the feeling that life is short, it can be cut even shorter, and you should pack in as much as you can while you're here, and try to make a difference.

Friday, September 20

I spoke to Anji about the GB/JP/PM situation. I think one of the reasons TB is quite chipper at the moment is that he has just kind of reconciled that they are not going to work together very well and he'll just have to work around the situation as best he can. He seems to have decided mentally that there is only so much he can do about it so there is no point losing sleep. JP is there, has huge strengths but can be really hard to work with, so let's look to the strengths and manage the rest. GB is brilliant but difficult so let's allow him to decide when he wants to be brilliant and work around him when he's difficult. Peter M wants to be more engaged but feels rebuffed so let's make him feel more involved and get him to take the same attitude to GB.

Sunday, September 22

I went for a long walk with Calum and got a few more lines. My favourite was 'The first wonder of the world is the mind of a child.' I was getting some good stuff on the concept of the team/community as well. And I was trying to play around with the 'Give me the child at 7 and I'll give you the man at 70,' with something like 'Give me the education system that's 35th in the world today, and I'll give you the economy that's 35th in the world tomorrow.'

Saturday, September 28

Grace was playing up because she knew both of us were going to be away for the week of conference, and she wasn't happy. TB was in the bath when I got there, which was always a bad sign. It meant we'd be rushing. He then discovered that CB had sent to the dry-cleaner's the suit that had in his pocket the ribbon Sam

McCluskie [general secretary of the National Union of Seamen] gave to him, which he showed me on the day of Sam's funeral [in 1995]. But he calmed down and said right, let's get down to it. I had been up at six to draft his words for the youth event he was doing later and we agreed those. The problem was we didn't have a strong story to take us through the Sundays and into the start of the week. Then David Blunkett called to say he'd heard the *Observer* were leading on Robin C saying New Labour was in danger of forgetting the poor – bang on message for Central Office and the betrayal thesis. Peter M was in Blackpool and I asked him to get on top of it while TB and I travelled up by train. Liz [Lloyd] and I were working late in Room 223 and after 11, all of a sudden TB storms in, livid, having caught the 11 o'clock news, and he says 'What is wrong with these people? Do they have a death wish?' He meant Robin, whose words were going fairly big. 'It is all about how the party sees them as they strut around the conference, and got fuck all to do with whether we ever actually get the power needed to do anything for the country.' He said what drove him really mad was that it was all playing into a Tory strategy. 'Their plan is to say I'm unprincipled and all I'm interested in is middle-class votes, so what does Robin do but come along and reinforce their message? It is weak and pathetic.' He was really storming and eventually I thought I should bring the mood back a little and did a big calm down, calm down number, some of us are trying to work on the speech. The storm passed very quickly and we chatted a bit more about the speech before he went off back to his room. I found Robin downstairs by the press office. 'Another fine mess,' I said. 'Fuck off, Alastair, I have been totally traduced on this.' Eventually we got a transcript and to be fair to Robin, he had been. The words had been distorted through selective use. He was genuinely pissed off so we went upstairs and together knocked out a statement for instant release, along with the transcript showing he had been traduced. RC was in full 'pause and sigh' mode, and playing really hurt. But of course on one level it wouldn't harm his street cred for the week. TB had been to a couple of functions with JP and Cherie said there was a lot more warmth for JP and he was of course milking it. I said to TB that the worst-case scenario was a sense at the end of the week that the Big Three were offside to greater or lesser degrees and he was isolated and therefore New Labour weakened. It was not hard to see how that might happen. JP was always just one moment away from explosion, which is why we had to build him up through the week. RC was clearly in a position to be identified as being offside, whatever the denials. And if GB combined continued disengagement with an old Labour speech on Monday, it could all get tricky for TB. I also learned second-hand via Liz that GB had done a 'Labour's coming home' section in his speech for Monday. It was a bit of a coincidence that within a day of them seeing a full draft, we then hear that. I suppose it's possible they thought of it, in that it is a fairly obvious thing with all the football hype we've been having, but we would have to get it removed from GB's speech. Ed Miliband said GB was very loath not to use that section. I said I saw our Labour's coming home section as possibly the single most important passage for the tabloids and there was no way GB could pre-empt it. I could tell we were in for a battle over it. I suggested to TB that he invite RC up to his room for a drink, not least to remind him it was there that RC told him a couple of years ago this week that getting rid of Clause 4 would split the party and possibly destroy his leadership. He should tell him he was wrong then and he was wrong again now in saying that pursuit of middle-class support meant any weakening of commitment to the poor. Sally said she spent two hours with Clare who was totally offside, not least when she was held up by security and her 'don't you know who I am?' act didn't appear to impress.

Sunday, September 29

Still arguing with GB over Labour's Coming Home, and he said he was really pissed off about it. I said it was central to TB's speech and I saw it as probably one of the main headlines out of it, whereas in GB's speech it would not have the same impact. I didn't mean it to come out like it did and I could tell that he hated it. It was as if I was saying because TB was leader he would get more out of it than GB, which was of course true but he didn't like it. I said that the line was more central to the overall strategy of TB's speech than it was to GB's, which should surely be getting the focus on economy/social justice, rather than an overall political positioning. I don't think he liked that point either but eventually he reluctantly agreed, and made clear we owed him one.

Monday, September 30

The BBC were in full hype mode on *Panorama*'s programme on spin doctors but they made a classic mistake, responding to our pre-emptive stuff by saying they had a big surprise in there which would justify the whole idea, but it never came. We had basically fucked them over, and won the battle of expectations, so that when the programme came to be shown, the overwhelming reaction was 'What was the point of that?' When I went back upstairs the office said it was crap. I started to watch a video and gave up after five minutes. It was a not very well-executed hatchet job but I couldn't be bothered with it. TB was not very happy about GB's speech. Robin C asked me what I thought of it. I said I never say anything bad about Labour MPs. 'Ah, that bad, eh?' he said, looking very happy. TB was doing a few receptions and when he came back he suddenly said he wasn't happy with the speech and we would have to start from scratch. Oh don't be so ridiculous. He tore off his clothes, got himself a dressing gown, then sat down on the sofa with the look of a man who had just been told the world was about to end, and it was his fault. I said the speech was fine. 'I'll have to do it myself,' he said. 'Leave me now and I'll call you when I've done it.' One year, we'll get a decent speech without all this nonsense. He called us in at half two. He hadn't changed that much.

Tuesday, October 1

Up by 6 and in to see TB who was already at the table in the window, and in full flight. He had decided on the 'age of progress' and 'achievement' as a driving theme, which everyone but him thought was crap, and the first thing to do was persuade him to go for one or the other, and achievement it was. It was more aspirational and more in tune with the way the policy sections were done. We had to get the speech pretty much done by 11 so that he could do autocue rehearsal and we just about did it. I could tell TB was emotional and so was I. I felt emotionally drained and went to my room, sat down and started crying. Fiona came in and was worried something terrible had happened. I said it's fine, I'm just totally drained. A lot hung on the speech and it really had to be good. The ending was better now, as long as he paced it right. TB started slowly, and I was trying to work out whether people would be able to spot how nervous he was. The jokes went fine and it was clear the audience was with him. The middle section flagged a bit. He got a huge cheer for Dunblane. He did the commitments well. 'Labour's Coming Home' got such a good reception first time, better than I thought it would, which meant that the crescendo effect never happened. And the ending became a bit complicated, like there were too many endings within the ending. But the mood was good and they were with him. Some people thought it was tacky to use Dunblane in the film but as a performance it went down a storm.

Friday, October 4

The office in the hotel was a total tip. Smelly and dirty, and everyone seemed to have a hangover. It was definitely time to get home, but I was still working with JP, which was pretty exhausting. Late last night, with Pauline asleep next door, he had been literally bellowing the speech out to me, Rosie, Brian Wilson, Rodney Bickerstaffe and one or two others, as if we were a real conference audience.

Friday, October 11

Cape Town. I woke at 5, the plane landed at 6, and TB was fairly chipper about the work we'd done on the way out, and thought we had the makings of a decent speech for the business event. We went off to the Residence, which was in a beautiful setting, and like a very comfortable Home Counties six-bedroomed house. TB had a kip while Jonathan [Powell] and I worked on knocking what we had done on the plane into shape. We then headed into town to see Mandela, who for most of the meeting was on his own. His eyes were still as clear as ever, big smile, bright shirt, and firm, firm handshake. There was something almost mesmeric about the lilt as he spoke. You wanted the next sentence to begin as soon as one had ended. He was a lovely man. His office was immaculate, and that was more than the fact that someone kept it tidy. Everything was in its place, and I guessed it was the order and the discipline of his decades in jail that made him as tidy as he was. He said as much. He told a couple of Thatcher stories which showed her in rather a good light. But he said he was happy to go out and say Labour were his friends. He would have to be careful not to stand accused of getting involved in UK politics, but it would be clear where his heart lay. And it was. TB raised the idea put to us by Rick Parry of the Premier League of a PL team going out to play in South Africa. Mandela took a pen and paper and made detailed notes, and said he was really keen on it. TB asked him to sign a book for Michael and Gilda Levy, which I thought was a bit naff. He wrote in an immaculate, old-fashioned style, very, very slowly, then looked at the ink drying before closing the book and handing it back. He did everything slowly, thoughtfully, and with impact. We had lunch in the room where [Harold] Macmillan [Conservative Prime Minister, 1957–63] made his 'Winds of Change' speech [in 1960]. I feared we were not going to be making quite the same impact but we were nonetheless in OK shape.

Thursday, October 24

In his discussion with GB yesterday, TB had gone on about the need for a clear economic message and GB was insistent that there had to be a different way of doing this, through policy rather than message. This was a total non-argument, as the two had to go together. All we were saying was that people doing interviews and speeches need a clear and basic economic message. GB felt we should be trying to get sleaze up at the weekend. He appeared more engaged today. I walked back with Donald Dewar. We both felt the rift between Peter M and GB was so deep that it was impossible to do anything much about it. Major was vitriolic about TB, saying that he could not be trusted and we stitched him up on Dunblane. I told TB, and I knew that when it came to Major, the iron was entering his soul, but still he said he didn't want me to go too hard on him. We agreed that re JM the basic line was weakness, damage and drift. I later put out some vicious words from JP, including a jokey reference to Major being rejected by *GMTV* for an item on *Tom and Jerry*. *Express* and *Sun* were doing tax, saying TB had won the battle to rule out a new top rate. Fuck knows where these things came from.

Friday, October 25
Carole Walker of the BBC called and read me an *Everyman* interview with Cardinal Winning in which he said our handling of the pro-life conference stall issue two years ago was 'fascist' and that TB's refusal to condemn abortion meant his Christian faith was a sham. The guy was unbelievable. My instinct was really to go for him, but TB calmed me down and was instead blathering on about why the BBC were running it. I said it was a perfectly legitimate story if Scotland's top Catholic Church man was calling the would-be Labour Prime Minister fascist and saying his religious beliefs were fake. We agreed a statement in which we simply said he disagreed with Winning on abortion and it had always been a matter of conscience for MPs. It was a good measured statement, which we hoped people would contrast with the over the top way in which Winning had expressed himself.

Tuesday, November 5
I had a good meeting with Alan McGee and Tony Saunders of Creation Records. They could get Noel Gallagher [from Oasis] to do stuff for us, but also wanted us to take the music industry seriously as an industry, and agreed to organise a business meeting on that theme. They felt it was better to 'keep Liam [Gallagher] away from Tony, but Noel has got his shit together'. There was a real buzz about Clinton winning again and he was on great form. Pager message saying the *FT* and the *Sun* had run a story saying TB had changed his hairstyle to woo women voters. I got Tim [Allan] to put out a line

saying it was a black day in the history of *FT* journalism, but it was one of those pieces of nonsense that would run. The *FT* of all people, for crying out loud.

Wednesday, November 6

The phone went early and I knew it would be TB and I knew it would be about the hair. I said we just had to make light of it. But it was one of those irritating little stories with the power to connect and damage. I guess what had happened was that someone who was aware we were looking at the gender gap stuff had noticed a new hairstyle and put two and two together and made seven. More likely, a journalist had done the sums for them. Our suspicion fell on Harriet, Tessa or Margaret Hodge [Labour MP for Barking], because people had been talking to them about the strategy. Then we learned Margaret had recently had lunch with the *FT* and the *Sun*, so probably from that. So there I am, having to deal with some nonsense about TB's fucking haircut. He and CB were due to visit Great Ormond Street hospital so I went over there and he was seething. He said all anyone will want to ask me about is my bloody hair. 'I cannot believe the *FT* can run a story like that.' I said the last thing we should suggest is that we were remotely fazed by it. But all the way there, in the car, he was fuming. By the time we got to the office, the hair story was all anyone was interested in. I said humour was the only way out of this and we put together a press release saying the *FT* had gone mad. We put the same picture of TB on twice and did a 'before' and 'after' heading. We did quotes from friends of the reporter who wrote it saying they were worried about it and then changed everyone's name to have a hair connection – Trim Allan, Hilary Cropman, Tony Hair, etc. It went down well upstairs but of course what it all meant was on the day the US President was re-elected, the focus on TB was on his wretched hair. TB agreed to a quote saying his problem was not changing his hair, but keeping it, which by my reckoning was his first admission that he was beginning to lose it.

Friday, November 8

CB and I were getting on a lot better. TB was asking why he was having to do the Brixton thing.[1] Because it's a good idea and because you agreed to it. It was held in a pretty grim community centre but run by terrific people. Julie Fawcett [south London tenants campaigner

---

[1] Meeting young people in Brixton. Major had been raised in Brixton and had attacked Blair for his public school background.

A collection of Labour leaders: Gordon Brown, John Smith, Neil Kinnock, Margaret Beckett (who led the party briefly after Smith's death) and Tony Blair, in 1992

Decision time: on holiday in the Provençal village of Flassan in 1994, Tony Blair persuaded Campbell to work for him despite opposition from family and friends such as Neil Kinnock. Left to right, Cherie Blair, Kinnock, Blair pushing Campbell's daughter Grace in pram, Campbell with son Calum on his shoulders

Three Labour leaders: Kinnock, Jim Callaghan and Blair joined Campbell at his farewell party as he left *Today* newspaper to work for Blair in 1994

Domestic politic
John Prescott an
Blair finalising th
wording of the '
Clause 4' in Mar
1995. Prescott w
important in sec
the support of th
left for change

Campbell tries to combine babysitting
his daughter Grace with watching a Blair
interview on television

Fit for office: in Brighton for the p
conference in 1995, Blair shows of
heading skills with Kevin Keega

The defection in October 1995 of
Alan Howarth MP (centre) from Tor
to Labour was a big moment in the
development of New Labour, and
a huge blow to the Tories on the
eve of their party conference

rch 1996: Blair follows Prime Minister John Major (left, with his wife Norma) in laying ers at the scene of the Dunblane massacre. Scottish Secretary Michael Forsyth (right) had to persuade Major to take Blair with him

Moving onto the international stage: Blair in 1996 with Nelson Mandela, a political leader in a league of his own

Campbell works with Peter Mandelson on the latter's newspaper column

THE Sun

An historic
announcement
from Britain's
No1 newspaper

MAY
1st

Tuesday, March 18, 1997   28p   THE PAPER OF THE PEOPLE

THE SUN
BACKS
BLAIR

Give change a chance

Peter Mandelson, Campbell, Blair and
Brown, often described as the four people
who created New Labour

First day of the 1997 election campaign, and
the Blair team get a welcome front page

Blair sets off for a nationwide tour
after launching the 1997 manifesto

Campbell on his mobile. *Mirror* journalist John Williams observed that if mobile phone use caused ill health, Campbell was a goner

Blair on the campaign battlebus in 1997 with Cherie…

…and with Campbell. Both Blair and Campbell hated the bus

Getting the message out in Blair's Sedgefield constituency

Disgraced Tory MP
Neil Hamilton and h[is]
'anti-sleaze' rival
candidate Martin Bel[l]
face each other at
Knutsford, April 1997

The last weekend of the 1997 campaign. Blair talks to education adviser Conor Ryan,
David Miliband and Campbell

The press record a landslide win

May 2, 1997, and after 18 years in Opposition, Tony Blair leads Labour into Downing Street

Public enthusiasm was unprecedented

Blair speaking outside No 10, May 2, 1997. Campbell's sons Calum (left) and Rory get a front-row place

Fiona Millar an
Carole Caplin v
Cherie and Bla

Cartoonist Charles
Griffin had a habit
of putting bolts
in the neck of
his former *Mirror*
colleague, here with
Peter Mandelson
(left) dealing
with Humphrey
the Downing
Street cat

"OK, THERE'S HUMPHREY. HE'S ALIVE. SEE? HE'S WAVING. TAKE YOUR SNAP AND GO."

Anji Hunter wi
Campbell. Blair
confessed to fee
destabilised wh
prior to the 20
election, each
separately told
they were think
of leaving

and anti-drugs activist] was chairing it, and afterwards she told me she thought TB had been a bit patronising, didn't speak their language or answer their questions. The problem was there were too many media there, it felt stage-managed and he hated it. He had not been on form and it was a bit of a wasted opportunity. Some days he just wasn't up for these kind of things. I felt the people felt a bit used. Most of the questions were about education but one boy asked about sport and TB gave a real politician's answer – no connection at all.

Friday, November 15

Paris. The Elysée entrance was less grand than I expected, the rest of it more so. [President] Chirac was friendly, personable, and fond of looking around himself the whole time, smiles mixed with occasional angry flashes for no apparent reason. He did a wonderful diatribe against the US, saying the most outrageous things as though they were statements of fact blindingly obvious to anyone. Chirac pressed on the euro, and if we met the Maastricht conditions, and Robin C stepped in very quickly – no, not on the deficit – and Chirac raised an eye at him. He had a wonderfully expressive face. He was either saying that is interesting and surprising, or he might have been saying 'I'm surprised that you should answer a question I asked of your leader.' Either way, he made RC feel uneasy. TB did a good doorstep, quite sceptical on the single currency. At the lunch, I was sitting next to some French guy who said he thought TB was brilliant. 'You're going to win by a landslide.' Maybe. TB was doing the rounds of the politicians and then did Le Nouvel Observateur in the back of the car and they were trying to set him at odds with [Lionel] Jospin [First Secretary of the Socialist Party], who had just launched very different ideas, e.g. 35-hour week. Jospin was very old Labour and the body language between them wasn't great. I could remember him being quite a big fish when I lived in France, and yet there was something non-politician about him, quite cerebral, a bit prone to depression I would reckon. He was a big football fan, and knew what he was talking about. Robin was clearly a lot more at home here, whereas TB looked a bit uncomfortable. RC was on good form, and clearly enjoyed being with TB. He was not averse to a bit of decent banter.

Tuesday, November 26

TB was regaling us with stories about Robin and the Queen at the Speaker's Dinner. He said even with the Queen, Robin was 'Robinesque'. She said she was due to speak to a Church conference but couldn't seem to get the media interested. 'I can't say I'm surprised,' said Robin. Then the Queen said she was amazed the Speaker could remember all the names and seats of all the MPs, and Robin said 'Oh, I don't think it's that difficult.' All in all, a good day. The Budget didn't give them the bounce they wanted, our response was good and we could lock horns on the economy with confidence. I went for a meeting with GB to plan the follow-through for the next few days. We agreed we needed to work up to 'better off with Labour'. If we establish this as a tax-raising government, taking with one hand and giving with another, then do the VAT cut ourselves, we will be in a strong position.

Thursday, December 5

Very little coverage for the speech to Shelter. The leak of Scottish focus group reports, and negative remarks re TB, was massive up there, but apart from a piece on the front of *The Times*, it didn't fly much in the London media. TB was livid at the leak. He said only the Labour Party could whack the ball into its own net like this. Donald [Dewar] clearly thought TB was just looking for things that showed him to be strong. TB said 'I'm not doing this to be strong. I'm doing it because I believe these people could cripple a Labour Government.' TB did STV, which was all about his so-called 'smarm' post the focus group leak, and he was getting nicely boiled up re the Scottish media. He did a very good 'I am what I am' passage, and indicated a lot of scorn and a bit of steel, and gave as good as he got. Jon Sopel [BBC journalist] was saying [Kenneth] Clarke [Chancellor of the Exchequer] had threatened to quit, had also said to Major others would quit if the Europe policy changed, and that he might even defect to us. Dobbo [Frank Dobson] called me and said he was at Café Nico yesterday and Clarke was having lunch with Sopel so the source for this stuff was probably Ken himself. We moved into overdrive on it just before PMQs. Clarke put out a statement denying he'd threatened to resign. TB was terrific at PMQs, best ever, and he got JM on the rack, asking detailed questions which JM answered with waffle. TB was cheered massively twice and our side was really up and buoyant at the end, shouting at Major 'GO, RESIGN,' etc. As we came out, I was engulfed and they were desperate for any detail re Clarke – who saw him with Sopel, how did we know, blah. I went with TB and CB to the airport, DD in car 2 with Pat [McFadden] and Roz Preston. The flight was delayed so TB and I wound up Pat re the Scottish press and party. TB said our entire programme could be fucked because of the commitment to the Scottish Parliament and still they whine that we're not doing enough for them. 'I fully understand why Thatcher got to the moaning minnie stage.' We got to the Hilton, Tim [Allan] called to say there was a real sense of disintegration around the Tories re pensions and Clarke and he thought we needed new TB words to push it on. I knocked out a short passage which we got out in time for *C4 News*. I had a very nice chat with GB. Maybe it was because we were on his home turf, and at a jolly Labour event, but he was a lot more relaxed than usual and we talked to each other rather than at each other. Donald [AC's brother] came up and met TB. I met Billy McNeill and Jim Baxter [ex-footballers], which was nice. DD did a great warm-up, and then after a slow start TB did a good job too.

Thursday, December 12

We arrived in Dublin and straight out to meet President Mary Robinson, a really impressive woman who seemed to mix a genuine warmth with a hard-headed assessment of issues. Lunch with Dick Spring [Minister for Foreign Affairs]. Neil had said he was one of the loveliest men in politics and he was, but he gave a very gloomy prognosis of the peace process, and he was pretty sure violence would resume before the election. His finance guy, Ruari Quinn, came up with the quote of the day at lunch. 'Every Labour government has foundered on the issue of a sterling crisis – so why not just get rid of sterling?' TB said he was determined to be pro-single currency but they had to understand just how awful our press were. Then bad news – the *Mirror* called to say the BBC had said someone had been trying to rig the *Today* programme 'personality of the year' for TB. Peter M and David Hill had known all day and decided to be robust, say it was what the Tories did last year, big deal etc. I was not so sure and TB was in a real spin about it. I spoke to GB, who felt we should admit someone had done something wrong and apologise. PM and DH didn't agree and said it was a case of the BBC making a huge fuss about nothing to get some publicity for their poll. I was moving towards agreement with GB as it became clear some of the papers were going big on it and I felt we had to have some humble pie/apology in the mix.

Friday, December 13

A new record was set for a TB call waking me up. 5am. He said he woke bolt upright, worrying whether he had been too dismissive about John Sergeant's [BBC's chief political correspondent] question on the poll-rigging. I said Tony, it is 5am and even if you were, which I can't remember, there is nothing I can do about it, so go back to sleep. OK, he said, and put the phone down. Then I couldn't get back to sleep. The papers arrived and several had splashed on the wretched *Today* poll. It was a sign of how they would get into us if they could. We set off for the border. We met up with Jonathan Powell and Mo, who although she could be a bit OTT was incredibly good at the touchy-feely, chatty, meeting and greeting. To Portadown to meet the troops and a briefing from the RUC [Royal Ulster Constabulary] deputy chief constable, who was very gloomy and said he expected a major IRA bomb before Christmas. Then to meet David Trimble [Ulster Unionist Party leader] on a farm. There was huge media interest and they did a joint doorstep standing in front of the cows. TB drove with him to his office and said afterwards he was a difficult guy to talk to, very internalised and hard to probe. We had a rather more rumbustious meeting with Peter Robinson [Democratic Unionist Party] in Belfast, lunch, then to his speech at Queen's. It was striking how few women there were wherever we went compared with audiences in England.

Tuesday, December 17

We agreed early on we should do beef for PMQs. TB was running late and in a bad mood. He was virtually silent on the way in and when we got into the office I said for God's sake get a grip and stop behaving like a two-year-old. I don't know if he had had a big scene with CB or whether it was just general grumpiness but when he did speak it was to complain that he was doing Des O'Connor's [singer and chat-show host] show and I had to start the whole process again of explaining why it was a good thing to do. We had had very friendly conversations with Des's people and the aim was to ask friendly questions and get TB to deliver a few anecdotes, e.g. running away from school, about the time when he failed to recognise Queen Beatrix of the Netherlands talking to him in a queue, etc. I said I could not believe he could not lift himself into a positive mindset about it but by now he had the hump with me. I had a row with Anji about it too, but that was probably more because she thought I was taking CB/Fiona's side in their argument. She said I was mishandling him. He was nervous about it because it was out of the usual interview zone and I had to understand that. I said it had gone beyond that, he was behaving like a child about it. I stayed out of his hair for a while then we started talking again in the car to the studio, first re Major, then trying to get him to focus positively re Des. We met Barbra Streisand in make-up, which cheered him up a bit, then Des came through. He was much more charismatic than I imagined, had real presence. In the end, TB did fine, well even, and the audience really went for it. I said to him in the car it would connect with more people for longer than anything else he had done in ages. We left on better terms after a pretty fractious day.

Friday, December 20

A historic first. At the end of today, TB called to APOLOGISE. He said everywhere he had been today, people had come up to him and said they'd seen him on *Des O'Connor* and he was terrific. 'I owe you a big apology,' he said 'for doubting your judgement and being a pain in the run-up to it.' It had definitely cut through. Grace Gould [PG's daughter] said some of her friends had been talking about it. Victoria [Bridge, neighbour] said he was brilliant in it.

Monday, January 6, 1997

One of those rare moments of pure political pleasure. I was in the bath at half six when John Sergeant came on with the story about Hugh Dykes [Conservative MP for Harrow East] defecting to the Lib Dems. Another Tory relaunch, another total flop because we had managed events to turn against them. Sergeant did us proud and later paged me to thank me for putting the story his way. It pretty much led the bulletins all day. The thing was running perfectly for us. GB was at the morning meeting. I noticed for the first time that he referred to Tony as 'Blair'. I wasn't the only one to clock it. Fiona said Maggie Rae[1] had been on saying that she was fixing a dinner for TB/CB, me and Fiona to have a proper session with Diana. Maggie said she had said to Diana she was thinking of inviting me. 'Oh yes, I do like Alastair,' Diana said.

Wednesday, January 8

TB said he was worried about us seeing Diana, with or without CB and Fiona. Anji was against, and worried it would get out. I was dead keen, and probably for the wrong reasons. It would be fascinating and I'd love to know what she was up to.

Thursday, January 9

TB was still fretting about Diana. I spoke to Maggie Rae, who said she had said she was terribly excited about seeing me. I said she said that to all the boys. TB said he was at a loss to know what more to

---

[1] The Blairs, Campbell and Fiona had been invited by Alan Howarth (secretary of the Parliamentary Labour Party – not the Conservative turned Labour MP), and his partner Maggie Rae to dinner with Diana, Princess of Wales. Maggie Rae had been a legal adviser in her divorce from Prince Charles.

elcome to Columbia County Library!
r phone number is 706-863-1946
u checked out the followins items:

The Blair years : extracts from the
Alastair Campbell Diaries
Barcode: 31057010287434 Due:
2009-03-16

-CCO 2009-03-02 16:15
a nice day.

do to get GB and Peter M working better together. I said it could not go on like this. CB called and said TB was going to be asking GB if they could have the Number 11 flat if we won, as it was bigger and more family-friendly than Number 10. I imagined this came out of the security meeting. I said I thought now might not be the time to ask.

Friday, January 10
TB wanted a strategy meeting – his big concern was tax, and the need to get our explanation clearer. He took me aside afterwards and said that he felt I had been a bit tense and ratty. I needed to hang loose a bit more. Peter M stayed on too, and TB said to him 'We have to make it work with you and Gordon.' 'How?' said PM. 'I don't know,' said TB. But he was getting exasperated and he was worried about the possible impact on a campaign.

Monday, January 13
There was an awful meeting with TB, GB, Peter M and me. We had agreed GB was going to make a series of four speeches on the economy, and we were trying to establish what they would say, one by one. At one point, he said nobody but his office should talk to the press about tax. He was still angry about last week's coverage. I said was he saying that if TB was ever asked about tax, we should simply say that is not a matter for me? It wasn't realistic. There had to be an agreed approach. He said all enquiries should be referred to him. The whole thing was ridiculous. TB kept trying to get him back to his planned four speeches. But all he would do was pick on something someone had said earlier, and go on about that. At one point, TB just laughed out loud, obviously suddenly struck by the comic nature of the whole thing. CB told Fiona that Tony was actually now not sleeping well, because he was worried that if he could not get GB working with me and Peter, we would not really have a campaign.

Wednesday, January 15
I had a terrible dream about election night. The exit polls had us way ahead, and there was lots of celebration etc, and then the real results started to come in and we were losing seat after seat. I told Fiona, who said she had dreamt that we were made homeless. The main story was Diana visiting Angola, and doing landmines and being accused by an unnamed defence minister of being a 'loose cannon'. Everyone assumed it was Nick Soames but it turned out

to be Earl Howe.[1] The other press story running was re the Millennium Exhibition. TB had been worried we would get badly hit by serious opinion if we didn't commit to it. I suggested we get out now and say we were unconvinced it was a good use of public money. GB was adamant we must not support it. Only TB and Hezza seemed to support it. Jack Cunningham called after his meeting with the Millennium commissioners, which had ended in impasse. He had stuck to the line that we had to be able to review it if we were not happy with the plans.

Thursday, January 16

An interminable meeting on the Millennium Dome. Heseltine had asked to see TB. His people then briefed the *Standard*, who ran it as a challenge to TB, slanted in a very pejorative way. I briefed that he was being 'silly and improper', and repeated that we had supported it but would not do so at any price. Hezza came in and I was pissed off to learn he had asked to see TB one on one. It meant Jack C (totally opposed), me (a student of Hezza) and Jonathan (who would probably have to negotiate afterwards) were not in there, and we were worried TB would just sign up. I listened at the door. TB said that he was worried that the contingency money was not really contingency money but part of the indicative budget. Jack was in the background going on and on about the *Standard* attacking him, a bit thin-skinned about it. TB was saying we could not give a blank cheque. They agreed we would have to work on a new form of words about what actually we were agreeing. But it was clear from the first effort that we were miles apart. To be fair to TB, he had not conceded too much, but Hezza basically sensed TB wanted to do this, and that put them in a stronger position than they needed to be. We then heard the Tories were briefing that Hezza had really torn into him, gone nuclear blah. I briefed that silly words would not help. TB called him and told him to pack it in. Hezza played innocent. TB said to him, and this time I could hear it clearly, that there was no shifting on the budget – no extra funds – or on the review. He was pretty firm and said he was alarmed that people on the Millennium Commission were saying the extra lottery money was already committed. TB said that meant it was a fundamentally dishonest Budget and should not be sanctioned. Hezza and Jennie Page,[2]

[1] Earl Howe, junior minister at the Ministry of Defence, 1995–97. Described Diana as a 'loose cannon' who knew nothing about landmines when she called for an international ban during a visit to Angola.
[2] Chief Executive of English Heritage. Chief Executive of the New Millennium Experience Company (NMEC), 1997–2000.

January '97: Hezza and TB discuss future of Dome

with [Bob] Ayling[1] on the phone, were constantly coming up with new suggestions. Simon Jenkins[2] was desperately trying to be involved, and did some not very clever interviews. Eventually JC and I did a briefing, which was taken as a dump on the whole thing. We could have steered a neutral line but Jack probably went on a bit, and gave them too much body language to read. So the headlines would be pretty negative. TB still did not want to scupper it unless there was genuine and insoluble difference over a point of substance. The latest draft conceded all the points to us, but then Simon Jenkins went on *Newsnight* and looked so smug that people clearly felt we were going to back down. Jack C was clearly not happy. He felt TB should just pull the plug.

Friday, January 17

TB was on the phone at half six, wanting to know how the Millennium stuff was playing out. The politics were pretty clear too, with several of the front pages basically depicting Hezza as going cap in hand to TB. As the day wore on, it became clearer that though Hezza saw the £280m lottery money as contingency, the Millennium Commission did not. They saw it as part of the project itself. The Millennium Exhibition discussions were going on endlessly, and we were refusing to concede the main points. Eventually we agreed a tough statement. Bob Ayling and the commissioners wanted to be able to write to Hezza and TB saying they clearly expected it to overrun. It was clear there were tensions with Hezza and he was insisting they sign up to it but they were covering their own backs, given they and not Hezza would be in charge of it. We were probably moving to a deal but there was no way we could sign up to something that made clear the lottery money was already assigned to the main project. Jonathan was coming in and out with different wordings of this and that, but none were satisfactory. Then Major did an interview somewhere saying he was surprised we were 'creating difficulties'. We should have seized it as the opportunity to say sod it and pull the plug, but TB still didn't want to scupper it and instead I briefed that JM's remarks were silly, unhelpful and inaccurate and that the real problem was the wrangling between Heseltine and the commissioners. I went back with Jonathan for a meeting in the Shadow Cabinet room with Jennie Page, Simon Jenkins and Mark Gibson [private secretary to Heseltine]. Page

[1] Chief executive of British Airways and Chairman of Millennium Central Ltd.
[2] Former editor of the *Evening Standard* and *The Times*.

was very emotional. At various points I thought she was going to start crying. I said there was no point. It was a difference of substance not words. I said we had been given different signals. Heseltine said one thing. They said another. If they briefed up the contingency fund, it would look like TB was saying one thing in a public statement, but essentially agreeing to something else privately. Jonathan and I put together a very bald, tough note, short and to the point and clear on review and funding. They said it made their blood run cold. They wanted to write into their letter that we should talk specifically about the extra lottery money and we refused. Jennie Page went to phone Ayling, who was in Rome on a wedding anniversary trip, while Jonathan and I spoke to TB, who was travelling round Sedgefield. TB agreed we should not say anything that suggested we were prepared to go beyond existing budgets. Back in the Shadow Cabinet room Jennie said it was clear TB understood there may be the need to go over-budget, but there had to be a clear understanding everyone would do their level best not to. It could not be thought to be part of the plan. We were getting there and all that remained was logistics. As Jenkins had to square the commissioners, I said we should say that we intended to make an announcement tomorrow and that TB and Hezza were both now confident of agreement. We agreed that I would put that out. While Jennie was out of the room, Jenkins said what was important was that she and Ayling would make it work but they had to be in it to stay. Now it was Jenkins' turn to be emotional. He kept saying 'Thank you, thank you, so much,' very quietly under his breath, as though we had just saved the fucking Crown jewels. 'You won't regret this. It is a very brave decision but you won't regret it.' He struck me as a total wanker, very self-important.

Saturday, January 18
Whelan, on GB's instructions, was giving Paul Routledge [journalist] a briefing on the windfall tax, saying it would go far wider than previously expected. All Charlie had said was he was going to brief some general lines about the public spending speech. We knew nothing about this until we got the papers later in the day.

Sunday, January 19
TB was livid at the windfall-tax story. 'To get this up at this time, as we are about to make a concerted push on a business strategy, is frankly suicidal.' George Jones [Daily Telegraph political editor], for example, said he had been told by Ed Balls that £5bn was a

'conservative' estimate and he had given him very strong hints that a wider net would be cast. So he quickly picked up on the differences in what we were saying. I said it would be for the specific purpose of the jobs programme, stressed the limits, said final decisions would be made in government in discussion with the regulators and the companies, and tried to steer people back onto the business strategy launch. TB said to tell Whelan that unless he reined back, he would ask me to dump on the story big time, with his clear backing. I had pretty much done that already. I said to Whelan I could not begin to understand the logic of getting this running as we were about to do a business launch. He kept saying 'I'll talk to you later,' saying he had GB or someone else on the other line. 'I'm quite relaxed about this,' he said. Well, I'm not, I said, I think it is dumb. 'Well, Gordon wanted it up so you'll have to speak to him.' 'I can see why he wanted it done for his own internal reasons but the external reasons are non-existent.' TB finally spoke to GB at 1.30 and GB assured him he would rein back. But then came a quite extraordinary development. Peter M called me just before 10pm. He said are you aware that GB is going to announce there will be no rise in basic or top-rate tax tomorrow? I said I wasn't. He said he had only found out because Sue Nye [GB's assistant] had called Margaret McDonagh to say they would be needing a major operation processing the speech tomorrow, and Margaret had pressed her, put two and two together and made four. I called TB, who was having dinner with Roy Jenkins. CB answered and I asked if GB had sent his speech to TB. She said Ed Miliband had sent something through earlier but because TB had been speaking to GB, she was not sure if TB had read it. It turned out that he hadn't, and it had just been lying there on the floor. I said could she find it and fax it through to me. She did so and after pages and pages, there it was – no rise in the basic rate, no rise in the top rate, clear as a bell. It helped explain why he had been so monosyllabic and protective at the meeting of the four of us last week, and why he had talked about an element of surprise. I called Peter and we were almost hysterical with laughter. It was such a ridiculous way to go on. GB was doing what TB wanted him to, and having conceded on the substance, he was being difficult on the process.

Monday, January 20

GB had an enormous hit on the *Today* programme. The overnight briefing was leading the news and then, bang in the middle of his interview with Jim Naughtie, he dropped it in. He did it very effectively. It was a big hit, one of those moments that you knew mattered. At the morning meeting, he was firing on all guns and now seeking to be inclusive – what did people think, what should we do now? He talked as if we had been planning it all along. You had to admire it in a way. He asked for a private session with me and Charlie [Whelan]. We went into Jonathan's room. He said it had been vital to have an element of surprise. He had set up the windfall-tax story to give the Tories something to be angry about, and be commenting on so that they would have no hint of the tax announcement. I said that was all fine, and I totally understood a strategy like that, and he had to be in charge of strategy on tax, but it hardly helped engender trust if they operated as they had in the last few days. TB was a lot calmer about GB than I thought he would be, because he was happy with the outcome.

Tuesday, January 21

Another election planning meeting. Me, Fiona, TB, PM, PG, Anji, Jonathan, MMcD. We'd agreed the basic shape and key themes, and were now building in greater detail. Leadership and the future were the themes that best played to our strengths. TB felt the concept of the future was not hard enough. PG felt it was, provided we stayed focused on education. The mood was good. Peter M and I were both motoring, and he was terrific when he was like this, focused, but really insistent we fix down detail. When we started to go into the real detail for Day One, I felt a real sense of excitement. TB was happy to delegate a lot of the planning, was looking to Peter and me to shape the campaign, Anji etc to fix the detail. Peter had a real look in his eye today, totally up for it, and I think we gave each other confidence. Dinner with Diana at Maggie and Alan's. Fiona was resigned to me behaving like a teenager. TB was in a very jumpy mood on the way, really worried that it would get out, and that it would spark a whole host of enquiries we wouldn't be able to deal with. Most of all, probably, what was I doing there? Maggie's answer was that she wanted me there, and I'm not sure he liked that much. We arrived, and he wanted the door to be open so I got out while Terry drove a little bit down the road and turned back. I stood at the door while they got out and he raced up and into the house. It was a very ordinary house in an ordinary street in Hackney and I was confident nobody had seen him arrive. She was already there and looking more beautiful than ever. She had a magical quality that was almost there in pictures, but strongly so in the flesh. She was wearing a lightweight black trouser suit, almost like a man's dinner suit, and a white silk blouse, quite high heels, white pearl earrings, lips heavily glossed, hair looked a bit longer. We discovered we shared a loathing of cats and Maggie's five cats running in and out and always making a beeline for one of us became a running joke. The atmosphere was a little bit forced at first and I think we were all struck by what an abnormal meeting it was, and I resorted to humour early on, telling her about TB's paranoia about the neighbours spotting anyone, and saying I had tried to assure him we were now in the hands of the best media operator in the world, that our operation was hopeless compared with hers, and if she wanted it quiet, it was quiet, so he had no need to worry. TB couldn't work out whether to flirt with her, or treat her like he would a visiting dignitary. He ended up doing a bit of both, but was not comfortable. We started off upstairs in the sitting room, and she was very much the centre of attention. He said how well she had done in Angola, and how impressed he was at the way she had redefined her role. There was a fair amount of small talk about her life, what she did when she stayed in, the kind of mail she got, likes and dislikes. She said she had made lots of mistakes and tried to learn from them. She was overwhelmed by all the media attention at first, and shocked at some of the cruelty, but said she decided to take them head on. She had met just about every editor now. She said some of them were quite likeable, but she hated the rat pack. She then said 'Of course you used to say one or two not nice things about me,' and there were mock gasps around the place, like Cherie saying 'Oh, Alastair, how could you?' I remember Charlie Rae when he was royal reporter on *Today* telling me she used to get upset by things I wrote and I thought he was just winding me up, but clearly she did. I said I don't know if it helps, but I feel very bad about it now, and my only excuse was that I was writing in ignorance. Later, when the two of us were walking down the stairs to the kitchen for dinner, she reminded me I had also had a go at her on *What the Papers Say*. I said is it all forgiven? And she said yes. She was a curious mix of fun (with a lovely girlish laugh, a beautiful smile and the ability to take the mickey out of herself) and insecurity. There were moments when I sensed she felt the conversation was getting too political, or into areas she did not feel comfortable with, and there would be an almost physical reaction, pushing back into her chair so that she literally withdrew from the conversation. She could also, suddenly, look terribly, terribly sad, just look at the floor, or a fixed point on the table, just for a few seconds or so and then, again with some physical movement, she would come back. She was very flirtatious, big on eye contact, though Fiona said later that was less the case with women. Her self-obsession came through too, or at least an obsession about how she was seen. She said to TB at one point 'You have to touch people in pictures. They can take a lot from you, but they can never take away the pictures.' Later, to the astonishment of Fiona and me, who had been at the earlier discussion on campaign themes, he said that 'compassion' would be the key theme of our campaign, and we had a lot to learn from her. I pointed out this was the man who never gave to beggars. She talked about the boys, said they got very nervous at times, but said they had no trouble from other kids at school. If there was any aggro, it came from parents. She clearly felt something for Charles. She said she had spoken to him today and he had sounded a bit depressed. 'I said he should go away to Italy for a year and paint.' Later, she and I were alone in the kitchen because I had said, as a joke when talking about my teetotalism, how wonderful it would be to be able to say Diana made me a cup of tea, and she said 'Why not?' While she was looking for things in the kitchen, I asked about William, and she said she would have some influence over what happened to him and she was clearly determined he would be King. She didn't quite say they should go straight from the Queen to William, but it is what she was getting at. She felt there had to be a cutting down of the monarchy. Once the Queen Mum died, it should be Queen, Philip, Charles and William as the main people, others less involved. When she did go, it would be like taking a leg from the table. You could make do with a three-legged table for a while, but not for long. She despised some of the courtiers. She said yes, they had influence. But that didn't scare her. What scared her was that people could be so nasty. Over dinner, TB was hinting at her having a more developed role but she didn't bite. He said there would inevitably be a debate on a new modernised monarchy, but it would have to come from within. He said the British people are capable of great rebellion. He said 'You tap deep into the psychology of the nation.' I said 'You probably have the power to save or destroy the monarchy.' We asked her for advice on pictures and she said TB should go to meet the down-and-outs on the Bullring, go to the London Lighthouse to meet Aids victims, or visit a hospital. She spoke, in fairly calculating terms, of how she had 'gone for the caring angle'. But she also saw it as her work, to make people feel happier and better, and to support causes which didn't always get strong support. Fiona, CB and I were now asking pretty direct questions and she was giving pretty direct answers. Did she have an agenda against them? No. Did she like Philip? No. She felt they had to change fundamentally and she didn't think they were capable. No matter how many times they 'relaunch', it won't work without fundamental change, she said. 'I'm fascinated by what Charles will do,' she said. 'I'm with the public on that one. I want to know if he will marry.' She helped clear the table, very 'mucking in', she said, laughing, and Alan Howarth said 'Imagine a lad from Blackburn like me having his plate cleared away by Princess Diana.' TB kind of enjoyed himself but I also got the feeling he was glad to leave. On the way out, he said to me not to do or say anything he wouldn't. He said to her 'He's quite clever, you know.' 'You went all the way to France to get him,' she said. 'And it's ruined our lives,' said Fiona. After he had gone, she and Maggie were talking gyms and colonics and rubbish for a while. She said she never drank. She went to the gym but she swapped times and dates to avoid the press. She had a stalking case coming in court and she hoped she would be able to get in there and pan the press. Fiona said, but isn't it the case that there are times you have used them? And she kind of half bought that but looked a bit hurt and said she was in a no-win position. I said she was brilliant at pictures and I asked her, half in jest, to get in touch with me if she had any good picture ideas for the campaign. She said she might just do that. She said the first pictures of the campaign would be the most important. I told her about the speech I made to the staff, when I said all the pressure was on TB, and our job was to help relieve it for him, and she went 'aaaaaah' in a real mickey-taking way. She ate more than I thought she would, easily as much as the other women – a potato, egg and mushroom starter, poached chicken, bread and butter pudding and fruit. When she left, Cherie kissed her on both cheeks and then Diana looked at me and said 'God knows what this man will do.' I shook her by the hand, and she giggled. I loved her laugh. I loved her analysis of the press. She was funny when she chose to be. TB had gone back to the House, and Fiona, CB and I got a minicab home. They felt she was tragic. She would be laughing one second and then the next her head was pointing to one side, and her face a picture of sadness.

Wednesday, January 22

The quote of the day was from Maggie Rae to Fiona. She said when she was cooking last night, when we were all upstairs, Alan came down to the kitchen, and she asked how it was going. He said 'It's fine because Alastair is cutting through the crap and Tony's behaving like a dickhead, telling her how wonderful she was in Angola.' I went home and watched a video with the kids. I told them a bit about

Diana last night. She sounds like a devious cow, said Rory. Not bad for a nine-year-old.

Got home late and Fiona was on the phone to Maggie, who said Diana had written and called and said she would like to help us if she could. I spoke to Maggie, who said she'd said I was sweet and funny and she would like to repeat the exercise. Maggie said why didn't Fiona and I go and see her at the Palace? I said it might be more fun on my own. Fiona seemed worried about it, but she accepted if she somehow let it be known she was supportive, that could be very helpful. Diana had said to Maggie she had thought about it a lot, she knew it would be difficult but if she could help, she would like to. I said to Fiona 'What do you think she's after?' 'You,' she said.

Friday, January 24
I drafted a letter to Diana saying how much we had enjoyed meeting her, suggesting we meet again to carry on the discussion, and hinting I was aware of what she had said to Maggie. Fiona was very wary of the whole thing, and TB said 'Be careful.' We agreed it had been quite an evening. He said I didn't have to drop him in it so spectacularly when he was giving all that bullshit about compassion and I said he didn't even give to beggars. He put on a cockney accent, said 'There was I chatting up this bird and my mate drops me in it cos he fancies her rotten. I clocked that one.'

Saturday, January 25
TB said to me that the way to really do in the Tories was to announce during the campaign that we would make the Bank of England independent, and we would not be joining the first wave on the euro.

Thursday, January 30
I had a chat with Alex F[erguson, Manchester United manager] who said we needed to start thinking about mental and physical fitness during the campaign. He said he recommended getting a masseur to travel with us. And we had to make sure there were rest periods worked into the programme. If you have physical fitness, you get mental fitness.

Monday, February 10
A woman from IRN [Independent Radio News] wanted to ask TB about a *Sun* story about a three-year-old girl who kept a picture of

him by her bedside. He looked embarrassed and said he was lost for words. I suggested we did it again, and he should say that she should write to him and come to the House to meet him. In the car, I said can you imagine what Bill Clinton would have done with that story? 'I am not Clinton, I am me.' He was clearly in anti-campaign mode. I was totally fucked off with him and said so in a meeting with him and Anji. I said he was becoming self-obsessed and did nothing but add to the pressures on people working for him, often needlessly. At the strategy meeting GB sat on the sofa, leaning forward, half his papers on his lap, the other half on the floor by his feet, and he fiddled with them the whole time. We were back onto the discussion about the need for a clear economic narrative to counter the one the Tories were pushing. GB did not believe we had to campaign on the economy as we were suggesting. TB did. GB suddenly announced he was making a big speech about the windfall tax. I said why can't we marry his speech on the windfall tax with Tony's launch on tax pledges, but then we were off into a different non-argument. My speech won't be about that, he said. What will it be about? Not that.

Wednesday, February 12

Fiona and I discussed CB/Carole [Caplin]. She said she was sure she was seeing Carole a lot more than we thought, and she felt only TB could stop it. But when I called TB, he seemed to think there was no problem. He said she was only a personal trainer, did her hair sometimes and helped out with clothes. So what? I said I felt he was being a bit too relaxed. I went with Philip [Gould] to Watford, where he was doing two groups of women. PG wanted me to sit quietly at the back but I burst out laughing when a woman introduced herself as Jane and PG said 'My first girlfriend was called Jane . . . she went on to kill herself.' What on earth was he thinking of? It was the usual mix of hopeful and depressing. What was hopeful was the general mood against the Tories. But the level of ignorance and the trivia that consumed them were depressing. When he showed them clips of Major and TB, they thought Major was weak and TB strong. But none of them had seen any of it. At one point, a woman called Georgina suddenly said she didn't like TB's smile, and they spent 20 minutes talking about whether they liked his smile or not. They didn't like it when he really went for the Tories, which was interesting, and what he himself had been saying. There was also a feeling that he wanted to be Prime Minister for himself, rather than for the country. But the overwhelming impression was that they worry more about every detail of how he looks, rather than what he says or does.

Friday, February 14

I met Pete Gatley from the ad agency at 2.45 and he showed me his latest idea for the last five days, or even the whole campaign. It was just 'New Labour, New Britain' in a series of really bright colours. I liked it. It was fresh, clear, new, had a nice positive feel. But I felt if they were up with real weight, they could add to a sense of a mood changing, hope, energy, enthusiasm. I wondered if rather than NL, NB, we could broaden out to contain shorthand versions of the pledges too. Once I'd seen them at Millbank, I then went to the agency and we went through the charade of Pete presenting them to me again, and I had to react as if seeing them for the first time. This time they had one in claret and blue, and said they would put it up in Burnley. Peter M arrived late, and saw them for the first time. I didn't give him any indication of what I thought when he first saw them. He said he really liked them a lot. He went along with Pete Gatley that maybe they could be used for the whole campaign, not just the last five days. Whether the words were right or not did not matter for the time being. The idea was the bright colours, and it was brilliant. Simple and brilliant. Peter said he had never seen anything so fresh for a campaign. I knew he would like them and with the two of us signed up positively, we'd get it through. It was one of the best parts of working with him – he would decide on a view, with real enthusiasm, and we could get things done.

Friday, February 21

The *Sun* was definitely moving away from us. I called Stuart Higgins, who was out, and ended up speaking to a very stroppy Chris Roycroft-Davis [executive editor], who said he didn't take kindly to being told what stories to put in the paper. I asked if they would only print stories that backed up their own editorial line. We both got abusive. TB wanted Peter M to speak to Irwin Stelzer [journalist and adviser to Rupert Murdoch] to ask what the hell is going on?

Saturday, February 22

We were taking the boys to Chelsea v Man U, and I picked up TB at 11.30. He was still not sure about the *Sun*. 'There is only one eye that matters, and the trouble is that it's not an eye that is always watching,' he said. His brother thought the *Sun* would promote the Tory line without actually coming out for the Tories. We were met by Tony Banks [Labour MP] and Ruth Harding [widow of Chelsea vice chairman, Matthew], and taken up for lunch. Chelsea was so not Burnley, all a bit celeb-y, Richard Wilson and Angus Deayton [actors], Dickie Attenborough [Sir Richard: actor and film director] who was supportive as ever. Ken Bates [Chelsea chairman] was very Bates-ish. David Mellor wanted TB to do an interview on Radio Chelsea. I could sense he was tense, especially when a bunch of Chelsea fans started singing 'We'll keep the blue flag flying high,' with the cameras following us. The match was terrific, really high quality. Afterwards I had a good chat with Glenn Hoddle [England football manager] about the World Cup bid. Mellor basically felt the game was up for the Tories. It's all there for you to lose, he said. Alex [Ferguson] came up for a drink afterwards, and we talked about what he might do during the general election. He said he was getting 'slaughtered' by some of the board over his political profile. He was down in London during the week and we agreed to meet and go over it. He said he'd love to help, but just had to be careful. On the way home, TB said he had found it an odd experience walking through the crowds with the camera following him. He was now a kind of celeb whether he liked it or not, which meant people had views on him for good or bad, and it took a bit of getting used to. I think he was quite taken aback by some of the abuse, though I hadn't felt it was particularly over the top, and pretty good-natured.

Tuesday, February 25

Met Alex again who has a good feel for politics and campaigns. He said it felt like we were 2–0 up, and now we had to sit back, let the others make mistakes, probe their weaknesses. He met TB briefly and said he felt tax was still a problem. He said TB would feel stress levels rising and he had to learn to become vacant, only let those things get on his mind that really have to. He said in positions of leadership the appearance of calm was important and you had to work at it, by cutting out everything that didn't matter. Don't let the peripheries crowd in. Delegate as much as you can, do as little with the press as you have to, leave the rest to AC. Only do what matters. He said both his wife and Brian Kidd [assistant manager] regularly said he was not listening but if someone suddenly said something that mattered, he would be able to click in.

Thursday, February 27

Went to bed early and got up for the Wirral result.[1] It was better than

---

[1] Labour's Ben Chapman polled 22,767 votes, taking the seat out of Conservative hands with a majority of 7,888 and an 18 per cent swing.

any of the predictions. JP was on great form on the by-election specials, called me a few times to say was he doing OK? – which he was – and then he drove through the night to do the broadcasts in the morning. 'If we can win like this in a place like this, we can win anywhere,' he said.

Saturday, March 1

TB was on the phone from seven, worried that we were walking into a big tax story. He was worried because the news had said he was going to announce that there would be a Budget within weeks to announce the windfall levy. TB must have called seven times in an hour, so I knew he was fretting. My chances of a day off were gone. Most of them seemed more interested in the welfare to work angle than in the Budget line. TB spoke to GB, who said that though the headlines were not brilliant we could definitely turn it around. He sent me an excellent briefing note, saying that we should call it 'the welfare to work Budget', that an interdepartmental committee was already working on job and training schemes, and that the long-term unemployed would have to take one of several options, as with the young. It gave a real crunch to the broad brush that I'd done overnight and it ran big time. It was so frustrating that whenever GB and I were able to work together properly, it just clicked and we could keep the whole show on the road, but these days it was so rare that he engaged like that.

Wednesday, March 5

The morning meeting was all about pensions, but was all over the place, Harriet taking ages to make points that didn't quite gel, and I pushed for GB to take over. I got back and watched Major's live press conference and his announcement was far bigger than we thought, effectively ending the state pension as we understood it. Eventually, after a couple of sessions with GB and Harriet, we agreed we should be emphasising it was going to cost lots of money, it represented a tax rise, privatisation, and it would extend risk. Peter M, who was better at getting on with Harriet than I was, wrote out a simple straightforward clip for her for the lunchtimes, which was fine. The problem was that the press saw it as a big, bold move, that Major was back with the initiative and we were being forced to catch up. Earlier, JP had said to TB 'I heard the pensions story on the radio first thing and I was half asleep and I thought they were talking about us. I thought, the bastard's kept me out of the loop again.'

Thursday, March 6

TB's first call of the day came just after seven and he was furious at Robin C who had said to a *Tribune* newspaper dinner last night that we were heading for a landslide. Unbelievably stupid, he said. He wanted me to contact him. I called Anna Healy and she said he did say it, but in the context of Michael Foot and Barbara Castle being there, and he said they were part of one landslide, and we could be on course for another one. I said it was a pretty silly thing to say and TB was livid. Robin called and said he was probably saying something that was accurate, though it was not necessarily a clever thing to say. He was anxious we did not put him down. I told TB that Major had been very, very effective on *Newsnight*, very calm, relaxed, in control, apologetic. TB said it was clear that they were trying to become the underdog again, and we could not let them get away from being cocky and arrogant. That was why it was so silly of RC to say what he did. We went through the various areas which Richard and Judy [popular afternoon TV presenting couple] would want to cover, Leo [TB's father], Mum, Cherie, the kids. The pensions initiative got a good press for them, and Harriet was pretty badly savaged, but it wasn't as big as I thought it would be. *Richard and Judy* was fine. TB was a lot more relaxed, especially in the phone-in. Amazingly, we were pretty much allowed to choose the questions. They were an interesting couple. He had a touch of the Kilroy-Silk [ex-Labour MP turned TV show host] about him, but I reckon that beneath the permatan exterior is a fairly decent bloke. She was very down-to-earth and friendly. TB was at his best on the phone-in, much more relaxed, lively and frank about Cherie.

Friday, March 7

The *Scotsman* ran a sniffy editorial saying he should not do things like *Richard and Judy*, but by and large we got great coverage for it. TB was seized all day by his 'underdog' worries, and felt we had to rethink how we dealt with the Tory strategy. I lost count of the times he referred to Robin C's 'stupid' landslide comments. He was so fanatically anti-complacent it was becoming a bit ludicrous. We had a poll showing us 26 points ahead but we had to go around with long faces saying woe is us. He said this was all part of getting to a dividing line of 'cocky Blair' v 'underdog Major'. I said 'Blair dares speak of victory' was hardly Sheffield rally time [see note on p. 103].

Sunday, March 16

TB called at 9.30, having spoken to GB, and they'd agreed it would be good to remind people that the election would be about the condition of Britain. Meanwhile I called Stuart Higgins and he said, clearly having spoken to Murdoch, that if we gave them a piece on Europe, saying the kind of things he'd said last time they met, they would put it on the front. I spoke to TB and after we chewed it over, we agreed to go for it. TB felt it could be the last thing needed to swing the *Sun* round. So did I. We agreed it was important not to change in any sense the policy, but in tone to allow them to put over the message that TB was not some kind of caricature euro-fanatic. It was fantastically irritating on one level that we had to go through these kinds of routines, but with an election looming, we would be daft not to try it. *Sun* piece was on the front, though not the splash. Higgins had spoken to Murdoch. He was clearly not going to back the Tories but they had to be careful in how they went full circle.

Monday, March 17

At last we were up and running. The *Sun* piece ran as the second leg to the main overnight story. It was seen as a significant event. TB and I didn't know just how significant until later today. The election was clearly, finally, happening. Terry collected me and we set off for TB's. The photographers were already there. I got in, and TB was worrying, as so often at real pressure moments, about his bloody hair. He was right that it was looking even wilder than usual, all over the place. He scribbled a few points on a scrap of paper – the choice, New Labour, Alan Howarth's selection as a Labour candidate in Newport East, the business survey showing that 50% of businesses want a Labour victory. I said a long campaign could benefit us as it would allow us to do the three Rs – reassure, remind, reward. We went back and did a few interviews in the garden. Cherie came out and started talking to them and said she was off to Gloucester, but they didn't seem to twig so were they. She and I were getting on a lot better, which was good as we were going to be together an awful lot in the next few weeks. They posed for pictures in the garden before TB and I set off for the office. Once it was obvious Major was going for it, we hit the buttons for the visit to the south London school and then Gloucester. While everyone was fussing around outside, TB and I had a quiet 10 minutes, and he said Alex Ferguson was right, we had to play our own game, we know what we're doing, and then we sit back and let them make mistakes. Over six weeks, they will. I thought they would regret such a long campaign. Once it was clear Major was on his way to the Palace, we set off for the school. TB was very quiet in the car, nodding to himself as he went over what he was planning to say. Occasionally he would tap me on the arm, look over and whisper a few lines and ask what I thought. He wasn't really looking for an answer, it was just part of the process of self-reassurance, rehearsal and memorising it. He was on good form. I always knew when he was going to be. He wasn't fretful. He was just focusing on what he was going to say, how he was going to say it. I said demeanour would count for a lot today. More than possibly any other part of the campaign, people would latch on to what he was saying, so it had to be clear and strong. We arrived, were taken into a classroom and we listened to Major's declaration, me intently, TB almost disinterestedly. He didn't intend to react. He was sticking to what we had decided. I didn't think much of JM's statement. He sounded tired and it felt flat. It felt like lines written for him by someone who had more energy than he did. TB did a round of interviews in front of a group of well-behaved kids. His down-the-line live ITN interview was brilliant, really strong, word-perfect, great body language, confident and clear, pushing the line that we wanted to frame the debate from day one – can Britain be better than this? We believe it can. He pushed it in interview after interview, and I did feel our lines, attack and defence, were stronger than theirs. He did a big doorstep on the way out, lots of nice pictures with the kids, then we set off for Paddington. Brilliant, I said. Fantastic start. He said he felt really relieved we were finally into it. We went to Paddington to meet Cherie, Fiona and Pat [McFadden]. I was by now briefing hard on the choice, and saying a long campaign suited us fine. I was talking to Derry about the TV debate. He was strongly of the view that we should get out our conditions publicly – on the audience, the panel of commentators, and the minority parties. He too thought there was little for us to gain in doing it but we must not be seen to scupper it. We changed trains at Swindon and TB asked if I thought we would win. I said I did. So did he, but he felt six weeks was a long time and he worried about the quality of the Shadow Cabinet and their capacity for making mistakes. He felt tax and spend remained a problem. The main mood around us was one of calm, which was good, and people like Jeremy Vine [BBC journalist] were commenting on it publicly. There was a good crowd to meet us at Gloucester, then we were driven to a hotel and country club. TB did a round of live interviews before going into a filmed meeting with 28 switchers. Paged to call Higgins urgently. He said they were going to come out for us in a big front page tomorrow. There will be things they criticise us for, but it is unequivocally backing Blair. I said I was really pleased. He said yesterday's article was important and Murdoch had said he was sure. I asked how Trevor [Kavanagh, political editor] had taken it, and Stuart said RM was sure, and laughed. I called Peter M to tell him, then told

Fiona, Anji and Pat. As soon as TB finished the Q & A session I took him to one side and said I had some good news. I said you remember in 1994 when I said we should try to get the *Sun* on board and you said you weren't sure it was possible, well, they are. He thought it was good news in its own right, but was good in the effect it would have on the other side's morale. I tipped off Mike Brunson at ITN. On one level, it was ridiculous that it should be seen as a big event, but the reality is that is exactly how it is seen. I felt it was a fruit of three years' hard work, and there will be many more. One of the sweetest moments of the day was phoning Montgomery [see note on p. 10] to tell him 'as a courtesy' that the *Sun* was coming out for us, and so would be the main media story for the start of the campaign. He didn't say much, said he would act on it. He said they clearly thought we were going to win. I felt the *Mirror* had been so lacking in politics of late that it was no wonder the *Sun* felt able to move in. Then Brendan Parsons came on from the *Mirror* and wanted to do a 'Blair backs the *Mirror*' piece. They really don't get it.

Tuesday, March 18

I got round to TB's early and he said the big problem was under-doggery. We were felt to be so far ahead that the press would want to hit us hard. He said 'I can't tell you how much my stomach churns when I think we've got six weeks of this. I barely slept last night. I've also been racking my brains for any skeletons that might still be clanking around.' At the press conference, with TB doing the core script, and JP coming in from Falmouth on a video link, which was excellent, GB was pressed on the levy. He would not say which companies were involved. At no time had he mentioned BT, BAA or Railtrack. However, in his body language he indicated they might be and this was confirmed by Ed Balls afterwards. So the lunchtime bulletins showed GB refusing to answer followed by 'aides' being filmed doing exactly that. It was the last kind of issue we needed up on the first full day of the campaign. Earlier Alan Sugar [businessman] called and said he wanted to see me to discuss our strategy. He said he would give us money, and come out for us in the last two weeks if we needed it. He would not work for the other lot, he said, but he seemed to know a bit about their plans. He said Major was going to try and take his time, not get too worn out, use the others a fair bit, then have a two weeks' crescendo. They had a lot of money for direct mail. He said my advice is don't shoot your bolt too soon.

Wednesday, March 19

I woke up, joyously, to the Tories leading the news on their suppression of the cash-for-questions report.[1] CB and Norma [Major] were both at the *Daily Star* gold awards lunch and the word was that Cherie stole the show. The *Star* put out a picture of the two of them laughing their heads off together. The windfall story got very little play, which surprised me because if they had wanted they could have done the contrary briefings going on. The *Guardian* carried my very heavy knockdown. GB's press conference was mainly on sleaze/Hamilton, and the Tories were very much on the defensive, but Philip [Gould] felt it didn't do us much good to be seen to be driving any of this, and he was probably right. It was good to get them on the defensive, but TB was strongest when pushing on a positive agenda for the future.

Thursday, March 20

The *Star* scored a hit with their CB/Norma picture, which played just about everywhere. Cherie was looking good. Sleaze was the main story but the thing bothering TB was his *New Statesman* interview in which he was promising not to do in Murdoch. By and large though the news was about as good as we could ask for. I think the scale of what lay ahead had dawned on TB, not just the length of the campaign and what it entailed, and all the pressure on him, but also what followed if we won. It was odd, both of us remarked, how just a few weeks from now, he could be Prime Minister. Yet because we saw it as our job to keep the party totally focused on the no-complacency message we didn't allow ourselves really to think about that, in case the public felt we were taking their support for granted. But he was looking more anxious and I said he really had to try to look more confident when we were out and about.

Saturday, March 22

Got home to a message to call Alan Clark. 'Congratters. It's going to be a bloody rout. If we carry on like this, we will be lucky to get 100 seats. I have never known morale so bad. You guys are just running rings round us day after day. There is no other way to describe it.' I told him we were doing our main poster launch in Kent and was

---

[1] In 1994 the *Guardian* alleged that the Conservative MPs Neil Hamilton (Tatton) and Jim Smith (Beaconsfield) accepted cash to ask questions in Parliament. The Conservatives sought to delay a report into the allegations until after the election.

there any chance we could use the grounds of his castle? I said I wanted a big field. He laughed away and said 'Why not? I love black humour.' He really felt Major had been stupid to back Hamilton and Smith because they were so clearly indefensible.

Wednesday, March 26

TB was doing an interview with David Baddiel [comedian] at Millbank, which was excellent. It was a more reflective interview than usual and TB put a lot more of himself into it. Ulrika Jonsson [TV personality] was doing Major for the same series. TB said to Baddiel 'How come I get you and Major gets Ulrika?' Mike Brunson said on *News at 10* that the *Sun* had a sex scandal, a Tory MP[1] who had an affair with a 17-year-old girl. I called Higgins to see who it was. He totally had me for a moment when he said it wasn't a Tory, it was Robin Cook.

Thursday, March 27

Sleaze was big again. I had the thought that we should field a single anti-Hamilton, independent, anti-corruption candidate in Tatton. I rang around for a few thoughts and most people were up for it. GB said he had been thinking of the same thing. TB thought it might work. I called Margaret McDonagh and asked her to check what the local party might think. She came back and said it was doable. It would be a terrific story for the weekend, and keep the Tories where we wanted them. I was desperate for it to happen, felt it would be a big blow to them.

Friday, March 28

I felt we were ending another week on top. I missed the morning meeting, and earlier I had cross words, because it was mainly about Tatton and the plan, agreed yesterday, to pull out our man and get the Lib Dems to do the same and try to get a single anti-corruption candidate. But I didn't think they were seized of the urgency. I had sensed a bit of a vacuum, and with a fair while to go to the manifesto, we needed something now. The problem was the Lib Dems were unsure. I spoke to Dick Newby, Chris Rennard and Jane Bonham-Carter [the Lib Dems' senior campaigns and communications executives], and tried to get over to them that it was a win win situation.

[1] Piers Merchant, Conservative MP for Beckenham. Merchant's liaison with a 17-year-old nightclub hostess (while his wife was canvassing for him) was vehemently denied, but later proved to be true.

We would pile the pressure on the Tories, get days of good coverage out of their problems, and if we got the right candidate it would become one of THE stories of the election, run the whole way through and Hamilton would probably lose his seat at the end. Compare and contrast a traditional three-way fight which you might win. I went off to start drafting a joint press release but then spoke to GB and suggested we did it unilaterally, pulled out our man on his own and then see the pressure build on the Lib Dems. He agreed, felt it was a risk worth taking. I spoke to TB, who was fine about it, squared David Evans [Labour Party North-West regional secretary] and the candidate [John Kelly] to be ready to do media, then went off to do a briefing on it. The moment I said we were withdrawing, the hacks just smiled. They knew it was a stunt but it was compelling copy and they would all go with it. When I said it was the candidate's idea, obviously, they fell about laughing. It went straight to the top of the bulletins. The Tories said it was a gimmick but I could tell on their faces they were worried about it. Margaret McDonagh had forgotten to tell Tom Sawyer and Co and Diana Jeuda [NEC member] came on and said if the candidate was pulling out, we would have to impose one. Talk about totally missing the point. JP called in a bit of a stew because he had got the wrong end of the stick too and was worried we were pulling out for the Liberal. I said the aim was to have no other candidate but an independent. He said I should have discussed it with him. He said he had talked to GB a minute ago and GB had said 'It's one of Alastair's crazy ideas.'

Saturday, March 29

The Hamilton scam was a rare total triumph, the splash I think in all the heavies, and a good show in the tabloids, big on the broadcasts today. Peter M was worried it would unravel at the candidate's press conference, but I had a long chat with him and with David Evans before they did it, then set off with the boys for Burnley. I felt bad taking a day off but in truth I was on the phone most of the way up and most of the way back until the phone died on me. John Kelly by all accounts did fine, and while on the one hand he was disappointed not to be fighting the seat, he was never going to win it and this was a way of landing a big blow on them. I felt sure the Lib Dems would have to follow. TB spoke to Paddy [Ashdown], who said they were doing a survey of local opinion before deciding what to do. The problem was many of their people loathed us and loathed the idea of cooperation with us.

Monday, March 31

I slept in because I forgot to set the alarm. JP said as he got back onto his bus that re Tatton 'you can't just pull out and leave it to the Libs.' We HAD to get the Liberal out. I wrote up a briefing note on the nature of the tour, emphasised that we would have a raised platform that came out of the bus and TB would be doing lots of impromptu speeches. For want of a better phrase I called it 'the people's platform'. What a lot of bollocks.

Tuesday, April 1

To College Green to launch the buses. They looked OK, and I liked the run of messages down the side, but they were better outside than in. Anji had done her best with the bus people but I suppose there is a limit to what you can do. Because the windows were tinted and covered in slogans, and the seats were a kind of dogshit brown, the atmosphere inside was really dingy. The toilet was incapable of being used by anyone above five feet six, and the little kitchen space was poky and every time we turned a corner, cups and stuff went flying. The thought of spending weeks on here was not a happy one, and TB felt exactly the same. 'I know we have to do a bus tour, but do we have to be on the bus to do it?' The TV didn't work but that was probably a good thing. I was more convinced than ever that the last thing we needed on top of all this was Robert Harris [writer] sitting up front taking a note of every spit and fart. As we headed off through north London, we both settled into a bit of a despond. The only way we were going to be able to survive the bus was through black humour. This is our prison, I said. We will be allowed out for exercise periods from time to time. We will get visitors, mainly reporters from local papers, and we will tell them we are happy, and then the powers that be may feel they should consider us for parole. TB said we should form an escape committee. Shadow Cabinet members who screw up should be forced to come in here as punishment. By 4.30 we had a statement on the Lib Dems pulling out of Tatton, which was great, and meant another day of that, plus a good running story for the campaign. We now had to find the right candidate. After the meeting, TB and I got driven back by car, thank God. News came through of the *Guardian* poll in which we were down two and they were up two and I briefed it was helpful for the gap to narrow and for people to know we had a fight on our hands. On the drive back, TB said he was worried we were not prepared well enough if we really came under attack. I called Anji and asked if it was too late to get a different bus.

Wednesday, April 2

Tory manifesto launch. Out before six and made the 7am Millbank meeting. TB had said he wanted to get to as many as possible before we went out on the road. I had a chat with Derry, who said things were very fragile whenever we came under pressure, and alliances within the building were not strong. The Tories' main initiative was a new tax allowance to let people stay at home. Again, they were trying to look like the party of ideas. We had a run around the block and then agreed that we had to go on trust. Major cannot be trusted because of his record. We had to get up the promises made in '92 that were broken. I said we should release the 'contract' section of the manifesto in advance, as it contained the meat of the main arguments in the manifesto. We needed a device so I got TB to write it out in his own handwriting. We would give that out and get fresh coverage for it. The Tories had hired a chicken to follow TB around, which wasn't a bad idea, and I wrote to Charles Lewington [Conservative Party's communications director], and released it to the press, saying the real chicken was Major in failing to deal with Hamilton. If the Tories stuck with the chicken, it could be embarrassing so we had to use humour to deal with it. It also helped us make clear they were not serious about negotiating over a TV debate, so the debate idea was well and truly dead. Piers Morgan [*Daily Mirror* editor] called to say he was hiring a fox to kill the chicken. Philip [Gould] called from the groups to say there was a real sense that TB had the energy and the drive to get Britain going. That was the same message coming through on the phone banks in the Pennine belt. I said to TB later 'So much of this hangs on you.' He sighed. 'I know, and the only people who don't know it are in the Labour Party.' The chicken was getting huge coverage.

Thursday, April 3

Today was manifesto day. I woke at about three and never got back to sleep. I was reasonably confident we would have a good day, and felt more and more comfortable on the agenda, but I was nonetheless really anxious. I got into that terrible state when you start to panic because you think you need sleep, because the day ahead will be tough, but the more you think you need it, the harder it seems to get it, and your mind races and races and races. I finally got up at five and worked on TB's words for the press conference. The Tories didn't do very well out of their manifesto, all a bit flat, but the *Mail* was vicious, a piece on five union leaders headed the 'conspiracy of silence', saying the union barons were keeping quiet in exchange for deals in government. They were going to go for us big time. On the way in, TB agreed we had to make a real virtue of there not being much new in the manifesto, that we were going to do the basics, deliver on our promises. The advance people were saying the chicken was waiting at the main entrance. There was a massive turnout, maybe 300 journalists, huge numbers of foreign crews, and a real sense of occasion. I remembered the '92 manifesto launch and Mike White [*Guardian* political editor] saying to me that it just didn't quite feel right. This time, it felt right. Yesterday's Tory launch had been flat, there was no real buzz. Today there was a buzz. TB was nervous beforehand, went for a pee a couple of times in half an hour, and both times asked me to go with him and just go over some of the lines and some of the tough questions again and again. Then we sat down with Peter M and GB and did the same questions again. We told him not to smile too much, to look serious. He felt the tricky questions were unions, tax and Scotland, but he was fine in the answers. We had a quick photocall with the Shadow Cabinet and then in he went. He looked strong, sounded confident, no trouble with the questions, was very confident, totally in control, and you could sense the room was impressed. We then did the usual round of interviews, and they all said they felt a real sense of occasion, which is exactly what we wanted. We got out through a fair crowd outside and onto the bus and set off for the Whiteleys shopping centre. Then to Battersea to get a helicopter to Stansted. We flew over the Matthew Harding stand at Chelsea. TB scribbled a note to me – how did I think it went? He knew the answer. Really well. Hard to know how it could have gone better. The plane was fine, much nicer than the bus, and would also be a place of work. I was getting on really well with CB at the moment. We were able to have a laugh, take the mick out of each other, and she was constantly asking how I was, and saying how important it was I got rest and was able to look after him. The flight was fine, though I sensed the journalists travelling with us would get fed up pretty quickly if they didn't get much in the papers, and would end up just writing process crap. We got to Edinburgh and George R said we had to get up a different story, otherwise the chicken would be the story. I said we had launched the manifesto and I suspected that would carry rather bigger. As we waited in the VIP lounge, I suggested inviting the chicken to dinner, and got an invite sent to it. Then its minders suddenly said no, he was going back to London, so I put out a line that the chicken was being held against its will, and it was actually a Labour chicken that wanted to switch to us but they wouldn't let it. I'd decided the only way to deal with it was humour, and smothering it with love. If we took the damn thing seriously, as GR seemed to, they would achieve what they were trying to do, unsettle us. TB got a great reception and as the chicken moved in on him, a few of our people turned on it, and were drowning it out with 'Tony, Tony.' It was probably the biggest day of the campaign so far, and we had won it. Re Tatton, tried to get Jill Morrell[1] to do it, but she said no.

Friday, April 4

Scotland, as ever, was a disaster waiting to happen. I had only been half listening when TB did his interview with the Scotsman, who went on the line that sovereignty would be staying at Westminster and claimed that TB compared the Parliament to a parish council. It was totally dishonest – he had been making a pro-Parliament point, saying that if a parish council could levy taxes, why was it such a big deal if the Scottish parliament could? But they twisted it against us, because they were determined to portray him as anti-devolution, and it was an immediate fucking nightmare. We should never have done the Scotsman. I should have followed my instinct and not listened to George [Robertson] and Jack [McConnell]. I should have remembered Alex [Ferguson]'s maxim about not taking risks. It was so ridiculous, it was funny, but the trouble was the rest of the Scottish media were now fixated upon it. We flew from Glasgow, where he wasted God knows how long listening to Harriet complaining about [her husband] Jack Dromey not being selected.[2] Later, TB, his dad and I went to the club in Trimdon for a drink. Leo and I had a lovely chat about things. He is such a nice man, and was effusive, thanking me for helping him and all that. He talked about Hazel and how proud she would have been, how she would never have imagined this was going to happen. 'Her son – Prime Minister. It's just incredible, isn't it?' He had a little tear in his eye and he said the reason he didn't believe in God in the same way that Tony did was because Hazel was not here to see him win. Tom Stoddart [photographer and adviser to AC on pictures] had some fantastic news on the Tatton front. He had bumped into Martin Bell [BBC journalist, particularly known as a war correspondent], who said he would like to be the

---

[1] Former fiancée of John McCarthy, a journalist kidnapped and held hostage in Beirut from 1986 to 1991.
[2] Dromey had been shortlisted for Pontefract and Castleford. The selection meeting chose Yvette Cooper, policy adviser to Labour's Treasury team, 1993–94, columnist on economic affairs and leader writer of the Independent, 1995–97.

anti-corruption candidate. It was perfect. I shook Tom by the hand so hard I almost took his hand off. I spoke to Bell, who said he would love to do it if we would have him. He said he had had his fill of the BBC. He was down to do Edinburgh Pentlands on election night, so they clearly didn't think much of him. It was time for him to do something and this would be perfect. I said I thought he would win. He was perfect for it. I got Jonathan [Powell] to speak to Paddy's people and they were fine, so it was all systems go. It was a real stroke of luck. It would break right through.

Saturday, April 5

I got up very early, went down to make a cup of tea and then Leo came down too. We talked for a while, before I started working on TB's words for his adoption meeting. The press was pretty grim. There is no doubt we had taken a hit and I felt responsible for having agreed to the *Scotsman* interview which kicked off the whole thing. Even the sensible ones, who could see at first glance what he had meant, felt they had to go with it. TB wasn't too fazed about it, said he certainly didn't blame me, and if it hadn't have been this, it would have been something else. The Tories were now broadening it out to the wider issue of trust, saying TB could not be trusted. The ease with which the Tories could get up lines was shown again when we got to the adoption meeting and TB was being doorstepped by them all asking about trust. We ignored it and went into the little side room, where I suggested he take it head on at the top, and we drafted a line, yes it is about who you trust – the man who said he would modernise the Labour Party and did, or the man who promised tax cuts and put up taxes, promised to sort BSE [bovine spongiform encephalopathy – mad cow disease], NHS spending etc. It worked well and straight onto the bulletins. The speech went fine, and the Sedgefield crowd were always terrific with him. Good pictures with TB and Leo at the bar. As TB toured the hospital in Middlesbrough, I was trying to sort out Tatton. It had got a bit messy, because some of the party and unions had got a bit grumpy about it, and David Evans said he was not sure it was deliverable. I spoke to Bell a few times and we agreed he would go up tomorrow to see the local parties and then we would put out a statement. I couldn't believe the local parties couldn't just do this.

Sunday, April 6

Major was on *Frost*, quite effective on trust, and he did a very effective sound bite on our manifesto unravelling. It was fine on one level, but not enough. TB said if all he could do was attack me, it wouldn't help him. There had to be some sense of the future under him, not him going on about the future under us. That was borne out by private and public polls. I tried to explain it by saying it was obvious there was a struggle going on re the policy, and Ken Clarke was clearly in charge, and he was ideological about this, whereas we were practical. But I felt I had fucked up. I felt ill. The phone never stopped, mainly about Tatton. Dick Newby said there had been a very bloody meeting of the Libs' local executive, and the vote was won by 6–5. He said Bell was terrific, really hit the right notes. Then David Evans called at 6 and said our people had backed it too. He said Bell had been terrific and won them over after a pretty bloody meeting. Anyway, it was a done deal. Newby didn't want to put the name out yet. I felt there was little chance of it holding because the circle of knowledge had widened. But I said we should try. I tipped off a few people without the name, said we had an agreed candidate. When I finally gave out the name at 7pm, they loved it. PA snap, change of bulletins, Major interview blown out of the water. I briefed on some of the background and again it helped that we had managed to keep it quiet and we were able to shape the story on our terms. Bell called and said he was not intending to go home and was intending to stay at La Gaffe in Hampstead. We arranged to meet there at half nine. There was an ITN camera outside but I found a way in where I wouldn't be seen. He was having dinner and was clearly very excited. He said today had been like a Le Carré novel. He said before he had spoken to the Libs' meeting, he could hear them arguing through the wall and 'it was worse than Bosnia'. He clearly felt our people were the nicer lot, but he said both meetings were hard, and he was glad he was able to swing them. I asked if he had any skeletons they were likely to find. He said he thought not. He was a friend of Bob Stewart, head of the Cheshire Regiment, and the Duke of Westminster. He was a bit batty, and very wandering from time to time, but it was hard to imagine a better person for the job. I said he could easily win. He said he thought he might be a 48-hour candidate, that Hamilton would go. He said it was weird to be the story like this, but I could tell he liked it and would do it fine. 'I'm not really a political animal,' he said, 'a floating voter.' Perfect.

Monday, April 7

The papers and the broadcasters were mainly leading on Bell. He came round to our house at 7.15, then Newby and Jane Bonham-

Carter arrived five minutes later. We went over some of the process points – that it was a joint initiative, that he had been put in touch by a mutual friend. We emphasised he had to show some real passion for doing it, and anger that drove him to it. Otherwise it would look like an ego trip. He was convinced that Hamilton would walk, and he would be the shortest-lived candidate ever. The rest of us were not sure, because Hamilton was neuralgic. Over to TB's. He wanted to work in the garden as we went over the difficult questions for *Panorama*. I said to the 3.30 meeting that we needed to fight back harder on this trust/betrayal and talk of their five years of betrayal, not our so-called two days. There was agreement on this, but I realised GB was still far happier away from anything negative. I spent a fair bit of the day talking to Martin Bell and getting him settled before his press conference. I could not quite tell whether the insecurity was a bit of an act. He did fine by all accounts though the Tory papers were going to go for him big time. We agreed to use *Panorama* to do a simple explanation on New Labour, that it was real, deep. David Dimbleby [TV presenter] came at him from the line that he had basically changed all of his beliefs to try to get power. He was sneering and rude but TB stayed calm and dealt with it OK. But the idea that these interviews are the key to healthy democratic debate is ridiculous. They've become a game. I'm not sure it was worth all the preparation, but it was another one ticked off, and basically fine. It would have settled our people down quite well. Seemingly the party got a good response in terms of phone calls etc.

Tuesday, April 8

TB was fretting a bit about *Panorama*, felt it had been ragged. Most people I spoke to thought he did well, but Philip G said later one or two in the groups thought he got a bit flustered. One man said 'If that's what he's like with an interviewer, what would he be like with Kohl?' [Helmut Kohl, German Chancellor] We stopped at a little café on the way and TB and JP got a perfectly good reception. You could often tell more by the mood at these impromptu stops with no press than you could on the planned visits. I said to Pat [McFadden] in the car afterwards that 70 per cent of those people would vote for us, or not at all. There was definitely a growing warmth to TB though. Then we had a silly little incident when some wanker in a Range Rover tried to cut between TB's car and the Special Branch car behind, and wouldn't take no for an answer. Only when they put on the sirens did he bugger off. There was still a lot of planning to do on Tatton, and we had the Pennington report on E. coli[1] coming out. I had them all laughing – including GB according to Philip – when I called into the meeting and said we were running Tatton like a military operation, and today the candidate would be accompanied by Colonel Bob Stewart [British UN Commander in Bosnia]. The walkabout was good, very warm, very few people not interested, none abusive. The mood and the body language between TB and JP was good, and with Basildon[2] the symbol it had become, good pictures out of here would be good for party morale elsewhere. Bell called me a couple of times, and sounded more nervy than yesterday. I said he was doing really well. TB and I drove back and listened to a dreadful *World at One* special. GB had read out a list of people and companies endorsing our welfare-to-work programme and Nick Scheele [chairman and chief executive of Jaguar Cars] was one of them, but they got hold of him to say he knew nothing about it. It was a classic unforced error, something clearly not pinned down and double-checked. I got called out to see an encounter on Knutsford Heath between Bell and Hamilton, surrounded by a media circus, in which Bell said he was prepared to give him the benefit of the doubt. It was a big mistake. He must have known that because he called me. I said it was a problem because it had been a struggle to get the two local parties to stand aside and they had done so in the end because they thought he was going to take Hamilton apart. He said he was not prepared to get into slanging matches and he wasn't a Rottweiler. Tim suggested we get Bell to write to Hamilton at least getting the admitted wrongdoing down in print. We drafted the letter. He took out one line but was otherwise fine. He just had to be coached in some pretty basic politics. He said he felt vulnerable and didn't know where to start. He was staying at the Longview hotel. He said he needed help from the other parties. I said we could organise Labour and Lib Dem help, but he should also appeal directly for disgruntled Tories to help him. Meanwhile, Anna Healy took me to one side and said she needed to speak to me about Mo. She explained that Mo had a brain tumour, which had required radio-

[1] Report of Professor Hugh Pennington's inquiry into the 1996 outbreak of infection with E. coli O157 in central Scotland.
[2] The marginal seat of Basildon had become a key indicator of which party was set to win a general election. The Conservative MP David Amess had been expected to lose the seat in 1992, but, like John Major's government, he held on. By May 1997, Amess had removed to Southend West.

therapy, and steroids which were making her put on weight. She had managed to keep it quiet for around three months but she thought people were beginning to notice and wonder. Mo wanted to talk to me about it. I spoke to her for ages, and she was really worried about the whole thing, not just for obvious reasons. She said she was worried if it got out, the Ulster Unionists would somehow use it against her. I said I was sure she was best to get the whole story out there, on her own terms, rather than wait for it to dribble out and she be forced to react. It reflected nothing but good on her and even the UUs would be forced to express some sympathy. Also, if we briefed it, we could accompany it with a statement of absolute support and approval from TB. She said she was fine but it had been a bit of an ordeal. [Lord] Snowdon [photographer] called me, angry that one of the papers had said the manifesto picture was Tom Stoddart's.

Wednesday, April 9

The papers were totally dominated by Tatton. We got up the Bell letter quite well and when he called, I said he must stay on the central allegations, again and again and again. He could not afford to be nice for the whole campaign. We agreed TB should do a clip on Hamilton, saying he was not fit to be a candidate. The polls were narrowing, inevitably, but it was alarming TB a bit. I hadn't realised how bad it was at Millbank until tonight. I phoned round several people and everyone said there was not enough communicating or making decisions unless we were there, and the minute we went, it slid back. Fiona's view was that I was a victim of my own success, that they were so used to clearing things with me; if I wasn't there, they just talked and drifted. I was beginning to think I should be at Millbank full-time. CB said she really thought I should be where he is, because I could keep him calm and take a lot of the pressure.

Thursday, April 10

I spent much of the day agonising about whether I should be on the road or at Millbank. I had a long chat with Derry, who said the factors were these. 1. Would it upset the GB/PM operation? 2. Was it a bad media story? – probably. 3. Who would replace me on the road? My view was that 2 and 3 effectively fucked it, but as the day wore on, most people came to the view that I should be there. Only Cherie was really against.

Friday, April 11

Alex [Ferguson] called, he said he thought we were doing OK, avoiding big mistakes. He thought TB looked strong and confident, and they were looking desperate. He said it was vital that we stepped outside the bubble and tried to see the big picture from outside. TB told me he'd had his first really sleepless night, his mind just racing and worrying about all the things that could go wrong.

Saturday, April 12

The days are now really rolling into one. Writing this a day after the event, I'm struggling to remember much at all about where he went or what he did. I can't remember much about yesterday's papers, which is probably a good sign. The BBC was a problem. The stuff through the day was bad enough for me to call John Morrison [editor, BBC News] at home to complain. Unions, Portillo whacking TB as phoney. I got the usual 'hear what you say' mantra, and I don't know if it had any effect, but the later bulletins were marginally better. The Tories were not really being pushed on forward policy. Another problem came with the *Sunday Times*, who had [John] McIntosh [head of the Oratory] doing his usual criticism of our policies on education. I said to TB he should blow him out of the water. Even TB, who normally defended him, was livid and called to complain. According to CB, who was in the car listening to the conversation, he left him in no doubt. I called McIntosh and said he had to put out a statement making clear he was not attacking TB or the policy. He claimed the press were interested in his views long before Euan went there.

Monday, April 14

The Times and the *Telegraph* had a story about Lewington complaining to BBC Radio 1 about playing 'Things Can Only Get Better'. TB was in the hotel dressing gown, working on his speech and generally fretting about Philip's focus groups last night. PG said later TB sounded pathetic when he filled him in. He had to get a tougher skin for this stuff. He felt he had taken a bit of a hit in recent days. There has never been a general election in which the focus is so much on one person, he said. This election, when you boil it down, is all about me, and whether I am fit to be Prime Minister. It's kind of scary at times. We discovered Major was doing a big attack on the Oratory, which even though it was a bit of a neuralgic issue for us, I felt was a mistake. TB was a bit down by the end of the day, said he was just a bit discombobulated. I said he had not been on form today. He said his mind was on GB/PM and whether they could hold things together.

He could not let them drag him down. His great strength was that he could get up in the morning and go out with a smile on his face. His optimism was key and he had to get himself back up again. We were beginning to think they were landing blows on us and we were not fighting back properly. We had to get better capacity at fighting them. That was confirmed by Philip, who said that while women liked the TB empathy, men wanted a bit more toughness from him.

Tuesday, April 15

Southampton. We visited a pub over from the hotel and a bit of a haranguing from a group of blokes who were the worse for wear. TB was a bit shaken. He said it was weird when everyone had a view about you. It was only just dawning on him that he had gone onto a different level and was in all likelihood soon about to go onto yet another level. He said rather plaintively, do you think I'll ever be able to be a normal person again?

Wednesday, April 16

JM did a big press conference setting out the whole position on Europe, which on one level sounded daft, but he was by all accounts very personal and passionate and he was getting marks for being bold and gutsy. Some thought it was mad, others that it was a real tour de force which brought the campaign to life. TB was meanwhile beating himself up, rightly felt his *Today* programme interview and his doorstep were crap and to make matters worse we were not even getting the speech on the news because JM was going so big. I complained to them all and they assured me it would get something on the late bulletins. As ever, they were following JM's agenda, and he was getting far too good a press for this morning. JM was ditching the planned PEB [party election broadcast] to do an 'address to the nation' type thing on Europe. He was clearly trying to turn his weakness into a strength, and we had to make it unravel quickly. I watched his broadcast and he did pretty well. As the day wore on, the papers were beginning to say the Tories were imploding on Europe but apart from *Newsnight* that wasn't coming across on TV. We had Robert Harris with us now and I really did feel it was just one more pressure we didn't need.

Sunday, April 20

TB was on much better form, more relaxed, had lost the tension and hyperness of the last few days. He said what had been nagging at him was the idea that it would just go away at the last minute, like in '92. The difference was that in '92 he didn't really think we would win.

This time, give or take the odd bad day or low moment, we thought it was going to happen. We flew up to Manchester, went straight to the hotel and Alex F came over for a drink. He asked TB how he was feeling. Tired and a bit stressed. He said we were doing great, and he reckoned we were on for a majority of 100 plus. 'Just take it a bit easy. You're way out in front, let them come after you more and watch them make mistakes and then punish them for it. Don't be taking risks yourself.' He thought we should lay off JM personally because he did better under attack. He said believe in yourself, know that you're here because you deserve to be and now just stay focused and calm. He and I went off for a drink and I told him I was getting more and more stressed out because as we got nearer more and more people thought TB was going to be PM and they were treating him differently. He said you have to be ruthless. Put the blinkers on. Don't let anyone into your space unless you want them there. If someone says only you can deal with it, give them a few seconds and if you decide someone else can solve it, move on. We went out into the street for some fresh air and I could sense in him the excitement at the idea of us winning and the Tories being out. He said you're home and dry, just carry on as you've been doing, and avoid mistakes.

Monday, April 21

TB was back saying I should be at Millbank more, but the last couple of days had persuaded me I was more good out with him, getting him over the humps and being able to react and respond to what he was thinking. He said he felt he had taken a hit out of last week and what was galling was that it wasn't really down to him. But he said if the British people put this lot back in power 'they want their heads examined'. Worse was to come. He did lots of radio interviews including one where he was asked whether he picked his nose a lot and who was his favourite Spice Girl. Mike Brunson was buying the Tory line that Europe was playing well for them. TB felt constantly putting the case for New Labour, in very personal and passionate terms, was what mattered in the next few days. We had to have a very simple last few days that motivated our core support to come out with the new support we were getting.

Tuesday, April 22

TB really had to let rip today. His instinct was that where the undecideds were was asking themselves if they really wanted the Tories back, and he was sure they didn't. So that was the question he would be framing through the day. Do people want to wake up on May 2 with these people back? Even on Europe, he was more optimistic than I was that the overwhelming sense of division would hit any bounce they were getting by being much more sceptic. He thought the Tories were kidding themselves if they thought Europe was turning things their way. That is what happens when you are behind. You start to delude yourself that things are better than they are. There was a rumour of the lead being down to single figures in a *Guardian* ICM poll. I hassled them for the figures and eventually got them from [Alan] Rusbridger [editor] around 6. Con 37%, Lab 42%, Lib 14% – only 5 points in it. It didn't feel right. Gallup had us on a 21-point lead, which felt wrong the other way. But clearly the *Guardian* one would get the attention. He was a bit thrown when I gave him the figures at the hotel, wondering whether in fact they were getting momentum on Europe. I felt we had to use it to hammer the anti-complacency, point-of-voting message.

Wednesday, April 23

The *Guardian* poll was going pretty big. The *Telegraph* even led on it, even though their own poll gave us a massive and growing lead. But we were still in good nick and I woke up feeling confident and strong. TB and Jonathan [Powell] were due to meet Robin Butler at Richmond Crescent. Again, it brought home how close it all was now, just over a week to go. I got home reasonably early but all the kids were in a bit of a state. In their different ways they were picking up on the extra pressure, and there was a lot of change in the air. I must try to give them more time but it's going to be hard for the rest of the campaign, and then for the first bit after that even harder if we win. TB said of his meeting with Butler that it was obvious the Civil Service had pretty much given up on the idea of the Tories coming back. There is so much to do the minute we get in, he said, and we'll be knackered. I still didn't want to focus on the day after. I had become almost superstitious about it, as if we would get punished for taking it for granted. I said to TB that as the day nears, the focus will get ever harsher on you and Major, and it's now shit or bust. 'God, it's terrifying,' he said. 'One week from now, it's happening, and if we win, it's life changing.' I said it's pretty life changing if we lose too.

Thursday, April 24

We had agreed yesterday to go really hard for them on pensions as part of the fifth-term attack. We had a rebranded set for the last-week launch, and it was fantastic – Tory pledges against Labour pledges, dark against bright. It was as if the hacks had decided we were going to win, so why were we hitting them so hard? One of them said it was like being cruel to a puppy. Do me a favour. We were dealing with a proven and ruthless political machine and so long as they thought they had a way back, we were going to make sure the way back was blocked. Stuart Higgins called in a fury because the *Mirror* had a decent picture spread on family snaps, and he said he wouldn't mind if I was honest and open, but I was devious about it. It was a nightmare, managing the *Sun* and the *Mirror*. Both thought they should get special treatment at the expense of the other. I asked him to understand the pressures I was under from all the papers, but he wasn't having it. I promised him a decent story by the end of the day.

Saturday, April 26

We were holding up really well in the polls. Richard Branson [head of Virgin] was going to be the big thing today. Again, it would help in terms of mood, the sense of things going in our direction. My favourite story was 'Major takes charge of campaign'. Where the hell had he been up to now? Meanwhile, TB was getting stronger all the time. I got there just before 7 and he stunned me straight out with the boldest plan yet. 'How would people feel if I gave Paddy a place in the Cabinet and started merger talks?' Fuck me. I loved the boldness of it, but doubted he could get it through the key players. He had the Clause 4 glint in his eye. He'd hinted at it a few times in the past, but this sounded like a plan. He was making a cup of tea, and chuckling. 'We could put the Tories out of business for a generation.' He felt if we won, we would never have a better chance. Jonathan told me later he'd sat in on his last Paddy meeting, and Ashdown was 'moist-eyed' about the prospect. First, we had to get through the Branson event. It was being seen as a great coup, but we had to watch him. We travelled down to Euston with TB and CB, a great media crowd on the platform and they walked to the podium. Branson spoke first, though TB was meant to. He said all the things he was meant to say, support re the lottery, tobacco ban, consumer protection, but then slipped in that obviously he supported rail privatisation. He was wanting still to point a little bit in two directions. I could see TB tense up. As we travelled up north, TB asked me several times if I thought Branson's words had been a problem. I thought they were just about OK and association with him was still broadly positive. Branson himself made me feel a bit uneasy and I felt there was a side to him that his image and marketing managed to hide. TB was not sure about him either. 'I thought today was meant to be about promoting me, not him,' he said. Never mind, onwards and upwards. Phil Hall [editor] called at 12 to say the *News of the World* was coming out for us, which was great. We flew back in a little jet. TB was visibly relaxing, said he felt the end was in sight. He said to the Special Branch guys that he was now thinking as much about Friday as about Thursday. I imagine they were too. Some of them were now likely to be staying with us, and it was amazing how quickly we had got used to having them around. I got home about six. Rory was being really difficult about me being away so much and Calum and Grace were very discombobulated as well.

Sunday, April 27

We had the last slot on *Frost*, and I was keen to get up education again, but it was bloody hard trying to keep finding stories for these big interviews. TB didn't really hammer home the message, which was a shame. He was fine but not brilliant. Interestingly enough, though, JP called and said he thought it was the best he'd ever seen him. Joe Haines had given me a line on grammar schools being the politics of rejection not the politics of selection, which he used without much conviction. Joe had sent me unsolicited a really helpful note about Downing Street and even though it would have changed since his day, I was sure a lot of the lessons still apply, most importantly that they got a sense of authority straight away, and that the system understood quickly who TB relied on. We flew to Derby in what was apparently Al Fayed's helicopter, the most comfortable we'd had. Cherie was looking good, all in white. I had to hand it to her and Carole C on the clothes front. She was looking good and Fiona was making a real difference to keeping CB on an even keel. Cherie has some terrific natural campaigning skills. I think both TB and I did better when our other halves were around.

Monday, April 28

We flew back by helicopter. TB asked me repeatedly if I thought he could put Ashdown in the Cabinet. 'It makes sense politically,' he said, 'and it stops them peeling off.' I couldn't see it happening, in either party. He said 'You imagine two years in if we are getting hammered by both Opposition parties.' CB was getting worried that he was tired and wanted us to see if we could cut some of the stuff out of the diary. But I felt we had to be pretty much flat out now. The slightest sign of coasting would be punished. There was a good mood in MBT [Millbank Tower] though GB looked exhausted and Peter M was very subdued and withdrawn. Robin Butler had done a selective briefing, to the *Mail*, *Express* and some of the heavies, in which he appeared to have given up on the notion of Major coming back, he'd talked about the process of the transition, the children moving in, etc. David Hughes [*Daily Mail*] said it was absolutely extraordinary. It was also deeply unhelpful. What on earth was he thinking of? I got Tim to put out a line that it was inaccurate, unhelpful and inappropriate. I would rather have at this stage a row with Butler than a story about TB/CB measuring the curtains. TB was sure that it was the right thing to do, rather than feed the idea the thing was all over, and he said so pretty strongly to Jonathan and PM. Butler later complained when he heard that the papers were reporting TB as furious. I had to go home for a while because Rory had been kicked out of football club for being rude to the guys running it. TB felt really fucked. So did I. The travel was the worst bit, but we were nearly there. Two full days, polling day, then a new job. I wished I could will the next few days away.

Tuesday, April 29

I called Butler. 'I must be in trouble,' he said, laughing. I apologised for the harsh words yesterday but said there were strong political reasons. I said I had not initially been aware he had done the briefing himself. He was apologetic but the more he talked about the reasons for the briefing, and what he had actually said, the more I doubted his political skills. He was unbelievably naive about the press, thought he was just being helpful to give them a sense of what would happen if. It all ended fine and amicably. TB had backed me yesterday but said I would have to get a new modus operandi with the senior civil servants. I couldn't just expect them to jump when asked as I did with party staff. CB was in a terrible mood, said she didn't want to go to Sedgefield and why couldn't they vote in Islington, which was ridiculous. I got the feeling they had had a row about what Anji would do in government. CB didn't want her there at all, and I was not sure if TB had confronted it. Tim [Allan] and Jonathan were in Downing Street discussing with the press people what we might want to do on Friday if we won. We wanted to get party and public into the street. They had said they would not allow crowds on both sides of the street. We had another round of interviews, including Jon Snow [*Channel 4 News*]. Jon said JM wouldn't be interviewed in Downing St because he wanted to stay in Huntingdon. He said the feeling was he had given up. He said TB was Prince Hal becoming Henry V and he would be a great leader.

Wednesday, April 30

I was up at half five to get round to TB's and do *GMTV*. There was a real last-lap feeling. It wasn't a great interview. He was tired and slightly going through the motions and I said afterwards we had to force ourselves, lift ourselves for one last push. The problem was everywhere you went it was being taken for granted we would win. There was a good feeling at MBT and we had a job to do to keep people's feet on the ground. Just as yesterday GB tried to get into the middle chair, and Peter and I had to indicate to TB to move over. Mary Ann Sieghart [*The Times*] had taken to bringing her daughter to the press conferences and she was trying to ask a question. GB ignored her though the two of them went over to talk to her afterwards. I said to TB I thought we came over as a bit cocky and in the bag, and he said it was hard not to be jocular today because it would have been po-faced not to have been a bit more up than usual. We met up with JP at Teesside and drove into Stockton. JP and I had a long chat at the airport. He didn't look tired at all, which was amazing because normally he did. He was handing out Prescott Express badges to passers-by while talking about the day after. His ideal was DPM [Deputy Prime Minister] including transport and environment and he wasn't too bothered about chairmanship of the key committees. He feared Robin would be a problem, and TB needed to get hold of him straight away and warn him about messing around. He said Robin was at it the whole time. I said I would do a briefing note that gave credit to all the key players and I would put it around so that we tried to get one narrative. He said shall I arrive on the bus on Friday morning? I wasn't sure if he was joking but said no, come by car. We then picked up Helen Mirren [actor] and did a visit to Cleveland police. There too the mood was good. A copper said to me 'People like winners and you lot have won.' It was a bizarre feeling, almost flat, certainly a developing sense of anticlimax. CB said she might stay the weekend at Richmond Crescent and then move in a few days after once the fuss had died down a bit. TB had never really let her speak to Butler properly, but these were going to be real issues and if they weren't handled properly, would just add to the pressure on him. It was true that TB had been as obsessed as I was about not giving out signals to the Civil Service that we felt it was in the bag, so it meant some of the family preparations had not been done. We finally got to Myrobella [the Blairs' constituency home] and everyone was totally whacked, almost in a state of collapse. But we still had a few hours to go. TB went for a nap while I watched the news, which was terrific. Fantastic pictures from the visit to Dumfries and with JP in Stockton and the messages we'd planned weeks ago were the ones they were

April '97: Last day, everything going Labour's way

focusing on. TB had campaigned bloody well in the final five days and we were nearly there now. Maybe there were things we could have done differently but it felt pretty much like we had done what we set out to do. Jeremy Vine did a piece in which he said his overwhelming memory was of our professionalism and the flawlessness of our campaign, that we were always on message and on strategy. It hadn't always felt like that, but it was about right. We'd known what we needed to do, we'd had lots thrown at us, but we'd pretty much kept to the plan. Jonathan arrived. He had a draft of the Queen's Speech and it was weird to see all the things we had been banging on about for so long set down on paper as a legislative programme. Jonathan had his critics, and he wasn't the most political of animals, which meant he got whacked in the party a bit, but while we had been campaigning he had been steadily getting the whole thing in place ready for government, and done a bloody good job. TB's last event was at Trimdon Labour club, where the atmosphere was buzzing, and he did a brilliant little speech, bringing together the story of them, New Labour, the campaign, and change for the country. We got back for dinner, TB, CB, me, Jonathan, Leo and Olwen [his wife], Gale [Cherie's mother], Ros [nanny] and the kids. The mood was fantastic. Kathryn was joking and constantly sticking her tongue out at me. Cherie was less fussy and stressed than she'd been. Leo was just looking at Tony with this great beam of pride and happiness on his face. TB said afterwards he would never have been able to do it without me. I said I'd loved every minute, then said 'That's a lie by the way.' I called home and spoke to the kids and I could tell the boys had a big sense of what was going on. I said life is never going to be the same again, because this is part of history and we're all part of that, our whole family. Calum said 'Are we definitely going to win?' I loved the 'we'. I said yes, I think so, and we might win big. After I put the phone down, I sat down on the bed, put my head in my hands and cried my eyes out. I don't know what it was. Relief it was over. Letting go of the nervous energy. Pride. A bit of fear. It was all in there. But I felt we'd done a fantastic job. We were going to win and we were going to make a difference. I'd felt the emotion welling up in me for days and had been keeping it in check for fear it spilled out in the wrong direction. I'd been worrying about Dad's health and was glad he and Mum would both see this happening, but sad that Fiona's dad, who'd always said one day Labour will get back, wasn't there to see it, or even know that Fiona and I had been involved. And I thought of the visits I'd made to John's grave[1] and all

---

[1] Since his death the grave had become a place for contemplation.

the questions I'd asked him there, right back to when I was agonising about whether to take the job.

Thursday, May 1

It was a weird feeling. It was as if we had been fighting a 15-round fight and as the bell rang for the last round, the other guy just didn't show. I had barely slept, even though for the first time in months, there was no reason to get up early. I gave up trying to sleep just after six, got up and read through the papers. They could hardly have been better. The *Sun* and the *Mirror* were terrific. The Tory papers didn't really do the business for them. A young snapper from *North News* got the best picture in Stockton yesterday and it made a few of the front pages. It was weird having time on my hands. At Myrobella, someone had turned on Radio 4. I switched it off, said we didn't have to worry any more, there was nothing we could do, and I twiddled the knob to find a music station. I got one, playing Abba – 'Winner Takes It All'. John Burton [Blair's Sedgefield agent] and I fell about. André Suard was up to do CB's hair, and cut mine while he was waiting for her. TB got up late, then was starting to deal with people re Cabinet and junior jobs. CB had said she wanted the kids to go with them to vote, which was great, but getting everyone ready was all a bit stress-y, like going to a wedding or something, but they looked good walking across the field at the back of the house to the polling station. Carole had clearly chosen all the clothes. Hilary had got them all lined up, good pictures, then TB set out to do a tour of polling stations. The weather was good, the mood was good. I went round with him for a while but then went up to the hotel for a swim. I was starting to get inundated with calls re logistics etc, and also editors who seemed to think I would have some magical insight into the result. TB was fretting on the Ashdown situation, and spoke to him later. Paddy baulked at the idea of the Cabinet post but felt a couple of places on a serious Cabinet committee might be doable. 'Are you sure?' said TB. Paddy said he was. 'He's not really bold enough,' said TB afterwards. I started to get word of the early exit polls during the afternoon and it looked like it was going to be big. TB didn't believe the figures and nor did I. When he came back from his tour, he said 'Do you really think we're going to win?' I said it looked like it. John Burton told him he had to go and open a factory, and TB was not happy. For God's sake, John, do I have to? John was amazing, the way he just fixed things for him to do. I was glad Fiona was coming up, but wished the kids were coming too. I tried to sleep but it was impossible, the phone never stopped. TB had a couple of bad-tempered conversations with GB. GB wanted to know all the junior ministerial positions he was planning, but some of the key ones he hadn't finally decided yet. TB said he did not want Whelan 'rolling round the Treasury'. They discussed the possibility of Whelan working to me in Number 10, but with Tim and Hilary I was already taking two special advisers into the press office. My mind was racing and I was starting to focus on tomorrow. Fiona arrived with lots of TB and CB's family, and the house was filled with noise. Fiona said the journey was pretty chaotic. TB was locked away in his office. All around us, everyone was incredibly jolly but TB and I were feeling flat. We kept getting updates on exit polls and we still didn't believe them. I went out for a walk and bumped into the BBC lot at the end of the road. I was worried they would see JP arrive, and kept talking to them till he did, engineering them so they were talking with their backs to the road. As he drove in, he was laughing, with two fingers up. He and TB had a long session first to sort his job, then go through the government. By now there was a lot of coming and going, but also problems. We watched the exit polls and again TB found it hard to believe. He went back into his office. It wasn't until we got the call from Number 10 later saying JM wanted to speak to him that we dared to believe it for sure. TB sat in the armchair by the fireplace, was very quiet and polite, as Major conceded, said it was clear there would be a considerable Labour majority and congratulations. Jonathan and I were watching him from the chairs by the door, and I think we both had a sense of the history of the moment, despite the cluttered setting and TB's clothes – he was wearing a rugby shirt, dark blue tracksuit bottoms and his ridiculous grandad slippers. TB paused, thanked JM for the call, said he had been a strong opponent and history would be kinder to him. In truth there was little love lost between them and I could only imagine how much JM hated making that call. Alex [Ferguson] called at one point to say they were filming me and TB live through the curtain. I looked over and he said yes, that one, and I went and closed the curtain. TB got a huge cheer as he arrived at the count. He was meant to be doing some interviews but he said he didn't want to. I did them instead and wished I hadn't. I was still doing no complacency when the votes were already in. I couldn't explain why I felt flat. I'd called David Hill earlier and said TB felt they were being too exuberant when the cameras were on them. David said it is very hard to persuade people that a landslide victory is a reason not to be cheerful. TB said we probably felt flat because we had to start all over again tomorrow. Imagine preparing for a new job by working flat out travelling the country for six weeks and then go a few nights without sleep. There was a TV in the bar and we stood together at one point as more and more Tories were falling. 'What on earth have we done?' TB said. 'This is unbelievable.' We'd decided that he would emphasise the family in his speech to the count, and be very measured, emphasise the party at Trimdon, and the country when we got to the Festival Hall. We got to Trimdon Labour club and they were all watching on a big screen the broadcasters had put up. The mood was fabulous. I really liked the Trimdon people. Fiona Bruce was there for the BBC and she noticed I had a tear in my eye. TB did a speech saying how important they were to his politics and his political journey. I'd said at the briefing earlier that what the media found hard to understand was that he was New Labour out of conviction, that he'd made the changes out of belief, and they were beliefs shared by these people. We were driven out to the airport and listened to the radio and the fantastic news that after a series of recounts Rupert Allason [Conservative MP for Torbay] had lost. Even that didn't lift me out of my flat mood though. Fiona asked what was wrong. I said it was probably the anticlimax and the worries about the future. We got on the plane, TB and CB across from me and Fiona, the cops, John Burton. Tom Stoddart was snapping away and we also had a TV camera for ITN. It was a really comfortable plane, better than the ones we had used for the campaign. There were bottles of champagne there but TB was still not really in celebratory mood. Just after take-off, he and CB had a very private chat across their little table. This was him telling her how important she had been and her saying how proud she was, what a great prime minister he would be, she would always support him, etc. I said to Fiona, it may be tough at times but it's quite something to be here, on the plane flying a new PM to London, to know we helped. He was quickly back into work/focus mode, wanting to discuss tone and feel for the Festival Hall. He was scribbling a few thoughts, as was I. More and more seats were coming through on the pager. TB at one point asked if I should have it on. 'Doesn't it interfere with the mechanics?' Dunno. It was now that the full extent of the rout became clear. Portillo lost while we were in the air. Sue Jackson was paging me all the results and seats were falling that we would never have imagined standing a hope in hell of winning. I would get the result, tell the rest and TB would say 'You're kidding me.' We were working on his speech – one nation, the extra sense of responsibility a big majority gives. We landed and I sought out Terry to give him a big hug. How many times had I sat in the back of the car and asked him if he thought we were going to win, and now we had. We headed into London, all quiet really, and then the Special

Branch had a nightmare as we got to the Festival Hall. Somehow they ended up down a wrong road and we got stuck, the whole convoy. We could hear them playing 'Things Can Only Get Better', again and again, and on the radio they were saying TB is only moments away, but what they didn't realise was we were stuck, and the whole convoy was having to do three-point turns and get TB's car up ahead of all the rest. Eventually, we got there, stopped briefly at the bottom of the ramp to get TB miked up, then up the ramp to a wall of noise as the cars pulled up. Fiona and I were in the car behind the police back-up and I suddenly realised I had his speech notes in my inside pocket. I jumped out while the car was still moving and the wheel went over my foot. There was a great carnival atmosphere, thousands of people, hundreds of journalists, Peter M, Neil, JP. TB worked the crowd then up to the lectern and 'a new dawn', and they cheered every word. We had been really flagging, but he was in great form now. The only time I got emotional was seeing Peter Hyman and Tim in the crowd and giving them a huge hug. Then seeing Philip and Gail, who said 'You were so, so brilliant.' And yet it was weird. I felt deflated. All around us people were close to delirium but I didn't feel part of it. I wanted to get to a quieter place. We were taken up to a room after-wards, and I said to TB, this is so weird, you've worked so hard for so long for something, it comes, you're surrounded by people who are so happy because of what you've achieved, yet you don't feel like they do, and you just want to get home to bed. He said he felt exactly the same. Maybe it was too big to take in. More likely was that while the crowd were focusing on now, we were thinking about the job ahead. I got home at 6.30, had an hour's sleep, a shower then to Richmond Crescent.

BOOK TWO

Power
May 1997–June 2001

Who's Who
May 1997–June 2001

The Cabinet

Tony Blair	Prime Minister (TB)
John Prescott	Deputy Prime Minister and Secretary of State for the Environment, Transport and the Regions (JP, John P)
Gordon Brown	Chancellor of the Exchequer (GB)
Robin Cook	Foreign Secretary (RC, Robin C)
Jack Straw	Home Secretary (JS, Jack S)
David Blunkett	Education and Employment Secretary (DB)
Margaret Beckett	Trade and Industry Secretary 1997–98, Leader of the Commons 1998–2001 (MB, Margaret B)
Jack Cunningham	Minister of Agriculture, Fisheries and Food 1997–98, Chancellor of the Duchy of Lancaster 1998–99
Donald Dewar	Secretary of State for Scotland 1997–99, Scotland's First Minister (Scottish Parliament) 1999–2000 (DD, Donald D)
George Robertson	Secretary of State for Defence 1997–99, NATO Secretary General 1999–2004 (GR, George R)
Frank Dobson	Secretary of State for Health 1997–99 (FD, Dobbo)
Ann Taylor	Leader of the Commons 1997–98, Chief Whip 1998–2001
Chris Smith	Secretary of State for Culture, Media and Sport
Harriet Harman	Social Security Secretary 1997–98
Mo Mowlam	Northern Ireland Secretary 1997–99, Chancellor of the Duchy of Lancaster 1999–2001
Ron Davies	Secretary of State for Wales 1997–98

Clare Short	International Development Secretary
Lord (Derry) Irvine	Lord Chancellor
Lord (Ivor) Richard	Leader of the House of Lords 1997–98
David Clark	Chancellor of the Duchy of Lancaster 1997–98
Gavin Strang	Minister of Transport 1997–98
Alistair Darling	Chief Secretary to the Treasury 1997–98, Social Security Secretary 1998–2002 (AD)
Nick Brown	Chief Whip 1997–98, Minister of Agriculture 1998–2001

Additional Cabinet Changes 1998–2001

Peter Mandelson	(Minister without Portfolio 1997–98), Trade and Industry Secretary 1998, Northern Ireland Secretary 1999–2001 (PM, Peter M)
Baroness (Margaret) Jay	Leader of the House of Lords 1998–2001
John Reid	Minister of Transport 1998–99, Secretary of State for Scotland 1999–2001, Northern Ireland Secretary 2001–02
Stephen Byers	Chief Secretary to the Treasury 1998, Trade and Industry Secretary 1998–2001 (Steve, SB)
Alan Milburn	Chief Secretary to the Treasury 1998–99, Health Secretary 1999–2003
Andrew Smith	Chief Secretary to the Treasury 1999–2002
Helen Liddell	Minister of Transport 1999, Secretary of State for Scotland 2001–03
Gus Macdonald	Minister of Transport 1999–2001
Alun Michael	Secretary of State for Wales 1998–99, First Secretary of Wales (Welsh Assembly) 1999–2000

Downing Street

Alex Allan	Principal Private Secretary to August 1997 (AA)
Tim Allan	Special Adviser, Press Office
Philip Barton	Private secretary, Foreign Affairs

Mark Bennett	AC's researcher
Alison Blackshaw	AC's senior personal assistant
Cherie Blair	Wife of TB (CB)
David Bradshaw	Special Adviser Strategic Communications Unit
Julian Braithwaite	Press officer, Foreign Affairs
Sir Robin Butler	Cabinet Secretary and Head of the Home Civil Service to 1998
Alastair Campbell	Chief Press Secretary and Prime Minister's Official Spokesman (AC)
Magi Cleaver	Press officer, overseas visits
Hilary Coffman	Special Adviser, Press Office
Kate Garvey	Diary secretary
Bruce Grocott MP	Parliamentary Private Secretary (Bruce G)
Jeremy Heywood	Private secretary, Principal Private Secretary from 1999
Robert Hill	Policy adviser
John Holmes	Principal Private Secretary and Foreign Policy adviser 1997–99
Anji Hunter	Presentation and planning
Peter Hyman	Strategist and speechwriter
Tom Kelly	NIO Spokesman, later Prime Minister's spokesman
Angus Lapsley	Private secretary, Home Affairs
Liz Lloyd	Policy adviser
Nick Matthews	Duty clerk
Pat McFadden	Policy adviser, later Deputy Chief of Staff
Lucie McNeil	Press officer
David Miliband	Head of Policy Unit (DM, David M)
Fiona Millar	AC's partner, aide to CB
Sally Morgan	Political secretary
Paul Murphy	Northern Ireland Office minister
David North	Private secretary
Allan Percival	Deputy press secretary
Jonathan Powell	Chief of Staff
Roz Preston	Assistant to CB
Lance Price	Special Adviser, Press Office
Terry Rayner	Driver
John Sawers	Foreign Policy Adviser to the Prime Minister 1999–2001 (John S)
Godric Smith	Press officer, later Deputy Press Secretary
Sir Richard Wilson	Cabinet Secretary 1998–2002

And Others

Gerry Adams	President of Sinn Fein (GA)
Bertie Ahern	Prime Minister of Ireland (Bertie, BA)
Lord Airlie	Lord Chamberlain, Royal Household
Paddy Ashdown MP	Liberal Democrat leader to 1999
Ed Balls	Adviser to GB
Sandy Berger	BC's National Security Adviser
Betty Boothroyd MP	Speaker of the House of Commons to 1992–2000
George W Bush	US President from January 2001 (GWB)
Andrew Card	GWB's Chief of Staff
Dick Cheney	US Vice-President from 2001
Jacques Chirac	President of France
Alan Clark MP	Conservative politician, diarist, friend of AC
General Wesley Clark	Supreme Allied Commander Europe (SACEUR)
Bill Clinton	US President to January 2001 (BC)
Hillary Clinton	US First Lady
Catherine Colonna	Chirac's press secretary
John de Chastelain	Chairman of the Independent International Commission on Decommissioning
Charlie Falconer	Barrister, close friend of TB
Sir Robert Fellowes	Private Secretary to the Queen
Alex Ferguson	Manager, Manchester United, friend of AC
Frank Field MP	Social Security minister
David Frost	Broadcaster
Al Gore	US Vice-President to 2001
Philip Gould	Political pollster and strategist, adviser to TB (Philip, PG)
General Sir Charles Guthrie	Chief of the Defence Staff, British Armed Forces
William Hague MP	Leader of the Opposition
John Hume	Leader, Social and Democratic Labour Party
Saddam Hussein	President of Iraq (SH)
General Sir Mike Jackson	Commander, Kosovo forces to Macedonia and Priština
Sir Robin Janvrin	Deputy Private Secretary to the Queen

Tessa Jowell MP	Health minister
Charles Kennedy MP	Liberal Democrat leader from 1999
Helmut Kohl	German Chancellor to 1998
Stephen Lamport	Private Secretary to the Prince of Wales
Joe Lennon	Press secretary to Bertie Ahern
Michael Levy	Businessman, Labour Party fund-raiser
Mike McCurry	BC's press secretary
Margaret McDonagh	Labour Party General Secretary 1998–2001
Martin McGuinness	Sinn Fein chief negotiator
Ken Maginnis	Ulster Unionist MP
Seamus Mallon	Deputy Leader, SDLP
Sir Christopher Meyer	British Ambassador to Washington
Slobodan Milosovic	President of Yugoslavia
George Mitchell	Chairman all-party peace negotiations, Northern Ireland
Estelle Morris MP	Education minister
Rupert Murdoch	Chairman, News Corporation
Ian Paisley	Leader of the Democratic Unionist Party
Colin Powell	GWB's Secretary of State
Prince Charles	Prince of Wales
Princess Diana	Princess of Wales
Vladimir Putin	Russian President from 1999
Queen Elizabeth II	UK monarch
Condoleezza Rice	GWB's National Security Adviser (Condi)
Geoffrey Robinson MP	Paymaster-General (Treasury)
Lt Col Malcolm Ross	Comptroller of the Lord Chamberlain's Office
Donald Rumsfeld	GWB's Defense Secretary
Gerhard Schroeder	German Chancellor 1998–2005
Jamie Shea	NATO spokesman
Javier Solana	NATO Secretary General to 1999
John Taylor	Deputy Leader, Ulster Unionist Party
Paddy Teahon	Adviser to Bertie Ahern
Margaret Thatcher	Former prime minister
David Trimble	Leader, Ulster Unionist Party
Ben Wegg-Prosser	Assistant to Peter Mandelson
Admiral Sir Alan West	Chief of Defence Intelligence, British Armed Forces
Charlie Whelan	Special Adviser, GB's press spokesman 1997–99
Boris Yeltsin	President of Russia 1991–99

Friday, May 2

Just a short sleep had bucked me up, and I had a session with some of the hacks in the street [Richmond Crescent] before going in. It was another lovely sunny day, and there was a good crowd outside. Inside, the usual frantic activity. Carole was there fussing around Cherie. TB was up in the bedroom working on the speech for the street. 'Practical measures in pursuit of noble causes.' Not sure about that. He got dressed and Jonathan and I went out to be met by Trevor Butler, who I knew from my *Mirror* days when he was looking after Thatcher and Major, and who would be taking over protection. He talked us through what was going to happen, the drive to the Palace, what Jonathan and I would do while TB saw the Queen, the drive back to Number 10. TB came out, did a little walkabout and then off we went. Jonathan and I were in the car behind the back up and the whole journey was fantastic, people coming out of houses and offices to wave and cheer. Going down Gower St, it was almost like watching a cascade. We were looking down the street and people following the car on TV were coming out to cheer. I had a surge of emotion almost on a par with the one in Sedgefield on Wednesday night. I said to Jonathan 'This is unbelievable.' We agreed that expectations were going to be way too high. There were big crowds outside the Palace, huge cheer as he went through. Then he was taken off to see the Queen while Jonathan and I were taken into a room with Alex Allan [PPS to the Prime Minister], Robin Janvrin [deputy private secretary to the Queen] and Geoff Crawford [press secretary to the Queen]. It was all very friendly and relaxed, and I couldn't quite take in that it was all happening. Alex Allan seemed a really nice bloke. It was odd to see people who didn't look exhausted. I was talking about how hard it had been to be away from the kids so much and then Janvrin said oh, look at those children at Number 10, and I turned round to the TV to see Calum and Grace sitting on the steps of Number 10, looking bemused, Calum playing with some sunglasses. I called Mum to get her to watch, and she already was. TB was in for half an hour or so, came out and we set off for Downing St. As we turned into Whitehall, we could hear the crowds. The cars stopped at the bottom of the street and we got out and the noise was deafening. Ton-ee, Ton-ee, Ton-ee. Labour's coming home, Labour's coming home. TB and CB got out, started the walk up. Jonathan and I followed on behind. The noise was almost like a sporting event. I caught sight of Fiona holding Grace up the street, and Rory and Calum standing there near the door. Tim was in tears in the crowd. It was fantastic to see the party people and the people from the office who had all worked their rocks off and were now able to enjoy this. David Bradshaw [campaign colleague] and Kerry [his wife], Liz, Peter H. It was brilliant. We got to the top and TB went to the lectern, did his speech, a few more pictures and then inside to meet the staff. Jonathan and I, Sally and David Miliband, followed. I'd been through that door so many times as a journalist. I'd stood in that hall dozens, hundreds of times, waiting to be called through with the rest of the hacks to Bernard Ingham's briefings. But this time it felt very different, walking in behind the new Prime Minister, knowing that for some years I would be spending more working hours here than virtually anywhere else. I felt a mix of confidence, but uncertainty too.

TB went off with Robin Butler to the Cabinet room for a security briefing. Jonathan, Sally, David M and I went up to the dining room, where a buffet lunch had been laid on. Jonathan Haslam showed me around, introduced me to a few people, and it was all a bit weird. Jonathan was being very pleasant and doing what he had to do, but I felt for him. He was being kicked out of the job, and having to guide me as to what to do next. I sensed very mixed feelings in the staff. The messengers seemed friendly and helpful. The press office people were nervous, I could tell. They also sensed, rightly, that I had not been impressed by the JM press operation and would want to make changes. Jonathan had left me a note on the strengths and weaknesses of all of them. It was odd having such a big office, PAs and the like, when I had been pretty much used to operating anywhere from a mobile phone. I was introduced to Alison [Blackshaw], my new PA, who seemed a bit dizzy, told me how much she had liked Major, and every time I wandered off, she said she had to know where I was and she was worried I would be too 'independent' for her to be able to do her job. TB seemed to be in his element. We were in the Cabinet room, working through the Cabinet and some of the junior jobs, and he was clear and decisive, had found new reserves of energy. Butler and Alex Allan seemed to take to him. Butler said later all the machine wanted was clear direction. I told him I had not been too impressed with the way the government media machine worked, and nor had TB. I asked if I was within my rights to get them all in and emphasise the need for change and he said no problem. That was what they expected. I was still feeling a bit flat and deflated, and the atmosphere of the place didn't help. The children helped lift things a bit, Euan and Nicky in particular running a bit wild. Butler was fussing around the whole time. Once lunch was out of the way, TB started to see everyone to appoint the Cabinet. JP came in first and was really happy with his lot. Robin went straight out and did a doorstep and TB said we had to keep a very wary eye on him. 'He is playing the old games.' Derry was happy enough. Blunkett came in and I introduced him to Haslam, who was going to be his top pressman. It was interesting how quickly the idea settled that they were now in government and off to do real jobs as opposed to all the shadow stuff we had been doing for years. Margaret B and Jack S in particular made the point they just couldn't wait to get started.

Saturday, May 3

TB was pretty knackered but he had to keep going on appointments. We started at 9 and he was keen for a very New Labour element to the reshuffle. He called Frank Field and offered him Number 2 to Harriet at Social Security. We were in the Cabinet room, TB, Jonathan and I on one side, Butler and Alex Allan on the other. Those two seemed absolutely fine about me and Jonathan, no problem at all. I got the feeling that Alex had found the last stages of the JM government really draining. He has a very quiet, unassuming manner, but there is a sharpness and energy there and I sense he really wants to help. RB is very smiley and friendly, but more old-fashioned, more naturally establishment. The one I was keeping a close eye on was Mark Adams [private secretary with responsibility for Prime Minister's Questions], who I sensed trying to get barriers up early on. I took a pretty instant dislike. He was cocky without having the obvious talent to justify it and when he was giving it large about how we should prepare for PMQs, I couldn't help pointing out that Major's PMQs was one of his biggest weaknesses. We got through the appointments quicker than any of us thought possible. Mo and I had a very friendly chat before she headed straight for Northern Ireland. TB had been slightly dreading telling Derek Foster, Tom Clarke and Michael Meacher that they would not be in the Cabinet, but they all took it as well as they could be expected to. We talked about Charlie [Whelan] who had come to see me earlier to say he was alarmed that TB didn't want him, that he would work as my deputy if that was what I really wanted. I said TB was wrong to suggest that, because I had to have a civil servant as a deputy. GB asked me to agree that Charlie stayed at the Treasury, but kept in regular communication with me. Charlie looked very low.

Monday, May 5

It was a bank holiday, but a normal working day. I went round to TB's, who was livid at Robin who had briefed hard on the Social Chapter. 'I could cheerfully kill the little bugger,' he said. He called him in the car on the way in and said he was now involved in running the country and representing Britain, not winning a few rounds of applause at a conference. These things have to be done according to an overall plan, not just spilled out when people feel like it. As he came off the phone, he said 'Unbelievable,' and laughed. 'He said "You are going to need me as much as I need you."' I had a meeting with GB, Ed B, Charlie W, Jill Rutter [Treasury head of press] and HMT officials to go over tomorrow's plan on the Bank. It was going to be big and bold and I said to GB he really had to capture the sense of history, set it in the bigger context of making Britain strong and competitive for the long term, building long-term prosperity. He was scribbling madly and I could see some of the Treasury officials realising they had never worked with anyone like this before.

Tuesday, May 6

I went over to GB's office for a pre-meeting on the Bank independence. There was a real buzz in there, and GB was tense and fidgety, firing off questions and then answering them himself. It was genuinely exciting, a really big moment. The Treasury officials looked a little bit shell-shocked. I sensed GB was taking far less care at keeping them sweet than TB. He was making very clear, in word and deed, who was in charge. The room was packed, GB had a real authority there, and dealt well with questions. GB was much more relaxed than he had been in the latter stages of the campaign. He was clearly taking to the Treasury like a duck to water.

Wednesday, May 7

GB got a terrific press re Bank of England independence, deservedly, though there was too much 'It was Ed Balls's idea' around. The Civil Service had done a not bad job writing the Queen's Speech based on

May '97: GB takes to Treasury like a duck to water

the advice we had given in advance re early priorities, but I rewrote it to make it a bit less frumpy and to get in a bit of message. The Palace were fine about most of the changes but one or two they pushed back on. Jonathan told me that Butler had said he did not think I should attend Cabinet. I did a little note to TB saying if we were to get clarity of briefing out of Cabinet I had to be there. He said in writing there was no question of me not attending Cabinet meetings. I was unimpressed that Butler had tried to get it done through Jonathan, rather than come to me or raise it with TB.

Thursday, May 8

I sensed we were really beginning to motor. In less than a week, we had established momentum and a sense of competence and we were getting broadly positive reactions to most things we were doing. TB was seeing Ashdown who, helpfully, volunteered the view that there should be reform of PMQs. This was great news because TB was intending to announce change tomorrow, and it was good that Paddy raised it rather than being pushed into backing it. Elsewhere, however, TB was unimpressed, because Paddy was not keen on merger talks and was instead asking for stuff like a Privy Counsellorship for Bob Maclennan [Lib Dem MP and party president], more peers. The Cabinet started arriving fairly early and there was a good mood around the place. They gathered outside and were drinking tea and chatting. I agreed with JP that he would do clips in the street afterwards, but nobody else. We had to stop the notion Robin had tried to start that people just wander over and talk to whoever is out there. We did the official photo, and it was only after they were all there that I realised there was only one woman in the front row, which didn't look great. GB looked very tense and bunched up. There was something about team photos that made people nervous and a bit silly. Alex Allan told me TB had said he would dispense with all the titles in Cabinet and just use Christian names. TB told me later it had been AA who first suggested it. TB said the last government had been a shambles and we had to learn from that. He said we will sink or swim together. He was serious about proper coordination through the centre, on policy and on press. Clare asked if every interview had to be cleared through me and he said yes. GB raised the pay review bodies and said he thought it was difficult for the Cabinet to take their full salary rises when they were urging restraint on others. TB and JP (less enthusiastically) weighed in with support. Donald [Dewar] said he needed more Scottish bills. TB said 'You'll have to drop the referendum bill to get them,' and DD laughed and that was that.

Friday, May 9

GB was in better form than of late, and a bit more engaged. I relayed the call I had from Nick Brown re BSE, who said 'Don't let TB take charge of it because it is insoluble.' GB said he was more worried about the public finances. Also, that he feared there was too much ill discipline among MPs. And he was worried, as ever, about JP. 'Why on earth did you give him the regions as well?' 'That was your idea,' said TB. 'No it wasn't.' GB said Robin was fucking up on Europe. I'd had words with RC about the TV shots of him kissing Oskar Lafontaine.[1] TB said our objectives for the IGC[2] were to protect borders, relax veto where we said we would, not allow inner core of countries to go ahead at different pace, reweighting of votes, flexible labour markets, CAP [Common Agricultural Policy] reform. I did the Sunday lobby at 1.20. I said I did not intend to have a fixed slot for them every week, and it would depend on whether there was anything to say. They were by and large not a serious bunch and it was largely a waste of time. The serious ones would demand more time outside the briefing anyway. It went on a bit and I was late for the [Wim] Kok [Dutch Prime Minister] lunch. TB was saying we intended to be constructive but there were certain things we could not cede. The Dutch (presidency) were publishing a new draft treaty in the next few days. The current game appeared to be that we would get it into the new treaty that we kept border controls, something the last government failed to get. TB emphasised no weakening of the veto on foreign and defence policy. He said the whole third pillar (justice and home affairs) could not become intergovernmental. It was like learning a new language and TB took to it easily, better than I did. Variable geometry? IGC, multi-speed, third pillar. He said it was important we stamped our mark on the IGC. Kok and TB had a private session then Kok came out to do a doorstep. We left our media to RC, who was so puffed up it was comic. TB was heading off to Chequers [Prime Minister's official country retreat]. We had a chat before he left and he said I had to try to get some rest.

Monday, May 12

TB said he reckoned he could see a way of sorting the Northern Ireland problem. I loved the way he said it, like nobody had thought of it before. I said what makes you think you can do it when nobody

[1] Chairman of the Social Democratic Party of Germany, 1995–99; later Minister of Finance in Gerhard Schroeder's government.
[2] The 1996–97 intergovernmental conference led to the signing of the Treaty of Amsterdam in October.

May '97: TB reckons he can sort out Northern Ireland

else could? I had a long session with him and John Holmes [foreign affairs private secretary at Number 10]. He was not your typical Foreign Office man. He was from Preston, had a very dry sense of humour and had been totally grown up about the main changes. He worked fantastically hard and quickly established a rapport with Tony, and an ability to speak his mind without bullshit. I could tell he was a bit quizzical about TB's optimism, but willing to give it a good go. I had a look round the Number 11 flat with Fiona and Roz. It was a bit musty and not terribly homely. The main living room felt more like an overpriced hotel than a home. The pictures were pretty dire. The kitchen was awful. I felt a bit sorry for them, having to move in but the kids seemed fine enough with it.

Wednesday, May 13

Queen's Speech day. TB went off, first to the Commons, then to the Lords, where they all watched the Queen deliver the Speech. I watched on TV and I loved hearing her read out the more political bits we had added in: for the whole nation . . . education the No. 1 priority . . . excess profits. She didn't look at all comfortable reading out the bit on banning handguns. The debate in the House was pretty flat. Major's heart wasn't in it, for fairly obvious reasons. We had a meeting in the Cabinet room on Ireland – TB, Jonathan, John H, RB, AA and me. JH had done a draft and it was in tone very Unionist but I felt the offer of talks with Sinn Fein was sufficiently big and bold for that to be the main story out of it, and so it was OK. TB said he was sure we had only a brief window of opportunity and we had to take it. He said he intended to sleep on it before making a final decision to do it. He was seeing Paddy in the morning and he would speak to JM tomorrow night, and tell him he intended to get officials to talk to SF. He admitted that the effect of what we were proposing was that SF would get into talks without a ceasefire. It was hard to see how the Unionists would do anything other than go mad at that, which is why the tone had to be heavily weighted in their favour.

Friday, May 16

I really enjoyed today, for all sorts of reasons. Northern Ireland was a big story, announcing government officials talking to SF without delivering a ceasefire. A bold move, full of risks, which by and large we handled pretty well. We spent a lot of time getting the words right, the details of the visits; there was a lot of sophisticated spinning had to be done, and it paid off. The Northern Ireland Office had been far too gabby about the visit, but nobody had a sniff of the scale of what he would say. Terry collected me at half six and I got in to hear the visit leading the news, but without much detail. I wrote a briefing note and Q & A based on the conversations with TB, JH and Jonathan. The difficult balancing act would be to reassure the Unionists while signalling a major change. Before we left, he spoke to Trimble [UUP leader] and he was pretty candid with him, but he seemed OK-ish. In the car to Northolt, he spoke to John Hume [SDLP leader], who was fine. TB met what Mo called 'the holies', namely the Protestant and Catholic top guys, then did a fantastic walkabout, really good mood, really friendly and warm. I called Denis Murray [BBC's Ireland correspondent] on his mobile just before the lunchtimes and briefed him fully on the speech. 'Bloody hell,' he said. He was impressed. He said it was a great story. I liked Denis, had always liked his reporting, and I felt I could trust him to put both parts of the equation. The first reports were important, and they were word-perfect for us when I listened down the phone a bit later. TB felt buoyed up after the walkabout. He said those people are desperate for something good to happen. He did the troops, then back into the helicopters to head for the Agriculture Show where he was doing the speech. By now there was an enormous media presence to match the expectations. We were as happy as we were ever going to be with the text. I was a bit alarmed hearing Trimble's overwhelmingly enthusiastic response, so briefed Denis again, who emphasised at the end of the lunchtime bulletin that the big thing here was the offer of talks, and Mo would be writing to Gerry Adams. Again, we were getting credit for being big and bold and ballsy. TB did another walkabout on the way out. It was a very rural, very Ulster event, but he seemed to have a natural empathy. As he walked along shaking hands I told him Hume and Trimble had been fine, Ian Paisley [Democratic Unionist Party leader] very hostile. TB put his foot in an enormous cowpat but just carried on till we got to the car. None of the media seemed to have noticed. Bill Lloyd [protection officer] gave him a packet of tissues and I said what a glamorous life I led, sitting alongside the Prime Minister as he cleaned bullshit off his shoes.

Wednesday, May 21

First PMQs day. TB went over the areas we needed lines on. He decided to do it without notes, though he had all the briefing from Mark Adams, which was working well. I felt quite nervous about it but TB was on good form. We left for the NEC where Greg Cook [Labour Party official, an expert on polling] did a polling presentation. TB said we must not lose sight of why we won – New Labour, good organ-

May '97: Blair's dramatic Northern Ireland move

isation, a united party, a clear message. He said the Tories would rebuild themselves, however long it took, and we had to remain united and disciplined, and always ahead of the game. No doubt we would have disagreements, but the tone of disagreement matters. The One Nation message was even more important given the size of the majority. Nobody should get drunk on power. We are here to serve. TB denied he was nervous pre-Questions. We left for the House. In the car on the way over, he was starting to go over some of the possible answers. He was more nervous now. He locked himself away in the office to write out answers on the tough questions, calling me in every now and then to try them out on me, then asking for help on sharpening lines. The civil servants told me Jonathan Haslam always said 'good luck' to Major as he went through to the chamber. I said my job was not to say 'good luck'. It was all of our jobs to make sure he didn't need it. It went fine in the end. If anything it was a bit of an anticlimax. Our lot were quite excited and there were maybe too many soft questions. The Tories' hearts weren't really in it. At the 4 o'clock briefing, they were all a bit disappointed. I got back for a meeting with the next Clinton advance team. It was hard to make progress because Clinton had apparently said he wanted to go shopping, eating and didn't know if he wanted to make a speech or not. They're all very nice, but very vague and didn't really know what they wanted. They thought Clinton wanted to go for an Indian meal. Then to a meeting with Peter, Jonathan, John Holmes, Brian Bender [Cabinet Office] on Europe and our plan for Noordwijk.[1] I was keen on the big picture messages. Europe was a total minefield, and I was concerned to make sure it was not the one that blew me up. I had been reading as much as I could to get on top of the detail, but it was really complicated.

Thursday, May 22

The honeymoon was still going on, with the press overwhelmingly favourable again. Cabinet was mainly Europe, Ireland and discussion of draft bills. TB gave them another little lecture about coordination. Robin said we were making progress on border controls and he was confident of the deal we would get. He said we had legal authority for retaining border controls and so achieving something the Tories never had. Defence was the other tricky area, with the French–Germans pushing for something that we would regard as undermining NATO. He said the smaller countries were on our side. TB said there were

[1] EU leaders conference, June 1997.

all sorts of areas for greater cooperation but we should not roll over and have our tummies tickled. On spending, he said he did not want a great outbreak of departmentalitis. Then we had a meeting with RC re Noordwijk. I then did a briefing with Nigel Sheinwald [Foreign Office press secretary and head of communications] and Paul Lever [Foreign Office senior official]. There was a huge turnout and a lot of interest in what approach he was intending to take. I was emphasising a more cooperative approach, but also saying we would argue for Europe on Britain's terms. Yes to more QMV[1] in certain areas, but border controls sacrosanct. We had a meeting of the Big Four. They had come from a Cabinet committee meeting on Bosnia where Clare had apparently said to the defence chiefs that our policy was 'shameful', and she spoke for the PLP. JP said she was bonkers. Then I got back for the end of TB's meeting with Thatcher. Nobody saw her go in though there were people – e.g. GB – who saw her inside the building. I doubted it would stay quiet. I had real doubts about the need for it but he was adamant it made sense to involve her, make her feel her advice was valued. She was over-hamming it all a bit, reminiscing loudly. Then the two of them went off for a session on their own, where he picked her brains on foreign affairs. He said afterwards she was still very sharp, though sometimes her determination to make a point got in the way of a broader understanding. I went in at the end to move him on for the next meeting and she was in full flow. Don't trust the FCO [Foreign and Commonwealth Office]. Germany will follow if TB gives a real lead. The French cannot be trusted. Then a long lecture on single parents, illegitimacy, etc. They were sitting on the sofas in the Green Room and she was complaining at the way loose threads were hanging off. To be fair, they did look a bit shabby. She told him he should do lots of receptions for the voluntary sector, then paused as if she was about to make a huge point, looked him in the eye and said 'And don't forget to invite the Lord Lieutenants.' We agreed that if we had press enquiries we should simply say he wanted to talk to her re foreign affairs. 'Quite so,' she said, and off she went. 'God, she is so strong,' he said as she went. I was more struck by how obvious it was that she missed the place. Her reminiscences had been less about the big things than the little routines that she got into. There was a group of party people waiting to see TB and their eyes almost dropped out when they saw her walking past the Cabinet room with TB.

[1] Qualified majority voting. Each member state has a fixed number of votes. The number allocated to each country is roughly determined by its population, though favouring smaller countries.

Tuesday, May 27

NATO summit, Paris. I didn't sleep at all well, and went down for break-fast just after 6, soon afterwards joined by TB. The first big thing of the day was the bilateral with Yeltsin at the Russian Ambassador's residence. I took an instant liking to him. He was all the things you expected – big, a bit clumsy, a bit gauche, larger than life, but a few things I hadn't expected – witty, very warm, tactile and sensitive to mood and moment. We had been warned he would be very vague on detail but that wasn't the case at all. He started the meeting by saying he was pleased TB had won the election, which was a good start. He said 'My heart is open to you,' that he wanted to have friendly relations, that Europe was stronger if Britain and Russia were together. TB praised Yeltsin's transformation of Russia, and said that as one of the youngest PMs on the scene, he looked up to him. 'Not one of the youngest,' barked Boris, 'THE youngest.' We were served up with blinis and caviar and great mounds of salmon. 'Eat,' he said, something he did with difficulty. I noticed he had a finger missing. On trade, he said he had brought in new people, Anatoly Chubais and Boris Nemtsov [pro-capitalist reformers and supporters of Yeltsin]. TB said he admired the appointments and the manner in which they were made. 'Fast,' said Yeltsin. They joked about sacking Robin. 'Your foreign minister is excellent – so let him work.' They spent a lot of time on NATO–Russia and Yeltsin asked if he favoured him going to Madrid, which TB did. Chirac supported it too, said Yeltsin. He said he would talk to Clinton and do some hard thinking. He asked TB to visit Moscow, then asked for support in moving from G7 to G8, with Russia a full member. Then they agreed to a joint agreement on dealing with organised crime. RC said he and Jack Straw would meet opposite numbers. Boris suddenly looked at TB and said 'You have good eyes, very bright. That says a bright mind. You are the right age. I think Great Britain is in good hands.' TB tried to steer it to economic reform but Boris was back on the personal – talking about his grandson at Millfield. TB said he played tennis near there. Yeltsin said he would get fit and challenge him. 'I used to beat other leaders.' He could not have been warmer or more friendly and they genuinely seemed to hit it off. TB said the leaders' lunch was an extraordinary event. 'If people had seen it, they would be terrified these people were running the world.' At one point Clinton, clearly in jest (or so TB thought), said to Yeltsin that he would get on with Ian Paisley and it would be a good idea if they met. Yeltsin appeared to take it seriously and twice asked TB when he wanted him to go. He said a lot of drink was taken, not just by Boris, and that Chirac could not stop making grand little speeches.

May '97: Yeltsin tells TB Britain is in good hands

Clinton told TB that Kohl said he saw TB as his natural successor as the main leader in Europe. Boris and Bill were all over him for the time I saw them together. Chirac was looking a bit unsettled, probably by the elections but I don't think he much liked having TB as the centre of attention among the big guys.

Thursday, May 29

The Clinton visit was well set up, with papers and broadcasts pretty much set according to the overnight briefing. I got in early to work on TB press conference words, when Cherie called and said André [Suard] was there and I should go up and get a haircut. TB was in the bath but came through and we went over what we wanted to get out of today. As ever he was keen to get a phrase that summed it all up. I quite liked 'new generation politics' because it suggested the generation was not so much about age as about a change in politics. In truth, we were getting such a good press at the moment that the Americans stood to gain far more than we did, especially as Bill C was being done in by the Paula Jones sexual harassment case[1] again. TB wanted it to be a day of definition so we went through the various areas where we could say a new politics was being forged, neither old left nor new right, and once I'd had my hair cut I went down and worked on a whole stack of lines beginning 'This is the generation which . . .' It was OK if a bit heavy on the cliché front, but as a device it could carry a fair number of strong policy messages on jobs, growth, inclusion. There was a real sense of anticipation at the idea of Clinton speaking to the Cabinet in the Cabinet room. We waited for him to arrive and got word he was a few minutes away. Cherie came down, looking great. She was on good form at the moment and had got a good press in the run-up, largely because of comparisons with Hillary. Fiona had to get a lot of the credit for the advice and for the outcome in the press. TB was nervous, fussing about tiny details, like where on the step to stand when he arrived, should he kiss Hillary – we decided not – whether he and BC should stand in the middle or put the wives in the middle. He was talking very quickly, a sure sign of nerves. I had a brief chat with JP re the choreography for Cabinet, and we agreed they should applaud but stay seated. Then the car pulled up. It was a lovely sunny day, there were hundreds of photographers there and the mood between them was great. The pictures went straight onto the front of the *Standard* – 'best

[1] Jones, a former Arkansas civil servant, filed a sexual harassment case against Bill Clinton in 1994.

of pals' – which BC loved when he saw it and later he asked if he could get a copy. By then we were at Le Pont de la Tour restaurant, and Hilary Coffman had to go and buy one from a punter for ten quid! TB's kids had come down to say hello just inside the door and he chatted to them as the rest of the American party piled in. There were too many of them and it was a bit crowded and hard to manage. BC's operation was overmanned and there were too many people claiming to have his ear who didn't. We had had the nonsense about the Indian. Now we were reliably informed he wanted the four of them to go to a pub. Anji even got Jon Mendelsohn and Ben Lucas [Labour campaigners] to stay in the Anchor Tap pub literally all day, and when TB mentioned it to BC, just as when we had mentioned the Indian, he looked at us like we were mad. He sparkled at Cabinet. 'I'm so thrilled to be here. It is very exciting for an American president to be in this room.' He spotted Mo and said he had seen her speeches on TV, and you could see her melt. He said he had read the policy handbook and went into the mantra – many not the few, future not the past, leadership not drift, education the Number 1 priority. I said to him afterwards I wish our own people could express it as fluently. He could hold a room with a pause and a nod, and so control events. He had enormous, beautifully manicured hands and he used these too to powerful communications effect. TB was very nice about me in public again. I don't know whether this was just flattery or whether it was a way of sending a signal to the Civil Service machine. He said to BC that I was 'something of a political legend', who scared our opponents. Afterwards I said to TB I was surprised how formal it was at times, Mr President, Mr Prime Minister. He said if it had been any less formal, it would have seemed gimmicky. But at both the meetings and the press conference he felt there were times when what they said was interchangeable. He really felt he was someone on his wavelength. Jobs, welfare, education, citizenship, that whole agenda he felt was shared by a kindred spirit.

Thursday, June 5

On the way to the morning meeting, I was locked in the lift with Alex [Allan], Charlie [Whelan], Nick Brown, Allan Percival, Siobhan [Kenny, press officer] and Jonathan. We were stuck in there for five minutes before rescue. Jonathan and I learned we had identical thoughts afterwards – how unpleasant it would be to die stuck inside a lift with Nick Brown. Meeting with TB and Alex Allan, and we agreed it would be bad news for him to see Diana before Charles.

Saturday, June 7

Interesting little interlude today. It was the day Diana was supposed to go to Chequers. She had been insistent that it was there, rather than at Maggie Rae's house as before. She had also been saying to her office that she would bring Harry. But it turned out in fact she was intending to bring William. Yet when Alex checked with the Palace, the time of the meeting did not coincide with a time when she would be with the boys at all. It was all a bit odd and reinforced me and AA in the view that he would do better to wait. TB felt we were being harsh, did not think she would exploit it, but it was not a risk worth taking. If it emerged he had seen her before Charles it would set off all sorts of bollocks. Alex and I both pressed him to cancel and eventually he agreed. In the end we got the duty clerk to call her office and to say there had been a message from Germany that he had to cancel.

Monday, June 10

I went over to the FCO to a meeting Robin had called on the IGC. I remembered the office from interviewing [Douglas] Hurd [ex foreign secretary] in there years ago, but somehow it looked even bigger and grander with RC in it. He was absolutely loving it, surrounded by public schoolboy diplomats he could order around, dealing with huge issues on which he could pontificate at will. I like to think part of him is overdoing it out of a sense of self-parody, but you can never be sure. But for all his diddling and pomposity, I find it hard not to like him. He was also clearly on top of the detail, and clear about what we needed to achieve. RC went through his own plan – win on borders; focus on jobs; aim for more votes for Britain; keep the veto on CFSP [Common Foreign and Security Policy]; NATO established as bedrock of European defence; tough action on fraud; CAP reform; fish. The Tory leadership results came through – could hardly have been better. Clarke 49, Hague 41, the other three split. So it looked like Hague would win. TB on balance felt Clarke would have been better for us, and that Hague was about the best choice they could make, but I still felt we would get the better of him. I went to Murdoch's do. TB was seeing the Queen, then called Clinton re Northern Ireland.

Wednesday, June 11

Paris. We arrived and were driven straight to the Elysée. Chirac was so over the top in his welcome it was almost comical. He slightly exaggerated everything. Handshake firmer than most, and longer than most. Hand movements slightly more expansive than most. He was a slow walker so he walked very slowly. He read from notes printed on little postcards and when he consulted them, he really looked at them, picked them up slowly, read them as everyone looked at him, put them down, then spoke. He said everything as though it was a grand statement. TB at times looked like he was about to burst out laughing. By comparison with TB, he was very much a no-detail merchant, even after looking at the cards. So the impression he gave, on JHA [Justice and Home Affairs], defence, anything, was that he agreed, but in fact most of the time he was saying something slightly different. TB said we wanted to take a new approach in Europe, but emphasised the importance of keeping border controls. TB said in passing we had no ID cards in Britain, and Chirac was shocked. 'No identity cards!! You have no identity cards. Mmmm.' Exaggerated nodding and shaking of head. TB said he was in favour but they were considered a breach of civil liberties. On *'cooperation renforcée'*, and some of his QMV areas, Chirac said *'C'est une bonne idée. Si non, je ne la proposerais pas.'* Exaggerated looking around for amused responses. He did have a fine sense of humour. When TB raised jobs, Chirac said *'Ah, là on va nous accorder, nous les hommes de gauche.'*

Monday, June 16

Amsterdam. News came through that two RUC officers had been killed in Lurgan. TB looked sick at the lunch. He said it was clearly a deliberate sabotage, that they knew the plan we had to get them into talks with a date next week and this was the signal that they intended to scupper it. It was pretty grim.

Tuesday, June 17

TB was preoccupied by Ireland and the shooting and wondering whether to reveal the exchange of letters he had with Sinn Fein. He met [Jacques] Santer [European Commission president] to tie him down on exchanges of letters re fish/quota hopping. Santer struck me as a particularly flabby character, dull and drab, rather surprised to be in the position he was. They were due to leave for the lunch and we discovered for the first time that the leaders were expected to ride a bike. I grabbed TB as he came out and said he should grab a proper-looking bike, get out there, turn it into a race, and win. We had to walk over a bridge to where the bikes were and on the way there were a number of girls screaming at him, Tony, Tony. The others looked on incredibly jealous, including Kohl. TB said how the hell is he going to ride a bike? This is a bit ridiculous, isn't it?

I said it may be, but they will be fantastic pictures, if he wins. Winning in Europe, get it? He went for it, pedalling away madly while trying to look cool, and he got over the bridge first. We then watched the others come over, including [Lamberto] Dini [Italian foreign minister] who fell off. Kohl didn't go on the bike and looked thoroughly pissed off. But he and TB had a good one-on-one re defence, and again, TB was winning on NATO, and watering down the commitment to the WEU [Western European Union]/EU merger. The lesson was to state bottom lines and stick to them. I enjoyed it a lot more than I did covering summits from the other side. It helped that we had pretty much won everything we had come to win. TB was tired, as we all were, but it had gone really well.

Thursday, June 19

We started the day thinking TB was going to make a statement on Northern Ireland, announcing that Sinn Fein had a timetable for coming into talks. We ended it saving the Millennium Exhibition. TB was now against an NI statement, not least because there was a possibility it would clash horribly with yesterday's funeral of the policemen, one of whose sons was absolutely heartbroken on the TV news last night. On the Dome, he had pretty much decided to go ahead. He seemed genuinely split but felt the pros outweighed the cons. Peter M was in favour, not least because he was going to be centrally involved in the relaunch, and had helped get us to where we were. He was less bullish than before, however, which unsettled TB. I had moved marginally in favour only because everyone else had come out against and I didn't want him to be seen to give in to pressure. TB was due for a bilateral with JP and he was clearly in favour as well. He went into one of his great loud speeches in a quiet, small room, a mix of mania and enthusiasm, said it will be great to pull it off, it will be made to work, he was leader and if his instincts say do it, we should do it. I called Heseltine to ask him to be around to say something positive. TB then, pre-Cabinet, squared GB, who came up with another approach. He said that rather than say we were going ahead per se, we should say there were five tests that had to be met. Costs, legacy, new management structure, educational role, the whole nation enjoying and taking part. I sensed this was a sensible media strategy, but also that he may be suggesting it as a way of slowing and then scuppering. But it became clear in Cabinet there was going to be a real problem. TB spoke, gave away one or two little doubts, but basically made clear he thought it was a good thing for Britain, provided costs, legacy, etc were all sorted. GB said it was fine, subject to the tests. Chris Smith agreed with the overall approach. Jack Straw said he remembered the Festival of Britain and the great impact on kids at that time. 'Absolutely,' boomed JP. Then Blunkett said he was deeply against it. Dobson said on balance, so was he. Ann Taylor thought there should be some independent cost analysis. Jack Cunningham said people are against it and the management is crap. Donald D said it was a leap in the dark. George Robertson was more supportive. Harriet was in favour. Clare said she was vehemently opposed. Ron Davies couldn't see how we could make it an event for the whole nation. Robin was worried it would be seen as a white elephant and every time anything went wrong, it will be our problem. Darling was against. Mo came over to me during the discussion and said 'He's not going to get this.' Coincidentally, TB had to leave early to go to the church blessing of Parliament, so JP took the chair. I could see TB was thinking he would not win, and seemed resigned to it. JP chaired the rest of the meeting in a very JP way, let everyone ramble on for ages, but it was very effective. It meant enough supportive points were made for him to sum up by saying that he would say to TB that there was a long discussion, but they recognised the decision had to be his, and the clear message from Cabinet was they would support him whatever that decision was. GB summed up in a very different way, saying that the five tests had to be passed. JP said 'Hold on, let's be clear in this. Are we saying yes if, or yes but? I'm for telling Tony it is yes but.' In other words, we are going ahead and we will do everything to make sure those tests are met. JP was not going to be budged. I think he was showing two things – his loyalty to TB, but also his ability to swing decisions. The truth is that he could easily have taken the discussion and said to TB sorry, Tony, there is no way we can do this. TB came back from the church, saying he had been worried leaving JP in charge, but the truth is that it was JP, helped by Margaret B above all, who really swung it round. TB said he was less bothered by the press reaction, than whether the thing could actually be made to work, whether we will be left with a white elephant or not. We agreed I should brief at 2pm, announce we were going ahead, and that TB was going straight to Greenwich. It went OK, though some were incredulous. George Pascoe-Watson [*Sun*] just sat shaking his head. I came back and Anji told me Peter M and Chris Smith were also going, which I thought was madness. I felt at this stage it was best left restricted to TB. He had not even sorted PM and CS respective roles. I went to TB's room, where he was talking to Peter. PM was already in full flow, protesting that we used him but did not treat him like a politician. He was winding himself up more and more and eventually directly accused me of trying to keep him off TV and undermine him. I said I thought it was wrong for him to be there when TB had not yet told Chris Smith that PM was to get the single share that would put him in charge of the project. Peter said nobody would even notice if he went, at which point TB said he was being absurd and ridiculous. He went on and on. TB was tearing his hair out. Jonathan had a smile on his face that said this is a madhouse. Eventually, Peter went to the door as if to walk out. TB warned him not to, and told him to come back and sit down. The Hague result came through. I said we should do him as being in charge of two parties, not sure which one he was leading. GB thought we should go straight for him as extremist.

Saturday, June 21

G7–G8, Denver. We had the bilateral planned for 11 with Clinton, and I was trying to fix up a picture and joint doorstep. The main G8 discussions were leaders plus sherpas, so hung around for the meeting to break. TB and Bill C were talking about the aide mémoire and what Bill C called Adams's 'stupid response' to the killings. Jonathan and John Holmes joined us and Clinton said to me 'OK, what do you want me to do?' I said what would be great from our point of view, as the aide mémoire is now public, is if you and TB stand side by side, say the same message, and that you in particular say 'The ball is now in Sinn Fein's court.' He said that sounded right to him. By now, a rather nervous-looking Mike McCurry had joined us. He said 'Mr President, don't you think you should discuss this with your policy advisers first.' BC said get them down here then, and someone went to get [Sandy] Berger and [Jim] Steinberg [senior Clinton aide]. They went into a little huddle, but I think I had won the argument with Clinton that this was the right thing to do. He came back and said OK, where are we doing this? He did it brilliantly, looked the part, sounded the part, and it led our news all day. I could tell that Sandy was pissed off that we'd got Clinton to do it, but if it was the right thing to do, and as the President thought so, I couldn't quite see the problem.

Sunday, June 22

I was up at 6 to prepare for ABC. TB was full of himself again, especially having met Chuck Berry with Clinton. Kohl clearly saw him as a kind of successor in Europe. So did Chirac, which is presumably why he had not taken to him. We went over some of the tough questions then left for the interview. I saw the questions by accident, knew they were going straight in on Northern Ireland. He was relaxed, competent, no real story but he talked about a letter he got from a young Northern Irish girl, and I knew the press would be on to it so we were tearing the Garden Rooms[1] apart trying to find it. He was tough on Bosnia, strong on Hong Kong. He didn't deliver one of the lines he wanted to push about us being a bridge over the Atlantic. I then went to Gordon's press conference, where I inadvertently turned the lights out leaning on the wall. I went back to the library where our private office was based to work on the environment speech for the Earth Summit at the UN tomorrow. BC asked me how I thought yesterday went on Ireland. I said it went well. Media-wise, could not have been better. I said he had carried the thing. He said TB was all over the US networks. I said he was all over the British ones. Of all of them, he was the warmest and the friendliest. Mike M told me he had been really appreciative of how we handled his visit to London, and managed to blow the Paula stuff away. Maybe the stuff yesterday was a bit of a payback. TB pointed out it was interesting how Bill asked my view on media stuff. I really liked him. Clinton was clearly a great politician and communicator, but had not been that impressive chairing the meeting. TB was thinking more and more about Ireland, trying to find a way forward.

Tuesday, June 24

We were back in the office just after 8 and the day was mainly given over to Northern Ireland. Both the briefings were almost exclusively about that, even though TB had a Commons statement on the G8, Hague's first as leader, after which he met TB to get briefed on Ireland. The main meetings were with Trimble, John Taylor and Ken Maginnis – not great but outside they were not as bad as they were in the meeting – and John Hume. Trimble was pretty difficult though, at one and the same time said he did not like the document, while claiming he had not been allowed to see it, and said we were conceding too much to the IRA because there was no mechanism to throw them out. The UUs were overemotional and saw conspiracies everywhere. 'It's all a pattern, always the same pattern,' said DT. TB said it was a moment of decision. He wanted to make a statement saying it was

[1] Downing Street home of the Prime Minister's secretarial staff, familiarly known as 'Garden Room girls'.

time to get substantial negotiations under way, leading to a devolved Assembly plus North–South dialogue. He said the mood in the US vis-à-vis SF had changed. It was time they got a move on. TB said they had to recognise there had always been the prospect of them getting into talks without giving up actual weapons. He talked up the independence of the commission on decommissioning under de Chastelain,[1] which would review the situation every 8 weeks. He had always felt the Tories bound themselves in too hard on decommissioning, and DT kept coming back to it, again and again, saying the mechanics were not strong enough. TB said there had to be inclusive talks with SF, and meanwhile build from the centre with the SDLP. He said there was a brief window of opportunity with the Irish and US governments together with us on this now. Trimble said the paper gave the IRA most of what they wanted and they would now push for more. There is no real pressure on them to pursue only peaceful means. TB said there was an emergency brake. Maginnis said they would not be thrown off once they were in because the pressures would be to keep them on board. DT said they needed 1. a firm commitment to decommissioning happening alongside talks, 2. machinery put in place to prevent SDLP and the Irish government putting a spanner in the works, 3. no 'guns for concessions'. Once we got on to 'confidence-building measures', they were all 'another sop to the IRA'. Prisoners, plastic bullets, changes to policing, they saw them all as a sop to the IRA. Any change must have the acceptance of both traditions. DT said we cannot survive in the same room unless SF are in parallel building confidence through decommissioning. Maginnis said Paisley would be able to create mayhem with this. TB said there would be sanctions on SF. DT said they were too weak. TB said if we didn't go for this now, we would miss the opportunity that was there. He knew it was a risk. He knew that SF had acted in bad faith. He knew all the obstacles, but he felt they had to move it forward now. Maginnis kept underlining just how deep the mutual suspicions were. The IRA had infiltrated many parts of their national life. This proposal would let them infiltrate top-level political life without any real demand being made on them. DT said Hume would never cut his links with Adams and McGuinness.

On one level, it was a terrible meeting in that every time TB made a specific point, they had strong arguments against it, and put them

---

[1] General John de Chastelain. Canadian former soldier and diplomat, head of the Independent International Commission on Decommissioning in Northern Ireland. Born a British subject and, like Blair, an old Fettesian.

very emotionally. On another level, they were positive in public and TB felt they wanted to do something. Some of the civil servants found the UUs a pain to deal with, but TB said he thought Trimble was fair. He said it makes quite a powerful impact when Maginnis tells you that he has personally met people who he knows had plotted to kill him. Taylor was keen to have the documents and in the end we gave them, and they did a pretty positive doorstep in the street. Hume came in, was just as emotional, said he was authorised to say he could set up a meeting between Martin McGuinness and Quentin Thomas [senior Northern Ireland Office official]. TB said that was not possible and he had to say that if SF did not come on board as a result of the decommissioning paper, and the IRA declare a ceasefire, he would acknowledge that we had to move on without them. Hume felt we were close to something, though John Holmes warned me he always said that. But he had seen Adams and McGuinness and they had not dismissed the decommissioning paper out of hand. The prisoners issue was important. He said one meeting between him, Quentin Thomas and McGuinness would lead to a ceasefire. 'The prize is enormous but so is the danger.' TB felt he had gone as far as he could in pushing the UUs. He would tip them over the edge if he went much further. 'I'd get torn limb from limb.' It was again, on one level, a good meeting, on another it was not. They were miles apart, but the one thing TB took out that was positive was a shared desire to make progress, even if both sides were basically saying the other would make it impossible.

Wednesday, June 25

Ireland statement day. We had agreed yesterday to get in the 12-year-old girl TB mentioned in America, so that was the focus early on. I was in late, having taken the boys to school for once, and worked on Ireland most of the day. TB was in a fury over the story about their new £3,500 bed, which was on the front page of the *Sun*. Following her shopping in New York, there was a touch of the Imeldas about the coverage surrounding CB. He knew nothing about it, was livid and said he would pay for it himself. It can't have been easy moving into a new 'house', and then finding you have very limited control over what you can and cannot do in there, but I think the problem was it is only just beginning fully to dawn on CB how un-private her life is going to be. Then another Clare Short fiasco to deal with. She had 'accidentally' invited Adams and McGuinness to a reception at Lancaster House. This only came to light when Adams called to say he could not make it and could he send someone else? I told TB, who said he needed an explanation. I said we should announce what she had done, and how, and at such a sensitive time, and he should sack her. He said no. My view of Clare was that she was nothing but trouble, had virtually no redeeming features and would give him more grief than any upside from her merited. But he had a more favourable view.

Monday, June 30
Hong Kong. We left for a meeting with Prince Charles on board *Britannia*. He struck me as a fairly decent bloke, surrounded by a lot of nonsense and people best described as from another age. He and TB had a private session while the rest of us were taken on a tour of *Britannia*. Then TB got the same tour as well, 'Oh you must, Prime Minister, it's fascinating,' while we made small talk with Charles. He said the more I travel the more I realise how marvellous Britain is. We drank very weak tea in very thin china, and little cakes that looked nicer than they tasted. There was something a bit sad about him. All his life, even on big issues, he had to make small talk, surrounded by luxury, as here, people fawning on him, and yet somehow obviously unfulfilled. People might look on and think how fantastic to live on a boat like that, waited on hand and foot, but if it is all you know, and you are basically not fulfilled, and your private life is a mess, it did not strike me as a very happy existence. I travelled with TB to the meeting with CH Tung [Tung Chee Hwa, Chief Executive of Hong Kong], and TB said as we drove away 'We must keep *Britannia*.' I knew he would. 'What an asset,' he said. The show at the handover ceremony was poor, a mix of orchestral and military music. [Chris] Patten's [last governor of Hong Kong] speech overdid the emotion, and as he sat down, he was close to tears and his daughters behind him were crying. TB looked embarrassed. Eventually we escaped and were driven to the police launch taking us over the river to the meeting with Jiang Zemin [President of the People's Republic of China], Li Peng [Chinese Prime Minister] and others. It was quite a dramatic journey, as the weather was now pretty stormy. On their side, the crowds were smaller and less enthusiastic. TB got quite a good reception, but it was not a good meeting. We went in, TB met him, shook hands, posed for the cameras, and then it began. There were a lot of hangers-on. Jiang had a fixed look on his face, half-smile, half-frown. TB did his now well-rehearsed line – new start, adhere to JD [Chinese–British Joint Declaration in 1984 on Hong Kong's future] – a few clichés on it being a historic day, how we wanted to build

bridges between each other, between China and the future. As the tea came round, Jiang said the handover removed a shadow from the relationship. The Labour Party does not have the historic burden. He said there was a Chinese saying – we can all wear our light uniform or march forward in a light manner. We all nodded knowingly, without having much of a clue what he meant. They did a bit on the economy and trade, again not very deep though. TB slipped in a very brief mention of human rights, and John Holmes wrote 'phew' on his notes as I had been briefing for days that obviously he would press them on human rights. Robin C and Derek Fatchett [Minister] looked very unimpressed. We all gave each other little 'was that it?' looks. He did it so gently it was barely noticeable, added to which Li Peng kept spitting loudly into his hankie, and one of his spits coincided with the human rights bit. TB knew he had not been at his best. He said later he had suddenly felt jet-lagged and tired, a bit disorientated.

Wednesday, July 2

I had a brief meeting with GB on the Budget, at which we agreed the key strategic lines to push in the immediate aftermath. We wanted to get the focus on health and education spending while also making clear the goal was long-term stability and old-style tax and spend was gone. We should emphasise that we were always going to do something with the windfall tax other than the jobs programme. He was pretty hyper. He briefed the Cabinet and got a good response, particularly for the extra money on health and education, and for the shift on pensions. He rattled through the figures and the forecasts, and then emphasised the key themes – investment, welfare to work, stability, education and skills. Some of the tax changes were straightforward, like petrol prices, and others less so. You sensed he was using the Cabinet presentation pretty much as a warm-up to his performance in the House. His style was very rat-tat-tat, very little light and shade, powering his way through it as if he was desperate to get it over with. But the Cabinet liked it.

Thursday, July 3

GB got a pretty good press though the BBC were still running it fairly negatively, focusing on the opposition and the scrapping of tax credits for pension funds, which [Peter] Lilley [Shadow Chancellor] had used to call 'the Robert Maxwell budget'. TB felt it had gone brilliantly in the press, though he still worried about some of the long-term issues. He gave a lecture to the Cabinet about where we were going with this. We had to emphasise that the government approach was to make

Britain 'fair, modern and strong' and he wanted them to make speeches on that theme, related to their own briefs. He was very warm re GB and then said the four things to emphasise were 1. prudence, financial responsibility for the long term, 2. schools and hospitals, 3. it was New Labour – pro business, pro enterprise, 4. it was a one-nation Budget.

Friday, July 4

I left with TB for Sedgefield and worked on the speech for tomorrow. Myrobella had changed markedly. There were armed police at the barber's shop as we approached, new fences, a new little police station, cops everywhere. CB and I travelled back to London together and had a nice enough chat about things. CB talked very loudly on her mobile and as she came off it I said I hope nobody in the carriage is a hack. She said she was finding it hard to get her head round the fact that anything they said or did was considered fair game, and also all the stuff that wasn't true.

Sunday, July 6

TB was at Chequers entertaining Diana and William. We chatted about it briefly. 'Yes,' he said, 'before you ask, she did ask for you.' But he admitted the conversation was hard and it might have been better had I been there to jolly things along. She had been a bit miffed that we had suggested she might leak. William played football with the boys and went for a swim with them, while she and TB went for a walk.

Tuesday, July 8

Madrid, NATO summit. Unbelievably gorgeous hostesses. During the break, it became clear that Clinton and TB felt exactly the same. There was a bizarre scene during a break, in the Gents. Several leaders, including Clinton, TB, [Romano] Prodi [Prime Minister of Italy], Kok and Kohl, were all having a pee in a row of stand-up urinals. Clinton turned around and said 'Isn't this the greatest picture that was never taken?' TB told him the story of the time Churchill moved away from Attlee while they were peeing together. Attlee looked hurt. Churchill explained: 'Every time you see something big you want to nationalise it.' TB said we were winning the arguments on NATO and you could see there was real panic among the French delegation, with Chirac having clearly overstated what he intended to get out of this.

Friday, July 11

We had a policy awayday at Chequers but were late leaving and then stopped for a cup of tea at a takeaway near Paddington, people gob-smacked to see us walking in to get a cup of tea. TB was worried about definition and the Fox Hunting Bill. He wanted us to get Mike Foster [anti-hunting Labour MP for Worcester] to agree to push it to a joint committee of the Commons and Lords. Chequers was a good place for these kinds of meetings. Very quiet. Mobiles didn't work. Good food. Long walks and all that. Geoff Mulgan [policy adviser to the Prime Minister] and Peter Hyman were going through some of the big questions coming up, particularly on welfare, education, and the economy. There were various presentations by Mulgan, Roger Liddle on Europe. TB was impressive but it was notable that he would react instinctively with a right-wing response. Geoff Mulgan threw up some moral choices we had to face, and TB instinctively leaned to the right. E.g. TB said he was in favour of gay marriages but would skirt around it in public. What about cannabis? asked Geoff. TB shook his head. During the health discussion in the after-noon, led by Robert Hill, he was very interested in whether we could do more with charges in the NHS. But when someone suggested defence cuts, it was a clear no-go. On schools, he said we were not being radical enough. On Europe he was really concerned about the politics of it all. On EMU he was clear the French and Germans were going to go ahead and we had to work out a strategy re the criteria. Down on the European institutions, CAP a total disgrace. It was a good lively discussion and there were some bright people in the policy team. Lunch was interrupted by a call with Bertie Ahern. The news that the Orange Order had agreed to reroute the Drumcree march vindicated Mo and gave a real sense of lift and hope[1]. The big disagree-ment with BA was still decommissioning. Bertie did not think [George] Mitchell [Independent chairman of the negotiations that led to the Good Friday Agreement] meant decommissioning during talks. TB did. We had a football match, my team against TB's, and we lost 3–2. TB missed a totally open goal though. After the fuss over a new bed, TB was worried re the new kitchen plans for Number 10. He told me

---

[1] The troubled annual parade by Orangemen from Drumcree Parish Church, Portadown (Co. Armagh), through the Catholic Garvaghy Road area. The parade was a key event in the Protestant marching season, marking the victory of William of Orange over the Catholic James II at the Battle of the Boyne, culmin-ating on July 12 each year. In 1998 the Northern Ireland Parades Commission banned the Drumcree march because of the Protestant–Catholic clashes. In following years the march was prevented from using Garvaghy Road as a route.

to tell the office it should be middle of the range not top of the range and no more than 15K. But he didn't speak to CB so when someone spoke to her about it, she thought it was me laying down the law on her bloody kitchen, not TB.

Friday, July 18

Discussed whether TB should go to the Uxbridge by-election.[1] The convention was PMs did not do by-elections, but was it a sensible one? The argument was you got the blame if you lost but that happened whether you went or not. JP was in favour. Philip said it was neck and neck and he might tip it our way. TB said we needed a shake-up of the private office. He was minded to put Anji in charge of a plan to get Number 10 going, get a bit more energy through the place. He decided we should go all out for Uxbridge. He and Anji were both at me for not involving Peter enough. Anji said it looked like we were in some kind of war about who got the credit for the election victory. I said it was more that his profile was becoming a negative because it was about him not the government and what we were trying to do. TB said he was getting fed up with the inability of his key people to work together and he was looking to me to sort it. PM was in Paris at a seminar to assess the election. I got home in time for the news and there was 14 minutes on the BBC re Northern Ireland. The ceasefire was clearly coming, which was good news, but I agreed with Mo we should say nothing until it was announced.

Saturday, July 19

The ceasefire was the main story. It finally came at 9.30 and I called TB, who was unaware of it. He was worried about the line being run at us that we were giving too much to IRA/SF. He asked me to emphasise that the approach on decommissioning had not changed, that we were clear there must be some decommissioning during negotiations. John [Holmes] told me John de Chastelain, the Canadian general, was probably going to chair the independent decommissioning body. I talked that up as something that should reassure the Unionists, but the noises coming from their briefings all day were not good. TB said Trimble was not good at standing up to his own people. But he had to be kept onside.

[1] Parliamentary by-election caused by the death of Conservative MP Sir Michael Shersby on May 8 1997. In the event, the Conservatives held the seat with a 3,766 majority.

Sunday, July 20

TB called early, worried about Ireland. He felt the way the coverage was leaning could add to the pressure on Trimble to pull out. There was a sense that the IRA ceasefire was a tactic to secure exactly that, so that the Unionists would be the ones blamed for screwing it up. TB suggested that I sprinkle around references to the UUs surely not wanting to be seen to throw away the best prospect of peace for years. He wanted it made clear that we had not changed the line on decommissioning, and there was far too much of that around in the Sundays. We had both to reassure the Unionists but also make clear how much was at stake if they pulled out now.

Monday, July 21

Ireland was leading the news in the morning because of the Trimble meeting. I briefed very hard on him not wanting to be the man who scuppered the peace talks. But we were in a difficult position. You have the sense that DT brings his own enemies with him, meaning John Taylor and Ken Maginnis. TB was worried about the whole thing, but said that at the 11 o'clock briefing I should be robust, making clear that we resented the suggestion by Trimble that we had done a deal with the IRA. I stressed that decommissioning meant during the negotiations. TB was becoming more and more preoccupied with Northern Ireland. He felt that if Trimble showed more strength, he could blow out Paisley. The mood was cautious and realistic. The problem was that the Irish government probably did tell Sinn Fein there would be no need for actual decommissioning, and we were saying the opposite to the Unionists. I didn't flam up but I didn't flam it down either. I spoke to Mo to suggest a doorstep hitting back at Trimble over the 'deal with the IRA' suggestion. We should stress that two weeks ago we were being accused of betrayal by the other side, because of Drumcree. The meeting with Trimble and Co was friendlier than the noises around suggested it would be. Maginnis was the only one who lost it really. The problem was that Trimble was not really in charge of the show, and you sensed he was constantly worrying what they were thinking. He had a naturally red face which turned redder and redder as the meeting wore on. He had a mildly priggish smile which got more priggish the more nervous he got. Jeffrey Donaldson [UUP MP for Lagan Valley] was the quietest but he spoke with considerable force. Taylor was quite languid. Maginnis was the ranter today. But he too could be subtle while being tough. When we were discussing the decommissioning line, he said very nicely, but menacingly, 'I'm very worried that if we take that approach, it will be very damaging to you personally, David.' TB was pretty firm, admitting he could not deliver the Irish government to say what we understood by decommissioning happening. He started the meeting by saying it was 'high noon' and laughing. He said the problem was they wanted a guarantee that SF would be kicked out after a certain period if there was no actual decommissioning and he could not get the Irish signed up to that. They said that it was intolerable for them to have to sit round a table with these people, knowing that they would not give up a bomb or a bullet and yet there would be no way of kicking them out. Trimble said SF were making it clear they had a guarantee they would not be kicked out. They do not believe they need to decommission. TB said there had to be some acceptance of good faith. Maginnis scoffed. DT said you can be acting in good faith and not reach an agreement. TB said the principle of consent was paramount. The greatest difficulty for SF will come when it is clear this is not necessarily going to lead to a united Ireland. He said decommissioning had become symbolic. He said he wanted a timetable. He did not want this dragging on for ever. He said it felt like swimming through blancmange. TB was looking exasperated at points and explained that two weeks ago he had the SDLP telling him he was guilty of the most monstrous betrayal, and now they were saying it. In the end we felt it might be better if Wednesday's vote on decommissioning did not take place and we got more time. Donaldson said it was always the Unionists being asked to help out, and there was nothing to show for it. He said he had lost members of his family to the IRA. 'We understand these people. They will go back to violence any time they feel like it.'

Tuesday, July 29

TB was worried that Noel Gallagher was coming to the reception tomorrow. He said he had no idea he had been invited. It had been Jonathan's idea to put him on the list, and TB felt he was bound to do something crazy.

Wednesday, July 30

I spoke to Alan McGee at Creation Records, who was coming to the No. 10 reception with Noel Gallagher, and said can we be assured he would behave OK. Alan said he would make sure he did. He was not going to mess around. He said if we had invited Liam, it might have been different. Gallagher arrived with his wife Meg, McGee and his girlfriend, loads of photographers outside, then Cherie met them and took them upstairs to see Kathryn and Nicky, who was pretty gobsmacked when Gallagher walked in. He said he thought Number 10 was 'tops', said he couldn't believe there was an ironing board in there. He was very down to earth, very funny. I took them up to do pictures with TB, then Lenny Henry, Maureen Lipman [actors], a few others.

Friday, August 1

We woke to defeat in Uxbridge. That fact itself was not surprising but the 4,000 majority was, even though we had been talking down our prospects. Still, we had the arguments to explain it, and in any case we had taken a decision not to do the usual Tory excuse-making, just take it, accept it, explain it, move on. TB called me in the car and was in fairly jocular mood, said provided we stuck to messages about the long term, the media would quickly move on. We also had the announcement of Richard Wilson as Butler's replacement as Cabinet Secretary, which at first we said should be embargoed but then agreed it should be done as a straight-up announcement at the 11 o'clock. TB wanted him sold as a moderniser. I got a message to call Phil Hall at the *News of the World*. I said I hope you are not going to unleash a scandal while I am on holiday. He said no, I'm going to do it now. I said what? He said 'Robin and Gaynor.' He said a couple of free-lances had come in with a set of pictures which showed they had spent several nights together last week. He said they were bang to rights. I let on that I knew nothing. He said he didn't know whether to run it, in a way he didn't want to, but if he didn't these guys would take it somewhere else, so it might as well be him. He said could I talk to RC and say they could either do it as an exposé, or they could do it with something from him, and they would do it as sympathet-ically as they could. I said I promised him a proper response of some kind tomorrow if he would give me a guarantee not to approach any of the people involved, or their families. He said that was fine. What was extraordinary was that I called him immediately after coming back from a meeting with TB, Butler and Jonathan, where we said it was going to be very hard to do a reshuffle of the Big Guns unless one of them had to quit. I went back to see TB, who was with Jonathan. I said I bring you your first sex scandal. I went through the facts as Phil had told me. TB said what are the chances of persuading them not to run it? I said somewhere between zero and 5 per cent. The chances of it not being run somewhere were closer to the zero end. We called Butler back and went over various options. He said the [David] Mellor[1] drama was not the main blow, it was the later ones. We made

---

[1] Details of the Conservative Heritage minister's extramarital affairs were made public in July 1992, but he did not resign his position until September, after a number of other stories about him were published.

a lot of bad-taste jokes, which is the usual sign of nervousness. Butler's main advice was to be aware of the clear difference between private and public morality, and the need not to make a rod for our backs. If he were to resign over an affair, that might seem the right thing now, but it might not always be so. He then left the room. TB was clearly a bit thrown by this one. He hated this personal stuff. It was why he was always so loath to get involved in Tory sleaze stories. 'What the hell do I do about this?' he said. We talked it round and round. Maybe RC would make our minds up for us. Maybe he would want to go. I doubted it. So did TB. Maybe he would be able to make a case for it being ludicrous even to think in those terms. TB said what is clear is that there will be a lot of interest in how we handle it. I called Peter M, who said we should dig out TB's *Spectator* lecture in '95, which made clear that morality to him was not about private lives.

I checked out RC's whereabouts without letting his office know why I wanted him. He was on the flight from Scotland to Heathrow to get the connection to Boston as he was going off for a holiday with Margaret.[1] He was due in London at 4.15 but the plane was delayed by half an hour. I said a lot will depend on how RC reacts and what he himself feels about this. We did talk over some of the worst-case scenarios, and were chewing over who should be Foreign Secretary if he went. Jack C, Beckett, JP possibly. TB and I then went round the entire Cabinet thinking of skeletons we either knew of, or could imagine. I said if you're not careful you'll be left with Dewar and Strang. I had left messages for RC and he called on his mobile after landing at Heathrow. He was being driven from the shuttle to the Boston plane. I asked if he was alone. He said no, I'm with Margaret and Dave Mathieson [special adviser to RC]. I said given what I am about to say, you might want to go to a private phone and call me back. I said a bad story was about to break and I needed to speak to him privately. 'Is it about me?' he asked. And I said yes it is. I could now hear Margaret chatting away happily in the background. I said are you sure you don't want to find a private phone. He said no, you speak, and I will listen. I suspected he knew what was coming. I said it's you and Gaynor. A freelance has seen you coming from her flat, having staked it out through the night, and they have pictures. He asked me to go through the dates, which I did. 'Yes,' he said, 'I can see how that could be a

[1] Margaret Cook, married to Robin Cook from 1969, and mother of his two sons. The couple divorced in March 1998.

problem.' I was, I must say, quite impressed at how cool he was. There he was, just been told he was about to get done over for an affair, his wife was sitting next to him, and he was successfully communicating to me in a weird kind of code. 'Mmm, I can see why you think this could be a problem. Just remind me of the dates you have in mind.'

I explained the deal I had made with Hall, that nobody would be approached until I got back to them to explain how he intended to react. He said I assume you've discussed it with Tony. I said I had and I was sure he would be supportive, that it was not per se a resignation issue. We had to decide how to handle it. He said that was good to know. He said what would your own advice be? I said I didn't know what the situation was, with Margaret or with Gaynor, but in pure media terms, and I think in political terms too, the most important thing was clarity. He said it would be hard to maintain a clear line for long, which I didn't fully understand, but I took it to mean something dramatic. He was then cut off, clearly going through a bad mobile area. He came back a few minutes later and sounded a lot less confident. He had told Margaret and he was with her as he spoke. He sounded very emotional. I said I really feel for you. He said we are swimming in a fair amount of emotional turmoil. We are talking things over, and I cannot be precise when I will get back to you. You must give me some time. I said that was fine. TB was with me and had a word. He was very sympathetic but also firm, and backed my view that the best thing was to have a clear line. We then sat around for ages, talking it over. Then the FCO called – clearly still unaware of the whole thing – and said the Foreign Secretary had cancelled his holiday and was on his way to London. I called him again and he said he could not go away at a time like this 'and leave Gaynor to face two weeks of hell'. That was a pretty clear signal he was going to leave Margaret. In the way he talked, he certainly seemed to be thinking more about Gaynor than Margaret. He said it was much more than a fling, more than a romance. He said he was planning to talk things over with Margaret and he would call me in the morning, hopefully with a decision. He said Margaret did not want him to leave. TB spoke to him again, and said that if he wanted to remain Foreign Secretary, he would support him. The most important thing, whatever the emotions flying around, was that he was clinical about this, and clear about what he intended to do. He [TB] said elements of the media were ghastly, and this whole thing would be horrible, but AC would negotiate as sympathetic a time as could be achieved in what were bound to be horrible circumstances. RC asked me again what I thought. I said I felt we should have something clear to say tomorrow, and then follow up with a Paddy Ashdown-type bare-all statement, then say no more will be said. I said a lot depended on what they decided, how they felt, but we would support him whatever, and help make the story as unsleazy as we could. I told him I was due to go on holiday. He said he would really appreciate it if I could help him through the next few days. I said I would.

TB was more relaxed about things once RC explained that he and Margaret had not really been man and wife for some time, that Margaret knew about Gaynor, though not that it was still going on, that he had been trying to end things, but it had been very difficult. I spoke to him a couple of times through the evening, trying to cheer him up. I said he had been unlucky. No, Alastair, he said, very firmly, I have been incredibly foolish. He asked me to get a pledge tonight from the *News of the World* that they would not approach Gaynor. TB and I were drafting RC and TB spokesman statements for tomorrow, but the truth was it entirely depended on their decision. I was pretty clear he was going to call and say he was leaving Margaret and setting up home with Gaynor. In my last call of the day, he said something that made that pretty clear. I said presentationally that was the cleanest, easiest way. He said he was doubtful he could persuade Margaret to go along with it. He sounded very down now. He had gone from the emotional to the rational and now the painful. Tim [Allan] said we did not have so many good ministers that we could afford to lose RC. TB said it was ridiculous. He said maybe it is possible to love two people at the same time. Oh yeah, I said, and Cherie would accept that, would she? What would Fiona do if it was me? I said. Mmm, he said, chew your balls off. Kill you probably. Cherie would be the same. I felt for Robin though. I had only met Margaret once as far as I could recall, at Will Hutton's [political commentator], and I really hadn't taken to her. It was clear Robin had been with Gaynor for some time, and kept it fairly quiet, but now he was in a different league and these things would get out.

Saturday, August 2

I made one last call to Robin at 1 Carlton Gardens [official London residence of the Foreign Secretary] before going to bed. He sounded even more depressed. He said he expected to say his marriage was over in the morning. There was no real way of knowing where this would go but we were better placed with the *NoW* than the Tories were during their sex scandals. Fiona and I were up by 4.30am and we were on the road by five. By the time we got through the Channel tunnel, I called TB, who was in the bath. He had not changed his basic view. I then called Robin, who had Margaret with him. He said that he was going to have a statement by 9, in which he would be saying his marriage was over. I said that was exactly what I expected. He said Margaret was insisting that the statement said 'I am leaving my wife.' He said they had both had a wretched night for obvious reasons but they had sorted things out and he had drafted a short statement setting out the facts, making it clear he was to blame and calling for the privacy of others to be respected. I said I would alert the *NoW* and underline that they should approach none of the other parties. I called TB, who by now was in the car on the way to the airport and had been talking to Peter. I read him the statement and later read it to PM. Neither of them liked those parts of the statement which admitted blame and responsibility, and TB wanted it to sound much more like a formal announcement. TB was also looking to say they had been trying to sort things out for some time. I fed all this through to Robin and also made one or two changes myself. By now, Margaret was leaving so he said he would call back.

During the day, we spoke several times, as we drove through France. The kids in the back were following it like some kind of soap opera. Where's Gaynor, what's Margaret doing now, is Robin going to live with Gaynor? It all made the journey go by a lot quicker than it otherwise would have done. Margaret got the 11 o'clock shuttle to Scotland, and Robin got the 3 o'clock, wanting to see his son, his mother and others up there, and also to get some things out of his house before coming back. He veered during the day between being very matter-of-fact and very depressed. There was a little part of me sensed that he was almost enjoying the fact he was involved in something like this – I don't mean the facts of it, which were grisly, but the fact that it was clearly going to be such a big thing reflected on his new status. For example, when I said we had to sort out the *News of the World*, and then deal with the fallout, he interrupted 'Which will be very considerate of course.' He also spoke somewhat in the language of another age, like he was delivering lines in a drama. 'Will you move in with Gaynor' I asked. 'My future is Gaynor,' he said. There was something almost surreal about me and TB talking on mobiles en route to holidays, with RC back in the UK wanting me to do all the dealings with the paper. TB and I agreed I should do the statement on the record, named, as a way of making absolutely clear this was TB sticking by him. It also helped me in the moves I was beginning to make to put my briefings on the record. As the day wore on, Robin seemed to get himself into better shape, maybe relieved Margaret was gone, perhaps just psyching himself up for what was to come. I had got a deal from Hall that they would let me see the copy in advance, and consult on headlines, even if I couldn't change them. It barely read like a *News of the World* exposé at all. It was very sympathetic, the headlines were basically onside, and totally based on the statements. They allowed us to make a couple of changes. The inside pages consisted of Robin's statement, my statement, the background and then a glowing profile of Robin. It was so not the *News of the World*. I spoke to him after his arrival in Edinburgh and said that it was about as good as we could hope for. For what seemed like the 100th time he thanked me for the help I was giving him. I said he had been unlucky. He repeated that he had been very foolish.

Tuesday, August 26

TB was onto the notion that our biggest enemy was cynicism. Once the mood really turns, they'll all turn together. Re the reshuffle, he had decided on Clark and Strang pretty much, but it didn't give him that much room for manoeuvre. He still had his mind on getting a couple of Liberals in. He was musing re the Millennium and felt maybe Peter M should be full-time in charge of it. He said he had written to Margaret Cook to say how sorry he was and how he hoped she would rebuild her life and she wrote back an odd letter saying she found it odd that he didn't say he was sad the marriage was over. He was clearly worried she would come back to cause us trouble at some point.

Saturday, August 30

A pretty extraordinary weekend, dealing with MI5 and the *Mail on Sunday*, then Diana's death in the early hours. The day started with Calum in tears when I said I might not be able to go to Burnley v Bristol Rovers. I was worried I would not be able to deal with the [David] Shayler[1] situation properly, but he was so upset so we set off. We then learned that in the exchange of letters [Jonathan] Holborow [editor of the *Mail on Sunday*] was saying that I threatened to 'call in the heavies'. TB was a bit exercised that I was 'tootling off to a football match' and it was hardly ideal. I spent most of the journey on the phone. We prepared a statement on the injunction and got people lined up. As the injunction hearing began at 11.30, we started to get

---

[1] A former MI5 officer whose 'revelations' to the *Mail on Sunday* led to the government seeking an injunction to prevent publication.

out the line that far from being heavy, we had done everything we could to help them publish, but they had not cooperated. I was so busy and distracted that I missed the M6 turnoff, and we took ages to get there. News of the injunction came through just before the kick-off, when Nick, the duty clerk,[1] called and said Government 1, *Mail on Sunday* nil. I spoke to TB at half-time, and we agreed that Jack [Straw] had to go up and be robust. It was the first game I had been to, part of which I had missed, because of constantly being on the phone. We were home by half nine, and the *Mail on Sunday* had a ridiculous account of my conversations with Holborow.

I got to bed, and at around two I was paged by media monitoring[2]: 'Car crash in Paris. Dodi killed. Di hurt. This is not a joke.' Then TB came on. He had been called by Number 10 and told the same thing. He was really shocked. He said she was in a coma and the chances are she'd die. I don't think I'd ever heard him like this. He was full of pauses, then gabbling a little, but equally clear what we had to do. We started to prepare a statement. We talked through the things we would have to do tomorrow, if she died. By now the phones were starting from the press, and I didn't sleep. Then about an hour later Nick called and said simply 'She's dead. The Prime Minister is being told now.' I went through on the call. Angus Lapsley was duty private secretary and was taking him through what we knew. But it was hard to get beyond the single fact of her death. 'I can't believe this. I just can't believe it,' said TB. 'You just can't take it in, can you?' And yet, as ever with TB, he was straight onto the ramifications. By the end of the call we had sorted all we had to do practically. There was also the issue of the chasing photographers. He said we should say that is not for now. We agreed to say nothing until a formal announcement but then Robin in Manila was about to get on a plane and was unable to resist making the announcement first, and raised the issue of the press. TB's mind was whirring. We had I don't know how many conversations, and they went round and round, veering from the emotional – I can't believe this – to the practical – what we were doing in Paris, when should he speak to the Queen? – to the political – what impact would this have? He thought he should probably speak to the Queen and Charles. 'Those poor boys.' It seemed an age between us being told of the death and the French interior minister and Michael Jay [UK Ambassador] announcing it. PA

[1] Nick Matthews, senior duty clerk. The Number 10 duty clerks handle the Prime Minister's most confidential filing, calls, etc.
[2] Labour Party media monitoring. The civil service did not have 24-hour monitoring at this time, an innovation Campbell was to introduce.

finally broke it through 'British sources'. TB had been late learning of the actual accident because he hadn't heard the phone and then when the cops were asked to wake him up, they thought it was a hoax. Number 10 had to go through Scotland Yard to get on to Durham and explain it was serious and the cops would have to bang on his door.

Once we knew she was dead, we were into a seemingly never-ending round of calls. At about 4, Angus and I had a conference call with Robert Fellowes. 'You know about Diana, do you? She's dead.' We were sorting when TB should speak to the Queen. It was all very matter-of-fact and practical, though he too, like TB earlier, said 'Those poor boys.' TB and I agreed a statement to put out as soon as it was confirmed that she was dead. It was pretty emotional. TB was genuinely shocked. It was also going to be a test for him, the first time in which the country had looked to him in a moment of shock and grief. We went round and round in circles about what he should say, and also how. I didn't like the idea of him walking out to do something just for this purpose and we agreed to do nothing until he went to the church in Trimdon in the morning. Anything before that would look tacky. I didn't want TB to pile in too much. I was pissed off with RC at having jumped the gun on the official announcement. The phones were going all the time and then at around 4 I got a rash of calls asking if it was true that she was dead, then the dreadful wait for the official announcement. I didn't like the position of knowing she was dead and having to fob people off the whole time. The journalists calling were breathless with excitement. Eventually, I turned off the phone, and just used the other one to speak to TB and Number 10. Just after seven TB called again. He'd been working on the words for his doorstep at the church and he was going over some lines he'd drafted. We agreed that it was fine to be emotional, and to call her the People's Princess. Talk about the good she did, how people were feeling. He kept saying 'I can't really believe this has happened. People will be in a state of real shock. There will be grief that you would not get for anyone else.' He said that if the Queen died there would be huge sadness and respect but this will lead to an outpouring of grief. 'She will become an icon straight away. She will live on as an icon.' He felt that it happened as she was fairly close to the height of her appeal. Dodi[1] was probably a step too far for a lot of people. Had she got married, had another child maybe, she'd have started to fall in popularity. But this will confirm her as a real icon. He kept coming back to his words. 'What I have to do today is try to express

---

[1] Dodi Fayed, who died in the crash with Diana.

what the country is feeling. There will be real shock.' We talked about the last time they met at Chequers and the letters she sent afterwards. She was a real asset, a big part of 'New Britain'. But somehow he knew it was going to end like this, well before her time. He asked me to fix up for him to speak to the Queen and Charles. Nick [Matthews] called to say the Palace was saying official mourning and a state funeral. I started to get calls from the FA about whether Newcastle against Liverpool should be cancelled.

I went down for breakfast and seeing it on TV made it harder to take in. I was tired and felt really emotional now, and drained, and started crying. TB called again, and said he felt absolutely devastated. We went through what he would say one more time and he headed to the church. I called Phil Wilson [Labour organiser, Sedgefield, and friend of TB] to go with him and get the cops to organise barriers. TB spoke to the Queen. Then he came on the TV as he and the family arrived at church. It was a very powerful piece of communication. The People's Princess was easily the strongest line and the people in the studio afterwards were clearly impressed, and felt he really had caught the mood. The question about the role of the press was gradually moving up the agenda. Chris Smith called and we agreed he would not do interviews. John Holmes was worried about the doorstep, felt it was too close to Di. We have to be careful, he said. I took the kids to Audrey's [Fiona's mother], riding their bikes, me trying to talk to people on the way, and we then had a series of conference calls, e.g. TB, Donald Dewar, Angus and me. Donald was reluctant to cancel campaigning on devolution because of the proximity. Hague had said he was suspending campaigning indefinitely and we agreed that we would say we were suspending now and would assess later. The Scots were not so wound up by it all. The word had come through that the royals thought it would be appropriate for TB to be there when the plane came back with the body, so we had to sort the logistics on that. Very careful thought was going to have to be given to every detail of the funeral and already some of the problems were becoming apparent. There was a suggestion the Spencers [Diana's family] might want a private funeral, which people would inevitably take as a bit of a hit on the royals, and in any event the public were clearly going to be expecting a really big event.

I got home to change and then left for the office. The cab driver was a Jewish woman, in tears. I had a catch-up meeting with Angus at Number 10 and then we left for RAF Northolt, to be greeted by an extraordinary array of Establishment figures. Several were in uniform but the only one I recognised was Field Marshal Bramall [former

Chief of Defence Staff]. The Lord Chamberlain [Lord Airlie] arrived in his enormous Rolls-Royce. He had quite the shiniest toecaps I'd ever seen, impressive white hair. The mood was a bit edgy. I sensed the concerns they all had about where it was heading. TB arrived with George Robertson, and again I was struck by how, in this company, they emanated a sense of being very different. Yet in these circumstances they knew that they maybe lacked the skills to navigate through. The LC said as much. Diana's former private secretary, Michael Gibbins, came later and he seemed a bit upset and withdrawn, and said she wouldn't have liked all these people sitting around talking about her funeral. He spoke to her a few days ago and she was really happy. 'This Dodi character may have been a bit odd but he certainly made her happy.' I was hovering near TB as he chatted to the Lord Chamberlain and they called me over. The LC was clear that this was an extraordinary situation and they would find it useful if we could be involved in the discussions about this. TB volunteered me for the next few days, and said we would do whatever they asked of us. They had been discussing the idea doing the rounds of a private funeral. I said nobody would understand. Some would think it was her family putting up two fingers to the royals. Some would say it was a royal plot to do her down. But basically people wouldn't understand. On one level, I found it odd to think I would be helping the royals work their way through a difficult public opinion situation. On the other hand, it was bound to be a fascinating period, and a genuinely interesting professional challenge.

Finally, the plane arrived carrying the body. There were hundreds of journalists kept behind barriers. TB et al went out onto the tarmac. There was absolute silence as the coffin was carried from the plane, and then driven away. Charles came in with Diana's sister. He looked sad, and not surprisingly was finding the never-ending small talk difficult. TB set off for Chequers, then Angus and I headed back to London. TB called from the car and said it was clear they didn't really know what had hit them, and genuinely wanted help and support. He felt we had to make sure the funeral was not a classic Establishment event, but a different kind of funeral that united the country around her personality. Today, he said, his job had been to express the feelings of the nation. Tomorrow it would be setting direction and shape. He said the Lord Chamberlain at least understood it had to be different, but none of us yet knew for sure what that might mean. He said he felt drained and cancelled most of his meetings for tomorrow, though he would be seeing GB there.

The *Herald Tribune*'s main headline was 'World Mourns the People's Princess'. The phrase had really taken hold, and was becoming part of the language immediately. We have to be careful though that it doesn't look like we are writing our script, rather than hers. TB said the two things that people saw in her above all were compassion and modernity. But what was clear was that we would shape the event. He called from Chequers early on and said it had to be clear quickly whether it was a state funeral or not. It needs to be a real memorial to her. There was a fair bit of play in the media for the fact they had not said prayers specifically for her at Balmoral. He felt they would be reluctant to stray far beyond what they know, and what tradition would dictate but it was important they did this differently. He felt the Queen and Charles were the key to this: that they would actively have to want to do something different. Allan Percival said later he was worried it was looking like a Labour thing, not a people's thing.

Angus Lapsley and I were called to a meeting at the Lord Chamberlain's office. We walked down through the growing crowds who were laying flowers and just milling. I don't think we were spotted going in, though later some of the photographers saw us coming out. Airlie chaired the meeting, which was also attended by Robert Fellowes, Michael Gibbins from Diana's office, Mark Bolland [adviser to Prince Charles], Penny Russell-Smith, Dickie Arbiter and Lieutenant Colonel Malcolm Ross, who sat to the Lord Chamberlain's left and appeared to be the main man. I was asked to sit opposite the LC, with Fellowes to his right. It took some time to get going as they took ages to link a conference call to Robin Janvrin and Stephen Lamport at Balmoral. It was clear that everyone was already thinking on the same lines, that there must be a mix of tradition and modernity which captured her uniqueness. There was no way they were just going to implement a 'dusty old plan'. They were clearly desperate to do this right and felt it could be a great healing event. We agreed on a gun carriage, not a hearse, and that there should be a procession of 300 or so people from the charities behind it. I said it was important they were not just the suits, chief executives etc, but people at all levels of the charities, above all the beneficiaries. We discussed a possible Pied Piper effect, the idea that people should start behind barriers then come in behind the procession, but this was later vetoed by the police. I stressed the need for a racial mix. I had noticed on the way down how many black people were paying tributes. The crowds were growing through the day. Every detail was going to have to be thought through. Every issue had the potential to bring its own difficulties. Who should go to the interment at Althorp [the Spencers' family home]? Who should walk behind the coffin? Would the boys be able to do it? What would happen if Charles walked and someone in the crowd turned on him? Then there were the questions of balance and tone in the service itself. Who should be invited? Stars? Children? Someone asked if all the Lords Lieutenant would be asked to the funeral and there was a fairly immediate chorus of NO. Do we invite the Al Fayeds? Yes. We discussed foreigners. It would be hard to stop world leaders and diplomats wanting to come but we should send out discouraging signs. The referendum campaign issue was getting difficult. Hague called for a delay, opportunistic little sod. The pressure to do something about the press was growing. Major did an interview and said as much and one or two MPs were clearly thinking we were staying out of this because of closeness to Murdoch.

Back at Number 10, I did a briefing on the discussions re funeral arrangements, and they were pressing for every little detail they could. I had been seen coming out of the Palace so there was no point pretending we weren't involved and we had to make sure people understood we were there because they asked us to be. I got up the People's Funeral line, and stressed they had been thinking on the same lines and that we were just offering help. I didn't sense any political difficulty in the briefing. I was in a seemingly never-ending round of meetings with Angus, John Holmes and people from the Palace. John came through with news the driver may have been drunk. At the second Palace meeting, Anji came too and we went to the meeting where Malcolm Ross briefed the relevant departments on thinking so far. He said 'the People's Princess' was the main theme and it would be a People's Funeral. He emphasised the role of her charities, said they wanted a proper ethnic mix. The pressure for a minute's silence was growing and we could put it into the service at the end. Re overseas visitors, I said they should feel free to use us to put out the signal that we did not want countries to send people for the sake of it. There was a case for inviting Clinton, Mandela and Chirac for special reasons but making clear it was not a traditional all countries to be represented event. We also agreed there should only be a small number from government, TB and JP perhaps, CB the only spouse. There must be as much space as possible for the non-traditional. Wandering around the building, it was bigger than Number 10, quieter, with fewer people. It was better kept in many ways but once you were into the working bits, very old-fashioned. They had a little tower of baskets as their in and out trays. The staff tended to be of a certain type, women with alice bands and big skirts.

Fellowes struck me as a kind person, but one who had worked out this had to be different, and had to be successful, and he had no qualms about letting us take the lead where that might help make it happen.

Tuesday, September 2

As I feared, there were the beginnings in the coverage of problems. For example, the *Telegraph* editorial suggested that we were politicising the funeral, and I wrote to Charles Moore [editor of the *Daily Telegraph*] to explain how our involvement came about. TB was clear that how they dealt with this now would dictate the extent of any problems they faced in the future. We were meant to be seeing Murdoch but after a bit of dithering, I felt it was a risk not worth taking. He was already on his way when I called Jane Reed [News Corporation executive] while TB was seeing Lord Alderdice [Lib Dem front-bench peer, Speaker of the Northern Ireland Assembly 1998–2004], and said I thought it was a bad idea, that it would get a whole thing going about privacy/paparazzi etc if we were not careful and it emerged he was there, which almost certainly it would. Janvrin asked where I thought they were in relation to public opinion. I said slightly ahead of the game but we need a few more big announcements as the days wear on. I also felt it was important that Charles made some sort of gesture towards the boys, a touch, a hug, something that said father and son, not just royal family. The problem was the diet on the royals had been so negative for so long that people didn't believe in good royal stories as they used to, but there was a basic sympathy there at the moment. I spoke to Penny Russell-Smith and agreed our office should take a back seat on the briefing re the funeral. Yesterday had established a legitimate role but they should be doing the basic briefing on this. I could sense some of the civil servants were not happy at our involvement but TB clearly felt we had to stay on top of this the whole way through. He wished he had got on to Clinton and asked him to come. The White House had picked up on our signals and said Hillary would be coming, not BC. It was a good signal though, and would help as we persuaded others not to feel they had to come. They were happy for us to take the diplomatic hit by effectively saying people were not wanted if they were purely representative. There had to be a connection.

At the 10am meeting, the police explained why we could not do the Pied Piper thing. The Lord Chamberlain stressed that it was not a state funeral. He said the theme had been agreed. Condolence books had been organised. We would have screens along the route of the funeral procession. We had got through a phenomenal amount in not too long – general outlines, theme, who would sing, condolences, other services, etc. Ross went through the groups that would normally be expected to attend and it was huge so we had to pare it down where we could. The media were already moving into a more questioning mode and there were lots of rumours doing the rounds about splits between the families, between the Palace and the government, etc, and it will be a job to see them properly addressed. We had to watch the politicisation problem. They seemed fine but it was clear there were those who felt TB was cashing in. There were some worries about how it would look if TB did a reading and Charles didn't. Michael Gibbins was clear that TB should do it, and she would have wanted that. Also the issue of the flag not flying at half-mast was beginning to pick up.

Robin C called, worried that the Ministry of Defence were pushing for us to exempt JP 233 bombs from the Oslo landmine talks. These were like bomblets, landmines dropped as part of another bomb. When Anji and I were having lunch with TB in the small dining room, Angus came in and said the family wanted RC to go to the funeral because of his work on landmines. I went for dinner at David Mellor's, where he was meeting his Football Taskforce people. He was an enthusiast and had got a good group of people from the sport, police, media, etc and I said TB really wanted them to think big on this, and come up with big ideas for change. Everyone was saying how well TB did yesterday, and how badly Hague had done in his tribute to Diana. 'People's Princess' was the phrase everyone was using.

Wednesday, September 3

Some of the papers were beginning to turn against the royals. The issue of no flag at half-mast, the family staying in Balmoral, it all had the *Sun* fulminating for example. I felt we had to keep making major announcements about the planning and build-up towards the funeral as a healing event. Today, for example, we would be saying that we were having to reroute the procession to meet the size of the crowds expected. They had clearly put to the Queen the issue of lowering the flag but it was a broken tradition too far. I put out words putting pressure on the Scottish Football Association, who were refusing to put off Saturday's game against Belarus. I proposed that TB do some media, maybe *Frost*, maybe a doorstep later. But every step of this was fraught. What looks like helping can look like interfering. Also, there was a sense of there being Di people and Charles people and it was not easy to bridge.

September '97: Diana's death/the mood turning nasty

I went to the LC morning meeting and Paul Condon [Metropolitan Commissioner of Police] was there for the Yard. He said they could handle anything really but they did have to know if the Princes were going to follow the cortège. They were having to work out how to ensure the dignity of the event while also ensuring security. The problem was the route had to be long to let the crowds see the cortège pass, but that created extra policing problems and also meant if the Princes followed it was a very long walk. I asked if there were any religious or protocol reasons why if the coffin was followed it had to be followed the whole way. Michael Gibbins got the point straight away and said it could go from Kensington Palace. Then pennies dropped all round. Problem solved. It would be put to the Queen then we could announce it later, along with all the extra detail that was being firmed up. Penny Russell-Smith, Sandy Henney and Mark Bolland kept me back and said they had a real fear this was becoming 'the people against the family'. Sandy said that somebody should go up to speak for the family, to say they were grieving and sharing the grief of the people. Sandy said who do we put up? 'What about the Lord Chamberlain?' said Penny. 'Dare I say wrong image?' I asked. Everyone fell about. We agreed Sandy should do it in the first instance, say the press were being unfair, there was no reason why they should not stay at Balmoral, it's where the children want to be etc. I spoke to TB several times to go over whether he should say something. I felt there was a case for it, that I should do a briefing ostensibly to announce the government attendance, but also to bolster the Palace. The Palace agreed and then we had a ready-made excuse for TB doing a doorstep as he arrived back from Chequers, namely the rerouting announcement. I walked back through the park. Flowers everywhere. It was heaving with people, yet quiet. The piles of flowers were now vast. I talked to a group of five youngish people, three men, two women, who had come up from Croydon. It was as if they knew her, like there was some kind of intimate bond. I couldn't work out if it was all about her, or all about them, or all about a desire for a new way of doing things. Heaven knows what she would have made of it. She knew she touched people, but she can't ever have imagined this.

Meanwhile I had a meeting with Philip, Margaret McD and Peter H re conference and a few new ideas involving real people, coordination, and they bemoaned the lack of an overall strategy and felt I should do more in relation to overall coordination. TB had met GB and GB had asked for me to go and see him re overall strategy. He was in good form, relaxed and friendly. He said that August showed up personality and presentational weaknesses. He clearly wanted an alliance against Peter and wanted to take a more active role in strategy.

I did a 3pm lobby on TB and JP representing the government at the funeral, and Robin going in a 'personal capacity'. The press were really trying to push us into the story being the royals remote and stiff, and I deflected all that, as did TB in his OK doorstep. He had a phone call with Charles and said afterwards he sounded really done in. Stuart Higgins [*Sun*] called. He said I had to persuade TB to get Charles to persuade the Queen to put a half-mast flag up there. Also, Sandy Henney was OK in what she was saying, but it was not enough. There was a lot of pressure building against the Queen and the family. Given some of the things I've written about the royals in the past, it is bizarre in a way, finding myself in the position of not only defending, but also thinking ideas to build them up. TB said they could sense that there was real change among the public. They would have to respond to it. We could help only if they went for it and realised they had to respond. In a way, while some may have seen Diana as their problem, in some ways she had been like a shield. Now she's gone they are suddenly exposed to this harshness. In the media, the feeling was that we could do no wrong and they could do no right. Only Charles Moore was really speaking up for them. Philip [Gould] called and said he felt TB should go to the crowds in the Mall.

Thursday, September 4

In an extraordinary week, this was in many ways the most extraordinary day yet. The mood was really turning against the royals and everyone seemed helpless in the face of it. It wasn't just the media, but the mood out on the Mall was dreadful. I called Fellowes and Janvrin and said it was becoming dangerous and unpleasant. The press were now fuelling a general feeling that the royals were not responding or even caring. The ugliness of the mood was growing. Today's media would make it worse and it had to be addressed. TB's intervention yesterday got good, straight coverage. But there had to be more big announcements to fill the vacuum and also the royals had to be more visible. In an ideal world, they would come back early to London and mix with people.

Geoff Crawford was back from Australia, which was good news. Hilary C was now with me at the 10am meeting, as well as Anji and Angus, and she suggested another giant screen in Regent's Park. They liked the idea of tickets for some of the people signing condolence books. Anne from Diana's office was in a real fury about the fact so many tickets for the service were going to the media.

September '97: Diana's death/she was 'the royals' shield' – TB

And the Spencer family were livid at James Whitaker [*Daily Mirror* royal correspondent] claiming he had been invited in a personal capacity. We had already agreed to cut media from 100 to 50 but they felt even that was too many. Anne said there should have been real consideration of this, and it had not happened. Without sounding offensive but clearly giving offence, Penny Russell-Smith said the problem was that the Princess did have her links with the tabloids and Anne snapped back that was completely irrelevant, the family should have been consulted about which media came. We then discovered, to Fellowes' fury, that Charles Spencer [9th Earl Spencer, Diana's brother] had 'disinvited' the editors.

We discussed screens, disabled access and then the Lord Chamberlain asked me and my team to stay behind for a conference call with Balmoral. They had agreed something of a 'fightback' plan. They would issue a statement authorised by the Queen to explain why it was best to stay at Balmoral. Today and tomorrow members of the family would start to visit the Chapel Royal. The Duke of Edinburgh has suggested that they go to church this evening before the boys head south. The Prince of Wales comes down tomorrow and visits Kensington Palace, Buckingham Palace and the chapel. The Queen and Queen Mother would come back and also visit the chapel royal and the Queen would do a broadcast. Even as they told us what the plans were, I could feel tension dissipating a little. It would all help. I also felt the various visits should involve seeing and talking to people in the crowds, particularly the Queen and the boys. And I felt that the broadcast should be more conversational than the usual, Christmas broadcast. LC seemed fine with all that and said she was keen to discuss it all with the Prime Minister. It was clear they were hurting at this idea that they were just up there, uncaring. It was still not clear who among the Princes would walk behind the coffin, and I suspected it would not be clear until the last minute. But what they were proposing would certainly help deal with the mood outside.

I had another discussion with Fellowes and said again it was a matter of mixing announcements with expressions of grief and feeling. TB was at the education summit at Number 10 and I filled him in later. Mike Brunson called and I said there were major changes to come. He called back and said they had picked up hints, via David English, re the broadcasts. I confirmed and explained some of the thinking, and his lunchtime 2-way was fine. I was worried the Palace would think I was jumping the gun but it was important the first pitch on it was right. TB was not in an easy position. He was fully aware of the public mood, which he too believed was more than just a media thing. His role was to give advice, frankly, but in circumstances where the Queen was clearly feeling sorely treated, and that people were not being reasonable. They would be feeling terrible, and there can be few things more terrible than feeling like that but also having your motives questioned. TB said the thing was Diana was a personality who made people feel they knew her when they didn't, so there were many people out there feeling loss and wanting to blame. As he told her, it was unfair that it was being directed at the Queen and the family. He saw his role as offering advice and doing what he could to unite the country in its support for her and the family. It was so important that the funeral service was healing. It was pretty clear that William really felt strongly about the role of the media vis-à-vis his mother, and would not want to be doing anything that he felt was for them. But as TB said, they were just one of the things he would have to deal with as King. I asked him where he thought we as a government needed to be at the end of this. He said 1. people saying we handled it well and captured the national mood, 2. Diana still there as a symbol of modernity and 3. the royals modernising a little.

The Palace did their briefing at 3, and then the Met had theirs. I was constantly pushing the line that the Palace were very much in the driving seat and we were there with help and support. Yes, we had ideas but they were in the lead on it all. We were never that far away from an interference/politicisation/exploitation line, and we had to stay the right side of the line. It was complicated by the fact that the *Standard* second edition had a line that Peter had come back to help, and cancelled his holiday to do it. I showed it to TB as he and I were working on the Queen's broadcast for tomorrow. He was angry, said it was damaging because it made it look like the whole thing was about presentation, and our presentation at that, rather than theirs. Up to now, they were fine with the help we were giving, and there was an understood mutual benefit, I guess. This took it to a different place. In briefings I specifically denied it. The main briefing problem was the press going too hard on the notion that Blair was saving the whole show. In truth, they had pretty much delegated a lot of the judgement on this to him, and he to me. The exact line-up behind the cortège was still not clear. There was an idea the family should just stand together at the Palace as the coffin went by but that would look like they were separate from the event, just part of the crowd.

Friday, September 5

Things were definitely turning their way. There was huge interest in the fact she was doing a broadcast to the nation. They got a far better press than on any other day this week. There were a few pieces on the TB link and the general feeling was we pushed them into all this. Nobody believed us when we said we didn't. TB was still fretting about whether he'd become too involved and was now unsure re doing *Frost* on Sunday. I wanted him to do it because there was a job to be done settling the country down, give the message that there must be hope and confidence for the future. There was a far better mood at the morning meeting. We went over some of the logistical issues, like the fact there would be 1 million bunches of flowers to deal with. They read out a series of engagements and walkabouts the Queen and Charles would do, and it was clear they were really motoring. We went over the Crathie church[1] visit. There had to be some expression of emotion from Charles. The main picture was Harry reaching for his hand. The morning meeting was fairly quick and then Airlie thanked everyone for their contribution. He then asked me to stay behind for a smaller meeting. We agreed that things were better and the broadcast and walkabouts will improve things further. The mood was definitely turning a little against the media, a trend Charles Spencer had helped. Airlie was very relaxed, and very nice to me and my little team. He said he genuinely appreciated the work we had done. He was hopeful that all the Princes would walk behind the coffin, alongside Charles Spencer. We agreed there had to be involvement in the procession itself, that the idea of watching from the road was a non-starter. The mood had really improved, but it was important they got the broadcast right. We agreed it should be done in the room where we had been meeting, so that the shot would capture all the people in the background. Fellowes said he felt we had all worked well together and were getting there. We were a day off the pace but we recovered, he said. We walked back through the ever-growing crowds to Number 10 and there was no doubt the mood was improving, and the ugliness would melt away once they came back and did their stuff.

The afternoon could not have gone better for them. As the Queen walked around in front of the Palace, looking at flowers and talking to people, you could sense the pressure lifting, the mood changing. Anna Ford [TV journalist and newsreader] was doing the live stuff and said as much. William and Harry did well, so did the others and the mood was changing totally. The broadcast script was fine. They sent it through and we made a few final changes. I persuaded Fellowes she should put in 'speaking as a grandmother'. I had a long meeting

[1] The Royal Family's place of worship when they are visiting Balmoral.

with TB and Peter to go over the reasons for and against *Frost* and sort out logistics and difficult questions. The press, Camilla [Parker Bowles], memorial, what it all meant. TB was getting into the black humour, said he should do the interview with two thumbs up as a way of seamlessly moving into the devolution campaign. TB had to leave for the Abbey for a rehearsal and he met Charles Spencer, who was really fired up re the media. Both William and Harry had done really well on the walkabout and my sense after the reaction they got was that they would want to walk behind the coffin. Piers Morgan called and asked me to do all that I could to stop Charles Spencer attacking the press. As if. The combination of the Queen's broadcast, William's walkabout and her walkabout had got things back on track.

I went back to Downing Street, having decided it made more sense to stay there overnight than fight through the crowds in the morning, so I borrowed Euan's room. TB and I sat down in the kitchen and went over everything for tomorrow. I was telling him about the Airlie meetings. He said Spencer had suggested TB see William. He also thought I should be seconded to the royals. They must be grateful to you for what you've done for them this week, he said. I felt the people had moved the royals, that it had been a genuine public response that they had been forced to respond to. I also felt privileged to have been part of events that would represent a moment in history. I watched the news and as the crowd surged towards the hearse along the extended route, which had been our idea, I couldn't resist saying to him: 'I did that.'

Saturday, September 6

I was up early and the only other person up was Carole Caplin. We just about managed to make polite small talk. We were both wary of each other, and she knew I really didn't think she should be there, but we got by this morning. TB and CB came through and CB made a joke about whether Carole and I had spent the night together. At least I think it was a joke. TB was continuing to fret about *Frost*, feared we lacked a real message. We were back to the days of testing a line again and again. The basic message was that good must come out of bad, we must be able to build from this a more compassionate Britain. Part of the stress of the day was trying to persuade him it was the right thing to do. My feeling was that there would be a big down tomorrow and we had to lift things. There was a big crowd at the gates so before they left for the Abbey, just as the coffin was leaving Kensington Palace, we went to the bottom of the street and he said hello to a few people. There was a ripple of applause, which I felt

September '97: Diana's death/funeral planning complete

was odd and I was worried people would say he was milking it. Once they'd gone, it felt very odd watching it all on TV. It was all happening very close by, but as I wasn't there I felt very remote from it. Yet I also felt some sense of authorship. The longer route. Some of the details of the service and procession. The way the mood had softened to its current state. I watched mainly on TV but then went upstairs to watch it come across Horseguards, then out to Whitehall as it came past Downing Street and there was more noise than I expected. There was a good mood in the crowd and several moments I found particularly moving. The card from the kids. I thought Elton John was tremendous. TB's reading was OK. The main event though for me was Charles Spencer's tribute, in which he directed barbs both at the press and the royal family. TB was sure the attack on the press would be the main thing. As soon as he came back he asked me to go and see him, even though he had a stack of kings and queens and others coming for lunch. Hillary Clinton arrived and the three of us went into the duty clerk's office. He asked her how she thought we should respond to what Charles Spencer had said about the press. She didn't seem to think it was much of a problem, said we should play it long, say obviously there were issues to look at but we would not get rushed into anything. Fairly obvious stuff. She talked about how hard it was when photographers physically invaded your space. Jackie Kennedy hated it. But she was clear this was not a legislation thing. TB asked me to speak to GB and Peter, which I did. They were more relaxed. GB felt, rightly in my view, that Spencer's attacks on the royals would be far more newsworthy. Once lunch was over, we prepared for *Frost* full-time, first on message, which was about the legacy of a more compassionate Britain, then worked through the more tricky questions. He asked me to speak to Dominic Lawson [editor of the *Sunday Telegraph*] and David English and ask if they would chair a committee of editors to look at the issues arising from this. Both were fine, though English pointed out that that was what the Press Complaints Commission was meant to be doing so we dropped it.

I got home at six and we went out for dinner. Fellowes called and said he wanted to say how grateful he was for the support and advice we had given. He said he didn't believe Spencer meant his speech as a great attack, he was just very emotional. On the royal train up to Althorp, he was struck by the camaraderie and the warmth. He was in an unusual position as he was both a royal employee but also, through his marriage to her sister, part of Diana's side. He said the burial was both sad and beautiful. It was one of the most beautiful places in England yet the event was so, so sad. He was clear the whole week would see the royal family change. This was echoed in a call later from Robin Janvrin, who said he felt a relationship had been forged in days that would normally have taken years. The barriers were broken down now, he said, and that meant they could push on for change. The fact that the Queen had said herself lessons must be learned meant that they really were intent on change. The funeral was absolutely wall-to-wall, every aspect of the service and the day. There were a few pieces on TB and the royals and he didn't much like them but they were more or less drowned out. He particularly didn't like a story that he had been going to make her a kind of ambassador. This came from a Tina Brown piece in the *New Yorker*, based on a conversation with Diana, which Godric [Smith] sort of confirmed, and it went too far.

Sunday, September 7

The *Frost* interview went pretty well and the story they were most interested in re Government was the committee with GB in the chair, to look at ideas to commemorate Diana. I was feeling stressed all day, but also feeling I had been part of a historic moment, and one which might lead the Royal Family to change. We had a Scotland visit tomorrow for the devo campaign and TB was able to go via Balmoral, and it meant the usual long stay was cut to a few hours. I flew up with Roz Preston. It was the first time I had used an airport without TB for ages, and what a difference. It was worrying how quickly I had got used to just being driven to airplane steps and never seeing a passport or ticket. I was picked up by Jack McConnell and we headed for the Caledonian. TB arrived, did a quick doorstep, a photo-call with Elizabeth Smith [widow of John] and then we went upstairs for a drink with GB. He was in very good form, regaling us with stories of how [Kenneth] Kaunda and [Milton] Obote[1] had responded to a display of Scottish culture at a CHOGM [Commonwealth Heads of Government Meeting] during the last devolution campaign. 'Are you sure these people are ready for self-government?' TB said the Royals were very pleased with the help we had given, but whenever he tried to raise any suggestions of future change, the blinds came down. He said they are very different people in a very different age. They don't know what to make of me, he said. They think I helped, but they also wonder whether my calling her the People's Princess didn't fuel the public feeling. They know I'm not left wing but they also know I'm Labour and want to change things. They believe things

[1] Presidents of Zambia and Uganda.

should pretty much stay the same, and they want them to stay the same.

Friday, September 12

TB called very early re the Scottish referendum.[1] 'Quite a result,' he said, but we must get the message out loud and clear that there must be no pandering to nationalism, and we must stress that it's good for the UK, not just for Scotland. The papers were full of it. TB was worried about English nationalism, a worry exacerbated by the questioning from the London hacks when we got there, all on the lines of why should Scottish MPs now have a say re English health or schools when English MPs have no say in Scotland. On the plane, he went through the conference draft and thought it was OK, but we still had a long way to go.

Tuesday, September 16

I had fucked up on pay. As TB said, for some reason my populist instincts had deserted me. I had been warning since last Sunday we had a potential problem but for some reason had not properly focused on it. So once it appeared in a couple of papers (that they would take the full salary) I said just confirm it, though both Tim and Godric were warning it could be a problem.[2] TB, I think for the first time I can remember, said I had fucked up. We were going to try to get away with the line that TB was different, and would not take it, but he believed other Cabinet ministers should. He broke the news to Cherie as we left the building. Peter was still there and she turned on him. 'It's OK for you, swanning around with friends who don't need to worry about money.' Peter, not surprisingly given he had actually supported the decision, looked a bit taken aback. This would take to well over £100,000 what TB had given up.

Monday, September 22

Stan Greenberg [pollster and political adviser, American associate of Philip Gould] called with the latest polling. TB's ratings were pretty much stratospheric. 93% positive job approval, 20% higher than before.

[1] The historic referendum had taken place on 11 September. 2,645,308 Scots had voted – 60.4 per cent of the electorate. 74.3 per cent agreed that Scotland should have a parliament, and 63.5 per cent agreed that a Scottish Parliament should have tax-varying powers. The Conservatives were the only significant party to campaign for a no to both referendum questions.

[2] In fact the Cabinet would be heading for significant pay restraint, urged by Brown and agreed by Blair.

He was strong on leadership, direction and trust. The most important areas the public health, schools, and getting inflation and interest rates under control.

Friday, September 26

David M, Peter H and I set off for Chequers and we did a run-through on the speech with TB. The opening was much better now. TB said he was panicking because he wasn't panicking. I said that meant the panic would come later, which was a screaming pain. We were honing the argument now, trying to strip it right down to a simple message. I briefed out the private polls – 93 per cent approval, Hague dying on his feet.

Monday–Thursday, September 29–October 2

Writing this on Thursday, that makes it the longest period for ages when I have not recorded stuff day to day. The Conference period has gone like a blur, most of it lived out in two hotel suites, his and mine, as we endured the worst part of the speechifying process. We came down on Saturday and though TB was having to do the usual round of receptions and meetings, I spent most of the time holed up in the hotel until we left for the speech. We had the argument right I think – that modernisation is the only route to Britain being a successful country. The rest flowed easily from that. The main last-minute struggle was a search for a phrase that brought it to life, the notion of Britain as a 21st-century model nation. I picked brains around the place and GB came up with the best – beacon, Britain as a beacon. We also had the Giving Age stuff I had done on the Heath, but the women in particular felt we should not mention Diana. TB and I went round in circles on that one and finally agreed, late on Monday night, to take it out. For some reason the end didn't work any more. The only time I went out from the hotel was to go spinning for Peter on the NEC elections. PM had come round to the little office that had been set up for the speech team and he asked me to go and brief. I said I had the speech to do and if I went out I would get swamped by people wanting stuff on the speech. But he really feared it was going to get out of control if I didn't. So at 4pm I called a briefing on the speech but it was really so that I could try to shape the coverage on PM. I didn't mind doing it because he had taken a big hit and we needed to use it to build him back up again. It was great having Fiona down and she was doing a great job with CB, who seemed a lot calmer than usual. I felt sorry for TB at having to traipse around so many receptions. His only respite was a tennis match on Sunday when JP had wanted him to go to his thing at the races. TB said he went for

October '97: No mention of Diana in conference speech

a shower and there were three guys there who practically collapsed when he suddenly walked into the shower area.

Sunday, October 5

TB said he'd been thinking over the weekend of three things. Single currency. Murdoch told him he was not theological about it but was not convinced it was in Britain's economic interests, to which TB said fine, as long as people accept it is economics not politics that will decide. Second, Lib Dems. He was now moving towards an April reshuffle in which he would like to bring two Liberals into the Cabinet, with some kind of full-scale merger after the next election, with an electoral commission on AV[1] for this time, 'proper' PR afterwards, at which point the Tories would be wiped out. Third, family. It was not clear where this was going but he felt we had to get to a modern position on this. It was possible to be pro gay, but also pro traditional family. He felt we had to move, and fairly quickly.

Monday, October 6

Moscow. We set off for the Kremlin and once we had driven through the old parts, Yeltsin's working quarters were very different. All new, a bit nouveau kitsch, lots of high white walls and fake gold leafery on furniture that didn't quite do it. I couldn't work out whether it was meant to say grandeur or modernity or both. It didn't do it for me, added to which the floors squeaked terribly and there were so many hangers-on that at times all you could hear was squeak, squeak, squeak outside the meeting. Yeltsin was a huge physical presence and he did everything in an exaggerated way. Big, big handshake, big grin. Spoke loudly. When the cameras were in, he made sure to do a great warm tribute to TB. The one-on-one session went on a lot longer than the protocol people had planned. At the lunch, I had to lose the vodka so as not to attract attention during the toasts, at which Yeltsin got ever warmer and more ostentatious. 'To a young energetic leader who is so popular in his country.' He cited lines from TB's speech. 'Britain not the biggest, but can be the best – good, good. Good speech.' Tony Bishop, the interpreter, was wonderful to watch. He had done every Russian leader since Stalin and he seemed to take on some of the mannerisms of both sides as the conversation unfolded. At times it felt a bit stilted but TB and BY seemed to get on fine. TB

[1] 'Approval voting'. System where voters can show 'approval' by giving one vote (but no more) to as many (or as few) candidates on a ballot paper as they wish.

said we were trying to leave the things Thatcher improved, and change the things she didn't, keep a spirit of enterprise, but invest more in education, infrastructure, technology. BY said he was going in the same direction. He said Russia had buried Communism for good, but China had not. TB said China uses the language but not the reality. BY said Thatcher had a quick mind and a quick wit. 'Talking to her, you must always be on your guard, or she will have you.'

Thursday, October 9

I went in late and saw TB who wanted to discuss Anji. He said he had persuaded her to stay and hoped Fiona could help smooth things over with CB. I said I doubted it. I felt with Fiona the hostility was because she [Fiona] had felt excluded in opposition in particular, with CB it is because she [CB] senses you are a bit dependent. He said he had always got dependent on people. He said he was dependent on me for certain things, but because I was a man that didn't bother her so much. He felt in his current position he needed different sorts of people with different sorts of skills around him and Anji added a huge amount.

Friday, October 10

We arrived at the Council of Europe, and at the lunch Chirac pronounced 'Tony is a modern socialist. That means he is 5 miles to the right of me.' Everyone laughed. 'Et j'en suis fier,' said TB ['And I'm proud of it.']. He said Chirac remained very chilly, while Kohl and Yeltsin were all over him like a rash. After we left, Yeltsin announced three-way summits annually with France and Germany, which was needless to say reported as a snub, but we believed it was Chirac who was behind it, not BY. Chirac thinks we're too cocky.

Monday, October 13

Flying to Ulster, we went over how to handle the Sinn Fein meeting. As we arrived, it was still not clear it was definitely happening because SF were so pissed off there was to be no camera present. They were big on visuals these guys. We did a brief doorstep so TB could say why he was meeting Adams, the importance of trying to move from violence to dialogue. We then had a short helicopter flight to Trimble territory. DT was his usual self, veering between smug and downtrodden, which was an odd combination. At the main meeting he sat on the sofa with TB and just whispered to him, making sure nobody else could hear, and he was clearly contemptuous of Mo, and was trying to signal that she didn't matter, that only TB did. She just looked over at me, smiled and shook her head as if to say it happened

October '97: TB persuades Anji Hunter to stay

all the time. DT gave him a little lecture on the history of the hand-shake – it was to show you had no arms, which could not be said of Mr Adams and Co. 'I'm sure my hand will be tainted,' said TB. TB also had a couple of little speeches to do and we had to do some careful footwork to avoid a meeting with a group of SF councillors who were clearly trying to ambush us.

We flew to Stormont, where he had maybe ten meetings with different groupings. In most of them, we were just going through the motions and everyone knew that. He had a good session with [George] Mitchell and his colleagues. He said they had one of the most difficult and thankless tasks and we were incredibly grateful to them. George M said that SF were skilful and articulate and worked the process well. The SDLP were hurt. DT was getting hit every day by Paisley. DT took TB to meet his staff. Seamus Mallon complained that TB was letting Trimble control the negotiations. He said every time DT went running to him for special favours, it undermined the whole process. We kept TB in there longer than planned because Adams was due to come down the corridor and for now we were avoiding him. As he worked his way through all the parties, I could see they were impressed at his grasp but also the determination. He was basically saying he wouldn't stop till they sorted it. As Gary McMichael [leader of the Ulster Democratic Party] left and shook TB by the hand, he said 'Is this the one that will shake Gerry Adams by the hand?' TB smiled at him and shrugged. Then, after a brief interlude to go over what he would say, we went in to the talks administration office, Adams, McGuinness, Pat Doherty [Vice President of Sinn Fein], Siobhan O'Hanlan [Sinn Fein negotiator], TB, Mo, Paul Murphy, John [Holmes], Jonathan, myself. They all shook hands with TB, who was steely but welcoming and warm at the same time. He said it was good they were in the process. He believed in equality of treatment. He knew there had to be change. The question was what kind of change. He emphasised there could be no return to violence and no change that does not carry the consent of the people. It will all require goodwill. 'I understand history better than you think. We have an opportunity which, if we do not seize it, will not come again in our lifetime. I feel a deep commit-ment to make it work. All the energy and dynamism I have will go into this if need be. It is a very rare thing for humanity to make sense of history but that is what we must try to do.' It was powerful stuff. They hung on every word, but very steely-eyed with it.

GA and McGuinness were both impressive in different ways, Adams more prone to philosophizing, McG always sizing things up, with a smile that veered from charm to menace. He said to TB he was the only man who could take this forward but he had to understand they had taken more risks than anyone. TB said he wanted to make this happen but it meant he had to get inside their minds. GA gave him a gift of a small harp. He said he acknowledged we had moved the process forward. But it is hard to build peace when the playing field is not level. The biggest cause of conflict is British involvement in Ireland. 'I want you to be the last British Prime Minister in this jurisdiction. Do you have any idea what it is like to live in your own country without proper rights?' He said he was still stopped by police the whole time, and asked what his name was. I was trying to gauge their sense of TB. They were impressed. GA said he would like to meet him often and talk more. 'I think you can be the person that brings peace to Northern Ireland.' TB said both sides had to try to see the other side's perspective. It's pointless to go back to the old ways. You need to unlock the better side of humanity among your people. He made a joke about how he was attacked by the Orange Order for marrying a Catholic. These things don't stop you. There is no point just going into all the old feelings. McG stressed the risks they were taking, said he saw no reason why there should be any more lives lost. He struck me as more pragmatic than GA, which surprised me. 'I know we won't get everything we want.' They pushed on Bloody Sunday, said it needed an international investigation. It was a running sore. GA said I know British people have died at the hands of the IRA and I regret it but we have people who were shot by Soldier A and Soldier B. TB said he could not stress enough how unique was the opportunity we now had. The political will is there from us, but it has to be matched.

Friday, October 17
EMU was our main problem of the day. Charlie Whelan and Ed Balls wanted GB to do an interview 'clarifying' the situation, saying policy was unchanged but making it clear we were clearly not going to be in the first wave, and therefore it was unlikely for this Parliament. Jonathan called and said though TB was not sure of the need, GB was trying to push him into agreeing to the interview. With all the chatter there had been around, I agreed with CW it was probably the right thing to do. It was not really an interview so much as a form of words which would be given to Phil Webster [political editor of *The Times*]. The Treasury drafted the words and I made a couple of changes to tone down the pro-Europeanism in a couple of places. I spoke to

Webster and agreed that the intro was that he was effectively ruling it out for this Parliament while saying it would be folly to close options. God knows how we had got to this, or to the headline at the end of the day, Blair rules out single currency for this Parliament, because while CW and I both believed we were doing what TB and GB wanted us to, they having discussed it earlier, it seemed they had not really gone over the line in any detail. GB was pushing where he wanted to go, I'm afraid I was keen to push my instinctive anti-EMU feelings because I didn't want TB outflanked by an impression that GB was keener on EMU. The words went to Webster, the spin was applied, and away we went.

It was all quiet until after 10, when TB called after he had seen the news and said what the hell is going on? 'We never agreed this,' he said. I said I thought they had. Peter M came on too, amazed. I said I couldn't understand, given this would run for days now, why GB wanted to do it like this. He said because he didn't like being seen to do things under pressure so it was a way of trying to do it on their terms. I suddenly realised that because I had not really checked and double-checked with TB, we had briefed an enormous story on the basis of a cock-up. TB could not get hold of GB – 10.15pm – so he spoke to Charlie, who professed himself 'gobsmacked' by the conversation. TB asked if we had ruled out EMU this Parliament. Yes, said Charlie. 'Is that not what you want?' No, it is not, said TB. 'Oh,' said Charlie. GB was also now on the rampage, saying this had all gone too far, as if suddenly the headline he had been asking for was not what he had asked for at all. Even today, writing this one day after the event, I cannot piece together exactly how we reached the point we did.

Saturday, October 18

Pretty much a weekend from hell, at the end of which I was totally unrested as we went into another week. I was beating myself up too because I knew I had screwed up. We had all screwed up but I felt I hadn't done what I normally do, which is double-check every base. Writing this on Sunday, I still think Charlie and I were doing what we thought our respective bosses wanted us to. TB wanted GB in line, GB wanted to stop all the split stories by spelling out the logic of our position for the Parliament. TB thought we could get by a while longer, GB felt we had to clear it up now. CW and I took those different positions and thought we were merging them to mutual benefit. Big mistake. TB called early, a bit more relaxed about things, because he felt we had reached the right position, even if we had done it at the wrong time and in the wrong way. 'What actually happened is that you and Charlie thought you had an instruction, after which GB and I were out of the loop about how you went about it.' Some of them were trying to run the line that TB had overruled GB and made him do it. When I told TB he said 'I wasn't even aware of it. What the press are saying about this is bad enough – but the truth is even worse.' He knew I felt pretty sore about it and was pretty fair considering, but I knew he was really pissed off at the whole thing.

Sunday, October 19

TB said we should say there would be a statement next Monday, ruling out the first wave for economic reasons, and saying that makes entry this Parliament unlikely. But there is no need formally to make a renunciation. GB said we should try to shut it down before Parliament returns. The danger was that in trying to end the confusion we create more confusion. He felt we should brief the outlines of what we would say next week, the five areas for assessment, then park on that. Anything that looks like a new line will just be another U-turn. We agreed to give out his Stock Exchange words today as a way of signalling the forward process to next week's statement. TB was happy with that, said we then say Parliament will have the full position set out next week. He did say, though, 'If the markets go haywire tomorrow, we are in deep shit on this. We will be subject to extreme and justified attack.' So after endless calls we agreed – we will not be bounced, and a full statement will be made to Parliament first, setting the issue in long-term national interest not short-term politics. Catherine McLeod [*Herald* journalist] said the problem for the government was Whelan. She said I should go totally on the record and be named so that people knew when a government spokesman was me rather than him talking some rubbish to his pals. TB said pretty much the same thing, and was now pretty sure we should get rid of the old lobby system and do proper on-the-record briefings. 'We get the worst of all worlds. The press make up anonymous quotes and say they are from us. We'd be better off if everything you said was on the record.'

Monday, October 20

I got a rare queasy feeling in the morning re 'Brown Monday'. GB spoke at the Stock Exchange and had the ultimate horror backdrop, the screens behind him going red as he spoke. The press were all unanimous we'd had our worst weekend since the election. I spoke to TB as he waited for Kohl. 'What I can't stand is the incompetence. I don't mind if we are attacked for what we do or stand for. I can't stand the incompetence though.' Whelan was beyond repair, but I felt I should support him because we had both been involved. The one good thing to come out of it was that PM and I agreed it would probably not have happened if we had been working together properly. I wrote him a note saying it was vital we worked together and we should let bygones be bygones. He sent back a very nice note.

Thursday, October 23

Cabinet was mainly on EMU and most of them were saying how important it was to keep the option open. It was striking how pro the majority were. GB was not saying much. TB set it in a political context, said there was a mood to change the climate, knock us more, and we had to be on our mettle. He said GB would go through the outlines of his statement and he did not want anyone discussing it outside. GB did a very chunky briefing on the background to the assessment and the five tests. On convergence, we were clearly in a different cycle. We were not convergent now and would not be in '99. On flexibility, and the ability to deal with shocks, he also felt there was more to be done on skills. He ran through investment, impact upon City and financial services, gave a fairly balanced picture but concluded we would not be joining in 1999 but we should be preparing to join later. At 12.30 we had a two-hour meeting, the first of several planned, on GB's EMU statement for next Monday. TB had done a draft. So had GB. GB liked the line – prepare now, decide later. The sense we would be giving was preparation for a referendum in the next Parliament if the economics were right.

Friday, October 24

Edinburgh, CHOGM. Mugabe [President of Zimbabwe] arrived with a little posse of expensively dressed officials. He said in the past he used to get invites to Labour Conferences in Scarborough, but it was so far to travel, and how Labour was always on their side against colonialism and imperialism. The Tories always looked at them as elements to be avoided. TB said our colonialism is something we now read about in history books, it does not define what we are. They ran around the main issues on the G8 agenda, talked on land distribution, during which we had another history lecture. TB was in better mood and quite enjoying chairing the summit. I asked how the Queen had been with him. He said she was fine, and brilliant at the way she handled all these very different characters. She got terrific coverage on the news, though she looked a bit bemused at the modern rendition of the national anthem. The news was fine on EMU. TB spoke to GB a couple of times and drafts were now flying back and forth. Geoffrey Howe [Conservative former Chancellor and Foreign Secretary] wrote to TB pleading with him not to rule out EMU.

Saturday, October 25

The main story out of CHOGM was Mandela saying the Lockerbie bombers should not be tried in Scotland. After a visit to the NGO [non-governmental organisations] Centre, I went to the Queen's reception. I was hanging back just keeping an eye on things when Fellowes said I ought to meet the Queen. He took me to where she was listening to a gaggle of Heads, and as she turned from them, Fellowes said to her how much help I had been to them in the week after Diana's death. She looked deeply unimpressed, nodded a little and then said 'Do you always travel with the Prime Minister?' I said yes, usually, and that was about it.

Monday, October 27

The statement was now clear and there was no question that we had not thought through. CHOGM finished on time, TB telling us how brilliantly he had chaired it. TB was regaling us with a few stories from the receptions. One of the African leaders pinching Cherie's bum and asking her who she was, then him jumping a mile when she said she was Tony's wife. Mandela being difficult on a couple of issues and TB saying to him 'You are so revered you can come out with any old nonsense and nobody is allowed to say it's nonsense,' Mandela laughing. We got back and went through the final final version, which was fine. GB was excellent in the House. All in all, it was another big occasion which had gone well. We'd done exactly what the strategic briefing said we would – turned setback into opportunity, shown clarity, direction and leadership, wrongfooted the Tories. What they didn't know was that we had also laid the ground for another defection – Peter Temple-Morris [Conservative MP for Leominster].

Tuesday, November 4

At the Lib–Lab committee meeting, Jack S sent me some very funny notes translating some of TB's words to the Libs e.g. 'Treat this confidentially = this has been in the FT for weeks.' 'Treat this as being between ourselves = I imagine you'll be straight onto the Guardian with this.' I think JS and I were the least enthusiastic about this exercise, though to be fair to Paddy he was on top of things policy-wise.

Robin C did a number on where we could work together on Europe. Paddy said he greatly welcomed the commitment to step up preparation for EMU. TB focused on jobs, crime and the environment as the three areas we should be focusing on re Europe. He also felt we should be explaining better what the single market would mean for people, the advantages it would bring.

Wednesday, November 5

I awoke, as feared, to tobacco and Formula 1 climbdown leading the news.[1] TB called, pissed off and denying that he had agreed to the change. But in truth Max Mosley [president of the Fédération Internationale de l'Automobile] and Bernie Ecclestone [president and CEO of Formula 1] had been lobbying and TB immediately sensed real danger because of course Ecclestone had given the party £1m before the election. Whatever the rights and wrongs of the policy, which had been worked out by people unaware of the donation, it would look absolutely dreadful, and it was bound to come out. I felt confident in the arguments though, and we had to argue the policy case on merit. TB suggested we give the donation back to Ecclestone because if it came out it would look so awful, or get [Sir Gordon] Downey [Parliamentary Standards Commissioner] to look at it, but Derry and I persuaded him that would be a mistake and would not help.

Thursday, November 6

We were taking a big hit on tobacco. At Cabinet, Robin C ran through plans for the Anglo-French summit, and then did Iraq. He said it was dangerous and nobody should underestimate Saddam's determination to develop weapons of mass destruction. TB and I had a long chat about Ecclestone. It was going to be bad. The question was how bad, and what could we do to minimise the badness? My instinct was it would be really bad, and the best way to deal with it would be to get everything out in the open, soon. I felt for TB, because I knew this was the kind of issue he hated most of all. He hated anything to do with funding and though in truth there was nothing wrong about the way the decision was reached, people would not want to believe that. The Chirac dinner was fine on one level but they really disagreed fundamentally on Iraq. He was totally dismissive of the US and any suggestion of bombing. 'What does bombing achieve except it pleases the US Congress? Nothing.' TB was emphasising the UN inspectors

[1] Formula 1 had originally been exempted from Labour's ban on sport being sponsored by tobacco manufacturers.

had to be able to do the job properly. Chirac said there was no way he could support bombing. They were a long way apart. He said threatening force was not the way to treat Saddam. He said we had to persuade the US to be reasonable. 'We will explain and you will translate.' TB said the least we needed to do was agree he must hold to the UN resolutions. He was also scathing re the Yanks on the Middle East, and about [Binyamin] Netanyahu [Prime Minister of Israel]. Chirac was more supportive re our position on EMU as outlined by GB.

Friday, November 7

We set off for the Anglo-French summit, and after the first exchanges TB and I had a conflab re Ecclestone. I felt we could not hold off much longer and I went off with Anne Stenson from the Garden Rooms [see note on p. 215] and drafted a briefing note, all the facts re the donation, making clear we have nothing to hide, that it would have been published in due course anyway, that the policy on banning was made after donation received, which blows the idea he bought a change, that the recent change was about making the policy workable without losing F1 from Britain. Anne let out a big whistle when I dictated the point about the million, but I felt totally comfortable in the argument, that it would be a rough ride but one we could tough out. We would also announce he planned to make future donations but TB felt in the light of all this, that might not be appropriate. I spoke to GB and Peter and at one point during the day, all four of us were agreed. One problem was that the circle of people who knew was widening. I had asked Tim [Allan] to check out whether Dobson and Jowell had known, and they hadn't. 'Cor fuck me' was Dobbo's response and of course at some point he would be bound to talk to others as a way of getting his line out properly.

Monday, November 10

I slept really badly. I was dreading being grilled on the who knew what where when, and I knew this thing was going to hit us. The papers were low-key and there was not yet any real heat in this. I went to see TB and Jonathan. I was getting more worried not less. TB was sure though that the best course was to let it dribble out. I felt we were in danger of ending up with the worst of all worlds. Sally M told me that [Lord] Neill [chair of the Committee on Standards in Public Life] had replied to Tom Sawyer's letter on Ecclestone and he was saying we should give the money back. I thought this was really odd. It meant very few donations were acceptable, because very

November '97: Formula One tobacco row

few major donors would not be affected by a specific government policy at some point or another. And who the hell was he to decide? But decide he had, having been asked his view, and it was going to have real implications. Then to a meeting with TB, Peter, Jonathan, Sally M, Robin Butler and, later, David Hill. We went through the tough questions, and drafted a briefing but we were still holding back re the size of the donation, which in the end was what made it the problem it was. Butler spoke to Neill to try to get a positive response to any decision to hand back. TB felt we had right on our side but that it was very unlikely to come out like that. GB felt we should give the money back straight away, but it meant state funding was inevitable. Through the evening the broadcasts were not as bad as we expected them to be. Indeed they were far better than we dared to hope. We now had to get the money back and get the thing dealt with finally. We got Blunkett to do interviews on it and he was fine. Also, the BBC still went on TB's speech as second item. With the Louise Woodward[1] verdict wiping everything out, there was a chance the Ecclestone story would die.

Tuesday, November 11

I woke to the BBC saying the Labour Party was 'still refusing' to reveal the size of Ecclestone's donation. TB called a couple of times, angry that they were not even reporting Neill's view that we had done nothing wrong. My own view was we had no option but to get out that it was £1m but Ecclestone was opposed to that and Jonathan said we had to wait until he agreed. It was beginning to look and feel worse. TB first agreed we should get out the figure but changed his mind after speaking to Peter M. I felt the whole strategy had failed, badly. TB rightly said this was bad for him and his reputation. I said there would obviously have to be a closer look at state funding if donations like this were not acceptable. TB was taking a real hit and there was a problem with his mindset, in that he was thinking he could do no wrong, and that people would therefore not assume he could do any wrong on issues like this. But in part because of the way we had handled it, it looked like he had done something wrong. We had made a big mistake in not going upfront, but he would not admit it.

---

[1] On October 30, Woodward, a 19-year-old nanny, had been sentenced to life imprisonment by a court in Massachusetts for the murder of a baby, Matthew Eappen. On November 10, on appeal, murder was reduced to involuntary manslaughter with a sentence of 'time served'. Having served 279 days in custody thus far, Woodward was controversially freed.

Wednesday, November 12

Tobacco/F1 had been running for a week now. The £1m was big in the papers and we were looking shifty and shabby. We agreed the tough questions were: why didn't we refer to Neill until it was clear the media were looking into it, and what was the policymaking process? I'd got Bevins to do the story re Hague pushing for a knighthood for Ecclestone and that was running a bit. PMQs was fine until Martin Bell got up and had a go, to pretty devastating effect. I was really not enjoying this at all. I felt things were on the mend a little until on the way home I got a call from David H that Phil Webster had got hold of the Neill letter, presumably through a Tory MP, which made clear there was an offer of a second donation after the election. I told Jonathan and TB, who went straight into head-in-sand mode. 'How can that be a story, that there was not a donation. This is getting absurd.' He was blaming everyone – Michael [Levy] for getting Bernie in, Jonathan on the policy, Jonathan for having a baby – Jonathan and I fell about on that one – and GB for persuading him it was the wrong thing to get all the facts out early. I said I blamed him for being persuaded. TB had wanted to pay the money back straight off, but didn't follow his instinct. I had wanted to brief straight away, but he was talked out of it. GB had started off agreeing with me, then changed his mind and with Peter's help changed Tony's. Then day after day we were forced to reveal more and more, look like we had more and more to hide. It was a disaster and getting worse and worse as the days wore on.

Thursday, November 13

Gallows humour was starting to come into the conversation. I was desperate to move things on, but this was the only story in town and we were handling it badly. At yet another meeting on it, I argued for openness. I also thought we should say we had made mistakes in the handling of it. Again, TB and GB were against on both fronts. He left the room and said to me and Jonathan 'Get it sorted out before Cabinet.' Unbelievable. Derry was also adamant we should be more open. 'How the fuck have we managed to bugger what is actually a good case?' he said. Then came the news that Ecclestone told the *Mirror* he never offered a second donation.

Friday, November 14

This nightmare would not go away. Every time we thought we were through it, something else would come up and hit us. It was one whole week since I wrote a memo that, if we had followed it, would

November '97: Ecclestone disaster makes us look shabby

have put things in better shape. TB called around 8 as he was heading north. I said what I thought of it all, and he said I should not get myself into such a state, as we would tough it through. I said I had done nothing else but tough it through. I said we were in a problem entirely of our own making and we had badly handled virtually every move to get out of it. Derry called. He was worried TB was believing his own propaganda on this. I went over to his office to review the situation. We gave the right advice, he said, and he ignored it. Derry felt the problem was the way TB worked, the decision-making process, a lack of clarity. He could not believe how badly we had fucked it up. He wanted a proper meeting where we could go through the whole process and work out where mistakes were made and why. Derry called again and said he intended to have a very heavy conversation with TB tomorrow. 'He thinks he's invincible. It happened to Thatcher after 10 years. It's happened to Tony after six months!!'

Saturday, November 15

TB called me and said 'I'm really sorry about all this. You have taken a lot of the heat on it and I really do apologise.' TB had the idea of saying we would publish all donors from the last five years if the other parties did the same. The problem was we were in government and they weren't and nobody really cared about the other parties. TB apologised again for the misery of the past fortnight. We agreed he should do *On the Record* tomorrow. We were up till half twelve going over the difficult questions. We had the answers but I was more worried he would not learn anything from this. Cherie said he would. He had obviously told her how pissed off I was because she came in and gave me a big kiss and said he knew he had handled it badly and should have listened to me and Derry last week, because the advice given by GB had been wrong.

Sunday, November 16

I got up just after six and went for a swim, then to breakfast with TB. Derry came down to help go through the tough questions again. He said TB's mistake was to think we could spin our way out of anything. This was a straightforward claim of malpractice, he said, for which we needed legal not media minds. He was at his most overbearing, but he was right, and had been from the start on this. The setting for *On the Record* looked fine, though his make-up was a bit odd. I said he had to reconnect on the basis of trust, make clear he was the same person they elected. TB did well on tone, and on fact. I watched it in the lounge with Cherie's mum. He was especially strong towards the end. The weakness for me was that we were apologising for the handling of it, rather than what we did, which made it seem like it was only about presentation. [John] Humphrys [BBC interviewer] was full of himself and I was probably a bit too rude to him, but he was so up himself it was hard not to be. Over lunch, CB and I both emphasised to TB he had to change modus operandi and learn lessons from this, get proper decision-making structures. TB said there had been a failure of decisiveness on his part, both on the policy and on handling. I said I was fed up with all of them and he said 'You love me really though,' and laughed. The problem had been lack of precision and lack of candour.

Thursday, November 20
I got in early and TB was already working on his speech on the Queen's golden wedding anniversary. He took these big Establishment events seriously, and also knew that he was always on the at-risk register with them, as people were always so ready to criticise the politicians by comparison with Her Maj. There was a lot of interest at the 11 in the people attending the banquet, and again they were probing on how much of the planning was ours and how much the Palace's. Cabinet had been brought forward to 9.30 and was mainly George Robertson reporting on Iraq and GB going over the general approach for the pre-Budget report. He did not like it when TB summed up the discussion. TB went off to the Abbey, then back for a meeting on the jobs summit, then hanging around waiting for the Queen and the Duke to arrive. They got some nice pictures out in the street. As they came through the door, TB said he was surprised that even with the Queen, the photographers showed no respect at all, just yelling out at her like she was a singer or something. The staff had lined up and TB took the Queen on a little tour. She stopped for a chat with Alison [Blackshaw], who was beaming. The walkabout went well, though TB was maybe a bit too enthusiastic and should have hung back more. Also, Geoff Crawford and I were in the shot far too much when I watched the news later.

Monday, November 24
Virtually the whole day was taken up dealing with Humphrey the [Downing Street] cat, because it was being put around that because CB didn't like cats, we had done away with it. Alan Clark, knowing I hated cats too, also got stuck in. It was raised at the 11, and I could tell that Brunson wanted to go big on it, and it made the lunchtimes.

'Is Humphrey alive?' I asked Hilary to set up a photocall in Bromley, and we had the ludicrous situation of me and the Cabinet Secretary both having to spend a large part of our day dealing with it. The bloody thing was retired in Surrey, and a bit old now, and Robin B wanted to be sure we would not be bringing any undue stress or attention on his new owner.

Thursday, December 4

BSE was massive in the press.[1] It had been decisive public health policy, but led to a lot of alarmist coverage. TB was not too happy but Jack [Cunningham] felt that having had the advice he'd had from the Chief Medical Officer, we really had no option. TB was looking tired, and too thin. A bit of weight had fallen off his face and he looked too gaunt. Having taken a succession of hits, we were all a bit tired and we were definitely lacking firepower at the centre. Philip came in to see me and said TB looked like someone not in control at the moment. TB kept insisting he was in command, consulting colleagues, but in reality he was finding it hard to keep on top of everything at the moment. We lacked capacity when the unexpected came up and hit us. He lacked people he could turn to, and feel reliant and confident. Richard Wilson called round. He was very odd-looking, with huge great ears and a face that didn't quite map together. He was obviously making friends around the place pre Butler's departure. He repeated the line about me having enormous power and influence because I was so clearly so close to TB. He felt the Cabinet Office was not giving TB enough support, also that we used him too much publicly. TB was seeing a number of journalists and was OK. But I felt he looked a bit diminished. He was down at the moment. Both of us were and neither seemed capable of lifting the other, which normally we could do. I said we had agreed to try to get him back on the domestic agenda but he was pretty much the whole time foreign affairs, defence, Ireland.

Monday, December 8

TB was looking tired. Fiona thought he was ill, and CB told her he had a bit of a turn on the tennis court, and that he hadn't slept at

---

[1] Tony Blair and Jack Cunningham had announced a UK ban on beef on the bone, because of potential infectivity in bone marrow and dorsal root ganglia in older cattle. The advice of SEAC (Spongiform Encephalopathy Advisory Committee) had been followed but provoked media hysteria.

all well. TB had another GB meeting later and although he was more on top of things than before, I was getting worried at how he looked, very tired, a bit yellow. I ran into Alan Clark, who said [Nicholas] Soames would give up his seat if we could get him the Paris Embassy. Couldn't tell if he was joking.

Thursday, December 11

TB spoke really nicely at the funeral for Sylvie [his former driver], and you could tell everyone was really touched he had gone. It was a really sad do, and her grandson Jack was distraught.

Adams and his team arrived 15 minutes early, and he did a little number in the street, where the media numbers were huge. This was a big moment, potentially historic in the progress it could lead to. They came inside and we kept them waiting while we went over what TB was due to say. Mo and Paul Murphy were both there and Mo was pretty fed up, feeling she was getting shit from all sides. They were hovering around the lifts and were summoned down to the Cabinet room. We had agreed TB should be positive but firm. He actually came over as friendly, welcoming them individually as they came in. I shook McGuinness by the hand, who as he sat down said, fairly loudly, 'So this is the room where all the damage was done.' It was a classic moment where the different histories played out. Everyone on our side thought he was referring to the mortar attack on Major, and we were shocked. Yet it became obvious from their surprise at our shock that he was referring to policymaking down the years, and Britain's involvement in Ireland. 'No, no, I meant 1921,' he said. I found McGuinness more impressive than Adams, who did the big statesman bit, and talked in grand histor-ical sweeps, but McGuinness just made a point and battered it, and forced you to take it on board. Of the women, I could not work out whether they really mattered, or whether they just took them round with them to look a bit less hard. They were tough as boots all three of them. TB was good in the use of language and captured well the sense of history and occasion. He said we faced a choice of history – violence and despair, or peace and progress. We were all taking risks, but they are risks worth taking. He said to Adams he wanted to be able to look him in the eye, hear him say he was committed to peaceful means, and he wanted to believe him. I was eyeing their reaction to TB the whole time, and both Adams and McG regularly let a little smile cross their lips. Martin Ferris [Sinn Fein negotiator] was the one who just stared. Mo got pissed off, volubly, when they said she wasn't doing enough. TB was maybe not as firm as we had

December '97: McGuinness more impressive than Adams

planned, but he did ask – which I decided not to brief, and knew they wouldn't – whether they would be able to sign up to a settlement that did not explicitly commit to a united Ireland. Adams was OK, but McGuinness was not. Adams said the prize of a lasting peace justifies the risks. Lloyd George, Balfour, Gladstone, Cromwell, they all thought they had answers of sorts. We want our answers to be the endgame. A cobbled-together agreement will not stand the test of time. He pushed hard on prisoners being released, and the aim of total demilitarisation, and TB just listened. TB said he would not be a persuader for a united Ireland. The principle of consent was central to the process. Adams said if TB could not be a persuader, he could be a facilitator. He said we would be dead in 40 years, but in the meantime this was the biggest test of TB's time in office, how he deals with the displaced citizens in a divided territory. A lot of people believed the armed struggle was legitimate. They have to be shown a different route to the same goal. There are two blocks – British policy, and the Unionist veto. He gave a series of history lessons on the way, including the industrial carve-up against the Nationalists. McG was the more aggressive of the two, inside and outside. He said this was the most important meeting in 75 years, but it would pass quickly. There were things in our power we could do now, if we stopped the securocrats from stopping us. He said the next meeting has to be with Trimble and TB must encourage it. Mo mentioned an escaped prisoner. Adams said 'Good luck to him.' Mo snapped back 'That is not a very helpful comment.' But there were flashes of humour. Mo slipped me a note saying she found GA sexier than McG.

On the way out GA took TB to one side, and clearly wanted to be able to brief they had had a one-on-one session. All he said was 'Merry Christmas.' I said we needed to agree a briefing line. He said why don't we say we've agreed to withdrawal of all troops by February and a united Ireland by spring. Fine, I said, I like a good clear line. TB roared with laughter. They were clearly trying to hang around and, added to their early arrival, exaggerate the length of the talks. I'd already learned how much these things mattered in relation to their impact on the other side. The three women went to the loo, and our security people were getting antsy at how long they were in there, while Jonathan and I chatted to GA and McG re holidays and Christmas and kids and stuff. Vera Doyle [messenger at Number 10] was on duty and came over to chat to them, and within seconds McG was charm itself, checking out where she came from and where she went on holiday. Vera was clearly a fan, but said to them as they left 'Now you two just behave, and help out our man here.'

Saturday, December 20

The papers were full of Hague's wedding. I had been hoping for a quiet day, but a letter from Blunkett to GB, attacking a number of DSS [Department of Social Security] proposals in the CSR [Comprehensive Spending Review], was about to hit us hard. I didn't react quickly enough and it was not really till late in the day that I got a grip of it. Welfare reform was running away from us as an issue. TB's speech went OK, though for some bizarre reason unknown even to him, he didn't actually deliver the line on the new ministerial group, which I had been pointing the broadcasters to as the main news in it. It led the bulletins anyway but it would have helped if he had actually said it. JP called and said he had had Simon Walters [*Mail on Sunday*] on saying he understood JP had asked TB to sack Harriet. We were travelling up to Mum and Dad's, and with the kids in the car I didn't really bother with the Blunkett business when I first heard of it. Godric was handling it and he called me several times through the day, sounding more and more alarmed. 'This is beginning to feel like the last government,' he said. That was the thing that shook me and got me motoring in trying to sort it out. 'Blunkett declares war on Brown' was the headline. I emphasised the commitment to reform, but GB called and said I had to dump on Blunkett, make clear that the entire Cabinet had signed up to welfare reform. Then I had Robin C on, then Dobson, because they were getting called. GB said I should put out a statement saying the CSR was a collective decision and DB had to stick to it along with everyone else. He believed someone close to DB had leaked the letter to portray him as a hero, fighting against GB for the poor. He said 'You cannot let him get away with it.' He said neither he nor TB had seen the paper he seemed to be reacting against, and this was the kind of ill discipline we could not accept. It was a tough call, because of course any kind of attack on DB would just inflame it even more. I spoke to TB, who was livid. 'What is David playing at, writing in those terms, e.g. saying we would lose our right to be seen as the party of social inclusion? It is as if it was written to be leaked.' Maybe it was but what do we do? He agreed the line should not be intemperate but should come down clearly on the side of reform. I tracked down DB and he, TB and I had a conference call. TB had calmed down but DB was apologetic. We agreed he should do the radio tomorrow, reaffirming his commitment to welfare reform. He was adamant he was not behind the leak. We were facing a real problem of leaks in this area at the moment. Godric said the day had been a nightmare of Majoresque proportions. After setting up the broadcasts and doing the overnight briefings of ministers and hacks, I finally got to bed at 1. Another fucking day off gone.

Monday, January 5, 1998

TB said he was rested, had had a great time and was really up for the battles ahead. We also needed a strategy for the party. He was worried about whether Frank Field had the political skills needed for the welfare job. Ireland was a major problem with the talks in danger of collapse. TB agreed to see Trimble and John Taylor, hopefully privately, but it leaked. TB was determined to get a Heads of Agreement tabled by Monday, preferably with the two governments, UUP and SDLP, but it looked pretty remote. Taylor went through the problem areas – the Billy Wright killing,[1] documents being given late, prisoner release, and the feeling that the Nationalists are getting too many concessions. TB was pretty strong on the idea that you cannot allow murderers to dictate the flow of the process. 'It would be crazy, if the extremists start to kill each other, for the moderates then to say the process is at an end. It gives them a permanent veto on progress.' When TB said that Sinn Fein had to be able to point to progress on their terms, Taylor raised his eyebrows very ostentatiously and coughed loudly. DT said it was impossible to engage [John] Hume in a serious discussion about an Assembly. TB said what would Hume do if you showed him a draft Heads of Agreement? 'He would certainly pick his nose,' said Taylor. 'No, he doesn't pick, he rubs it,' said Trimble and there followed a discussion between them about whether he was a nose picker or nose rubber. John [Holmes] and I exchanged looks of bewilderment. I could tell TB was avoiding looking at me in case he got the giggles. He was totally gobsmacked when Taylor said that Maze prison officers have to go through metal

[1] Wright, leader of the Loyalist Volunteer Force, was murdered by Irish National Liberation Army prisoners while imprisoned in the Maze top-security prison.

detectors but prison visitors don't. Taylor said it was good to see scales falling from eyes.

Tuesday, January 6

The Maze was the main focus of any news today, because UUs and others were going inside to see some of the paramilitary leaders, and came out having failed to persuade them it was the right thing to stay in the talks. TB was busy on the phone, to Ahern and Hume. Adams came out and said the whole thing was a ploy to stop any further engagement from the Unionists. I had a meeting with TB/CB in the flat at 6.30. They were horrified that they had been sent a Cabinet Office bill for private use of his car, e.g. going to play tennis or going to church. It was ridiculous, given that he HAD to use that car, and for security reasons could not go out on his own, and yet he was being charged for it.

Wednesday, January 7

Fresh from the row over TB having to pay for the use of his official car, Fiona was now embroiled in a row over whether CB could use Number 10 notepaper. Apparently she could if she signed them Cherie Blair, but not if she signed them Cherie Booth. It was antediluvian.

Thursday, January 8

TB was a bit down as we drove to Lancaster House for the meeting with the European Commission to launch our EU presidency formally. 'It is going to be tough this,' he said. 'They talk the language of being up for reform but they baulk when it happens and vested interests get upset.' The commission meeting was the usual long-winded Euro-crap, pompous statements being made back and forth across the table, and as yesterday I was going out of my way to be nice to everyone. Stephen Wall [Ambassador and Permanent Representative to the European Union] commented that the Rottweiler had become a pussycat. We even got TB to wear the presidency tie. TB then had a meeting and a lunch with Santer. I guess it was a nightmare job trying to marry different positions, compromise the whole time, but he was so vague and indistinct. I was called out to see Donald Dewar who had told TB he was going for a seat in the Scottish Parliament and wanted to announce it today.

On the way to the airport, Ben Wegg-Prosser [political adviser to Mandelson] called me to say that Paul Routledge's book on GB had found its way to the *Guardian* and they were splashing on a story about the TB–GB 'pact', claiming TB went back on his word. It was the usual stuff – also that TB was out campaigning when John Smith's body was still warm. I called Whelan and said he had to deny it was done with GB's cooperation, though the *Guardian* said otherwise. He also had to make clear GB knew there had never been a pact. If he WAS behind this stuff, it was ridiculous. We arrived in Tokyo at 3pm local time.

Friday, January 9

Magi [Cleaver] called with the cuttings, including one in *The Times* saying that I had ordered Robin C to end his marriage. It came out of an interview with Margaret Cook. It was fairly buried in *The Times*, but I was the nose of the story and it was one of those that would stick. It was also totally untrue. What a cow – though I suppose there was the chance it is what RC said to her at the time, as a way of making his decision easier. I don't know. Got a message to call RC urgently. I did so. There was not a word of apology that I was getting this in the neck, just irritation that it was up in lights again. I said to him I was not totally sure how we dealt with this. He was clear that if she carried on like this, it would be hard to reach any financial settlement with her. He was also clear she had the potential to do more damage to him. I said one of the names being mentioned and he didn't exactly demur. 'I'm well aware this has the potential to damage me,' he said. 'If I speak to her, I'll make sure she understands any settlement rather depends upon my career surviving.' He feared Margaret had given the media 'gold dust' by hanging out the bait of 'other women'.

Saturday, January 10

Ireland was a problem again. Someone had leaked to the *Telegraph* the details of negotiations between Trimble, us and the Irish over the latest paper, which included proportional representation for Assembly elections and a new idea, the Council of the Isles. Worse, he had done it to the one paper more hostile than any other to what we were doing. They featured the idea of keeping Mo out of it because TB had to take over and they also said, rightly, that the SDLP and SF would be unhappy. This was all very irritating and John Holmes was deeply pissed off. TB was fairly calm about it. I feared Trimble was trying to scupper it. It meant that from 8am London time, with Jonathan negotiating there, and John H here, every spare minute was going into trying to fix it. If ever peace is secured in Northern Ireland, and a film is made, then one of the key scenes will see TB in a posh Japanese restaurant, cross-legged and barefoot, with our hosts serving course after course as he tried to talk to Mo, DT and others and get it back on track. Even now, he was very optimistic. John thought he was overly so. He did a doorstep on Ireland, FEPOWs,[1] Japan generally. Siobhan in London said the pictures were fantastic. I had a meeting with the Japanese Ambassador to London, and introduced him to some of our more serious journos to discuss how we could try to get better coverage for the Emperor's visit to London, which did not just revolve around the usual old clichés.

Monday, January 12

TB had been up till 3, arguing with various people in the Irish situation, the main stumbling block being the UUs on the wording for the cross-border bodies. As soon as he was up, in between the meetings in Tokyo, he was on the phone again, first with Ahern. The other distraction was Robin C, who announced he and Gaynor were getting married as soon as his divorce came through, which led most of the tabloids. I sent him through a note saying I thought he was better to say nothing from now on. The nonsense about Peter and I spreading rumours that GB was gay was still around and I had totally lost it with Whelan over the Routledge book. It was the denial of all knowledge that really got my goat. I phoned him 3am UK time and said I don't know what your strategy is re the book but it isn't working. Other than being bemused at being woken, he went into his all innocent, nothing we can do to stop people writing what they want mode. I said they were pumping this stuff out the whole time. TB said of GB that on reflection he would not like the way it had all played. He would not like all these headlines.

Wednesday, January 14

One of the first things I did back in the office was speak to Whelan. I had totally lost it with him, and in between screaming abuse at him, I said we needed a written strategy paper on how he intended to get us out of the mess into which they had led us. I said I was not prepared to put up with his nonsense any more, that he had not been able to make the transition from opposition to government and his efforts to pursue a pure GB agenda were pathetic and doing GB more harm than good. He interrupted several times and I said if he had been in my line of vision in Japan I would have taken his head off.

[1] 'Far East Prisoners of War' and former civilian internees objected to the planned visit to London by Emperor Akihito, and demanded an apology for their treatment during the Second World War.

Thursday, January 15

The GB situation was worse because a Routledge article in the *Scotsman* said it WAS an authorised book and also that Nick Brown was a key source. The other interesting development was the Tories (Iain Duncan Smith) signalling they would support us on welfare reform if they felt it was the right thing to do. David H went round saying this was mischief-making but TB wanted to welcome it, say it showed they recognised the failings of their policies.

Friday, January 23

Clinton's problems were getting worse. The problem was not his affairs so much as the charge he asked Monica Lewinsky[1] to lie. Philip had spoken to George Stephanopoulos [senior adviser to Clinton] who said they all felt totally betrayed, that he had promised once he got to the White House, all this kind of stuff would stop. We were being pressed to say we were rethinking the visit, but on the contrary we were expressing strong support for him despite his difficulties. TB said he intended to be very supportive when we went there and maybe say he thought it was ridiculous to have this system where someone like Starr[2] was appointed at massive public expense to go fishing for dirt on the President. I went home, then to the *Mirror* party at Kettner's. Charlie was there, pissed, and told Anji he knew he had fucked up and eventually would have to go.

Monday, January 26

Clinton was mega in the press and it was looking pretty bad for him. Clinton, Hillary and Gore did a press event on childcare, at the end of which BC said he did not have an affair with Lewinsky. He did a pretty good job.

Tuesday, January 27

TB took a call from Clinton. He said he and CB were thinking of them and anything we could do to support him, we would. BC was straight onto Iraq and the need for firm action against Saddam because of his latest challenge to UNSCOM.[3] It was pretty clear to anyone listening

---

[1] White House intern who had an affair with Clinton.
[2] Kenneth Starr, American lawyer and former judge, appointed as Independent Counsel in 1994. His investigations led to the impeachment of President Clinton.
[3] In December 1997, inspectors from the United Nations Special Commission, investigating Iraq's development of non-conventional weapons, were denied access to a number of presidential sites in Iraq.

that what Tam Dalyell offensively was calling 'the war of Clinton's penis' was about to begin. He said I hope you can support us if it comes to military. TB said the bottom line was that Saddam could not keep flouting international law. He said it would be better if we stayed together with a UN resolution. They talked over MEPP [Middle East Peace Process] and NI but the purpose was clearly to get us focused on bombing of Iraq. He said it was vital we were together, got the French onside and the Chinese and Russians to abstain. TB said afterwards that the last time they spoke, BC was less hawkish than TB, but that had definitely shifted. They were preparing for an attack, no doubt, and we had to be out there setting the ground for that, because there is no doubt we were going to take a political hit on this.

Thursday, January 29

Cabinet was largely Iraq, which was all pretty worrying; Ireland, and a discussion on Bloody Sunday; pay and welfare reform. Mo thanked George R re agreeing to the Bloody Sunday Inquiry, said he would take a lot of flak in the military. Dobbo was pretty solid on pay, saying more money for pay meant less for services, and GB did quite a good number emphasising the long term over the short term. He said the settlements were relatively generous but phasing in was necessary to avoid wage inflation. I had another go at the trivialisation of the media at the 11, as the Robin C questions kept coming. You had Ireland, public sector pay, welfare, serious issues and they went on endlessly about his bloody secretary. I called McCurry and we agreed to float the idea of a joint radio address. I gave it to *The Times* and the *Sun*, *The Times* because they would do it properly, the *Sun* because I wanted to fuck the *Mirror* for the way they were doing in Cook. I went over with TB for the Bloody Sunday statement, which went fine, as did the briefing afterwards. Even though some of the Irish experts were in there, I felt on top of all the detail.

Sunday, February 1

I went to see Ellie [Merritt].[1] Lindsay [Nicholson, her mother] wasn't there and we had a really long chat about John. She said she missed his funny drawings. She used to say something and he would turn it into a drawing. She said she missed his cuddles. He always wanted to cuddle her and rub noses. He could always make her laugh, even when she was feeling a bit fed up. She remembered the day he died,

---

[1] Daughter of John Merritt, Campbell's best friend, who died of leukaemia, Ellie was diagnosed as also suffering from the disease.

February '98: Remembering John Merritt with daughter Ellie

and couldn't understand how she would never be able to see him again. She remembered being worried about Lindsay having the baby without John being there, and how she would have to remember everything really hard so that she could tell Hope what he was like. I said I tried to do that too. She asked me to read her a story. Then she asked me to tell her what John was like and I told her the stories of the Boy George night on the town we had, the royal carriage story, how he turned over the private ward when he was in hospital, the silly pranks in the office, how John could jump onto the desk from a standing start. I told her how he once doorstepped a group of terrorists and she suddenly had a look of panic on her face. 'Wasn't he scared?' I said probably but he was very brave. She looked so much like him when she laughed. She laughed the loudest when I told her about the pig-out in the South of France and she wanted to know everything he ate. She wanted to hear everything we did on holiday together. She was perkier than last week, and really sweet. It was the longest conversation we'd ever had, just the two of us, as usually there were other people there. She said I like talking to you about Daddy, because it makes it like he's here again and we were both blubbing in no time.

Monday, February 2

The Bill and Tony show was starting to hype up a lot. Iraq was the main focus with the French and Russians trying to get a diplomatic solution, but TB was pretty clear where it was heading. At the office meeting, TB said he was determined to exempt the military from the minimum wage and also he was amazed that the Low Pay Commission was recommending from £3.50 to £3.75. He was off on one, ranting that they were all going native and not understanding the bigger picture and have they thought of the effect on business? He said just because we have some superhumanly mad people running the unions does not mean we are obliged to meet them halfway in their madness. Sally M slipped me a note – 'Has he been seeing Thatcher again?' We had a brief meeting with the US Ambassador, who had a weird and very American, over-firm and over-friendly handshake, a bit like Levy's. Then we started the rounds of US interviews, with Diane Sawyer [US broadcast journalist; a former press aide to Richard Nixon]. I really didn't take to her. The worst type of TV blonde confection, gushing smile. She was obsessed with questions on marital fidelity, which TB non-answered. When they changed tapes, the producer started asking her to do more on Clinton/fidelity and I stepped in and said please stop wasting your time. They did Clinton, Iraq, Ireland, Diana. TB liked her a lot more than I did. He had been worrying how best to express support for Clinton but in the end it was fairly easy. It was all about emphasising the big picture, the importance of the transatlantic relationship, the leadership BC had given to the centre left. News came through the Russians had been invited by Iraq to inspect eight more sites and we said it was all game playing. Robin C was to go to Saudi Arabia on Wednesday, and we met and agreed we should use his speech on Wednesday to get up the message on Iraq. The ABC producer told me there was massive interest in TB's visit, more than he could remember for any leader.

Wednesday, February 4

We turned the factual briefing into a paper for the media showing the extent of Saddam's capability and the damage he could do. Iraq dominated the 11. I chatted to Mike McCurry again and it was clear they were worried about how we would handle questions on Lewinsky. I said TB would be very supportive, but they were more worried about the direct questions to BC. On the school visit, for example, they were worried the press would get a child to ask him a question on Lewinsky. Mike had a nice turn of phrase and said this would be 'double parking in a no comment slot'. We agreed to a mixed pool as they came into the White House so that the questions were likely to be varied. TB did a call with Yeltsin, who sounded a bit slurred and mentioned World War 3 breaking out. He said we all wanted to avert a strike. Russia had influence on Iraq. We could get into their sites. TB was pretty hawkish, saying Saddam had to be stopped from developing these weapons. He [Yeltsin] said France, Germany and Russia favoured the same approach. If 'England' could come with us, you could persuade the Americans maybe and we could resolve diplomatically. On the way to the airport, I had a chat with Chris Meyer [British Ambassador in Washington], who had done a round of TV clips on the visit. On the plane, we took TB through the detail on the trip, but he was worried about Philip's recent groups. He kept asking me 'How much trouble do you think we're in?' I felt it was win-backable but we had to see it as a warning signal if we wandered off too much. It was nice having Fiona on the trip but I was working till 4am UK time and was knackered but unable to sleep. They'd also put us in a room with single beds, which I hate.

Thursday, February 5

TB was really quite nervous as we left for the White House, wanting to go over every detail again. Bill and Hillary looked a little bit pinched and the body language between them was cool to non-existent, except when Bill tried to be warm, and she sort of responded because she knew she had to, for the sake of form, but there was none of the chemistry that was normally there. He seemed a bit diminished by it. He was still phenomenally charismatic and I could see the impact he was having on people who had met him for the first time, but I also sensed that slight diminution. The mood between the four of them was excellent. Bill was clearly grateful for the support. They went off for a private session, then came back and as we settled down in the Oval Office, the two pools came through. The American pool was half on Monica, half Iraq. The British were three-quarters Iraq and the rest Monica. Boris Johnson [*Daily Telegraph* journalist; later a Conservative MP] annoyed TB with a question asking if he was jealous of Clinton. The news came in that Lewinsky was to get immunity. Clinton was starting to get a bit more steamed up. He, TB and I started talking about how we would deal with it all at the full press conference they were going to have to do. He was steamed up about some of the commentators, going on about stuff in *their* private lives. I said he was crazy to engage on the detail. He is so much bigger than them. Keep going on the big picture. He said there has to be a change in the way the media operates, that politics will become impossible if media trends carry on as they are, into this stuff the whole time. They went off for lunch, mainly Iraq, Iran, N Ireland. The Yank media liked our Iraq document. I had prepared a line Educate, Diplomatise, Prepare, which we kept coming back to. These big long-running situations always needed that kind of strategic line. BC was definitely more relaxed when HC was off with CB and again that was totally understandable. I asked him what it was like having the whole world thinking and talking about your sex life. He said as long as he couldn't hear them all at the same time, he could get by. He said Hillary had been great, considering. There was still an awful lot that bound them together and she knew he was no saint, but somehow they kept going. I got the impression he was quite pleased to be talking about it in a very normal, human kind of way. His staff were close, and supportive, but I had picked up a lot of anger against him. Also, they were far more deferential to him as President, and I'm not sure any of them had the kind of really personal conversation that I could have with TB. I think TB was worried I was being a bit forward even raising it, but the fact BC kept coming over for little chats made me think he welcomed it. He said I can't tell you how good it is to have you guys in town right now. Then right at the end, I made the announcement about the Bob Hope knighthood, which went down well.

Fiona came back from the Hillary/CB event and said Cherie had been brilliant at it. She had spoken really nicely about Hillary without undermining Bill, and some of the women there had been moved to tears. Mike McCurry and I were working really well together and I felt personally close to him, and we were able to watch each other's backs pretty well. He said they really appreciated what we were doing, but said it was important for TB that he tried to establish a good relationship with Gore. He was right to be supportive of the President, but he needed to be careful. The general view was that there had been some kind of physical relationship, certainly some kind of infatuation, and his worry was that this could still end in a bad place. Hell, he said, he's a 50-year-old man and what is he doing chasing a girl like this? He said Monica had always been hanging around trying to be close, and Hillary had even got her moved to the other side of the building. They were all touched by the tribute from TB but be careful. We had a good chat on the nature of the job and the impact on family life.

The only time during the trip I felt Hillary was really looking at BC was when, during one of the wonkathon sessions, he appeared to be nodding off, and she really stared into him. He opened his eyes, nodded forward, saw she was looking at him, and smiled weakly, then she just looked away. There was a real strength and dignity to her, but the hurt was there. After the dinner there was a glitzy event with Harrison Ford, Spielberg-type people. Elton John and Stevie Wonder did a double act, and again I found Fiona and me seated right behind the principals with the press all looking on as we arrived, and I felt uncomfortable. Bill and Hillary looked great as they arrived. He still had the ability to turn it on and sparkle. TB was looking a bit tired by now. I was desperate to get to bed, and felt a bit of a heel, thinking how many people would love to be sitting five yards from Stevie Wonder and Elton John doing a double act. I think Elton was meant to be a surprise but we had heard him rehearsing during a session on Turkey.

Friday, February 6

TB and I were going over how to handle the press conference. It was going to get massive coverage and we decided there was no way to finesse, we just had to be shoulder to shoulder. The tough question was whether he thought BC was telling the truth, and we agreed the best answer was to say Bill Clinton had always been a man he could trust and do business with. Clinton came down with Sandy Berger, Mike and one or two others and we started to go through difficult questions. The breaking story was about a secretary being told to lie. He said he would deal with it, no need to bother Tony on the detail. The others went away to take their seats with the press, leaving the four of us there for five minutes or so. BC was in a fairly vulnerable position. This had built up and up and up and he was more nervous than TB. TB took me to one side before they went through, as he often did, just to restate everything we had agreed, and get that final reassurance he was on the right lines. Total support. Big picture. Important relationship between our countries. BC took a few deep breaths, cracked a joke about asking how many of the press could claim hand on heart to be faithful, then off they went. Mike and I went in on the side, and got there just as TB and BC got up to the lecterns. There was an explosion of camera clicks, they waited till everyone was settled. Both did good introductory words and closed down the Monica stuff well. TB could not have been clearer, nor BC more grateful. There was the odd flash of humour, as when Phil Murphy [Press Association] asked whether Bill appreciated TB's support and he said no. TB was even more warm and supportive than we planned, and Bill really appreciated it. As theatre, it was virtuoso. As they came out, Bill said TB would increase his standing because of what he did and was effusive in his thanks. He and TB walked down the red carpet and met us in the room where we had done the briefing. BC took us to one side and said I'm going to make sure you will always be proud of what you did out there. 'It was a noble thing to do.' He was on a bit of an adrenalin rush, realised it had gone well, and was glad it was over. The others came through, Berger etc, and everyone was pleased. There had been a real sense of foreboding, that the whole thing was going to be humiliating for him, and it was fine, in fact better than fine, though the reality remained. Fiona had been up in their flat with Hillary and CB and said it was really nice compared with Number 10, very homely but really smart.

Monday, February 16

TB chaired the first meeting on the Iraq media management group I had suggested, which would then be chaired by Derek Fatchett. TB was alarmed at how poor the FCO/MoD propaganda effort was, and I certainly felt we were not really ahead in the PR battle. Charles Guthrie and Alan West, the Chief of Defence Intelligence, were doing a briefing and Guthrie was good on the military objectives.

West was strong on the factual account of Iraq's capability, and on missing weapons post-UNSCOM. When he started saying that the presidential sites so called would stretch from Greenwich to Streatham or Wapping to Hyde Park, they finally got some idea of what was going on. They ran though some of the WMD [weapons of mass destruction]. Charles looked at his most menacing when he said very quietly 'You wouldn't want to bomb a tank full of anthrax.' They were both impressive in different ways, Charles very soldierly, upper-crust-sounding but not remotely twerpish like some of them, while West had a very quiet authority. They both emphasised the aim was to get the inspectors in, and there was a diplomatic route. But if the Iraqis were watching, they'd have got a pretty heavy message put through to them.

Thursday, February 19

The Iraq meeting was quite bad-tempered. Cabinet was mainly Iraq and Ireland. TB said it was not an option to do nothing. We either got the inspectors in or we had to take action. TB said the fear was Saddam would pitch a response perfectly to Kofi [Annan, Secretary General of the UN] to get the French and the Russians into a different position to the rest of us. After the 11, I went to the JIC [Joint Intelligence Committee] briefing room with TB, Jonathan and John [Holmes], joined by [Richard] Wilson, [Roger] Liddle [European policy adviser], Edgar Buckley [Senior defence policy adviser, MoD], Air Marshal John Day [Deputy Chief of Defence Staff (Commitments)], Guthrie and a few others, and we got the presentation on targeting plans. 96 missiles from B-52s, 300 from ships in the Gulf. They envisaged 1,500 to 2,500 casualties. What struck me was not just the detail in the aerial photos, and the quality, but the extent to which they calculated where the mosques or any historical sites were, and the lengths they went to to avoid them. They whizzed through with a very straightforward approach. It was an odd feeling to be shown all this, to know where bombs might be heading, and to know people were going to be killed. I wondered if you ever became immune to that thought, and suspected you did. The plan was to use B-52s, cruise missiles, wave after wave over a relatively short period, but non-stop. The main targets would be the Iraqi Republican Guard, command and control, air defences in the south. The planning documents stretched to about four dense books the size of *Yellow Pages*. TB raised re-attack if not all targets were taken out and Guthrie said there were no re-attack plans because the US were worried about 'Hanoi baggage'. I sensed he wasn't totally taken with the Yanks. TB said he would speak to Bill. He agreed with Charles Guthrie you may need a second wave. Guthrie was clearly keen to get going. Robin C was not. RC said if we did not get another UNSCR [United Nations Security Council Resolution] we would be politically and diplomatically isolated. He was a lone voice pretty much, but kept going. Charles said it was not helpful to think we needed to go for another resolution because it could take up to two weeks. He also said he was clear about what they were going into. There was tension with Robin on this and TB sided with the MoD. Later, Guthrie, out of uniform and wearing a very smart suit and the shiniest shoes I had seen for yonks, came over for a cup of tea and a chat. He wanted me to know the MoD had a lot of time for TB, and for me. He knew the MoD had traditionally not done media well and if I needed help in changing attitudes, he would provide it.

Sunday, February 22

I had to go to a landline to listen in on the TB–Clinton call. The only place I could find was the foyer at the Sobell centre [leisure centre in north London] and it was a bit surreal, kids wandering around in skates, and at one point the cleaner mopping around my feet as I listened to TB and Bill C talking about military action. Both were deliberately sounding a bit vague. The main thing was that they wanted to get a new resolution, which would allow a military attack for material breach of the resolutions. They were both worried that Kofi would get a deal that would split the big five, and allow Saddam to diddle around. The bottom line was still unfettered access. Then Kofi called TB and gave him a not very satisfactory briefing. He said he had an agreement, hoped that we were happy with it, that he got all that he was asked to get and now he was very tired. He said he would be leaving tomorrow and would be back in New York on Tuesday. TB did not press on the detail, assuming Kofi would not be able or willing to speak freely. Kofi sounded exhausted, TB sounded nervous, as if he was hearing behind the words a bit of a problem which was looming. There followed another call with Clinton, and this time both of them sounded a bit nervous. Bill said I don't like this delay. One and a half days, not knowing the detail, and he says it's a deal. But the problem is Saddam does know the detail and he could outspin and outsmart us on this, and I don't like that one bit. TB said a lot of this now was about who got their line out first and Saddam had the upper hand. We had to keep the focus on repeat inspections, not just a one-off inspection regime. TB said he got very little out of Kofi, and Bill said he was worried. Neither Clinton nor TB liked being in this position where it was being said a deal was done, that Kofi had got everything he wanted, so we were meant to look and sound pleased, but we had no idea what the deal was. TB was worried we would get to Tuesday and then not be able to sign up to it, which would be incredibly embarrassing for the UN. The UN were briefing the deal being done before we had any detail at all. The news was fine in terms of TB's role, lots on his calls etc, but it would all look a bit silly if we ended up not signing up to it. The danger was clear, that we end up being isolated with the US, everyone else agreeing to a deal we are not sure about.

Tuesday, February 24
Peter Hyman had done a very good draft for TB for his speech at the big Dome event, which was aimed at winning financial support and turning some of the media. He delivered it brilliantly and you could feel minds being changed. He pitched it as good for Britain, and really managed to enthuse people with it. David English said the *Mail* would find it much harder to criticise blindly now. Hezza was there, looking a bit old I thought.

Thursday, February 26
Cabinet was Iraq followed by GB going through the outlines of the Budget. Robin said there were really worrying signs about what UNSCOM can do. We were pursuing a balanced twin-track approach – light at the end of the tunnel on sanctions, allied to clear warnings if Iraq breaks the agreement. TB said we can only tell if it is a good agreement by whether it holds or not. He said he was assured by Chirac he agrees the language makes clear military action will follow if Saddam breaks the agreement. JP did a number saying how well TB, George Robertson and RC had done. Clare piped up: 'Robin has played it beautifully.' On the Budget GB started by saying that we were into a stage where the press seemed to know more about the Budget than the Treasury. JP fell about and was chuckling away for ages, thinking like most of them that GB was the last person to complain about the Budget being briefed out in advance. TB and I left for Paddington and the train to Reading. In the car, as ever, he went over his various current angsts. He was not sure we had a proper grip on the Budget. Chirac was being difficult. The Iraqis were making pretty clear they would not deliver. He was alarmed about Harriet. Frank [Field]'s White Paper was crap. He told me he was thinking of a reshuffle before Easter. He was wondering whether to add Harriet to the list. I said I bet you don't. He was also disappointed with Chris Smith.

Tuesday, March 3

There was a real sense we were losing our grip and another real problem developing, that we were in danger of being seen as a soap opera not a government. It was why the Budget and the welfare reform programme were even more important. The press were warming up for Derry at the select committee,[1] which we finally managed to find on TV, and I settled down to plough through some paperwork while watching a PR disaster unfold. It was so bad that it was comic, and he seemed to have no sense whatever of how it would be seen. Yes, he conceded, it was a lot of money to spend on wallpaper [£59,000]. But that was the total extent to which he followed the briefing. Then came a succession of extraordinary remarks, which would be panned all over the shop. He said the refurbishment was a 'noble cause'. The whole thing was a storm in a teacup, and he had this hysterical line that the wallpaper would last 60 years, because it was not like something from your local DIY. It also became very apparent that he didn't know what B&Q was. I love him dearly but even I found him arrogant, overbearing, pompous. I told Derry he had fed all the preconceptions they wanted till they were stuffed with joy. He was having none of it. He said 'I am totally unrepentant. It was important to get the facts on the record, I have done so and I'm happy about it.' I said the tape will be played again and again. 'Well, be that as it may, I am absolutely convinced it was the right thing to do, and I'm glad I did.' I said we will have to agree to disagree. Indeed we will, he said, good day, and he put the phone down. TB called Derry and was very firm with him. I sat opposite and so could only half hear Derry but it was a pretty tough conversation for TB to have. He said we have a problem and if you can't see it's a problem, then that means we have a bigger problem. It's not what you said in terms of the facts, it is the manner and the expressions used. DIY stores are used by millions of people, and what they will see out of that is a snob. It cuts right through to them. I thought we got the message through last week that if you are going to be in this game, you have to be political. Derry then said that his officials said he had done well. TB said in which case they are completely bonkers. It pains me to talk to you like this but you are being damaged and in turn that is damaging the government. Derry now sounded hurt. He said I can send you the transcripts. TB exploded, I'm not interested in the transcripts. I am interested in what the public are saying, and the problem

[1] Lord Irvine was called before the Commons Public Administration Committee to explain £650,000 spent refurbishing his official residence.

March '98: Danger of being seen as a soap opera

that poses to their understanding of the government. You may have right on your side, but how on earth can you call the refurbishment of an official residence a noble fucking cause? As he spoke, he was pulling faces at me, looks of ever greater exasperation. I couldn't remember the last time TB swore so much in one conversation. He said he hated going over the top but he felt it was the only way to get it through to him. Otherwise he would not take it seriously. He said what really worried him was that Derry didn't seem to realise it was a problem. He asked if I thought he was rescue-able. I said it was difficult.

Wednesday, March 4

TB was incredibly rough with Derry, almost losing it at points. He swore several times, and said that he was in no doubt yesterday had lost us council seats. 'You are doing yourself and the government real damage. Maybe some people think it is good to tell the public to fuck off, but I am not sure it is entirely sensible. They think we got rid of the Tories because they were out of touch, pompous, up themselves and couldn't care less about ordinary people, and then we have this and they think what's different?' Derry asked him if he wanted him to leave the government and TB said no, but he had to be rebuilt, and that would only be done if he took advice. He must not do any media without talking to me. I advised him not to do any interviews for a while. He said it would lead to stories he had been gagged. I said that was preferable to more interviews on the wallpaper.

Monday, March 9

TB was very funny, joking about all the little gifts that he got. He said he loved Chirac's watch. He liked the pen from Germany, so Helmut was a top bloke. Japan gave him a kite.

Thursday, March 19

I took the planning meeting on the welfare reform Green Paper. We agreed Frank [Field] would do the statement and no briefing of the press before on the detail. The argument was about whether we should try to get coverage on the principles or have a single policy with a hard edge to take the communications lead. TB saw Frank and Harriet before Cabinet and went through the last bits, while also bollocking them for talking to the press the whole time. For example, the FT today had a big story on compulsory second pensions. Cabinet was OK, but very general. First on agenda 2000, then Robin on Israel, who are asking us to play a greater part. RC was back and said his visit went well despite the obvious. Harriet went through the welfare stuff, and JP's eyes rolled straight away as she managed to get New Labour and the Third Way into the first sentence. Then she threw in rejecting Old Labour by simply putting up benefit levels for good measure. Actually the principles were fine. First, helping people into work. Second, public-private partnership. Third, greatest help to those in greatest need. Fourth, the role of public services of high quality. Fifth, strengthening families and tackling poverty. Sixth, openness and honesty. Seventh, streamlining services. She then set out the success measures we should judge ourselves by. TB said it was not a blueprint but signposting and setting direction. He stressed welfare to work, pensions and disability as the most important areas. Work for those who can, security for those who can't. Donald [Dewar] was a bit dubious, and asked where is the beef?

Tuesday, March 24

The main thing today was TB's speech to the National Assembly in Paris, and he was pretty hyper about it. But we were also moving to the final stages of planning on the welfare Green Paper. TB had been practising his French on and off all day and was nervous. On arrival we went straight to the British Council but he was irritated at having to do lots of stuff before the main event, which he really needed to psych himself up for. There was a big scrum in the street as we walked to the National Assembly, a band playing 'Land of Hope and Glory'. We were met by an army of flunkeys and lots of twittering. TB was more nervous than I've seen him for ages. As Jonathan, John Holmes, Brian Bender [Cabinet Office] and I were taken away to the public gallery, TB was taken by Laurent Fabius [President of the French National Assembly] through a line of really loud drummers. 'They're going to execute you,' I said and he smiled a bit weakly. It was a fantastic building, very French, incredibly atmospheric. It was terrific to watch the way the members responded to different parts of the speech. The left went for the obviously left bits, but there were lines the French left would never say, and the right rose up in over-the-top cheering. At times it was comical, but the overall effect was strong. He was tired by the end. He got Brownie points from the French for doing the whole thing in French. Re ECB [European Central Bank] Governor, Chirac said he would veto [Wim] Duisenberg [former president of the Central Bank of the Netherlands]. Kok would veto [Jean-Claude] Trichet [director of the Banque de France], but a third man would be acceptable to Kohl. 'Or woman?' said TB. On Iraq, they were in very different places, TB claiming a success for diplomacy

March '98: TB speaks to French National Assembly

backed by force, Chirac basically saying we were killing children through sanctions. It was all in all a good visit. On the plane we worked on the Green Paper.

Wednesday, March 25
We got good coverage out of France but we had a real problem re Blackpool, because the NEC had decided we would not go there in the next three years, and someone had briefed it was because the hotels were tatty. It was a real problem and nobody had a grip on it at the party. After Questions, Peter M, Richard Wilson, David M, Robin Young [Cabinet Office] and I went to the DSS to sit down with Harriet and Frank and their people. It was like a start from scratch lesson. Relations between the two of them were poor, and they had lost confidence while also still coming over as arrogant. Frank's statement was all over the place and we agreed I should try to rewrite it and make the argument clearer. Again, he was a curious mix – grateful for the help, but hurt because we were making it pretty obvious he needed it. We flattered away about his credibility as a radical etc but that too was a piece of spin now, and I think he knew that's what everyone in the room thought. As I worked on the statement, I felt myself getting angrier and angrier. Why the fuck was I having to do this on top of everything else? Why was I having to deal with Blackpool for heaven's sake? I was feeling under more pressure because so much was falling upon me, because there were so few people able or willing to take responsibility for sorting anything out. I got TB to do a clip for BBC North West and also when I heard the *Blackpool Gazette* were delivering some rock and some copies of the paper with 'Blair betrayal' headlines, I got the reporter and photographer to come in and see TB. The reporter almost fainted. He was a young kid called Vincent and he was literally dumbstruck. The photographer ended up trying to help him ask the questions.

Saturday, March 28
The main problem in the Sundays was the *Mail* getting hold of two letters from me bollocking Frank F and Harriet. They were a bit OTT and meant more bollocks about me in the Sundays. I was becoming the story again.

Sunday, March 29
I felt gloomy all day. I called Tom Bostock [AC's GP] in Ireland. He said I had to heed the signals. I had been going without a proper break for four years and three times in my medical history I had three

major upheavals because I ignored the signals when first they came. Acute asthma, a nervous breakdown and a serious stomach complaint. He felt all three were connected to anger. You get all of the shit, none of the glory, and you spend a lot of the time taking seriously people you despise. You would not be human if that did not make you angry. But I was becoming the story again, and didn't much like it. Nor did Audrey [Fiona's mother] or Mum, who phoned and said what was this committee [the Public Administration Select Committee] all about and I could tell she was worried. She also volunteered the same view as Bostock – you get all the blame and none of the credit, and I don't know why you do it for them.

Monday, March 30

Richard Wilson came to see me, said he was worried because everyone seemed to be miserable. I said we had to get better people into the GICS [Government Information and Communication Service]. He said Peter M and I had been brilliant dealing with Harriet and FF, but I said it was ridiculous we had to get involved at that level. We discussed what to do re the PASC inquiry.[1] Alan Clark called and said fuck the critics – you're doing the right thing, shaking things up.

Tuesday, March 31

I woke up, tired, and was running as the second story on the news. I was the big story all day and frankly too knackered to deal with it properly. I spoke to TB who had not really been aware of how it had built up in the preceding days. He said don't worry, just be calm about it. Understand that they are building up to knock you down, because they know you are an asset to me. That is all this is about. The *World at One* did 20 minutes on me, Kim Howells[2] doing a good job. Because he had nothing else to do, William Hague stepped in. I got a stack of calls of support, which meant it was out there big time. Skinner called and said it was absolutely right that I bollock ministers like Frank and Harriet where they were not up to the mark. Tam Dalyell called to say I should not have bollocked ministers in my own name. Bernard Ingham was all over the place saying how awful I was telling ministers what to do. Philip said in the focus groups I was 'out there' with Peter as an issue. TV and radio were going mad,

[1] Among the issues it was to consider were the 'boundary between effective presentation and party political advocacy', and the 'special treatment' of some journalists.
[2] Minister for Lifelong Learning at the Department for Education and Employment.

March '98: Campbell becomes the story

political journalists interviewing each other about their feelings about me.

Wednesday, April 1

Alan Clark, who always managed to cheer me up, was the first call of the day. He said he was really pissed off he hadn't got more coverage for his comments supporting me. He said the whips were giving him a hard time but fuck it, I was his friend, I was under attack and the Tories needed to know they would get nowhere with it. The cartoonists were into me as well now. TB said he didn't fear them coming at him about me, but about the relationship with Murdoch. And he didn't fancy a sustained set of questions about whether Murdoch lobbied him.

Monday, April 6

TB called me into his meeting with Robin, talking over his wedding. TB was worried he was becoming a devalued figure because of the Gaynor stuff. We said it would be better if he could do it quietly. I told Robin that he was being panned in focus groups, because they felt he was vile to Margaret. He said they would like to get married privately but if you got a register office licence for a private residence there had to be unfettered access for the public. We suggested he get a quick marriage and do it privately and he agreed to do that but was clearly not sure he could do it. He looked very down. TB said all I care about is that we have a Foreign Secretary back and not some extra in a soap opera, which is what the press are trying to do with you. I couldn't agree more, said Robin.

Tuesday, April 7

Mitchell finally tabled his paper around midnight and though it didn't leak, it was clear there were going to be problems. TB was furious when he came down from the flat because he felt both Mitchell and the NIO had not handled the UUs properly. He said they didn't understand how, because the Irish government had such a close relationship to the SDLP, we had to give the UUs the sense that we were there for them, at least keeping an eye on things from their perspective, even when we were pushing them in a certain direction. I was still having to deal with Robin and his bloody wedding. He had established that he could get it done this week but was still going on about photos, and some kind of photocall on Friday. He then called me about whether his bloody mother should go. His judgement on this was becoming awful. We left around 3.30 and I briefed Denis Murray and John Irvine [BBC's and ITV's Ireland correspondents] from the car. On the plane we went through the paper in some detail and it was obvious what Trimble's problem was. The areas for cooperation were too numerous and too all-encompassing. TB was a bit fed up with it because he and Bertie had not actually negotiated all this, but Mitchell insisted it was all in there. He had been angry with DT before, but felt he had a point here. He discussed plans for a doorstep on arrival at Hillsborough [official residence of the Secretary of State for Northern Ireland], and I drafted a few lines. But he pretty much did his own thing. This is not a time for sound bites but I feel the hand of history upon my shoulder. Hell of a sound bite. The press loved it. DT arrived at Hillsborough and was perfectly friendly but a bit detached, as though this was all happening around him but was not directly in his control or even relevant to him. It was his coping mechanism, one I had noticed before, that he was almost like a commentator, but then something would spark him into seeing the total absolute relevance to himself and his situation, and his temper would go, and the face would go puce. Tonight he was calm and lucid, and said simply – and repeatedly – that he could not do a deal on this basis. TB said effectively that he would negotiate for him. We were not going to get the UUs signed up to this as it was. Mo seemed a little peeved that TB and Bertie were taking it over, but this was inevitable. I went in to see TB as he was getting ready for bed. He said his gut feeling was very negative. He couldn't see how to fill the gaps. Adams had been pushing for another meeting. The SDLP had been on, saying we must not give in to blackmail.

Wednesday, April 8

I got a message to go and see TB before I was even up. He was in the bath, and said he was worried. I knew he was worried anyway because he was playing the fool the whole time, putting on a thick Irish accent, pretending he was a newsreader announcing that Cherie was going to become a Protestant and he was going to speak with an Irish accent as part of a deal to secure peace in NI. Bertie's mum had died and he was coming up for breakfast before then going back for the funeral. TB said what was important was to get Trimble pointing in a more positive direction. He said my task for the day was to get DT out there being more positive than the neanderthals, who were doing most of the media and pushing the worst-case scenario for the UUs. Paddy Teahon [senior adviser to Ahern] said Trimble was asking for the Holy Trinity to be replaced by the Almighty God in the Irish Constitution. Even Bertie managed a laugh. Bertie said if he was exposed to either of them too much today, he would be worried he would end up thumping them. At Stormont, TB was having to see all the parties regularly just to keep them on board but the focus was DT. He came in on his own just after lunch and this time TB really tried all the charm and the cajoling and DT was moving, but then moved right back again. We were also a bit stuck without Bertie but he came back around 6.30, looking even more knackered than before. I felt really sorry for him. It was obvious the way he talked about her that he was close to his mother, and she was barely buried and he was back taking a whole load of grief from the UUs. They talked to him, and about him, with something close to contempt, and it was terrific the way he took it. I did a reasonably optimistic briefing and then afterwards came the key meeting of the day, with TB, BA and the UUs, at which Trimble and, more implausibly, John Taylor suddenly signalled they were ready to do a deal. Bertie started, speaking very quietly, said it would be a great tragedy if we could not reach a deal now. Joe Lennon [press secretary to Ahern] scribbled me a note saying DT had too many enemies for this to work, but the mood was fine. It was when Taylor suddenly piped up – 'There is room for manoeuvre here' – that we thought there was a sign of change. Bertie had said before he would walk out if he started up on his usual record. He said he couldn't be arsed listening to it all again. But this time Taylor was significantly different. It was the first time he had ever been anything remotely approaching positive. It was a big turnaround and they agreed to go away and sort it with their people. It cheered us up no end, because we had been half expecting the opposite, but something had clearly happened in their discussions to trigger a switch. After the main trilateral, we had a long session with Adams and McGuinness and later with Adams alone. They were both very charming in their own way, also very clever, and always making points at various levels. I liked McG better of the two. Whatever he had done in the past, there was a directness to him that I liked and he was driven by the genuine sense of grievance about the way people were forced to live. I guess Adams is too, but he also strikes me as more interested in his own place in the firmament, more a politician than a people's person.

TB and I went for a walk out in the freezing cold. We didn't want to be seen so just found this little garden and walked round for a few minutes. 'This is like prison exercise,' said TB. But he had perked up. 'Do you think we can do this? It would be amazing if we pull this off. I think we can pull it off, I really do.' DT came to see us again, and said he had a UU solution that he thought would do the trick.

We went down to the Irish Office and TB tried it on Bertie, who was very gloomy. We bumped into Mitchell on the way back and he looked pretty fed up too. He said he felt we were living through a Greek tragedy. Maybe the UU shift had been bollocks. Also, TB was a bit spooked by Adams saying the shift on policing wasn't enough. He was very pissed off. 'They don't really want these implementation bodies at all,' said BA, who was really tired and gloomy by now. They want consent principle enshrined, an Assembly, the Irish constitutional claim on the North gone, and they want to give fuck all in return. We had been up and down all day, but were ending it very much down.

Thursday, April 9

Writing this on Saturday, back at home, just random thoughts really, with the main notes done as the discussions happened, and a real sense I was recording history. It was an extraordinary time, and felt like it. It showed TB at his infuriating best. Once he got the bit between the teeth, and decided to go for it, he always knew best, there was no one else could put a counter-view, he was like a man possessed. He would ask to see someone and then ten seconds later shout out 'Where the fuck are they? I need them here NOW.' He would pace up and down, go over all the various parts of the analysis, work out who was likely to be saying what next, work out our own next move. We had room for the usual black humour in there. Jonathan was putting on weight and I christened him 'five bellies',[1] which stuck, and whenever TB was in need of a laugh he would put on a Geordie accent and ask 'five bellies' to get him a cup of tea and some pork scratchings. As the days wore on, he started to take on a grey-green tinge, and looked exhausted, but he was brilliant throughout. Mo did a great job keeping people's spirits up. She and I took it on ourselves to keep a bit of humour going through the proceedings. Even though it got on her nerves that she was largely kept out of the TB discussions with Trimble, because DT didn't really want her involved, she didn't allow it to get her down. One of the cameramen said he picked up Mo saying something she shouldn't – Maginnis and the Irish being in a paddy – so he suggested we do it again and wiped the tape. He had also caught her belching on tape, something she did rather too often for most people's taste. The midnight deadline we had set just came and went without people really being bothered. TB said how

[1] A reference to footballer Paul Gascoigne's rotund friend Jimmy 'five bellies' Gardner.

bad is this if we fail? I did the better to have tried bollocks, but truth be told it would be bad to come this far and fall at what now felt like the last. Come the early hours we started to feel that it was going to fall into place, but none of us quite knew how. There were lots of ups and downs but the mood most of the time felt doable. Nonetheless he asked me to sit down and work out an exit strategy. It would have to be based on the idea of returning for intensive talks. Mo came in and had us falling about with the story of Plum Smith [of the Progressive Unionist Party] asking whether he would get out in two years if he went in and wiped out Trimble. So the black humour was all around us.

TB at breakfast not very optimistic, and convinced maybe we should have kept going last night to get the thing done. When Bertie arrived we were straight back to could we get Strand 2 agreed or not. Trimble had said he was ready to compromise and do a deal but Bertie was pretty sceptical, said I'm not sure I trust these guys. North–South bodies, police and decommissioning were going to be the toughest areas.

1.05pm, TB ranting and raving because he wanted to see BA, who was locked in discussions in the SDLP office. His problem was he wanted everyone to work at our pace and to our agenda. E.g. there were times he was suspicious of Joe Lennon giving Bertie the wrong advice, but I pointed out the BBC ran a dire package for the Irish, full of vox pops saying they had to keep articles 2 and 3 of the constitution. When the Irish came in, I suggested to TB that he 'turn off the charm tap' and he start to get a bit heavier. The problem was they wanted clear Westminster legislation to set up implementation bodies; otherwise, said Paddy Teahon, it would be just like Sunningdale,[1] built on sand, all too easily collapsible. Bertie said on the one hand they are expected to change their constitution – to give up the claim to the North effectively – and yet there is no 'on the other hand' of equal clarity. Bertie said he saw them last night and he knows they will use every trick in the book to stop the N–S bodies happening. We went round in circles. By prior arrangement, TB asked me what the reaction would be if we didn't do a deal. I said Bertie would be crucified. 'They think the other lot are mad anyway, but they think you guys are sane so it would be you that gets crucified if we fall apart over this.' Decommissioning was still a problem. Next

[1] An agreement (signed in 1973 at Sunningdale) between the UK, the Republic of Ireland, and the UUP, the SDLP and the Alliance Party of NI to set up a Council of Ireland.

meeting was DT and Taylor and we had an interminable discussion about N–S bodies, what areas, what they would actually do. TB called up Bertie for a meeting, during which Siobhan O'H came round for a chat. More gallows humour, Jonathan said we'd better get rid of the Taoiseach (meaning finish the meeting). SO'H: 'You don't need to get rid of him.' Jonathan: 'I didn't mean it in your sense of the word.' George Mitchell came in and said he had a document ready for tabling pretty quickly but now Trimble was away with his executive for 2 hours. Mitchell wanted to give them half an hour to read it and then have a plenary. He said to TB the difference he had made was in forcing the pace through deadlines. Major would never put a deadline, which meant they would keep us here for ten years if they could.

5.55 Adams, McGuinness, O'Hanlan. In to do some more chiselling. They were not happy. All the big concessions had gone to the Unionists. A changed Irish constitution. NI Assembly. Right to veto implementation bodies. McGuinness said what can we point to? TB said changes to UK constitution, nationalist identity recognised, implementation bodies, changes to policing, prisoners, equality agenda. And he said everything was protected by mutually assured destruction. If the Assembly failed, the whole thing failed. If the implementation bodies didn't happen, the Assembly falls. Adams said the UUs were the perceived winners and them the perceived losers. TB said they had to get over this thing with the spin on it, as if it was a zero-sum game. Everyone could win, but everyone had to compromise. He said 'I've got blood out of a stone from the Unionists, and the points you're making are not persuasive.' Paddy Teahon put his head round the door and said the SDLP were going wobbly. TB said in the past 48 hours I've been wondering whether I understand politics at all. Sinn Fein went away then came back, no doubt influenced by *Channel 4 News*, which had too much of the pro-UU spin, and said they would not be able to sell the document as it was. They could not accept the Unionist veto on the implementation bodies. Policing was also a problem. TB said 'I don't accept you can't sell this. This is a programme for change and a lot of the change is to the benefit of your community.' GA said he was a British Prime Minister speaking. Their audience didn't listen to British Prime Ministers. TB's voice was rising as Adams's was getting softer. We have dealt with decommissioning on your terms. We did Bloody Sunday – Mo: 'And we applauded you.' TB: 'I appreciate the pressures on you, believe me I do, but this is fundamental change and you would be mad to turn away from it – N–S bodies, consent, new policing, prisoners, equality.' GA said we want to do the best for our people, to end the conflict with hope. TB: 'I cannot tell you how difficult this has been. If you pull out of this now, I don't know where that leaves us.' After they left, Jonathan, optimistic as ever, said it was just a good cop bad cop routine to drag a bit more out of us. TB was downcast, said he felt they weren't able to get it through their heavies and they were going to fall off the end. 'You have to remember they are negotiating with at least a modicum of worry someone will come along and blow their brains out if they go too far.'

7.30 SDLP, Hume worried about the feasibility studies re N–S bodies. No, no, said TB, it means the six bodies will be set up by the time of the Assembly. He gave them the same line re mutually assured destruction but they were not convinced. TB asked me to get out a briefing for the later bulletins that there is a battle between an irresistible force and an immovable object. 'The irresistible force is the legacy and the baggage. The immovable object is me.' Seamus Mallon had a good line. 'Enough is never enough for those who think that enough is too little.' I said get Clinton engaged. TB – To say what? To tell them nobody will understand if they walk away over this. TB said we weren't cooked enough yet. 'They're deciding everything according to the spin of the others. It's pathetic. Yesterday the Nationalists' tails were up. Why? Because the UUs were going round with long faces and saying everyone was against them. Today, one good headline in the *Belfast Telegraph* for Trimble and the other lot are going round like the world has ended. It's ludicrous.'

8pm I drafted an exit strategy, two notes, one from TB, one from Mitchell, saying how far we had come and how we would come back to it soon.

8.10 Trimble, Taylor, Reg Empey [Vice President of the UUP]. They were in better mood, which John [Holmes] rightly took as a bad sign, because the other lot would be falling off the end. Rumours started of another DT triumph – Assembly to decide the implementation bodies, and it was running far too much in their favour. I got in Mike Brunson and Denis Murray and for the third time in a day did a very greenified briefing, stressing the implementation bodies could be up and running at the same time as the Assembly itself. I also reduced them to hysterics by saying, with a straight face, that they had to ignore the spin and just listen to me. All our problems today were really started by the headline in the *Belfast Telegraph*. The UUs reacted too positively and SF too negatively. It was just another fucking story in the end, I said to McGuiness. He said at one point to TB 'Believe me, this is not a threat, but they could return to violence.' Murray's reports were brilliant today, got the balance and the nuances and the little shifts. Bertie went off to a Mass, during which Paddy T came in with some more changes on Strand 2. 'No, no, I can't,' said TB. Bertie said he had to be sure SF were going to be on board. TB was worried Bertie was not getting enough out of the media stuff so I tried to correct it with Brunson, re the point about Westminster legislation, but he went OTT and said the UUs had made a massive concession to the Irish, so then we had a counter-problem with DT. I called Joe Lennon to make sure he had seen it, and make sure he understood we were trying to push the boat out for Bertie. He said SF were trying to persuade them the point about legislation is that it was a concession TO the UUs, not by them. It was like walking a connecting web of tightropes. I called Siobhan O'H and said we were trying our best to get the spin in the right place for them to do what they had to do.

10.30 TB very down again because they were all off doing their own thing. John Holmes had come back with a whole load more Strand 2 changes from the Irish. He had a list of 20 implementation bodies they wanted. John lay down on the sofa, just shaking his head. TB: 'I've been wasting my time.' John said it has all been about keeping SF on board. TB said they will push the UUs off board again.

10.40 Bertie and Mo came in to go through the list. TB just listened, pretty stony-faced. Again, we had the odd light moment to help us through. An Irish official called Wally came in and said we should remove food safety from the list 'because the Irish government is not quite ready for it'. Bertie: 'We are going to poison everyone instead.' TB sat shaking his head with his arms folded as we went through them one by one. Arts. It's out. Language. They won't wear that. Paddy suddenly piped up. 'It's all quite simple. 1. Get Strand 1 sorted. 2. Do the deal with Trimble on Strand 2. 3. Get Clinton to force Sinn Fein into line.' TB just sighed and looked like he wanted to curl up into a ball. John H was almost asleep on the sofa. Jonathan was still smiling. Nick Matthews was in and out with food and drink. After they left, TB just said 'Fuck, fuck, fuck.'

11.28 DT came back. John Taylor was with him and rather cheerily announced there was a new death threat out against him. They had had a good meeting with the SDLP and felt we could make progress. Again we had to listen to the minutest detail of the smallest ideas for the bodies we were talking about. But at least the mood was better. They left at 11.50 and TB and I fell into hysterics again, putting on our best Irish accents and wondering what new bodies we could come up with – the waste-paper bin emptying body, the screwing tops off bottles body. They had been banging on about closing the Maryfield office block[1], and I set TB off, saying why has Scotland's rugby ground suddenly become a crucial part of the negotiations? It was all designed just to keep us going through the low moments, of which we sensed there were more to come as we got tired. Mo's private secretary, Ken Lindsay, called me and Jonathan out to tell us Paisley and 400 of his friends were in the grounds and marching to the press tent to be there at midnight. It would actually serve as a good media distraction for a while as the deadline passed. We called Clinton and asked him to be on standby to make calls to Adams and Hume and maybe DT.

Friday, April 10

12.15 John H and Jonathan met with Dermot Gallagher [Irish Diplomat] and Paddy Teahon and the Irish were saying they couldn't change a word of Strand 3. They were spooked by Sinn Fein. TB suggested a 4-way meeting with Bertie, DT and Hume. He now believed SF were pulling the plug because they didn't want a deal at all. They were holding the whole thing to ransom. Mo was trying to calm him down, but he was really aerated. GA has gone right down in my estimation.

12.30 TB spoke to Bertie. SF were stuck on three years for prisoner release. There was no way we could do a deal on prisoner release without SF being on board for the rest of it all. I suggested we make it clear prisoner release only applies to groups who are fully signed up to the deal.

1.10 DT and Taylor in to argue about the size of the Assembly.

1.45 Bertie plus his key officials, to discuss the weight of voting in Assembly. Mo said 18 x 6 plus a civic forum was fair and just. TB: 'We'd better reject it then.' Laughter. Joe Lennon: 'He's learning.' We were still arguing re Irish language.

2.15 Hume and Mallon re the size of the Assembly. TB asked Hume what SF were up to. He said it was all about prisoners. They basically want them out in one year, and think they will end up with two. TB said this can only be sold as a meaningful agreement if they are signed up to all of it.

2.30 David Ervine [PUP] et al. UUP were saying voting weight 18 x 5, Ervine 18 x 6. TB was suddenly worried that we had told Hume we were prepared to offer one year for prisoners. When he

---

[1] Maryfield, location of the Irish secretariat in Belfast, became an issue in the talks. Campbell thereafter referred to it as Murrayfield, Scotland's rugby ground.

told Bertie he had done it, he panicked a bit and got Hume back to say he was worried and, for now, forget he had said it. Mo was also of the view that we were giving away too much too soon. [Jeffrey] Donaldson was being pretty difficult about everything. TB asked me to go with him to see their people, and said I should interject at the right moment that they will be crucified if they suddenly throw in new problems now. George Mitchell said even for these guys, they were being ridiculous. I asked him if he intended to write a book about the talks. 'No, the truth would be too awful for words.'

3.10 TB finally said get Clinton.

3.15 UDP. Gary McMichael said they wanted 18 x 5 plus a top-up.

3.25 TB and DT, Trimble for once without his other people. TB had another go at getting the Irish-language promotion in and equality of treatment out. We had a long lecture about the history of Ullans, the Ulster-Scots language.

3.37 TB spoke to Clinton. 'Where are we?' asked Bill. TB said we had been going non-stop for three days. We were close to a deal, and had been for some time. The problem is every time we get close to a bottom line, a new one comes up. SF have an issue on prisoners, and on language. They want their prisoners out in a year. They want to put together a long list, which they just want to throw in at the last minute. They are playing silly buggers. They have suddenly come up with a new list of amendments days and days into the negotiations. He said he was worried they were getting nervous about doing a deal at all. Nothing has changed except the UUs are on board and when they're on board, SF feel they can't be. BC asked about the language issue and as TB tried to explain it to him, it was clear there was no way we could let this be a stumbling block. It was crazy. Bill asked if TB wanted him to call. TB suggested he call Bertie and emphasise the big changes they have won here. There is no way we can do the deal on prisoners unless SF sign up to the whole agreement. Our public opinion would rightly say what the hell is going on if we gave them that, and still they were not recommending the whole package. TB said the Irish and SDLP were happy. It was now about putting the pressure on SF. TB ran through the areas we had conceded on and it was a long list. But he still felt best to hold BC back from SF for now. Bill said there is nothing more important to me right now than this. Call me whenever, even if it means waking me up.

3.50 Clinton was ready to call Bertie. Paddy T was still pushing on language. For the first time, I detected Mo being pretty down, when she said she wasn't convinced they were serious. Adams was still holding out on some of the stuff they put in at the last minute. TB asked Mo to go and see him and tell GA he was 'staggered' at the way he was behaving. Paddy said there was no need, it was better we left the Taoiseach to deal with him.

4.10 John H called Sandy Berger and briefed him for the Clinton calls. John was worried that if the side letter to DT on decommissioning was leaked we would be accused of playing the Orange card.

TB decided not to see Adams. Nick Matthews came in with a huge plateload of bacon sandwiches. Mo was doing the toing and froing between GA, who was clearly pissed off TB was not doing it himself. Mo had six issues they were still concerned with. They wanted a department of equality. TB was eating bacon sandwiches and bananas, and beginning to look a bit grey.

4.18 TB–BC. Bill had made some calls and said it was time to move for it. He said Adams was nervous about being blamed for collapse. He was trying to squeeze down to 6 months. TB said we were always at two years. He said DT was 'really tight-assed'. He had slept so was rational. He had more energy. He was looking for something because he felt Adams had done better.

4.30 Another Clinton call: 'Hell, I'd rather be on holiday with Kenneth Starr than hanging out with these guys.' He said SF were moving to the deal, thought TB had done a great job, but we had to watch the UUs running away once GA said yes. TB called DT and said we have to do this now, otherwise it is going away. DT was in one of his distant modes, not really engaging. We had a problem when it seemed Donaldson was trying to engineer some kind of vote against DT but Trimble called and said he was going for it.

5am. John Hume in for a chat. He makes TB nervous re prisoners. After he's left, TB says he's worried how DT and Alderdice will react. Mo, now looking exhausted, said her officials were saying the prisoners deal would be really hard to get.

5.35 We agreed BC should call Adams, and we briefed he should set out how difficult the prisoners issue was, unless they signed up to the whole deal. Bill got the point straight away and was on the phone to him immediately. It felt, finally, like it was falling into place. We were now working with Bertie on Adams and McGuinness with the officials kept out. They finally left at 7.30. Mitchell McLoughlin [chairman of Sinn Fein] was being a bit more positive at the press briefing, and again the press got a sense we were going the right way. TB just about persuaded them on prisoners. Then Gerry read out another list of demands and TB laughed and said he was not prepared to negotiate any more. 'You are a compulsive negotiator, Gerry. This is a balanced package and you know it.' We then sat down to try and pin him down re his public reaction, which was going to be important. He was fine, if tricky. They said it was important I do my best to spin it positively for them, and said several times they would have to get it through their conference. McG was not saying much and I detected a little bit of anger directed at Bertie, but BA was brilliant at taking flak from the lot of them.

8.10 If you had to pin me down and ask me to explain how it suddenly came together, I couldn't, but I was in the press tent briefing that basically we had a done deal, that it was huge, historic, ginormous, all that stuff. I felt really quite emotional and had to hold myself together. I could see in some of the NI hacks too a real deep emotion, and a desire for this to be true. I actually felt like crying but held it together. The final TB–BA–GA–McG meetings were crucial and I did my best to spin for the Sinners without pushing the other lot too far off the other side. The whole thing nearly came unstuck over a fuck-up over the wretched implementation bodies, because by mistake the Irish-language promotion (Trimble's staff's fault) and export promotion (our fault) were back in the fucking list. We then had another history lesson from DT on the importance of Ullans. TB could not believe what he was hearing. I said why can't we just say it is promotion of Celtic languages? Because Ullans is not a Celtic tongue, said DT. We had effectively announced the deal was done, give or take a bit or two at the edges and here we were, with DT ready to unpick the whole thing over this. As we got into the helicopter Jonathan said the Queen wanted to talk to TB but we couldn't make the call pre take-off. TB thanked his staff for once, said everyone had been terrific and should be proud of what we had done. I got home, wired and exhausted, and still trying to remember how it all came together at the end.

Wednesday, April 15

Paisley was dominating the news all day with the launch of his No campaign. He still has the capacity to put over a point with real force, and he was not to be underestimated. At the moment he was on big picture, but there was detail he would get into as we went along.

Saturday, May 2

Holland. TB spoke to Chirac, who was totally against Duisenberg, said he could not countenance him in that ECB job without a specific date

Leaders at Blair's first G8, Denver, June 1997, included Helmut Kohl,
Boris Yeltsin, Bill Clinton and Jacques Chirac

Clinton addressed the Cabinet in Downing Street in 1997 then sent this jokey note
offering to swap Campbell with his own press secretary

Leading in Europe:
Germany's Helmut Kohl and
President Chirac of France (right)
opt out of the EU leaders'
bike race, as the Young
Pretender roars off to win

Blair shares a joke with Noel Gallagher
after his initial alarm that the Oasis star
been invited to a No 10 reception

The handover of Hong Kong, June 30,
1997, and China's President Jiang Zemin
was more comfortable with the idea than
Prince Charles and Tony Blair

‘The People’s Princess’

The Queen broadcasts to the nation, September 5, 1997, seeking to calm the growing anger at royal handling of Diana’s death

The end of an extraordinary week planning the funeral of Princess Diana. Right to the last, it was uncertain whether the four Princes – (left to right) Philip, William, Harry and Charles – would join Charles Spencer (centre) in walking behind the gun carriage

A historic moment: Gerry Adams and Martin McGuinness lead the first ever Sinn Fein delegation to Downing Street December 1997. When John Major was No 10, the IRA landed a mortar on the

Three very different personalities in the for peace – David Trimble, Tony Blair Mo Mowlam

Yet another flight from Belfast after yet another negotiation. Campbell is wearing Mo Mowlam's wig, which she regularly removed in meetings

A warm greeting from Blair for Bertie Ahern. The two leaders worked tirelessly on the Northern Ireland peace process. During the Good Friday Agreement talks, Ahern had to leave at one point for his mother's funeral. Hence the black tie

Gladhanding
at the G8 in
[B]irmingham 1998

[Fe]bruary 1998, the Clintons made an
[eno]rmous effort to ensure Blair's first
[vi]sit to the White House as Prime
[Min]ister was a success. Elton John and
[Stevie] Wonder provided the entertainment

[A]bove right, Clinton and Monica
[Le]winsky in a TV grab of a White
[Ho]use lawn party. The scandal came
[close] to bringing him down but his own
[res]ilience and the support of others
ensured his political survival

Clinton visited Omagh with
Blair to offer support after the
bombing in September 1998

26 June 1998: TV of Campbell's first appearance before a Parliamentary committee, investi charges of politici the Government Information Servi

A real Tory toff: Campbell worked with Viscount Cranborne on a deal to reform the House of Lords, the Tory peer acting at odds with his leader William Hague's position

Peter Mandelson leaving the home he bought with the help of a loan from Geoffrey Robinson, which would lead to his first resignation from the Cabinet in 1998

lav president Slobodan Milosevic
ssing his nation on television in
h 1999, as NATO was poised to
. His ethnic cleansing policy was
reversed by military action

Ethnic Albanian refugees wave at
lair's helicopter above Stenkovec
camp near Skopje, May 1999

nd Cherie listen to the stories of
s of Milosevic's policy of ethnic
ng. His visit to the refugee camps
Blair's zeal for action even more

Some light relief was provided when Manchester United lifted the Champions League Trophy to win a historic Treble in May 1999. Campbell had the task of telling his friend Alex Ferguson, the team manager, that the Cabinet Secretary wanted to rush him immediately into the next honours list for a knighthood

NATO Secretary General Javier Solana General Wesley Clark, Supreme Allie Commander Europe. Campbell was aske Clinton and Blair to 'fix' NATO's comn cations during the Kosovo conflict

Millennium Eve at the Dome, and everyone was trying hard to enjoy it

for his departure. TB said later he couldn't believe he would kibosh the whole thing over this. It sent a dreadful message to the markets around the world. Chirac was a big character and a big showman. We set off for Brussels. TB wanted to see Kohl on his own, which he did, but at the expense of deeply pissing off Chirac waiting outside, who then stormed off. It was going to be a fraught day. The issue was basically how long Duisenberg stayed in place. Chirac insisted it was clear he was gone by 2002 and Trichet gets it. Chirac was so contemptuous of Duisenberg. 'Who is this man who says we must waste all this time talking about a few weeks longer he stays in the job?' Kok said the Bank's credibility depended on Duisenberg being able to set the time himself. He then turned on Chirac: 'You say who is this man? He is not someone who just turned up off the street, you know.' Chirac did one of his 'boeuf' snorts. Kohl stepped in. 'I don't like the tone of this conversation. I'm assured this is a man of quality and honour. It is important we discuss this honourably.' He said we risk creating a terrible impression. Chirac did not change his demeanour. He said we learned about Duisenberg through the press and I will not be treated like that. He said they had already accepted the Bank would be in Frankfurt. TB said 'This is not very productive.' Chirac said 'Nor dignified.' He said to TB: 'You are a very clear and precise person. This is a not a clear and precise process.' Chirac said Duisenberg must agree to 1.1.2002 'as a matter of dignity'. This was going in circles. TB then saw Duisenberg on his own for 20 minutes. Chirac was getting more and more up himself. 'A mere civil servant is keeping 15 heads of state and government waiting for hours and hours. This is a mad situation. Do you think Churchill or Queen Victoria would wait for someone like this?' Through the day, Duisenberg's position strengthened as Chirac's weakened. TB asked WD to speak to the leaders, and explain his case, and the mood was dire. He said he was honoured to be appointed, but added a man of his age would not want to serve the full term. It just about worked as a formula. TB emphasised it was our decision. WD said it was a decision made of his own free will. I reckoned TB had had some 20 or so really tough meetings, the toughest and longest of which had been Kohl–Chirac, but we got there in the end.

Sunday, May 10

GB was on *Frost*. I suggested he really push to get up the NI economic package as a broadcast story. GB said it would be more than £100m. He was also asked about the Routledge book and for the first time he said there was no deal and we reached the right decision when

TB became leader. It was a good strong interview for all kinds of reasons – good on general message, good on personal, and he did the NI stuff really well. The Irish government had let out the Balcombe Street gang[1] for 48 hours and they got a heroes' welcome, while Mo had let out four as well, including the IRA leader in the Maze. The sight of Adams and McGuinness out with the Balcombe St gang was awful, even if the overall effect was 'The war is over'. But their refusal to say it was a continuing problem.

Monday, May 11

Ireland was a disaster area. A combination of the Balcombe Street gang plus the IRA leaders out of the Maze was about as bad as it could get for the strategy we were trying to pursue. Mo had let the Maze guys out without us knowing, which was ridiculous. It was a side favour Mo did for Adams, I suspect, but it was disasterville for the Unionist votes we were after. David Kerr [Trimble's spokesman] called from Trimble's office. Even though DT could be very old-womany, he had a point when he said this was as bad a move as we could have made. It had prisoners, past outrages, SF confidence and two fingers to the rest of you all wrapped up in one. Mo was not nearly sensitive enough to the UU side of things, because she found DT irritating. But this showed a lack of judgement, also evident on the *Today* programme when she made a crack about how people were let out if their granny died, and that this had been necessary to get the vote up for the Agreement. TB was livid all round.

Wednesday, May 13

I started the day in a foul mood and it got worse as the day went on. The lobby worked themselves into a mini-frenzy re a story in *The Times* that Prince Philip had opposed the Order of the Garter for the Emperor of Japan. I spoke to Robert Fellowes and agreed a robust denial. At the 11, I gave the line and they kept coming at me on it and I got totally fed up with it and started really going at them. I could see Godric and Hilary out of the corner of my eye trying to get me to slow down but I was in total 'fuck it' mode. I went for Liam Halligan [FT political correspondent], totally over the top, was horrible to Patrick Wintour – so horrible I later apologised – then took a pop at George Jones [*Daily Telegraph*]. Robin Oakley said on a point of order that I was there to answer questions. I said I was there to answer questions

---

[1] Martin O'Connell, Eddie Butler, Harry Duggan and Hugh Doherty had terrorised London for two years in the mid-1970s.

as I saw fit and if they didn't like the answers, tough. One or two tried to talk to me as I left but I couldn't be bothered with them. Don Macintyre [*Independent*] took me for a cup of tea and said I had to calm down. I said I was sick of dealing with wankers. Why should I pretend to respect them when I didn't? There were only half a dozen I would give the time of day to if I didn't have to see them every day. I told him the politicians were getting on my nerves too, and I was thinking of quitting. It was the first time I had articulated that. I had a cup of tea with Betty Boothroyd [Speaker of the House of Commons] up in her residence. She was really nice, said she was very pro me, and not to worry about all the MPs who were having a go, they were basically doing it because I was good at my job. She advised me to play a very straight bat when I appeared at the PASC. I couldn't really get a feel for her take on TB. I got the sense she was being as nice to me as she was because she basically thought I was more old Labour than TB. It was a really nice meeting though, and I felt my batteries a bit recharged. She had been very nice about what she saw as my role in getting us elected and I suppose I should always hang on to that when the press and the politicians were getting me down.

Thursday, May 14

I woke up tired and fed up, and wishing I could just stay in bed and tell the whole lot of them to fuck off. I knew I had screwed up yesterday. I had gone totally over the top and was now beating myself up. I did real damage to my own relations with the media yesterday. Most of them I didn't care about, but I actually lost it with some of the good guys too, which was just daft. I knew I could recover it, but it would take time and it would take energy I could be putting elsewhere. I hated making daft mistakes like that, and letting my mood drive me to make them. I went to see TB in the flat. He said he was worried I was exhausted and I would make mistakes and I had to get more support, and have the odd day off. I said every time I tried to take a day off, he created a stack of work.

Friday, May 15

Birmingham. G8 summit and the Heads' dinner. The row over dinner was whether to 'deplore' or 'condemn' the nuclear tests. Yeltsin and Chirac – the latter loudly, and the former barely making sense – were arguing for a softer line. Clinton's people were worried he would take a big hit if they were too soft. The dinner was almost comic though. Chirac was at his most Chiracian, grand gestures, saying '*la France*' when he meant 'I', generally huffy if anyone disagreed; Boris was laughing loudly when nothing had been said; TB looked over at one point and mouthed the word 'madhouse'. One of the advance people told me that some poor sod had removed the stamens out of two and a half tons of flowers because of Clinton's allergy. I told Bill, who said it was bullshit. 'Everywhere I go this happens and it's bullshit. It's got into one of those State Department notes and it's wrong.'

TB was totally obsessing re Ireland, said we had to have story after story after story to keep the momentum going our way. I asked BC if he would do *Frost* with TB. He said he would do anything we thought would help. I said it would. 'You decide,' he said, 'I'll do whatever you want.' Jim Steinberg again looked a bit antsy at my just asking BC straight up to do stuff, but I said a big joint interview on Ireland would help ease his worry about BC being whacked too hard on India. I called to tell Frost and Barney Jones, who were orgasmic at the thought. Back at the hotel I put together a briefing note on India, Indonesia, MEPP and Kosovo, taking in the main points out of the dinner. I suddenly felt tired, deflated and depressed again. It was probably just overwork. Clinton cheered me up a lot, because he was such a laugh just to chat with, and a real pro to work with. Mo threw a wobbly because we were pursuing the prison medal[1] from Number 10 not NIO.

Saturday, May 16

G8. We set off for Weston Park, which was a lovely house in a beautiful setting, and just right for the more relaxed atmosphere we were trying to get. The Japanese were in a bit of a state over the *Mail* story which said the Emperor would express regret over the PoWs issue [see note on p. 271]. Nishimura [Japanese government senior official] said this was for the Emperor alone to say and it would cause problems if this kind of media coverage gathered pace. I drafted a line with Philip Barton [private secretary to Blair] which we gave out to PA. We were talking to [Ryutaro] Hashimoto about it as TB was writing a Good Luck letter to Newcastle for the Cup Final and, bizarrely, Hashimoto said he would like to do one too. So I was sitting there with the Japanese Prime Minister translating his hieroglyphics on a Number 10-headed piece of paper to send to the Newcastle dressing room. God knows what Kenny Dalglish [Newcastle United manager] would make of it. In the break, TB regaled us with stories from last

[1] A medal was to be issued to recognise the services of members of the Northern Ireland Prison Service.

May '98: The vexed question of Japanese PoWs

night. He said at one point it was like being in bedlam, with interpreters getting more and more unable to cope. Yeltsin was shouting and yet had a quietly spoken interpreter. Chirac had an interpreter who was louder than Yeltsin. Clinton just giggled and Kohl looked pained. TB was now worrying the Hashimoto letter would look like a stunt by us and piss off Londoners. We then heard there was a panic on because Clinton and [Jean] Chrétien [Prime Minister of Canada] had escaped the Secret Service and gone off somewhere and been spotted climbing a fence together.

Sunday, May 17

It was interesting to watch BC around the place. Of all of them, he was the one with the most natural empathy with e.g. the stewards and waiters etc, and it was that basic human touch allied to his intellect and communications skills that made him the ultimate modern politician in many ways. I started to wind up TB about how much better BC was as a communicator. They did a bit on the Millennium Bug, then Indonesia, then Boris suddenly made a passionate plea for it to be renamed the G8 in 2000 'as a personal favour to me'. Nobody seemed to know how to react, but TB made positive noises then wound everything up. Bill C was saying how he would like to go up in a hot-air balloon fuelled by all the discussions at summits. 'Hey, we could stay up there for days.' On the way out of the hotel one of the hotel staff had asked if I could help her to meet Clinton. I arranged for her to be in the lift. She was a little old West Indian woman and by the time we hit the ground floor, he had her whole life story out of her. She practically collapsed as he left the lift and later we heard she had been in tears for hours, moved to bits.

Tuesday, May 19

Geneva, for the WTO [World Trade Organisation] meeting. We had the briefest of meetings with [Fidel] Castro [Cuban Leader]. TB just bumped into him, literally, and they found themselves standing toe to toe, shaking hands, and not a photographer in sight. He was taller than I imagined, also looked older but had a wicked smile. He said he admired TB and he had read all the third-way speeches.

Wednesday, May 20

I had the idea of a series of handwritten pledges which we would put up as a poster backdrop when he spoke in Northern Ireland. I called the NIO to get an ad van and agency on standby while John [Holmes] and I worked on the wordings. TB was not totally sure about it, and said the wordings had to be very, very careful. TB sat with Hague on the plane and they mainly talked Ireland, Europe, Chirac. Hague was very proper in these circumstances, always called him Prime Minister, didn't push too hard, listened and then spoke briefly.

Thursday, May 28

Peter M said he thought I was fed up because I had a proper job and as one of the few people capable of making decisions, I was being leaned on by everyone. He said he was fed up because he didn't have a proper job and as one of the few people capable of making decisions, he was not being asked to make any.

Tuesday, June 2

We left for Belfast in the smallest and most uncomfortable plane the RAF could provide, the 146 having been taken off us to take Prince Charles somewhere. It was noisy, both of us did our necks trying to get in and drinking without spilling was virtually impossible. We headed for Parliament buildings, did a big doorstep, where it became apparent there was no clear narrative for the day. As the meetings went on, the marching season was the main concern for most of them. Sinn Fein turned up with a couple we had not seen before, introduced by Adams as from a residents' association. One of the security guys told me they were in fact fairly high up the IRA ladder, so do not be taken in by the label. TB seemed to have the measure of them early on. John Hume had made the point SF could pretty much turn the violence on and off like a tap, and Adams virtually admitted as much when he said he thought they could calm it if TB managed to get them a meeting with Trimble. They also reminded TB of his exact words on one year and prisoners. DT was much more confident. He had Donaldson with him but was not deferring at all. He said the Parades Commission was damaged goods. Ian Paisley was missing from the DUP line-up because he was in Scotland, and there was a very funny moment when the fire alarm went off as TB was trying to persuade them re the principle of consent. 'It's a lie detector,' said Peter Robinson. TB laughed, glad to be able to stop talking under pressure when they clearly weren't buying it.

Thursday, June 4

At Cabinet, TB and George Robertson were making it pretty clear that intervention in Kosovo was an option. He said it was a classic Bosnia situation and we could not let it deteriorate. It was clear we had to start preparing the ground and I wrote a briefing note stepping up the possibility of military action. The FCO, in the form of Emyr Jones-Parry [deputy political director in the Foreign Office], were not keen. Several of the papers were claiming TB changed his accent for his Des O'Connor interview. What were they on?

Friday, June 5
Kosovo was definitely moving fast, and I adapted the briefing note I drafted last night with the view to giving it to the Sundays, drawing on what TB had said to the Cabinet, warning troops may have to be used. Jones-Parry said we were going for a new UNSCR, which the Russians would block, and we would end with the threat of air strikes, possibly strikes for real. TB was worrying re NI again. Far from moving to decommission, SF–IRA were looking for new arms the whole time. The meeting with [Romano] Prodi went fine, though he was hard to follow at times. There was a broad measure of agreement on the main agenda, and he seemed sound on Kosovo. Prodi went as far as saying he thought military action may now be inevitable. [Viktor] Klima [Austrian Chancellor] was in pretty much the same place on Kosovo when we landed in Vienna later.

Tuesday, June 9
The [Jean-Luc] Dehaene [Prime Minister of Belgium] meeting was long and dull and I became mesmerised by how often he said 'er'. At times he was doing it between every single word. The longest he went without a single er was nine words. There was no love lost between them. TB didn't like his manner, and of course Dehaene never forgave the Brits for blocking him for the top Europe job. Chirac was in pretty patronising mode the whole way through. 'Je ne sais pas si tu as apprécié ma lettre, mais elle mérite d'être appréciée, Tonee.' He said Europe was becoming unwieldy, and needed leadership, which meant Germany, France and Britain. If we all had the same dynamism, Europe is strong. TB said afterwards he could not help liking him. He was at times a rogue and could be full of bullshit but he had such natural charm and beneath it all there was a part of him laughing at the whole thing.

Thursday, June 10
Some silly story about the minimum wage and tips was leading the news. I got in and was working on a couple of briefings, one on post-Cabinet CSR [Comprehensive Spending Review], another pre-Cardiff, when Alison put a call through. She said Terry Tavener [friend] is on the line, and I don't know why but the second she

said it, I felt sure it was about Ellie. 'It's Ellie,' she said, and she was crying. 'She's dead.' It is so weird how people can sense these things. Alison had put through God knows how many calls but she knew as well, and came in and said are you all right, and I just collapsed in tears. At the hospital, I bumped into Terry in the corridor and we just collapsed again. There were a few kids running around, but around the main desk nurses were crying. A nurse stopped me and said she had just haemorrhaged and it was awful. I walked on and there was Lindsay, looking all cried out, but she started again, and as I hugged her she talked over the last bit in the minutest detail, and said she felt guilty she wasn't there when she finally went. She had gone home last night because she was finally to get a bed at last, and got a call at 9 to say come in because Ellie was ill. She got in to learn she was dead. Now she was worrying about Hope [her younger daughter] who was on her way to Cornwall and she had no way of contacting her. She wanted us to see the body, and I steeled myself. Fiona cracked though and then so did I. I so wanted John to be there now, because I had always had this feeling when he died that she changed and something dreadful was going to happen. She looked a little pained even now, the poor little darling. Her eyes were closed, her mouth a little bit open, her skin so fair but a bit puffy. Lindsay just sat there, stroking her hand and her hair, occasionally talking to her as though she could hear, then remembering, and crying again. I don't know how on earth she could cope this time. The hospital's priest was there, and really nice, and Father Anthony came in. The psychologist who was there to help Lindsay cope was a friend of Jonathan's. After a while we more or less managed to have a conversation, but by then I had that pain that follows crying, throat, eyes, chest, and also the feeling you were doing nothing useful. Lindsay decided she had to get to Hope and the only way to do it was to go there herself. We organised trains while I spoke to Geoff Lakeman [long-serving West Country reporter for the *Mirror*], asked him to meet her and look after her and try to find the place where Hope was staying. He was a real trooper, straight into it, dropped everything else. It was odd how someone like him, who had played a part in that period of our lives when we all met, should suddenly be involved like this. Then as we left the hospital, we bumped into David Hill of all people. People were really nice back at the office but of course life goes on and all that had happened after several hours out was that a stack more work had piled up. And of course suddenly you felt none of it mattered. I went over for GB's CSR statement, which went fine, and afterwards Ed Balls and I did a lower gallery briefing and I let him take the lead and just wanted to disappear now. One or two of them knew John, lots knew of him, but in the end what was it all? – another story they had to file, another briefing we had to do, and it all felt like total bollocks really. I was home by eight and talked to the boys, who couldn't really take it all in. Calum asked question upon question. Rory was just a bit quiet.

Wednesday, June 17

Richard Wilson was giving evidence to the Public Administration Select Committee inquiry into the GICS and he was fine. The only stuff making the news was hinting he was keeping an eye on me. He came to see me afterwards and I said what he had said was fine. He said he was trying to present a different image of me, make clear I'd done nothing wrong but obviously as head of the Civil Service he would keep an eye on me.

Monday, June 22

All the bollocks about my appearance at the GICS was really starting to crank up. At the 11, I could sense how excited some of them were about it. I spent a lot of the day just reading through all the briefing and the previous evidence. Peter M came over and said no bravura, just be very polite and charming and answer their questions thoughtfully. Bruce [Grocott] said just be yourself. Hilary said do not lose your temper. That was my only real worry, that one of the Tories really got under my skin and I lost it. I was also worried I might go over the top re the BBC. I stopped Bernard Ingham from coming into the street to be interviewed. Petty maybe, but why should I help the silly old fucker land one on me?

Tuesday, June 23

GICS select committee day and some of the Tories had successfully got up the notion that I should hand over tapes of my briefings. The build-up had been pretty steady and clearly the media were hoping for some big explosion. I had a lot of good-luck messages, including from David Davis [Conservative MP] who said his advice as a select committee chairman was just to stay cool. They will try to rile you, and you mustn't let them. You are cleverer than they are and the only hope they have is you either show contempt for them or you lose your rag. TB called me up to the flat. He said he hadn't realised how big this thing was being built up. He had much the same advice. Just stay calm, and be polite at all times. Be as greasy as you like. He said they would be more scared of me than I was of them because having built it up as an event they will want to have something out of it mediawise, whereas you do these kinds of events every day, just without cameras in. I called Richard Wilson to say I wanted to be able to do some politics, namely say the reason the Tories were obsessed with me was because they were in a state of denial about how they lost. I felt I needed at least something to be able to divide them politically and also hit back when the nasty boys started. RW was fine. Alison had put together a big folder for me, whittling down all the official briefing, but I was by now clear about the main lines, and memorising some of the big points I intended to put over. I avoided the press on the way out, got driven over and then went up to the committee corridor. There was a big crowd outside, loads of hacks, researchers, students, all the sketch writers who en masse always looked a sad little bunch, Routledge muttering something about me meeting my match. I said Christ, if you're here it's even more trivial than I thought. Tosser. The little shit Parris[1] was to my left with that perma-smirk on his face. Brunson was the other one out of the corner of my eye which I didn't mind. I made a mental note to block them all out. There was a strong element of it being showbiz and Rhodri[2] was loving the fact his committee was getting all this attention. Quite a few non-committee MPs came in. RM announced that there was a World Cup-style screen in an overflow room for those who had not been able to get in here. After a slow start I got into my stride quickly. I got all the points out I wanted to make and I didn't feel the Tories had worked through their questions rigorously. They were looking to get coverage for their questions rather than probe properly on the answers. They started up on 'psychological flaws' but then it fizzled. I was worried they would go at me re TB saying I attacked the Tories but I got round it with a joke about 'Campbell attacks Blair headline' and it went. They had one or two specifics I thought they would go on, but they didn't sustain a line of questioning and I was always able to bring it back to bigger points. Added to which I was thrown the odd full toss by our side. I was conscious of getting tired as it went on, but felt on a winning run. I damned Ingham with faint praise. It ended with an exchange about whether I supported England or Scotland. [David] Ruffley [Conservative MP for Bury St Edmunds] was the one they had expected to land a blow and he didn't really get near. I shafted him by pointing

[1] Matthew Parris, sketch writer for The Times.
[2] Rhodri Morgan MP, Chairman of the House of Commons Select Committee on Public Administration, 1997–99.

June '98: But all goes well

out the inconsistency in his argument – at one point my sin was doing too much with ministers, at another not enough. I was followed back to Number 10 by camera crews and photographers. The reaction back at the office was really positive, that I had done better than most ministers and mandarins do, but I was glad it was over. TB came back from his audience with the Queen and watched the *C4 News* coverage, which he felt was fine.

Wednesday, June 24
The 'media obsessed with itself' line was made flesh with the *Sun*'s attack on TB as 'the most dangerous man in Britain' running as the second news item on the BBC. These people were never happier than when talking about themselves. Newspaper attacks politician because he disagrees with their line on Europe – so fucking what. I bumped into Alan Clark, who was in mega-mischief mode, stirring against Hague. His other insight for the day was that I should use my select committee appearance as the basis for a pitch for the top job. 'Get yourself a safe seat now and you're the next man. Blair is the only one who could get near you.' And with that he roared off. John Birt [Director General of the BBC] said he had watched my appearance and I could have my own BBC show whenever I wanted. Even among my enemies the feedback from yesterday was pretty positive.

Wednesday, July 1
Got a nice letter from Betty [Boothroyd] on my select committee appearance. Today was the first day of the NI Assembly, which was a fantastic achievement, but with a tough backdrop now. TB then did two interviews on England going out of the World Cup, BBC then Sky, and came out with one of the worst soundbites in history – 'a mountain of courage and a molehill of luck'. Yuk. I was almost tempted to start a coughing fit in the hope they would have to do it again.

Thursday, July 2
Jeremy Paxman had written a letter to *The Times* having a go at my latest whack at the media, and revealed a pretty thin skin. The problem was every time I had a go, the media loved it because it was another excuse to wank on about themselves and how important they were, especially the big-name guys. TB told me to watch I didn't end up fighting too many fights on too many fronts. He said I was in a different position to him. He had protection, not least through people like me, but above all of course because of his position. But I was in a way more exposed and there were a lot of people desperate for me to fall,

and people who would help to push if the fall began. I said I understood that but you had to engage with these people, otherwise they would roll you over.

Friday, July 3

The media picked up on Jonathan being in Belfast. It was an irritant but of course the real downside was it would send Mo into a mini-meltdown. Trouble was TB just didn't think she had the skills needed to hold all the different sides of this together. He felt she just didn't understand how you had to deal with the UUs, and that to call the NIO civil servants 'a bunch of clods' – in front of some of them – was not very clever.

Tuesday, July 14

CSR day. TB and I were both still worried about spend spend spend, especially as Whelan was planning to accumulate the spending figures. TB met GB a.m. for a long meeting to finalise the statement. They were definitely working better at the moment. Both TB and I made suggested changes to the text, which he accepted straight away. He even asked before Cabinet if I could look at the final draft and write in any changes. I faxed them over and he called to say he had got them. It could be he was just looking to get me in the right frame of mind to push for him after the event. At Cabinet GB rattled through it all at pace, good figures on the surplus, debt–GDP ratio improving, interest rates by the end of the Parliament £15bn lower than we inherited. He said the main themes were investment for reform, money for modernisation. He said AD would be setting out an internal process of continuous scrutiny of spending. There would be tough efficiency targets. There would be an expansion of public-private partnerships. He set out the tough package on welfare reform, the new deal for communities, a pilot of Educational Maintenance Allowances, Sure Start. More money for the key public services but it had to be tied to reform. TB thanked them all for the cooperative approach, at which some of them – especially those who felt bounced – had a little look at each other or a shake of the head. He reiterated the key messages, especially money for modernisation. He said the Tories have opted out of the policy debate, but we still have to take on the difficult choices and explain them. He said we had to be emphasising the long term. We were being tough for these two years, laying the foundations and we had to set out that narrative clearly, be clear where it was all leading. There were strong political dividing lines that had to be laid out. Public spending can be good not bad. But people need to know where money is being spent, what it is delivering. We have to get definition out of this. After Cabinet I briefed some of the best lines out of it, and they were beginning finally to get a feel for the scale of what he was planning to announce. If anything, there was as much as in a Budget but because it was a new process, they were not quite onto the scale or the breadth yet. The official Treasury background papers, as ever, were detailed and impressive. So was GB in the House. He had real reach, and the thing hung together well. Our side liked it and the Tories did not respond well. They were totally wrong-footed by the sheer scale of it, the numbers, the number of issues covered, the changes being made. The only thing I found difficult, which I had spotted in advance and agreed the line with GB, was the fact that social security spending would rise in the third year. We had to work up an argument about spending on waste and investing in the fight v poverty.

Wednesday, July 15

We got a great press for the CSR, mainly on health and education but the big-picture narrative was there too. TB did half a dozen interviews, all of which were fine. We did a school visit, then a phone-in, and he warmed up as it went on. A nurse and a teacher gave him a really hard time and I felt he was a bit defensive and non-empathetic, but it was OK. We reckoned Hague would do welfare at PMQs, and he did. TB had all the figures, but it all ended up a bit statty and yahboo and we didn't get the big message booming through. It was a score draw, though TB did a very enjoyable splattering of Michael Fabricant [Conservative MP]. TB and GB wanted me to push the line that there was bad welfare spending and good welfare spending, we were dealing with one and expanding the other. There was a fair bit of TB–GB-ology in the papers, but TB seemed fine about it. We were definitely back in charge of the agenda for a while.

Monday, July 20

Re the reshuffle, TB was now thinking Jack Cunningham at the Cabinet Office, with Charlie F below him. He said if he pushed out four, with the prospect of another five next year, that was a pretty big reshuffle. I sensed he was getting cold feet re getting rid of Nick Brown, because of GB, and also because he didn't want Nick's organisational skills being run against him. He didn't really know what to do with Frank Dobson, but hadn't been impressed with how he had handled Health. He was thinking he should leave Steve Byers and Alan Milburn where they are. He wanted to give Field some kind of all-party welfare fraud job.

Philip had also said he was worried we were going a bit cold on welfare reform, which people really wanted to see. PG had done another poll in Scotland, which confirmed that TB and New Labour were what we needed there. TB popped round on his way up to the flat and ran through his current concerns – economy, GB/PM, reshuffle, CSR fallout, conference. He said conference had to be effectively a relaunch of New Labour. That was how we should be thinking over the holiday.

Thursday, July 23

Reshuffle meeting, where Anji was pressing for a much bigger reshuffle, but TB felt it was big enough already. He had settled on Harman out, Field out, though he was still thinking about giving him something outside government, which we were all against. The real discussion was how GB would take it, particularly the move on Nick Brown. We were pressing him to be bold but he said 'I'm just telling you there is a case to be cautious if it all ends up with GB offside.' TB said you have to remember we are co-creators of New Labour, and I do not want him offside. We have come this far together in part because of his nous and political skills and I want to keep them inside the operation. With PM and others in, and 4 out, you are talking a big reshuffle and I do not want a war with GB out of it. If we lose Geoffrey Robinson, Nigel Griffiths [Labour MP for Edinburgh South], Tom Clarke, Harriet H, and Nick Brown moved, the PLP will see it as a bit of a hit on GB. I do not want them to see it as an all-out attack. He was clearly dreading the day. I hate reshuffles, he said. You just have to steel yourself but they are horrible.

Sunday, July 26

The general response from the hacks re Jack C at the Cabinet Office was very positive. TB asked me to call Ann Taylor and ask her to be down by 4.30 to see him. I had done a detailed note on logistics and also on key messages, e.g. re women, TB strong centre, New Labour. It was a strong reshuffle and would be seen positively for TB but he was worried re GB's reaction, particularly the move for Nick Brown. JP called and asked if it was true re JC. I said yes. He said 'You're not expecting him to do much work, are you?' TB went to see GB at 8. I was called up at 8.45. TB was in the kitchen getting a drink so GB was sitting alone in the falling darkness in the study. He looked really gloomy, and said nothing. I tried a few pleasantries but he was not engaging. TB had just told him – Nick B moved, Geoffrey, Griffiths, Tom Clarke out, Ann Taylor chief whip. TB said how do we stop this reshuffle being seen as a blow to GB? I said it needn't be because there were enough big stories in here. The problem was less the reshuffle than the backdrop of the GB–Peter stuff. I said Charlie [Whelan] had made it worse by getting so involved in the pre-briefing, saying what GB did or did not want. TB said he and GB were getting on better but it still didn't come over like that. Again I said Charlie was the problem. GB didn't argue, but he was clearly worried the reshuffle would be portrayed as a big negative for him. We agreed TB should see Nick tonight and GB said he would work on him to accept it as a good move. He wasn't really arguing with the decisions, and even said he had reached pretty much the same conclusions, but he was worrying re his own place in this. He was pacing around the room, and picked up a bit as we went on, because he could at least see TB and I did not want to use it to do him down. TB also spoke to Peter M and said he wanted him to meet GB tonight and sort a few things out. He said if they did not work together he would have to take drastic action, because he was not prepared to let them bring the whole show down. He also agreed I could brief that he had told Peter he had to knuckle down and do a proper job properly. JP came in and we went through the junior ranks all over again. TB was now having a wobble re Harriet, said that it would seem really cruel given she had been basically loyal the whole way through. He wanted me to indicate she still maybe had a future. Likewise he wanted to be nice to Frank [Field] and try to avoid him attacking us in the *Mail* and the *Telegraph* every day. We were thinking of some grand think tank on fraud that he might be able to run.

Monday, July 27

I told GB I could not trust Charlie at all and he had to understand that and make a judgement about whether that mattered. He said the press liked him. I said that was because he was a rival source operating against the centre, so of course they liked him. I said even if Peter was at it, we weren't, and I wasn't, despite a lot of provocation. I said I protected him as much as anyone. He said Nick Brown was a victim of a phalanx of people telling TB he was a problem when in fact he had a lot of ability. NB had described himself as a 'victim of war', which was a bit dramatic. I said he was also a combatant. TB had been talking to Nick till 1am. He said he was hurt and disappointed that he was being moved from chief whip. He said he had stayed loyal. Went over to the House and managed to avoid the media. First in was Gavin [Strang], short and sweet, and he left with a smile which failed to hide the hurt. We then couldn't get hold of

David Clark, which held things up. When finally we did, he was reasonably fine about it. Then Harriet and TB thought it best I stay out of sight so I went into GB's Commons office till she was gone. He told her he liked and respected her but felt she needed a breather from the front line. She asked only two things – 1. that I didn't brief her down, and 2. that TB wrote to her kids to say she had done a good job. I respected her for that, but I couldn't pretend to feel we had lost a huge welfare reform talent. Then Ivor Richard, who left quickly and without looking at anyone. Trouble ahead, said Jonathan. Jack C was absolutely loving the attention. We agreed he should go wall-to-wall today. He said I want you to know I owe nothing to JP or GB, my loyalty is 100 per cent to Tony, and nobody else.

Saturday, August 15 (holiday, Flassan)

Wendy Abbs [Downing Street duty clerk] came through on the other line to say there had been a huge explosion in Omagh, 12 thought to be dead, the PM was just being told, having just arrived at the house in France. I asked her to fix a conference call with him and Philip Barton, who was manning the office as duty private secretary. PB had already done the basics you'd expect, but the details were all a bit patchy. As we spoke, reports were coming in that the death toll may be higher and all the holiday ease that had been in TB's voice at the start was gone. I said he would have to do TV straight away. There was a problem in that he had arrived ahead of his clothes and he was scruffily dressed. I asked which cops were with him, and he ended up using Bill Lloyd's suit and a shirt borrowed from one of the neighbours. We also had a conference call with John McFall, newly appointed NI minister, who was on duty. 'What a baptism,' said TB. It was clear John was nervous and I was worried he would hit the wrong note in extended interviews. For example, when I said what do you say if they ask if it harms the peace process, he said it's too early to say. I said we had to get over that the peace process is bigger than a group of fanatics who want to derail it. TB weighed in, saying we had to be making clear every peace process always faced disruption from people who wanted to destroy it. TB said this was the last resistance, and if we saw it off with public opinion there totally on our side, it could be another turning point. But how we react now will dictate that. It was pretty clear if the death toll was as bad as feared, he would have to break his holiday at some point, but I suggested for today JP went there. I spoke to JP, who said he

August '98: Omagh bombing

would do whatever we thought was required, and we fixed it for the afternoon. I said the line we wanted to push was that we would not let a small bunch of psychopaths disrupt the will of the majority. We also had to get SF up on the right side of the argument. I called McCurry, who was playing golf with his son, and said BC would be key in making the kind of noises SF would want to echo. PB called Berger and Steinberg to brief them and try to get Clinton engaged early. We had to pull out all the stops to make sure SF said the right thing. Adams was on holiday in Italy but announced he was coming back. McGuinness put out a very strong statement. TB said that what we had to engineer was a situation where people felt the IRA were isolated from these people, that they were seen as a rump, that there was now an internal battle between the democratic process and renegades. TB said there will be obstacles along the way but the forces of good have to prevail. He had got over the initial shock and was now working on next steps. After church TB got ready to go back and called from the car to go over the basic line – peace process can prevail, we can be stronger than these evil people, etc. TB went to the hospital and then met Trimble at Hillsborough. The scale of it was becoming clearer now and it had definitely been the right thing to go. Indeed I was worried Mo was going to take a hammering for still not being there, with the world waking up to the enormity of it. There was also the fear TB would look a bit cruel ducking out after a day or so. Prince Charles was due to go on Tuesday. At the moment the main focus was on the carnage.

Monday, August 17

Again, I didn't sleep too well. I was just dozing when TB called around 1am. He had been up till 12 with Trimble but the real reason for the call was he said he was deeply affected by the visit to the Belfast Royal. He described some of the scenes he saw, the wounds and the scars and the mutilated bodies, and all the human suffering around them. But basically they were all giving him the same message – keep going, don't give up, work for peace harder than ever. He said it was really humbling. TB said it was vital that we came up, whatever the legal hurdles, with a security package that gave people confidence we were on top of things. TB said he was not convinced these people had intended to do quite as much damage as they did, but I doubted that. They had totally set the agenda on their terms and in different ways made life difficult for every part of the political debate with the possible exception of Paisley. What was amazing was that even before I had told Fiona or anyone about the new security measures, Rory said to me 'Why don't you just pick up the top man on phone-tap material, then the other top people, and find excuses to keep them inside until you find all their weapons, then break the organisation?' At 5pm I listened in to a TB–Mo call. Mo read through the joint statement she planned with the Irish justice minister [John O'Donoghue]. It was wordy and woolly and with no specifics to drive things forward. TB said he wanted to see the police chiefs' ideas and then take half an hour to redraft and get back. I said to Mo the press can wait. Mo sounded like she always did when we were involved – pissed off and sullen, but the truth was it was a second-rate piece of work. Then another extraordinary conference call with him and Mo. The police chiefs want to leave, the justice minister wants to leave and they cannot renegotiate because Bertie is in a meeting in Dublin. TB was pretty firm with her. He said 'I'm very sorry, Mo, but I am going to have to press you and you are going to have to press them because the statement is not adequate. It needs a strong intro and it needs three specific areas that have to be addressed: 1. Proscription and a specific criminal offence. 2. Measures to make it easier to secure convictions. We do not need to go into detail here but people will know this is phone-tap material. 3. Specific operational measures, where there has to be a sense of detail. We then had the ludicrous situation of TB having to ask Mo for her fax number, and her shouting out 'Anyone out there who knows the fax number?' and then saying the officials had disappeared. It was the Mo manner that was fine when things didn't matter, but deeply irritating when they did. She sounded more and more exasperated. 'I'll say whatever you want, Tony,' she said, at which point TB exploded at her 'It is not a case of saying what I want. It is a case of doing the right thing and then explaining it to the public, who may have cause to be concerned about recent events.' She then lost the plot completely. 'You cannot do this to me. I'm sick of the long-distance control. You are making it impossible for me. I can't do it any more.' Well, you're going to have to, he said. Ronnie Flanagan [Chief Constable of the RUC] came on the line and was like a voice of reason and sanity. He did not sound like a man trying to charge out of the door. TB took him through some of the changes and he sounded fine. But Mo was getting near hysterical. TB said to her if you went out and read that statement as you read it to us earlier, you will be dead. I mean dead, totally out of the game. Nobody would take you seriously. She said 'I'd rather be dead than carrying on like this. I don't care any more.' TB said 'Yes you do, and that is why we do the extra bit to get it right.'

Tuesday, August 18

I listened by phone to Mo's doorstep, which was pretty grim stuff. She got the three areas for action mixed up and had to be rescued by O'Donoghue and she got muddled with the Irish on internment. She was clearly in a bit of a state. Then I learned she wanted to resume her holiday tomorrow, which would be a disaster area for her locally. TB called, having been told by Mo that her statement went fine. 'It was tough but I did it.' I told him what actually happened, that she had got things in the wrong order and did not even get out the line that PIRA [Provisional IRA] were not involved. He said 'You are going to have to take charge of this, and do a lot of one-on-one briefings.' I was genuinely worried about Mo, and what she might be saying. She said she wanted to go back to Greece because it was a waste of time constantly being second-guessed by remote control.

Wednesday, August 19

The right-wing press was starting to be difficult, trying to link RIRA [Real IRA] and IRA as pretty much the same thing. Their desire to fuck us over on this was pretty powerful. The GA–DT situation was going backwards, SF rejecting the language we had tried on them. It was making the UUs uneasy again. The RIRA called a ceasefire which we rejected in contemptuous tones, saying it was an insult to the dead and an attempt simply to stall the new security measures. The RIRA were intimating it had been intended as a big commercial hit, not heavy loss of life. That had been TB's view, that it caused more damage than intended. Mo was still intending to stay only until tomorrow, which was worrying me.

Friday, August 21

The last week of the holiday pretty much wiped out. Fiona had done a brilliant job keeping the show on the road while I was busy, and I think understood I felt there was no choice. People had said when I first started that NI would get to me, and it had.

Tuesday, August 25

I was picked up at 6.40 to head to Northolt to get a plane to Toulouse to meet TB. TB felt Bill C was in some genuine trouble but the only option for us was to stand by him. I asked CB if she would stand by TB if he got involved with a Monica Lewinsky. She said probably, but she would make his life hell. TB said he was confident she would kick him straight out, and Fiona would do the same to me. TB had a different kind of concern re the Parliament recall, namely that we would face a lot of opposition from the judiciary. We dropped CB and family off at Northolt and then headed for Belfast.

TB drafted his own press statement, which was strong. He focused on the emotions aroused, the recall as agreed by the Speaker and the general thinking behind it. He was worried though that the political situation was fragile. Trimble and Mallon were barely speaking, DT was vile about the service he was getting from the Civil Service, Sinn Fein were attacking everything we did and saying Trimble's sole aim was to ensure the GFA was not implemented. DT was a very difficult personality to deal with. When he was good, he was very good, but at times he could become very distant and disengaged and not focus. Mo and Tom Kelly [NIO spokesman] were both worried that Mallon would quit if things did not improve. We were flown by helicopter to Omagh, where the atmosphere was very subdued, as expected. TB did a meeting with local leaders and then groups of emergency services in little knots, all very friendly but some of them clearly shaken up. He talked to some of the locals in the street and though there were one or two difficult questions, he handled it all well. He was saying the measures we planned were tough but I thought he was wrong to say draconian. We had an unbelievably awful helicopter flight to Belfast, foul weather, low flying, dodging pylons, etc. We arrived for the talks, first Trimble, who was clearly under pressure and not very friendly. Several of the UUs were making clear they would not sit on the executive with SF. They were also – in part fuelled by the Tories and the *Telegraph* – driving decommissioning up the agenda again. TB was seething afterwards, felt that whenever we took our eye off the ball, things slipped. We had an equally difficult meeting with McGuinness, Doherty and Bairbre de Bruin [Sinn Fein's policing and justice spokeswoman], who felt Trimble was stalling while they were constantly being asked for more. TB felt if we did not get progress going soon, the thing was in danger of collapse, and he was worried about the attitude shift on both sides. Over dinner at Hillsborough, TB agreed he should do a statement on Omagh on the day Parliament came back, both to set the tone and to give a broader context. DT came back for another meeting and TB decided to do it mainly tête-à-tête to try to get him to get a grip. They agreed to work towards a series of steps e.g. 1. SF say something indicating the war is over. 2. DT calls a meeting of all parties, including SF. 3. McGuinness agrees to speak to the decommissioning body. 4. Trimble–Adams bilateral. Over a massive bowl of raspberries and strawberries, TB said he felt DT was a curious mix – he wants to lead but is needy about how to do it. It was as if he needed lessons – for example, he should bind in Donaldson and then

August '98: Face to face with Omagh tragedy

every time Donaldson slips outside the net he diminishes himself not DT. He felt Donaldson was the one person who could really damage DT.

Saturday, August 29

TB called and said he felt that with Clinton in trouble because of Monica, and Yeltsin now hit sideways by the Russian economic crisis, there was a bit of vacuum in world leadership and we had to do something. He instigated a series of calls to different world leaders in his capacity as chair of G7, starting today with Chirac and Prodi, tomorrow [Keizo] Obuchi [new Prime Minister of Japan], Kohl and Chrétien and a further conversation with Clinton, who was keeping a brave face on things but sounded down when you listened closely. The main message TB was driving was that we were willing to help Russia but any help must be tied to economic reform. In most of the conversations, there was a concern that Yeltsin had pretty much lost it and didn't really know how to handle what was happening.

Thursday, September 3

I was up just after 5 to get to Number 10 for the convoy to Northolt. It was pouring with rain. TB and John H were getting anxious Trimble may stall right through. On the way to the airport, TB and I were discussing how he should handle Bill. I said there was no mileage in any distance and he should be close. The speech should be a mix of where we are in the peace process, but also talk up BC's role. Trimble was waiting for us on the plane. TB was working on the speech for the Waterfront Hall, while DT read the papers. I made sure he didn't see the *Independent*, which was the most firm re a meeting with Adams. We then had a discussion about what DT might say. Trimble said he didn't intend it to be a big deal, as both TB and Clinton were around and bound to take the headlines. We persuaded him there was an opportunity here and TB asked me to draft a few lines for him. I did, including a further clear hint that he would meet Adams. I never imagined he would deliver them, especially when he just folded the paper and put it in his pocket without comment, but later he did deliver them, as drafted. He told us he was having problems with Ken Maginnis and also with his executive but he believed it could be done. We got TB's speech finished, arrived and waited for Bill C to arrive. There was the usual over-the-top security getting on everyone's nerves. I told the advance guy he should get hold of a copy of the *Independent* for Bill to see. They took it a step further, gave it to Sandy Berger as he landed and he had it under his arm as he walked across the tarmac. But they were clearly desperate for a success story with all the other stuff going on back home.

We left for Stormont, good pictures of TB, BC, Trimble and Mallon on arrival, then upstairs for a meeting. Bill asked a great question – 'What can I do to help?' TB said 1. show the three governments working together, 2. put pressure on SF re weapons decommissioning, 3. isolate pro-violence opinion in the US and 4. economic help. DT was pretty churlish throughout and afterwards BC said to me 'Someone should tell him that part of the art of politics is smiling when you feel like you're swallowing a turd.' He also used that great line from Mario Cuomo [former Governor of New York]: 'We campaign in poetry but we govern in prose.' It's about who clears the drains, he said. The Yanks were keen to be seen to be doing something for Adams. But now the US and SF wanted more – they wanted GA on the platform, claiming that is exactly what would happen with a constituency visit, and he should speak for a minute. John Holmes and Jonathan seemed surprisingly relaxed but TB and I were both worried that would wipe everything else out and send real bad waves through the Unionist community. But the Americans were really pushing, and Adams was pressurising Mo. It was a classic last-minute SF bounce and I felt we had to resist as we had not thought through the consequences. Jim Steinberg came to our offices but after ten minutes of toing and froing we couldn't agree so went to see Bill. I explained why we thought it was a bad move and said instead it would be better that TB said some warm words re GA and his role when he was making his remarks introducing Margaret Gibney.[1] Bill, who was a bit distracted as he was working on his speech, was fine with that. Mo did a little speech, then a young boy, then TB, who went off the cuff and called Adams 'Gerry', I think for the first time in public, which John H hoped nobody would notice. Berger said to me I looked pained when he said it. I said we were always pained when we saw and heard things which we knew would see the other end of the see-saw tip over again. Bill had a little cat nap in the holding room, and looked pretty shattered when he woke up. Hillary looked tired too. This was the deep freeze but he was bearing it well.

We were taken by helicopter to Omagh. We went straight to the local leisure centre to meet families of the victims. There was a little

---

[1] As a 12-year old in 1997, she wrote to the Prime Minister asking him to continue the search for peace, and imploring terrorists to give up violence. After Blair read out her letter on US TV, she caught the imagination of many Americans, including Hillary Clinton. Subsequently became a UNICEF Young Ambassador.

boy there, wearing a Leeds shirt, who was the double of Calum. It was very quiet, a few sobs around the place, but as BC and TB toured the tables, the noise levels picked up a bit and people started to pour out their stories. But it was pretty harrowing. I chatted to a policewoman who was helping some of them through it and she said she had never known anything as bad as this. There was no media at all, just a sound feed for TB and Bill's little speeches. Then they went round every single table and by the end people were mobbing Bill asking for photos and autographs. The atmosphere lifted as time wore on, but you knew it would fall back soon after they left. They set off to the scene of the bombing, laid flowers and then walked slowly down the street. The crowds were warm and friendly, and Bill was clearly getting a lift from the crowds and their reaction to him. TB said to me later he felt Bill was very down, but hiding it well, and also feeling very damaged. A role in the peace process meant a lot to him, for lots of different reasons. We flew to Armagh over some stunning scenery. There was a big crowd – up to 11,000 – waiting for them and the US team had told Bill he had been a bit down in his earlier speech and this was the one to get pumped up for. He did, and got the best reception yet. Mallon spoke really well. Trimble was flat and unyielding as ever. TB said later he had the worst personal skills of any top politician he had met. He just couldn't rise to these big occasions. DT looked gobsmacked for example when TB said he should try to develop a good relationship with Adams. He was still avoiding any official acknowledgement of a meeting. Both TB and BC felt today had gone well. We saw him off, then set off for home ourselves. It was getting massive and positive coverage here but a lot less so in the US, which is where he needed it. TB was anxious for him.

Thursday, September 10

Pressure on Clinton was now really intense, with a lot of new voices saying he should go. I left early and headed for the Cabinet awayday at Chequers with Jonathan, Peter H and David M. We had to deal with a problem on the way down, a US agency having put out a story that TB told Congressmen we would demilitarise in exchange for decommissioning. We put out a line making clear there were no such trade-offs. We got there by 9 for a pre-meeting with TB. The meeting itself started with a PG presentation, the numbers OK, doing well on values, TB strong though worries about arrogance, doing better on delivery but not getting the message on social disintegration. Hague was picking up a bit. TB was on OK form, did the usual thing about how few of them we ever heard putting out a broader government message, stressed modernisation for conference, but with fairness as the purpose. He said he had a letter the other day which began 'Now you have been in government for a few years . . .' expectations were still very high. Economic strength has to be the focus, and it requires tough decisions for the long term. Modernisation of schools, hospitals, welfare, fight against crime. There is no point us just being the party of more money for public services. We have to be the modernisers too. The values come through in messages about fairness – new deal, tax credits. He said ministers had to drive their departments harder, force them to be more innovative. JP kept talking about the CRS when he meant the CSR. Margaret Beckett said the Tories and the media were redefining the promises we made so they could say we had broken them. GB was good on basic message. Ann Taylor said some people were scared of change and we had to be careful modernisation did not become a concept people were fearful of. Peter M said he felt we had to be more challenging to the public about the need for the country to raise its sights higher. Clare did her Mother Teresa bit, said we had to stop all the briefings against each other. 'We actually all like each other so why all the stabbing in the back?' Chris Smith warned not to underestimate Hague. John Reid was excellent, really got the big picture and put it over. Ron Davies warned of farmers rioting. Dobbo said we had to present ourselves more as a team. Sitting there listening, you had no real sense of a discussion leading to a conclusion, more a group of people who felt they had to speak and who made essentially random points. After lunch, GB did a presentation on the economy (MPC[1] left interest rates unchanged) and did a number on his productivity spiel. He said we had to develop national policies for a global economy. We had to build a national economic purpose, become a rock of stability in an uncertain world. TB summed up rather differently – focus on macro-stability, micro-dynamism, welfare reform, skills, education, transport. We were clearly moving towards a conference more workmanlike than visionary. But the mood was OK.

Friday, September 11

With the Starr report due for publication, pressure was really mounting on Clinton, and there was a lot of interest in how TB would handle it. I spoke to him at Chequers and he said though we should keep out of it as best we could in relation to the detail, basically we had to stand by him. There was no merit in distancing ourselves at all. The Starr report was published, and was grim for BC. It was wall-to-wall on the

[1] The Bank of England's Monetary Policy Committee.

September '98: Frustration over ministers

media all over the world. At 9.30, with the world just digesting the whole damn mess, TB's call with Clinton went ahead. Considering what was happening around him, he was amazing. It was as if nothing was going on. 'Tony, hi.' If he was acting nonchalant, he did a great job. TB said we were thinking of him. He said he was confident, people were rooting for him, Starr was just a politically motivated rumour-monger. Then they were onto Northern Ireland and Russia. The DT–GA meeting had gone better than anyone expected, 45 minutes instead of 10, and with at least some engagement. TB stressed again how important decommissioning was going to be, but it was difficult for Adams. BC suggested token decommissioning plus – as it was assumed SF knew who was responsible – an Omagh arrest with briefing that SF were helping with the tip-offs. Then Russia. 'The good news is they have a new government, the bad news is they have put troglodytes in the economic portfolios,' said BC. He said [Yevgeney] Primakov [new Russian Prime Minister] was smart but knew jack all about the economy. TB was straight on after the call ended – what a guy, that was not someone who was going down. He believed the process would start to turn in his favour, that people had heard all the reasons why he should go and would now be looking for reasons why he should stay. I spoke to McCurry, who was literally counting down 'x briefings to go.' Mike said BC was more confident than he had been, felt Starr had overplayed his hand.

Sunday, September 13

TB said re Bill C, of course he can deal with these things but the question is whether this is what politics has now become. He said if you looked at any sexual relationship in the context of a report like that, it could be made to look terrible. Likewise, he said, if every conversation you and I ever had was published, we would be dead. Every leader had to be able to let go a little. TB called again later to say he had informed Ashdown, by letter, that he did not feel able to deliver on PR before the general election, that there was so much constitutional change going through we had to watch out for overload, added to which we needed to see how it worked elsewhere. Paddy wrote back to say he was virtually finished if he could not deliver PR. TB was not convinced and in any case could not get it through Cabinet.

Wednesday, September 16

TB and CB were meeting Prince Charles for lunch, which meant Lizzie McCrossan [secretary, Garden Rooms] and I were separated off as the cars hit the driveway at Highgrove, TB taken to the front, us to the back. Then, it seemed, I was supposed to eat in one room, Lizzie in another. I suggested we ate together. We had wild pasta, salad and vegetables served by someone with a real smell under nose problem. I had asked the cops earlier to check out whether there was a pool I could use and they had said there was a pool, but not for use (except by PC) so I had another go when I got there. A man in uniform came through with two towels, gave one to me and one to Lizzie, who politely pointed out she wouldn't be swimming. It was a journey so far back in time it felt extra-planetary. Not only were Lizzie and I expected to eat in different places, but the drivers and cops were even further down the table, out in the barn according to Terry, with a sandwich. The cops were in different rooms according to rank. The rooms were comfortable without being over the top, but totally unwelcoming, though Charles's watercolours brightened things up a little. I swam for 20-odd minutes and the pool was warm and a bit manky with too many leaves floating around. It didn't feel like it was swum in very often. TB was heading off to Coventry and I was due to come back with CB. We met up at the shop, where I had a brief glimpse of Charles, who was showing them some of his organic produce. She said organic farming had taken up most of their conversation at lunch. The rest had been a meandering around foreign affairs. TB was always pretty discreet about his royal dealings, CB less so. She said when she first met Princess Anne, Anne had called her 'Mrs Blair', to which CB said 'Call me Cherie.' 'I'd rather not, Mrs Blair,' said Anne. She said she didn't bother to protest when Charles called her Mrs Blair today.

Friday, September 18

Clinton was the big running story. TB was at Chequers and called a few times, ostensibly to talk about the speech, but I could tell he was worrying about New York. I said it was going to be a bit of a nightmare but we just had to get through it. Richard Wilson came to see me, worried about his profile, and how he was seen to be clearing everything we put forward. On GB, he agreed we had to get Whelan out. He said Peter M was a 'star – he will transform DTI'. He then raised what was probably the reason for the call in the first place. He said Major had called him and claimed that the story about legal bills for Wills and Harry was leaked by Mark Bolland to Peter M and that Peter or I leaked it to the *Guardian*. This was paranoid nonsense but he was adamant, said RW, and had been 'ranting on at me about it'.

And so to what, in a note to TB yesterday, Jeremy Heywood called 'the day trip from hell'. There was only a little bit of 'why is he still going?' and TB was strongly of the view now that strong support for BC would stand us in good stead for the long term, not just with Clinton but with the US more generally. But he was dreading the seminar. 'How did we get into this? We have lost control of it.' He was exaggerating how bad it would be and from Clinton's perspective, there was something to be said for just keeping on keeping on. David M was trying desperately to be serious about the Third Way seminar, but TB and I were in messing around mode. We called it 'le sommet surrealiste', with the world watching BC's videotaped evidence while he, and we, were locked in a policy wonk discussion about the future of the world with Romano Prodi and the President of Bulgaria [Petar Stoyanov]. TB started off embarrassed about the seminar. By the time we reached NY he was obsessed with the idea that we now turn it into a big positive thing about the rebirth of progressive politics. By now, they were one hour into the BC tapes and the initial judgement was that they didn't add much. Doug Senior (Clinton staff) told me they were totally confident he would get through OK, that the worst had been thrown and he was still standing and there was a backlash in his favour. The public totally got why he lied about it, and didn't think it meant he was a liar in his political life. Bill and Hillary arrived, and he was in pretty upbeat form. 'Hey, buddy, we just had a good day,' he said to me. Sandy Berger said it would be very good if TB could at some point make a reference to the importance of BC's leadership, which I passed on to TB. Sidney Blumenthal [former journalist; adviser to Clinton] said it would be 'appropriate' for TB to talk up BC's leadership! Then in they went and le surrealisme began. Prodi was just Prodi, meandering away, Bill and TB were fine but it was all a bit samey and heard it all before, though TB did his progressive rebirth line perfectly well. But there were no hostages and it didn't feel as bad as it might have done. Afterwards Hillary led him through to meet some students. Bill C arrived a short time later and got a terrific response, which seemed to cheer him up. We then had the TB–BC bilateral – NI, economy, G7–8, Kosovo – then to the reception. BC told him that Prodi had done a big number for him yesterday and it would be good if TB did the same, which he did with the students. Jim Steinberg felt he was still in difficulty. On the way out, Clinton asked me how it all felt and I said I thought he was through the worst and he needed to keep doing what he was doing. In the airport, TB was beginning to unwind.

The whole day had indeed been a bit surreal, he said, but it could have been a lot worse. TB was by now on his world-celeb high, felt the day had gone a lot better than it might have done.

Thursday, September 24
Although Chequers was not my cup of tea, I could see why TB liked it on days like this. He spent most of the day just sitting out in the garden, surrounded by papers, taking an occasional phone call, the Wrens who work there serving him tea whenever he wanted it. The food was good and the atmosphere relaxed, and he did at least get a lot of work done on the conference speech today. He was a bit worried that he was not in his usual panic. Panicking about not panicking, I said, is hardly leadership. In any event, he has the Sunday Q & A to panic about instead.

Friday, September 25
We discussed Bill C again. TB said he totally understood how it happens. He likes women. He needs release from the pressures of the job. He wants to be a normal person. He said he still found it hard to deal with the fact that everyone has a view about him, that people talk about him as though they know him. Though I didn't much like Chequers, I felt that today we broke the back of the speech. We still had two drafts but they were merging into one.

Tuesday, September 29
TB was up around 6 and when I went in at half past, I was pleased to see he was reading through it calmly, rather than slashing out great swathes or scribbling madly. He made a few changes, and some good cuts, but by and large we were in shape. We ran the final fact and policy checks with the office and departments, then did the autocue rehearsal. TB was very happy with it now, said he felt, on going through it, it was the best exposition of the third way he had done. We made only tiny changes as we went through it. He was much calmer than at this stage in previous years. I briefed the evenings and the broadcasters. They clearly didn't like the reference to 'Zeitgeist' so we took it out. We headed for the Winter Gardens, with the usual live coverage all the way, and into the little office upstairs for a final read-through. There was a fantastic buzz around the place and I felt it was well set up. It was 90 per cent there and the last 10 per cent would all be in the delivery. He looked very calm just before going on. The audience took to it pretty much from the off. I watched from the back of the hall, next to Roger Berry [Labour MP for Kingswood] and Maria Fyfe

September '98: TB on Clinton and pressure

[Labour MP for Glasgow North], and even they were very warm about it. It was very much the argument he had set out in his draft note coming through, and the redrafting process had definitely turned a strong argument into a good speech. He delivered it brilliantly. There was an extraordinary standing ovation for Mo when he paid tribute to her in the middle of the speech, which added to the sense of occasion. He got a good response re Stephen Lawrence,[1] women and children, Lords. Later, I couldn't face going out so I just stayed in my room, cheered only by the fact the cop on the door was a Burnley fan and we nattered a bit about that. I watched the main bulletins and the speech coverage was fantastic.

Tuesday, October 6

China. We landed 7.30 local time, 12.30 body-clock time and I was exhausted. We set off for Tiananmen Square for the welcoming ceremony, which was really hot and muggy. But they had put on the full works. TB was much more comfortable raising human rights than the last time with the Chinese. There was clearly post-Clinton a greater degree of willingness to engage. TB liked Zhu [Rongji, Prime Minister of the Republic of China] and warmed to him as the meeting went on. He liked the way Zhu said he had a reform programme and then just took him through it, state enterprise by state enterprise. TB and I both felt we lacked any real oomph in the main Chinese speech. TB wanted a specific China story. I wanted something more general that would resonate more at home. John H and I both felt his ideas on the world economy were not substantial enough to make the speech fly, but he and GB both felt they were onto something. We set off for the banquet at the Great Hall. TB wanted the speech to be seen as an international explanation of Blairism. If we were to make anything of the international financial changes we were proposing, we had to build him up.

Wednesday, October 7

Talks with Jiang Zemin, which were a lot more formal, and a lot more small talky than with Zhu. He told TB he was jealous of his youth. He also treated us to a lecture on Tibet. He was pretty scathing about the Dalai Lama, suggested he was influenced by young people in his entourage and said things he wasn't sure of. Zhu came up to the Guest House to do a personal farewell which was meant to be a fairly

[1] A black teenager, whose murder in south-east London, in 1993, was racially motivated. An inquiry into the way the murder investigation was conducted began in March 1998.

significant gesture, designed to mean a lot. It had 15 minutes in the diary but extended to 45. TB said he felt it was in their own best interests that they moved faster and further on human rights. Zhu invited the family out for a holiday there. TB had a surreal phone call with Yeltsin. The interpreters seemed to give up at one point.

Friday, October 9

Godric called at 7am, midnight UK time, to tell me Clare Short had said on *Question Time* that Clinton was not fit to be President because he lied. My instinct, as so often with Short, was that TB should sack her. His argument was always that she would become a martyr and cause more trouble outside. But I wasn't convinced she actually had a following. She had got herself into a position where the press lauded her publicly, because she gave us a headache, but in truth did not see her as a very credible figure. Of course Clinton had done things that were hard to defend, which is why it was best to be in a position of defending in general while avoiding the specific. When I told him about it, he just said what a silly woman she is – does she have any redeeming features? Then he added 'I'm probably asking the wrong person.'

Tuesday, October 27

Jonathan came into my office and shut the door, which usually meant there was a problem. There was. He said Jack Straw had just called. He had had a call from John Stevens, Deputy Commissioner at the Yard, who said Ron Davies had been cruising on Clapham Common last night and had been picked up by a black male prostitute who later robbed him. This turned out to be an OTT account of what happened, but clearly something had and we had a real problem. Jonathan and I went to see TB. We took him into the dining room and told him what we knew. He looked surprised but not shocked and then, as I had, laughed. Bloody hell, he said. We arranged for him to come in around 11. I did the 11 o'clock. By the time I got back upstairs, Ron had arrived and was in with TB and Jonathan who was taking a note rather more completely than usual. Ron looked absolutely shattered. He ran through the story, how he had been driving back to London from Wales, wanted some fresh air, stopped at Clapham Common, went for a walk, met a guy, got talking, agreed to go for a drink, met up with some of his mates, agreed to go for a curry, got into a car, got robbed of cash, wallet, car phone, went to police, and here he was. He set it out in a very matter-of-fact way, as though every step was in its own way logical, but clearly TB, Jonathan and

I all felt exactly the same thing – what on earth was he doing there, how on earth did he get involved with a group of complete strangers, and how the hell do we explain this one? I could tell looking at TB's face that he had pretty much decided this was a no-hope situation for Ron, and that the only way for him to salvage anything from this was to get ahead of the curve, resign before anyone knew the first thing about it, and maybe get some sympathy and understanding. TB was in clear and decisive mode. Right, he said, the more I hear of this, the more convinced I am that as soon as people hear of this, they will think it all very odd and it will be very hard to explain away. We agreed I would go back to the Welsh Office with Ron and draft an exchange of letters.

We drove over together and in the car he was 'business as usual', as if nothing had happened. When we got there, there was a sullen atmosphere. He called in June Milligan, his private secretary, and told her he was probably going to resign. It was perfectly clear to me that she was pleased to hear it. I asked if he had spoken to his wife, Chris. He hadn't. He called her and told her, in the most perfunctory way imaginable, that he had seen Tony, who had been 'very nice', and he was probably going to resign and something might be on the news. 'All right, love?' And that was pretty much it. Earlier, TB had said to Ron 'I am not going to ask you about your sexuality,' which of course was a way of asking about it, because if Ron had wanted to come back at him, he would have. He didn't. I was doing it longhand and getting it typed up outside. We sent over the drafts to Number 10. TB made a couple of changes including reference to 'foolish error'. Ron got in his senior staff and told them what was happening. I didn't sense any warmth there either way, no real sympathy, and he struck me as being lonely in his private and public lives. He was trying to be matter-of-fact but must have known he was about to have his reputation shredded. TB saw the Queen for the weekly audience later. We arranged for Ron to head off as soon as the interview was done, as the story would be around the BBC in no time, while I went back to Number 10 to brief on it. It was not easy. As I knew they would, they got straight to the point – what had he done wrong? – and I didn't particularly want to dump all over him, so I was avoiding a lot of questions.

Wednesday, October 28
I wanted TB to speak to Ron, but he was holding back. Anji was of the view that nobody would understand if he stayed and we may have to go for him. TB eventually spoke to him and it was a difficult

conversation. There was a hint of menace in Ron's voice now. He said he felt the wrong decision was taken. He had gone along with 'your' strategy but the Welsh party will not dance to the London media tune. He was not going to be kicked out by a kangaroo court. TB held pretty firm, said in a way the easier thing would be to leave him, and let events take their course but we needed to know 1. that there would be no other stories coming out about his private life and 2. that the Welsh party genuinely wanted him to stay. TB said there should be a special executive of the Welsh party. Ron said fine, let's go for Monday. TB said Friday, to avoid days of chatter about it that would damage the party. Ron said he had to have time to prepare his case and there had to be justice. 'If we stand for anything, we stand for justice and fairness. The Welsh party elected me and London cannot force me out.'

Thursday, October 29

Another day from hell. Jonathan and I were both anxious about the inconsistencies emerging, not least in me saying we knew nothing else and that the police had not been in contact. Ron said he was now thinking of stepping down. He hadn't slept again, he had thought about it all night and he was sure it was the best thing. He said he would probably just give a letter to his chairman.

I helped Ron draft his letter over the phone before going for the [President Carlos] Menem lunch. He had a bit of an ageing Spanish pop star feel to him, but the talks went fine. He invited TB to the Welsh-speaking part of Argentina. 'Wales is very much on my mind at the moment, as you may have read in our papers,' said TB. Menem laughed, too loud. The Falklands discussion was really just going through motions, though TB was good on the improving mood music. We went a lot further on the arms embargo than they expected. I briefed the Argentine media in the street and found myself banjaxed by a Jeremy Beadle-type character for one of the comedy news shows out there, yelling and shouting about David Beckham and Diego Maradona. The *Guardian* were in seeing GB and as they came out I grabbed Mike White and introduced him to this guy as the Chancellor and got him to do an interview and get the guy off my back.

Ron was now at Devizes nick doing his statement and had to leave at 6.30 for an identity parade at Brixton. We couldn't get the Ron letters sorted so we needed a statement to make clear what was happening. I persuaded Ron that the sooner this was done the better. TB spoke to Ron again, then I went through the statement with him and he was fine. 'OK, let it go,' he said. I called Jon Smith (PA) and said he should describe me as a spokesman for Ron. I also gave him a reaction from me. Endgame. I felt totally drained and I felt incredibly sorry for Ron. He said to me just before we did the statement 'I'm not sure I can take much more of this.'

Monday, November 2

Betty Boothroyd's office had indicated it was by no means certain she would grant Ron a resignation statement, but he was heading to London pretty determined to do it. His draft was basically a long attack on the media, with nothing to add on the detail of events, and both Bruce and I spoke to him to say as it stood it would harm not help his case. TB was still very unkeen for him to make a statement at all. I was suggesting Ron should be left in peace but by the time I got upstairs, he had been granted the statement. Ron's statement was in some ways quite powerful but it was hard to get away from the unanswered questions. The press basically took it as an admission he was gay. He called me later and said he was going away for a few days.

Thursday, November 4

The *News of the World* had apparently trapped Nick Brown with rent boys – pictures, tapes, etc. As TB said later, with a touch of black humour, we could get away with Ron as a one-off aberration, but if the public start to think the whole Cabinet is indulging in gay sex, we might have a bit of a political problem. I could feel another weekend going away. I drove with TB to the *Guardian* for lunch. We had a chat about pressure. He said the fact of being at the interface with the media was a pressure in itself, added to which they were always looking to have a go at me. He said I was a buffer for pressure on him, but ultimately the real pressure was on him. Take Iraq, he said. You have to help me communicate decisions. I have to take a decision that may lead to people losing their lives.

Wednesday, November 11

We had a big Iraq meeting at TB's Commons office with Robin C, George R, Jonathan, John H and Charles Guthrie. TB said it was clear we were on for Saturday and we should be totally supportive. Equally, he had told BC he must accept the offer of support from others and we should be continuing to build support. Guthrie said that in the 52 hours of planned attack, it was possible 2,500 people would die, and UK planes and bombs would be responsible for about 250 of them. TB nodded, but looked nervous. Charles also said he could not rule out casualties among our Tornado teams. He took us through the plan of action from midnight Saturday. TB was clearly on for it, but worried, and felt we needed to keep building the diplomatic cover. Charles, who is a top man, and absolutely clear in the way he spells things out, said we would be responsible for 20 per cent of the flying, while the US would be doing most of the hits from elsewhere. He circulated secret papers on it which he took back at the end.

Thursday, November 12

On Iraq, the main message at Cabinet was that air strikes were looking likelier, sooner rather than later. TB said Saddam was not moving. GR described it as the gravest crisis since the end of the Gulf War. Saddam had broken the ceasefire agreement, broken his word to Kofi, and was rebuilding chemical and biological weapons programmes. He was weaponising nerve agents. These are 'ferocious weapons' and his neighbours believe there is intent. TB made clear this was the US demanding and us complying, but that our own independent judgement was that he must be forced to comply. He said there was a real breach, not a technical breach. GR talked through the British likely involvement – 12 Tornado teams and 600 troops based in Saudi.

Saturday, November 14

Jonathan and I got in at 9 to see TB, then the first main meeting at 10, TB, RC, GR, CDS [Chief of Defence Staff], RW, Jonathan, John H, AC. The operation was being launched at 4pm, air strikes plus cruise missiles. I drafted a full statement, which TB then rewrote while I fixed for him to speak to Group Captain Alan Vincent [commander of the RAF's Tornado force] in Kuwait. Joe Lockhart [new White House press secretary] and I had agreed Clinton would go up around 4.45 our time, so TB should aim to do something around that time. We put together a list of the world leaders and foreign ministers TB and RC would call. We agreed TB would do a statement in the street and then lie low till tomorrow.

Then John Holmes came through and said Clinton was putting a pause on it. Iraq was sending a letter making clear they were ready to have the UN inspectors back in. The military were still keen to go but BC felt he had to order the pause at least until we had seen the letter. When it came, it was full of holes and at the end there was an annexe that was basically a list of THEIR conditions. But Saddam had managed to sow doubt and confusion and division and over the next few hours there were a few difficult calls with Bill C and Sandy Berger

November '98: Air strikes likely on Iraq

in particular. Clinton wanted a 24-hour delay. I immediately redrafted the statement to say TB had authorised use of force; that SH only climbed down because he feared attack; that the forces would now stay there until this was all tested and bolted down, and compliance clear. But the US did not want to refer to the authorisation of force because they did not want it known the operation had been about to begin even though we said – rightly as it turned out – that it was bound to leak in the US, where they had a much leakier system, and where the military were likely to be annoyed at the delay. TB said he understood why Bill did it, but our general view was that we should have gone ahead without the pause but that now the pause was ordered, we would have to test the letter until a further breach. Our strong view was we had to be out there saying this attempted backdown was only the result of him thinking he was about to get hit – which he was. That was the only cover we had to the charge of dithering. We should now be setting clear conditions and if they were not met in full, immediately, we hit him. But the US – particularly Gore, Berger and Bill Cohen [US Defense Secretary] – felt we had to hit him anyway but instead of doing it Saturday, let's do it Sunday. We sensed Bill felt he had taken the wrong decision re the pause and was now looking for a way round that. It was a bit messy. They seemed now to be making the argument there was no way to do a deal with him. So why pause in the first place? we asked. TB was worried we would end up diluting the support we had. Clear breach would get us support. If we were signalling we weren't sure, or it didn't matter, we would dissipate it. That was his game. Why were we letting him play it?

In all TB had eight calls with Clinton over an 18-hour period up to Sunday 4.30am, when he finally went to bed. He felt BC had taken the pause decision alone and was now under pressure from everyone else to go for it. TB felt Bill had slightly lost faith in himself. On one of the calls, around 5–6pm, Gore and Berger did most of the talking. TB was getting exasperated. If the pause was to test the sincerity of intent, but now we were going ahead anyway, but 24 hours later, what was the pause in the end for? GR and Guthrie came over to get a face-to-face briefing on what was going on. Charles said we should have gone ahead, and said the letter came too late. But now the decision was taken to pause, it was sensible surely to wait, till SH broke any aspect of the deal, and then hit him straight away. That seemed obvious to everyone at our end, but in the States there was obviously a big argument going on. I couldn't understand why they didn't see the one thing they seemed most worried about – a charge of weakness – was best addressed by promoting the fact he had responded to our strength. TB was clear we should have gone the whole way. The truth is they unilaterally reversed the decision to go and now they were trying to wind back the reel. It was a nightmare, but TB did say we should keep close with them, and was clear we did not want any hint of division spilling out. TB said whatever we thought of their handling of it, we should not peel off from the US.

Sunday, November 15

I got to bed at 12.30 and at 4.30 TB called again, wanting me to get briefing again re the Iraqis making further concessions at the UN and making clear we were worried our conditions were not in fact being met. He called again at 8. By now it was already out there that B-52 bombers had been in the air when BC withdrew the order, so a day late I started to brief that TB had given the authority for military action, and that he had spoken to commanders in Kuwait. TB was now worried the whole thing would seem like a backdown by us not SH. The answer was that we were prepared to hit him, and had authorised the action to do so – that was the difference with February. We were also making clear that in the event of any further breach, there would be no warning at all. I went in and TB was up in the flat. He said we had got the assurances from Iraq – whether meaningless or not they had been given – but the US were still talking about going in today. This was a nightmare, he said. Having taken the wrong decision, they think they can put it right by taking the decision they should have taken in the first place. But the circumstances have changed and they may be making the wrong decision again. Then word came through from the MoD that the US were preparing plans based on the assumption that the UK would not take part. Jonathan and I went back up to tell TB. We cannot let that happen, he said. Whether we think they are in the right place or not, it would be disastrous for the transatlantic relationship if we pulled out on this. George Robertson, Robin, Charles Guthrie and officials arrived. GR and Charles were totally sound, and absolutely of our view. RC clearly felt there were no circumstances in which we could support, let alone take part in, military action. When I said later I would be very pissed off if the Americans briefed that we had talked them out of action, Robin said 'It would go down very well on the Continent.' In fact, one of the last calls of the night had been a three-way call between Bill, TB and Chirac and Chirac basically said that only the US view mattered, but indicated if there was a further breach, he would accept we had to go in. So we actually had quite a strong position but RC was being very weaselly, saying if we went in after the events of recent days, we would be isolated and it would take at least a year to recover our European relations. TB said he did not accept that. But if we pulled the plug on the Yanks, it would take a lot longer to recover. He said we still needed to persuade the Americans to get going with a public line that a combination of diplomacy and the threat of force had forced a climbdown and we had to maintain that pressure with a real threat of force at any breach. I did a briefing to push that line, gave out loads of detail on all the calls etc, but a lot of them were starting to see it as a win for SH because he averted the strikes and split the international community again. TB was pretty exasperated at the way the US had handled things in the last couple of days. They had allowed the obvious division and dithering to get out on the public radar. Their body language had also been dreadful, especially as we were now getting pictures from Baghdad of the 'celebrations' of yet another triumph for SH.

Monday, November 16

The press here wasn't bad. A lot better than the States, where there was a lot of scepticism and the feeling SH had diddled and won. At DOP [Defence and Overseas Policy Cabinet Committee] GR and Charles [Guthrie] made clear we could not keep troops there indefinitely, that it was fine to say we were maintaining the pressure, but it was a very expensive option. We could be there for weeks if not months. TB spoke to Kofi and Bill later. BC sounded a bit fed up but did keep saying – so often he was protesting too much – that he thought he made the right decision.

Monday, November 23

At the Queen's Speech reception for ministers, I had a nice chat with Betty Boothroyd, who was supportive of me, and said not to worry about all the attacks, but she said she felt TB was attacking the Tories too much at PMQs, and he had to watch it.

Tuesday, November 24

Queen's Speech day. The overnight briefing had gone not bad, with welfare reform high up in the mix. But the story was bound to be Lords[1] after the reaction in the chamber when the Queen read out the relevant section and there was a mix of hear, hears alongside grumbles of

---

[1] The speech announced that the right of hereditary peers to sit and vote in the House of Lords would be removed, as the first stage in the democratic reform of the Lords.

disapproval. TB was working on the speech mainly on his own and particularly after what Betty said last night, which I passed on to him, I was a bit worried we didn't have a big enough theme. We had been hoping to walk as per last year but the police advised against because of an animal liberation protest, so we went by car and with the streets all closed that would lead to more bollocks about being more remote and aloof. I briefed the broadcasters as the Queen was doing her thing, and then TB came back to carry on working on his speech. He was in a bit of a grumpy mood. TB said he needed to talk to me about the Lords. He said Derry had had a lot of contact with [Robert] Cranborne [Conservative leader in the Lords]. How would it be, he said, if we cut a deal with Cranborne under which one-tenth of hereditary peers would stay for the transitional period; that three cross-benchers put down an amendment that made clear all of them would go apart from this block, that there would be a limited number of appointments to balance it up, and then we and then the Lib Dems would back it? TB seemed confident we could get Cranborne to do the deal without Hague, who was, seemingly, not expressing a view while others were totally opposed. I said it sounded fine, and if it was doable, the sooner the better. It would be even better if we could say at the same time that as a result there would be more space for other bills of greater relevance to people's lives that we could bring in. Lords reform was dominating the news coverage and it was becoming a PR battle. We really had to go for it now.

Wednesday, November 25

Hillsborough. TB was worried that the process was in danger of moving backwards and felt we had to make progress soon on the North–South implementation bodies. He was also concerned at the feeling in the security services that the Real IRA would be going for a big assassination soon. We headed for Stormont and there was a lot of tension between Trimble and Mallon at the first meeting. Then Adams, and TB trying again to push on decommissioning but getting nowhere, with GA constantly moving back to DT being obstructive. I ducked out of some of the meetings to work on the speech for the Dáil,[1] marrying John H's draft with TB's comments overnight. It was a strong speech which I started to brief. I particularly enjoyed briefing the 'new positive relations with the Republic' line with Ian Paisley sitting on the edge of my desk looking at a newspaper. He looked around at me, shook his head. I winked and he laughed.

[1] In the first speech to the Dáil Éireann (the Irish Parliament) by a UK prime Minister since 1922, Blair appealed for nationalists and unionists to work together.

Thursday, November 26

TB saw Cranborne and [Sir Alastair] Goodlad [former Conservative chief whip]. They pretty much did the deal – amendment would go down in the name of 3 cross-benchers. They would support it whether Hague liked it or not. Very odd.

Friday, November 27

I was at a loss to understand how Cranborne felt he was in a position to say he would go ahead with it regardless of whether Hague supported it or not. TB said Cranborne seemed adamant, that he was so fed up with Hague's lack of judgement and leadership. TB was sure Cranborne could deliver. On timing, I said the optimum was 1. crossbenchers announce, 2. we welcome and say it could mean room for the Food Standards Agency and Rail Authority Bills, 3. Cranborne welcomes and says Tories in the Lords will support. I spoke to Derry to say this was what we need to happen. He came back after speaking to Goodlad, who said nothing could be done until Wednesday, when Cranborne was seeing his hereditaries. I spoke to Cranborne, and agreed we should both micro-manage. I think we were both surprised to be dealing with each other. He said 'I hope you understand my need in this is to cover my arse. I am committing high treason just talking to you.' He said he had to put the proposal to his own people before we could progress, but he was confident of support.

Saturday, November 28

Derry called, clearly suspicious that Cranborne no longer wanted to deal with the cross-benchers. He was also worried about leaks, as I was, with the circle of knowledge widening. TB had told JP, who was happy because if the deal was executed as planned, it would mean room for his Rail Authority Bill. He had also spoken to Margaret B, who was not happy because she felt the party would expect there to be no hereditaries left at all.

Monday, November 30

I had a meeting with Cranborne, who Mark Bennett [AC's assistant] brought in through 70 Whitehall. I could tell the minute he walked in that he was enjoying the drama of it, the plotting, and the fact of consorting with an enemy, a subject he joked about frequently. He was wearing bright red socks and a very smart suit. We talked a bit about how brilliant the Number 10 switchboard were, and what secrets they knew, and got down to it. I said I didn't understand why he wanted me to be the one speaking to the cross-benchers. He said they would enjoy the drama of it, but more importantly it was part of him covering his own arse with his own side. He could not be seen to be a prime mover in this. I said I felt they might think it odd if I did it because I am not a peer, let alone a minister, and I suggested Margaret Jay. He said he could see what I was saying, that I was a 'big juju', whatever that is, in the eyes of the Tories and maybe non-Tory peers too, and he was happy with Margaret. Later I spoke to Margaret and squared her. The loop was widening the whole time and the earliest we could do this was lunchtime Wednesday – the cross-benchers' statement, with Cranborne reacting. I drafted the statement for the cross-benchers while he was there, with Mark quietly typing it up from our scribbles. TB and Derry were both happy with it. Cranborne took a copy and said there were still a few people he would need to square but he was confident we could get support where we needed it. I still could not fully understand why he would do this – he didn't know me from Adam, and what he did know he probably didn't like and yet we had just sat down and agreed a line-by-line plan that he must know would damage his leadership, help us through a difficulty, and no matter how much I tried to take a rap and protect his arse, he was going to be implicated. He was certainly a different breed to what I knew, but I remember Alan Clark once saying to me the Tory toffs were fascinated by me because they thought I was brutal and understood power and its use. Cranborne had power going down through his family line, and was enjoying the game. As he left, after an hour or so, he said to me 'You do realise I am committing high treason, don't you?' 'Good,' I said, and he left. But I still could not fathom what was really in it for him. He didn't really care what Hague thought about this, said he was doing the thinking for him.

Tuesday, December 1

On more and more days, I was waking up and wondering how we were going to get through the day. There just seemed to be too many high-octane issues flowing through the system at once, and too few of us dealing with them. On the Lords, TB was having to be fairly devious, as we all were. My most devious piece of deviousness was probably saying at the top of the draft note that all this was subject to agreement by the PM and Lord C, which should it leak gave us the option of that being Lord Chancellor or Cranborne. I spoke to Cranborne a couple of times. He said he was seeing Hague in the morning and he would be 'no trouble, I promise you'. TB was moving to the view that Hague might feel he had to sack him when it became clear, as inevitably it would, he had been negotiating with us direct. Cranborne also mentioned on a couple of occasions he might get the chop. Back to see JP, and I got the impression he was on board. He was a bit like me, in that he liked these big hits. His worry was that Cranborne would make a big deal of being left with more than 100 peers in total, that he had stuffed us and would say they could stay beyond the second stage. Derry was very excited by the whole thing, said that if we pulled it off we 'deserved the order of Bevan'.

Wednesday, December 2

Cranborne called, said he had seen Hague, who was 'reeling – but not sufficient to sack me yet'. He asked me what he should advise Hague to do, and I said take credit for the idea. I got Jo Gibbons [Margaret Jay's special adviser] to start tipping off the press re the [Lord] Weatherill [Convenor of the Cross-bench Peers] press conference. Now Hague knew, TB and I discussed the outside chance he would raise it in the Commons, oppose it, and leave Cranborne out to dry. TB felt that would still leave us in a win-win situation, because we would say we still had the deal with Cranborne, who was confident he could get it through his people in the Lords. Over to the House and, hey presto, Hague did it. At first TB, like me, thought he was supporting the deal, but it turned out he wasn't. TB was very quick on his feet, said even Hague's own people were supporting him, was he on some kind of suicide mission etc? He hit him again on how he always got the strategic questions wrong. It was a clear win in House terms, but obviously there would be a battle in the briefings to win too. Of course, apart from Charles Reiss [*Evening Standard*], who we had briefed, the media were totally bemused by it all, which meant we had to get straight out explaining. Gregor Mackay [Hague's spokesman] and I were both swamped at either door out of the gallery, and I was at a big advantage knowing so much of the background. He looked flustered when I looked across. Clearly the whole thing raised the question of whether Hague had sacked, or was sacking, Cranborne. I briefed in very factual terms and did so again at the formal briefing at 3.45. Cranborne called Alison [Blackshaw] at 3.20, while we were still in the chamber, and left me a message 'apologising for Hague's behaviour and saying he felt he has let you down.' They are a totally different breed these people. He had just shafted his leader and he was apologising to me because he had refused to take the shafting. Hague seemingly went to Cranborne's meeting, which went in Cranborne's favour, but then Cranborne was sacked. He called me afterwards, apologised re Hague.

'I'm really sorry. I made the mistake of thinking we were dealing with grown-ups, which sadly we are not.' He was very chatty, sounded a bit high. 'It has been very good doing business with you,' he said. 'We are doing the right thing, I'm sure of it.' Alan Clark called, said 'You've lit the fucking touchpaper, and my party is in flames all around you.' I did a note for the file on the various chats with Cranborne. Hague wanted to appoint Strathclyde as Cranborne's replacement, but Lord S said he would only do it on condition he could support the deal. Hague agreed, so looked like he was weak and climbing down. I was beginning to worry we had destabilised him too much. The more I thought about it, the more shocked I was that Cranborne had consorted with us the way he did. It was always going to end in tears for them.

Monday, December 14

TB was called by Bill C early, his second call in 36 hours, and it was pretty clear he was gearing up for action on Iraq. [Richard] Butler [Head of UN arms inspection team, UNSCOM] was due to report for UNSCOM tomorrow. If he said he was being obstructed, BC was clearly on for a strike. The problem was Ramadan was due – Saturday – so the strike would have to be soon. TB was supportive but worried that the public would simply think the whole thing was a diversion from impeachment; or that Butler would not be crystal clear, and we would be going to war on an ambiguity. TB said if the US were going in, we would support them and Guthrie was told he could put out a secret signal that we would be with them. The latest intelligence suggested Saddam did not believe he was going to be attacked. Guthrie said the US were being less open with us because of what happened last time. We reckoned Butler was going to say there had been clear and unambiguous obstruction. TB said he wished the background was not impeachment, but having said that, the Americans had been on record as saying that if he [SH] did not comply, he would be hit without warning. People will understand and support that, though there is no doubt Clinton's domestic problems complicate things. Guthrie was clearly up for it. He said there would be lasting problems if people felt they were led up to the top of the hill again.

Tuesday, December 15

We had a draft of Butler which TB did not feel was as clear as we had been expecting. I disagreed, felt it would be seen by any fair-minded reader as a clear obstruction and a clear breach of his November undertakings. So while there were undoubtedly problems because of Bill's impeachment situation, which was worsening, equally you could not hold back from doing something in the international sphere out of fear of how it would be seen in relation to the domestic situation. The President called TB from his plane around 9pm and at this stage was still basically asking for views. TB and I were both sure they were going to go for it, and Bill C was clearly being advised in that direction, but he was very sensitive to the allegations there would be re impeachment and diversion. Of all the meetings through the day, the most important was DOP which should have been in the Cabinet room but for some reason ended up taking place in TB's overcrowded room. Things weren't helped when JP arrived late and sat at the back, which made him grumpy and probably more quizzical than he otherwise might have been. He was pressing on whether anyone had got Butler to harden up the language. TB had to massage him a fair bit during the meeting, and I could spot Guthrie keeping an eye on him the whole time. Robin C was a lot more bellicose than yesterday, and clearly felt Butler was reason enough. In the end, TB gave explicit authority for Guthrie to instruct the Yanks, and our own troops, that we would be there if the US decided to carry out the strikes. George R warned of the likelihood of loss of British life. RC talked through what we had to go through to try to get UK nationals out.

Wednesday, December 16

The briefings overnight went well and the sense in the morning media was that Butler was damning and now we had to show we were serious in the November pledge to hit without warning if he carried on obstructing. So by the 11 o'clock, the questions were all about why we hadn't hit him already, as the breach was so clear. I fed this through to Joe Lockhart, who was very different to deal with after Mike [McCurry]. The US were absolutely paranoid about security of information and I had to be vague bordering on misleading with the press. Charles Guthrie had really had to push to get the plans, said only five people in the UK knew and he was doubling the size of the net. TB spoke to Bill C again and it was now very much when not if. Guthrie was furious at leaks – we think through the FCO – of yesterday's meeting. He told me he 'got the horrors at the thought of Cook talking to his European cronies about all this'. He had a strong face, big expressive eyes and a wonderfully conspiratorial way of talking. I sensed him as someone who was a great ally and a terrible enemy, and I liked him instinctively. You would certainly go into the jungle with him. TB was more nervous than usual, and wanted to do a proper run-through for once, and was constantly asking for reassurance we had the words and the tone right. I thought the statement was strong. He delivered it well. The MoD and FCO had produced a very good briefing pack which I took over to the gallery, full of drunken hacks who had been out on the Christmas party circuit. Everything went according to plan – operation launched, brief announcement from Lockhart at 10pm our time, TB 10.15, Bill 10.40. The general feeling was TB got the tone spot on. He was less worried about the impeachment situation now than the possible loss of innocent civilian life. He said he worried about our forces losing their lives, and he worried about the people on the receiving end too. 'I think if ever you lose that, you risk making the wrong decision, and you cease to do your job properly.' It was at moments like these you got a proper sense of the enormity of his job. Dealing with this, on the same day as the Irish were pressing him to get more involved in their problems, and with a stack of difficult domestic issues too, it was pretty impressive the way he kept these different issues under some kind of control, and was able to move from one to the other and box them off where he needed to. I could tell he was worried and would stay so until he got word the operation had gone well. He called some of the Europeans. Schroeder was basically supportive, Chirac iffy while Klima said 'I will offer understanding or support depending on the outcome'!!

Thursday, December 17
I saw TB first thing and he went through the main points for me to take to the meeting at the MoD bunker, chaired by George R with CDS alongside. I spoke to Guthrie earlier to make sure toppling of Saddam was not on the list of military objectives, as it would require tens of thousands of land troops. Likewise we should be making clear no threat to Iraq's territorial integrity. We had a lot of material to get out re Saddam's actions in previous crises, the way they faked evidence etc. Charles did a very good job at the press conference, then we went up to George's room. He is a great guy but he has a real problem on the blather front, and it meant we kept having the same conversations to go over things already agreed. At Cabinet, too, I could sense him and Robin vying as to who was the minister most involved and most knowledgeable. TB said Saddam had had 'umpteen' last warnings and what happened overnight was the response to his latest deliberate and clear obstruction. He went through the Ramadan sensitivities. He said he had tried as hard as anyone could to avoid being in this situation, but he was sure we had to act in this way now to

uphold the inspections regime. Robin said it was in no way a breach of the UN Charter. He warned the Iraqis would mercilessly play pictures of poor Iraqis being targeted by our bombs, and we had to point out past fraudulence and also the reality of the penury of their lives under the SH regime. In came Clare with a real stomach-churner: 'We know he is a bastard but can we help the poor people too?' She was calling for a new sanctions regime.

Peter M, out of nowhere, asked me if Geoffrey Robinson was being sacked. At lunchtime, it became clear why he was asking. Ben [Wegg-Prosser] called me and said Routledge's book on Peter was going to reveal that he had given PM a 300K loan to help buy his place in Notting Hill. Peter felt they should get it out through e.g. Bevins as part of a story about dirt being dug on Peter. I said hold fire. There was no way the story would be anything other than the existence of a loan that most people would find very odd. 'Do you think it is a problem?' asked Ben, knowing the answer. I do, I said. A big problem? Well, it sounds like it. I went round to see TB, who was in the loo. I took Jonathan into TB's room and waited for him to come back. He was in upbeat mood, which I was about to deflate. I told him the facts as I knew them, and he was horrified. First, what on earth was Peter doing taking out that kind of loan from Geoffrey, who was not an uncontroversial figure? Second, we were immediately onto the angle that Peter was ultimately in charge of the DTI [Department of Trade and Industry] investigation into Geoffrey. Third, it was bound to be – or certainly seen to be – part of the ongoing GB–PM nonsense. We assumed Geoffrey had told GB's lot, and someone had fed it to Routledge as a way of doing in Peter if Geoffrey was going to go down anyway. And all in the middle of a bloody difficult international situation which required us to keep our eye on a very different kind of ball. TB was not best pleased, but quickly calmed down and went into his usual 'we need the facts' mode. I found it astonishing Peter wanted to brief pre-emptively, which would never work on this. He wavered between anger and exasperation. 'I hate this. I cannot believe this. The Tories will murder us for it.' Yet when I spoke to Peter, he couldn't see it, or at least pretended not to. It was a loan between old friends who go back a long way. What about the DTI angle? I would not be making the decisions. Charlie F came to see me, and asked me what was wrong with Geoffrey lending him money? Possibly nothing, but the politics are fairly obvious and you can't just ignore them.

In the car on the way over, TB said 'Christ, I hope our pilots are OK.' TB was constantly asking Jonathan and me to find out what was happening re our pilots. He was also a lot more concerned than I imagined he would be re Iraqi casualties. Calum brought that home to me when I got home and he had been watching the news, and asking why we were killing Iraqi children. I tried my best to explain, and also to point out that in the past they had faked pictures like that. But the truth was you could not escape the reality of bombs and deaths, and some of them unintended. By now the second wave of Tornados was under way. Oona Muirhead [Director of Information Strategy and News in the MoD] called with the idea of TB doing a briefing tomorrow from the MoD crisis management centre. In between Iraq, we were beginning to think through the Peter M situation, which had the makings of a disaster area.

Friday, December 18

TB told me he had spoken to Peter and warned him his instinct was that the Geoffrey Robinson loan story was potentially very dangerous. We had asked Charlie F to do a report on the facts, and when I spoke to him later, he seemed to think it was pretty serious. Peter was still of a mind to brief on his terms, and later Ben W-P told me Tom Baldwin [*The Times*] knew about it. Then Wilson came to see me, said Michael Scholar [Permanent Secretary, Department of Trade and Industry] had only been informed of the loan once PM knew the book was going to divulge it. So there would definitely be questions about non-declaration as well. I felt it was a no-hope situation for him. It could easily be seen as bad as anything the Tories did, and it showed poor judgement, first to get involved, and then not to be upfront when there was the possibility of a conflict of interest re the DTI investigating Geoffrey.

PJHQ [Permanent Joint Headquarters] gave us a rather gloomy assessment of bombs that didn't work, or missed their target. It was 'potentially disappointing', they concluded, which probably meant a bit of a disaster area. Around half of the command and control targets had been hit, 55 per cent of air defence targets, only 2 out of 11 WMD targets definitely damaged. All the airfield attacks were successful. TB and I both emphasised that with the Iraqis now playing their usual games re engineering Western media coverage, we had to engage fully in a propaganda war. There were some excellent pictures of successful strikes which would form the centrepiece of the press conference. SH had been taken by surprise, and there had been clear damage to his command structure. It was possible there would be a terrorist response, probably bin Laden. George Robertson and Guthrie took TB down to the ops room for a morale boost visit. In many ways, it was just like any other Whitehall office, only they were deep underground and tracking military action hundreds of miles away. TB was a bit downcast when we got back, felt the picture had been a gloomy one.

Saturday, December 19

The press was turning. The right wing so hated Clinton for winning twice that they were now going at him over this, and the *Guardian* were now going down the usual mealy-mouthed route. There was the chance we would get politically hurt by the damage to BC. I didn't think it was very wise that he was out dancing last night. Bunker meeting at 8. CDS and PJHQ explained what had happened overnight militarily. There had been a 75 per cent strike rate. When I said the main problems today would be diplomatic, Robin came in on cue, and was in a very spiky mood. I had real trouble with the FCO yesterday getting them to prepare proper briefing material on the regime. Finally, after a lot of resistance, I got Robin to agree it would be done, and he would front it. But he was in very difficult mood. At one point Alan West, who probably irritated Robin because he had a bowler hat, was going through his brief and RC kept asking snide questions and then looking away. He asked the significance of one destroyed target, a Republican Guard maintenance area near Kuwait. West said it was to stop Saddam invading Kuwait. 'Was there any sign that he was going to?' asked RC. 'Not today,' said West. The updates were much better than yesterday, though the MoD guys were getting angry, feeling the Yanks were not being as open as they should be re overall targeting strategy. Clinton's impeachment hearings were about to begin, which was an added complication. There was a mildly comic moment when George Robertson told us they had successfully hit Republican Guard targets and destroyed his radio jamming capability. I said we should announce re jamming at the press conference and TB should do a World Service interview. Julian [Braithwaite, FCO official seconded to Campbell's team] called the BBC WS to fix, and they said there had been no jamming for a year!

I had a long chat with Peter M, who claimed not to see what the problem was re the loan. He said what is wrong with a friend lending money to someone? I said it had the potential to be a big bad story and surely he could see that. He said I was overreacting, I had always been a bit of a Calvinist, and it was all a bit 'Alastair and Fiona-ish'. He was adamant it would not be much of a story. I said it had the potential to be the worst thing to hit us yet. 'Would it be the same if it was Sainsbury?'[1] he said. Probably not, I said, but politics is not

[1] Lord Sainsbury, Under-Secretary for Science and Innovation. Until July 1998, chairman of J. Sainsbury plc.

science. So it is a Geoffrey problem, he said. I said it is a Geoffrey problem, but it is also a Peter Grand Panjandrum problem, and it is a GB–PM self-destruct at the heart of government problem. He was adamant I was overreacting. I began to wonder if I was and checked out how the others who knew about it saw it. John H, whose judgement was pretty solid, thought it was indefensible. Wilson, Charlie Falconer, Jonathan and most important TB all saw it as a major problem, and very hard to defend. John said to me he had noted in politicians that no matter how talented they were, they tended to be useless as their own advisers on their own personal affairs.

Bill C was due to do a press conference at 11 calling it [the attack] to a halt. TB was worried that Bill was now going too far in terms of carrots – e.g. sanctions. They spoke and agreed the threat of force had to remain in place. They agreed they would go out soon, but Steinberg came on, very clear BC would take it amiss if we went out first. We had TB at the door at one point, but John H came though to say hold fire. By the time he went out, flanked by Guthrie and GR, RC was on the phone complaining he wasn't there. I said he should have asked, like the others did. It was all a bit messy and scratchy.

Sunday, December 20

I stayed overnight at the flat and woke to a set of papers that were not that great. There was quite a lot of 'poodle-ism' around. TB said if this had been a Tory government supporting the US, the media would have been overwhelmingly supportive. They cannot stand a Labour government and a Democratic presidency working together. He felt we had done the right thing. He said he had found it really difficult to sleep these past few days, and he had worried the whole time about our pilots. It is one thing to make a decision in the comfort and safety of Downing St, but you always have to remember there are people who then literally put their lives on the line. He was just relieved they were all back safe and sound. Peter M called, said he was worried the *Guardian* were about to do the Geoffrey loan story and he felt it important he get on record that he was removed from any responsibility in the inquiry into Robinson. He was still refusing to accept it would be an enormous story. TB said if Whelan had given info to Routledge he intended to have it out with GB when he got back from the States. Peter felt he could tough it out. TB called around 10, as I was going to bed, and said he was now really worried about it. He thought it was possible, but unlikely, that we could tough this out. I could barely bring myself to think about the next few days if this was about to land on us.

Monday, December 21

The BBC was grim, with the Baghdad line being swallowed pretty much wholesale, and though the print news media was OK, most of the comment, *Sun* and *Mirror* apart, was pretty hostile. Also the Tories were moving into a more difficult position, saying there was no long-term strategy and we should be going for Saddam personally. I spoke to TB and we agreed he should do Christiane Amanpour on CNN and TF1 [French TV channel]. He was less down about the reaction than I was. I felt there was very little sense of military success, a lot of international isolation, and more re impeachment than during the strikes. We had to keep up the arguments. I called Robin C and said he had to go wall-to-wall again, and agreed with Guthrie he would do an article for the *Sun*. A draft came over which we knocked into decent shape and David Yelland [editor of the *Sun*] took it.

I went to a meeting on the planned Freedom of Information moves, which I feared were going to be a disaster, an excuse for the media basically to clog up the whole government machine with ludicrous enquiries the whole time. Charlie F leaned to my view but Derry was driving it very hard. The 11 o'clock briefing was long and difficult. I felt real public opinion was more or less with us but for their different reasons most of the press had decided to go hostile. Added to which some of the questions were difficult to answer for anyone but the Americans and they had not thought them all through. I did OK, and felt comfortable with the big arguments, but it was tricky. I went then to a briefing for the foreign press, which was less hostile, but more focused on how we rebuild some of the diplomatic relations damaged over this. TB was back just before 4, went straight into the interviews, which were OK though for some reason he said we hit every target, when we hadn't. And we were still struggling to get over the lines as to why this had been necessary now, because it was so easy for the media to compare negatively with the Kuwaiti invasion.

Then, the other problem was upon us. The *Guardian* put a series of questions to Ben W-P re Peter's loan. Charlie F and Lance [Price] went to see Peter, and then Geoffrey, and came back with a draft Peter statement, while I worked on a Number 10 line. TB was angry, at the bad judgement as much as anything, but also the way the thing had clearly been used in the PM–GB battle. Charlie said that when he went to see Robinson, Ed Balls came in in the middle and went through what CF was sure was a great charade of not knowing anything about it. Charlie, Lance and Ben came over to my office, where we were joined by Jonathan. I sent the draft line round to Richard Wilson and spoke to Scholar. Our only real point of defence was that Peter was not directly involved in the Geoffrey Robinson inquiry at the DTI, and had insulated himself from it. Apart from that, we didn't have much ground to stake out. The *Guardian* were asking about breaches of the code, and registration rules, and would doubtless get hold of Tories, and some of our own, to fuel it along. Derry joined us, and like the rest of us thought it was going to be difficult. Both he and Charlie F felt our major vulnerability was that PM did not tell the Permanent Secretary about the loan when he was appointed to the job. I said you could also make the argument he should have told TB prior to accepting the appointment. The press and the Tories would be onto that angle in no time as well. Wilson's view was that it would be better if Peter were to admit he should have declared it earlier, and also to announce that he would pay back the loan. Peter was going to say that his mother would help him do that. He was dreading her being dragged into it, and also dreading the press hanging round the house.

We all kind of felt he was not going to survive, but also felt we owed it to him to see if we could fight it out. That was going to mean him leading the fight, explaining himself, and seeing how party and public reacted. His problem was there would be a few enemies out to sort him. I told him I felt it was rocky but we would support him in a fight. We took an hour or so to sort the final statement, then heard the *Mirror* were onto it too, presumably via Routledge. I had a number of calls with Peter to go over the tricky questions. He was a curious mix of nervous and steely. We were agreed it was going to be awful. The question was how awful. I fixed for him to go and do the Millbank rounds and given how sticky the wicket, he did OK. But Yelland and [Piers] Morgan were both straight on, saying it was a political and presentational disaster, which of course it was. All we could do was set out the facts, say it was a private loan, and emphasise the insulation from the Robinson inquiry. TB said either he goes, or we defend him robustly, there can be no in between. But he accepted it was likely to end in him going. I called Whelan and said I did not want to hear of a single Treasury comment, and I intended to ask every single journalist whether he was briefing on it. Needless to say he denied having anything to do with Routledge getting hold of the story in the first place. I persuaded Peter to say that with hindsight, he wished he had declared it earlier, but that did not change the fundamentals. He was in for an almighty kicking, and the next 24 hours would be crucial. Richard Wilson was making it clear he did not want to be set up as a kind of judge on this – ministerial conduct was a matter for the PM, Sebastian Wood [Cabinet office] reminded me – while Michael Scholar was equally not prepared to say he had 'cleared' it. The truth is he did not know until the press were onto it, and only then did Peter declare it to him. It was a very weak point and Peter knew it. I was beginning to lose the will to live, first days and nights on Iraq and now this when I was hoping to wind down pre-Christmas.

Tuesday, December 22

The Iraq fallout was bad enough but the Peter M situation was a wall-to-wall disaster area. Every paper led on it in later editions, and it was grim. Though Peter did OK on his broadcast interviews, as the day wore on the thing felt worse and worse. I went to see TB in the flat. Should we cancel the end-of-term meetings with editors? No. TB had seen GB last night who was on, finally, both for Geoffrey Robinson's dismissal, and Whelan too. But Robinson was fighting hard, saying it was absurd if he was to be dismissed for being generous, and was angry with GB every bit as much as TB now. Whelan was saying he would go if we could get him a job at the FA. TB said his antennae were twitching, the damage to be done was real, and he could not see a way through it. He felt the line to hold was the avoidance of conflict of interest, and that maybe Peter himself should ask for the registrar of members' interests to look into it. I spoke to Peter and Charlie F to go through the tricky questions again. Though the press scented blood, I felt the briefing went fine, I knew the ground to stand on and just stood there, and let them make their own judgement about everything else. I agreed Peter had made an error in not being open about it, but he had moved to avoid a conflict of interest.

After the lunchtimes, which were pretty ghastly, I went to see TB in the flat, where he was making lunch for the kids. He said he sensed the Tories and the media would not let up, and there was enough here to drive Peter out. I felt the Tories were missing the point – they were so mesmerised by Peter, but that story was taking care of itself. They would have been better going on the notion that Geoffrey survived everything because he provided TB with holidays, GB with funding and Peter with a loan to buy a swanky place to live. The party would hate it. I went to see GB and he asked what I thought was the worst part of it. I said choose any angle you want – Robinson problem; PM liability; TB–GB-ery; cronyism; sleaze; no better than Tories. There were a lot of hits in one go. He knew I would be gunning for Whelan again and was being very nice and charming, saying we had a problem, what did I suggest for getting out of it? I asked if there were any other ministers Geoffrey had given money to, also whether he had paid Balls' and Whelan's wages at any time. He said most of Geoffrey's money went into the leader's office and campaigns, in opposition. I said it would be better all round if he resigned. GB said he had already put that to him, not saying it was what TB wanted, and he got very difficult about it. He felt he had done nothing wrong and was not prepared to be sacrificed.

I got a call to go back to Number 10 and TB asked me to go and see him, upstairs in the flat. He said wouldn't it be better if we asked both to go? I said you could make the case for that. Geoffrey had become more and more of a problem for the government, Peter had shown bad judgement, this had brought it all to a head. They could always come back at some point, he said. He then put the counter-argument as though he were now trying to talk himself out of it – Robinson had merely loaned a friend some money. It did not add to the difficulties he was already in, over which we had consistently defended him. Peter's judgement may be called into question but he had avoided a conflict-of-interest situation. And so on, then the other side, circular conversation time. Charlie F joined us and thought it was a bad idea, felt it was better to see if we could hold the line, not give in to hysteria. He was against Geoffrey going because that would make it much harder to keep Peter. I called JP. He said Peter's weaknesses were vanity and arrogance and they were the cause of his downfall. He used the word downfall, which suggested he felt he was a goner. I asked if he thought that. He said on balance I don't think TB should sack him, but it is bad and it could get worse. DB and Mo both called in, both appalled and clearly on the tough end of the market. JC agreed to do interviews but even he found it a tough wicket. He said the party would be appalled. He would defend him because he was a loyal team member, he said, 'but I find it very hard to defend at all'. It was interesting, however, how few of the hacks were saying he should resign. Little did they know that TB was getting to that point before them. TB said 'I blame myself for this. We should have got rid of Geoffrey earlier.' I felt TB would wake up and decide he [Peter] should go.

Wednesday, December 23

The papers were absolutely ghastly for Peter, massive coverage and relentlessly negative. Sadly – and it was never going to be any other

December '98: Both Mandelson and Robinson should go

way – people's basic reaction was the same as ours had been, and with the usual venom on top. Yet despite all that the balance of opinion was that he should stay, which was a surprise. But I had dreadful vibes about the next day or so. I had a doctor's appointment, came back and Fiona said Ben W-P had been on the phone, there was some problem re an aspect to the mortgage that Peter thought could be a resigning issue. Could I go to a meeting at 10.30? I spoke to TB, who, as I thought he would, had pretty much made his mind up. 'I'm worried what this is all doing to the public, never mind the press,' he said. He said in the end it was the concealment that was the main problem. Everything else was secondary but they would pick away. I said if Peter went, Geoffrey would have to go too. I know, he said. We had a conference call with GB, who was still asking if Geoffrey could stay. Re Peter, he was saying maybe an apology and a reprimand would be enough. TB said that didn't do enough. He felt Peter could only rebuild from a fresh start. He had spoken to Peter late last night, and he sensed PM was coming to the same view. Peter had spoken to GB this morning too, and one of the odder aspects of this was that as it got worse, he turned to GB for advice and support, despite being pretty sure his people had been involved in setting the whole thing up.

I got a lift in with Fiona, feeling pretty stressed and depressed. I met up with Jonathan and Lance and we went to the DTI. Jonathan was scruffily dressed as he was due to go to the Lake District. Lance was due to be heading to Chile for a break. We were driven into the underground car park, met by a very pretty girl who took us upstairs to an outer office that was deathlike in its atmosphere and then in to see Peter, who was at his desk, reading the papers. He had done the office very much to his taste, modern and brightly coloured furniture, a minimalist desk, nice pictures. A Christmas card from Prince Charles had pride of place on his desk. I asked everyone else to wait outside and told him TB wanted to talk to him. I didn't listen in so only heard Peter's side of the call, that he knew he had made a mistake, wished he had handled it differently, but was it really a hanging offence? I could tell from the vibe coming back that TB was in steely mode, and saying that it was. His argument was that an apology would just be seen as a piece of spin. There had been a deception, or at least a concealment that could be construed as such. Added to which neither party nor public could really grasp the scale of it. I was pacing up and down by the window and after a while Peter's tone changed, became one of resignation. He said 'You have clearly made up your mind and

I have to accept your judgement, which of course I do. I'm obviously very sorry.' The call ended, he looked at me, shrugged and then went out to see Ben.

I spoke to TB and began drafting resignation letters. I told Lance to put out a line that the PM was looking at the detail. I called Jack C, who was still manfully doing bids on it, and warned him it may end with his resignation, so change the tone. I spoke again to TB, who said we now just had to put sentiment to one side, and deal with it. He wanted it made clear that we were not the Tories, and never would slide to standards as low as theirs. He, Jonathan and I worked out the reshuffle and agreed the sooner it was done the better. I felt desperately sad for Peter, who came back in looking wretched. I said this is not going to be easy, but we are just going to have to do it, and be professional about it. I know, he said, I know. He had clearly been crying. He collected himself and then amazed me by saying he felt he ought to call Gordon. Again, I only heard his side, but it sounded as though sympathetic noises were coming from the other end. PM said he had been foolish, he was desperately sorry it was ending like this, and he hoped they would maintain some kind of relationship. It was extraordinary considering all that had gone on. GB was clearly saying he could trust him because Peter said on more than one occasion 'Yes, I know I can trust you, I know that.' I wanted the letters done and dusted and out by the lunchtimes, and started to read the draft of PM's letter to TB. The first line was 'I can scarcely believe I am writing this.' We were both quite emotional by now. I went over to him, said this is all absolutely dreadful but we just have to get through it. He kept saying why, why, why, but I was unsure whether he meant why did he do what he did, or why was he being forced to go. He felt if it was anyone else, we could have fought on. He made a few small changes, I got Lance to type it up outside, and then spoke to TB re his reply. Again, Peter startled me re GB. 'It's important Gordon sees them before they go out,' he said. He saw my surprise. I sat alongside him as he read through the letters, tears cascading down his face, and I gripped his shoulder and told him he had to be strong, and just get through the next ghastly few hours. I watched the news with Peter, who was calmer now, more focused. 'Please do your best,' he said. 'Don't let them portray me as some kind of felon.'

Michael Scholar popped in to say he was sorry, and seemed genuinely moved. Peter was fine when someone else came in like that but when it was the two of us, he kept breaking down. 'You don't deserve this, Peter, you really don't.' Yes, I do. 'Well,' I said, 'even

December '98: Mandelson consults Brown as he resigns

if you do, you don't really, if you see what I mean.' How many times had I warned him that what I called his 'lifestyle ambitions' would do for him? His desire to be famous and mingle with the rich and the great and the good. What the fuck was Charles's card doing there like it was the biggest thing in the mailbag? I really felt for him though, and felt wretched that I was having to act like some kind of undertaker to his ministerial career, doing the letters, shaping the media, telling them it was all over and soon he would be gone. We had had so many moments, good and bad, but when push came to shove, he was still one of the best and it was a dreadful fucking waste. I'd done Ron Davies's letters, and others, and it was just a job really, just helping sort things tidily, but I really felt this, and felt dreadful for Peter, for whom politics was wrapped up in everything he had.

As we left, I took him to one side and hugged him, and he me, and my mobile phone went off inside my jacket. We laughed. Be strong, I said. Do not let those bastards take any joy in seeing you broken. Stand tall and give every sense that one day you'll be back. I left feeling absolutely drained. TB called to go over the lines we should be pushing. It's grim, I said. Yes, he said, but we just have to get on with it now. I spoke to Peter again, who said he felt better. He said 'I've done the right thing so I feel better about it.'

Saturday, December 26

Amid the fallout, some of the papers were saying PM would lead the euro campaign, or go for London mayor. TB was trying to calculate whether we had been really damaged or whether this was a one-off quickly forgotten. I felt there was a cumulative effect building at the moment re out-of-touchness and this was a part of that. He felt Peter personally was badly damaged but if he learned the right lessons, and changed his ways, he could emerge stronger from it. I didn't like these friends and family social dos, because truth be told you were never really off duty, and I didn't like the atmosphere at Chequers anyway. I think we were both glad to have a 'proper excuse' to go into TB's study and prepare for his BBC interview and talk things over. He played tennis for a bit then we went up to their bedroom to talk over the interview. He was in the bath, and CB was lying in the bed throwing out lines of argument, until he said it wasn't helping him and could she be quiet.

It went fine, short fairly factual questions, pressing mainly on why he didn't sack Geoffrey earlier. He managed to get some big-picture message into it and was reasonably happy. The top line was Peter had done something wrong and now we had to move on. That was a bit inconsistent with Peter's resignation letter, which TB had not actually read, but had had read to him by me.

Peter was changing tack a bit. He was clearly being told by some that he should have toughed it out. He told TB he was getting lots of supportive letters and the feeling was we had allowed the media to force him out. TB told him he could only rebuild if he accepted he had made a big mistake and learned from it. He had to be more honest with himself. He said afterwards he was worried. Peter had gone from contrite to feeling somehow we had wronged him. I suspected it was just the after-effect. He had been hit by a truck and was now feeling the bruises. JP was very down on him, said he was pretty much a busted flush and had shown poor judgement. Little friendship and loyalty at the top. Peter was discovering that TB could be pretty ruthless when he had to be. Indeed, his only worry after the interview was whether he had been too obviously too ruthless. Then he did his jokey northern accent bit: 'Right you are, Ali, what a triumph, eh?'

Monday, December 28

I had spoken to one or two people re Whelan yesterday and the *Sun* were going for him today, while the *Mirror*, no doubt organised by Routledge, were starting what looked like a mini-campaign to save him. I sent a note through to TB saying the problem here was weakness. Everyone knew we wanted him out, and yet we appeared unable to shift him. That was a very weakening position. TB called on receipt and said the difference now was that GB accepted he had to go, but we had to get the timing right. If we did it now, it would keep the PM story running and look like a minor form of disintegration.

Thursday, December 31

GB called. He felt we could only get back on the front foot through major policy, but it may be the climate would not take it and we just had to let this period pass. He then raised Whelan. He said where are we with the Charlie situation? I said 'You tell me.' He said that Charlie would not accept responsibility for the Peter loan story and if he was forced out on those grounds, he would put up a real fight and cause us real trouble. He said he had told him that when a press officer becomes the story, he ceases to be effective. I pointed out that a day earlier a survey showed I got more coverage than virtually every member of the Cabinet. He laughed and said I was in a different position, but got the point. GB was in his warm and friendly, almost pleading mode – you have to understand I am with you on this, he said, but we have to be careful how we handle it. He felt we should try to help get him a job, though of course he was getting a pretty bad press, which was unlikely to help.

Friday, January 1, 1999

I called TB on holiday. He said he was having a great time. Having virtually lost my voice, I said I was so pleased for him. He banged on again about the need for me to get more time off, but I couldn't see where it was coming from. Would you have been happy if I had gone away as well? Probably not, he said. I said if I had buggered off like everyone else, I suspect we would be in an even bigger mess. There was a fair old rash of Whelan stories around the place. He was banking on something at the FA but I had spoken to David Davies [chief executive of the Football Association] who did not sound very encouraging.

Saturday, January 2

TB sent through a note saying he wanted a major focus on domestic policy as soon as we were back – Frank Dobson on nurses' pay, Blunkett on minister for inner-city schools. I called them both and they were on board for major statements. They were also totally supportive of any agitating re Whelan. I spoke to Frank while I was out on the Heath. At one point I said the way things stand, Gordon has allowed Whelan to alienate so many of his colleagues that if Tony fell under a bus tomorrow, it is hard to think of any who would positively want to vote for Gordon to be leader. 'That's interesting,' said a passer-by.

Sunday, January 3

I finally had a very difficult call with TB. He was out on a boat and it had taken an hour for switch [switch is the familiar name for the Downing Street switchboard] to get through on a line decent enough to have a proper conversation. I said he was getting a dreadful press, there was a sense of drift and he was being weakened and damaged. 'What am I supposed to do about it from here?' he asked, sounding irritated to be bothered. I said one thing he could do was call GB and tell him it had to be resolved re Whelan. There was a boil to be lanced and it was time to lance it. He said that was difficult when there was no actual evidence he was responsible for providing the info which brought down Peter. The main call was ridiculous and summed up the nonsense of the whole fucking situation. He was out on a fishing boat and halfway through the conversation suddenly said 'Hold on, I think I've got a fish.' He handed the phone to Bill Lloyd [protection officer], who then gave me a detailed running commentary as he brought the fish in until I said 'Bill, I could not give a flying fuck about his fish.' I then listened to shouts and hollers and 'wows' until TB came back and said 'You should see the size of the fish I've just caught.' I said I was so pleased for him. 'Yeah, OK,' he said, now sounding hurt. GB came through. Another difficult conversation. I asked what was happening re Charlie. He said – nothing, he was due back tomorrow. I said I was not prepared to work with him any longer. It was not just one thing – it was a modus operandi over years that made him an impediment to effective and professional politics or communications. Whelan had to go. I called GB again. He said he was surprised TB had not called me. He said he had persuaded Whelan he would make a statement saying he had worked in Labour politics for several years, now he had become too much part of the story and it was time to move on. He said CW was feeling very bitter and hurt. There were loads of media outside his house when he got back from Scotland tonight. He said it was vital the story was not sacked but moving on. I said I could assist in that. The second I put the phone down, it rang again. It was Charlie. 'Happy New Year' – you had to hand it to him.

Monday, January 4
I called TB at 6.30 after a sleepless night. He said Whelan was going, but it was important we did not do him in, and that GB was not damaged. This was as much about a media obsession with spin doctors as anything else. With a mix of friendliness and sarcasm, he 'thanked' me for the cuttings I had sent out, and said he was grateful I had waited till his break was almost over before ruining his holiday. He knew it was right for Whelan to go, but coming after Peter and Geoffrey Robinson, he was worried the press would start to think they could decide who survived and who didn't. I pointed out that we had been arguing for Charlie to go. Most of the press wanted him to survive. He said GB had said to him 'We must not let this kind of thing happen again, and in future I will do what you say on these issues.' GB called as CW arrived. Charlie was remarkably cheerful, though if you looked

closely, you could sense he was both hurt and nervous. Despite it all, there was something likeable about him. He kept his coat on for some reason, and stuck his feet on the table, an odd mix of relaxed and can't wait to get out of here. We were both pretty businesslike and perfectly civilised to each other. I said there was no point going over old stuff, we just had to sort today as best we could with minimum damage to him or GB, or TB. He denied briefing against ministers. 'Come off it, Charlie,' and he did his look of injured innocence which I had seen so many times. We finished his statement and I got GB on the phone to go through it. He said it was important we got through today with Charlie's integrity intact, and with him being seen as effective and thus employable. My briefing went OK. Endless questions on Whelan. They clearly felt he was pushed and I did my best to play it down and go on about the absurd priorities of the modern media.

Tuesday, January 5
Richard Wilson was back after a break in California and he said I was TB's main person and I had to be protected. 'All the main tensions come down through you, because you are the one they all speak to.' He said I really had to watch for exhaustion. He was worried that TB did not involve his colleagues enough, which would leave him prone to isolation. He felt Whelan's departure meant we could finally leave the ways of opposition behind us.

Wednesday, January 6
Seychelles. We arrived after an 11-hour flight. Philip Barton, John [Holmes], and I got off the plane in 30-degree heat and were taken to a waiting room. TB and CB arrived soon after. We had exchanged some fairly heavy words in the last few days, but as ever the tensions subsided pretty quickly. He came in, made a big beeline for me and said to the lounge staff 'Can I have some of your best coconut milk for my friend Mr Campbell, who has had a bad few days while I've been away.' Peter Wilkinson [Downing Street press office] was told by the *Sun* that Prince Edward and Sophie Rhys-Jones were announcing their engagement. We knew nothing about it. I called Geoff Crawford, who confirmed it. I said it was a shame they hadn't announced it two days ago. TB and I worked through all the basic arguments and upcoming problems on the plane. There was no doubt we had taken a hit, he said, and people would be looking to see how we responded to that. It was all about perspective and staying focused on the right priorities. He was worried about the NHS and the talk of bed shortages for the flu epidemic, which was provoking the usual

'winter crisis' talk. We worked on the South Africa speech for the rest of the flight. We arrived to a pretty impressive welcome and were driven to the presidential guest house. TB and CB had a private dinner with the Mbekis.[1] TB felt he was charming and friendly but it wasn't easy living in Mandela's shadow. TB felt there was too much attachment to the policy of affirmative action to promote blacks and he wanted to get Mbeki to say black South Africa would not become rich by making white South Africa poor.

Thursday, January 7

I worked on a proper briefing note for the speech, which was coming into shape. TB read it and okayed it in the car on the way to see Mandela. He was looking pretty good, if walking more slowly. His ankles were visibly thicker than the last time we saw him, and his hearing was clearly going. They went straight into a tête-à-tête on Lockerbie. And when I got him to sign a book for Monica [Prentice, Downing Street messenger], he took an age to write it out in his elaborate, old-fashioned handwriting, then looked up halfway and said 'It's not THAT Monica, I hope.' The atmospherics at their doorstep were good but NM having dropped Lockerbie on them, we had to get our act together on it. It had been a difficult discussion because Mandela wanted to tell Gaddafi [Libyan leader] that sanctions would be lifted for good if the suspects were handed over for trial. Gaddafi's worry was that the two suspects would say he ordered them to do it and the US–UK would then have to go for him. They were looking for assurances that the Libyans would not be interrogated by our police over other crimes.

Friday, January 8

TB was feeling dreadful, and looking not too good either. He was performing heroics in public for it not to be noticed just how ghastly he was clearly feeling. TB did a session with the two black journalists travelling with us and one of them, Steve Pope, said he couldn't believe how awful the British travelling press were. He said it had made him wonder whether we deserve a free press. Once we reached Cape Town, TB called GB, who was back thinking he needed a non-civil servant to do his media. We went straight to Nazareth House, the home for kids with HIV, where the staff were absolutely superb. The nuns didn't want the press to name Ntombi (the girl they sponsor)

[1] Thabo Mbeki, Mandela's deputy and leader of the ANC, was due to succeed Mandela in the spring.

but Reuters did so and it was obvious from the way she stuck to them that she was the one. TB seemed genuinely moved talking to her, and did a very good clip on the whole Aids situation, the figures on which were mind-blowing. We got to the Parliament building for the reception, followed by the speech, which went well, and he did an excellent off-the-cuff peroration about noble causes/glittering prizes, the need to challenge cynicism, politics as soap opera. Robin Oakley managed to get three clips out of the speech onto the bulletins, and said the riots had helped take the trip higher up the news agenda. TB had done well to get through the speech, and by the time we got to the residence was in a bad way. He sat picking at a salad, with just a towel around him, muttering how crap he felt. I went for a swim, then spoke to Peter, who said the Britannia building society were going to be clear he had done nothing wrong. On the plane to Kuwait, I had a session with some of the more grown-up journalists to get their take on the current media prism. Oakley thought things were getting worse not better, and it was becoming harder and harder to get serious coverage. I took a sleeping pill, slept for a few hours, and woke to find the crew really worried about TB, and even talking about diverting to land and get a doctor. He had been sick and looked wretched, but we agreed we had to plough on and just get through the next visit and then home. I half jokingly said the public have no sympathy with illness in politicians so we just had to get on with it.

Saturday, January 9

TB was looking like death warmed up but still the press hadn't latched onto it. We were driven to the Emir's palace for an odd meeting, in which TB did his best but provoked fairly monosyllabic responses, mainly re Iraq. TB said he was trying to build a consensus for a policy of containment. The Emir said Britain always helped Kuwait. They chatted about South Africa and the euro, but without much energy. TB did a sales pitch on a defence contract we were chasing against the US, and then we were gone, a meeting that was neither friendly nor unfriendly, neither substantial nor insubstantial. Sally [Morgan] called and said there was a lot of anger around re Peter being back in Number 10 yesterday doing the Hombach meeting (Labour–German SDP group). JP and others were up in arms about it. She said the *Indy* was running a story too that JP, GB and Jack S were uniting to oppose the Lib Dem strategy. TB was livid with Peter. It had not been necessary to meet there and the whole thing was just to get him back in the political picture, he said, when the time was not right. 'He should just disappear for a few months.' He was getting exasperated again, not least by JP's overreaction – he had been on to Jonathan to say it was undermining of him as DPM that Peter was in there holding meetings! He was still feeling really rough, sweating profusely but just about managing to hold it together when he was in public. It was only the tan he had developed in the last few days that stopped it being obvious he was in a pretty bad way. I really felt for him having to do all the official stuff and the glad-handing. We went to see the pilots out at the airbase. They were a lot younger than I had expected, very friendly and professional, but when you got them talking openly, admitted it was a pretty tough place to work. On landing, I had a message to call Robin C re the Margaret stuff. I still felt it best he stay right out of it. 'Is this survivable?' Robin asked. 'For fuck's sake of course it is. Stop being so melodramatic. TB will not give this a moment's thought. He backed you when it mattered and will back you now. It is personal and unpleasant but it is certainly survivable.'

Tuesday, January 12
Philip called from a focus group in Edgware to say 'Shagger Cook is a hero, and they think she (wife) is fucking ghastly.' I called Robin, hoping to cheer him up a bit, and it seemed to cheer him up a lot. He said he felt 'she' – underlined four times – had gone too far and would have little public sympathy. I said the most important thing was he stopped thinking and talking about it, and got on with the job.

Saturday, January 16
Peter M and Ben W-P came round for dinner. Peter said he was in no doubt he should come back, because he saw politics as a vocation. He could not see himself doing anything else. I said if he did a book that was self-indulgent, or too controversial and provocative, there was a danger it would kill him in the party. He would not be able to control how it was perceived as easily as he might think. He said he would listen to advice on the book, but he had to do something to fill his time. He could not vegetate. Ben wanted him to quit altogether but that was clearly a non-starter as far as PM was concerned. Fiona asked if he thought he could change his ways. The answer suggested not – he said he was confident party and public felt he was different and special, lots of them thought it was wrong he resigned and they want him back. He denied leading the glamorous social life the press chronicled and of which we so obviously disapproved. The friendliness to GB on the day of the resignation had now totally gone.

Monday, January 18

Kosovo was the main story of the day, with RC doing a statement and TB took a big meeting on it. They agreed we could not bomb at the moment because there was no political process and the KLA [Kosovo Liberation Army] were not much better than the Serbs, and just looking to NATO to be their defence arm and bomb [Slobodan] Milosevic [President of Yugoslavia] for them. George Robertson said there was a growing overstretch problem, with 27 per cent of the army currently involved in conflict somewhere. The US are at 11 per cent. Guthrie said it would be difficult to sustain a long-term UK ground troop commitment if we ever get to that. The US are in any event opposed to ground troops, GR said. He said Wes Clark blamed everything on the Serbs. Guthrie said he didn't mention the Kosovars once when he briefed the NAC [North Atlantic Council] yesterday. TB said everyone accepts Milosevic is a dreadful man, but if we bomb as things stand, what is the process we are trying to bring about? If the KLA move back in and take over, what then?

Wednesday, January 20

I did a line on Paddy A's standing-down announcement, which we'd managed to keep quiet. Only TB, Jonathan and I had known so it was a bit of an 'oo-er' moment when the Press Association snapped it. It got far bigger coverage than I predicted all day but then Paddy always said I underestimated the importance of the Libs.

Thursday, January 21

There was huge coverage of Paddy Ashdown stepping down and a lot of 'end of Lib–Lab' speculation, which TB didn't like. We arranged for him to do a doorstep as he arrived for the volunteering speech. He said people underestimated what a serious figure he was, how popular he was, what a good communicator, and he was sure any successor would realise party and public wanted a more mature politics. At Cabinet, they went over Kosovo, Lords and general politics, with a bit on the Libs. JP kicked it off with a laugh by suggesting we had a minute's silence for Paddy's career. Jack S was reasonably positive re the Libs, which was a surprise. But one or two, e.g. Dobson and Blunkett, said people were not sure what the purpose of the Libs' strategy was, and David was unsure our people meant it when they said they wanted a new politics. Robin was unbelievably pompous and overbearing when he went through Kosovo, but good on substance. TB said the situation was serious, RC that it was 'very grave'. War crimes were being committed. There was a humanitarian crisis. Everyone including the Russians was united against Milosevic. I left with TB for the European Publishers' Conference lunch. TB and I were seated either side of Murdoch and as the lunch wore on, he got more and more right wing – tax, competition, BBC, Europe, pretty full-on mode come the end. I don't think Murdoch much enjoys these big shindigs, even if he is the main man among them all. I noticed how quietly he talks when he is in little groups. I couldn't decide whether it was shyness, boredom or a way of forcing them to listen hard. TB and GB had dinner with Murdoch, Les Hinton [News International's executive chairman] and Irwin Stelzer. When TB called later, he said it had been a bit small-talky and when they did get to Europe, he quickly realised it was pointless because Murdoch's position was so fixed and OTT Murdoch said at one point he thought Britain could be like Switzerland. It was faintly obscene that we even had to worry what they thought, but we had to do what we could to get a better debate going on Europe. TB said he was 'really irritated' at the idea of Murdoch comparing Britain to Switzerland.

Friday, January 29

Vienna. TB came over and said he would like to boil in oil the person who decided to come to this meeting. I said it was him. In which case I will boil myself, he said.

Monday, February 1

As expected, the *Mail* and the *Sun* were hostile re what we were saying re the press, and the ante would be seen as being upped with TB doing *Richard and Judy* today. The interview started on the stories about us taking a new media approach, then a bit of nurses, then Glenn Hoddle's comments on the disabled,[1] where he went a bit further than we had agreed and as far as the press were concerned strayed into 'Hoddle must go' headline territory. I knew as he said it that he had gone further than he wanted and that the last thing he would want to do was fuel a frenzy about Hoddle, but that was what he did. He rowed back a bit by saying Hoddle must be given the chance to put his side of the story, but it was hard to balance it up. When he came off, re the strategy of going on programmes like this rather than the more conventional political outlets, he said 'God, the press will kill us for this.' 'Fuck them,' I said, 'we have to reframe the terms of the debate. They

[1] The England football manager had been quoted in *The Times* saying disabled people were paying for sins in a previous life.

believe that they helped do for Thatcher, did for Major, and that they can do for us, and we have to stop them.' The *Standard*, predictably, went on 'Hoddle must go, says Blair,' so I called Hoddle to say he had said no such thing, and it had been taken out of context. Glenn said he had never said what he was quoted as saying. I spoke to his agent Denis Roach as well, who then went on Sky to say TB had assured Hoddle he was not calling for his sacking. TB was not keen to get too involved, but did not want to pile any more pressure on Hoddle, who he thought was basically a decent bloke. The lobby were also getting agitated re our 'new media strategy'. I made the point that a lot of people were turning off from the Westminster Village coverage and we would not be doing our job properly if we didn't try to get our message out to people who were switching off from politics. I said as well that they could give it but they couldn't take it and they better get used to us drawing attention to the reality of modern political coverage. I pointed out that a 50 per cent fall in youth unemployment did not make a line in the national press, so forgive us if we tried to get it covered elsewhere. When did you ever feature people benefiting from the minimum wage or the WFTC [Working Families Tax Credit]? Never. Bevins was about the only one who openly agreed.

Tuesday, February 2

Comment on TB was critical, feeling he should have kept out of it. I sent the full transcript to Hoddle last night so that he could see the full context, but Godric had a pretty torrid time at the 11. Also, Tony Banks had said Hoddle's position was untenable, and the feeling was TB had given him licence to get involved, and raise the pressure. I called Banks in Lausanne and said no more interviews. I met up with TB at Paddington, then we waited for Wim Kok. He asked what I was in a previous life. I said I was a German shepherd. I was beginning to feel sorry for Hoddle, as the firestorm continued on the media, and with no real understanding yet as to what if anything he actually said. On the way to Wales, I was gently ribbing TB, suggesting his intervention against another Christian had not been very Christian. David Davies called to say Hoddle would be gone by 7. We had a few calls saying TB should never have got involved, which was right. Jim White of the *Guardian* was suggesting I was engineering Hoddle's downfall. Twat.

Wednesday, February 3

I had a sleepless night. Fiona woke up at 5 and said not to worry, but I felt I had overcooked the row with the press, and the new media strategy, and that the overblowing of TB's comments re Hoddle was a kind of revenge. Peter M called, said I should put it behind me, but he was unsure where we were heading with our media strategy. He was sure we were right to take them on, but what was the endgame? TB felt wretched that he was in the story, let alone the thought he had done for Hoddle, and kicked him when he was down. So we were both very down when we were preparing for PMQs.

Thursday, February 4

Apart from the *Mirror*, we didn't get too badly hit re Hoddle, but the truth was we were saved by Hague being so dreadful. TB was still feeling a bit raw and we were both pissed off at having handled it badly. I had a meeting with Donald Dewar pre his TV debate with [Alex] Salmond [leader of the Scottish National Party]. Salmond was vulnerable to a sense of being slippery. I suggested to DD he find an opportunity to say at one point 'You are not being honest, Alex,' but DD, as ever with anything involving risk or conflict, was ultra-cautious and reluctant. At Cabinet, DD gave a pretty downbeat assessment of the situation, despite a very good poll for us today, at the end of which TB said 'For those of you who don't know Donald, that was a very rosy assessment for him.' DD said the SNP were doing well to establish themselves as 'Scotland's party'. There was a lot of cynicism about politics generally. And we had suffered a few self-inflicted wounds. Having said that, the polls were moving our way and support for independence was falling. Our aim was to put over the cost of separatism.

Sunday, February 7

TB called to say it was about to be announced officially King Hussein [of Jordan] was dead. We were taking Hague, Seb Coe [Hague's Chief of Staff] and Ashdown out to the funeral with us. JP said 'Keep TB away from Paddy.' The flight out was fine, and I got through a stack of work, including the speech I was doing to a BBC seminar on Tuesday, which I had to get right. TB was reading through the GM papers [on the genetically modified food question] he had asked for, and getting more and more agitato re the Opposition. Derek Plumbly [FCO director, Middle East and North Africa] briefed TB, Hague and Paddy over dinner re what was likely to happen in Jordan. Hague looked very low and out of place. I could tell his confidence was a bit down and ended up feeling a bit sorry for him. I could remember from opposition what a pain these 'tag-on' events were as well, but he seemed particularly down.

Monday, February 8

We were out and about at 8. There was a fair bit of hanging around, and when you saw the list of leaders attending you realised the enormity of the logistical and security effort. We set off for the residence to meet Prince Charles. I thought his suit was a bit light for a funeral. After a bit of small talk he and TB travelled together to what can only be described as a 'holding palace', where we spent two hours just wandering around bumping into people and having a mix of small-talk chats and vaguely useful bilaterals. If a bomb had been dropped on there it would have been quite a hit. Clinton and Chirac on the stairs, TB chatting to them, then the Emir of Bahrain, then Crown Prince Abdullah, Crown Prince of Kuwait, then Jimmy Carter dropped by, there with [Gerald] Ford and George Bush [Sr] [all three former presidents of America]. We were one of a tiny number of countries who at least had our own room, and once we settled in there, a succession of people came in for a chat, including the King of Spain and Sultan of Brunei to see Charles. Charles taps his feet on the ground the whole time. He has very stubby fingers, which he is always tapping together, and he is constantly fiddling with his pinkie ring. Hague and Ashdown pretty much stayed in there and Hague looked very fed up. TB wandered around the place now bumping into all sorts – Kok, then [Poul Nyrup] Rasmussen [Prime Minister of Denmark], a proper sit-down chat with Yasser Arafat [leader of the PLO], who was boasting he had personally stopped two attacks on Israel.

Once the word came to go to pay respects, the atmosphere was almost like kids being let out of school. Clinton said it was like a world leaders' day out. I watched Chirac jostling the whole time, and he clearly understood if he was around BC he was likely to get in a lot of the TV coverage. TB tended to hang back a bit. There was a long rambling queue up to the coffin and when we got to the top of the stairs I realised they were going to usher all of us in there to pay respects, including officials. Hague was hanging back and I grabbed him and pushed him up with TB and Paddy. Partly it was for him, but also the last thing I needed was for me to be in the shot and him out of it. The young King and the old Crown Prince, who must have spent most of his life thinking he would one day be King, had to stand there and watch delegation after delegation go by. Neither was really allowed to show emotion, other than a certain steely hurt. As we went out, the first people we met were the Israelis – [Ezer] Weizman [President of Israel], [Shimon] Peres [former leader of the Israeli Labor Party], [Binyamin] Netanyahu – which must have pissed a lot of the Arabs off. There was a bit more hanging around as the other leaders paid their respects,

February '99: World leaders gather for funeral

then we were corralled again to follow the coffin on a fairly long passage up to the burial. Chirac got himself in pole position next to Bill and some of the others were starting to notice and make little jokes about Chirac's new-found pro-Americanism. It was warm now, and fairly dusty, and the combined noise from the feet shuffling along was fairly loud, so people had to raise their voices a little to be heard in the little chats taking place as the snake wound up the hill. Prince Charles introduced us to the 'King' of Yugoslavia [Alexander, Crown Prince of Yugoslavia], exiled of course, who was giving us his views on Milosevic.

Clinton had suggested a bilateral so we went up to the American room, where he was having a nap, but his people felt he wouldn't mind being woken up. He was the one most into the whole atmospherics, 'What a day, what an amazing event, how many bilaterals you done, Tony?' kind of thing. We did Kosovo then Ireland, with BC clear the IRA had to decommission real weapons before Trimble should be expected to have Sinn Fein on the executive. He thought it was 'amazing' they would not even think of doing something symbolic. We were called out because we now had a session with the new King, Abdullah, so we walked up the winding hill again, and in for a fairly brief session. The poor guy must be having to do every world leader going, so TB did not stay too long, talked about what a great man his father was, how important Jordan was, and how we would do whatever we could to help. Abdullah was short and stocky, less impressive than his father, but that may just be an age and authority thing. He had a mild twitch, but he definitely had the makings of it and it was easy to see why Hussein had chosen him ahead of his brother, who was looking really hurt and sad. The policy guys later briefed us on Libya. TB asked how Gaddafi stayed in power: 'Terror, a better economy and a pretty useful secret police.' 'Sounds OK,' said TB. Hague laughed, Paddy shook his head. Hague went back to his seat, leaving TB and Paddy to have a bit of a chat on Lib–Lab cooperation, wanting to take it into areas of health, education, pensions. I asked Paddy who would get his job. 'Charles [Kennedy] – it's his to lose,' he said. He said he was a very attractive personality but he could be lazy and foolhardy. He surprised us later on by saying he had kept a diary and he would like to publish it at some point, and would I like to see it? I said I would. He said he had done 30 minutes every day, and that he did it so his grandchildren would know what their grandad did. 'And there's the serialisation,' I said.

Sunday, February 21

We had a meeting in GB's room at Number 11 – TB, GB, Nigel Wicks [Second Permanent Secretary to the Treasury], Jeremy Heywood, John Sawers, Ed B, Jonathan, AC, re the changeover plan re preparations for the euro. We were still not totally decided when we would do the statement, or who, TB or GB. TB had done his own draft statement, which was definitely a shift to a pro position. GB, who was clearly anxious at the thought of TB doing the statement, felt it was too pro and would be seen effectively as a change of policy. TB's argument was that it articulated the policy according to current events. GB felt the policy he had set out on October 27, '97 was a robust position and one that would get us through the next election, given there was next to no chance of us going in before. I proposed that we speak about a change of gear, not a change of policy, and they both seemed OK with that. We had to admit that we were warming up on the issue, because time was passing, but still the basic policy framework set by GB applied. TB kept saying he felt we needed greater clarity about the direction of travel, whereas GB was wedded to the position as he had set it out. We agreed it would not be sensible to set a date but the fact of TB fronting it, and the fact we would be talking about public expenditure implications, would be seen as a pretty big signal. GB felt it would be enough just to set out what the preparations were. There was a clear difference of emphasis, but also I sensed GB basically trying to maintain control of a process that he rightly felt TB wanted to push along now.

Monday, February 22

The *Sun* front page said we were the most arrogant government in history. A lot of this was still payback for my whacks at the national press. I felt we had to keep going, ensure the public conditioned their response to media attacks with an understanding of the game being played, but TB was losing his nerve a bit. He called me at 7.20, said the front pages were ghastly. 'We are in trouble on this.' He made the same point at the office meeting, said he wasn't sure where this war with the media ends. I said it doesn't end, you have to fight the whole time, or they make sure you never get heard properly. Philip was the only one totally supportive of where I was, saying the public would be with us over time, and there was never a better time. But people were getting jumpy. They were finding lots of things to kick us with and kicking hard, and TB was feeling a bit scarred. He said PG and I were so anti-press we were beginning to sound like constituency surgery cases. 'It's reaching the point where John Burton pops his head round the door and says "You have another appointment."' I argued for confidence and boldness, taking them by surprise, always staying a step ahead of them. He asked me again if I was sure about taking on the press in the way we were. I said he had to show who was boss, him not them. Later he spoke to Murdoch. Anji listened in and said it was a very chilly conversation. Trevor Kavanagh had clearly been pouring vitriol into Murdoch's ear and they had decided tomorrow meant we were going into the euro whatever, regardless of economic reform. TB said he was worried my sense of injustice about what they did was clouding my judgement about how to deal with them.

Tuesday, March 9

Donald Dewar came to see me before Cabinet. He looked tired and was hobbling more than usual and he seemed just sad really. His sparkle was going, which was sad to behold, and the more we tried to raise his spirits or generate stomach for the fight, the closer to collapse he seemed to be. At Cabinet, GB rattled through the outlines of the Budget, basically a shortened version of the speech, as ever firing figures at them, so fast those who were taking notes could barely keep up. As ever, the overall impression was strong. He knew what he was on about, and he was confident. Their reaction was pretty good. TB let most of them have their say but it was all a bit otiose, given the thing was a done deal and had been at the printers for days.

Tuesday, March 16

Schroeder arrived [for the EU conference]. He seemed to understand we were not going to shift on the rebate. TB said the private session was perfectly friendly 'but it's not much fun having your balls squeezed by a German who is being wound up by a Frenchman'.[1]

Tuesday, March 23

We agreed early that TB should do a Commons statement on Kosovo, so that dominated the morning briefing. Sandy Berger had sent over a good note on arguments for getting involved, and we worked some of that into the statement. TB had a meeting to go over the whole

[1] Urged on by Chirac, German Chancellor Gerhard Schroeder (as holder of the EU presidency) was pressing to scrap the £2bn British rebate from the EU, arguing that EU spending patterns had changed since the rebate was negotiated in 1984 by Margaret Thatcher.

scene – RC, GR, CDS, RW, Jonathan, AC – and it was pretty gloomy. Charles Guthrie made clear it was a difficult operation being considered and nobody could be quite sure when or how it ended. It could be very bloody indeed, he said. TB's statement went fine and Hague was poor again. They were beginning to look really pissed off behind him now. The Germans briefed that they would be looking at the UK rebate regardless of this being about the costs of enlargement, which TB took as a worrying sign. We had another session with Donald D, TB and I trying as gently as we could to get him to understand the need for a clear message in Scotland, a clear and agreed strategy, and some energy and aggression. TB said afterwards he felt dreadful, so downcast did Donald look. But we had to grip it. TB spoke to Bill C re Kosovo. He said afterwards it is ridiculous trying to juggle all these things – Kosovo, NI, Agenda 2000 – every one of them required real care and attention. I said that was his job and we just had to do it. But the pressure was intense at the moment, and it was affecting us in different ways.

Wednesday, March 24

Berlin. Kosovo was still the main story. I spent part of the afternoon working on TB's Kosovo broadcast. John Sawers took me to one side and said Kosovo was definitely on and action was set to start at 7pm. SACEUR [General Wes Clark NATO Supreme Allied Commander, Europe] had the key. We went back to the hotel and TB worked on the draft I'd done, and wrote a strong ending. Chirac and Schroeder were sound. Once it started, we were nervous until we heard the four Harriers were back safe and sound.

Thursday, March 25

TB was trying to talk to Schroeder for ages after he woke up, but even by 8 we were told he was in bed. This on the day he was meant to be solving the mass of problems still outstanding. I think Schroeder had felt TB might give something on the rebate, but wasn't, and TB was now pushing in other areas, and looking for a bit of help. GB was taking part as well and was good, spraying the jargon all around to show he knew what he was on about, VAT/GNP, own resources, no windfall gains, which is where we ended. We were winning on most points. We had reshaped what we were asking for and where we saw how others could change and Schroeder seemed pretty on board but some of his people were wheedling at him. Later, when TB had another go at Schroeder, he totally lost it, basically told TB to fuck off, and stormed off, and his interpreter turned to me and said 'I don't think we need to translate that one.' TB said 'I think we've pushed him as far as he'll go.' Chirac was digging in re CAP and at one point TB was asked to have a go at Chirac, which he did, though to what effect was unclear. Chirac was playing hardball and gently doing in Jospin at the same time. Kok stopped short of really going for Chirac on CAP. Truth be told though, a very good deal for us was emerging, and it was others who were in trouble now.

Friday, March 26

The feedback from the Kosovo attacks was not great. As well as the Harriers failing to hit their targets, our TLAMs [Tomahawk land attack missiles] from *Splendid* failed too. The Yanks who sold us the missiles were not surprisingly in a bit of a flap about it. I suggested we just say it was a joint operation and not get into who did which bit of the operation. The summit coverage was going well, but dwarfed of course by Kosovo. On the plane back, we had the usual joking re the other leaders. TB felt Chirac had really hung tough, Dehaene had been tough, Schroeder had been pretty cool apart from his fuck-off moment. 'I thought he was going to hit me,' he said.

Saturday, March 27

I slept solid for 12 hours then took the football club at school. The US fixed a TB–Bill C call for 7pm so I had to leave the kids' school disco to get home and listen in. They agreed to an intensification of the campaign and I briefed that TB had said we would increase our contribution. They also went over the yardsticks by which they would judge it right to talk to Milosevic again. There was no real clarity about an endgame at the moment. Good call, and he sounded a lot more sharp and clear than last time they did Kosovo. Then we heard a stealth bomber had been shot down and there was a race on to get to the pilot first – thankfully won by the Americans. But because the stealth bomber was supposed to be undetectable by radar, it would have a bad effect on morale. The press was not so bad, but we had a real problem with the BBC and we talked over whether we should go for them publicly. They made no effort to balance the fact that they were reporting democracies and a dictatorship, virtually taking the dictatorship propaganda at face value while putting everything we did through a far more intense scrutiny.

Sunday, March 28

The news was dominated by the stealth bomber, more UK planes being deployed and NATO saying it was the worst genocide since WW2. Paddy A went up on Kosovar Albanians not being heard. TB called, worried at the delayed reaction to the Budget, felt GB should have been more open about some of the changes now out there.

Monday, March 29

Another day from hell really. The refugee situation was getting worse, and there wasn't much sign the military campaign was getting better. The question had really moved from justification – there was widespread support for the idea of action – to competence and efficiency and ability to deliver the policy. At 9.30 RC, CDS, GR, RW came over for a meeting and Charles gave a pretty gloomy assessment. Bad weather and poor weapons performance meant we were not really hurting Milosevic as planned. TB looked pretty downcast. CDS was fulminating re the TV armchair generals and later vowed he would do none of it when he retired. I was asking why they were not hitting transmitters, if our argument was that his media machine was part of his military machine. Charles said even if the Yanks had the stomach for a ground war – doubtful – the Italians wouldn't. TB said we had to do such damage to Milosevic, the regime and the personal assets that he would sue for peace. He too couldn't understand why we were not taking out his transmitters. [Alex] Salmond made the mistake of comparing the air strikes – targeted at a dictatorship – with the Blitz of London or Clydebank. Silly boy. Bad judgement and we went for him. Plane to Belfast. We helicoptered to Hillsborough, where TB did a fairly downbeat doorstep, less 'hand of history' than 'we have come too far to stop now'. TB saw Bertie, then Trimble, then Mallon, then he and Bertie met Adams and McGuinness together. Everyone seemed to think we were in the shit. I had a chat with McGuinness re Kosovo. He said he would be a hard nut to crack and 'bombing into submission' isn't always a sensible policy. Pots and kettles. The only breakthrough of sorts came when Adams said to us 'Look, we know the score, there has got to be decommissioning.' It was the first time he, rather than we, had been that blunt. It had also been announced where nine of the 'disappeared' were. The downside of that was it reminded people the IRA were killers. As TB said, are we really expected to be hugely grateful that years after they did it they told us where they killed and disposed of a few people?

Tuesday, March 30

Kosovo was not looking good. The humanitarian crisis was becoming a disaster, and another night of bad weather meant another night of military failure. He said we had to start doing some real damage. He felt we had two days before things turned against us. TB said

Milosevic will only move if he senses we are in a position of overwhelming strength. He saw the Orange Order before we left for Stormont for talks mainly with the smaller parties. He and Bertie saw de Chastelain, who must live a very weird life, backwards and forwards to NI, with large periods of literally nothing happening to bring him into the picture. But TB stressed de Chastelain's credibility was vital to the process. He felt we might get something, possibly an act of decommissioning, videotaped by SF, verified by them. Paisley was out and about rowing with the Irish, but the one TB really couldn't stand was Brendan McKenna [Garvaghy Road residents' spokesman]. He said he was making things worse and people could die as a result. I watched the GR, CDS, Clare press conference, which was OK but we really needed signs of the military campaign working. Joe Lennon and I suggested that we impose a deadline of midnight and that if there is no progress by then we leave. They were nervous. Then school visit, which was a way of trying to get through to public opinion direct. We flew back to Hillsborough and over lunch TB and BA agreed they would really try to work on Sinn Fein. GA and McG were basically saying they would decommission – not least because they knew they had to – but they could not be sure how the IRA would react to that idea. TB said if it was left to him and Bertie, they could sort a deal that most people would support in five minutes. There were meetings going on all over the place but the one that mattered was SF–UUs. Adams and McGuinness were always on their own, Trimble always with a huge entourage to keep an eye on him. About 9, they came through into the big lounge where we were just chatting and Adams said 'I'm afraid that rather than wasting everyone's time we thought it best to tell you we have a real problem.' Trimble said 'We are not in the same ballpark.' Very calmly, GA went through the main difficulties – the UUs need some kind of act, and we cannot deliver it in that way, while we cannot have decommissioning as a precondition for joining the executive, and political realities make that impossible for David. There was a long silence, TB a mix of frustration and anger, and he just sat there stony-faced for a while. TB's only hope was GA and McG were off seeing the IRA guys to say 'Do we really want to be the people who bring this crashing down?' There had been something pathetic about the way they came through to TB and BA to say they couldn't sort it. It made you worry they could never work in government together, which was meant to be the aim.

Kosovo had had another night of bad weather so military frustration. TB was worrying about that, and about NI, where he said at the first meeting he just felt we were too far apart. We're wasting our time here, he said. I had a brief chat with McGuinness in the corridor and said I thought TB was getting to the end of his tether on this, so they needed to work out their lines for failure. He said it was all down to Trimble (or Trumble as he says it). TB saw the UUs. BA saw SF and gave them a hard time, said TB had a 'war to fight' and they were keeping him here, buggering him around and getting nowhere. 'I told them in Dublin Central language to "stop fucking about".' Obviously nobody wanted to be seen to bring the whole thing crashing down, and they had to feel more pressure. That did require us to stay a little longer, whatever the frustrations. I agreed with Bertie that when we left we would say if left to the two PMs it would be sorted in minutes, and people had to face up to their responsibilities, to give the sense there was a solution but the two sides would not embrace it. TB was a bit worried leaving Mo in charge of the talks, as her relations with the UUs were so poor. Yesterday she asked him what job he was going to give her post-devolution. She was making clear she felt she deserved one of the big ones. TB felt Cabinet Office was probably the best he could offer her. He had not been impressed by the way she had let the UUs stray more and more offside. We had to leave for PMQs. Re the *Mail* and the Tories, he said their patriotism is as deep as the next opportunity to attack a Labour government. The word from Belfast was not good. McG had basically said piss off to the paper. Bertie was threatening to go home.

We had a Kosovo meeting. TB said he couldn't believe the weather could be such a factor when we were talking about supposedly sophisticated weapons. He said the generals had to understand they should really be going for it, no holding back. In fact [Javier] Solana [Secretary General of NATO] had vetoed plans to hit military buildings yesterday. Charles [Guthrie] was still trying to get them to hit broadcast transmitters. Robin was very gung-ho. TB said we had to do a lot more damage before we could even think about peace moves. CDS was raging about armchair generals again, 'rats who should be shot'. He told me as a result of his press conferences he was starting to get hate mail and fan mail. His favourite was one that said he was a hapless poodle to a demented Jock.

We left for Northolt again. We met Bertie at Aldegrove, got a helicopter to Hillsborough, then took stock. Clinton wanted to speak to Adams but he was away 'consulting' IRA members, which meant we couldn't get hold of him, as he went without a mobile, presumably because he knew he could be tracked on it. DT was at Stormont, telling everyone he intended to go to the opera. You sometimes wondered if they were serious. We started the next round around 8, first BA–TB, then the UUs and then a possible breakthrough meeting, just TB, Bertie, Adams and McGuinness. TB called us in after a while, saying 'I think we are in go mode.' Ken Maginnis gave me a real bearding about how awful Mo was, how she didn't understand where they were coming from at all. He said there was no way they would accept all these normalisation measures 'and remember I am relatively speaking one of the liberals'. They all later surrounded TB and monstered him with the same kind of message. John Taylor said Mo was a liar. TB said afterwards, I think now I understand better why Trimble is like he is. While SF were away again, I had a very nice quiet chat with Bertie and Mo. Bertie said even though it is all so frustrating, it is worth remembering that not long ago, people inside this building were trying to kill each other. He was right. TB was less sanguine than Bertie. Yet somehow I thought we would get there.

Thursday, April 1

We rolled into the early hours. Taylor said his troops were getting more and more fractious and wanted to go home. TB talked them into staying. I said to Taylor why don't you go up for a nap? I suggested he take TB's bed, to which he said 'I could not possibly use a bed reserved in the main for the Queen and the PM.' So he took my room instead, and Maginnis, clearly no possessor of false modesty, took TB's. When I wandered up later he was snoring loudly at the ceiling. Bertie was convinced there was a real and substantial discussion of the IRA Army Council, inside the building, and that GA and McG were genuinely trying to win them round. TB was looking a bit grey by now though, and the briefings on Kosovo weren't helping his mood or morale. TB had another session with Adams and McGuinness. I went in, and later got DT in, and said we had to publish something today, or else people would feel we were totally hopeless and this was all going nowhere. Mo and I were both getting really pissed off at the way the SF people were handling it all. Mo said they have got two PMs totally tied up in this, and a US president, yet they are giving nothing at the moment. It reached a low point when we got Clinton up at 5am US time to speak to Adams, who was busy delivering a history lesson to TB and too busy to take the fucking call. Berger was raging about it. We were moving to the idea of publishing the document and simply saying the parties would have to consult on it, and we would give them ten days to do so. Then, cheek of all cheeks, McGuinness said 'You realise we will be bound to oppose the delay.' Bertie, by now getting fractious, said 'That's a good one – you'll oppose it when you've been calling for it.' The important thing was to give at least some sense of progress and movement. People were reasonably upbeat apart from SF. What a crazy place to work. TB was still worried that if we pushed SF too hard, they would be unable to shift at all. I got home, and crashed out.

Wednesday, April 14

TB spoke again to Thatcher re Kosovo, who said she couldn't understand why Clinton was not more exercised and hitting the buttons harder. George Robertson and CDS came over to do a presentation on ground troops. Charles taped a map up to the mantelpiece above the fireplace and went through the three routes in – Albania, Macedonia, Montenegro? – and explained why all three were difficult. He said there were two options for invasion – limited, which meant three months and involving around 80,000 troops at least; or unlimited, which would mean 200,000 troops, and no idea yet where they would come from. TB was nodding silently, occasionally sighing loudly, and clearly taken aback at the scale of what it would require to be sure – and even then you wouldn't be that sure. He said we had to carry on making the preparations and in the meantime hope the air campaign improved in effectiveness and intensity. The Serbs were claiming NATO bombs had hit a convoy of refugees, killing many. I called Jamie Shea [NATO spokesman] and said while the facts were being established, we had to have ready a history of the lies the Serbs told about casualties. It was not clear at first whether the claims were true or not and it was proving hard to get the info out of the military. TB came out for a Clinton phone call. Both were now hitting the panic buttons quite hard. Bill said we had to work on Chirac to support attacks on Phase 3 targets, and we had to help Solana and Wes Clark on presentation. He felt Jamie was OK as a frontman but the operation needed building up. TB said the methods of operation were too diffuse and both of them needed to be driving this more directly. Yes, we have done some damage but we are not there and yet here I am, at an EU meeting where they are talking about the future of the Balkans as if this thing is won. Clinton said he would lean on Chirac, and say that if we ended up unable to take the decisions that the military believed were necessary, and the suffering went on longer than it should, we would all pay a price for that. TB said he would send me to see Solana re the presentation issue.

Thursday, April 15

The convoy attack, now virtually admitted by NATO, was clearly going to be the main story, and all kinds of different versions were flying around. I went to the MoD bunker meeting to hear another gloomy overnight assessment of military operations. I got back through the tunnel for DOP, where TB said there were two main problems: 1. a military operation with too many people able to call shots, and a resulting lack of intensity and effectiveness and 2. poor presentation, which was hurting us in NATO countries' public opinion. Jack Straw said we needed 'some good old-fashioned Millbank discipline instilled in them'. Quite, said TB. He was very fired up and I used some of the words and feelings to harden the line personally against Milosevic as being responsible for all the suffering. TB called Solana to discuss presentation, thinking they would resist a UK takeover. But Solana said, almost as soon as TB raised it, 'If you can send me your man Campbell, that would be best.' He said I was the best in Europe and, listening in opposite Jonathan, I felt myself blushing. TB said I would go out tomorrow. Cabinet was nearly all Kosovo, TB warning we were in for a long haul. The mood was fairly gloomy. I was now starting to get focused on tomorrow, working out the best way of ensuring I got Solana and Clark onside for change. I spoke to Jamie S again and he sounded genuinely pleased I was going out. He said Solana was desperate to see me, really wanted to put the thing on a different level. So at least I was entering what Charles Guthrie would call a permissive environment.

Friday, April 16

Brussels. Pretty extraordinary day. My main message for the NATO lot was that a military campaign had to be founded on simple concepts, and so did any supporting media campaign; that they should not be having to deal with media the whole time and needed to let professional media advisers take the strain so they could concentrate on the military; that the morale and effectiveness of the operation could be enhanced by the feeling of a strong and coordinated media message going out around the world. On the train back, I wrote up the meetings with Solana, Wes Clark, etc and then prepared a detailed plan to put to TB, CDS, GR, RC, etc. TB discussed it with Bill C, who said he thought I should base myself there until it was over. I told TB he was right to be anxious. They did not feel like they were in charge of a winning campaign. They felt they had hands tied behind their backs, and they struck me as a bit desperate and demoralised. I felt that Clark would be in a bad way if it went on too long like this. TB said we are going to have to take this show over.

Saturday, April 17

Peter M was worried my role would become too big a story and 'spin' would be a problem. TB said he was fed up with all the bollocks about spin. He said 19 democracies were at war with a dictatorship and we needed the best media operation available, which up to now we sorely lacked. He was desperate for some real grip and discipline. He was, however, telling me I had to get some rest, which as ever he followed with half a dozen ideas or instructions he wanted me to put into action.

Sunday, April 18

TB saw Guthrie and he basically levelled and said we were likely to have to put in ground troops. TB said he was aware of all the sensitivities but he wanted the preparations to go on. Guthrie called me later and said according to [General Sir] Rupert Smith [NATO's Deputy Supreme Allied Commander Europe] I had scored a direct hit with Clark, who told everyone he wanted my plan put into action, and every cooperation given. Charles's assessment was that Clark was not a 'proper' general, also that he was suspicious of Rupert because he was a 'proper' commander. I said I was reasonably impressed by him and Charles said yes, Tony said that, but a good general looks upwards and sideways, delegates and then protects the people he has delegated to from the politicians. Clark won't delegate so he risks being swamped by events. And he is not good at explaining strategy when there is one. Why those targets? What are we trying to achieve? You always need the answers to those questions.

Tuesday, April 20

Brussels. I left to meet TB. I briefed him in the car and he was alarmed at some of the points in my note – eg Solana and Clark being at odds the whole time, Clark doing his own media. We arrived at SHAPE [NATO HQ – Supreme Headquarters Allied Powers Europe], met by Smith, and TB was taken straight to the video-conferencing centre, where Clark talks daily to the commanders in the field. Clark 'compered' it, and asked TB to say a few words. He spoke really passionately, and powerfully, about the job they were doing, and I could feel a positive effect around the room. He also went out of his way to build up Clark. On the way out, Clark was effusive in his thanks. TB got the impression Clark was very nervous, and unsure about whether we were winning. Milosevic's military capability was at 70 per cent, so degraded but still fairly strong. As he had with me, Clark went on about Milosevic in a very personal way, and TB felt he saw it a bit too much as a personal mission, rather than a military leadership task. 'If we don't win, all our asses are on the line,' TB told him. They went over ground troop options, which was becoming the most talked-about likelihood, but one that was worrying the US in particular. Guthrie called and said the feedback from my intervention so far was totally positive. Rupert told him I had 'electrified' the place and that Clark had made it clear that when I said jump, they had to jump, so hopefully so far so good.

Clark took me in for a chat after TB left. I thought it would be about his meeting, or about his profile, on which I had sent him a note earlier. Instead he took me to a raised dais and opened a book that was lying on it. It contained satellite photos of targets. In particular he showed me various pictures of RTS Belgrade (TV) and the Socialist Party HQ, which was used as a broadcasting centre run by Milosevic's daughter. He said the French would let him hit one but not the other. Alongside the picture of RTS was a strapline 'collateral damage risk very high'. It was next to a church and other buildings. The party HQ was more open. He would like to hit both because his media machine was a legitimate target, but the French would be very iffy. He was intending to hit the TV station. I said we had been arguing for that for weeks. But he said there was another problem. This was the place where some of the Western journalists did their broadcasts. Ken Bacon [US Department of Defense spokesman] had been saying there were no safe places in Belgrade, which was as near as we could get to warning them, but how big a problem was it? he asked. It suddenly dawned on me I was being asked whether the significance of the target was sufficient to live with the fallout of outrage and possibly deaths among the Western media. 'So can I do it?' he asked. Not like 'do I have permission?' but 'is this doable?' He said: 'I need your answer within the hour if that's OK.' Then Solana called. Clark said 'Alastair and I are discussing whether to hit it. The French are being difficult but I'm in favour.' I said after the call had finished it was not difficult to make the case it was a military target, and that unless we feared there was a human shield situation, there was no difference between a working journalist and any other civilian who might be hurt. He said if he could hit TV today, electricity tomorrow, we would really start to make progress. I bumped into Rupert Smith, told him of the conversation, and he said it was typical of him. 'He should just do it. His decision, nobody else's. The right call.' I discussed it with TB. He said it may be he was just trying to flatter me by making me think I was centrally involved. Equally, I had clocked he couldn't resist telling Solana I was there and involved in the discussion. TB said I should say to him that I was there to be used but this was not a responsibility I expected at this time. Fortunately, in our party media monitoring report, I clocked a line of John Simpson [BBC's world affairs editor] saying he had been 'invited' to the TV station but didn't go, which suggested the media realised it may be a target. TB had had a pretty dispiriting chat with Smith, who said the operation wasn't focusing ruthlessly on the job in hand.

Wednesday, April 21
We got terrific press from TB's visit, right round Europe and the US. The press were also beginning to say the media operation was improving. I had a bit of a lie-in, took the kids to school, then straight to the Kosovo meeting. TB was now of the view, encouraged by SACEUR, Smith and [General Dieter] Stockman [Clark's Chief of Staff], that there was no way we were going to win without ground troops. The US were behind us on the issue. TB's only worry for PMQs was ground troops, but he did fine. He gave a good answer on Simpson – he should be free to report as he sees fit. We should also be free to speak as we find. Afterwards he said of Simpson 'What a precious arsehole. Thinks he should swan around criticising as he pleases but if anyone speaks back it is an attack on civilisation as we know it.' On the plane to Washington, TB said if we didn't win this, it was curtains for the government, and not just ours. He was going over the argument he intended to use with Bill – if we the politicians say we cannot afford to lose, and they the generals say they cannot do it without ground troops, then we have to go for it. Invasion. Simple as that. The politicians would never win a great briefing war with the military. They would say their hands were being tied. He asked if I thought Clark was up to it. I said he's the only one in charge so we have to build him up. He was worried if he pushed too hard on ground troops, he would risk his relationship with Clinton. Berger complained to Sawers about a *Wall St Journal* story that TB was flying out to stiffen Clinton's resolve. We were driven straight to the White House, TB and Guthrie in the back row of the car, John Sawers and I in front. John said they were very, very cool on ground forces and I think we all knew it was going to be a difficult meeting. Guthrie had just come from speaking to [General Harry] Shelton [chairman of the US Joint Chiefs of Staff] who was of the view they had to go for ground troops. TB said the bottom line was that all the military appeared to be advocating ground troops. TB said his goal was to at

least get commitment to proper planning of ground troops. Shelton also asked us to speak up for Clark. CDS felt Bill Cohen was muttering about getting rid of him, which would be a disaster at this juncture.

Bill C arrived, went round everyone shaking hands and then took us up in the lift to one of the bigger lounge rooms upstairs. Madeleine Albright [US Secretary of State], Berger and Steinberg were already there and the mood was pretty stiff, other than with BC. Clockwise, BC and TB in chairs, Madeleine, Sawers and Chris Meyer on a sofa, Jonathan and I in chairs, Steinberg and Berger on a sofa. The small talk didn't last very long. They went through the NATO summit agenda, then into the detail on Kosovo. TB laid out a very tough case. 1. NATO/SHAPE is a mess. 2. The air campaign is OK but not much more than that. 3. All the military seem to be saying air power alone won't do the job. TB said he knew how difficult this was, not least because we had all said we would do it without ground forces. But 'I start from the assumption we cannot afford to lose. So we must do whatever we have to do to win.' He thought Milosevic was unlikely to cave unless he thought there was a realistic prospect of a ground troop invasion. He was worried if we waited and waited and waited we would suddenly find we were close to winter and near impossible conditions. He said of Clark he was doing a heroic job but he needed help. He was swamped. They were very unkeen on ground troops, or even saying there were contingency plans. It would require an invasion force of 150–200,000, the bulk of them from the US. TB said the bottom line was he had to win, and if the military said it couldn't be done just by air, we had to listen. Bill was fairly mild throughout, chewing on a cigar, drinking Diet Coke, grumbling about the French a lot. Jonathan said it was win-win for the French. If we fuck up, our fault. If we win, they are part of a great victory. BC said he felt we were probably damaging Milosevic more than we thought based upon their public statements. We were hitting him harder than he ever imagined we would. The question was whether we could hit him so hard he looked for a diplomatic way out. BC was talking both about Milosevic being indicted for war crimes, and at the same time about whether we could do a deal with him. Bill said we had to bomb like hell, be more creative diplomatically, maybe arm the Albanians, sort the presentation. He was very nice about my plan, a copy of which Joe had shown him. Bill went off to get some drinks as it became obvious this was going to drag on a bit. TB said the worst-case scenario was we lost and the generals were out saying they were prevented from doing what was needed to win. Berger said there should not be a whisper about ground troops. TB realised we had to work on Berger more and at one point he was addressing him as much as Bill. Bill said at one point the Republicans would probably support him on ground forces 'because it might destroy me'. They may not think it is Vietnam, or Hitler and Tito, but they think we will be there for a long time and with a lot of casualties. BC and TB had a short session on their own, during which I filled them in on how bad NATO/SHAPE was, at the end of which Berger said 'I will now jump out of the window.'

In the car TB was very gloomy. He felt we were a long way apart, and there was a danger of a US–UK rift being the background, which of course Chirac would love. He said to me and Jonathan 'This could finish us. If we lose, or even if it ends in a messy deal, we are in trouble.' We had been in there for two and a half hours. 'I think I failed in my mission tonight,' he said.

Thursday, April 22

TB woke up more resolved, and quite angry. As far as he was concerned, this was a moral challenge and a moral issue. TB hadn't liked what he heard last night. Bill was rehearsing the pros and cons. Berger was trying to keep him on the cons. Madeleine Albright was trying to give herself room to negotiate with Milosevic. TB was back to being mega worried, constantly asking where do we stand, where is this heading? He said Bill seemed to be hoping Milosevic would just crumble and shove off but when Jonathan had asked how air power alone could make that happen, Berger just served out waffle. He kept coming back to the central point – if all the generals were saying we could not win by air power alone, we had to listen. The US press were saying not just TB but also Chirac was pressing Clinton. I raised this on the conference call, during which Catherine [Colonna, spokeswoman for the French president] said 'off the record' that Jospin could not deliver the government for ground troops. He would lose the Communists and others and he would be gone. We are not there 'yet', she said. It was interesting she said 'yet', and also significant that she sent me an advance copy of Chirac's address to the French people, which was very strong, 'Presque blairiste,' she said. The conference call was largely about ground forces. TB spoke to Yeltsin, who was banging on about World War 3, and we then left for the Senate to see Trent Lott [Republican senator and Majority leader] and the other ghastlies who run the place. But they loved Tony, absolutely, gushingly, totally over-the-toply loved him. He could do no wrong. Jesse Helms [Republican senator and chair of the Foreign

April '99: Kosovo/'a moral challenge' – TB

Relations Committee] of all people told him he was the greatest political leader alive today. Back at the hotel TB spoke to Bill C again by
phone and was more reassured afterwards. I was listening in with
Charles Guthrie, who had just seen Shelton and said he told him to
stiffen spines.

Saturday, April 24

At the NATO lunch, TB and Chirac had a spat re targeting. Primed
by Bill, TB raised the way targeting was agreed and both he and
Schroeder said it was crazy that we were not hitting him harder, and
pulling back from military targets the generals wanted to hit. TB said
it was ridiculous that the targets were subject to a kind of committee
discussion after the military had decided what was needed, and Chirac
said it was preposterous if we thought the military should have sole
decision-making power. TB said they didn't, they were given general
authority and specific authority where it was particularly sensitive,
but too many people were claiming a veto. TB was disappointed that
Bill having set up the row, he then positioned himself somewhere in
the middle, but it was probably sensible management of Chirac.

Sunday, April 25

There had been bad weather again so not all the planned targets had
been hit. On the conference call we agreed to get the focus on the
front-line states who were coming in to see the NATO leaders today.
TB/CB had been out at the White House dinner till 2.30am and Bill
had said to TB 'Don't worry, I'm not going to go wobbly on you.' TB
had replied he wasn't worried about him going wobbly, but he worried
the way the operations were structured meant there were too many
pressures to stop us really going for it to get the job done. Cherie said
that BC had said I ought to go out to Brussels and stay there till the
job was done, because the co-ordination was definitely improving and
it was improving overall performance as well. Jonathan and John S
felt TB was pushing Bill too hard, that the US system would rebel once
we had gone home, and that in the cold light of day Clinton would
resent the way TB had dominated the agenda. TB felt he should engage
Hillary C and get her engaged in pressing Bill to be more urgent. TB's
main focus now was 1. US urgency and ground troop preparations,
2. help for SACEUR, 3. maintain improvement re communications.

Monday, April 26

Jill Dando [TV presenter] was murdered, which was a real shock. I
had always got on with her really well when I did breakfast telly and

she was easily one of the nicest people in TV. The immediate assumption was that it was *Crimewatch*-related, someone her programme had done over, but then I worried whether it was Serb retaliation for our attacks on their media machine being part of their military machine. Given that Milosevic said much the same about the BBC, I wondered whether they were going to start thinking BBC journalists were fair game. When I mentioned it to TB, he said 'They would be far more likely to try to take out you.' Thanks.

Tuesday, April 27

Brussels. Wes Clark arrived at 4.45, was very warm and friendly, on his way to see Solana, then we walked together to the media ops room where he did the rounds, said hello to people individually, then said they were doing an important job, then off we went. His briefing was poor. I walked out of the side of the building with him and into the waiting car. The door was easily as heavy as the one on TB's car, possibly even heavier. He had moderate security and secure comms travelling behind. What did you think of that? he asked when we set off. 'No diplomacy required?' I asked and he said, sure. I said mobiles were ringing the whole time during the press conference. They should all be switched off and people should be listening. He should be got in and out without a scrum, no crews allowed to swarm. There had been no crystal-clear message so they fished around. He said he had read my note about his own profile and found it 'insightful'. I said but it wasn't being acted upon. You have to understand not everyone understands the media like you, he said. His big problem was the way the war was being conducted. Key principles of war are clear objectives – we don't have them; tactical surprise – we have lost it; and clear command structures – we have 19 countries who all think they can be boss. Clark's basic complaint was rooted in the reality of NATO, an essentially political structure running a military campaign. Yet he was sure we were going to win. As we drove along, I noticed again how much he jiggled his legs, which didn't fill you with confidence, but I found him likeable and open. He talked about his wife, who was clearly influential, his son, a scriptwriter in Hollywood, a bit about his politics. He had much kinder eyes than you would expect for a general, and a warm smile. He would not look out of place in American politics. He said the Serbs were masters at intelligence. They certainly tracked UK diplomatic traffic. He had studied Milosevic and the people around him, went through the key people, said they were weaklings, would never stand up to him, but if they had to kill anyone else they would, every single one of them. We carried on over a dinner of cheese salad, chicken and pasta, fruit salad, all pretty healthy and he wasn't hitting the wine hard either. He said war is about clarity, politics is about compromise and when they meet it can get messy. This is messy at the moment, but I promise you we're going to win. Solana had hinted to me about a possible deal and he had asked me to start thinking how we sell a deal with Milosevic still there. With difficulty I said, but that was clearly what Clark was referring to. Both of us felt, and I know TB did, that after all he had done, and after all we had said about him, our publics would not tolerate a deal that kept him there. Clark was pretty positive re Clinton, very impressed by TB, but said it was a nightmare fighting a war with so many politicians involved. I said Clinton showed the media mattered less than was assumed. If the media had real 'power', he would not still be there.

Thursday, April 29

Julian [Braithwaite] came out to meet me at Mons and we were driven to SHAPE. I had sold him effectively as Clark's special adviser and he had to establish himself pretty quickly as indispensable. We went to Clark's desk-side meeting, where the mood was a lot gloomier than yesterday. The weather had again affected operations and nobody really knew what Milosevic was thinking. After the meeting, Wes asked me to sit down, and said something very quietly, and very interesting. 'I like you, and I like your Prime Minister. And you and your Prime Minister need to be very careful. Because if I hear the noises out of Washington right, I can hear the sound of saws being sharpened. They are preparing to make a deal, and if they make a deal they will cut through the tree and you and your Prime Minister are going to be stranded on the bit they cut.' He said he totally supported our position, but we needed to be careful about the endgame. I wrote up some of the remaining problems on the drive to Lille. I got to the office and saw TB, who was still pissed off at the lack of US razor-sharp focus. He had not even had a reply to the note he sent about a US–UK nerve centre. He sensed no progress at all re ground troops and he was worried, particularly after I relayed Clark's comments, that there was some dreadful deal in the making. He said he could only live with Milosevic still there provided we then helped neighbouring countries to do him in and boost democratic forces there. He was stuck on this being a moral question which required a different order of response. We went out into the garden and strolled around a bit. His frustration was more intense even than when we had been at the summit.

Friday, April 30

During the evening conference call came news of a third nail bomb[1] in London, this time at a gay pub in Soho. TB called and we agreed for now he should leave the response to Jack [Straw]. I worked on TB's *Sunday Times* piece on race pre his speech tomorrow, as well as having to sort the bomb reaction.

Monday, May 3

On the way out to Northolt, I sent over a note to the MoD re their press conference, setting the line on the extra money for refugees and the defence of electricity as a military target. TB arrived half an hour later. He had sent another note to Clinton pressing on the setting up of a US–UK nerve centre in London, having received no real response to the last one. He said he was getting frustrated with them, felt the US system still wasn't responding with the urgency we needed. Chris Meyer had sent a telegram saying Bill had disengaged a bit from the Kosovo situation. He went through the military side of things with Guthrie, and then the humanitarian with John Vereker from DFID [Department for International Development]. He is a nice, kindly man, but whose compassion is also matched by a hard-headedness. He told me he was fed up with the Home Office, who were being very slow and difficult about deciding on taking more refugees. But I could see TB's eyebrows arch upwards when John said he wanted the UK to be getting up to 1,000 a week. He warned TB/CB how awful the camps were going to be. John S and I were working on the speech for Romania, which was fine. We landed and drove to 4 Armoured Brigade, where [General] Mike Jackson and Brigadier [Hamish] Rollo briefed TB inside what from the outside looked like a very ordinary tent but which inside was a major and very sophisticated military operations centre. The logistical skills of these guys is something else. Cherie had brought a hideous Nicole Farhi jumper for TB to wear, which would have been a hideous fashion statement to make touring a refugee camp. I was wearing a Gap t-shirt Fiona had bought in Washington and was going to suggest we swap. TB wandered round talking to some of the troops in their tanks and minesweepers and then went down into the middle of a field, they gathered round and he did a very good rallying speech. I met a couple of Burnley fans and chatted a bit about football. We then had a private session with CDS and Jackson, who was another one who had soldier written all

[1] David Copeland detonated nail bombs in Brick Lane, Brixton and Soho. The last explosion, in the Admiral Duncan pub, killed 3 people and wounded 70.

over him. He has a rich whisky-coated voice, bags under his eyes you could carry your boots in, and a wonderful clarity of view. He said there was no way in the world we would win without a build-up of ground troops. He was unimpressed by the way the war was being waged and we had to keep pressing them to get tougher and quickly. There was a threat, which was being taken seriously, that TB would be attacked if we went to Kumanovo[1] so instead we organised for him to speak to some of the people there by phone. I was briefed on [Major General Walter] Jertz's [new NATO Military spokesman] first briefing, which went well. But Julian still wasn't being listened to enough, e.g. he wanted to put out a strategic briefing re SACEUR's visit to Bulgaria and Albania but they couldn't see the point.

We drove to the Stenkovec refugee camp [accommodating some 23,000 refugees]. Anji had done a great job advancing it, with TV corralled properly. It was a vast sprawling place. Kids were swimming in what looked like pretty dodgy water. As soon as we arrived, TB was virtually mobbed, and the kids were shouting 'Ton-ee, Ton-ee,' smiling and really generous of spirit in pretty grim conditions. It was hard to walk around with the crowds following, and both he and Cherie were clearly moved by the whole thing. Anji had organised for him to talk to smaller groups inside some of the tents. They told heart-rending stories of relatives dead or missing, the long journey to escape, their worries about the future. But they were totally supportive of what we were doing. He then went up to the mike that had been set up to speak to them and announce the doubling of money for refugees and the plan for the UK to take more. He met the UNHCR and the NGOs to ask what more they needed and try to get a proper fix on things. We then left for Blace [refugee camp on the Kosovo–Albanian border], where even though the refugees were standing in queues, many exhausted and emotional, eyes glazed, clearly hungry, they started to applaud as he arrived, first a ripple, then louder as people realised he was there. It was close to 30 degrees. In the queue I spotted a little girl who could have been Grace's double. She had a huge great smile, yet next to her, her mother was crying, and looked as though she had been crying for days on end. An old man tried to press his papers into Tony's hands and asked us to take him to Britain. Then we walked across no-man's-land to the top of the queue, where there was a more palpable sense of fear, no crying, no talking, silence apart from the voices of the people from the NGOs

[1] Third largest city in the Republic of Macedonia, north-east of the capital, Skopje.

explaining the process by which they were taken in. We did a doorstep with the silent queues as the backdrop. We got into the car. It is a total obscenity, I said. It just makes me so angry, he said, that we have been so slow and still we are not going fast enough. He said it had confirmed him in his view there was no way in the world of doing a deal with Milosevic, whatever the deal they thought could be cooked up. It was hard to understand why Clinton, the ultimate empathetic politician, did not seem to get this in the same way as we did.

Tuesday, May 4
Wes felt TB was going to have to take on a lot of the leadership here, because he was the only one who could persuade the Europeans to provide the kind of numbers for a ground invasion – 100,000 maybe – that would persuade the US they would not have to provide them all. His wife said America would tolerate 40 per cent max.

Wednesday, May 5
Brussels. Clinton came down after his meeting with Solana and wanted to see the new media operations. He came over, was very warm and friendly, and said thanks for what you're doing. He wanted me to show him around, so I introduced him to a few people. He was working his usual magic on them all. I suggested he go to one of the camps. He said he would love to, but his people wouldn't let him because of the security.

Friday, May 7
The Scotland results were good, Wales and the locals indifferent, though it was the first time this century the party of government polled ahead in local elections.

The Serbs put out a claim that we had hit a hospital and we had the usual teeth-drawing exercise trying to find out from SHAPE exactly what had happened, if anything. We had a long and difficult conference call beating up [Air Commodore David] Wilby [NATO spokesman] to get a quicker response. It was more than 10 hours before we had a useable response. I got so exasperated I called Wes Clark at 11pm and he said he thought we'd already put the line out. But worse was to come. Julian warned me there were suggestions we had hit the Chinese Embassy in Belgrade. I went to bed, was asleep, when the phone went and it was switch[board] with someone from SHAPE. An American, very clipped and precise. 'Mr Campbell, General Clark asked me to call you and let you know that we have hit the Chinese Embassy in Belgrade.' He said it in exactly the same tone as he might have said 'General Clark has had his breakfast and is on his way to work.' Speaking quietly because I didn't want to wake up Fiona, I asked him to repeat that, which he did, word for word. I assume it wasn't deliberate, I said. No, sir, came back this robot voice, it was an accident. Fucking hell. 24 carat disaster time. There was nothing to do but admit to a terrible error. Depending on how the Chinese react, it could be absolutely disastrous.

Saturday, May 8

PJ Crowley [US National Security Council spokesman] called and said he felt Wes should do the briefing today, as this was going to be heavy. I worked up a script for him based on the lines agreed last night and got Julian working on him, but he wasn't at all keen. So the script went to Jertz instead. Meanwhile we were pumping out 'regret' in briefings in all the main capitals. TB called as I was listening to Humphrys trying to pummel Robin on *Today*, Humphrys doing his usual anti-war stuff, saying we had done nothing for the Kosovar Albanians. TB heard it too, was furious, said what would that man have been like during the Second World War? Jamie Shea said he would be 'funereal' at the briefing. I said don't overdo it. We have to make sure this does not dominate the agenda for days. We regret it, we move on. There was a lot of black humour flying around, Chinese takeaways etc, someone suggesting we have a sweepstake on what target we wrongly hit next. Berger called John S though and said Clinton was a bit shaky. TB said we had to hold our nerve. BC said that's right, this thing will turn soon. It is going to work. He sounded a lot better than in the last call. I called Clark and said both had said on the call how well he was doing. It wasn't strictly true.

Monday, May 10

The Chinese were being a lot trickier now. Hypocritically, given their own position on demos, they were now encouraging the demos to go on, and their media had still not reported NATO's apology and admission of error. So to the Chinese we had just decided to take out their embassy. TB was even more pissed off with the Russians, found their basic attitude that what happened inside other people's countries was 'their own business' disgusting when you thought what Milosevic was actually doing, added to which they were perpetually on the lookout for money out of it. Clark was very pleased with the George Robertson headline in the *Telegraph*, 'Wesley Clark is the man to beat Milosevic,' which would also get shown around Washington and hopefully bolster him a little. But CDS came to see me, said he knew I had to build him up, but the truth was a lot of the military weren't happy with him. He said ground forces were the only option but the Americans were terrified. I liked Charles, who had been 100 per cent solid throughout all this. He was also clearly a bit of a mover. Good meeting with Solana. He was almost Levy-like though in his hand-grabbing, back-stroking tactile ways. But he was definitely buying into what we were trying to do.

Tuesday, May 11

Wes and I discussed Hillary's visit. Over dinner at the castle, he said he felt it was important she become a kind of spokeswoman for the refugees. He said don't forget New York has more Kosovar Albanians than anywhere outside the Balkans. Hillary had agreed to do an event with CB on the way through, which we were planning. He felt Hillary had deep moral convictions. He had mixed feelings about Clinton. He liked him, but he said the reason most Republicans – and that meant a lot of soldiers – hated him was that when he became President he did gays in the military, and he used to say Wes was a friend of his as a way of trying to buy some cred with the military. But it did Wes a lot of damage inside the military. He thought he would have been a runner for the top job but for that. 'Also, if you are Oxford and Rhodes scholar, you are marked.' He was in a fairly mellow, reflective mood. He believed in the end the US would do the right thing, but they really wanted to test whether the air campaign could do it. I felt he had far more qualities than his critics, e.g. Charles, suggested. The politics attached to the job were hard, and he handled them pretty well. He was bright, had a really lively mind and was engaging, but he needed constant reassurance that he was a good leader.

Thursday, May 13

Hillary C was very friendly, said half jokingly that she was going to the Balkans for me. We had got together some refugee families, who gathered in the White Room, and both she and CB were terrific with them. Once the cameras were out, Hillary and Cherie got them all to tell their stories in more detail. She was a good listener, let them talk, didn't mind the occasional silence and the stories they told of their own escapes and family losses were genuinely moving. What was also moving was their clear gratitude that we were trying to do something. We are the lucky ones, we want to help the others was their basic position. TB felt Hillary's visit to the region was really important, because we were running out of time on ground troops, and Bill was going to have to shift things quickly.

Monday, May 17

I drove in with Jonathan and TB called to go through the reshuffle. He had agreed with GB, and Pat McF, that John Reid should get Scotland, Helen [Liddell] pissed off. At the office meeting, TB said there was little point talking about Kosovo as it was so obvious what we had to do, but out of our hands as to whether we would do it. This was crunch week and the media knew it, and we would get pushed harder and harder. TB was worrying re the domestic scene, felt that schools, health and crime were in danger of moving backwards, that when there was a big international thing going on, ministers and departments relaxed. Charlie [Falconer] had been to the Home Office in his delivery capacity and had found them pretty down about things. They said the best that could be done was to slow the rise in crime. They couldn't cut it, he was told. It had nothing to do with the economy and everything to do with the numbers and nature of young men. Berger made clear to John S that they had been picking up on the different signals re ground troops, and also some of the briefing re Cohen and him being the obstacles, and they were unsurprisingly pissed off. If they imagined it was a deliberate briefing operation, they were wrong. But the atmospherics had a way of getting out because so many people spoke to so many people. If anything, the media were understating the differences, and the frustrations TB felt. We tried our best to assure them this wasn't being briefed, but I don't think they believed us. TB and Bill had not spoken for more than a week, which was bad. I was asked about when they last spoke and just dodged it, said they kept in touch the whole time. Bulgaria went fine. Both [Ivan] Kostov [Prime Minister] and [President Petar] Stoyanov, not to mention their very attractive foreign minister [Nadedzda Mihailova], were supportive, said whatever doubts earlier they knew we had to win, while the speech was well received, particularly the long-term commitment to the region. Stoyanov said they had waited 120 years for a British PM to visit, but it was worth it. I couldn't believe that. 120 years! They were now terrified of a Milosevic who survived and was stronger and able to threaten his neighbours even more. TB did an OK doorstep but the interpreters interrupted so often to make it virtually unusable in packages. Mum was getting inundated with calls after a story in Nigel Dempster's column in the *Mail* that she plays bridge with Hague's aunt Mary. Ridiculous that was deemed to be a story. I told her to get someone to answer the phone for her and tell them all to get lost.

A combination of TB's and Robin's words of yesterday, while they said nothing new, was being seen, especially in the US, as a hardening of the position on ground troops. Added to which the Germans were briefing that they could not understand why the UK was pushing this out further than before. BC was getting a hard time and there was bound to be some blowback in our direction. Then it got worse when we heard Schroeder, visiting Italy, had said ground troops were unthinkable. Even before that, over breakfast, TB said he didn't mind admitting he was 'really worried now', and that he couldn't see a way out of this. I said Schroeder's remarks were the equivalent of his 'fuck off' at Berlin – it was deliberate and divisive. The US meanwhile clearly believed we were briefing against them. I tried to explain to Jonathan Prince [US official seconded to Campbell's team at NATO], and get him to persuade the White House, that it just was not in our interests to brief against the President, but that people knew there were differences. The thing was to resolve the differences, not fret and frazzle over who was saying what to whom. I said for us to brief against them would be dumb and counter-productive because they can always hit back harder. TB was really worked up by now, feeling the US had pretty much given up on the idea of ground troops and the Europeans, sensing no lead, just fell into the same position. He was half attracted to Massimo d'Alema's [Italian foreign minister] idea of a 48-hour bombing pause while the UNSCR was put together, calling on him to withdraw. TB was convinced we had at least to threaten ground forces, and make the preparations, otherwise Milosevic would think he could just sit there until our resolve weakened. I said he must speak to Schroeder tonight because he was due to be at NATO tomorrow and would be the main media focus for the day, and we had to get him in a different position.

In Tirana, we visited the refugee camp, and an old couple who had survived their escape and were very matter-of-fact but also very moving about how they did it. The kids were suntanned and cheerful and seemed to be getting enough to eat, though inside the tents it was unbelievably hot and clammy. Mothers seemed to be the ones finding the going toughest. One woman stopped us and said her husband came out with four broken ribs. They had all their money taken off them, and had left behind relatives they knew had been murdered or raped. TB did a little 'you will go home' message to them, and spoke of the basic need for humanity to prevail. TB was minded to try again with BC, to say he was now genuinely worried we were to be left with no strategy but air power, and Milosevic would just sit it out until we ran out of options. He knew that the more we bombed the more civilians we would kill and over time the resolve of some of our partners would break. The refugees were not going to go back if he was still there, and we were unlikely to get rid of him without at least the realistic threat of ground troops. Just before midnight, John Sawers woke me up to fill me in on a 'very difficult' BC–TB phone call. They had spoken for over an hour, and the first five to ten minutes was taken up with Bill in a total rage. He had seen the UK reports and the stuff in the US and he 'knew what was going on, it was deliberate and it had to stop'. He said it may play well with the UK media and public but 'there is a price to pay and you will pay it'. John said he was clearly suggesting I had been briefing deliberately to build up TB at his expense. TB protested as best he could, said he was appalled they would think we would undermine him when he was leading the whole thing, to which BC said in which case it is happening without you knowing – the implied notion being that was even worse. John said he didn't name names but it was obvious who he meant. He had never heard him so angry and TB was taken aback. On the substance, however, BC appeared to be moving. He shared TB's view that the d'Alema option could be a way of getting the ground force option out there. TB put it in terms – we have a 48-hour pause while we agree a new UNSCR, then if Milosevic does not comply, based on the 5 NATO demands, we bomb again and plan for ground forces. Bill leapt at it.

Wednesday, May 19

TB said BC's outburst was 'real, red-hot anger'. He felt he was just getting a lot out of his system, and TB was the only one he could really let rip with. He claimed that he had always been basically in favour of ground troops, but it had to be understood he could not be briefed against like this. All that was happening was that people were picking up the obvious differences of tone and emphasis. Our right wing of course, which hates a Labour government and a Democrat White House running a military situation, was stirring as best they could. Boris Johnson had a piece today suggesting we had a deliberate strategy to make TB look good alongside BC. They would be getting all this played back to them. Joe Lockhart called and said they were getting sick and tired of reading that Robin Cook was flying out to stiffen their resolve. I said these things happened, we understood why they were pissed off, but I would be very pissed off too if I thought they thought we had done this deliberately. Schroeder had another pop when he did the NATO briefing. Mark Laity [BBC] asked him where he stood on ground troops and he said he didn't want to take part in this exclusive British debate. It was a deliberate and pretty stupid statement. I watched the press conference and he went right down in my estimation. It wasn't just that he was putting a different position, but doing it in a fairly glib way. Joe called after the call, and said I should understand that though they were angry, it was a sign of how close they were that BC could lose it with TB like that. We had another round of NI talks today, as if Kosovo wasn't enough to be dealing with. At one point, TB's kids were trying to show Adams and McGuinness how to use a skateboard.

Thursday, May 20

The air campaign was doing a lot of damage but the worry was Milosevic was stringing us out to a time when it would be too late, because of winter, to mount a ground force invasion. D'Alema offered opportunities as well as difficulties. It was a way of getting the ground force option on the table. GB warned that the cost of the military operation, and the refugee crisis, meant there could be no room for anything else from the Reserve, and it all underlined the need for stability to be maintained, welfare-to-work programmes to be improved, other departments to ensure money is well spent. Alistair Darling gave a very tough message on seeing the welfare changes through. The *New York Times* had an account of the TB–BC call, clearly briefed, saying Clinton had told TB to get control of his people. I was worried it would get picked up and run here and in Europe, and form a new backdrop.

Saturday, May 22

Another bombing error. We hit a Serb command post which had been taken over by the KLA [Kosovo Liberation Army], and which had even been visited by Western media to be shown how the KLA were doing. There had also been some major hits overnight though, and again, the scale of coverage of the mistake was not as large as earlier. I did the Sundays by phone and they were pushing mainly on NATO divisions. I pushed the unity of the alliance as one of the great success stories. Ken Bacon [Pentagon spokesman] had talked last night of an expanded KFOR [Kosovo Force] and our press was seeing that as another step towards ground forces.

It was FA Cup Final day, and I took Rory and Calum into Number 10, and went upstairs to see TB. He was wearing a Real Madrid track suit and doing lots of different impersonations, much to the boys' amusement. We got an escort up to Wembley and on the way he had a couple of difficult calls with Trimble and Adams. I had fixed an interview with Jim Rosenthal [sports commentator] on the live coverage with both Bertie [Ahern] (Man U) and TB (Newcastle). He got a pretty good reception from the Newcastle fans, apart from one in a wheelchair, who yelled out 'Tony is a Tory.' TB and Bertie did a bit of NI in the margins, but they were pretty much on show here at events like this and expected to mingle etc. We were taken up to the wives' section beforehand and TB chatted to Posh Spice and her dad, while I chatted to Bertie and Celia. It was an OK match, without being storming, and I was chuffed for Alex [Ferguson] that he won. He was loving it at the end and when I spoke to him later, he said he had a feeling about the treble. TB called on his way home and said Newcastle just weren't at the races.

Sunday, May 23

TB was worried that with me almost totally focused on Kosovo, we were losing some of our drive and crunch on domestic policy issues, e.g. we were being run ragged on GM, and on welfare reform, and Scotland had not settled down. The problem was that though Godric could do the briefings well, as a civil servant he couldn't do the politics, and Lance [Price] didn't really fill the gap.

Tuesday, May 25

I was up at 6am local time and off to SHAPE. Clark looked tired and fed up. He wanted to go to the NAC[1] this evening and say it was time to get real, either we really go for the air campaign and stop whining about there being more collateral damage, or we go for ground forces. His leg was jiggling more than ever, and he was snappy with some of his advisers. As we walked to the video-conference room, he said he was getting fed up with the mood of apology surrounding everything. Did people really think you could run a sustained air campaign without civilian deaths?

Wednesday, May 26

I was really looking forward to getting away with Rory to Barcelona for the Champions League Final [Manchester United v Bayern Munich]. United didn't really click and Alex was looking more and more anxious towards the end. Bayern should have buried them in the second half. Then United scored in injury time and suddenly, all round the ground, people were saying they were going to do it again. And they did. The place went absolutely ballistic. Amid the

[1] North Atlantic Council, the key decision-making body of NATO.

celebrations, which seemed to go on for ever, I suddenly remembered that Richard Wilson had told me if they won the Treble, they would rush Alex into the honours list with a knighthood, but they would need to know tomorrow if he was up for it. We were needing to leave for the plane, so I jumped into the VIP section, found Cathy [Ferguson], explained the situation, and she said 'I'm against all that. And don't you think he's won enough already?' To be on the safe side I also told [their son] Mark, who was clearly keener than she was. I left a message on Alex's mobile and he called later, said he had been numb most of the night. He said he wanted to think overnight about the knighthood, talk to Cathy and one or two others. The question that mattered for him was whether his parents would be proud of it or not, and he thought they probably would. We got home at about 4am. Rory was fast asleep. A brilliant, brilliant night.

Thursday, May 27

Up at 7 telling Fiona everything about last night. I got in to see TB, who was doing another note to Clinton about how we would explain the ground force option. There was a real buzz around the place and everyone wanted to know every last detail about last night. Cabinet was mainly Kosovo, Robin more pompous than ever. He went through the whole process, which was not straightforward, and centred on the fact that we could not exclude the possibility of having to deal with Milosevic in the future. TB said there had been a mood shift, and that the resolve, including the possibility of ground forces, had strengthened. GB chipped in again with a warning about costs saying it could go to billions and have implications for every department's budget. TB spoke to Clinton again. He said Bill basically felt we had shafted him and we now had to help him get back to the position he wanted to be in.

To Paris for a socialist leaders' meeting. We had a bilateral with Jospin at the Matignon [French PM's offices]. He is a real football fan, and we spent the first few minutes talking about the Man U game. He was very strong on Milosevic, said he did not believe there were any circumstances in which he could stay as leader in Serbia. He thought it was good that [Martti] Ahtisaari [President of Finland] was speaking to him, but we should be cautious again. He indicated French military were very cautious about ground forces. We left for the utterly ghastly event, speech after speech to an audience that spent most of the time muttering. Schroeder, in shirtsleeves, was totally dismissive of the whole event and was absolutely crap. Jospin spoke really well on Kosovo but then waffled on for half an hour,

May '99: Kosovo/resolve strengthens re ground troops

meandering from one issue to the next without clear argument. TB sat there with a fixed grin throughout, clearly hating it. He said on the flight back that if ever he agreed to such an event again, we had to overrule him, no matter how forceful he was, on pain of death or dismissal. He had not been impressed by Schroeder again. He had seen in Clinton's posture the chance for Germany to do us in a bit and he went for it. I said the problem was that within NATO, the truth was we really were more like the Americans and we were not like the Europeans in the final analysis. 'That is exactly what Thatcher said when I saw her on Tuesday,' said TB.

Thursday, June 3

TB's education speech did fine. I had an early meeting with Robin, who was doing media, emphasising no compromise, real pressure still on, keep hitting them hard. Through the morning, news came that the Serb parliament had voted to accept the plan. I did a briefing and there was a real buzz in the media, an excitement building up that it was over and moving our way. I did a briefing saying Milosevic seemed to be getting the message, but we were absolutely clear all the conditions had to be met, nothing else would do. I called John Simpson, who surprised me by saying 'Congratulations, it looks like game, set and match.' TB did a very tough pooled clip – 'We hope it's true, if so, it's progress and now must be implemented.' TB was convinced that it was the fear of ground troops, and the apparent shift by the Americans, that moved Milosevic to where he was. There was an irony in the fact that this was all happening on Schroeder's watch, when had he been in charge of the overall strategy, the threats would not have been there in the first place. Although the afternoon session went ahead re economic reform, they were really just waiting for Ahtisaari. TB did an extended CNN interview. Everyone seemed to be presenting it now as a great victory. Jonathan said that Simpson's report had been superb for us. We had to resist any triumphalism, but it was clear they were already on to 'anatomy of a victory' pieces. Ahtisaari finally arrived, looked tired but pretty exhilarated for a Finn, limped in to loud applause and again I thought Schroeder misread the mood by doing a great bear hug. It sent all the wrong signals. The Germans were telling us to lighten up, but I agreed with the Americans that we should be cautious, not least because of Milosevic's record. Indeed, Ahtisaari was foremost in urging us to take nothing for granted. He and Schroeder went off to do a press conference. TB did some TV interviews before we left for the hotel and then later to the Schloss for dinner. It had all come pretty suddenly.

There didn't seem any doubt that we had won, though there was no jubilation. Chirac, who did a broadcast to the nation, complained that the Americans could have done this earlier if they had involved the Russians properly. TB was totally on the line that this only happened because of our resolve and determination. He was getting a great press.

Friday, June 4

Both the *Sun* and the *Mirror* did 'who Blairs wins' headlines. I met Robin, who said that TB and I should be more upbeat, that this was a huge success. But we felt that if the mood of celebration was over-done it would send Milosevic the signal that we had given up on further negotiation. The military to military paper had been worked up overnight, with various drafts flying around through the day and the final version sent to the Serbs at 4am Saturday. RC felt we had to be saying this was our victory but TB was still cautious. We started to focus on the job that we would need to do in the region itself once we got in there. In the meantime, stay cautious and the bombing continues until there is verifiable withdrawal of his troops.

Saturday, June 5

Julian [Braithwaite] called early, having travelled to Macedonia with the SHAPE team for the Blace talks. There was a problem. The Serbs did not want to come to the venue we had chosen. The talks were due to start at 9. The Serbs came up with another venue and after a lot of to-ing and fro-ing, NATO agreed we may have to move. This might be the start of all his usual pissing around. Milosevic was looking to get family out. My immediate reaction was to stay quiet but overnight changed my mind. We were now dealing with classic Milosevic. He did the deal on the principle, then screwed around on the detail in a way that made it look like he was winning on the narrow points he was defining.

Sunday, June 6

We had a real conundrum. The Serbs would not withdraw without a UNSCR. The Russians would not negotiate a UNSCR until we stopped the bombing. And we would not stop the bombing until they withdrew. Mike Jackson told TB that he didn't believe they were serious and we should tell them to get lost. Ahtisaari suggested he went there and in the final analysis said he would call Milosevic, say KFOR would have to go in and we get a UNSCR afterwards. TB said he feared Jackson was a great soldier but less good as a negotiator. I liked him, and he is a tough character, but prickly and impatient, and not necessarily aware of the difference between what was going on in reality and what it made sense to brief. What had to be clear was that the buggering about all came from the Serb side and meantime we had to carry on bombing.

Monday, June 7

I had gone to bed after my calls with Jackson, then woke to find he had gone out in the early hours and was now leading the news saying pretty much what we had agreed, plus a bit about intensifying the bombing. The story, though, was collapse in the talks. TB called at 6.50 – he was worried whether there was enough subtlety to these negotiations. TB spoke to Ahtisaari for the fifth or sixth time in 24 hours, at one point asking what is Schroeder doing and why are we having to do this? I put together a line for the 11 basically saying it was a test of how serious he was about implementing the agreement. I called Clark about 10 and, parodying the line we had been using for days now, said 'You're winning, he's losing and he knows it.' He said he still believed it was only 50–50. Milosevic was perfectly capable of playing several moves ahead of us. He was looking for a new game to play and we had to work out what it was. He said we were 'bombing the Dickens out of them' and doing real damage but Milosevic was just sending in more and more replacements. He just didn't care how many men he lost.

Thursday, June 10

At Cabinet, TB was not remotely triumphalist but pretty much everyone was saying he had done an amazing job. After Cabinet, TB took me, RW, GR and CDS aside and said he wanted to set up a small team to review the lessons to be learned. He said he would never have gone into this in the way we did if he had known how weak our allies would become. The story wasn't here but out in theatre and in Brussels, where we were waiting for Clark to tell Solana that withdrawal had begun. Clark spoke to a Serb general who said it would begin at noon. On the conference call, Prince said Solana wanted to announce it alone. We all agreed it would be better with Clark there too. More hanging around and then half an hour later, he was out. TB meanwhile was on the phone to Clinton and I was listening in and responsible for a near disaster. I didn't realise that whenever I pulled out of the call I cut off. Twice. Also, even though I had hit the mute button, for some reason they could hear me, for example saying 'God, this is fucking bollocks' as they were talking about Aids. The first time I cut them off was when I went through with a note saying that Solana was about to go out and they should go out soon after. TB was full of praise re Bill and Bill, I felt, less so in return.

Friday, June 11

What should have been an amazingly positive day for everyone was close to being a total fucking fiasco. We had been told last night that the Paras and the Gurkhas would lead the way into Kosovo today. We woke up to reports that there had been a delay. The suggestion being made was that we had to wait for the marines so that the US could go in too. This was clearly being said by people out there but was potentially very damaging. The delay became the story. And, mid-morning, the news that a small convoy of Russian tanks was on its way to Kosovo from Bosnia. This electrified the place. The truth was nobody was aware in advance. CDS [Guthrie] and George R came over for a meeting with TB and we agreed to try to put out a calm line, namely we had always envisaged working closely with the Russians. Everyone seemed to think they may go into Priština before us. Charles said the only way to beat them, and secure the airport, was to send in forces by air – helicopter – but it was by no means a risk-free operation. TB was very nervous about it, said he couldn't really send in troops at such a risk and we didn't even know what the situation would be, what the Russians were up to, where they would be going. So we tried to calm it. Then at 1.05, Wes Clark called me and said that Russian troops were moving and now he had learned they had asked for air space for six planes through Hungary. Either we go for a very risky military operation, or we risk partition, with the Russians just taking over. This is now a political-military operation. He said the Serbs were 100% in cahoots with the Russians. His instinct was that we should go in and take the airport. But Jackson was concerned. I said TB's instincts when Guthrie raised it were cautious but I would speak to him again. He said this was the result of diplomatic ambiguity at the heart of the agreement. We have to ask political leaders to give us clear cover. This is grand strategy stuff. He said he didn't want it known that he had called me, it was an offline call. I went to see TB, who was doing his policy unit awayday upstairs, took him out and just relayed what Wes had said. Don't shoot the messenger, I said. He said 'You are suggesting that I lose some of our soldiers in fighting with the Russians. That is World War Three. I could just about stand up in the Commons and say there's a bit of a mess about who controls the airport. But I cannot defend starting World War Three. Tell him we have to wait and see what their plans are and in the meantime they have to get rolling into Kosovo. I wish to God these generals would calm down a bit.'

I got to bed fairly late and then at 1.05, Robin Clifford [KFOR spokesman] called and said they had got an order down from SACEUR that they were to be put on hold for another 24 hours while the US continued to work on the integration of the Russians. This was unbelievable. We had looked ragged enough as it was, but this was ridiculous. I called John Sawers and also put in a call to Clark. John was asleep, unaware and said he couldn't believe it and would call Berger. He called back, Berger having said they were trying to tie down the arrangements with the Russians to be part of the US sector. CNN was showing Russians already in Priština. Strobe Talbot [US official] was asking the Russians what was going on and they claimed they had been deployed in error. Some error. Clifford, watching on CNN, said they were being greeted by Serbs as liberators. Wes Clark called and said he was told they were going to apologise and withdraw. The White House had asked for a 24-hour pause to talk to the Russians and sort out the integration question. He had one hour, maybe one and a half hours, to call off the deployment. The Russians will not talk to NATO, only to the US. We agreed that not only would it look dreadful if we didn't go, with all the media already lined up, but it would send the signal the Serbs most wanted – that the Russians could call the shots. The whole thing was dreadful. I called TB, who said that if we didn't deploy he would have to speak to Clinton. He said what earthly reason is there not to deploy? We can resolve the Russian question later. If we run into the Russians in Priština, so what? Either we overwhelm them or we can embrace them. And if they really are leaving, we won't meet them anyway. Everyone agreed we had to deploy KFOR for real reasons of substance as well as for presentation. John spoke to Berger again to say TB wanted to speak to Bill if there was no deployment. I spoke to Wes to say TB was fully behind the decision to deploy. Berger wanted a few more minutes to pin down the Russians. Wes said the plan was to send a couple of guys from SHAPE to Moscow, collect some Russians, get to Macedonia, meet Jackson, then discuss with the US if the Russians would deploy as part of the US force. That takes another eighteen hours. John came up with another very good idea which Wes leapt at. Deploy the French and the Brits and say to the Russians that we will hold back on the Americans – who were not due to go in yet anyway – and let the Russians discuss that. While I was on to Wes, CNN broadcast Igor Ivanov [Deputy Director of the Federal Security Service] saying that the Russians arriving in Priština was an unfortunate error. Unbelievable. Clark said this could be a tempest in a teapot but if they go from the town to the airport we have a problem. Just after 3am, Charles Guthrie came on. The US had finally agreed to go, delaying their own troops till later. He had spoken to Clark and Shelton, told them both they were a shambles and they would come out of it dreadfully if they didn't go now. This was crazy stuff. To be fair, Clark agreed. He said that if we thought Russia was a joke, Washington was not far behind. Anyway the deed was done.

Saturday, June 12

I got a couple of hours' sleep, up to see the news, pictures of the troops and tanks inside Kosovo and then to the lido for a swim. Wes asked me to do a script for his press conference later. I spoke to TB before he left for Trooping the Colour. He said it would sort itself out diplomatically. Wes did fine and I called him afterwards to say so. He said either there was a government within a government in Russia, or there was a good cop bad cop routine going on, but either way it was worrying. TB felt it was settling down, that the Russians were just trying to take the gloss off NATO's triumph by being first into Priština. [Igor] Ivanov having claimed deployment was a mistake, Yeltsin now promoted the general who took the troops into Pristina. There were still Russian tanks driving around the airfield, and some of the TV reporters described it as a farce.

Sunday, June 13

Lucie [McNeil, Downing Street press officer, seconded to NATO] called at 7 to say she was stuck in a convoy hemmed in at either end by Russian tanks. However much we said that the Russians were just trying to be noticed, there were real problems of substance here which would have to be addressed diplomatically. Later John S called to say Wes was suggesting we actually seize the airport, despite the risks of a firefight with the Russians, which would be a disaster. I put round a line that their understandable frustrations were not significant compared with the job our military had to do and the importance of getting the refugees back home. The Russians were making us look silly and we were unable to give a clear sense of who was in charge. TB found the Russians outrageous on this. They are party to the agreement and now they try to screw us up. Berger called Sawers to say they weren't happy with some of the things our military were saying out there, for example that we were happy to concede the airport to the Russians. It was true that a line went out from the MoD to senior Brits out there to say that we were not to take part in any Clark plan for an attack on the airport. It was a national red card job. Jackson, according to Sawers, had threatened to resign because he was being asked to do something he believed would involve shooting at Russians and he was not prepared to do it. George R confirmed to TB, Jackson was adamant that if the Russians were supposed to be part of KFOR, we could hardly start shooting at them. Clark, via US ventriloquising, was saying we had to take the runway with Apaches and para-troopers. Our public line was still that we were working it out but it was becoming near untenable. The worry about Clark was that years of pent-up feeling about the Russians was boiling up and he was spoiling for a fight.

By the later conference call, things were looking more ragged, a journalist shot dead, German troops killing Serbs, Albanians stoning withdrawing Serbs and making it very difficult to police the two sides, plus the Russian problem was still there. TB spoke to Clinton, who said Yeltsin was out of it at the moment and causing real bother. Wes Clark called at 1am, wanting to discuss the Russians. He wanted to send in air force to take it, including Brits. He was being overruled but said 'A beautiful victory is in danger of being lost because we were resolute for 78 days but we're being irresolute now.' The Russians would see us as weak and take advantage. They were ready to send 20,000 troops in because they wanted to screw up the whole operation and if we let them, it would be a real problem for the long term. They had raced to Berlin in '45 and that was what this was about. The problem for Clark was that Clinton had made clear he thought any notion of a battle with the Russians was crazy.

Monday, June 14

Richard Wilson chaired a meeting – CDS, Kevin Tebbit [Permanent Secretary at the MoD], John Sawers, John Kerr [Permanent Secretary at the FCO], Michael Pakenham [Cabinet Office], AC and Sebastian Wood. It got a bit rambling but the basic feeling was that we had been pretty lucky. Richard asked why we won and Charles said 'Because Milosevic caved in.' There was a fair bit of covering of tracks going on. Both John S and I felt there were times when we had just been stumbling, that we didn't have the fullest range of advice for TB. We didn't have a clear assessment of the politics of NATO, or of the politics of the US administration. But in fact it was only once the US engaged that things really moved, and at times it felt like we had been carrying the whole show. TB had been exposed at times and we had had to fly by the seat of our pants. There was a general feeling that after a dreadful start we had worked wonders in presentation, but Charles and I got into a rare shouting match when I said there had been too many soldiers doing interviews with potential policy ramifications. He said it was easy to sit watching television and criticise but it's very hard not to do interviews. I said that was rubbish. There was some talk about doing a White Paper on lessons learned, but I doubted TB would want to go that far. Clark called at 10 still worried about the Russians. He still wanted to go in and was confident it could be done without any deaths. I said I would speak to TB again but knew his view already, that he thought the whole idea was mad. If we suddenly sent UK troops to attack the Russians, he would have Clinton, Chirac and everyone else against him. It would be inexplicable. He hated what the Russians were doing, and was troubled by Clark's perseverance, but believed it would resolve itself. Wes believed the Russians were planning to get more troops in again tonight and it was important we stopped people giving them airspace. Yeltsin had told Clinton there would be no more Russian troops into Kosovo without agreement. Then again, he had also asked Bill for a US–Russian summit on board a submarine. TB said I needed to keep talking to Wes. He quite liked him and he felt there was something in what he said but it was politically impossible.

Tuesday, June 15

I was off at 5 to Brize Norton again. The plane was full of soldiers heading out there, some of them looking not much older than Rory. I sat at the back and worked on a note to TB on the lessons of the elections.[1] I did TB a private note on yesterday's Kosovo-lessons-learned meeting. His own view was that NATO had been exposed as ineffective and he had been shocked at the Americans. The way NATO worked was that the US basically ran it, sometimes we managed to get our hands up their back and sometimes the others managed to screw them over. Kerr had said TB's standing was so high he could probably get Ashdown as the UN civil authority person. We landed and to my amazement at the bottom of the steps was Julian, wearing the most extraordinary square-pointed shoes. I thought you would need some local knowledge, he said. We walked across the tarmac to a waiting Puma helicopter complete with machine-

[1] The European elections held on June 10 saw Labour's MEPs reduced from 62 to 29. Conservative MEPs increased from 18 to 36, and Liberal Democrats from 2 to 10. It was the first time proportional representation had been used for a nationwide poll, and saw UKIP [United Kingdom Independence Party] and the Green Party gaining seats for the first time.

gun protection guys hanging out of the doors and off we went, the sides open and the wind howling through. We were flying through some extraordinarily beautiful scenery, but so close to the ground that when we went through valleys, you could almost touch the trees on either side, and suddenly we would swoop up and be able to see for miles and miles. Through the headset I could hear the voice of the pilot spotting potential dangers, like Serb troop movements as they withdrew. We flew over some of the ethnically cleansed villages, homes that were shells of themselves, animals scavenging, lots of rough-and-ready graves. Ten minutes into Kosovo and there were people clearly walking home who were waving up at the helicopter. I was really excited to be there. I felt that I had been part of something important and powerful and deeply moving. What I couldn't see was much sign of beaten-up tanks or Serb military, and the Serb liaison officer at the talks apparently told Jackson that we only hit 14 out of 400. We arrived at the military base and met Clifford, who looked thunderstruck when he saw Julian. I'm not sure exactly what he had done to upset them but clearly he had. Clifford told me later there was a time and a place for clever people with briefcases but Kumanovo in the last few days was not one of them. He had just been too clever and pushy in constantly talking about his conversations to 'important people in London'.

Then left with a French driver, a very pretty woman soldier named Aude. We overtook a column of tanks and vehicles going over a bridge, then a line of Serb cars and lorries and the bandana brigade staring at us, giving us the finger, making obscene and threatening gestures. It was eerie. They had guns and were pointing them at us, finger on the trigger. Whenever they clocked Aude, they went into a kind of weird group grunt. I had never understood why stories of invasion and victory are always accompanied by stories of rape. But I could see the rapist in their eyes. They were among the most disgusting people I had ever seen and I felt all the more satisfied at what we had done. We parked the car by their old HQ, now occupied by the British Army. There was an overwhelming stench of burning of evidence. Jackson was excellent with the Serbs, very calm, polite, even-handed. As he finished, he came over and said what are you doing here? He was both gruff and friendly at the same time. He said who are you working for, the Prime Minister or Clark? I said I was working for him. He said good, he needed real help, not lots of bright boys. As we chatted, and I explained how I thought we could help him, the aggression disappeared and he became quite friendly. Jackson was growing on me. He had a great booming voice, took no crap from anybody and struck me as having done a pretty extraordinary job. I tried to get to the bottom of just why Julian caused him such offence. When I mentioned to Clifford that Clark had really taken to Julian, he said 'That says it all.' Jackson was even more dismissive, said that on Sunday, when he wanted to hit the airport, 'I said Wes, you're fucking barking. I'm just not doing it.'

Wednesday, June 16

I woke up at 5.30, tired and my bones aching. I had not slept in a tent for God knows how long. The helicopter flight to Skopje was even more extraordinary than yesterday. The scenery was stunning but then every few minutes we would fly over either a scene of joy, kids jumping and waving and giving victory signs, or scenes of desolation and devastation, communities totally wiped out, bodies, graves. I felt it was without doubt one of the most worthwhile things we had done since the election and I was proud of the job I had done. I had brought together a disparate group of people from different parts of the world and from Clinton and Clark down, I think they acknowledged that we had used communications strategically to make a difference on the military side too.

Friday, June 18

Clinton said we had to look beyond short-term relief towards a stability pact with south-east Europe and the Balkans but we have to get rid of Milosevic, get the people there to define their own vision of the Balkans and then work for it. TB was clear that we should be pushing money to the neighbouring countries while Serbia was getting none. They had to know Milosevic had totally screwed up. They were both worried about Yeltsin.

Saturday, June 19

I went out for lunch with Catherine Colonna, who had been brilliant in the last few weeks. She was very open about Chirac. She liked him, but he was not like he seemed. He was much more insecure than people imagined. Sometimes he lashed out and then regretted it. He found it hard to change a position or a view. He tended to develop an opinion of someone and not let experience change it, which meant he could be very black/white. He found it hard to get on with Jospin. He had noticed, and didn't like, TB's quote on page one of *Le Monde* saying we must never let the right back in Europe. We went back for a meeting with Bono and Geldof [about the Jubilee 2000 campaign to cut Third World debt]. First we had to get them there, because Bono for some reason told [Adam] Boulton he wasn't going. I called Geldof and got him to persuade him that it would be seen as total grandstanding not to turn up when the media were already there waiting. In the event, we had a very good meeting. I liked them both. They were really funny but also incredibly committed, and they knew what they were on about. They had facts at their fingertips. There was no way this was just a spray-on cause to help their rock-star image. TB said at one point that we were pushing as hard as we could but there was a lot of politics, different countries with different agendas, and it was like climbing Everest. Bono said 'When you see Everest, Tony, you don't look at it, you fucking climb it.' We got the cameras in and they went a little bit rock star-rish but it was impossible not to like them.

Sunday, June 20

The Cologne summit was big on TV but pretty low-key in the papers. TB said he'd had a fascinating chat with Chirac. He'd said he was impetuous and impulsive but we must never take it too seriously when he has one of his storms. He said he wanted to come to London to go to a nice Japanese restaurant that TB had mentioned, and he would take TB to one of his favourite Paris bistros in return. He was clearly, in general, in a fairly musing and whimsical mode. We bumped into him and he went off on a tirade about the music from last night, and then about nouvelle cuisine. 'I hate it when a big plate is brought ceremoniously to the table, and a huge silver thing on top, then the waiter lifts the silver thing and you are staring at three haricots verts.' He then told us a story about how Claude, his daughter, was called by someone she thought was Mike Jackson the soldier and it turned out to be Michael Jackson the singer. Yeltsin finally arrived with Schroeder. He was looking pretty unstable with an enormous fixed smile. It was painful watching him try to hold the smile together. He went round giving everyone enormous bear hugs. He and TB had a brief chat. Yeltsin said 'Anthony, I told you it would be a dangerous course and you should have got off it before. But now we must work together.' Clinton was laughing and joking with him, saying he prayed for him every night. Close up, Yeltsin looked really quite ill.

Tuesday, June 22

I sent my draft speech on Kosovo and the media to Wes Clark, who called back and said 'I love it. I think you and Jamie Shea should fly the press down to Kosovo, visit the mass graves and rub their noses in the dirt.' Charles Guthrie liked it and wanted me to deliver it as a speech to his commanders. Oona [Muirhead] and Jamie Shea had a few good comments to make, and Oona suggested and then fixed that I should do it at RUSI [Royal United Services Institute]. Jonathan thought it was self-indulgent. Peter M liked it but wanted to tone down the attacks on the media.

Thursday, June 24
Philip had done a couple of dreadful groups – no sense of delivery and re the war what a waste of fucking money. It made you wonder why we bothered sometimes. PG said he wanted to hit some of them. He said the *Mail* was a real problem, just poisoned some of these people against any understanding at all. They had no idea of anything we had done. On Kosovo, they thought Clinton carried TB as a poodle. It was ludicrous.

Friday, June 25
Jonathan and I saw TB to go through Philip's latest, unbelievably gloomy note. TB thought he was overstating it, that the problem was really lack of progress in public services. He looked tired and drawn though and I think felt that having done as much as he had to win a war people had said they supported, it was odd not to get at least some credit for it. Equally, they did not seem to want to give us credit on the economy.

Sunday, June 27
Trimble was putting out a less grudging line re SF/decommissioning, but when TB called, he said he was really worried about him, felt the others were getting to him big time. He was also worried Jonathan was getting too emotional about it, which I felt was a good thing. But TB was alarmed last week, e.g. when the Orangemen were attacking TB and Jonathan really went for them, saying you cannot talk to a prime minister like that. I don't know why but I felt we should be more confident. The engine was in place, the carriages were waiting, and it was just a question of getting the carriages in the right order.

Monday, June 28
TB was wondering whether he could send Peter to NIO. On the plane he mapped out the various approaches to take with the different parties. He was pretty fed up having to go through it all again. Jonathan had spent the whole weekend out there, poor sod, talking to the Garvaghy Rd residents' association and the Orange

Order.[1] On arrival we worked through a plan for the day with Bertie. We wanted SF to agree that they would say they would persuade the IRA to decommission, while the UUs would accept a statement that the war was over. But a lot of his time was taken up with the residents and the Orange Order re Drumcree, which was dire. Whenever we got on to these marches, even TB's patience wore thin after a while. Both sides just lectured from their different takes on it. He told them this was never going to change until at least they tried to see the other point of view, but he might as well have asked them to dive into a vat of burning oil. They were not listening let alone changing their minds. As Paul Murphy said, fighting for this was all some of these people felt they had, and they were not prepared to lose it.

Wednesday, June 30

Over breakfast with Bertie, TB said he feared real problems with the UUs today. They were imagining that by the end of the day, there would be a commitment to acts of decommissioning but of course even if we got decent words, there would have to be an IRA convention to get it agreed. SF were going to make a historic statement of intent of their commitment to decommission, without any guarantee of how it could be delivered. TB said we had to lower the bar for SF and we had to lower it for Trimble. We got DT in and he was pretty nervy. We tried to persuade him that the media was actually worse for SF than for him, and the pressure was still on them more than him. If they were to make a commitment as historic as the one we were working on, he had to seize that as major progress won by his side. We knew it didn't mean for sure all the weapons would go but it signalled a direction of travel that was surely worth seizing on. He didn't look so sure. A while back that would have been seen as real progress, but in the current mood it would be difficult. On the one hand it was remarkable SF were prepared to say 'total disarmament' but on the other, if that was the case, it would merely confirm and strengthen suspicion on the other side if they could not go further and talk about how, when, etc. It would be hard to take the UUs forward on the basis of what they were saying.

DT saw TB alone at 2pm, and left looking really downcast. I went in to see TB, who was now just sitting there looking out of the window.

[1] The Parades Commission that day ordered the Orange Order's annual Drumcree march to be rerouted away from the Garvaghy Road. In the end, despite an Orange Order protest meeting, the march passed off relatively peaceably.

He looked up, shook his head, and he said he could scarcely believe it – the UUs were about to turn the victory of the IRA handing in weapons into a defeat because psychologically they were incapable of getting out of defeat mode. If they see a Republican with a smile on his face, they assume they have lost something. They were incapable of seeing a bigger picture. At 2.20 Trimble came in, and alongside him John Taylor, Reg Empey, Jeffrey Donaldson and Ken Maginnis. TB was very curt with them, less of the small talk and the bonhomie he usually doles out. He said he was trying to get a statement from SF, and from the IRA, effectively that de Chastelain was the means of decommissioning, the process, and the failsafe. But it was clear from their faces, barely reacting as he spoke, that they would not be able to go with anything other than a 'jump together' – the executive set up at the same time as arms were handed over. Trimble said that with Drumcree rerouted, and with the Patten review on policing due, and bound to be terrible for them, they could not hold their own people with this. If we push too far, we risk the UUP falling to the extremists. Whether Donaldson, smirking a bit throughout, was the target of that one I wasn't sure. Maginnis said the release of prisoners 'cost us 45,000 votes and we have bugger all to show for it'. 'With all due respect,' TB said – which he tended to say when he meant to indicate a lack of respect on a particular point – 'I think you have a tendency to snatch defeat from the jaws of victory and you are in danger of doing that now. You have the IRA making a commitment to decommission and you are saying it is not significant.' Empey said it may be, but they were being asked to accept a post-dated cheque. 'We give them a whole load of cash now, but we have to wait to get anything in return.' Also they hated the failsafe idea because it suggested SF–IRA had a veto on the whole thing. Trimble said the people who were trying to make it work would be the ones who end up punished. TB said if we fail to reach agreement he could not defend spending days and days of his time trying again. 'People will not understand if we pull the plug at this point. There is a Rubicon to be crossed and you have to lead the way.' If we could get an agreement around this, and sort Drumcree, we are back on track. If we don't, we will never get it done. Empey said nobody doubted his commitment or seriousness of intent but it had to be a good deal.

We were in a TB–Bertie stocktaking session when Jonathan came over to me and said two of my best friends were at the door wanting to see me. I went over and it was Adams and McGuinness, with some of their other key guys behind them. 'Here's the guilty man,' said Jonathan in that wonderfully flip way he has. They claimed I had briefed they were going to get an IRA statement. I had done nothing of the sort and I explained they were confusing two things. I had briefed that there were SF–IRA meetings going on (which they later denied). I wasn't convinced they believed me, and there was something pretty heavy about seeing them lined up demanding explanations. They were jovial, but there was a real hint of menace. 'Look, Alastair,' said Adams. 'We live here. We know what is going on.' I said I wished to fuck I did, because so far as I could see, we were going nowhere. Back inside, TB was looking downcast again, but we decided to keep going through 9, then 10, then 11, when Adams did a pretty positive briefing, followed by Trimble being very negative, prompting me to go out and say de Chastelain was putting forward his report shortly, and that both GA and TB were keen to see the UU Assembly members. It was time to put the pressure on Trimble. I briefed Mark Mardell [BBC journalist] and Brunson that there was real movement from Adams and the pressure was all on Trimble now. TB had talked to both the Queen and the President by now. We regrouped with the Irish after 11, TB having done another sweep of the smaller parties to stop them getting too fed up. It was all getting a bit high-wire again, but we had rediscovered a third wind and we were determined to sort something. McGuinness had called de Chastelain to say they would be making a statement making clear their commitment to decommission, though not speaking for the IRA. He accepted it at least as a step in the right direction, but we needed an IRA statement. They had to accept the executive will only come into being once the process starts. The process must start, then the timetable will want weapons a few months later. TB said they will want to see if it beds down. Bertie said they still feared if they did this, nothing would change. Trimble would still not speak to them. McGuinness came to see TB. Their problem was going out and saying decommissioning will happen. In some ways it would be easier to do if they didn't have to say they were doing it. De Chastelain is the key to determining any progress.

As midnight approached, TB called me in and said what do we do by way of fallback? What do we say if we make no real progress? He was really tired and tetchy. 'I can't understand them. I am really scared about it this time because I don't have a clue what I would say to the country and I don't have a clue what the consequences will be if we have to walk away without real progress.' DT was seeing GA at midnight but was unable to get real detail on what they planned. TB set out for DT what we saw as a best-case scenario for him but even that wasn't good enough. He said to him he (DT) was the leader who was getting the IRA to commit to decommission, and he was walking away from it as though it were a defeat. All we could really do was let them sweat – put out details of the kind of deal on offer and let them consult. I worked on a draft failure statement, with the key line 'I believe the parties are sincere, but the parties do not believe each other.' Trimble took TB's best-case list to his people and reported back that not one of them supported it. He came back with Seamus Mallon at 1.05am for an unbearably gloomy meeting. Even Jonathan and I had given up on the black humour for now. Trimble said he had no support for what was being proposed. They did not believe we would kick SF off the executive once they were on, and they did not believe decommissioning would happen. TB was tired and saying little for once. Mallon quizzed Trimble, said there was never a good time but real opinion out there supported him more than he thought. Trimble said that didn't matter, because the Unionist Council would not support it. TB was getting close to the view that deep down they just didn't want to share power with Catholics. Mallon felt DT lived in permanent fear of political crucifixion by Paisley and [Bob] McCartney [leader of the UK Unionist Party]. Bertie was patient as ever, trying to coax out DT into a more positive position. TB said 'If I get them to agree to decommission within a month, would that do?' He said 'I wouldn't be there. They only need two weeks to get me out.' He was clear his Assembly people just wouldn't wear it. Mallon said 'David, think the worst the whole time and we all go down, but Adams goes out smelling of roses, while you are there with your party intact but you'll be wrecked.' 'I'm wrecked whatever,' he said. Mallon: 'Who dares wins.' Trimble: 'I'm always wary when others are urging me on to what I know will be my own destruction.' TB: 'At least give me a counterproposal.' Silence. TB turned to me and said what do we say? I said all we can do is say we have failed and you give an honest assessment of where we got to, what was on offer, and let people make their own judgement. TB said if we go out there and offer no hope at all, we have a bloodbath on our hands. But he also said he wasn't prepared to keep coming again and again to put in day after day on negotiations going nowhere.

Then at 1.55am, Adams came in and made clear there was no way he was going to sign up to a deal that had decommissioning prior to the executive, or to a shadow executive going nowhere. I had now drafted a three-page statement setting the context for failure but TB was for now determined to keep going. We cannot go out of here having failed, he said. Adams and Trimble had another meeting but as ever came out with totally different interpretations of what had been said. The problem was DT kept going back to his own people and instead of offering leadership around a position secured by him, he took all their criticisms like a sponge. We had another round, then TB spoke to Clinton around 3.45, gave him his assessment and got him to speak to both GA and DT to urge them on. DT was in our office when the call came through from the US and he was almost embarrassed, looking away from us, whispering and mumbling, humming like he did when he was nervous, then turned to us, wiped his mobile on his sleeve and said 'It's President Clinton.' BC took the line that the world would not understand if we failed to take this step forward now. As we left TB was pretty apocalyptic, could see it going nowhere fast, and then with dreadful consequences on the street as the blame games and the retreats started. In the car, he said he felt the Irish were not putting enough pressure on SF, whose position was a mirror of the UUs, and they were both as unreasonable as each other but because SF were cleverer negotiators and media operators, they got away with more. I reckoned he had about 80 meetings long and short behind him, and he was looking really tired. 'I have to find some verve and energy from somewhere. Otherwise this is going down.'

Thursday, July 1
Willie Whitelaw [former Conservative deputy prime minister] died. The other big event was the official opening of the Scottish Parliament and TB's absence was going noted without being too much of a story. The press was full of the knife-edge stuff re NI. At breakfast, he said it was time to put real pressure on them. He intended to say it was now or never, that the civilised world would not understand if we did not do this now, and that we agree the co-ordination of two historic steps. The IRA will disarm. The UUs will share power with Catholics. No sane person outside of this place would remotely understand how you can turn your backs on that. We had the full-cholesterol Hillsborough breakfast, which was one of the delights of NI, and then flew off by helicopter. He was fired up by the time we landed. We linked up with Bertie and they did the last bit of the journey by car together, TB spelling out his plan of action. We got inside, then they went out again to do a brief doorstep, during which Adams came down, very wired for him, close to hyperventilating, saying TB had to meet them because Republicans did not understand why the deadline passed, why they had made this huge shift on a commitment to decommission and they were still waiting for a proper response.

TB to DT: 'I need to know you can back me on this.' DT: 'Sorry, I can't.' It seemed we had Taylor in a better position than Trimble.

TB explained, as if they didn't know, that it took the IRA 6 to 8 weeks to get round all their people. To which Trimble replied – OK, let's wait a few weeks then. But he also knew that they needed to be able to take with them the power sharing. TB said that if they signed up to the 'possible sequencing' paper, that was an enormous step for them, and he couldn't ignore that. We went round and round in circles, having hit the absolute nub of the problem – they wanted decommissioning prior to the executive being established. SF wanted it the other way round. And neither trusted the other to deliver if they were meant to go second.

Trimble went off to see Bertie while we worked on Sinn Fein, just to see if changing the mix might produce something. One-hour-plus TB meeting with Adams and McGuinness, who was in full flow about how he and Gerry were being ripped apart for their 'peace strategy', their people feeling they were giving all and getting nothing. Decommissioning in days was not a runner, he said, it just was not possible. It was hard enough to get an IRA statement on the general commitment. They felt I had been pushing too far in briefings on the seeming progress they were making with the IRA. They lived in fear, he said. I said I know sometimes they thought I pushed too far, but they needed to understand I did nothing without TB wanting it done, so if he wanted the pressure shifted one way or the other, that's what we did. 'Alastair, that stuff (IRA statements re decommissioning is what I think he meant) is sacrosanct. Youse cannot get involved like that, and sometimes you scare the life out of me.' He said he would decommission 'the day before yesterday' if he could, but we had to deal with the realities we had before us. We pressed on and they finally agreed to put a proposal to the UUs. BA gloomy again. Trimble in again. TB said he was going to speak to Clinton and together the three leaders would put the deal to Gerry.

Friday, July 2

Breakfast was pretty gloomy. Jonathan reported that de Chastelain was getting restless and feeling messed around. TB was worried it was all going down the pan again. Bertie was equally gloomy. The date of an IRA statement and lack of certainty about decommissioning were holding us back. Trimble seemed on for it early on but Donaldson could see his moment and was trying to undo the whole thing. The good news was that Taylor and Maginnis seemed better than before. But TB was exasperated that they could not grasp the fact they were about to deliver the death of the IRA, if only they would seize it. SF were being difficult. McGuinness and Gerry Kelly came in while I was talking to TB and Jonathan. 'We're here about him,' said McGuinness, pointing to me. He said I was currently spinning the line that we were about to announce there would be legislation to exclude them if there was no decommissioning. I said it would be far better if he focused more on the talks inside and less what was said out there by the press. Kelly, sharp-eyed and sharp-suited as ever, flashed one of his looks. People still said McGuinness and Ferris were the real hardnuts, but Kelly could be pretty disconcerting.[1]

De Chastelain came over with his report and had half an hour with TB while we waited for Bertie to come back from Sinn Fein. De Chastelain, and perhaps more importantly Ambassador Don Johnson,[2] clearly did believe the IRA would decommission and that SF had moved. At 4.10 Trimble came in on his own and said he could not go for it. Then exactly half an hour later he came back and said he would go for it. He may not survive but he was willing to give it a go. TB said it was the right thing to do. It was better than the Hillsborough deal and there would be the legislative failsafe. By five I was telling the broadcasters we were on for a deal, that Trimble was hanging tough. Trimble came back in again and I gave him the line which he seemed OK with, 'Are we really not prepared to test for thirty days a process that could end thirty years of violence?' At 5.20 Paddy Teahon came in saying SF were having big trouble with anything that suggested days and weeks. Joe Lennon was pissed off I was briefing on the deal at all. But TB, who was now seeing the smaller parties, was keen to press the button. We gave the thing the title 'The Way Forward' and some new lines to inject forward process. Then at 7, Trimble came back in with Taylor and Reg Empey, said sorry but he couldn't do it. His party could not support it, they would split and he would be gone. TB said let me go and speak to them. They didn't want that. He said it was an own-goal of potentially historic proportions. They could be the people to end the IRA and see off violence for good but for the sake of a few days' uncertainty they weren't prepared to take a risk. He looked pretty close to despair. They all went over to shake TB by the hand, Trimble said nothing, Taylor said thank you for everything you have tried to do. TB said 'I fear you will deliver public opinion to the nationalists at a time they don't deserve it. It is a real error and you will take time to recover from it.' Then finally we were off, and on the car radio on *The World Tonight*

[1] Gerry Kelly and Martin Ferris, key figures in the Sinn Fein leadership, along with Adams and McGuinness.
[2] From the Independent International Commission on Decommissioning.

the reporter said he had a sinking feeling. So did we. On the plane Jonathan and I tried to keep up TB's spirits but he was as fed up as I've seen him, veering from silently looking out of the window to looking back and muttering about the UUs' zero strategy. In the car he called Clinton, who was also amazed they rejected the deal. TB said only the Unionists could throw that chance away.

Friday, July 9

Walked across Whitehall with Alison [Blackshaw] and Mark [Bennett] to do my speech (on the media coverage of Kosovo) to RUSI, which, needless to say, was seen as a scathing attack on the media, which is how they see anything I say about them, but in fact was much more rounded than that. Guthrie was in good form and paid a very nice tribute to me at the end. I enjoyed the Q&A. John Keegan [military historian] said he agreed with everything I said. The audience was mainly diplomatic, foreign media and defence experts. Iain Duncan Smith was there. I'm not sure I would have advised him to go. The broadcasters wanted interviews, but I felt best to leave it to text. *Channel 4 News* did a snide package but would have done anyway. I got back to work on TB's speech for tomorrow. The good thing about his 'scars on my back' was that it had generated renewed interest in modernisation and the domestic agenda. His stuff on nurses was going really well. Earlier, TB and GB saw Colin Marshall and explained we didn't think Britain in Europe[1] were yet in the right shape to do the launch and in particular needed more polling. They must have thought we were total plonkers.

Saturday, July 10

The coverage for my speech was totally predictable, dominated by John Simpson's self-serving attack. As Guthrie said, they showed themselves to be the thin-skinned wankers that they are. They only ever wanted to present one side of an argument, the side that fitted their agenda or prism. Lucie felt we should have organised supportive statements, but in the end I felt the argument got through.

Tuesday, July 13

Ireland was the main story again with the bill due in the House today. Jonathan, John S and I were called up to the flat first thing. There

[1] Cross-party pressure group chaired by Lord Marshall, chairman of British Airways.

was a sense of political crisis out of yesterday but the marches going well is a bonus. TB was worried that we were stumbling towards the end of the road and we had no real strategy. TB saw Robin to see whether he was interested in the NATO job. We were pretty confident the US would back a British candidate to replace Solana. TB was in two minds about losing Robin from the Cabinet but he did need some space for a reshuffle. He had a private meeting with Trimble and said afterwards he felt DT really wanted to help, and TB was the only person he trusted to deal with, but it was difficult for him. He felt we might need to park the whole thing for the summer, which would be a big disappointment.

Wednesday, July 14

Northern Ireland was still dominant. John Sawers had put together a number of amendments to the bill. There was a lot of excitement at the amendments plan though I was careful to say we didn't know if it would be enough and by now Adams and McGuinness were spitting fury. The briefing went on for an eternity. Now we were just waiting for the outcome of Trimble's meeting. Elinor Goodman [*Channel 4 News* political editor] called to say they had rejected the deal. It meant there was no longer a need to rush through emergency legislation. TB agreed with Bertie there was no point doing the legislation now. But Sinn Fein and SDLP were livid. Mallon sounded close to quitting. TB spoke to an as ever graceless DT, who sometimes spoke as though he wasn't actually involved in the process at all, as if his party was some kind of distant entity.

Thursday, July 15

It was descending into farce and chaos. Recriminations were beginning, with some of the blame going towards TB, but Trimble taking the bulk of it. Cabinet was pretty downbeat. TB said neither side was really ready for this. He said we would put those limited issues into a review process and the Assembly would effectively be in recess. But he believed there was something to come back to. He asked me to speak to Trimble and urge him to be more positive, at least give the sense there was some hope there. TB's view was that provided we could limit the recriminations, and give the sense there was something to come back to, it would not be so bad.

Wednesday, July 21

Jonathan called to say the IRA were putting out a statement. For one great moment, I thought it was going to be the statement we had been working for but in fact it was deeply gloomy, critical of the government and with clear veiled threat to return to violence. Denis Murray did a pretty breathless two-way. TB, who was seeing the Sultan of Oman, was pretty fed up.

Thursday, July 22

The IRA statement was leading the news. TB was due to see Trimble and Adams, and TB, John Sawers and I felt there was a case for cancelling the meeting but Jonathan was strongly against. Meeting with Adams, McGuinness and Ferris. John Sawers thought Adams and McGuinness had asked Ferris to be there to show they weren't patsies and could be really tough with TB. TB was pretty tough back and there was a fair amount of mutual fed-upness. TB said, re the IRA statement, 'Well, I get the message, and it's a pretty heavy message too.' McGuinness said 'Nothing to do with me. Not guilty.' In a different context, it would have raised a smile but on both sides, there wasn't much humour. Adams said, rather patronisingly, we think you are trying your best but the Unionists have no interest in sharing power. The Mitchell review is a waste of time. We have been sitting on the Agreement for 15 months and getting nowhere. He said that TB was the best guarantor of not going back to violence, but as an organisation they were not as disciplined as sometimes we thought. 'I know you may have doubts about us but we are the best you've got. We have our own reasons to do this and the main one is a better future for our young people, and the only person that can make it work is you. They have to know change is coming.' TB said both sides operated according to norms that they couldn't imagine changing. He believed the Unionists did want to make it work, but they had people capable of talking themselves into despondency greater than any people he has ever met. 'That doesn't mean they don't want to share power. You have a real understanding. I can put pressure on them as the Irish put pressure on you. I also know that if you go back to violence then I see none of you again. I'm a pragmatist but I feel things deeply. I felt Kosovo. I feel this peace process and if I get an IRA statement like that on the day Gerry Adams and Martin McGuinness are coming in, I don't like that. I don't like the threat. I don't operate like that. And just understand if you go back to violence, I see none of you again.'

McGuinness said their only strategy was to stop power sharing. TB was having none of it. 'The problem with you is that both sides have absolute clarity about the wrongness of the position of the other side. They say to me the IRA will never do it and I say, you're wrong.

Just as I'm telling you you're wrong about Trimble.' They seemed a bit taken aback by how heavy he was with them and Adams tried to soften it, said he accepted part of Trimble wanted it to happen. TB said so what the hell do you want me to do? Adams: implement the Agreement. TB: what the hell do you think I am trying to do? I am implementing the damn Agreement. McGuinness: the only person that can sort this is you, by making them do it. TB: you still can't see it from both sides, as I have to. Adams had a go as well. He said this is going to be bad long after me and Alastair have gone. It's a life-and-death situation. Jonathan made a joke about that being a direct threat to me, which again lightened the mood, and I said to McGuinness 'You're obsessed with this media stuff.' TB joked he would tell me to be nice and gentle with them, but then went back to being serious bordering on heavy. 'If there is a return to violence, just be clear I will have absolutely nothing to do with any of you. I will pursue the justice and equality agenda because I said I would and because it's right. But do not lose your patience so quickly. I will keep mine and get it done. I regard Unionist supremacy as an intolerable historical relic. But it won't go just because you will it to go. And it certainly won't go through more intimidation. My doubt about you is not that you don't want to do it but that if you do not get what you want, you can revert to a situation where you become an enemy when you don't really want to be. I don't want to sound like some kind of Relate counsellor but you should work harder at finding out what the other side is thinking and why. Retreat into your boxes and you will squander it all.' McGuinness said TB and Trimble have to come to terms with the fact that they have more influence on the IRA than him or Gerry. They hung around for a fair bit, obviously trying to work out how best to deal with it.

Over at the House, I bumped into Soames by the cash dispenser. He was raging at me about hunting. 'How would you feel if we got back into power and passed a law banning Burnley fucking Football Club?' He said he had told 'that fucking halfwit Grocott' it was war. To add to the lively scene, Trimble and his wife wandered by, Trimble saying he wished he had his camera, then Andrew Lansley [Conservative MP], who gave us a quizzical look, provoking Soames to yell at him 'Well you can fuck off for starters!' He said he was desperate for ten minutes with TB to talk him out of 'the worst decision he's ever made' re hunting.

Saturday, July 31

Priština. As word had spread, crowds had grown and the cops were a bit worried. As we left he was given a hero's welcome as warm and powerful as any I had ever seen. They were chanting his name: Tony, Tony, in a rhythm that got stronger as he walked through, kids waving flags and running up to him with flowers. One man went to shake his hand, took TB's hand in both of his, and wouldn't let go, just smiling and saying thank you. We then went to the military centre, which was well organised, and I introduced him to some of the Brits I had met when I came out earlier. We went out to the main piazza, where he did an off-the-cuff speech relayed to the crowd through an interpreter, and what with the translations and the cheering, it seemed to go on an awful long time, but the mood was terrific.

August Holiday 99

TB's holiday was coming in for the usual attention, and he wasn't helped by the police shutting down a beach for eight miles either side, to local uproar. TB ordered its reopening, but it meant parts of the press now felt the holiday was generally fair game. It was virtually impossible for him to have a normal holiday. George Robertson was endorsed at NATO. The *Sun* had been on asking if TB had a new marble bathroom. The press office had checked out the facts, which were that £43,000 was being spent on a rolling programme of refurbishment, £15k on the bathroom, of which £4k was marble bits. TB was immediately seized of what was going on, called me, said our opponents are struggling to get us on policy so will go for lifestyle and personality, knowing that's the stuff the press prefer anyway. He said neither he nor Cherie were aware of the cost involved, he had talked to her and we should just cancel it. There was no way he was having a four-figure sum spent on a few bits of marble. TB said at one point 'Last year it was the Omagh bombing, this year it's a piece of marble. It is crazy the time and energy we have to waste because of the media we have got.' We had both been pissed off to be bothered about it, but at least we had groped our way to the right decision.

Wednesday, September 8

We had a longer than usual office meeting, TB was quiet, didn't seem confident. He was warning against creating too many enemies. He was banging on at me again about freeing up time. It was a deeply unsatisfying meeting, unstructured, no clear purpose. Peter M suddenly launched into a big defence of fox hunting. Charlie [Falconer] went through the marketing strategy for the Dome, but didn't sound convinced. Afterwards I had a brainstorm with PM, Philip and Peter Hyman re conference speech. As per my note, I thought the key to the speech and to the next few months was for the government in general and TB in particular to be seen to be in a struggle against the forces that held people back. I had sent my note to GB for his views and went over to the Treasury to discuss. He said he agreed with it, but he warned that it meant taking on a lot of people, which risked creating a lot of enemies, and he was not sure how we did that successfully. He felt we should plan these challenges one by one, and bind in the Cabinet. He also felt our approach was too presidential, that too much of the focus was on TB. He was very good on one level, and unlike most of them at least thought strategically, but he could also be maddening, fixing on one point and going on and on about it.

Monday, September 13
Told Godric I felt like the Alan Shearer [Newcastle United and England footballer] of the Government, past his best, but no clear replacement. Four-hour session with Heads of Information. OK, but most of them didn't get it. I hoped some good came of it, but I doubted it. Philip said the last few groups had been dire. In one of them the only good thing that anyone could remember about the government was TB on Diana. PG said to TB and me that if we went to one of his groups at the moment, we would probably kill ourselves.

Monday, September 20
The serialisation of [Peter] Oborne's [journalist] book on me started in the *Express*, and the *Mail*'s spoiler said Dad died when I was 10. For once, we had them bang to rights. I sent a letter to [Paul] Dacre [editor of the *Daily Mail*], who replied in the most grovelling fashion imaginable. He agreed to run the apology I drafted, word for word, with a cheque for the kids' school.

Friday, September 24
I didn't sleep well. I got to bed about 1 and was up before 6. Briefing TB I mentioned a story that was running about the menopause and he suddenly looked pained and said Cherie might be pregnant. I laughed out loud, then said I could not imagine having a baby at my age, let alone his. Added to which, there would be the whole business of the media management of it, wanting to know every detail, and promulgating theories as to why, what significance, etc. It would also make the planning of trips involving Cherie even crazier. Nobody can complain you don't make news, I said.

Saturday, September 25

I went into the office first thing, then up to see TB. He was now sure. Cherie was pregnant. They worked out it happened at Balmoral. A royal baby! He said he felt a mix of pleasure and horror. Thank God I'm a Christian, he said. It allows me to assume there must be a reason. We discussed it on the train. At the moment, TB, CB, Fiona and I were the only people who knew, and I was winding them up as to how much money we could make by tipping off the press. There was a part of it that was just funny, but it was also clearly worrying him. Once we got to the hotel, any time the two of us were together, he would just want to talk about it, what impact it was going to have. Once we had arrived at Bournemouth, we had a session on the speech and agreed to restructure it. We had a very good laugh when we imagined what it would be like to go out and deliver a truth speech – Conference, Gordon and Peter really do hate each other. It's true that Robin never stops diddling. Philip did a couple of groups down there and reckoned our problem was that we had this great majority and a useless opposition and yet we appeared to be struggling to make change happen quickly.

Monday, September 27–Wednesday, September 29

Writing this at the end of a speech process which in the end seemed to work. It was touch and go. Philip captured the lowest point around 2am Tuesday when he did a note which began 'This speech has seriously lost the plot. The main argument is nowhere. What has happened?' What had happened, as ever, was that we had to go through the awful crisis of confidence that TB seems to need to go through before he can make a great speech. We had done it every year but this time, partly because he was struggling to settle on the central argument, and partly because I was struggling to find the words, it was worse than ever. We had spent two days with him repeatedly saying 'What is the argument? What is the main political point?' We sat down and wrote out different versions, ending up where we started with the idea that Britain had been held back by forces of conservatism which had to be overwhelmed by modernisation and reform to liberate the potential of all the people. Only a modernised Labour Party could do that, because we believed in it, believed in the equal worth of all people and had found our voice and our mission. Peter H and I worked relentlessly trying to get him to take more colour in the speech and be more personal. But it was hard. He didn't like exposing himself too much, didn't like the personal sections which everybody else thought made the speech come alive.

TB went over for the Gordon speech, which went well, really well, and when TB came back he was totally discombobulated. I had been watching it with Miliband and though both of us thought it was OK, neither of us thought it brilliant, so either there was an effect in the hall that didn't come over on TV, or this was just TB using everything and anything to wind himself up further to get him and the rest of us to dig deep and do better. He said it was the best conference speech by someone other than a leader he had ever seen. His worry now was that if we didn't do something special, the TB/GB mischief could get out of hand. There were also continuing arguments, e.g. GB refusing to let us say we would be switching spending from the DSS budget to schools and hospitals. I had never really seen him like this. It wasn't quite panic. It was more like he was trying to convince himself it had been a great speech as a way of putting on pressure, almost like he wanted a moment of panic. He said the pressure on him had been building since the non-reshuffle.

He had all this to deal with and also the business of the pregnancy. Cherie and Fiona had gone back to London quietly. On Tuesday morning, Fiona called as they travelled back down and said the answer was yes. At this stage, only the four of us in Bournemouth knew though TB kept dropping hints, enough for both Sally and Anji to ask me if something was going on. For example at one point, when we were going through the section on childcare, he said he understood about children and then just stared into the middle distance. At times, my jokes about royal babies cheered him up, at other times he was saying he couldn't believe this had happened. What I dreaded was having to deal with all the guff that would come with it. The media would have a field day.

The Monday night was awful. TB got back from his final reception, read the draft, said this is truly hopeless, we are going to have to start again. It was a total overreaction but by now even Philip and I were starting to panic. I was doing lines and talking to him the whole time to try to get him in a better frame of mind, not chuck out the whole thing for the wrong reasons. He wanted a couple of purple-prose passages, which I worked on. We worked through till 3am, and he said he was in a total panic about it. But by then we were going round in circles and needed some rest. We were back working on it at 6am Tuesday and actually we had got the argument back in shape but we still needed more colour and drama in it. The hunt demo was going big and we agreed he should start the speech by saying tally-ho. We had got a couple of half-decent jokes but more important I felt we had a really good argument, good lines, policy that actually knitted into the speech as a whole. The reason the press hadn't liked the overnight briefing was because it lacked the forces of conservatism line that would give edge to the whole argument. It would fly because it was about him showing himself to be confident, in charge of the landscape, really going for it. He was now worried there was too much purple prose, but it was too late.

The hall was gloomy. The set looked fantastic. Some of our best passages were brilliant, others not quite so good, but as a whole it worked and I could feel the party connecting and going for it. The personal stuff worked, and forces of conservatism definitely gave it drama and definition. The general immediate coverage was good but by Wednesday, the feeling was building that when we talked about the forces of conservatism, TB meant anything that went before him.

Fiona called to say that Bloomberg agency had been on to Tanya [Joseph] in the press office to ask if Cherie was pregnant. After we got back to the hotel, the four of us sat down with Sally and talked it through. CB just didn't want it public yet. Tanya had pleaded ignorance, and I felt we could just leave it at that for now. I think they were both, with the speech out of the way, more clearly seized of the nightmare that was about to be unleashed. It was perfectly possible that someone had seen her visiting the doctor, or that the news had got out from us talking on mobiles, but it was not going to be easy to keep it quiet for long.

Monday, October 11

At the office meeting, TB had still not decided re Ken [Livingstone],[1] but we were all growing increasingly alarmed about Frank's lack of any campaign. TB was getting more and more frustrated about delivery. When I pointed out that at these Monday morning meetings, we seemed to be saying the same things week after week, he said 'What do I have to do to translate what we say into action?' TB then saw JP and GB and the reshuffle began. TB said GB was not happy with it and had warned him, 'with a hint of real menace' said TB, that there would be an avalanche of criticism. Well, make sure it's not from you, said TB. Jack C was in first and came through with a handwritten note that he intended to put out as his resignation letter suggesting he offered to resign some time ago. I told him that the press team would really miss him because he

---

[1] Labour MP for Brent East and former leader of the Greater London Council. After Frank Dobson was selected as the sole Labour candidate for the 2000 London mayoral election, Livingstone stood as an independent candidate and was expelled from the party.

had been reliable and a team player and I hoped we could still call on him. Then Mo came round after seeing TB, all lovey-dovey, burbling away about how she saw herself as a coordinator rather than an enforcer and she wanted to go to Belfast with Peter tomorrow. I had to persuade TB not to move Charlie F, who would be essential to making sure that Mo didn't run amok. Then [Alan] Milburn, then [Chris] Smith, and then Peter to Northern Ireland. I was glad he was back. He looked genuinely shocked and wasn't himself at all. He went to the loo and when after a few minutes he hadn't come back, I went looking for him and found him, still in there, saying he had never felt so anxious. I took him back through to my office and then got Mo round again and suggested they went out together and travelled off in the car together. He said he was due to see Gordon and then said, as if an aside to Mo, 'In this government I am appointed by two people not one.' TB claimed that when he saw him one on one he had been very hard on him, told him that if he didn't really behave, not diddle, just do the job properly, he would be finished. That may explain why he was so shell-shocked. GB was pushing for his usual people, Yvette [Cooper],[1] Douglas [Alexander, Labour MP for Paisley and Renfrewshire South]. Bruce [Grocott] at one point said can't we just have an hour put aside in the diary at every reshuffle for pointless discussions about Michael Wills [Labour MP for North Swindon]. Like all reshuffles, there had been difficulties but this one had probably been easier than most. Mo's interviews were pretty hopeless. The 'hiya babe' approach had a certain appeal I suppose, but she was incredibly loose with language. I spoke to Peter later, who was settling in. He was seeing his new protection team and said 'I've just introduced them to the concept of Reinaldo.'

Monday, October 25

TB and I got stuck in dreadful traffic and got out to get the tube from Monument. It was interesting to see the reactions of people. Most were just surprised to see him, and there was lots of nudging and nodding. Lots, this being the tube, looked embarrassed to be looking. But the ones who came over and spoke were overwhelmingly friendly, though I think these days it is as much a celebrity thing as a leadership or political thing.

Tuesday, October 26

I had another problem with Mo. She'd told Richard Wilson she wanted to make public she'd taken cannabis 'and inhaled'. Pure self-indulgence,

---

[1] Labour MP for Pontefract and Castleford; married Ed Balls in 1998.

which would put pressure on other ministers re all manner of personal life questions. TB said we had to find ways of harnessing her popularity.

Sunday, October 31

The big developing story was Prince Charles taking William out hunting. Again, it seemed pretty clear it was a political act coming so soon after his attack on GM and the 'boycotting' of the Chinese banquet. Then, news that *The Times* were splashing on Prince Charles becoming a 'beef ambassador'. What seemed to be happening was that he was following through a strategy to put himself at the head of the forces of conservatism. The speech had clearly really struck a nerve. Charles's people were briefing the Monday papers that his meeting with TB was basically about hunting. TB said I should say the meeting was long arranged, they got on very well, and it was no surprise to anyone that he hunted. I agreed a line with Stephen Lamport to play it all down, but the fact of the meeting was out there and was going to be a big thing. When TB came back he was pretty shocked that the media had been staking it out.

Wednesday, November 3

We had a meeting on London. To block or not to block was the only question. Peter and I seemed to be the last two really to feel that the risk of him being a Labour mayor was greater than the wrath we would face for blocking him. But TB had definitely moved. He felt we would do real damage to ourselves if we blocked him now, that we would lose lots of members, and not just on the hard left. He was not confident that JP, GB, Mo would really support it in practice. They would just let us take the flak.

Thursday, November 4

Cabinet. TB said we were unprecedentedly strong for a government at this time, not least because of economic management, and also because the Opposition was so badly perceived. But there was an impatience and frustration on public service delivery. Added to which the Tories were successfully labelling us as arrogant and out of touch and they were making inroads on Europe. GB said we had laid foundations. The Tories had gone too far on Europe. We can portray them as ideological. On the economy, there too they had gone to the right. They were also becoming incoherent, making inconsistent noises on tax cuts in general and spending commitments in particular. He felt we were able to put the case for compassion and prosperity together.

But modernisation and reform was an important part of the argument. We have to be modernising public services and welfare and the Tory alternative is their dismantling. He also went through the argument for the PBR [Pre Budget Report]. The Tories would try and present us as arrogant and elitist, which was why we had to be always on the side of hard-working families.

Thursday, November 11

Beef was becoming a real disaster area[1] in the media but TB was still of the view we were doing the right thing. TB said the baby would be called Leo or Hazel. She was still keen to keep it all quiet but the bump was definitely beginning to show. On the plane out, TB and I had another chat about what I felt was his, and our, loss of cutting edge. I felt he was becoming a bit too remote from the public, and did think he was listening less and becoming prone to thinking he was always right. There were always things we could do better. My only chat with the hacks on the plane had led to stories about CB having to spend lots of her own money on clothes. This had come out as I was defending myself over an untrue story in the Sundays that I earned more than the Cabinet.

Tuesday, November 16

I went up to see CB to apologise for the wall-to-wall coverage of her clothes that had followed me trying to deal with the stories about my salary. She was very nice about it, even when the press coverage got so big the broadcasters felt obliged to follow it up. I had fallen for the oldest trick in the book and allowed myself to get verballed. She said 'To them, I'm just a picture.'

I was at the dentist for three hours, then back to more discussions on Ken. We had got the broadcasters lined up for 5pm but it was clear there was a problem. The transcript showed that Ken refused to say he would support a manifesto that included PPP [Public Private Partnership]. There was a clear case for blocking him, but then Frank called me to say he did not make a habit of threatening prime ministers, but if Ken was blocked, we could not take it for granted that he would run as a 'lone ranger'. He said Ken had to stand. He called me again later to make the same point. TB made the suggestion to Margaret B that we say they would call Ken back. It seemed that Clive Soley [chairman of the PLP] was for blocking him straight away

[1] The French had decided unilaterally not to lift the ban on British beef, imposed after the BSE outbreak.

whereas Ian McCartney wanted the party to see we were bending over backwards to be fair to him. But the hacks were all hanging around outside and it was beginning to look a bit farcical. TB felt though that he was slightly playing into our hands. JP was pretty wound up about him refusing to sign up to our manifesto and he agreed to go up tomorrow on the *Today* programme. He was very bullish about it. 'You can't run on a separate manifesto.' About 8, Soley finally went out and said that Ken would have to come back on Thursday and that he had not been clear and straightforward. TB was pretty exasperated. Our famed so-called news management was looking pretty ropy. On *Newsnight*, Glenda [Jackson, Labour MP for Hampstead and Highgate] and Ken united against the system. Ann Keen [PPS to Frank Dobson] called me to say Dobbo was really angry, close to quitting, and she didn't trust the people in his camp. We had really fucked this from start to finish. The only good thing coming out of it was the sense of Livingstone as a totally divisive figure. But it was pretty hopeless. Mo told me she would support blocking if he didn't go for the manifesto. Margaret B was not so clear. But all in all, it was a dreadful day, the best part of which was probably the visit to the dentist.

Wednesday, November 17

Queen's Speech day, and Ken fucking Livingstone was leading the news. I think what I hated as much as anything was that we looked so incompetent. It was like something out of the eighties. Cherie's clothes was still running as a problem. It was all a pretty grim back-drop for the Queen's Speech. GB and I had another go at TB, said that whatever he signed up to, he would just shift afterwards. Clive [Soley] was excellent on the media. On PPP, GB felt Livingstone had to go for more than just saying he would support the manifesto. He would have to retract what he had said. JP made clear he could not stand as an independent on a Labour ticket. Meanwhile Frank D, or someone on his behalf, was busy briefing what Ann Keen had told me yesterday, mainly that he would pull out if Ken was not put forward. TB thought it was a pretty asinine move. Meanwhile Glenda J was sitting there thinking she would benefit from blocking Ken. TB felt that it was possible to block him and he would go up and say why, but he had spent thirty minutes with Frank, who had said there was no way he would stand if Ken was blocked. But some of them felt there was some merit in that happening and getting both of them out. GB and I were the two most strongly arguing for him to be blocked. Lance came in with a statement from Ken which said he would support the manifesto and not withdraw halfway through if he was not happy with it. This felt like some of the nonsense Neil [Kinnock] had to put up with the whole time. TB was also worrying about possible legal challenges. At one point he said to me 'Would you mind refraining from just sitting there and shaking your head?' He felt the statement made it very difficult to block him. GB said if he won, as Labour but effectively as an independent, our transport policy is dead. I got Neil to speak to Frank but he called halfway through the football to say that it was hopeless and he just wouldn't go for it if Ken was blocked. I saw Ian McCartney for a meeting on the COI [Central Office of Information], after which we chatted about Ken. Ian felt that he was capitulating and we had to let him go through. I said my worry was you couldn't believe a word he said, but Ian, like Frank, felt he could be beaten in argument.

Thursday, November 18

At one o'clock, Piers Morgan called and said he had a story and if he told me what it was could he guarantee it would stay exclusive? I said I know what it is. He said 'How are your christening robes?' I said I would have to talk to TB. Then I had a meeting with Fiona and we agreed we would just let the *Mirror* run it and then confirm. But the *Sun* had heard something and Rebekah Wade [deputy editor] was paging and calling both of us relentlessly. Eventually, after speaking to CB, Fiona gave the story to Rebekah around 8, which was clearly going to be disasterville with Piers. There was no way he would think the *Sun* got on to it themselves. I got TB to call him to try to mollify him a bit but later Piers was absolutely fuming. 'Why do those two women (Cherie and Fiona) have such a problem with me? I don't get it.' CB was clear she didn't want her pregnancy to seem as somehow being owned as a *Mirror* story. Once the *Sun* were on to it, she wanted them to have the story. It was a one-fact story. Dealing with the *Sun* and the *Mirror* the whole time was like having two mistresses. It was a fucking nightmare. Both thought they were entitled to some kind of special treatment. It would probably have been better just to have announced it earlier, but Cherie had wanted to keep it quiet for as long as possible, which was fair enough. We had a statement out at 9.10, and it led Sky straight away. There was something amusing about seeing all these hard-nosed characters standing outside Number 10 going on about babies.

Friday, November 19

Philip sent me a message. Absolutely brilliant. He seemed to think the whole thing about the baby was a planned piece of news management to deal with Ken. I was able to disabuse him. News of the pregnancy led the *Today* programme, though Trevor Kavanagh said later that Tony Hall had issued an edict that programmes and bulletins couldn't lead on it. Piers was out and about on TV trying to milk it. I was in just after 7 and went up to see TB and CB. She was perfectly happy with it. There was a fair old media crowd outside. Hague and GB were both being very nice about it, but TB had a slight concern people would think the whole thing had been designed for media purposes. What, I said, like we told you to have a baby because we had a few gaps in the Grid [a calendar system instigated by Campbell in 1997 to coordinate government announcements]? We had a meeting with GB at 9. He said we would regret letting Ken go through. We also had a bit of an up-and-downer about spending because GB didn't accept we should put more into schools and hospitals for now, but wait. TB said they needed it now. GB said 'You just want me to shovel in cash every time they ask. I can't do it. It's not on.' TB said 'No I'm not, but if we have the money what is the point in getting hit on it?' I spoke to Dobbo to say he should get out and make a big thing about Ken having called for GB to be sacked. At the 11 o'clock briefing, it was all about the baby and there was actually a very good mood and less cynicism than I thought there would be. Mike White asked the funniest question – 'Any advice for the Hagues?' Fiona had come to the briefing, said she really enjoyed it.

Saturday, November 20

Money could not buy the publicity we were getting. Even the *Mail* and the *Telegraph* were feeling they had to be nice-ish about it. There was a fair bit of speculation round about whether I had put the story out there, Roger Gale [Conservative MP for North Thanet] having said as much yesterday. The Piers/Yelland rubbish was still going on. I got Hilary C to go in and organise TB doing some words in the street as we left Number 10. Took Calum and Grace out to the Heath and then went into Number 10. Cabbie, who said Cherie's dad kissed him when he was pissed, said the country was loving it. TB said he couldn't believe the scale of the coverage. He did a little mingle with some kids in the street. He was reading the papers for once.

Wednesday, November 24

We had a meeting re PMQs. I felt we still weren't using them to promote and drive strategy. And because Hague was still coming up with good one-liners, TB wasn't getting the political plus points he ought to be. We were giving him good lines but he was very reluctant to use them in the House. He didn't like doing things that were over-rehearsed. It was fair enough. But he lacked a killer instinct in there. PMQs was a bit all over the place, debt, Chechnya, euro, slavery. Philip said later that he felt at the strategy meeting TB had been very low and I wondered whether it was because I put through a very tough note saying the operation today had been woeful. That there was no killer instinct from him and the MPs and we had missed opportunities. I left at 5 to go to Reading v Burnley. Crap match. Nil-nil. TB called, I think a bit hurt by my note. He said part of the problem was that some days he just felt ground down and his instincts weren't always so sharp.

Thursday, November 25

At Cabinet, there was a good discussion on Anglo-French defence and then we waited for Chirac, and then Jospin upstairs in the White Room. Chirac was being helpful on beef but there were still problems in the text on the NATO-friendliness of the language. We were served Welsh wine at the lunch and Chirac did a brilliantly exaggerated approving tasting managing simultaneously to say it was marvellous while indicating through every part of his face that he didn't think much of it at all. TB told Chirac the Americans were very nervous about the defence initiative, and he had to understand NATO's centrality to it all. But he felt Europe had to improve its capability particularly re logistics and strategic lift. It wasn't on that Europe had to go for American help all the time. Chirac said the politics on this were very different. In Britain we were under pressure to be pro-NATO. In France there are many anti-NATO forces. So the balance we had to find was between not being critical and not being submissive. But he never missed an opportunity to have a dig at the Americans, at one point saying Clinton was playing golf when he should have been focusing on some issue Chirac was badgering him about. There was a similarly tricksy mood in their discussions on Iraq.

Wednesday, December 1

TB asked me why I was so fed up with him. I said because I was expected to do far too much, both by the politicians and by the press. He also expected me to do too much of the motivational stuff within the building, and not just with my own people. And it got very wearing when on the one hand he kept advising me to take more time off and on the other never stopped loading things upon me. Frank D had stood in for Jeffrey Archer at a media ball and I had a stack of calls from people telling me he had been absolutely dreadful. This thing felt worse by the day.

Thursday, December 2

Power was devolved at midnight. Gerry Adams called me and said he wanted to say thanks to TB and to all of us. He said it was a really emotional day which many thought they would never see. It was wall-to-wall on TB all day and Peter M was doing stacks of media and doing it well. Lance came in with the news, via Ann Keen, that Shaun Woodward was about to be sacked for refusing to support their policy on Section 28,[1] and he might defect. He was with Ann Keen and he wanted to talk to Cherie. I felt a bit uneasy at involving Cherie. I spoke to Ann and then to Shaun and said if he was going to defect, he must broaden out the issues and come over soon. Otherwise, no matter how strongly he felt on one issue, he would look opportunistic. He said he was also uneasy about Europe, their approach on the economy and tax, general illiberalism. He came over to see me at 8.15 and poured his heart out re what had happened and why it mattered so much. He said he couldn't support anything that in his view led to homophobic bullying, something that for family reasons he had cause to know about. He said several times it was about decency, what kind of society we want. I said that if he came over, though no promises could be made, he should look at the help we gave to Alan Howarth in trying to find a seat. Cherie popped in and saw him for about twenty minutes and she basically just said he should do what he felt was right. He looked like he had been crying. He had put on some weight and was very emotional. I'd say he started out forty per cent in favour of defecting and ended closer to seventy. TB was amazed by it but agreed with me he had to be broadened out from Section 28.

Saturday, December 4

TB called and said he was pretty confident Woodward would come over. He was genuinely impressed by his intelligence and thought his stand on Section 28 was definitely principled. But Shaun didn't like the comparisons with Alan Howarth because he saw himself as a much bigger fish, possibly even Tory leadership material. TB wanted me to go in for the meeting with him but Calum was in such a rage

[1] Conservative MP for Witney and Opposition spokesman on London. Section 28 of the Local Government Act 1988 banned local authorities from promoting homosexuality.

December '99: NI: Power devolved at last

about me saying I was going in on yet another Saturday that I ended up joining them on the speakerphone. I tee'd up Peter M to be the one to emphasise the need to broaden it out from Section 28, and that was how the conversation was going when I checked in. Shaun clearly felt very strongly that he had managed to get over the argument about bullying. He said that in his heart he had moved over already, but he felt if he did it now, right now, his friends would know it was out of character. Chris Patten's reaction, he was sure, would be 'This is Alastair Campbell at work. I can't believe you didn't think about it more deeply.' The press would say it was a fit of pique. My argument was that in a sense this should be seen as the straw that broke the camel's back, the last in a line of issues where he felt out of step with his own party, but actually he needed a bit of emotionalism in his explanation, and that the longer he waited, the more it might be seen as opportunism. TB and I then went into a bit of a soft cop hard cop routine. TB kept saying Shaun should take as long as he wanted, and think about it deeply because it was such an important step. I was saying that if he was going to make a career in the Labour Party, the Labour Party was going to have to take to him and he wouldn't get much better circumstances than resigning over an issue of principle like this, and then broadening out. He said he thought he should disappear for a while and then come back and do it. If he did it now, people would say it was a stunt. On broadening out, Peter M said that as he had been a frontbencher, it would be difficult because there would be very little on the record to point to. I said Shaun needed to go through all areas of policy and decide which he genuinely opposed. The conversation went on for about ninety minutes, and I suspected there were going to be plenty more. I took Calum to school for football and then went to pick up Mum at King's Cross. She commented that I seemed to be on the phone more than ever, which was bound to get the kids down.

Thursday, December 9
TB spoke to Adams about the bug that had been found in his car, a call we had agreed to simply to let GA say that he had raised it and protested. 'Sorry to bug you with this,' he said.

Tuesday, December 14
I went with Lance to Paul Gambaccini's [broadcaster and writer on music, friend of Price] flat at County Hall and waited for Shaun W. He had written out a speech which we went through and we also

had a draft-handling plan. He made clear again, less subtly than before, that he felt he was seen by some in the Tory Party as a possible future leader. We agreed that he would do the speech on Friday, and defect on Saturday after seeing his constituency chairman. I think he had pretty much decided but he still needed a lot of assurance so we were in for another long meeting. He was worried that the speech would be seen by Hague as so over the top that they would withdraw the whip, which would make it look like the defection was in response to that, rather than the obvious natural consequence of the arguments he had made. I didn't feel they would do that but we agreed to go through the speech with that in mind and soften if necessary. After an hour or so, I felt confident enough that he was going to do it and started to map out a detailed handling plan. He seemed to be assuming he would be Europe minister. TB said I should make no promises but make him feel there would definitely be a role.

Thursday, December 16

I went to join Lance with Shaun at Paul Gambaccini's flat. Shaun had gone through the speech and also his letter to Hague and the articles he was planning. He had done a really good job and the letter was very powerful. It was quite a big thing he was doing and I was reaching the view he was doing it more for the right reasons than for the wrong ones. He had done an article for the *Express*, basically an extract from tomorrow's speech, and later [Tony] Bevins asked him if he was going to defect. Shaun, taken aback, said no, which had the potential to be a problem later. His wife, Camilla, was very pretty, seemed genuinely supportive and very composed. He led us to believe she had all sorts of concerns, but she actually seemed quite comfortable with the whole thing. He was full of it now, said he felt totally happy about it, totally at home. I sensed they hadn't really gone through the detail, e.g. what they would do with the children when it broke. I felt it was important she was with him, and posed with him, with or without the kids. I liked her. I thought she was very calm and would be helpful in the next few days. He asked me to tell TB he felt 100% happy about it and was sure it was the right thing.

Saturday, December 18

The rumour mill was starting. Shaun saw his constituency chairman and it broke on PA around 12. It set the agenda for the day. There was a good response from the Tory reform group and others on the left of the party, and a very bitter response from Hague, who said

December '99: Woodward '100% happy' about going

Woodward had no honour. Their basic line of attack was careerism. Shaun called, said he was happy, felt great, felt that he was home. As well as careerism, the Tories were clearly trying to make it as much about me and Peter as possible, said we were more ruthless than the security services getting spies to defect. Shaun intended to use the line that their response showed how vile they were.

Friday, December 24

TB agreed with my analysis re the Dome, said we needed a real sense of excitement building, but it wasn't really happening. The *Telegraph* had a story that Prince Charles had a joke Dome at Highgrove made of Cotswolds materials.

Thursday, December 30

TB was back from Sedgefield. He was intending to do a note that would be 'positively compendious' over the next few days so we ran through the various problem areas we had to sort. Cherie had been trying to find out if they could get access to part of the Number 10 flat once the baby was born, and GB had written to say he was willing to give them the whole flat, which of course was not what anybody had wanted. Anji paged me to say there were difficulties with the big new wheel[1] that was going up on the river. And JP called to say it was not going to be possible to fix passengers for it tomorrow. I fixed a conference call with him, Charlie F, Bob Ayling and Anji. It was a bit of a disaster. Bob decided that the people who were coming would get a free flight to anywhere in the world, a party on the Thames, and be the first people to go on the wheel when it finally started. Added to the fact that thousands of tickets for the Dome event had still not gone out, we had the makings of a bit of a fiasco. Charlie was adamant the tickets would be sorted. We went out for dinner with the Goulds and even before I mentioned the wheel, Philip said he thought the Dome was 'on a knife edge'. Then Anji called after getting calls from both Trimble and Margaret Beckett that they didn't know what the arrangements were for getting back from the Dome. I did a conference call with Charlie and some of his people. They were far too trusting and assumed that when people said things were being done, it meant they were. Even though the wheel was not really our problem, we would cop for it, as we would if the tickets weren't sorted. Charlie said let's save the witch-hunt for later. I said let's make sure we don't need one.

[1] The landmark observation wheel known as the London Eye.

Friday, December 31

TB called, a bit agitato, said he could not believe that on the eve of a new millennium we could not get the fucking wheel to move. 'I just can't believe this. We'll be a laughing stock.' While we were speaking, the message came through that Yeltsin had announced he was stepping down ahead of time, but after a brief discussion on that, he was back to the wheel and the Dome. He spoke to Charlie F and later called me back to say he thought Charlie was doing everything he could. For the rest of the day, the phone never stopped re tonight's events, a case of people talking themselves into a state. We had to accept the wheel wasn't going to move but he was still due to say something at its official opening. I went into Number 10 with Fiona and the kids and briefed TB on the night's events. TB said 'This is worse than the election. At least then we had a fair idea we were going to win. Here, we don't have a clue what is going to happen, but we feel it in our bones something is going to go wrong.' There was a great atmosphere out on the streets for TB. There was a fair bit of hanging around, then over to the Lords, and down to the Underground, where Peter M was prancing around taking pictures of everyone. TB was in with the Archbishop and the Commonwealth Secretary General. There was something very Zil lane[1] about it all as we were whisked straight there. On arrival, we went up to the VIP room, where Marianna [Falconer] told me there was a problem at Stratford, where lots of the media people were being forced to wait for hours to get their tickets. The problem seemed to be there was only one scanner. Philip was there and said it was a total disaster area. Greg Dyke [new director-general of the BBC], Jon Snow, Peter Stothard, lots of them, going absolutely mental. I was going into an absolute rage, especially as nobody seemed to be taking it that seriously. Nobody was taking responsibility to sort it out. Charlie kept asking for assurances, being given them, but then they weren't doing the things they said they were. I said to Charlie we could not allow these people to get away with such incompetence. TB said I shouldn't lose it with them but this had the feeling of a bit of a disaster. He said my rage was a bit too obvious, not least because my ears had gone red. Fiona was showing the children around. Cherie had a dreadful cold but was soldiering on. Jennie Page showed TB around and he felt it had the makings of a success. But not if tonight was a disaster. There was a good atmosphere but there were a lot of empty

[1] In Moscow, high-ranking Soviet officials could take advantage of a separate lane for their Zil limousines.

seats, presumably those of the people stranded at Stratford. The Queen arrived with Philip, Anne and her husband. Apart from the Queen, who at least managed the odd smile, the others looked very pissed off to be there. TB worked away at them, trying to charm them into the mood, but Anne was like granite. Cherie even curtsied to the Queen, a bit of a first I think, but it didn't seem to do much good. The pre-midnight show was not that great. It needed a compere to get everyone wound up and excited, but instead we just had a few acts, some good, some indifferent, but the climax of two young choristers was dull, and the moment itself was upon us too soon. Fiona, the kids and I were sitting directly in front of Hague and Ffion. At one point not long before midnight, I looked round at Hague, who was probably listening to my continuing phone calls about Stratford, as the list of angry hacks grew longer, when he said 'It's all going very well then.' TB and CB tried to get the royals going a bit once 'Auld Lang Syne' came on but it was pretty clear they would rather be sitting under their travelling rugs in Balmoral. The Queen did kiss Philip and took his and TB's hands for 'Auld Lang Syne' but they did not look comfortable with the whole thing. TB claimed Philip said to him it was 'brilliant', but his body language did not radiate in that direction. Also, it would clearly have been better with the young Princes there but Charles was never going to let that happen. Afterwards the show was pretty spectacular and got people going a bit more than the build-up had but you would be hard-pressed to say it was the greatest show on earth. The fireworks outside sounded amazing and I sensed people feeling they would rather be out than in. At the party afterwards, again the mood was OK without being great. It just didn't feel that extra special that was needed to make it work really well, and create a mood that could give us a bit of momentum. The so-called river of fire, a flame down the Thames, had been a damp squib, barely visible. I enjoyed the boat ride back and the Dome itself actually looked quite impressive from that angle, all lit up. The mood around the place was OK, but there were a lot of people very pissed and it all felt just a bit debauched. It was clear Paris, Rio and Sydney were thought to have done best. In fact the picture of the night used as the headline caption picture was the bloody Eiffel Tower with fireworks coming out of it. Simple but brilliant, and better than anything that came out of the Dome in terms of single image.

Saturday, January 1, 2000

After a few hours' sleep, the phone went and it was TB, fretting about the way things had gone down. I said I felt it was about a 70 per cent success rate, but some of the other capitals did better. Also the Stratford strandings were going to hit us hard because they would all vent their own spleen. I also felt the show itself had been poor. I said I thought we were a long way from persuading people it had been a success, given all the fuss over cost etc. Charlie F was down at the Dome doing interviews and of course the big thing there was going to be the first paying customers, and what they thought. It was a real baptism of fire for Charlie but he seemed up for it. Charlie arrived fairly late and seemed to think the Dome itself was going OK. We gave him a reasonably hard time, but he was coping pretty well I thought. The great thing about Charlie is he always managed to see a funny side of things. I suspected this was a quality he was going to need in large supply. TB felt in reality it had been an 85 per cent success. The problem was that fuck-up at Stratford. He worried the papers would just go out to kill the Dome now.

Sunday, January 2

The press was definitely turning for the worse. TB felt that we must have it established within a couple of days that the Dome was a must-see, or we would be in trouble. It didn't feel that good, not least because the blame game was starting, between the police and NMEC, Jennie Page and Mike Lockett [Dome opening-night organiser]. They were already in defensive, damage limitation mode which was a real problem.

Wednesday, January 5

The first full day back. Jonathan told me that TB and CB were going to stay with Cliff Richard [veteran pop singer] in the Algarve. I called him and said I thought it would become a real problem, parody material, if it became public. He said he just couldn't see why. Why couldn't they just chill out without always having to see famous people. His argument was that they couldn't have normal holidays partly because of security. Charlie F called, said that Jennie was really down, and the blame game was going into overdrive.

Friday, January 7

Writing this at the end of a not untypical day at the end of which, when they called just before midnight, I told switch, in answer to their friendly 'How are you?', that I was both homicidal and suicidal. The Dome press coverage, with the exception of the *Mirror* poll, was wall-to-wall dreadful. I did a conference call with Charlie F, Jennie P and Jez [Sagar, Dome press office] to go through the script for the Sundays. TB later said he thought me doing a briefing on it was a bad idea because it would lay it all on us, but if it failed, we were the ones who would cop it anyway. I also felt if we didn't show real support, it would look really wounded. My main pitch was to try to divide real people, who were overwhelmingly positive, from the chattering class knockers. Jennie and Charlie were both getting more and more defensive. Also, I had been banging on for days about the need to get a few celebs down there, but it just hadn't happened. Dobbo's launch didn't really break through and by the end of the day Ken had turned it into a personal attack on him, which he believed Frank would regret.

Tuesday, January 11

The other thing that was coming up fast on the radar was Mike Tyson, who was due to fight in London, so there would be a big hoo-ha if he was let in, given his various misdemeanours.[1] I dropped a line to Jack Straw to say I thought he would be absolutely hammered if Tyson was banned. Coincidentally, the *Standard* splashed on it today with an editorial saying he should be banned. Jack's line was that rules are rules, and he had to play it by the book. I felt it was one of those where people who wanted him banned didn't feel it that strongly, and would be on to the next cause pretty quickly, whereas there would be a constituency that would really, really object if he was kept out of the country. I got a sense of the mixed views at the 4 o'clock. The sense they got from my briefing was that he definitely would be banned, because I was emphasising Jack's 'rules are rules' line. Frank

[1] The heavyweight boxer had served prison sentences for rape and assault.

Warren, who was promoting the fight, was out blaming me for breaking the rules re applications. Little did he know that I was fighting his corner.

Thursday, January 13

The World at One led on Tyson and a union guy saying it was dreadful that an immigration worker would have to decide. That was indeed the logic of Jack's rules are rules approach. I had finally got TB engaged and he agreed we had to get it sorted quickly. Otherwise, he said, it will be a shambles by the morning. Jack was feeling a bit hurt, I think, and made a joke – though without much humour – about how he would happily give it up and let me do the job for him. I said we had to have it sorted by the 4 o'clock, because this felt like a shambles and we had enough of those at the moment. Frank Warren made a submission and included the wider issues of businesses that would be badly affected if the fight didn't go ahead. After my briefing yesterday, he had finally realised that I was on his side and today invited 'you and your lady wife' to the fight! By the 4, Jack had discovered that he did after all have discretion and he was going to use it and review the situation.

Thursday, January 20

I told Dobbo about the dreadful *Mirror* poll but he showed no sign of wanting to pull out. I spoke to Mo, who came up with, even for her, an unbelievably up-herself statement, namely that TB was now so unpopular that 'even I might not be able to pull it off.'

Tuesday, January 25

TB was in a real state about Livingstone. Frank had refused to come out. His pride was at stake and that was that. Also Mo was not willing to push him too hard. TB said it was the worst of all worlds – we had a candidate in the ring who can't win and a candidate outside the ring who would probably walk it. I asked him if he could imagine himself campaigning for Ken.

Wednesday, January 26

I went home briefly before going back in to join TB to see Frank and Janet Dobson, to try to persuade him to pull out. Frank said he was convinced it was moving his way, but I said there wasn't much evidence of that. TB said what he cared about was the impact on the party and the government if Ken won. It would be a big disaster and he didn't want that. All the evidence suggested Frank wouldn't win, and Mo might. That says to us that we should get her in. Frank was adamant he could do it and that she would do no better. Between us, TB and I must have tried eight or ten times, but he wouldn't move from the basic point, that he didn't think she was the answer. TB asked him, if he carried on and things didn't pick up, whether he would pull out later in the contest and he said no. I felt sorry for him. He was almost certainly going to lose, and surely he must know that, and he'd be left with nothing. I had one last go, saying he could come out with dignity, but he didn't buy it.

Monday, January 31

Peter Kilfoyle's resignation [as junior defence minister] was going pretty big. TB and I agreed we should be nice about Peter, though TB felt nothing but contempt for what he had done. 'Two and a half years in, they all think they should be Cabinet ministers and they all want it to be easy.' Anji and I stayed at the end of the office meeting and had another go at trying to get an agreement on the strategy for the press. Do we make them an issue, and really go for some of them, or not? He said he felt the same about journalists as I did. The question is, is it sensible politics to be at war with them? I wanted to undermine them, divide and rule. He felt we could continue to woo them.

Saturday, February 5

I set off for Burnley and on the train worked on his speech for tomorrow on the politics of unity v division, which TB had trailed yesterday. Godric called to say some of the papers were clearly on to Jennie Page getting the boot. I set up a conference call with Charlie etc. and we agreed it was better to get out a more positive story, that it shouldn't just be about her, that the new Dome boss PY Gerbeau was coming, pay tribute to her and say different skills were now required. PY was a bit worried about our media. I said we would give him all the support we could, but it was really important it was all seen as their operation and not ours. Governments shouldn't run tourist attractions.

Wednesday, February 9

After I had gone to bed, I got an extraordinary call from Mo. She had seen Tony. She wanted to be Foreign Secretary but she realised it wasn't going to happen. She was not very happy where she was and she was going to be looking for something new. She *did* want to be Mayor, and she suggested to TB that maybe she could be an independent.

Two businessmen had offered her forty thousand quid. She said people were coming up to her the whole time urging her to go for it. She was looking for a way in. TB had grimaced at the idea of her being an independent. Amazingly, it was the idea I had put forward weeks ago and I still felt surely it was possible. Mo said whatever she did she was going to be a problem area for him and she needed to be out of it. She said the Tony crony thing was a real problem.

Sunday, February 20

TB was very agitato, called several times. The first was to say that Frank had won the Labour Party's mayoral nomination and that I needed to speak to him and talk him through the day. He had to rise above the process and get on to policy. Frank came round after Margaret B spoke to him and he was looking a lot more relaxed than before. We went over the script and I said he had to be policy, policy, policy and leave process to Ken. None of us really knew how Ken would play it. Frank felt he would go as an independent. I was suggesting to Frank that he didn't wear a tie, tried to be more relaxed and look a bit happier than of late, and also that Janet should be with him. She hated the idea because she didn't want to be the lady mayoress. The focus was all really on whether or not Ken would go as an independent. I was pretty sure he would.

Saturday, February 26

TB said he was willing to see Ken but I felt Ken would just use it for a few more days, limelight hogging and to remind people how badly we had handled the whole thing. The problem was that neither TB nor I were seeing this as the public were.

Thursday, March 2

I briefed John Reid for *Question Time* but then we agreed it was better to put on Frank as they had Ken, Steve Norris and Susan Kramer [the Conservative and Lib Dem candidates] on the programme. I had been very reluctant at first because I didn't like the BBC setting the agenda and dictating what programmes Frank should do, but there was now a danger Ken would run away with it. TB and GB both agreed he had to do it. Frank came in to see TB and me and we talked him through the best ways to get the focus on him as policy and Ken as process and trouble. Frank looked nervous again, nodded and made lots of jokes, but didn't really have the edge he was going to need. As he left, TB said 'He's not going to come out of it well.' We had to set it up with a statement from Frank which we put together and got out to PA and it was good attacking stuff which he would now have to see through. I gave him the line to use in the programme: 'Ken, make my day and stand.' Ken of course was enjoying the limelight and we had to burst the bubble quickly. TB felt Ken was no longer the problem. Frank was the problem and we had to improve his capacity and the team around him. I got home and after dinner watched Dobbo on *Question Time*. He did OK at the start, delivered the 'make my day' line perfectly well but then got very bumbly, didn't really go for Ken on crime, sometimes looked as though he was surprised to be there, made statements then looked around as though he was expecting someone to ask him to leave. Philip felt it had been a mistake for him to go on. Make my day would win him the head-lines, but he didn't really win the arguments. Stan Greenberg, watching in the US, felt that the process had hit TB hard.

Tuesday, March 7

Livingstone choosing to stand as an independent was wall-to-wall and he got a very good press without necessarily being endorsed. There was a sense running through it that we had really fucked it up. He was running rings round us. There was a poll in the *Guardian* which had him at 55%, but still somehow he was the underdog. TB felt that too much putting the boot in would play into his hands. The strategy had to be to build up the policy arguments against him. His credentials on crime in particular were vulnerable. We also needed business people to come out for Frank. Our big problem was the press and TV were doing his job for him. It was a conclusion of their desire to use him to kick us.

Wednesday, March 8

Philip had done some groups on London and had concluded it was a lost cause trying to build up Frank. He was too much of a plodder and just didn't inspire. Yet Ken was beatable with a good candidate.

Friday, March 10

Russia. We did a bit of schmoozing with the hacks on the plane. It was only when we got into reading the briefing and Tony Bishop the interpreter was talking to us that TB got a proper fix on just how bad some of the stuff in Chechnya had been. But on the big picture, though we knew it was difficult, we were defending the trip as being good for UK–Russia relations.

Saturday, March 11

We were definitely going to be getting flak from the human rights people. Rod Lyne [Ambassador to Russia] warned us we were likely to be bugged wherever we were so it was quite tricky to discuss how we intended to handle it. It meant whatever we said in private would be part of our message to them. TB agreed he would be reasonably tough but balanced. TB found the small talk quite difficult but Putin was clearly bright and very focused. He was clearly physically very fit, sharp-eyed but had a nice smile. He was definitely not going to be a pushover. Rod's basic advice was to be friendly without being overly chummy in case he turned out either to be bad or, in six months' time, in real trouble. He was a very good communicator, but worried about turnout at the elections. He took us on a long tour through the palace and then into a nice if rather dark room for talks. Rod broke his chair in front of the world's media. Once they were out, and we got on to Chechnya, it was clear he was definitely a believer in attack is the best form of defence. TB set out our line in reasonably moderate tone and Putin said at least we were more balanced in our views than France. His basic line was the Islamic conspiracy theory, and also that criminal religious elements were at work and if they weren't dealt with it would cause the break-up of the CIS [Commonwealth of Independent States] TB didn't really push him but the fact that it was the largest part of the conversation by far meant at least we could honestly say it had been the real focus, even if it was Putin who did most of the talking. He said extremism was based on a very narrow trend of Islamic thought but they were up against weapons from Pakistan, Afghanistan, the Taliban, Arabs and Muslims. They were facing criminals who pretended their motivation was religious. It was aggressive extremism posing a real threat to Russia. TB urged him to do more to get out to the West the reality of what was going on down there. But people also needed to know any response was proportionate and that any allegations of human rights violations are addressed. Putin pretty much point-blank denied there were any. He said Russia was prepared to accept some form of independence for Chechnya but they cannot be unlimited in the territory they choose. He was pretty fired up about it and it was a relief when they got on to the domestic front, economic reform, developing a market economy. He said he intended to be tough on crime and tough on the causes of crime. Soundbitesky. There were times when Putin looked thoroughly modern, but then suddenly he would revert and be very much the old KGB man.

We left for the Hermitage, had a nice tour there with some very good pictures and then the second round of talks, which we left to TB and Putin alone and which seemed to go better, according to Tony Bishop. He said he opened up a lot more without all the officials around him. His assessment was that for the first meeting with a Russian leader – and Tony had seen them all right back to Stalin – it was a very good first encounter. We organised some very good pictures on the staircase and drove back to the hotel in the Zil but TB had taken the warning about bugging seriously, and was saying next to nothing other than how much he had liked him. Later, he said Putin had told him he would be happy to see Milosevic go but didn't want that stated publicly. On his own programme, he was determined to be modern and reformist. His view was that their version of socialism had poisoned the mentality of the people and it would not be easy.

Monday, March 13
It was John Sergeant's first day as ITN political editor and his first question was about Dobbo's beard. I said 'Is that the debut story?' to which he replied 'Is that the debut insult?'

Wednesday, March 22
On the flight to the EU summit in Lisbon, TB said it was becoming a problem that I was seen as such a figure in my own right, because it made the straightforward job of briefing harder. They basically saw it as their job now either to trip me up, or to present things as news because I was saying them rather than because they were his views. I had been getting more and more concerned at the latter point. TB said he read the lobby notes and he could see the pitfalls and the traps they were trying to lay. I said I would be very happy to give up the briefings, but they were a means by which I kept on top of pretty much everything. We also discussed whether it might not be sensible for me to find a way of being more directly involved in Millbank, without it becoming just another great big hoo-ha.

Thursday, March 23
I did a couple of briefings through the day and felt that we were winning on all the main economic arguments but we were getting precious little coverage on that. The whole thing was overshadowed by the fact that TB, GB and Robin C all came out on different planes. The *Standard* splashed on it, which got them all thinking they had to do it. We were down to do an interview with Oakley, who said he wanted to do it mainly on TB's paternity leave and now planes. At least he looked embarrassed, but it was ridiculous that this was

their agenda. It was a big problem that we had a political press that wasn't really interested in politics and was obsessed with the trivia. I was more convinced than ever we had to take them on. But TB said it wasn't really possible before an election. At the second briefing, I said I would alternate between serious and trivial questions. George Jones eventually asked about the planes issue and I blasted him out of the water. It was ridiculous that we were sitting there having to explain different departure times etc. TB got bored in the afternoon session, came out to do interviews. He couldn't believe that the three planes story was their main focus. We went for a little wander in the press room and he got a taste of what I dealt with all the time – foreign media asking serious questions about serious things, our lot obsessed with trivia. I sent a letter to Tony Hall saying that the Beeb's coverage today was further evidence of press-driven dumbing down.

Friday, March 31

I was up lateish and then a car came to take us to Chequers. There was first a three-hour discussion where GB made an OK presentation on strategy, followed by the usual mix of different statements that didn't really stack up with the odd insight. Peter M and Milburn were OK. Jack S all detail, Mo all over the shop. TB did a very good summary on the importance of New Labour in getting us here, stressing this was the first Labour Cabinet for a long time with no ideological divide and we had to ensure we didn't lose that. Equally GB was absolutely clear there was no inconsistency between a strategy for the heartlands and a strategy for Middle England. JP said we were not motivating our core people like the other parties were their core people. Philip kicked the thing off with polling that listed as strengths the economy, TB, education, and a will to succeed. Weaknesses were in the areas of lack of delivery and trust/spin. But there was a hollowing-out of our support. TB said we had to keep the focus on reform and keep the coalition that built New Labour together. He said we had to stay absolutely focused on the possibility of a Tory recovery. Nobody thought we would win during the Thatcher era but they had still successfully made us the issue. The Tories may be weak but we still had to generate fear about them. JP did a number on turnout and argued for more politics and better organisation. GB said that what was missing was a big central message and that in its absence other things fell in – spin, Middle England v heartlands, individual policy areas. Between now and an election we had to be clear of the challenges, achievement in meeting them, and then the next steps. We have three enemies, he said. The Tories, the Libs and the smaller parties, and apathy. The Tories' weapon is not fear of Labour, it's cynicism. Read the *Mail* and see their strategy. It is an anti-politics agenda designed to damage us. Once the key players had said their bit, the others tended just to make random points rather than actually discuss what was said with TB trying to bring it all together. He said our opponents want to make New Labour, New Britain a devalued concept. Why? Because it is successful. We have taken political territory we mustn't yield up. He said he didn't just want to win next time but win well again and that meant we kept driving modernisation. We have the right values but we have to be the party of reform. I worked on tomorrow's speech. I sent Peter M a draft of a note for TB. He felt this kind of strategy work was what I needed to do more of. Like TB, and like me, he thought I should pull back from the briefings. But he felt as the note stood, it was too strong to send to TB, and might seriously undermine his confidence. Added to which, it might leak.

Thursday, April 6

TB came round and we talked through the argument re Middle England. He wanted the speech targeted very clearly at the country, not the party, where it would be seen simply as a response to Kilfoyle. He said we just had to accept we were going through a bad phase and we would come through it. But we had to woo the press a bit harder. I had to stop whacking them so hard. He said he understood how it was impossible not to feel contempt for them most of the time but it wasn't sensible to let them all know that's what I thought. I had to try to quell the anger. We had a meeting on local elections in London which was pretty dreadful. At Cabinet, Jack S went through what was being done re asylum. It was beginning to pick up as a political issue and Jack was setting out how many of our current problems were a direct result of how the Tories ran it. The sums of money involved were becoming ridiculous, but of course there was a sense in which the Tories were using this to play the race card. Robin gave a very funny account of Mugabe at the Europe–Africa summit in Cairo. He said Gaddafi spoke for forty-five minutes. Did he mention the Third Way? asked TB. Apparently Gaddafi's very big on the Third Way, he said. No, said Robin, but he did wear painted nails. He said that on day two, Antonio Guterres [Prime Minister of Portugal] rang a bell after five minutes of a speech. He said Mugabe had decided to cool the rhetoric against us for 48 hours but then went back to his usual potty ways and announced last night that Peter Hain was the gay lover of Peter Tatchell [gay rights activist]. 'Hain is taking it calmly,' said Robin. 'Tatchell is furious.'

Sunday, April 9
Asylum was really picking up and the Tories had briefed on the back of the local elections launch that they were going to make asylum the issue. This was going to be really difficult for us.

Tuesday, April 11
Anji was worried that the Cockerell thing was becoming *AC: The Movie*, that they would try to show TB couldn't cope without me.[1] I reminded Cockerell we had agreed this would be a film as much about the press as about us. If it went wrong, I'd be pretty isolated. Fiona was totally against it, so was Anji. So was Pat [McFadden]. Peter M had his doubts too.

Thursday, April 13
I wasn't sleeping well and I had a nagging feeling that Cockerell was a mistake and that I was heading for a fall. I went over to the Northern Ireland Office for a meeting with Peter M, Philip, Stan Greenberg, Bob Shrum [long-term campaign strategist for the US Democrats] and Ed Miliband. Stan took us through the poll and there were real problems beneath the top-line figures. I felt the real weakness was the sense that there was no well of conviction, that we needed to recapture the forces of conservatism concept if not the language. Peter M was totally opposed, said it was then that the big tent had started to fray and we should keep repairing. I said that only happened because we bottled out, we didn't stick to our guns, went back to being all things to all men, which has given us a different kind of definition problem. He said maybe he was still Blair 94/5 whereas we felt the world had moved on, but he was worried we were losing business. He felt a message focused on hard-working families was too class-based. I argued it meant working and middle class, but he felt many middle-class families didn't think it meant them, not because they weren't hard-working but because they thought it related to our traditional support. Bob Shrum was very likeable, red-faced, avuncular, chewing Nicorette very aggressively. He said our weakness was lack

[1] The film-maker Michael Cockerell was given unprecedented access to film AC's relations with the media over a period of four months, for a BBC documentary, *News from Number 10*.

of clarity about who we were for. TB and GB were more or less in the same place, but he felt TB's language was too abstract. I stressed conviction, and then direction and delivery as the key to TB reconnecting. Peter was fine on that but not at the expense of New Labour or new supporters. We must not risk alienating our first-time voters. I argued that they were the very people who wanted to see conviction, direction and delivery. PG was pretty down today, and so was Stan.

Monday, April 17
Putin day. I went up to the flat to see TB, who was worrying re pensioners. The babble industry was going into overdrive re human rights, which was getting more play than when we went out there. TB was clearly getting irritated about Cockerell being around, and I think John S was stirring it a bit, with Jonathan away in Belfast again. There was another example of the presence of the cameras changing the nature of the event. As we waited in the hall for Vlad to arrive, TB would normally want to chat with me just by the door, but I could tell he was sensitive to the possible thesis that he couldn't do anything without being directed. So he wandered off. Putin arrived, good pictures outside, then came in and made somewhat of a beeline for me, which I could see Cockerell lighting up at. I was having second second thoughts. We went upstairs for the first round of talks, which was very much Putin in lecture mode, first on the world economy, then Kosovo and then, briefly, on Chechnya. TB let him do most of the talking and said he would reserve his main points for the tête-à-tête, after which he reported that Putin was a lot more open on National Missile Defence, and less steamed up re Chechnya. TB said it was a very exciting time for Russia and we wanted Russia seen as an equal partner in the international community. Putin went through his economic plan, but when he went through the scale of some of the problems, and the restructuring he envisaged, it was clear he had his work cut out. Banking reform, pensions, housing, poverty and corruption, changing from Communist systems, it was a huge challenge and he made no effort to minimise it. I was surprised at the way Putin made the odd joke at Ivanov's [Foreign Minister] expense, who in turn looked a bit hurt. He had quite hangdog eyes anyway, whereas Vlad's eyes were real killers', piercing blue and able to move from sensitive soul to hard nut with one blink. He was not as aggressive on Chechnya as he was at the press conference later when he really got steamed up. He was now in slight jaw-jutting mode and he was also, a bit like Neil, someone who clenched his

jaw muscles if he didn't like what he was hearing, as when I said they would try to get him going on Chechnya and paint TB as being a bit soft with him on human rights. Vlad totally stole the show with a really strong and passionate defence on Chechnya. I did another interview with Cockerell and TB popped round, feigning surprise that he was there, and we had a not terribly natural chat about things before Cockerell drew him into a kind of interview, first re Putin, then re me, TB saying I was the best in the business but then, bizarrely, saying we never discussed policy. He was trying to downplay the media side of things and I stupidly undercut him as he left when I pointed out he had just wasted his time talking to Michael C. We then had the media reception upstairs, where the atmosphere was fairly relaxed, and they didn't seem overly to mind the cameras. Cockerell was interviewing and some were laying into me a bit.

Monday, May 1

After lunch we had a quick game of football, me, TB and Calum v Rory, Euan and Nicky, nine all. The news was totally dominated by the so called 'anti-capitalist' riots in SW1. Both Churchill's statue and the Cenotaph were defaced. I put out strong words from TB, but was alarmed later watching the softly-softly policing in the street where people were tearing up the lawns and wrecking anything they could find. It was unbelievably depressing.

Tuesday, May 2

I called Jim [Callaghan] who was for him very grumpy, to the point of being deeply pissed off. 'So someone is bothered with me after three years,' he said. He said he would never say anything because he knew how difficult it was to be in a position of leadership, but he didn't like some of the things we were doing, and he didn't like the constant repetition of New Labour as a deliberate foil to Old Labour, as though nothing they had ever done had been good. We chatted for a while, and it ended perfectly amicably, but I did a note to TB saying he really needed to keep relations with some of our big figures from the past in better repair. I think what pissed off Jim more than anything is the sense he would get through the media that TB would be more worried about Thatcher and [Roy] Jenkins. Whitehall was a sight after the riots, boards up, graffiti everywhere. We agreed TB should go out to the Cenotaph and do a clip. My routine was now see or speak to TB first thing, GB meeting, my own government meeting, see TB again, then do what was needed to get everything ready for the 11. I did both briefings today, mainly focused on Ireland, Rover[1] and the riots, all quite difficult. Peter M was working out of my office most of the day because he was not at the Northern Ireland meetings and very pissed off not to be so. He felt Number 10 and Jonathan in particular were not setting meetings up well, and also that TB was too prone to buying the line from Adams. There was a little scene at the end of the day when, in front of officials, TB referred to 'demilitarisation'. Peter M said 'We call it normalisation. Don't use your Sinn Fein methods just because you've been absorbing them all day.' Peter was clearly feeling a bit isolated and undermined.

Thursday, May 4

I woke up to the feeling that we had a bad day ahead, on the Mayor and electoral front and also re Northern Ireland. TB, having worried for so long about Ken, seemed alarmingly indifferent. But we all felt it was going to require a real empathetic response. I really felt the GB meetings were getting better, and GB was beginning to get back some of his old humour. Cabinet did Northern Ireland, Zimbabwe, Rover and then the local elections. JP had a terrific crack when Robin was reporting on Zimbabwe and said Mugabe's slogan was 'Down with British imperialism'. JP said it sounded like a variation of traditional values in the modern setting. Off to Belfast. Adams and McGuinness came privately for a couple of meetings before going off to get the IRA to agree a statement. Things felt a little bit more hopeful. Over dinner, which was pretty relaxed, Bertie said there were three options. They come back with a good statement and we go snap. A bad one, and we go home, or one somewhere in between that means a long negotiation. I felt a little bit unworthy that my principal selfish thought in all of this was how to make sure I managed to get home to collect Calum and get to Scunthorpe on Saturday for what was, after our recent run, Burnley's biggest game in years.

Friday, May 5

Adams and McGuinness came through with their IRA statement, which was fine though slightly watered down, Brian Keenan [IRA representative] having insisted on putting in a line about 'the causes of conflict' next to the line about decommissioning. But it was pretty good. However, it was becoming clear through the day that

[1] Rover would shortly be bought from BMW for £10, by a consortium headed by its former CEO.

Trimble, while reasonably happy on the decommissioning front, was desperate for something new on [Chris] Patten [chairman of the Independent Commission on Policing for Northern Ireland] to avoid problems being generated by David Burnside [UUP]. We had a whole series of arguments about the title of the new police service, with Trimble desperate to get some kind of reference to RUC in the title. The Northern Ireland stuff was really up and down and TB was getting a bit frantic. He was really getting down at the idea that this thing could come crashing down over what we called the police force. As the thing dragged on, eventually I left in an armoured police car that whisked me through to get the 9.40 flight. I felt personal pleasure at leaving and knowing that I would make the match tomorrow, but professional guilt because I could sense both TB and Jonathan felt I should stay. By the time we landed, it was all moving. They had pretty much got the deal. Trimble not too bad about it. Jonathan and Tom Kelly both sounded genuinely excited about it. TB sounded tired but the atmosphere had been transformed. The key was the SF/UUP meeting. It also allowed us to say that Peter M had done a real job in talks, getting the UUs to move. We could be pretty pleased with the last few days' work.

Tuesday, May 9

When I was working on TB's speech in the Garden Room, they were all going on about how hilarious the sketches of me and TB were in the Rory Bremner show [a weekly political satire programme]. Jack Straw was over for a meeting with TB and came to see me to say he was worried that TB's strength was being turned into arrogance, and also that I was being turned into a problem for him and had to retreat. In a way, he said, I was too good at my job, and too interesting, and it inevitably drew attention to me because they saw me all the time. He felt the Bremner programme was genuinely damaging to TB. It had taken them years to satirise Thatcher successfully, but this really captured something about Tony and it would weaken him. Also, he was worried that though TB was clearly the main focus of the government, there was little sense of him being the main focus for the party and we had to change that. I think he had been genuinely well-intentioned in saying what he was saying and I agreed with the basic thesis.

Saturday, May 13

Andrew Marr was replacing Oakley as BBC political editor. I called Marr, who was clearly very pleased. On balance, it was probably good

May '00: Straw worried TB's strength was turning to arrogance

news though it was slightly alarming the extent to which he talked about himself, rather than politics or the politicians. He said he wanted to give a leadership voice to the BBC. I said it would be inevitable that our opponents would try to present him as a Blair stooge and I was worried that might lead to overcompensation. We could also say in all honesty we knew nothing about it until today.

Sunday, May 14

Oakley called me, to say he was really angry that he was being described as a Tory in some of the papers and he wanted me to know how angry he was. His anger went way beyond that though. He said he had simply been summoned to a hotel at 10pm on Thursday and told he was going before his time. He sounded devastated, said he was devastated and felt betrayed and very bitter. I said I had always found him fair and reasonable and I was sorry he had been treated so badly. I asked him if he wanted me to generate people to say he was someone of independence and integrity, which he did.

Thursday, May 18

Phil Bassett did a very good analysis of the commentators which showed very clearly that most now saw it as their job to do in the government. I then left for the ad agency and was there from 2 till 8, going through the process, kicking around ideas. GB came down from 3 till 6 and we split into little groups to put together fifty-word mission statements. I was with Ed Miliband and we concluded on something like 'We exist to put power, wealth and opportunity in the hands of the many not the few so that lower- and middle-income families enjoy rising living standards and public services they can trust. And by confronting the forces that hold people back we liberate talent to build a fairer, more prosperous Britain.' It was quite a good exercise and what emerged was that people felt we were better at defining what we weren't than what we were, and had to work on that. GB was back on his goals. Peter H was arguing we needed more enemies. But it was a good session and I wished we had more time to do this kind of thing. GB and I were engaging well but he clearly felt that we played up new v old Labour too much and nobody really knew what the old v new Britain divide was. I wish we had been able to stick with forces of conservatism. We needed to be breaking more eggs for better omelettes. I also felt TB's fall in ratings was in part a consequence of a sense that all things to all men meant no conviction.

Friday, May 19

Fiona and Cherie were pretty sure the baby was going to be born fairly soon. TB stayed in the office till about 8 and Anji said later he had been really nervous, nervous about the politics of where we were, nervous about the baby and what it would do for him, Cherie and the way we work. TB called as he was going to the hospital. I called Anji to get Cockerell down there to film the media outside. Fiona kept me in touch through the night. It finally came at 12.25 and we decided not to put anything out until they got home. I was in bed when Fiona texted that it was a boy. I called through, spoke to TB, who sounded very happy about it. I heard the baby and TB said 'Here you are, Leo, talk to your spin doctor.'

Saturday, May 20

Fiona got back about 4 and was still out to swim at 7. The media was going into meltdown on it, leading every bulletin, every spit and fart. TB sounded elated and was pleased that he had been able to get home. But he was still talking about our political problems. He genuinely felt that our problems were as much of perception as of reality. I agreed with him that he would have to go out and say something in the street. Jonathan and his little daughter Jessica were all over the news coverage as the only people in the office to go through the front door. I thought it best to stay away, rather than have the whole thing seen as a spin operation. Fiona went in with Grace and said that before TB went out he was incredibly nervous but did fine, though they would no doubt have a field day with his mug, which was a picture of the kids. He still underestimated how much they gorged on this kind of stuff. TB and I must have spoken four or five times during the day but usually about the political scene, which he was really running around his mind the whole time. He said we had to stay bang in the centre ground. 'I know I am right. I am where the country is.'

Sunday, May 21

TB was boasting about how he had been changing nappies. Nicky and Euan both got followed by cameramen so we had to work out how to handle that. And we had a little drama at the start of the day because Cherie had put a picture of the baby on the Number 10 intranet which Fiona got taken off pretty sharpish. We weren't going to be putting pictures out until tomorrow. As the *Observer* said, I was in a bit of a no-win situation: do too little and we alienate the press, too much and they would say we were exploiting it. Mary McCartney [photographer] was going in to do the pictures today and we were going to put them out tomorrow. We agreed with CB that she would put out a few words in a statement. Fiona went in when Mary was doing the pictures and said it was very normal (!) family life.

Monday, May 22

I got in and went up to see TB. The baby was upstairs asleep. There was a lot of focus on what sort of paternity leave he might have and we agreed that he wouldn't be doing PMQs and Cabinet, but he would do the Queen. I put together a script on the photos, and Robbie Montgomery (Mary McCartney's agent) came in with an assistant and assured me they were able to cope with the demand. We quickly chose the one free photo we would send all round and then picked 14 others that could be used at £500 a time for two cancer charities, which was Fiona's idea. TB had decided that we were doing the right things and in the right place but we were not communicating properly. I felt that that was arrogant and wrong. He didn't buy the idea that we should emphasise we were for middle- and lower- income families, or working families, because these were exclusive messages. People basically think it means working class and we had to be careful. He felt all our problems came from where we were not New Labour – on crime not being tough enough, on asylum sending out the wrong signals, pushing on the anti-poverty agenda without regard to the impact on taxation with the result that we got little political credit for doing the right thing. At least we were having proper strategic discussion again. He also wanted me to have one-on-one meetings with all the key ministers and get them all properly fitted into a strategy. The 11 o'clock was mainly about the baby. Jonathan and I went up to see TB a couple of times and he was just sitting there holding the baby, all gooey-eyed.

Thursday, May 25

GB said he might say something about the girl rejected by Oxford[1] who went to Harvard when he spoke at the TUC equality conference. It was a bit of a risk not knowing all the detail, but he was very up for it. I stayed behind to talk with him about TB's note of last night which said that our problems were Middle England issues. GB said he feared that TB wanted to get us into a different position and that we would cede too much ground. TB's argument was that we ceded

[1] Laura Spence, a pupil from a state school in North Tyneside, was rejected by Magdalen College despite her predicted five A-level 'A' grades.

the ground in the centre if we shifted to the left. GB believed we had an alliance which meant we could focus on jobs and the social justice agenda while maintaining support for it in the centre ground. He felt that the way TB was crafting the argument for his speech to the Women's Institute risked it becoming the equivalent of Back to Basics [a moralising policy disaster for John Major].

Thursday, June 1

The Laura Spence issue had rumbled on and on and the internal opposition on the elitism row was pretty strong. Peter M, Anji and Charlie F were all winding TB up to varying degrees, but I was still very much with GB on it. Philip felt that TB was sometimes put off by the sheer weight of propaganda against us, and the power of basically conservative assumptions. TB said something interesting later though, when I was going on again about the need to isolate the *Mail* and go for them. 'I do understand that Dacre and his lot positively hate me. They think this is a conservative country full stop. And they know that we are changing it.' GB, probably for the first time, had had his eyes opened about just how conservative the press can be. He was facing criticism of an intensity that we had to deal with pretty much all the time. This was actually a rerun, with a bit of the same backlash, of the forces of conservatism argument which I was convinced we could win, and had to win.

Friday, June 2

TB was working on his speech to the Women's Institute next week, which I felt at the moment was too conservative. He wanted to balance new and old, put the responsibility agenda up alongside opportunity. His worry was that in what was basically a conservative country, we were being portrayed as anti-family, anti-tax cuts, anti-strong defence, all rights and no responsibilities.

Saturday, June 3

TB and I must have spoken a dozen times over the weekend about the WI speech. Independently, Peter Hyman, Philip and I reached the same conclusion, that this was not really him, that it was over-pandering to what he thought a certain constituency wanted to hear. He was adamant that he had to marry the old and the new and the key to that was opportunity and responsibility as the twin pillars of community. It was perfectly fine as an idea but the first draft was very defensive, almost apologetic about New Labour and about wanting to change Britain. Both Philip and I sent through notes which were pretty harsh. Mine said that the speech lacked focus and leadership, it didn't properly explain or defend modernisation and so risked being Majoresque nostalgia. Peter H, Philip and Sally [Morgan] all said as it stood it was far too right wing and would not go down well.

Sunday, June 4

TB called a few times and was still saying he didn't want to change the basic message in the speech, bringing the old and the new together. With the exception of Peter M and Anji, everyone thought it was ghastly. Peter H was so violently against it, I thought he was going to have a seizure. Philip thought it was dreadful. Part of the problem of course was that we were giving TB conflicting advice. I thought it would be sensible to get others outside the usual inner circle to read it. I got Godric, Hilary and Mark Bennett to have a read and none of them liked it at all. Mark said it was 'all wool, no thread'.

Monday, June 5

We had several meetings on the WI speech. Peter M and Anji argued that it really was TB's voice and would do the trick of connecting him back in the way we wanted. I felt it was too whimsical and there was a real danger it would be seen as whimsy and nostalgia and was open to parody. But TB felt strongly all our problems were Middle England problems and also that we had a problem with older people because they felt excluded from the 'new' the whole time. I don't recall a speech taking up as much time as any outside of party conference, and I don't recall a speech provoking as much division. I, Philip, Peter H and Bruce were totally against it. So, perhaps more unusually, was Jonathan, who told TB that it made him cringe. Anji and Peter M were arguing strongly in favour.

Tuesday, June 6

A potentially seminal two days. Ever since Saturday we had been doing virtually nothing but work on TB's speech for the WI tomorrow. We had a fundamental disagreement that was simply not resolving itself. TB was convinced we had to set out the old/new balance. The rest of us kept reading the changing drafts, where he wasn't taking any of the stuff we did to recalibrate the message. Paul Johnson [right-wing author and commentator] of all people was sending over his advice and it was drivel, including a paragraph, which at one point TB included, about the new being a glittering sword and the old a sturdy shield. We went round and round in circles all day and I was there till gone ten trying to get it sorted. We weren't helped by the fact that TB was getting diametrically opposed advice. He was definitely, post Laura Spence, of a mood to tack to the right. I felt if we lost our nerve on opportunity for all, we would get hit.

Wednesday, June 7

TB was upstairs in a dressing gown, writing away. He said he was sure it was the right argument. Amid it all, we did not heed a call from Lucie McNeil, who was advancing the visit, who said it must not be too political. We didn't think our way through that. The thing had now been built up over days into an enormous political event. We had been so worried about getting the message right that we had overlooked the fact they probably didn't want anything overtly political at all. Monica [Jelley] from the Garden Room said she had never done so much typing on a speech in all the time she had been there. TB set off with Tessa. I had decided not to go because I had a series of meetings, including one with JP. He turned up after TB's speech had started and which I was watching on Sky, having postponed the lobby. It seemed to start OK, and I turned the sound down a bit as JP and I talked over things. Over JP's shoulder, I could see there was a bit of reaction around the place and then the clear sound of slow hand-clapping and heckling. It was pretty obvious the speech was a goner. I turned up the sound and both of us watched as TB did what JP called his Bambi look, really startled but with the smile still there as he ploughed on and eventually scythed through the speech. This had the potential to be a disaster area. I paged Anji, who called back and said it was a very odd atmosphere. It was clearly the wrong speech for the wrong audience and we had a PR disaster on our hands in media terms. I said to JP it's a good job we've got lines in there about being more relaxed and chilled out. But it was clear to TB that he was no longer loved or even understood. The TV news people were loving it of course. He called me as soon as he got in the car and said it had been really bad. It wasn't just the slow hand-clapping. Every element had been wrong. Their main complaint was that it was a political speech, to which I said what did they think politicians were for? Of course there was no way we would win a war of words with the Women's Institute. I went round to see TB later and he was just sitting in his chair, with his chin in his hand, looking hurt and worried. He was really angry that we had spent so much time on a speech that was now defined as a disaster area. He asked if I really thought that people of this country were so stupid that they could kick us out and go back to the Tories. Is it such a conser-

The Downing Street baby: with his father. 'Nobody can ~~accuse~~ you of not making news,' Campbell said when told Cherie was pregnant

...nd Campbell spent hundreds of hours together travelling and talking in the backs of cars

Gordon Brown and wife Sarah at Donald Dewar's funeral, October 2000. The immensely popular Scottish First Minister had been a key figure in the devolution process

All change at the White House: in December 2000, the US media heralded the end of an extraordinary Presidential election process, and a decision that would have a major impact on UK politics too

Peter Mandelson in Downing Street, announcing his second resignation from Cabinet, this time as Northern Ireland secretary

Campbell's son Rory took this re of his father ter Mandelson going through he newspapers ing them to be in the wake of delson's second resignation

ction campaign unch day 2001: tack by an egg- owing protestor Rhyl on John Prescott, and his sponse, ensured our's manifesto unch was barely d by the media

'Wiggy.' A poster from Trevor Beattie's TBWA ad agency, which had Hague with Thatcher's hair, and successfully used humour to make a point

Campbell in grim mood as Blair postponed the election to focus on foot and mouth: this was the picture the press used of him more than any other

March 2001: foot and mouth was one of the toughest crises Blair had to deal with

The Blairs head back to Downing Street after Labour's second election win, 2001

September 11, within hours of the attacks on the
twin towers. Blair, alongside TUC general secretary
John Monks, prepares to cut short his speech and
return to London

Osama bin Laden

First Lady Laura Bush, flanked
by Blair and New York mayor
Rudy Giuliani, listen to
President Bush address a joint
session of Congress after 9/11

Blair in Gaza City with Yasser
Arafat, November 1, 2001…

….and with Israeli Prime
Minister Ariel Sharon in
Jerusalem the same day:
neither of them were ever
easy to deal with

Putin's visit to
Downing Street, June 20[

A cartoonist's take on Blair
being feted abroad whilst attacked
at home, which hangs on
Campbell's wall – even though
Martin Rowson cannot spell
Middlesbrough

SO THIS IS KABUL, GREETING ME AS ITS LIBERATOR! WHAT A BLIGHTED SCENE! LANDSCAPE STREWN WITH RUBBLE! PUBLIC SERVICES IN A STATE OF COLLAPSE AND INFRASTRUCTURE TOTALLY NEGLECTED!

ER.. ACTUALLY BOSS, THI[
IS MIDDLESBOROUGH.

Whatever problems Blair had
as a leader, Hamid Karzai's felt
greater as he sought to build
post-Taliban Afghanistan

Blair and Bush. The relationship
may have damaged Blair politically
but he always defended it as being
in Britain's interest

Kevin Spacey introduces Bill Clinton and Blair at a Labour party conference reception,
pool 2002. Later Clinton, Spacey, Campbell and Fiona had a night out – at McDonald's

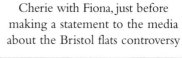

reapons inspector Hans Blix flew to London
n Iraq to brief Blair in November 2002

Cherie with Fiona, just before
making a statement to the media
about the Bristol flats controversy

Prime Ministers present, pas
and future. Blair, Thatcher a
Brown pay their respects at
Cenotaph, November 2002

Saddam Hussein

vative country that they will do anything to get us out? He was very down. I said it wasn't that bad, and that our real bonus was that people didn't like the Tories and wanted to keep them out, we really needed to come out now and show some fight. Hattersley was about saying it was the PR department's fault and we had to understand Tony could not please everyone all of the time. He felt TB would get more support if he made more enemies and people believed what he was doing.

Friday, June 9

TB said I was too angry at the moment, and being nasty to him. He said if we could get better people fine, but where are they? I also said there were too many people around who told him what he wanted to hear and he said 'For God's sake, who? Nobody does – you, Gordon, Peter, Jonathan, nobody does. That is ridiculous.' He said we simply had to hold our nerve and have balls of steel. I said fine but we should not pretend that because we defend ourselves the whole time, there are not things that we defend that don't actually need changing. He said on the big tent approach, he was insisting he was right and we had to back his judgement on that. There came a point when we couldn't keep having the same arguments, and in the end he had to make the final calls. TB asked me to go and see him and asked whether it was getting to me that there was so much shit about me personally in the press. I said I didn't think so, and actually you could argue that it could be worse. The things that annoyed me were having to deal with a media I didn't much like or respect, and from time to time the politicians expected too much of me, and sometimes that included him. I always felt I could justify to myself and the family working flat out if it was in a way and on an agenda that I supported. But when there was drift and disagreement, and I felt too much of the pressure fall on me to sort it, I did get angry. He said that in most organisations, lots of people would do things, but very few people could assume real leadership, and I was one of the people who knew how to step up to the mark. He agreed there were problems and said it was possible we were in trouble. His own feeling was that we could lose narrowly, though it was doubtful, or we could win again with a big majority, which he felt was more likely, but it did mean the key people sticking together. He also said if the biggest criticism they could mount was that he tried to be all things to all men, he could live with that. Cockerell was in for the Sunday briefing and I really went into the whole real world v medialand agenda, how much of what they wrote was actually spin, and they complained they were just extras in a film I wanted making. What was clear was that they were lining up for more 'Blair's worst week yet' bollocks. There was a very funny moment when I said 'I've seen some guff in my time' and was interrupted 'You haven't seen the background pieces we've done yet.' They were all men, and I wondered how many groups and organisations today were still all male.

Monday, June 12

TB had sent a note through on Saturday saying that he has absolutely decided on the big tent approach and he wanted it implemented, no questions asked. Peter M said, in a very Peterish way, 'It's very good that you have finally decided to agree with yourself.'

Wednesday, June 14

There was lots in the papers about me not briefing. Oborne was on *GMTV* saying Godric was boring and it was like replacing Botham with Tavare.[1] God, I hate these people. First they say we spin them too much and then when we take it away they say they need more spin. At the 4 o'clock, as Martin Sheehan [press officer] said, they were like a jilted lover. It was packed out, far more people than usual, very hot and sweaty. I was perfectly calm but made clear this wasn't for discussion, I had decided to pull back and do very few briefings myself. They were straight away on to the idea of it not being good for them but I gave no ground whatever. Godric and David Bradshaw [special adviser] had both warned they were not going to be very nice about this but I really didn't care what they thought. First they complained about being spun, now they complained about being snubbed. It was pathetic. I was followed down the road by ITN and said the fact they did me rather than the job figures as their lunchtime political story said more about the media than it did about us. I then literally, by an extraordinary coincidence, bumped into Gus O'Donnell, and swapped notes about the time he did my job for Major.

Monday, June 26

After another crap weekend ruined by work, I was in no mood for TB. GB cancelled his meeting again but asked me to go over for a one-on-one. He said we had to get a grip on Europe. He said because we hadn't slapped down Peter when he started this off, he was now taking advantage. He believed TB was limbering up for a change, possibly tied to

[1] Ex-England cricketers. Ian Botham had a reputation as a swashbuckling match winner; Chris Tavare as an obdurate blocker.

the inward investment figures, and it would be a dreadful mistake. Unless we got back to the kind of discipline we had in opposition, we were in trouble. It was becoming accepted we were divided. The press are going for us because we lack a big message and sense of direction. They sense weakness and when they sense weakness, they are merciless. He put the blame firmly at Peter's door and then at Tony's for allowing it, and then those who followed because they felt they should. He said 'I could go out tomorrow and say the Treasury won't foot the bill for the Patten reforms or that I want to rename the RUC – what would he say to that?' I said what are you saying, that all those Peter, Robin, Steve Byers, should be sacked? He said there had to be discipline and nobody should say anything unless it went through Number 10 and the Treasury. We then went over general message and he said again he thought the one nation message didn't work. He felt many not the few gave us more edge and took us to our issues – education, crime, health, poverty. I said we needed to get back to his daily meetings for the politics, and mine to drive decisions through the machine. He said he would, but wanted me to know how fed up he was with recent events. Everyone seemed fed up at the moment.

Tuesday, June 27

I woke up to Zimbabwe and more intimidation of the Opposition, followed by a story that Mo was calling for the Queen to move out of Buckingham Palace. Lucie called to ask if I thought Mo should go on. I said no. She went on anyway but with TB as the ardent monarchist, anything we said would take us to 'slap down' territory and so it duly proved. The full transcript was even worse. It was now becoming a given that we saw her standing ovation at conference as a problem, and also a given that there was a Number 10 briefing operation against her. Both were nonsense. We had pretty much organised the reaction during the speech, with Peter M deliberately sitting with her, and I was now pretty convinced the so-called briefing operation consisted of her and her friends just going around saying it. It just wasn't serious. Philip called, said he had just done his worst focus groups ever. They felt TB was weak and for the first time were saying they felt Hague could be PM. He said all the warnings we had been given were coming through – drift, division, lack of conviction. For One Nation, they just read all things to all men.

Thursday, June 29

We left for the trip to Germany, and on the way to the airport, he said he was thinking of splitting the Home Office to have a separate department dealing with crime, he would put Blunkett in charge, put Jack S to education, which we would rename Education and Sport. He was also thinking that we should have a department focused on work rather than unemployment, and a separate department dealing with the non-working age side of DSS – kids' benefits, pensioners, veterans, etc. The non-crime Home Office stuff would go to a beefed-up Lord Chancellor's department. Gaming to DCMS [Department of Culture, Media and Sport]. He was thinking maybe Byers for NIO, maybe Darling to DTI, maybe Mo to a new Pensions department. He was also thinking of coming out firmly for the euro, while on fox hunting saying it was not a priority and he was not prepared to let it get in the way of legislation on things that were. All pretty bold and he wanted to do it just before the CSR to get back to a position of strength. He felt we would go down further before we came up again. On the plane, we worked on the speech and I was trying to get the religion out and more politics in. We were working up on-the-spot fines as the top policy line. He had recovered some of his confidence, and I some of my confidence in him, by the fact he had at least come up with a few bold plans. We met Schroeder on the bridge where they used to exchange spies, which made for good pictures. They did their doorstep. As he walked over, Schroeder, who always liked to have a laugh and a joke with me, asked if I was always there when the spies were swapped.

Sunday, July 2

Mo called, bright as a bee, and said 'Hi, Ali, just to say if you want me to go up and say whoever's doing all this to me, it's not Tony, I will,' and I really lost it. I said the best thing she could do is what she should have done months ago and tell the truth, namely that it's total balls that anyone was doing her in from Number 10. She could say that she was too busy dealing with serious issues like drugs and social exclusion to worry about gossip, but no, we had to deal with this fucking rubbish every weekend because people were too self-indulgent. I spoke to TB, who also said to her she had to make it clear that the stuff about her being briefed against was rubbish. He was pretty forceful and she sounded close to tears. She later called Anji and said I had blamed her for the whole thing, which indeed I did. I knew TB hadn't said anything untoward about her, I knew I hadn't. Most of the journalists Jonathan spoke to complained he never said anything to them. I was convinced she and her pals were the ones putting it about.

Tuesday, July 4

TB called me in and asked if I was alright. He said there was so much anger in me at the moment and it's not sensible. He said there weren't many people he was dependent on but I was one of them and angry advice was not always the right advice. He relied on me for the right advice. He said my problem was that most Cabinet ministers, certainly the important ones, trusted and respected my judgement. He said in the end he had to take most of the strain because he was the top man. But when it came to taking the strain and the pressure, I was second in line and he knew that I was taking more than most people were capable of. But somehow I had to get more time off and I had to delegate more, and I had to try to rebuild some of the relationships with the media.

Thursday, July 6

At 2am, Godric called to say Euan had been picked up by the cops, drunk and incapable, and the *Sun* and *The Times* had been tipped off. I told him to emphasise he was still sixteen and try to get them to hold off. I got in, went up to the flat and saw TB. He said he hadn't slept at all, he was cross with Euan, and had been up all night dealing with it. The cops said he had been found alone, lying on the ground being sick. Cherie was in Portugal with the baby, so I spoke to her on the kind of line we were using, fairly light. She sounded very calm about it. Jack S came in and briefed Tony more fully, having been briefed by the Deputy Commissioner. The guy from the Met came through for a meeting with me and Jack and we put together a more detailed statement. Cabinet itself was mainly the legislation to deal with hooligans. JP had a bit of a go at Jack for not being tough enough. There was actually going to be a lot of sympathy both for TB and Euan. Fiona came down to see me after the briefing and said that Euan had seen the news and was distraught. I said it would be grim for a few days but then fine. I felt sorry for him because the press would now see him as a fair target on the socialising front. I called [Lord] Wakeham [chairman of the Press Complaints Commission] and agreed he would put out a friendly line, as we had accepted it was fair to report this.

On the train down to Brighton, we heard that Germany had won the World Cup bid. TB asked if things could get any worse. But the black churches conference cheered him up. There was real sympathy about Euan. They loved the speech. They loved the line about Britain one day having a black prime minister. There couldn't have been a better audience on a day like this. He spoke to Cherie in the car. TB said he wanted to stop for a pint, very rare, off the beaten track. The cops found a very nice little pub and the locals were gobsmacked, including a barman who was only working there for that day. It was interesting how people reacted. There was a couple in the corner clearly having an illicit meeting who scarpered the minute we arrived. Some of them just wanted to be left alone and ignore us. Lots of them wanted their photos taken, one or two wanted a serious chat. Cherie was really steamed up about how the press had got to hear about Euan before either she or Tony did, and going on about needing an inquiry. We were going to have to work out how to get Euan to go to the cops for his caution. By the time we got back to Number 10, and up to see Cherie and Euan, I was so knackered I was even nice to Carole [Caplin], who was looking tanned and pretty fit after their little break in Portugal.

Thursday, July 13
The press went in droves to a screening of the Cockerell film, which I watched in the office. It seemed fine, worthy, neither great nor disastrous. The only moment I cringed was when I seemed to be taking the piss out of TB. There was a real sense of access but some, e.g. Peter H, felt it made TB look weak and me look strong. Jamie Rubin [until May 2000, chief spokesman for the US State Department] did me proud on *Westminster Live*. It certainly wasn't a hatchet job, though the press were bound to go for the bits they wanted. TB seemed fine about Cockerell. He didn't watch it but had relied on Jonathan, Anji and Sally M for their views. Fiona felt it did me no harm but it still hadn't been worth the hassle.

Friday, July 14
TB's worry, that the Cockerell film stood up the Rory Bremner analysis, was slightly borne out by the press. The *Mirror* leader said I could take over, several said TB looked weak, but at least it wasn't meltdown and most people thought we came out better than the press. Peter M felt we had to sue for peace now. TB ditto. Jonathan felt we should go all out for on-the-record televised briefings. TB felt I had to go on a major schmooze. He did admit his dinner with the *Mail* lot had been ghastly and they were just basically right-wing shits.

Tuesday, July 18
GB did an excellent presentation to the CSR Cabinet and was well received. The figures on debt as a share of national income were impressive, 37% to 36 to 33. The costs of unemployment were down

£3.5 billion. Good growth delivered up an extra £6bn. 80% of the new money was for public services. He went through it all then department by department, and most of them ought to be able to do something pretty meaningful with what they were getting. He was on the right track on the big picture and he had some good individual moves to do with children. Bruce said the PLP feedback on Cockerell was totally positive, that they basically felt reassured there was someone in here who was really Labour.

Wednesday, July 19

Tokyo. We left for the G8 at a palace up the road from the hotel. Clinton was late because of MEPP [Middle East Peace Process] talks, Schroeder didn't bother, Chirac came last and in the end TB was in hysterics, said it was possibly the most pointless meeting he had ever attended, enlivened only by Chirac's extraordinary rudeness to Larry Summers [US Secretary of the Treasury]. He said Chirac went on for twenty minutes then when Summers started, Chirac leaned back in his chair, threw his head back, snored loudly, came to a couple of minutes later with what TB called a loud snort and then shouted 'Too long, too long' in English as Summers went on and on. TB said it was as impressive an exhibition of rudeness and anti-Americanism as he had ever seen.

Saturday, July 22

TB said over breakfast that in eight presidential suites in eight five-star hotels there are eight leaders asking eight sherpas and eight press secretaries 'What the hell are we all doing here?' We were staying in a beautiful part of the world, in spectacular and luxurious surroundings. But it was all a bit unreal. There didn't seem to be any 'real people' around the place, other than those brought in for a swim. The agenda was fairly big stuff, but it was doubtful much of it actually needed the leaders to resolve. TB was wearing one of the silly shirts they were all being made to wear. He said he was bored and we needed to get some muscle back into the deliberations.

Monday, July 24

We had an office meeting to plan August and September but it was pretty meandering. Eventually I snapped and said none of this will happen unless you get a grip of GB and Peter M, and unless we properly empower Millbank. I felt myself close to losing it and I could see that some of the others were shocked, but I really had had enough. The meeting ended OK but then after a few minutes TB called me back, and was a bit steelier than usual. He said you cannot talk to me like that. It's wrong and it unsettles all the others. He said this is not about vanity or amour propre because I am the least status-conscious politician I know, but that was bad. And the reason we have things like Rory Bremner is because that kind of thing gets out. I kind of apologised and said I felt completely stymied by the lack of follow-through from ministers and the lack of basic discipline and professionalism, and the extent to which he expected me and one or two others to pick up all the pieces. But I accepted I was too easily slipping into a mode of being critical of him. He said it was OK for me to go at him in front of Sally, Anji and Jonathan but that was it. I got round to my desk and a call from Fiona to say the kids were fighting and could I go home.

Thursday, July 27

TB was a bit hurt I think that we didn't want to go to the christening, but I explained that my children would be entitled to feel we gave too much by way of time to TB and CB already, and going away on Calum's birthday to do something with their kids might make them think that even more, added to which we didn't do the God thing. I was just tired and knew we all needed a break from each other.

August holiday

We had a house in Puyméras, a little village on the other side of Ventoux. We had an OK time, though there were too many party people around in one go – Neil and Glenys at the bottom of the road, the Goulds in the village, Jonathan and family about a mile away, and the Kennedys [Professor Ian (academic lawyer) and Andrea Kennedy]. Some days, I was chronically depressed. Philip's view was that I had moved from characteristic glumness to anger. We were all pretty much agreed by the end of the holiday that I felt I had to give my all and was asked to do too much and pick up too much of the slack. Neil could tell I wasn't terribly happy and after ten days or so we sat down at the bar in the village and talked it over. He asked what was wrong and I said I felt I had to work round the clock to hold the show together. I asked if he thought there were any circum-stances in which I could quit. He said no, because he worried it would fall apart. I said that was the pressure I felt. His view was that TB had to reassert a grip but it maybe meant understanding that GB and Peter M could not work together, and one of them had to go. He was pretty down on both of them but felt on balance Peter should go, or at least be told to concentrate on Ireland and nothing else. Neil recalled John Smith's death, when his line to them had been that they had to decide it among themselves. He was always clear it should be TB but that was an agreement the two of them had to reach. Six years on, it was extraordinary that the feelings aroused by that period were still felt to be so relevant. It was a nice chat but the bottom line was that he felt I just had to keep going. He also felt there wasn't that much I could do to change the way the press operated. I was conscious of my bad moods getting everybody down, though Philip and I had the usual good laughs. But he felt I had changed, become more introverted, less outgoing, angrier. He said he felt I was disappointed with TB. The kids seemed to have a good time, but I was beginning to worry whether I needed some sort of help on the depression front. I felt almost as tired when we got back as when we left, and it had been a strain on Fiona too. Her basic take was that all our problems stemmed from me going to work for TB against her advice, because in the end I always did what I wanted regardless of the consequences. She felt she had had to toughen herself to avoid being hurt by it. Philip's view was that even Fiona didn't fully understand the cumulative effect of months and months of sustained pounding against me, but part of her felt I had brought it all on myself. We agreed it would probably be best if I quit after the election and then looked to do something maybe in sport. I also went on a few runs with Rory, who was having a go at me for lounging around by the pool, getting fat and lazy. I got into it fairly quickly and by the end of the holiday was thinking about doing a marathon.

Tuesday, August 29
TB called me up to the flat when he got back. He wanted to say at some point why it had been right to keep the best of Thatcherism. Both Peter M and I said that one jarred a bit. I said I couldn't work out why he had to define himself against Thatcher rather than as his own man. He said we had to make people feel that just because they had voted Tory during the eighties, it didn't make them bad people. He was clearly rested, certain this new drive for the centre ground was what we needed. He was emphasising crime and the importance of respect. He was also a bit more abrupt with everyone, which was no bad thing.

Wednesday, August 30
TB said it was important I understood why parts of Thatcherism were right. Later in the day he came up with another belter when Peter H, trying to get him to be more progressive and radical, asked what gave him real edge as a politician and TB said 'What gives me real edge is that I'm not as Labour as you lot.' I pointed out that was a rather

discomfiting observation. He said it was true. He felt he was in the same position he had always been and we were the people who had changed to adapt. Re me, he said I had to learn to be less het up and emotional about this because in the end it was my political judgement he wanted me for. In another conversation later, he said the problem with schools was uniformity of teaching. I said the problem was the background of poorer kids and he just rolled his eyes at me.

Friday, September 8

New York. We had a meeting of the P5[1] at the Waldorf Astoria. Clinton was trying to tease out the idea of a specific proposal, which in the end was just that the five of them would appoint an official to work with Kofi on the implementation of the Brahimi report.[2] When we got to the P5, Sandy Berger sent me a note: 'For seven and a half years I have been trying to get Clinton to do what Blair just did at the UNSC. Fuck you!' I looked over and he was smiling and doing a thumbs up. Jiang Zemin talked about it being historic and that the P5 should try where possible to support the UN together. Even Chirac was quite supportive of what TB had been saying about conflict in Africa. Chirac said if there were no diamonds in Sierra Leone, there would be no war. He said it was only if we worked together that we would be able to deal with issues like drugs and money-laundering. But he was also very tough about the benefits we gave to countries that had no democratic rules. He said he had been saying this for years 'but it will not prevent me from repeating myself again.' Clinton had a particular problem because of the hostility of a lot of American politicians to the UN. He felt people were with him more than the politicians, but we had constantly to explain if we could prevent conflict and reduce conflict overseas, there was a relevance to our people at home. He cited what we had done in Sierra Leone, but also thought re e.g. Ethiopia and Eritrea that if we could resolve that conflict for good, and the two leaders be seen as models for the future, it would have a big impact elsewhere. The discussion went wider and wider, TB's next intervention being on the rise of extremism and its links to terrorism. Jiang Zemin said he felt it was possible we were entering a phase of peace, prosperity and stability and that if the five countries in the room stayed together, that was more likely. Putin said it was better to talk among five than fifteen. He said all our countries

[1] UN Security Council permanent five: US, UK, China, Russia, France.
[2] Report of the Panel on United Nations Peace Operations (chaired by Lakhdar Brahimi).

have a certain capacity so if we set our minds to do something, we can do it, we can make things happen. But it must not turn into a new bureaucracy. He said the world has more than enough big public organisations. Bill chaired it very well as ever. He loved meetings like this, wanted it to go on for ever. God knows how he was going to cope when he had to leave the job.

David M got back from Washington and said he sensed really big tensions between the Clinton people and the Gore people. He sensed the Hillary campaign wasn't going too well and that she might have to rely on him pulling in a landslide. We had a brief bilateral with Clinton but then Leo arrived and that was that. He was wearing a very cute Stars and Stripes jumper and Bill loved it so much he took him down to see Chirac, who was cooing over him as well with the usual Chirac guff, saying to TB and CB he was the most beautiful baby he had ever seen. There was a very odd incident at the airport when we learned that Andy Marr had told the airline staff that he would be sitting next to TB on the plane to do an interview with him. British Airways put the Secret Service onto it because they thought he was behaving oddly.

Saturday, September 9

TB was much more worried about petrol. GB was in Paris for the OPEC meeting trying to get the OPEC countries to increase production to get prices down. There was a lot of talk of more blockades coming to Britain with hauliers threatening to blockade oil refineries in protest at fuel prices.

Monday, September 11

In for a GB meeting. He was just skirting around the petrol blockades, which were clearly going to be trouble. I left to meet up with TB and head off to the station. Both of us were a bit worried to be leaving London. He said he regretted not having gripped this earlier. There followed a day of us, and particularly him, applying endless pressure on Straw, Jonathan and Byers, trying to get it gripped. We seemed unable to get the police to focus in the way they needed to. The oil companies were pusillanimous. Every time we spoke to Jack, he gave us all the problems, which we knew well enough, but little sense of solutions. TB said at one point that if this was Thatcher and the miners, the police would waste no time wading in. We were just pussyfooting with small groups of people threatening to bring the whole of the country to ransom. He felt the whole thing was political. We had another long round of calls but he wasn't happy about the way it was handled. Jack had gone to bed at 11, saying he wasn't to be disturbed. We were due in Hull for a dinner for JP to celebrate his thirty years as an MP and we arrived to the usual chaos. But JP's instincts were usually pretty sound and he was exactly where we were in terms of where the fuel situation was heading. We got to City Hall, where about 250 anti-hunt protesters, needless to say described as fuel protesters by the media, made a real racket. Security was pretty heavy. TB did an excellent little number on John for party members, after which the police took us into a side room and told us that all the streets on the way in to the restaurant we were due to be holding the dinner in were closed. I could tell JP was very disappointed, but the police were pretty clear that it was all getting a bit nasty and we should call it off. We were taken out by a side door, but even there TB and I only just made it into the car before a group of protesters found us and were chasing us down. This is getting ugly, he said. In the car, we had another long round of calls but again he wasn't happy about the way it was handled. We were staying at the Sheffield Hilton but as we arrived agreed it was probably best to go back and take charge tomorrow. There was a really nasty feeling in the air now. The hauliers were threatening to bring Leeds to a standstill. TB could not understand why the police were not stopping it. The go-slow of tractors earlier even had a police lead car leading them along. He kept banging on about the difference in their handling of the miners.

Tuesday, September 12

As ever, TB wanted fact rather than all the blather that departments pumped out. He was convinced that while there was not a conspiracy as such, a lot of the forces at work were political. When we got back to Number 10, he was appalled at the lack of grip. He felt the police were getting mixed signals. TB took a meeting at which we were given the same promises as yesterday that things were about to move. TB was looking nervous and was getting irritated. He decided personally to call all of the main oil company chairmen and urge them to raise their game on it. The police insisted that whatever problems there were re intimidation or access, they could deal with them. TB felt they had been getting very mixed signals but as the day wore on, it was clear we were not getting the movement we needed. It was obvious TB was going to have to front this until we had seen it through. We had another meeting with ministers and officials and ACPO [Association of Chief Police Officers]. I could sense TB's irritation every time David Omand [Permanent Secretary at the Home Office] tried to convey the idea that everything that could be done was being

September '00: Fuel protest; TB's anger at lack of grip

done. At the end of it, I said TB's voice had to be heard, we had to say that the oil companies could move, the police could police it. The protesters were still strong and they were playing quite a clever game in letting the odd one through and saying it was for emergency services. But it was clear the drivers were being intimidated. TB spoke to Bill Morris and John Monks and the unions were being terrific. It was business that was sitting on its hands while the Tories were just exploiting it as ever, and the media, claiming to represent public opinion, were supportive of the cause. But it was getting more and more serious by the hour and there was a real sense we were losing control. Milburn called me, and said we should play the NHS card soon because real problems were developing. He was probably right, but I said we should just wait a bit. TB did a press conference in the dining room at 5.30 and I knew as soon as he said it the 24 hours line would be a problem. But his tone overall was good and his manner prime ministerial. TB was now fully seized of the seriousness of it all, said it could be the end of him. 'This is a real crisis, make no mistake. I can't back down now and if we don't get things moving pretty quickly, I'll have to let someone else take it on.' I went out for a couple of hours to meet Calum and go to Fulham v Burnley, missing the first goal. By the time I got back to the office, the full horror of the situation was mounting. We weren't far off a crisis in the basic infrastructure of the nation. Fuel shortages leading to food shortages, and an inability to run public services. There was some movement of tankers but not enough to change things. TB was with JP and Gus [Macdonald] when I got back and we were now looking to step up the military options as well as putting pressure on the oil companies. I left just after midnight, TB's last words that it would get a lot worse before it got better.

Wednesday, September 13

I was longing to wake up and hear of massive movement of lorries and tankers, but it wasn't happening. For an hour or so it had looked OK, but then nothing. It was grim and getting grimmer. We were starting to get some focus onto the protesters, putting them under pressure for the first time. I went up to the flat to see TB, who said we are in deep shit if we don't get things moving soon. GB came on, said that the oil had to move but had no real idea how to bring that about. We called a meeting with the oil company executives, who came in at 10.30. They were not a very pleasant, compelling or impressive group of people. The only really strong voice there was [businessman] Jeffrey Stirling, who said the companies had to get the message to the drivers that if they didn't get out, they would get other drivers to do it for them. There was a lot of comic interplay between him and JP, but the BP and Shell people were not impressive. I guess part of them was happy for this all to be seen as a government problem. I said why didn't they operate in this together? TB said they had to get things moving. He left them in no doubt of his frustration. They all had stories of intimidation, and said the protesters were becoming more violent. They wanted police escorts, but they understood the police were stretched. TB said we could get out 200 military drivers. The guy from BP said he was worried they would be left holding the baby. I said don't worry, when the shit flies, most of it ends up here. They agreed at least to get a senior representative from every company into a room with government and police so we could finally get some proper coordination. I did a statement, no questions, leading to Jon Snow chasing them all the way down the street.

ACPO rather pooh-poohed the idea of intimidation. Through the day there were endless rumours of big breakouts which never really happened. The media was a big part of the problem here. TB said he accepted this was all about trying to break us undemocratically but he would need a second term to do anything about it. The entire pitch of the media coverage was to create rather than report problems. The protesters were treated like heroes, the government like villains. Jeremy Heywood was doing a brilliant job but Cobra,[1] defended to the hilt by Richard Wilson, had been useless. Milburn and I discussed a strategy to put the NHS at the centre of this. We got some excellent NHS people to visit some of the picket lines and directly accuse the protesters of doing real damage to essential services. Milburn put the NHS on emergencies-only red alert and went up for a round of interviews, and there was a real sense now of it turning a bit. We were having trouble getting GB to engage on the tax issue. We got Sainsbury's and BP out talking about intimidation. We felt better at the end of today than yesterday. Gus Macdonald had been impressive. The oil companies had got their act together a bit following the meeting. JP was fine though he lost his temper a bit too much. Byers was too zen-like. The polls on it were bad but I felt the Milburn interviews, and the NHS people out on the picket line, were a turning point.

[1] The committee intended to lead responses to national crises; named after Cabinet Office Briefing Room A.

September '00: Fuel: BP and Shell not impressive

Thursday, September 14

I woke up to news that the protesters at Stanlow refinery were calling it off. TB's bottom line was that we couldn't cave in. Although everyone had been caught up in it, we were actually dealing with small numbers of people who were vested interests, so the media labels of 'people's protest' and 'taxpayers' revolt' were misleading. He felt the media coverage had been an outrage but he didn't want to say so publicly. The oil crisis dominated a long discussion at Cabinet. TB was critical of the oil companies, and of the media and of the way the Tories had exploited it. Jack S went through the facts, reckoned we were operating on 15% of normal deliveries and prioritising essential services. Byers said we needed 900 deliveries even for that and we were facing real difficulties. As GB spoke, and spoke well, I couldn't help thinking how different it might have been if he had engaged earlier. But he was still not keen to make the arguments that we make it a tax issue. He said the press had become the opposition on this and the Tory Party were just echoing them. On the question of tax and spend, we had to broaden it out, make it about schools and hospitals, and the cuts they would threaten. He said it was limited the extent to which we could put pressure on OPEC. Nick Brown had met leaders of the food industry, who had basically said there was a danger the country would run out of food. Animals would have to be slaughtered. He said the oil companies were favouring their own in the distribution and intimidation was getting worse. TB said we had to get the focus on the impact on health, schools, the military, agriculture and business. He felt yesterday was the first time he got the public more on our side. We then had a meeting with the oil companies. TB said he wanted to read the riot act because he wasn't happy with their systems, and didn't really feel they had pulled out all the stops. Mark Moody-Stuart [chairman of Shell] was dreadful. He had earlier asked if TB minded if he sent his deputy. Yes he would was the answer. It was pretty tense at times, not least when JP had a go at their contracts system.

Friday, September 15

Though some of the papers were willing to acknowledge TB had stood firm, the sense was nonetheless of a victory of sorts for the protesters and a defeat for TB. Philip did some groups last night which were not as bad as they might have been. It had felt absolutely terrible at the centre, an almost palpable feeling of a gulf opening between government and country. Up in the flat, he said he felt as if he had been the one trying to shut down the nation, the way we were being treated. I was doing my usual rant about the press and he said I had to understand this was a power battle and it was only worth going for if we knew what the outcome would be. Under Thatcher, he said, they got drunk on the power she let them wield and then they tore Major to shreds, in part with our complicity. Also, for pragmatic reasons, we entered into a whole series of basically dishonest relationships with them and now they realised that. They realised that they actually have less power than they did and they see us as all-powerful and they want their power back. So there was no point in all-out war, because at the moment we have the upper hand. But I promise you, nobody despises them more than I do, but if you want to take them on we have to be sure that it's worth it.

Tuesday, September 26

Labour Party Conference, Brighton. We had been working till late but TB was up at 5, and me at 6. I did the final uplifting 'spirit of Britain' stuff and worked on a couple of jokes about Hague. Both Neil and Bruce were very against the section I had done as an apology. They worried if we went too far, it was all anyone would take and actually there wasn't that much to apologise for. I redid it, and then TB redrafted the section that tried to do a tone of apology without straying into weakness. TB had written a very powerful section on his 'irreducible core', which we thought would work best as an almost unscripted ad lib towards the end. He worked on that while I worked on the 75p line, admitting we'd been wrong to limit the inflation linked pensions rise to 75p, and I think we just about got the balance right. We had the usual rush of last-minute changes, fact checking, points from departments. Neither GB nor AD was happy with the 75p pensions passage because it would be used to throw back millions of words used against us. But it was clearly the right thing to do. We actually got things finished in reasonably good time and TB was panicking less than in previous years. We left for the conference centre by foot. We got JP to introduce him. TB was very quickly into it and as in previous years, I knew early on it was going to go well. I was standing next to Jeremy Paxman as we watched it and he seemed impressed, as did others when I did the rounds afterwards. The big trivia point was the amount he sweated. There was also a bit of forces of conservatism RIP but nonetheless you could feel things settling down. I went back to the hotel to watch the news and he had really done the business for us. However, the BBC reaction packages were bad, no doubt long planned. We had to start thinking though how to prepare for the fuel protesters' sixty-day deadline.

Thursday, October 5

The fall of Milosevic, which was brilliant. I had breakfast with Jonathan Faull, Prodi's spokesman. He said Prodi felt out of favour and was pissed off with the Brits. He felt we snubbed him in New York and didn't give him enough support. He was clearly a very prickly character. I went through TB's speech. It was clear that we were still seen as a bit of a back marker. He said there was a lot of talk around the place that we weren't that much different to the Tories, that we weren't really pushing the boat out on the euro, and they couldn't understand why a leader with such personal skills and a huge majority was not going for it. TB was wondering whether he could use the line about Europe becoming a 'superpower, not a superstate'. The uprising on the streets of Belgrade was growing and growing and we were witnessing a revolution that was fantastic to watch. I was hoping he was as scared as he deserved to be. We got TB out to say Milosevic must go before there was more death and that we would offer the hand of friendship to the Serbs if they embraced democracy. It felt great that Milosevic was so clearly on the way out and hiding in a hole somewhere, really panicking. We left for Warsaw. I got to bed late and watched events in Belgrade for ages. Needless to say, despite the significance of what had happened in Kosovo, we were getting zero credit, and indeed Robin's attempts to link us to events was being whacked by the commentariat.

Tuesday, October 10

I got a call from Brian Fitzpatrick [the First Minister's head of policy] that Donald Dewar was ill, that he had fallen and was now in hospital again. He said he would be kept in overnight and it was fine, but it was clear things were a lot worse and, as the day wore on, it became clear things were a lot, lot worse. I could tell from the tone of the calls from Fitzpatrick and David Whitton [the First Minister's chief spokesman] that he was on the way out. They kept us in touch through the day and virtually every call sounded a bit more desperate. I promised to take Grace and her friends to see Britney Spears at Wembley, and I was in and out the whole time taking calls about Donald. I was also hoping to avoid being seen but just as we settled down for the second half, Matthew Engel from the *Guardian* popped up behind me and said he was doing a piece on the crowd.

Wednesday, October 11

Donald was on life support and they were just waiting for Ian and Marian (his children) to turn off the machine. I called Ian and suggested they entrust someone like Jimmy Gordon [Lord Gordon of Strathblane, Labour peer] to take over the management of the funeral, and I offered Hilary C and Anne Shevas [Downing Street chief press officer] to help. He died officially at 12.18, while TB was seeing the Czechs. He did his own tribute. Everyone was really sad about Donald. He could be maddening at times with his old-fashioned ways, but he was a truly solid citizen and he had been a great help to me so many times. The *Record* called for an article and I said TB would also do one that we would offer to everyone and back came the answer 'Fine, but it would be nice to get a couple of gimmicks just for us.' And they wonder why I loathe them.

Wednesday, October 18

Normal politics was suspended for the day for Donald's funeral. TB was looking really tired, his face a bit grey and his hair clearly thinning and greying. Sally pointed out that if the plane had crashed, only GB and Peter would have been left. What a smooth handover. I said GB wouldn't know which Queen to call first. As we arrived I attached myself to David Blunkett and looked after him for most of the day. We were taken by bus to the Scottish Executive building and met by Henry McLeish, who shook hands with everyone and said 'thanks for coming' as though it was his event. John Reid was busy stirring. Wendy Alexander [Labour MSP for Paisley North] was clearly wanting to have a serious discussion, but I wasn't really up for it. I talked to Derry and Alison [Irvine], and it must have been a particularly difficult day for them. Alison looked very nervy. It was a nice atmosphere on the bus to the cathedral. Because of the security, we were in for a good hour or more before the service started. Douglas [Alexander]'s dad was conducting the service and I felt his welcome to TB was a bit patronising, and maybe I was too sensitive, but it was like he was welcoming him to a foreign country. GB's tribute was very powerful, very socialist, more of the old Labour than the new. I loved the Gaelic singing, which reminded me of our holidays in Tiree, but I wasn't as emotional as I normally get at funerals. We filed out to the Internationale and were back on the bus and then to the Kelvingrove Art Gallery. What I had picked up very strongly through the day was how virtually everyone in the Cabinet was really fed up with the GB–PM situation and that they saw the Robinson book as part of that.

Sunday, October 22

TB called, said we had to rebuild patiently, that it may be after Christmas before the mood starts to turn and we just had to accept we were going to be treated like any other government. 'Why should we be different?' he asked. Because, I said, the Tories were useless, we were better than them, and the vast bulk of our problems were self-inflicted. He said 'That's politics. There's not much you can do about it. If it wasn't me and GB, or him and Peter, it would be something else. What matters is that we know what we want to do and we get it done despite the difficulties.' TB was both buoyant and down. Down about some of the realities, and the basic unfairness of the way we were depicted, but buoyant because he felt we were doing the right things and making progress and also because he had resigned himself to the idea that if we lost, we lost, and it wasn't the end of the world. He had clearly been chatting to his maker again. I said if Britain was ready to elect the Tories again, then I was out of here. Deep down, I think we were both confident the mood would turn.

Monday, October 30
Violent gales again. TB saw Murdoch and Irwin Stelzer. He had asked them outright whether they were going to back us. Murdoch said the Tories were unelectable and that was that. TB seemed to take it at face value. I still felt we were using too much of his own time on journalists, time we could be devoting to him doing things that would make a difference and get a different sort of coverage. He did at least agree to do some phone calls to people in the emergency services dealing with the floods.[1]

Tuesday, November 7
Philip was more and more worried about the US elections. The TV was saying neck and neck but though Gore had closed strongly, it was not looking brilliant. They had been daft not to use Clinton properly. We had been right to stay out of it but now it was going to be important to be on the right side of the result, and there would be a real desire to present a Bush win as a disaster for us.

Wednesday, November 8
The US elections scene was unbelievable. I went to bed thinking Bush had won, then woke up to 'too close to call', then on the way in Gore seemed to be conceding defeat, only to retract as the day wore on amid suggestions of real jiggery-pokery going on. There was nothing we could do but wait before we could begin to put in

---

[1] Intense autumn rainfall had led to severe flooding in England and Wales.

place a strategy for either outcome, but it was going to be the only show in town for a while. Our daily fuel meetings were going fine and we were getting some good regional coverage and overall winning the arguments I think. GB presented the PBR to Cabinet, good on the big picture, lots in it on inner cities, youth unemployment. Obviously the moves on fuel prices would be important and the general feeling was that he got the balance right, that there was enough of a shift on prices to have an impact, without it looking like we were conceding too much. We had the usual bombardment of facts and figures on tax credits, but overall he did well. Prosperity for all, moving to full employment, rising living standards, the messages were in the right place. We went over for PMQs and then stayed for the PBR, which was fine. Ed Balls and I did the briefing afterwards. They were all very cynical and wanting to make the story the tax burden again so we had to push hard on fuel and pensions and the overall strength of the economy. Ed was good on detail but not good on message and he had a habit of just repeating what GB had said, when what they needed was a bit of nuance and the main strategic message hammered through. I had a meeting with Gus Macdonald re [David] Handley[1] who was now very much on the back foot and we had to keep him there. I got back to track the US situation, which was surely one of the most amazing election stories ever. Hillary Clinton did brilliantly in New York and we sent through a message on the q.t.

Fiona and I had dinner with TB and CB in the flat. TB knew I had not been very happy of late, and also that Fiona was pressing for a decision on how long I went on. I said I would probably want to go after the election, and he needed to understand others would want to do the same and so he should be looking around for new people. He said there was no way I would go because if we came to recommend entry I would not be able to resist the challenge of a euro campaign, and if we went for it, he would want me around. I said I was not that bothered about the euro. It didn't move me like a Labour v Tory battle did. He said if he could get new people, that would be great, but he didn't know where they were. He accepted that GB and PM could not really work together but even with that, they were still brilliant. He accepted that part of GB's strategy was that he put himself in a slightly different position to TB. But even that was worth bearing to keep his input. I said that was all well and good but it was incredibly draining because I had to deal with so much of the fallout.

[1] Monmouthshire farmer, chairman of the People's Fuel Lobby.

It was different for him, because he was Prime Minister and when all was said and done would get the kudos, the place in history, and the knowledge that in the end he had made so much difference. I sometimes felt like I was just picking up the shit left by everyone else. He said he would love to rely on more people, but he came back to his basic point – GB was special, Peter was special, I was special, there were plenty of very good people but very few who could just take you to a different level, and I had to understand he would not let go easily. In between the heavy stuff, we had a lot of laughs and Cherie was back to her old self. Between us we gave TB a bit of a hard time, said he *was* becoming a bit out of touch, that he was no longer seen as having North-East connections, that he spent too much time at Chequers, that he didn't get the empathy stuff. But as he said himself, he was about as normal as any politician could be given the weird circumstances of his existence. 'There aren't many prime ministers who could sit and listen to their missus, their spin doctor and their spin doctor's missus all telling him how useless and out of touch he is, and still keep smiling.' He then pretended to call through for executioners to come and take us out and hang us on Horseguards for rank insubordination. The upshot was he was determined I should stay but accepted we might have to do things differently. As we left, he said that in politics today you need intellectual ability, nous, judgement, a thick skin and a very strong personality. He came back to his point – though we were all flawed in some way or another, he, GB, PM and I were the ones that had that and he wasn't going to let go of that talent lightly.

Thursday, November 9

The daily fuel meetings were going well, showing again that if we had an agreed message, and systems for communicating it, we could usually win arguments. ACPO put out a very tough warning to anyone thinking of fucking up the motorways. York police said they were up to their ears in floods. Handley was clearly looking for a way out from the kind of protest they had been planning. The police told Gus that if Handley met TB or GB, they reckoned he would call it off. GB was reluctant to see him, which was right, and TB certainly shouldn't see him. We arranged for Gus to see him tomorrow. Blunkett praised the work we had done centralising operations in response to the fuel situation, and en passant described Handley as an obnoxious little individual. Gus was still pressing for GB or JP to see Handley. I felt both were too big for it. Maybe Jack.

Friday, November 10
The US elections were still confused. I felt the Democrats should really go for it and not give in. There were more and more stories of how people thought they voted Gore and in fact voted Buchanan.[1] The whole thing was a mess and whoever finally won was going to be weakened at the start, at a point they should have maximum strength. The best news was that the lorry convoys were basically fizzling out. Handley had virtually gone into hiding and Brynle Williams[2] was asking them to call it off.

Thursday, November 16
I woke up to another load of balls on Europe and the euro. Peter M had said to a dinner of business people that we had made a strategic error saying that we just had to win the political and constitutional argument, and the *FT* were on to it. TB said if it happened again, he would reprimand Peter. I was with GB on this. At Cabinet, TB was pretty tough, saying that he was fed up that we agreed an advance grid, and then so much crowded in to make it completely different at the last minute. He wanted ministers to get a proper grip of their departments and he didn't want to have to keep coming back to the same message. Otherwise it was pretty quiet. He called in Peter at the end, said he was fed up with all the diddling and he had to understand he did not want Europe up as a big election issue, he wanted it shut down. Peter gave an unconvincing account of how it all happened, that he had been trying to prevent one story and inadvertently created another. He said it was ludicrous that the Foreign Secretary was not supposed to make speeches about Europe. TB was getting more and more agitated and finally said 'I am losing patience on this. I want it shut down, end of story. You had better understand that I am the Prime Minister, and the Leader of the Labour Party and you do what I say.' Peter looked a bit taken aback but eventually said 'I sometimes have to think of my own interests too.' TB: 'You are going to have to listen to my judgement in this and I want an end to it.' This verbal tennis went on for a bit longer. Eventually I said 'It is

[1] Pat Buchanan, the Reform Party candidate, received an unexpectedly high number of votes in Palm Beach County, Florida. It is possible that this was caused by a 'butterfly ballot'. The list of candidates was laid out in two columns, divided by a single row of holes. Punching the second hole did not register a vote for Gore, the second name in the left-hand list, but for Buchanan, the first name in the right-hand list.
[2] The Flintshire farmer led the fuel blockades at Stanlow. Later became a Conservative Member of the Welsh Assembly.

November '00: Peter M in hot water again over Europe

fucking ludicrous in a week we had an agreed plan to get up investment that I'm now about to leave for 40 minutes of questioning on the single currency.'

Friday, November 17

I drove down with TB to Chequers, to go over his spiel to the political Cabinet. There was real anger at GB and Peter and TB could strengthen his position. We arrived, and I was the subject of considerable piss-taking over the photo in the *Sun* of me arriving at the Britney Spears party, clearly trying not to be seen. The meeting itself was good. TB was on superb form. He was clear, determined, didn't pull his punches in saying they had to raise their game. He laid out the strategy and the dividing lines, the need to take things to a choice and a personal offer of prosperity. GB was also more New Labour than usual. Philip did a polling presentation, 54–37 wrong direction–right direction, floods and fuel creating a bad mood, but we still had an 8-point lead. Hague was being hit on opportunism and poor judgement, but the Tories could make inroads in standing up for Britain. TB emphasised the need for people to be given a personal offer about their future, that we had to be less general and more specific. And he warned that patriotism was an area the Tories would try to take back. He said it was a stupid mistake that a week after the PBR we were arguing about Europe. We have to be far more focused. We also had to expose the Tories' backdoor strategy, which was to make people as cynical as possible, depress the vote, and get their own vote out. He felt the dividing lines were clear – stability v boom and bust; investment v cuts; prosperity for all v social division; opportunity and responsibility together v social disorder; leadership v engagement. On all the big arguments, we were on the right side of them but we lacked the capacity for explaining them. Ministers were too departmentalised, lacking in politics. Hague is dangerous because he is weak and he has bad judgement, and people have to know that. He ended by saying we have to go into this fight as though our lives depended on it.

Sunday, November 19

I watched Rory Bremner with the kids. I ended up being fired, kicking the Queen's corgis, ending up working for her and getting a knighthood. Although the bloke playing me was overweight, it was uncanny how he got some of my mannerisms, and the nature of some of the exchanges between me and TB.

Monday, December 4

I had a meeting with Richard Desmond [new owner of the *Daily Express*]. He looked and sounded a bit wide boy, but was pretty bright. I gave him an assessment of how I thought they should take on the *Mail*, be campaigning but from a spirit of optimism, promote what's good, don't just run everything down. He was not a fan of Clive Hollick [of United Business Media, previous owner]. He was clearly going to sack loads of people, would ideally like to run newspapers without journalists. His grasp on policy was pretty tenuous. It was all really about himself – he hated Hague because he hadn't returned a phone call.

Saturday, December 9

EU summit, Nice. The Chirac–Schroeder relationship was bad, and Chirac–Jospin was even worse. There was clearly very little trust between them. The Dutch were angry because they were given too few votes, Spain were happy enough to be lagging just behind the big four but everyone else was pretty fed up and felt that the French were basically losing the plot. Our big worry had to be that the French cut a deal with the Germans and then come after us together on tax. But it was clear the French were finding it hard to see a way through. Lena (Schroeder's interpreter) suggested we speak to Schroeder and at lunch he, TB and I went out on the balcony and agreed we should try to work together with Italy to try to put together a proposal people could live with. Schroeder was sufficiently fed up to go for it. Schroeder agreed Chirac had made a mess of things by setting such store on the issue of parity[1] and by making the point earlier that as they had been on the winning side in the war they had nuclear weapons. 'It's not easy for me to say to 20-year-old Germans, dear German citizens, because your grandfather occupied France we got a very bad deal from President Chirac at Nice.' Top man, really, tough and by and large straight.

Monday, December 11

We were now down to 29 votes for the big four, which was cutting down on reweighting, and the whole thing was not brilliant at all. It was taking a fair amount of strong-arming to get the medium-sized

---

[1] Votes on the EU Council were allocated according to the size of population, with weighting in favour of smaller countries. Proposed changes favoured larger states, but France wanted to retain parity with Germany, despite its smaller population.

and the smaller countries to go for it. At one point TB and Schroeder literally had [Guy] Verhofstadt [Prime Minister of Belgium] pinned into the corner of the room, his smile getting thinner and thinner as TB did the charm and Schroeder did the exasperation bordering on anger. Chirac was even more aggressive, at one point telling the Belgian foreign minister he was a coward because they wouldn't take the deal. His handling of the whole thing had been bizarre, making such a totem of French parity with Germany without regard to some of the long-term friendships and alliances that were bound to be affected by the nastiness at the end. At one point, though he was meant to be chairing it, Chirac asked his staff to get some letters to sign and just sat there working at his desk on his own. Schroeder was sitting a bit further round the circle, just staring out, looking tired. [José María] Aznar [Spanish prime minister] and Guterres walked out. The last bits of haggling were done in the margins and largely by officials. Finally around 5am it was all done. It's ludicrous that these negotiations were sorted in this atmosphere of frenzy, with everyone exhausted and losing their tempers.

Wednesday, December 13

I went for a run in the pitch black round the grounds of Hillsborough, falling over once or twice and landing really badly on my shoulder. After breakfast, TB had a session with Ronnie Flanagan and the new head of the army in NI. They were reasonably helpful in trying to get some moves on demilitarisation but the big symbolic things Sinn Fein wanted were not going to be possible. Peter was a bit odd at these meetings. He was obviously so used to being the main man here and lording it and found it hard to adapt when TB came in and was clearly the focus. He was very good in describing other people's positions, usually in exaggerated and sometimes disparaging terms. TB was getting more and more exasperated by his manner. We left for Stormont and were left hanging around for ages waiting for Bill Clinton, who was seeing Adams and Hume at the hotel. He finally arrived 45 minutes late and did the rounds of Assembly members and we then met some of the leaders. We did a photo call, TB, BC, Trimble and Mallon, before a meeting of the four of them. Trimble was worried about Patten[1] and the effect it would have on the Unionist community. Seamus was clearly worried that Sinn Fein would outflank

---

[1] The Patten report included recommendations that the RUC be abolished and that recruitment to a replacement force maintain parity between Catholics and Protestants.

the SDLP. TB was worried later re Seamus, felt he was a lot more difficult than before, that he was being driven by the SDLP not being clear about their purpose in all this. The politics were clearly in flux and all of them seemed a bit unsure how to deal with it.

It must have been odd for Clinton to be trying to help us deal with all this, in what was ultimately a fairly small part of the world, albeit one that had a resonance elsewhere, and back home there were pretty seismic events going on. I spoke to several of the Clinton people about the Gore situation. They obviously felt the campaign could have gone better if Bill had been more involved. The Supreme Court judgement had basically been that a recount was unconstitutional so that was basically that. Gore was planning to concede 2am our time, then Bush would speak an hour later. Clinton was reasonably discreet but he clearly felt his legacy was at risk, that they lost by allowing the Republicans to neutralise the issue of the economy, by allowing their basic message to move leftwards, and by not using him properly. He was right on all three counts.

TB saw the UUP, SF and SDLP, and the meetings were more convivial than usual, which sometimes meant progress was not being made. Ken Maginnis was pressing for proper recognition of the RUC and said we were playing a very dangerous game if we were going for an amnesty for the 'OTRs' [on-the-run terrorists]. Then Sinn Fein. Martin McGuinness said he liked doing education and he felt most people felt he was doing his job. But we kept coming back to all the old impediments to progress and it pissed him off. He said he would welcome it if more of 'our people' joined the police but they are not convinced that a new police force genuinely represents a new beginning. He said he was the guy going out to Republicans saying Blair is a good guy, different to every other prime minister, but they laugh at me if I say that policing is a good deal for us. Patten did not go far enough for them. He said we don't come from where they come from and we have to understand the psychology. People hate the RUC even more than the British Army, but there is an appreciation that there must be a policing service. People are up for that but are badly disappointed. TB said what's your beef? We've done everything the SDLP asked for in the implementation plan. Bairbre de Bruin said their people just weren't going to join as things stood. It was interesting that McGuinness did more of the talking this time than Adams. Gerry Kelly and Ferris did the strong silent bit as usual. Policing, demilitarisation and decommissioning were coming together as real problems. Clinton seemed more tired than usual, at

December '00: Wrangling over future of RUC

one point nodding off on a long black sofa in the holding room. Hillary was also clearly having to really fight within herself to put on a brave face about what was happening back home, and she was if anything even more discreet re Gore. But they were very anxious about the future.

Thursday, December 14

I went in with Philip and chaired a meeting on next steps but the only thing that mattered today really was Bush. It must have been so weird for Clinton, who was down at Chequers and giving TB a tip or two on how to make sure he got in with Bush. We got flown up by helicopter to Warwick University. There was something almost weird about us sitting there in the office waiting for the Bush call, while outside everyone was getting very excited about Clinton. Bush came on, and made a point of saying it was the first call he was making. Neither of them mentioned the recent turmoil. There was lots of laughter and joking, then the standard stuff about the special relationship and the importance of working together. They didn't really get into substance at all, it wasn't that kind of call. He sounded friendly enough. Bill arrived and we were put into a very poky little holding room before they went down to do the speeches. He was going out of his way to help. I had been trying to get their speeches to work together to show the Third Way as being something more than just an electoral device. He spoke really well. As he came off the stage he said 'I hope that did something for you.' I said I wasn't the biggest Third Way fan in the world, but we may as well try to get something out of it. He said he always preferred the first way. There was definitely an end of era feel to things. He said he wanted to thank us for all the help we had given him. I said he was the best political communicator I had ever seen or heard and he said thanks for everything. I reckoned he would find it quite hard to adapt out of power. Hillary looked sad as well. She said say hi to Fiona and keep in touch. Then they walked out, smiled and waved at the small crowd over the road, into the car, and off they went. There was something about a presidential motorcade that looks both impressive and sad at the same time. Impressive in that it sweeps all before it, but sad that they need that kind of support and protection, and for an outgoing president what was once a symbol of power becomes a symbol purely of status of what he once was. You could feel that the power was no longer there, but had moved.

Friday, December 22

The *Mail* splashed on Prince Charles 'privately' expressing opposition to our position on European defence. As TB said when I told him about it, 'I'd be amazed if he's even looked at what the real proposals are. Mark Bolland will just be trying to get him big licks in the *Mail*.' The Tories were straight onto it.

Thursday, January 4, 2001

TB was getting more and more hyper and putting me under more pressure. Fiona was putting on the pressure from another direction, wanting me to leave. She had talked to CB, who had mentioned it to him, and he was pressing all the buttons – about commitment, about his fear that he'd find it much harder if I wasn't there, above all the appeal of the scale of the challenge. I also knew that Anji was telling him she wanted to go.

Friday, January 5

Working at home, I did a conference call to generate story ideas for *Frost*. I had an eighty-minute chat with TB on the phone. He said to have me and Anji telling him we were thinking of leaving was really unsettling. I said he had to understand the pressure I was under, and also my fear that I wasn't really motoring like before. Fiona had never wanted me to do the job in the first place and yet found every day of her life effectively run by that decision. At the very least she wants a date that we can start to think about as a point of departure. He said he believed things would be easier in the second term because we would be more experienced, it would be much more our mandate, the press would have to see the country had changed. He was clear about the agenda for the second term – public service reform, the euro if the conditions are right, international leadership because there was a vacuum. He honestly didn't know if he would go for a third term. But he felt he would be very exposed if he lost his key people. He felt both Anji and I gave him something nobody else could. He said the reason he was like a cat on a hot tin roof at the moment was because this was worrying him. It was a mix of flattery, threat, black-mail, an appeal to my better nature and also his insight that I was committed and wanted to be part of this for the long term. Just as he had made it impossible to refuse in the first place, so he was making it hard to leave.

Tuesday, January 9

I spoke to Clare Short, who we wanted to do a speech that would surprise people by being more New Labour. I had forgotten how stressful it was being out on the road with TB, his constant agitation. Got the train down to Bristol. We were warned by the cops that there was a hundred-strong demo but they would be OK. We arrived, at a college, and were immediately showered with tomatoes. TB was hit by one on the back but he just kept walking. Inside he did a Q & A, toured about and then we left, the crowd having dispersed. He was all for making a joke about tomatoes, but I couldn't see the point. The speech was strong, and the Q & A was tough and he did well. All the main political editors were there, and had to acknowledge he was very good at these events. We got the train back and he was angry at security being so badly organised. He was pretty sure that if we pressed on with hunting, we would be dogged by protesters everywhere we went. I still felt that if he tried to do a U-turn on this, the risk was enormous. His big problem with it was that he felt it was basically illiberal, and not him. Despite the tomato, he had enjoyed getting out and about and said he wanted to do more visits outside London. Chris Meyer came to see me re [George W] Bush. He said Bush was determined to make every effort with TB. Meyer thought [Donald] Rumsfeld would be a problem for us and also he wasn't sure whether Condi Rice would have real clout. He was assuring me that Bush had no interest whatever in helping Hague, that on the one occasion they had discussed it he referred to him as Jim Hague.

Thursday, January 11

On hunting, TB was still trying to think of a way out. One idea now doing the rounds was that it would get blocked in the Lords and we could then put a middle way in the manifesto for the next parliament.

Friday, January 12

I went to the agency, where Trevor Beattie [creative director of the TBWA advertising agency] presented some really good stuff, including a terrific picture of Hague with Thatcher's hair. TB would be nervous about it but it was funny and he would buy it if we ran it alongside something positive. The recent groups were mixed but there was no doubt we were getting some traction with the Tory attacks.

Tuesday, January 16

TB was still banging on about hunting. The Tories thought he was being very clever and cunning. In fact he was agonising because he did not feel comfortable about the position he was in. You could argue that we would never win the support of most of those who opposed our position, but that we would lose a stack of support if he tried to shift the position back. But he didn't like doing things he didn't instinctively feel were right. Anji was as ever whispering in his ear what all her right-wing friends were saying, and the whole thing was unsettling him. Peter M was pressing for us to go to NI tomorrow. Maybe he wanted to miss the hunting vote too.

Wednesday, January 17

Even though we had trailed it, there was inevitably cynicism at TB heading off for NI on the day of the hunting vote, even though we made clear he would have maintained the same position as before – voting for a ban – had he been there. Philip had the latest poll in, which was pretty good.

Thursday, January 18

TB said he was really worried, that he had not quite realised how much ordinary Unionist opinion had moved away from us. He had been alarmed by the meeting with the DUP. Even without Paisley there, they had been very chipper, cocky even, and he sensed that they sensed things were moving their way. They told him straight out that Trimble was going down the pan and he'd better get used to dealing with them. I didn't like the tone or feel of it one bit. TB now felt that unless there was decommissioning – and that meant product not words – then he feared Trimble was dead, and without him there was no peace process as things stood. He felt that was confirmed by the Alliance and the women's group, who though not big players were very good barometers. He really was worried, more worried than I had heard or seen him for ages. He said without Trimble there was no peace process and no Good Friday Agreement worth saving. He was getting irritated by the way the Irish officials overstated where we were with SF. They were saying what they wanted to be true, rather than what they knew to be true. He said he feared we were going round in circles. He spent hours with SF, then said to us he wasn't actually sure what they were saying any more. TB was trying to persuade the Irish and SF that electoral disaster for Trimble would not be good for any of us. He called me through to a meeting with Adams, McGuinness and Gerry Kelly, who all seemed very relaxed and jolly given the circumstances. TB asked whether we could get away with a meeting at Chequers without the media knowing, and I said of course. We ended up talking about TB's neighbours, and chatted re Jackie Stewart [former Formula 1 champion] and somehow we ended up discussing whether we liked Des O'Connor, and Adams said maybe in the absence of anything else concrete to report, I could go out and brief that there was agreement that we all liked Des O'Connor. I said you just like his surname. I had to fish TB out to meet Ronnie Flanagan and the new GOC [General Officer Commanding, Lieutenant General Sir Alistair Irwin] who had been flown in by chopper to avoid being seen either by the media or SF. TB was very upfront with them about wanting to concede something on the demilitarisation front, provided we got something back, but he also wanted to assure them if they had genuine security concerns, he would not press. I sensed Flanagan was more up for doing something, but this was very tricky stuff.

Saturday, January 20

TB was very buoyed up by the talks yesterday, which, amazingly, hadn't leaked, even though Gerry etc were seen in Amersham. He felt they made real progress and felt that if we could pull them off some of their demands on policing, and above all get actual decommissioning, it would be the biggest thing since the GFA [Good Friday Agreement] itself. Bush's inauguration provided a news sponge for the day. We were planning another possible NI trip on Monday to keep the thing moving. TB was saying if we went we may need to stay to Tuesday too, if we felt progress was being made. He clearly thought yesterday had turned things. Yet again, the lack of the 'crisis talks' spotlight had helped. TB called after his Chequers dinner which must have been a collectors' item – Bono and Geldof, Jackie Stewart, Polly Toynbee [journalist] and her dreary bloke [David Walker, a journalist], John Denham [Minister of State for Social Security], Kate Garvey. He said it was totally surreal, but the real star was Dickie Bird [former cricket umpire], who was singing my praises all night, saying I was a good lad because I stuck with Burnley, and how he was so honoured to be there he would happily have walked all the way from Barnsley. TB said he arrived two hours early and was mesmerised by the place. He asked Bono whether he had had many hits. TB said Bono and Geldof were a good double act, and deadly serious on the policy front.

Sunday, January 21

I went for a run and then was playing tennis at Market Road when I finally got hold of Peter to get a line on the story in the *Observer* that he tried to help the Hindujas[1] get a British passport. He denied it but I could tell he was in a real state. There was something bizarre about the sound of tennis balls getting whacked all around me as I tried to concentrate on what he was saying. He didn't want to talk about that story, but the page 2 story in the *Sunday Times* re him and GB criticising each other. There was something about it that really got to him, which was odd in that there had been a fair few stories like this before. He said 'these people' had destroyed 'half my life, half my career, half my future, and they would not rest until the whole job was done'. He said I had to understand that ultimately it was the Prime Minister they wanted to destroy and they would stop at nothing to do it. I said the problem was that the media was on autopilot on this. He said he had no desire to destroy GB, but he had no doubt whatever GB was determined to destroy him. He said these stories only appear because GB and his people want them to. Routledge's book happened because of GB, so did Robinson's. I said here we are talking about a page 2 story unlikely to be followed, and nobody knew for sure they briefed it, and he just exploded. He said it was unacceptable to have a group of people determined to destroy him and all I could do was say that it was six of one and half a dozen of the other. He said he did not know when, but he intended to remove himself from the situation before too long. I tried to pin him down a bit more re the Hindujas, but he just said the story was wrong.

Monday, January 22

Hinduja/Peter M was low level but had a bad feel to it. I didn't do well at the 11, because I think they sensed my worry about Peter M, and I was not sufficiently on top of the detail. PM had been very dismissive yesterday and I did not follow my own instincts sufficiently to get to the bottom of it. It went on for ages and had a bad feel to it and they clearly sensed something here. Then it emerged that we having said it was all handled by a private secretary, Peter M seemingly did speak to Mike O'Brien [Home Office immigration minister] about it. So we were heading for a process/handling drama that would have them obsessing. Peter M had been adamant yesterday

[1] It was claimed that Mandelson had helped Srichand Hinduja's application for a British passport. A subsequent inquiry found he did not make representations but by then he had lost his job.

re non-involvement. The Home Office finally told us there had been a call with O'Brien at 3.45 and we went into a stack of conference calls, the most important of which was me, Tom Kelly, Godric, PM and Mike O'Brien, where I said we had to get all the facts. The position was defensible but not if we were saying different things or the story was changing and we had to get the facts quickly. It was another wretched weekend situation, where departments had not bothered to grip until the next day when things were often too late. I should have done so myself yesterday. TB was adamant we must not let the press create a false firestorm if Peter had done nothing wrong at all. Even if he had pressed for citizenship, there would be nothing wrong with that provided the normal rules and procedures were followed. The problem was the changing line, Peter having first said it was all handled by a private secretary, us sticking to that, but then the Home Office saying there was this phone call. It was not good. I called Peter M to say I was really worried about the Hinduja story and we had to get it sorted.

Tuesday, January 23

There was an odd feeling to the Hinduja story, which on one level was going away but I still feared the damage to be done if it came out later that Peter had spoken to O'Brien. Worse, we had known about it yesterday and indeed Jack Straw and Mike O'Brien both told us they had reminded Peter of the call last week. Jack felt we had to get it out because we were bound to be asked about it. I felt my own position was difficult because inadvertently I had already misled people. TB was worried an admission out of the blue would simply set the touchpaper alight. Peter agreed that we brief that he had asked for all the facts and had not recalled the conversation but Mike O'Brien had. It was a bad scenario and he sounded worried. He was also not consistent, for example trying to say that what he told me at the weekend was consistent with what he was saying now. TB wasn't helping much because he was going into his righteous indignation lather, saying what mattered was whether he had actually done anything wrong, not the press trying to present the handling as wrong. But the fact we had to change our story meant we were going to be lacerated. TB felt it was a classic firestorm and we should not concede. But he had to accept Peter had not given us the whole picture on Sunday, or at the least had been vague and unclear when we were asking for clarity. The Home Office were useless at setting out the facts clearly. Only when TB was asking for the facts did they start to get going. PM came over for the Northern Ireland talks and was nervous. I did my best to appear calm and controlled but it was going to be grim, as was clear with the BBC now leading on it, and by the 4 o'clock they were in full cry and the facts were getting lost. Peter was in and out of my office. TB now felt the situation was bad but we had to get the facts out. Peter and I agreed he should do the rounds at Millbank and defend himself, but he opened new loose ends, for example saying he had not forgotten anything, alongside unravelling the Home Office version too. He was strangely detached through the day, almost as if he was talking about someone else, not himself. TB was by now irritated we were having to spend so much time on this, which he said had nothing to do with real people and real lives and yet would get millions of words devoted to it. He accepted it showed a loss of judgement by Peter, who had damaged his chances of a top job post-election. I meanwhile was fed up having to pick up the pieces and draw so much of the blame. This was going to do us real damage. The press could sense how bad it felt. I was also sensing that if Peter was moved on, I would be the next target, and I was going to take a hit on this stuff anyway.

Wednesday, January 24

I slept really badly and woke up with a strong sense that Peter was a goner. I felt there was no way out. I went up to the flat where TB was going through it all. He had spoken to Derry and asked him to look at all the facts and Derry later joined TB, me, Jonathan, Bruce [Grocott] and RW. It was clear that even if there was no problem with the application issue – and Derry was not convinced of that, feeling there was too much information about it in the July 2 memo – there was an insurmountable problem with the stuff about Jack reminding him last week that he had spoken to O'Brien. Jack also told Jonathan and me that Peter's office had called Jack's private office on January 11 to say Peter didn't see why the existence of the phone call had to be acknowledged. Peter had earlier called me and said we needed a chronology of the last few days squaring all the different statements. I said the problem was he did say to me that his sole involvement was via a private secretary and that I had passed that on to the media, as had Chris Smith in interviews based on what I told him. Also, his statement on TV last night, that he hadn't forgotten anything, did not sit easily with what Jack and O'Brien were saying. His friends, particularly Robert Harris and to a lesser extent Anji, felt I was going for him. I simply said that he had misled us. It was all so piddling in one way but he had made it a big problem because of the way he had allowed us to handle it on Sunday. Again, as on Sunday, he was strangely disengaged but now there was just a hint of panic. He asked if I was still hating my life and I said at times like this, yes. I said to TB that the worst-case scenario was that he was asked direct in the House whether he had been aware of any evidence that PM did know about the call. TB would have to say yes. TB spoke to Jack himself and I could tell from his tone of voice was satisfying himself that there were grounds for Peter going. He was asking whether he could stay for the duration of the next part of the process but we all agreed that wasn't possible. Also, whether he should say he was satisfied there was no wrongdoing in relation to the application but in any event we should have an inquiry. That's what we did in the end, and Richard Wilson got hold of Anthony Hammond [QC, asked by the government to carry out an inquiry]. I was clear we had to get this sorted before PMQs, preferably by the 11. Derry was clear we either had to get rid of him or have an inquiry, or both. The mood was ghastly and it was pretty much curtains. TB said I cannot believe we are going through this again. The guy is finished. Is there nothing we can do for him at all? If not, it's his life over. PM came to see TB at 10.45. I went in at 10.55 and said I needed a line for the 11 o'clock. Peter said things weren't resolved. He was resisting the idea of going. I said we had to be clear that if any new information came out, for example Jack's call last week, it was curtains, and I feared that was where it would end. TB said can't you just busk your way through it? I said no, I had to have something to say. He and I popped out and agreed I should say Peter was here because TB wanted to establish for himself the facts before being questioned in Parliament.

I did the 11, was as calm as I could be, maybe too calm, because they read from the body language a mix of feeling down and accepting inevitability re PM going. I hadn't deliberately signalled it, but they sensed something was going on. After a while I said I was no use to them down here, I was better off upstairs, establishing what was happening. I went back up and TB looked absolutely wretched. Peter looked becalmed. TB said he had made clear to PM he had to go and that though he wasn't sure, over time he would see why it had been necessary. TB seemed much more emotional about the whole thing than Peter. TB was writing what PM might say. Peter went up to Anji's office to do the same. Up till now, I had pretty much dealt with it like any other difficult handling issue, but seeing him sitting there, looking pale, almost poleaxed, but trying to keep a very brave face on it, I was suddenly hit by how awful the whole thing was. Also there was a line emerging, e.g. via Andy Marr, that what this was all about was a blazing row between me and Peter, that I had said to TB it was him or me. It hadn't been like that, but here I was again, just me and Peter, drafting resignation letters, statements to the press, etc. Peter was far less emotional than the first time, much more matter-of-fact. I said he was a good thing, and he didn't deserve this happening to him again. He said maybe I did. He was strangely quiet and unmoved. We agreed he should be allowed to do Northern Ireland Questions and we went round to my office with Tom Kelly to prepare for that. In between I was backwards and forwards to TB to agree lines and letters and help him prepare for PMQs. Peter finally went out to the street to face the media. It was windy and his hair was flapping about but he was pretty dignified and his fears that he would fall apart were unfounded. Fiona and Cherie came into my office to see him, and again he seemed strangely unmoved. In the House, Hague was too shrill and misjudged it. Because it had been Northern Ireland Questions, Peter was on the front bench alongside TB and only now I think started to realise this was probably the last time he would be there. The 4 o'clock was packed, standing room only, and I think I did OK. I tried to kill the stuff about Peter and me falling out. TB wanted to do interviews but I felt the stuff in the House was better than any interview, and he could always do more tomorrow.

We now had to work on the reshuffle, John Reid to NI, Helen Liddell to Scotland. Brian Wilson was really unhappy about it. In the end, TB got Hain to move to DTI and Brian into Hain's job. In all of the calls, TB said it was a tragedy for PM, that he had paid a terrible price for a small sin. Peter called me from the airport and was perfectly nice. There was a delayed reaction to come, I was appalled at Robert Harris going on TV effectively saying I had pushed him out. GB was advising TB to use the cover of the reshuffle to get me to go to Millbank, which was positive on one level, but TB was still worried it would make it impossible for me to go back after the election. There was a real sense of vengeance in the media, PM getting his comeuppance. TB said Hague would regret being as lowlife as he had been today. TB said he was heartbroken for Peter but now we just had to pick up and move on. Peter H said I must get Tony to look a little less like his child had been run over by a bus. The only good thing out of today was people saying we had acted decisively, but by the time I got home, I felt drained and low, and Rory and Calum were both sad for Peter.

Thursday, January 25

Papers totally crucified Peter as expected. There were loads of predictable inaccurate pieces about me being the assassin. TB said all we could get out of this now was a sense of government as normal straight away. Peter, having slept on it, was now feeling a sense of injustice and was penning a self-defence that was wrong. At Cabinet, TB opened by saying there would a political Cabinet on Tuesday, and there then followed a totally political Cabinet anyway. He dealt with the PM business fairly quickly, said it was a tragedy for Peter and serious for the government, but provided we moved on quickly, and got back onto the fundamentals, we would not sustain lasting damage. I was always struck at how quickly Cabinet business returned to normal, got over the shock of something like yesterday. I was worried that my profile was going to be up again. Sky were running a piece again and again. I spent most of the day talking to various ministers doing interviews. I felt I had not done as well this week as I should have done, that I should have picked up on Sunday with the way PM was deliberately distracted by the GB stuff and skating over the thin ice of the Hinduja story. I had too much on, and hadn't focused properly. For Peter too, NI was the main thing. If we had been thinking properly, we should have found a way to get out the facts re the Jack calls as soon as we knew. As I was running later, up on Kite Hill, Jack called to say *The Times* had asked whether he spoke to PM re the PQ [parliamentary question] and he was minded to say yes. I agreed. It sent Godric into a real stew. He feared it would end in a dreadful situation for me, but I felt we just had to get all of this out there and done with. The Sundays would be in meltdown. I did a conference call with Jack and advisers to pin down all the lines we needed for the Sundays.

Friday, January 26

Another bad night on the sleep front. The press had now moved on to Keith Vaz,[1] who was accused of all manner of things. TB disagreed with me and Jack re our approach of getting out the stuff about Jack speaking to Peter. I said it would be a disaster if it came out as a new fact. Through the day, we had a series of conversations about whether to divulge or not. He and I were in favour of disclosing both that Jack spoke to Peter pre the PQ, and that Jack's revelation to us had been what tipped it towards being a resignation issue. But Derry, TB and Richard W were all in favour of saying the inquiry would establish the facts and leave it at that. TB was more worried about Vaz, though

[1] Minister for Europe, also accused of assisting the Hinduja brothers.

again felt a lot of it was media nonsense. I chaired a handling meeting and made the mistake of mentioning the JS–PM call, and became worried it would come out not on our terms.

Peter then called on the mobile and said his ex-assistant private secretary, Emma Scott, had called him and said she was absolutely sure that it was she who spoke to O'Brien's private office, she did not recollect Peter speaking to O'Brien and therefore she vindicated his account. He had recovered himself, and was now convinced he was the victim of an injustice, not the perpetrator of a resignation-worthy mistake. He said there had been funny business at the Home Office and he intended to speak to Richard Wilson. He had been treated unfairly, his career and his life had been destroyed and he had to get his side of the story out. He said it was possible that everyone was telling what they thought to be the truth. There were funny things going on at the Home Office, but I couldn't ignore what Emma Scott was saying. He said I had a responsibility to sort it out. I said I had thousands of things to do. He said this is my life, my reputation, my future and you have to grip it because nobody else can. I said this was why I hated my life, because everyone told me only I could grip these things, but how was I to make sense of the conflicting stories, the Home Office clear there had been these calls, him denying it, not recollecting fairly recent events. I said I will try, but he had to understand why it was difficult. He said he got some-thing wrong but was it really such a bad mistake? He said he was in there seeing Tony and he hadn't even marshalled all the facts, then you come in saying you have to have a line for the wretched 11 o'clock, a bunch of total bastards, and we didn't have all the facts, hadn't examined all the facts, and on that basis I am destroyed. You have to believe me, I've been telling the truth. I said OK, I'll try but please understand the pressures I am under. He then called Derry and RW, both of whom called me to say they were worried enough to want to shut Jack up. We had various calls on it ending at 8pm with TB, Jonathan, Jack and I agreeing we should just say the Home Office handled it properly and we would now leave things to the inquiry. We got Richard to ask Hammond to make clear he did not want potential witnesses to give interviews while he was conducting the inquiry. Peter agreed to that and also said he was thinking about his future. TB had said to me PM might not stand again but when I put that to Peter, he said it was nonsense. I said he definitely needed a break from it all, but he was talking about fightback. TB felt I was being too brutal with him and that as a result PM had refused to take our advice. He had to feel we were on his side. Peter called late in the evening and was very different to earlier, calm, friendly, asking about the kids.

Saturday, January 27

TB called, having just spoken to Peter, who was now really angry, believed we had forced him out without allowing him to put a case. TB said he was genuinely worried about how far he might go, that he really felt deeply aggrieved. There were still a lot of difficult questions in this. TB felt that Peter had a case in saying we hadn't properly marshalled the facts, if it hadn't been Peter, and we lived in a different country without our mad, wretched media, Peter might still be in government. I still felt we couldn't square the different versions of events. We were having a birthday party for Audrey, and I had asked Peter to come round. To our amazement, around half nine, he and Reinaldo arrived. Shortly afterwards, the papers arrived, full of stories about me and him being at war. Rory took a very funny picture of the two of us reading papers with big headlines about us being at war. Some of his oldest friends, like Chris and Illtyd,[1] were there, but partly because he had not been so close recently, they weren't as sympathetic as they might once have been. But he was on pretty good form considering the nightmare he had been through, and was very nice to Audrey. Given how bad the Sundays were, it was not unhelpful for us to be able to put out a line saying that far from being at war, he had been here for a family birthday party. The problem was I had said he was curiously detached and had been unfocused and for the tossers of the Sunday lobby, that was enough for them to flam it up as me saying he was off his trolley. Some of them were amazed at his nerve in being there at all. They arrived just as Grace and some of her cousins were doing a dance and so had to stand and watch, while some of the other guests were muttering about them being there. But the boys were very nice to him and having a laugh, particularly once the papers arrived. He asked me why I said he was detached, I said because he was, but I shouldn't have said it to that lot. It was a surreal evening. TB was at a Holocaust memorial event and called on his way home. He too was surprised that Peter had turned up, but on balance he felt it was a good sign. We actually spoke very little about recent events and he seemed to want to talk about other things and be with other people. Reinaldo said they were just about coping but it was hard.

---

[1] Christopher Downes, theatre dresser and critic; Illtyd Harrington, former chairman of the GLC.

January '01: Peter M believes was forced out

Sunday, January 28

The broadcast media were still talking about little else and there was endless stuff about my relationship with Peter. I felt I had to do something to correct the dreadful coverage of my Sunday lobby briefing, Number 10 knifes Mandelson kind of thing. I put together a statement after an early-morning run making clear I had been misrepresented. The truth was I should not have got involved in their amateur psychology games. I called Peter and he too felt they were worse in the cold light of day than when we had first seen the papers last night. He said he was determined to rebuild his reputation. He repeated that there had been funny stuff going on at the Home Office. TB, Jonathan and I had a conference call. TB felt it was all going to move to questions about me and Peter, and they would also be piling in on Vaz. He said Peter was in a dangerous mood and would be assuming we were advising him for our purposes not his. TB said he intended to have very sharp words with Richard Wilson on the quality of factual material that came back from departments. TB was clearly beginning to doubt whether he should have gone. He said it may have been he genuinely forgot, and it may be it was O'Brien who placed the call, and a private secretary who made the enquiry.

Monday, January 29

The broadcasters were desperate to keep the story going. There was reams of AC–PM stuff. I had the cameras filming me leaving home. Philip felt Peter had just lost it in recent days, and would now move against us unless he felt we were genuinely advising him in his own interests. TB felt it remained a difficult situation, which we had to close down as best we could. We must not play the games the press want us to play.

Friday, February 2

The press were using Peter's departure to talk up GB again. TB said he would happily hand over once he felt he had done the job he had set out to do. I felt for TB at the moment. Peter gone, me under pressure to go and not performing at my best, Anji going, GB rampant. The twin pressures, one set at work, another at home, were doing my head in. Fiona felt the problem was my basic perfectionism, that if things weren't happening entirely on my terms, I wasn't happy. So at work, I kept taking on things I thought needed to be done, without regard for the knock-on effects. Kosovo was the worst example, she said, where for four months, I might as well not have been here.

Sunday, February 4

I dreamt that I had my left leg blown off in a bombing, and at the hospital where I was being treated, they didn't allow family visits. They said they only made exceptions for people who could sing like Barry White![1] Philip had spoken to Peter who was by all accounts still very much on edge and determined to prove he had been wronged.

Monday, February 5

The papers were in full cry on Vaz and most of us had a sneaking feeling it would end in tears. But with Robin C having stood up for him yesterday we had to do the same today so I was very dismissive and curt at the 11. Any positive agenda was just being submerged at the moment. Peter Hyman, who had been working for weeks on next steps, was exasperated with TB, who was even hinting he would drop Thursday's speech if it wasn't big enough. He wanted to do meritocracy as the big idea, both Bruce and I felt he was tilting at windmills, for example re modernising comprehensives, he was saying schools have to stop treating all children the same, which they don't. It was all geared to a right-wing prism so a bit depressing. PH said that while GB was powering ahead with a real values-based agenda, TB looked like he was the pragmatic manager of different day-to-day problems. Forget what we knew, said Peter, GB was doing well on the economy, had a message on society and was delivering, had taken over debt and Africa. He looked like someone with vision and drive whereas TB looked and sounded destabilised, felt isolated re Peter M and let down by the Civil Service. It was an interesting take, and at TB's office meeting, it did strike me how much he was currently focusing on short term, day to day. He knew he wasn't on form but said he would get through it.

Thursday, February 8

TB was trying to persuade me of his idea for a revamped Prime Minister's Office with three big departments. Jonathan looking after policy and what you might call government issues, Anji doing politics and people, and me in charge of communications. I felt he was trying to revamp systems according to people and in the case of two of the three, it was not clear we would be staying. That was something he was not even acknowledging now. Also, though Anji had many skills, she was seen as being of a very particular strain of Labour, namely his. He would be lucky to hold on to Sally if

[1] Gravel-voiced singer, nicknamed 'the walrus of love'.

she was meant to be a subordinate. On Hammond, TB was hoping that we would end up in a position where it was clear Peter didn't lie but he had been responsible for creating a real muddle, According to Charlie [Falconer], Richard W's basic line was that we panicked.

Monday, February 12

TB was still pushing me re his new office plans. I said I still wasn't sure I wanted to stay. 'I can't believe you said that,' he said. He said he agreed I should keep pulling back from direct contact with the press, that I was too big a figure to be doing it every day because I was seen as doing it in my own right rather than as his spokesman. He felt we needed to get a civil servant doing it while I did strategy.

Tuesday, February 13

My 'bog standard comprehensive' comment got the schools story up rather larger than I intended. TB pointed out that he had used it before and nobody batted an eyelid. It was the headline in several papers and on TV it was a debate about where the phrase bog standard came from. There was a terrible irony in me being the one who said it, as the one who was constantly defending comprehensives, and going at TB about it. I had also been the one always defending Blunkett. Andrew Adonis [TB's education policy adviser] told me DB was going to denounce the comment if asked about it, which he would be. All I had been trying to do was make a point in favour of modernised comprehensives, with the emphasis on both parts of that. But it was too colourful a phrase for them not to turn into an attack. Blunkett was very pissed off, wrote me a pained letter saying his job was difficult enough and this didn't help. I apologised to him when he came over for a meeting with TB. It was going to be very tough to get it back on the terms we intended.

Wednesday, February 14

David B said the PLP was up in arms. Party members were resigning. The cartoonists were getting in on the act, which was always a sign we were in trouble. TB was supportive, though said I had to be careful re language, and said as ever the real problem was the party over-reacting to something that with a few moments' thought could be justified. Bruce was sympathetic, said that he knew what I meant, that it was saying all comprehensive schools should be good schools, and he felt I had enough cred in the party on the issue for it to blow over fairly quickly. He said it was amazing I didn't make more mistakes given the pressures I was under at those briefings, and the problem in his view was not the phrase but the policy. TB said the problem was not the policy but the phrase, because it sounded insulting. I had a stack of meetings to get through – GB, office, TB, Group of 6, Cabinet Office lot re regional communications. But 'bog standard' was following me wherever I went. Some got it, most didn't, but the net effect was bad.

Thursday, February 15

Richard W came to see me, said TB had asked him to establish whether I was going to stay on after an election. I said it was ridiculous he had to do this. For me to stay, I had to be committed to this heart, body and soul, and at the moment I felt demotivated because I felt things would never change, because he would never change his ways and nor would I. RW said what he really values is my opinion and my judgement and we have to find a way of him getting those without me then having to execute the outcome of our discussions. Maybe if Godric was PMOS [Prime Minister's offical spokesman] I could do strategy and communications and general troubleshooting. I told him Fiona was also very unlikely to want to stay, so Tony and Cherie needed to start thinking about that too. I said we had to think about what kind of life we were going to lead long term. I was also beginning to wonder whether I was as good at the job as I used to be. I'd done it for a few years at a heavy pace, and it may have taken its toll more than others, even people close in, always saw.

I then went off down Whitehall to see Hammond, who had been given an office over the road to conduct his inquiry. He surprised me a little by going through a rough sketch of what other witnesses had said. The impression was that most did not buy Peter's story, but he was alarmed that there was no hard evidence of phone calls at the Home Office. We didn't spend that long on the weekend. He was pressing me on what happened on the Wednesday, and why TB had felt it was necessary for him to resign. I was determined not to dump too hard on Peter, but I did say I found it odd that he didn't tell me about Jack Straw's call to him the week before the PQ. He asked me if I thought he should see TB and Jonathan. I said maybe Jonathan but my own view would be against the PM having to do this. I wasn't convinced this was the place for inquiry into whether it was right or wrong he left the government. The issue was whether there had been wrongdoing re the application. I was there for over an hour, and felt it went OK, but strongly sensed it was not going to come out as well as we would like. I didn't get the impression he was too impressed by the Home Office. He was clearly baffled, as was I, that PM did not tell us everything at the outset, as it would probably have been defensible even if there had been a call. I said I could see why he said he didn't lie, but I didn't feel we got the whole story, which was a pity. He seemed to be casting around for my views on what happened and why. I stuck pretty much to what I had said at briefings, was perfectly nice about Peter, but had to convey the view that he had not been full and frank.

Friday, February 16

Later the balloon went up over US–UK attacks on Iraq outside the no-fly zone. None of us in Number 10, including TB and John Sawers, had known the exact time it was going to happen. It would clearly overshadow the spring conference. I had to scramble together a usable line. JP called from Glasgow, said he was cancelling interviews because he was bound to be asked whether and when he knew – this was like the old days when 'Prescott excluded' was the first headline they thought of. It wasn't much comfort to tell him I had been excluded too. He didn't change on this kind of thing. I stopped short of telling him TB had been unaware it was happening tonight too. We just had to deal with this. Geoff Hoon was reluctant to go up on it but I persuaded him he had to. Robin C was equally reluctant but said he would do the morning media. He said he felt the MoD did not quiz the US sufficiently on their military planning and added 'I'm not sure the US military planners really gave much thought as to whether their actions would wipe out your well-laid plans for the Labour Party's spring conference. You might wish to make them aware of your displeasure at this.' He can still make me laugh can Robin.

Saturday, February 17

The media was totally dominated by Iraq. What coverage there was for GB's speech was OK but his disciples seemed to think we had deliberately bombed Iraq as a way of minimising coverage. They really seemed to believe it too. JP was still in a rage at not knowing about the action in Iraq. The only minister who knew the truth about how we too had been in the dark was Jack S. He had been on the phone to TB and had seen the news of the air strikes on TV. 'How long is the bombing in Baghdad going on?' 'What bombing?' 'You are bombing Baghdad.' We did our best at explaining it, saying simply it had gone down the military chain of command and as there was no change of policy there had been no need for a TB–GWB call on it. But it was seat of the pants stuff and clearly someone inside the MoD had fucked up.

Their political antennae were hopeless. It was perfectly clear the Yanks were cranking this up. Mum was down staying with us for the weekend and said why do you work so hard for people who turn on you when the going gets a bit rough? Good question.

Tuesday, February 20

I went up to the flat on my own, and once we had settled down in the sitting room I told TB I was feeling tired and demotivated. I felt I had given him my best for several years and I no longer felt on top form, and I wasn't convinced I would recover it. He said he went through phases like that too, and felt election years always produced this kind of mood, particularly at the start of the year. He said the problem was a quality-of-life issue, and we all felt our quality of life was poorer than it should be. He said I was key to the election and after that we had to make sure I had less pressure, less to do with the media, became more strategic. He was sure we could make that happen. He said I was underselling myself. I may have had bad days but he felt my bad days were more use to him that a lot of people's best days. I was a politician not a pressman. I had a mind that gave him something extra and he was loath to lose it. He felt I had become too big a figure to be seeing the press all the time because they were as interested in me as they were in most of the politicians. But he promised things would change. We would be strengthened by a second mandate. He was not at all sure he wanted to fight a third election and so he would go for it on his own terms. We would have new better ministers, a new chief whip, a new chairman, Charles Clarke, who would take a lot of the weight. I said that was all fine for him but I did not believe my job would change. He said it would if I let it. CB came in and he picked up his guitar and started strumming it, which clearly irritated her. Fiona and I had a row in the car home, because she said it was clear I was going to stay. TB called as I arrived home and said 'Be nice to her.' He was taken aback at how angry she was. He said she probably felt totally boxed in and subservient, and I had become such a big thing in politics that it was difficult for her, and I had to be more sympathetic to that. But the scene was bad all round.

Wednesday, February 21

TB said in the end, there are big people and little people. The big people do big things and the little people do little things. You are a big person and this is a big project, changing the course of a country and it's better and more important than anything you will ever do.

February '01: TB not sure he wants to fight third election

Thursday, February 22

It was minus 27 degrees in Ottawa, sunny but freezing cold. I went out for a run but my asthma kicked off so I used the gym. TB was all over the news. He was up at the crack of dawn to work on the speech, which was in good shape and had a good section on the false choice for Britain between Europe and America. He had had a good time with [Jean] Chrétien, who told him the hilarious story of how Opposition leader Stockwell Day made a pledge that if 3 per cent of the population wanted a referendum on any issue, they could have it, so the Liberals got a TV station to organise a 3 per cent write-in campaign for Stockwell to change his first name to Doris. It really took off, to the point the Liberals even adopted 'Que Sera Sera' as their campaign song. There was a case of foot-and-mouth back home and the Tories were blaming us for it. This could become a real problem if it becomes another farming crisis. Chrétien heard Godric and me briefing TB about it and came over all concerned, said be very, very careful. That is the kind of issue that can quickly get out of control. He was a real wily and interesting character.

Friday, February 23

I was up before 6 to prepare TB for three US interviews. The first big meeting was with [Dick] Cheney at Blair House [official guest house]. He was very dry, quite quietly spoken. If he was a Brit, you'd say total Tory. TB did OK but Cheney was clearly very sceptical about European defence. Oddly he managed to seem relaxed while at the same time emanating tension. He was very well informed about pretty much all the issues they covered. And in a way straight warm-up man for Bush, who would later seem warm and friendly and personable by comparison. TB kicked off with a bit of US–UK, then on Iraq said he took the view that Saddam was a significant threat to the region. On the Middle East, Cheney was clear they would not rush in but get involved at the appropriate point. He was clearly sceptical about Arafat's commitment and ability. TB likewise felt we may have reached the limit with Arafat. Nor could he see a way round the Jerusalem problem. On NMD [National Missile Defense], Cheney set out their concerns on Iran, Libya, Korea, Iraq. TB said that if the capability existed to improve defence, we understood the reason for wanting to develop such a capability and that nuclear and WMD were clearly concerns.

We got driven out to the helipad for the 50-minute helicopter ride to Camp David. Bush was out to greet TB and the rest of us, all smiles, very warm and with a nervous laugh at the end of his first few sentences. We were given little bungalow-style huts, pretty plush without being over the top, mainly named after trees it seemed, with Laurel the big one in the centre where most of the work would get done. Jonathan and I were in Maple, TB in Birch, Bush in Aspen. Bush himself took care of the introductions to [Colin] Powell, Condi, Andrew Card [Chief of Staff], Ari Fleischer [press secretary], Steve Hadley [Condoleezza Rice's deputy] etc. Bush's style was very informal and relaxed, and he was clearly one of those leaders who made a point of talking to officials on the other side almost as much as to the leader. He was very solicitous of TB and you had a strong sense of both of them making an effort. On European defence, TB again set out the reasons why we were keen on this, the lessons of Bosnia, Sierra Leone and Kosovo. Again he stressed it would be NATO-friendly. Again, Bush was less subtle than Cheney in his response, said he appreciated the commitment to NATO and said the US was sick of having to do so much peacekeeping in the world. Bush said he was pleased with some of the things Putin had been saying. He said that 'we owe it to humanity' to get a system that works and the ABM Treaty[1] stops us doing it. He let Powell again do a fairly long spiel on the Middle East. Bush said they were going to take their time. TB thought Arafat was a problem and did quite an interesting read-across to the Irish situation, said the Israelis were the Unionists, the PLO were the Republicans, for the Irish read Egypt, for the Americans, read Britain. Bush wasn't as up to speed on the NI detail as Clinton, but he asked the right questions and said if we needed help, pick up a phone. He was a curious mix of cocky and self-deprecating, relaxed and hyper. He liked to see everything in very simple terms, let others set out complicated arguments and then he would try to distil them in shorter phrases. He was very clear about his own positions on the big foreign policy questions. After lunch, they went out to do some pictures and there was a dreadful moment when Bush clicked his fingers for his dog to follow him and the media were trying to make it look like Tony turned and walked towards him.

Saturday, February 24

TB clearly felt yesterday went well, that Bush pushed the boat out both in inviting him to Camp David, and also in the way we were treated. They had had a couple of fairly long conversations alone and he said he found him clear and straightforward. But also, for example

---

[1] The Anti-Ballistic Missile Treaty, of 1972, agreed between the US and USSR as part of the Strategic Arms Limitation Talks.

on Putin, willing to listen and adapt. When they first discussed Putin yesterday, he was down on him. But TB had opened his mind to a different way of looking at him, and it was interesting that Bush probed him on that this morning. On Europe, TB was also trying to show him a different way of thinking about it, that it was silly for us to keep having our views of each other negatively defined by wars. He just didn't want to let the French run European politics, which was why we had to engage e.g. on defence. TB said that on one of their little walks they talked about God and about their kids and Bush, clearly having read the potted biographies, asked TB why so many of his senior staff weren't married, and TB said he was constantly trying to persuade us. Breakfast was a kind of help yourself set-up just down from where we had dinner, and Laura was more visible, very chatty about her kids and quite prim and poised. When he came in, I was sitting in his rocking chair and he asked if I liked it. I said yes. 'It's yours.' He was clearly pumping out the personal charm but beneath it you got a real sense that if he didn't get his way he would be, to quote himself, a tough son of a bitch. We had come out fine from yesterday, having effectively traded support on NMD for GWB backing on EU defence, and the general feeling was that his words of support for us were stronger and clearer than TB's for them. He wasn't a big fan of the press, but wasn't really buying my line that they had it easy compared with us. He said the reason he thought we were right to avoid TV debates was that the press made them all about themselves. Every now and then, he or one of the others would say something that exposed just how much further to the right they were, but he was obviously on his best behaviour. Cherie and I had both felt a bit uneasy at times, but you couldn't deny he had a lot more charm and nous than the caricature. TB said he liked him, thought he was straight. As ever, there was disproportionate interest in TB's terrible sense of style, e.g. the awful pullover he wore on his walk with Bush and the dreadful creation he wore on the plane. He was hopeless at casual clothes.

Sunday, February 25

Up to Manchester with Rory. United thrashed Arsenal. I had a good session with Alex [Ferguson] afterwards and asked for his advice. He fully understood why I was pissed off but said there were two questions I had to ask. One, how many people could TB really trust? He guessed not many, and I was one of them. Two, how many jobs are there that really matter? Again, not that many, and I had one of them. If you took my main interests, it was probably the best job there was. He said you are working for the most important man in the country in one of the most important positions and if you left it, you would regret it. You do it well and your future is taken care of. The reason why people go at you all the time is because they want to stop you doing it well. He felt that Fiona could leave if she wanted to but shouldn't make me feel I had to. We chatted for half an hour or so and it helped clear my mind before we went for a drink with his boys.

Monday, February 26
Foot-and-mouth disease was getting worse and was clearly moving towards a sense of crisis. TB was anxious Hammond would over-shadow the Budget and remained of the view we wanted Peter effectively cleared of wrongdoing, even if it meant we took a bit of a hit. He did his FMD interview and both of us were having alarm bells ringing louder and louder.

Tuesday, February 27
More cases of FMD, racing cancelled and a growing sense of crisis. I told TB I had no sense of it being gripped properly and no confidence in the machinery of government. Though Nick Brown was getting quite a good press, he was beginning to look strained and I wasn't convinced MAFF [Ministry of Agriculture, Fisheries and Food] could handle it, despite all the assurances. We agreed he should do a ministerial meeting and a webcast. FMD was not only bad in reality but also now damaging the government on the level of competence.

Wednesday, February 28
FMD was massive throughout the media and if that wasn't bad enough, then came news of a train crash in Selby. It would have the effect of further demoralising everyone. People were starting to talk about whether you could have an election with FMD. I went to TB's meeting on Hammond. He said he didn't mind ending up with a bit of egg on his face providing the thing went away quickly. The problem was if Hammond said clearly that the PM–O'Brien call took place, we were in the clear but Peter would be in the stratosphere. If Hammond was unclear, Peter was in the clear and TB was left having to explain why he resigned. He also felt let down, that the Civil Service had been cavalier in saying there was a record of the call when in fact there was not.

Thursday, March 1
A combination of FMD, the rail crash and the weather meant we were in for a bad period. Cabinet was obviously dominated by FMD and

rail. Nick Brown said that any hopes of FMD being confined to one or two regions were long gone. He said the tough conditions put in place were having some effect but what was emerging was that it was well incubated before the restrictions were put in. The Chief Vet [James Scudamore] thought we might be able to announce limited movements tomorrow but even if some trade were possible it would be nowhere near normal and the movement restrictions will stay. He had been to the council of ministers and there was enormous pressure to blame Britain for exporting another disease. TB said Nick and the Chief Vet had handled things well, but I think both of us thought they were close to being overwhelmed. TB was talking about cancelling his visit to Gloucester and Wales because he wanted to stay on top of this, and also on the Budget and Hammond. The Hammond report came in. Jonathan basically said a call took place but Peter M wasn't happy with it. It was actually not that bad and probably got the balance about right. Peter had not been dishonest but had created a bit of a muddle and a call probably took place.

Friday, March 2

TB's apparent attack on the supermarkets last night was going big.[1] It had not been planned and when the supermarkets came back at us through the day he got a bit discombobulated. We learned through the day that Peter M was seeing Hammond again and did so for three hours in the afternoon. If this went wrong, we could have Peter back on the rampage soon. I spoke to him later and he sounded relaxed but he had clearly convinced himself the call with O'Brien never took place, also that I had hardened up things at various crucial points and therefore that my role as the person responsible for his downfall was not crystal clear in the report. He said Hammond was reeling from it all. I said the next few days were not going to be very nice but we had to get through them as best we could. He said the Sundays – not briefed by him – were going to say he was cleared, which wasn't very good, or at least wouldn't be when he reported that a call took place. He said he had tried to get Hammond to be more inconclusive. The supermarket thing was really running and we had to put out a line making clear we were not saying that they caused the FMD epidemic.

Saturday, March 3

I had a long chat with TB re FMD, which still did not have the feeling of being under control. Peter M called re Hammond. He was working

[1] Blair had said supermarkets had farmers in an 'armlock'.

on a note about handling, but it would be totally from his own perspective. TB clearly didn't mind taking a bit of a hit, but we had to be careful it wasn't too big a hit. TB called, felt we had to get deeper into the FMD situation.

Monday, March 5

I slept really badly and was genuinely worried both about Hammond and FMD. Peter clearly wanted to push us into presenting Hammond as a vindication, which would mean saying we took the wrong decision on his departure. TB was clearly giving him the impression that was OK. FMD was still raging and TB had had a six-page letter from Prince Charles suggesting it was all down to closed abattoirs, lack of understanding of the countryside, etc. TB said this is likely to be down to one farmer who didn't boil pigswill and should be prosecuted. Peter M sent over his suggested Q & A script on Hammond, which started 'Q: Does this exonerate Peter M? A: Yes.' You had to hand it to him. He had thus far been pretty successful spinning the whole thing to his benefit and had pretty much persuaded TB that he was victim not perpetrator. I did feel that if it had been anyone but Peter, we could have got through it. It was in many ways a perfectly sensible note but there were still a few circles we were finding it hard to square. Bruce told me he was leaving at the election, Sally that she was leaving to go to the Lords. I said I was probably going to stay but Fiona was totally against and it would be difficult.

Thursday, March 8

Peter M called first thing as I was looking out over the gardens at Hillsborough and he asked 'How exactly is my castle from which you evicted me so forcibly?' It was a joke, but he was pretty focused when we got on to what we intended to say about Hammond's report tomorrow. I said we had to give a plausible reason for his resignation and that was that people came to be misled and he had taken responsibility for that. The final report had come through and it was clear Hammond was trying to be fair to everyone. Peter had now redrafted all the lines, so many times that I didn't know if I was coming or going. There were bits in it that would cause problems for him, e.g. in relation to intelligence advice and also a suggestion that he had helped them before, and that he himself spoke to a private secretary at the Home Office. But he felt it was effectively a total vindication. Derry went through it with a legal mind and he thought we came out fine, Peter less so. Later in the day TB spoke to Peter from the sitting room upstairs at Hillsborough and when he said he intended to say it cleared Peter but that he had inadvertently caused the public to be misled, Peter became quite menacing. 'I see where you're coming from. It's all about saving your face. You say what you have to say. I'll say what I have to say.' He said the whole thing was a squalid exercise, that he had been pushed out for the sake of expedience, that I had hardened up the line and created the problem. TB listened for a while, then lost his rag, said 'Just listen to me for one second. I have bent over backwards to help you and I have to tell you I don't think you come out of it as well as you seem to think.' PM said there was confusion, that's all, and he should never have been made to leave the Cabinet. TB said whether he liked it or not, people had been misled but Peter would not accept that. TB eventually hung up but, showing Peter's intimidating manner can work, TB did take out some of the more critical parts of the draft statement. They spoke again later. Peter said the top line had to be that he had been cleared. He said you have given me no adequate explanation as to why I left the Cabinet. 'Liable to misrepresentation' is hardly a hanging offence. He said resigning was the biggest mistake of his life, that we should have waited for the inquiry but that we had pressed him. If a bit of confusion was the problem, why am I alone in being blamed?

Saturday, March 10
Papers were full of the Peter stuff but things could have been worse. And despite the media focus, I didn't feel this was going through to the public much. We now had to shut it down. Peter sent through a fax, almost comic, saying that he could not guarantee that 'friends of Peter Mandelson' may not be out causing us trouble and pointing the finger of blame at me but he would do all in his power to ensure that didn't happen.

Monday, March 12
Philip said he thought Peter had detached us from the public again. He also felt since GB became more involved in strategy, TB had slightly lost his voice and his power. There was definitely too much in the press at the moment about the inevitability of GB taking over and I didn't like this notion of GB being the big ideas powerhouse while TB took control of Ireland, foreign affairs and things that went wrong.

Wednesday, March 14
A number of councils were now urging us to call off the local elections because of FMD. Part of me felt the whole thing was a political

ploy by the Tories, but TB was anxious we did nothing that could be seen or thought to be insensitive. He called twice before I had even got out of the house and was also desperate to speak to GB, who later came over to Number 10 for a meeting about it. GB and I felt we shouldn't get drawn, should basically just shut it down. I felt that only if it was genuinely logistically impossible should we call them off. I said there was no doubt we could manage the local elections and we had to be careful not to send out a signal that life as we knew it had come to an end. Also, the implications for tourism of the message that the countryside was effectively closed were pretty grim and had not been sufficiently understood at the start of the outbreak. In Cabinet, FMD was the main focus and TB said it was serious, the number of cases growing day by day, the future unsure. Most of it was traceable back to one farmer and two dealers and it was now affecting large parts of the country. He said the farming sector was in difficulty even before this and we were going to have to provide a lot of help. Tourism was also being badly hit. He felt some of the restrictions on movement may be over the top but we had to be at the tough end of the market. He said Nick Brown was doing a terrific job in desperately difficult circumstances. Nick did a more detailed factual briefing. Blunkett was the first who pointed out the sheer emotional power that this was unleashing. He said there were industrial, employment and political problems arising from this and the government had to keep its nerve. Nick was looking tired. He was doing a statement tomorrow announcing massive slaughter of sheep. Later I asked the boys what they thought about me packing in the job. Calum seemed to think it was a good idea. Rory was appalled, said it was the best job I'd ever get and added 'You have to understand that it's good for my image at school.' Fiona was really piling on the pressure though and said she just couldn't understand why I would not give it up when she was asking me to do so. Also, as I had ended up pretty much hating the press, being driven crazy by the politicians, she didn't understand why I didn't want to leave anyway, and she was totally unconvinced his planned changes would make any difference at all.

Thursday, March 15

TB was up north and must have called half a dozen times in the morning, like a phone-in caller making random points to a radio station – about FMD, Vaz, anything that came into his head. Prince Charles was leading the news with the Prince's Trust £500,000 donation to rural charities. It's amazing he can lead the news with small change given their wealth and we can get fuck all for spending billions.

Saturday, March 17

FMD was becoming more and more of a problem and despite all the promises, it was clear MAFF didn't have a grip. We were certainly going to have to take over the presentational strategy. TB called, said he wanted a strategy to put the scientific case for the cull, and also get up the message that the countryside was not shut. He was beginning to sound a bit panicked. This was our opponents' last shot at moving us off strategic course. I did a conference call with him, Nick, David North [Blair's private secretary, agriculture, food and rural affairs] after Jim Scudamore had warned us it could go on for months and months. I felt we had to start to identify some of our opponents and their arguments as politically motivated, e.g. the Duke of Devonshire. David Handley's mob were also now getting involved. TB felt MAFF were incapable of subtlety. The key now was to do whatever it took to knock out the disease. There were some suggestions of farmers moving livestock illegally, which was likely to spread the disease. But for us to get too heavy on that risked playing into the town v country divide that our opponents were trying to grow. The pressure to suspend elections was growing. The 'countryside is open for business' message was sitting uneasily alongside the fact we had to kill hundreds of thousands of healthy animals.

Sunday, March 18

TB was working on FMD all day and did a very good note setting out a forward strategy. Nick Brown had done well early on but it was getting more and more ragged and though the NFU [National Farmers' Union] was still trying to be reasonable with us, a lot of farmers were getting more and more critical, while the public imagery was bad. Tourism was really getting hit hard now. We were going to have to take over the whole of the presentational strategy and a good deal of the operational management as well. TB wanted a subtler differentiation approach – focus relentlessly on areas where it was really bad but try to get restrictions lifted on other areas. Philip was getting very nervous about the impact of FMD on public opinion more generally.

Monday, March 19

TB did a 75-minute meeting with Nick Brown and Meacher on FMD. Everything depended on us doing everything possible to knock out the disease, to re-establish a sense of basic competence and develop a forward strategy for the countryside. He said we must have a sense by the end of the week that it's turning. We need to be promoting tourism alongside. I felt we had been far too sensitive early on to MAFF's concerns that a Number 10 takeover would spark the feeling of a crisis. If there was one thing we should have learned by now, it's that once you are in crisis mode, you need more not less centralisation. With TB clearly signalling we were taking it over, I now sensed relief rather than alarm across the table.

He was still keen on May 3 for the general election, and felt it could be possible. What was clear was that the Tories wanted to put it off.

Wednesday, March 21

We were getting badly hit on competence re FMD and also the sense that we were more interested in the election than dealing with it. As GB said, we should shut up about elections and get on top of it. Both TB and I were moving to the view that any talk of election would look like putting party before country. Hague had helped in a way because he was making the case that would allow us to postpone both local and national. We had pretty much lost confidence in MAFF now. David North and Jeremy Heywood were pretty much full-time on FMD. TB felt we could only go for May 3 if it was absolutely clear we were on top of the disease. I tried to pick his brains on whether the Queen was 100% happy at the way Prince Charles was piling in. He was unbelievably discreet though.

Friday, March 23

Major had done a letter to TB on the election timing and was now embarked on his little media operation which included the *Today* programme 8.10 slot, going on about TB's disreputable spin machine. I really wanted to go for him but wiser counsel prevailed and we ignored it. But it all added to the sense that May 3 was impossible. TB felt it would be insensitive. We had breakfast with [Giuliano] Amato [Prime Minister of Italy], which was a total waste of time.[1] I spoke to Vaz about how to do his media. TB travelled to the summit centre with Amato, thereby totally screwing up the protocol order. His mind was never far from FMD with the epidemiological report due out, which contained some pretty gruesome material likely to cause a bit of panic. TB had to be in the main meeting most of the time but was calling us in and out wanting information, and wanting to feed in ideas.

---

[1] In Stockholm, for an EU leaders' summit.

March '01: TB takes over FMD crisis

Saturday, March 24

I was hoping that yesterday was the real low point in media terms re FMD. Godric was doing a good job. GB was still pressing me to send him [Godric] to MAFF, but that missed the point. TB was up early making a series of phone calls on FMD before we had a meeting to go through the summit conclusions then breakfast with Bertie Ahern, before we left for the summit. Schroeder stole the show when somebody lobbed in a football during the photocall and he did fifteen kickups. The summit stuff was reasonably straightforward though we just about lost the energy row with the French. I did the Sundays with a couple of strong lines Godric had worked up on pigswill and 21-day movement of sheep. For the first time in days, we were pushing our own story. I spoke to Nick to try to get him to push on the same lines. I slept on the flight back to Devon while TB did a couple of boxes. We were driven to Exeter. TB met NFU leaders, businessmen and hoteliers, and said he wanted to hear for himself any changes they thought we needed to improve operational effectiveness. The NFU guys went through some of the hurdles they were facing. They had some pretty desperate stories to tell. As well as the emotional and economic trauma, the constant imagery of burning pyres was really hitting tourism now. There were constant complaints about communication, which meant rumour was too strong a currency. Again, TB was left feeling that things had not been done that should have been, there was too much red tape, that we were pulling levers but not always in a way that made things happen. Rural MPs were getting really jumpy. TB said that with the media as it was, demanding instant solutions to complex problems, we were always going to be behind the curve on an unexpected crisis as bad as this, and the Civil Service had not covered itself in glory.

Monday, March 26

I still had a sense we weren't really on top of things and that was confirmed at the 9am Cobra meeting. The MAFF people were tired and lacking in clarity. The things TB had asked for yesterday were still being promised for tomorrow. He pointed out for example that a decision on the Solway cull was taken ten days ago and we were still talking about it while the farmers were all saying get on with it. Scudamore was giving reasons why things couldn't happen rather than explaining how they could. TB later told Wilson the Civil Service had shown itself very good at setting up new committees but we kept announcing policy approaches which they could not implement. On election timing, Jack Straw was still urging May 3, TB was pretty convinced we had to go for June as a way of taking out some heat. At Cobra, we agreed to try to implement a policy of 24 hours from diagnosis to slaughter, 48 hours for contiguous farms. TB was going to have to front much more of this, and we needed to see him out there dealing with it, as well as running it from the centre.

Wednesday, March 28
If people knew had hard it was to crank our machinery into gear, they would be appalled. We saw Chris Smith, then Nick Brown and Scudamore and the argument was all pushing towards vaccination, maybe Cumbria and Devon first. Scudamore had the eyes of a man who had been shot to bits. NB was tired and deflated. I sent him a note re my assessment of the MAFF operation which he clearly copied around because soon after Robert Lowson [MAFF's director of communications] called and asked if he retained my confidence. I said yes, provided he accepted the need for more support. I was in fact losing patience with him and with Mike Granatt [head of GICS] because I kept being told things were being done but by the next meeting I was being told the same thing. Godric did the 11 and did fine considering we were so badly armed on the figures front. I had a GB meeting on pledges, manifesto format and timing, where the argument was becoming more open and public. We went over to the House, where again despite a lack of proper facts and figures TB did fine. He was so much better at the tone than Nick or anyone else. I got a call about a *Times* poll which still had us 19 ahead, so that would get people thinking May was still a possibility but TB was pretty much settled against it. I was trying to be objective, and concluded it was probably my own situation that was pushing me to May, and he was right to delay. To go for May would mean calling it in days and it just wouldn't be right. It would also be the worst possible back-drop for the launch of a campaign. I used the poll to brief the line that all he cared about was getting on top of the disease, and that re local elections, what mattered was whether logistically they were impossible because of all the restrictions on movement.

Thursday, March 29
Philip had done some groups in Shropshire last night and said people were appalled at the idea we could be considering a general election with FMD as bad as it was. Then tonight he did some groups in South Norwood, who said go for it, so there was clearly a rural/urban divide on it. But TB had pretty much decided. He had a number of NFU meetings today re vaccination, and later with a group of scien-

tists. The NFU were clearly reluctant on vaccination. David North had been clear from the start we should be going that way, but they were leaning more to vaccination plus slaughter, which improved compensation. Ben Gill [NFU president] said he wanted to stay plugged in to all our discussions re vaccination. Cabinet was all FMD. GB gave a little lecture on the potential enormity of the public spending implications as the bill was running to the billions. Nick Brown did a presentation and then TB went on even longer. He had become an 'expert' and went into so much detail some of them started to glaze over. There was no mention of election dates, apart from a couple of jokes at the end. After Cabinet, Jeremy H and I discussed with TB whether David King [chief scientific adviser], who TB had taken to, and was affectionately calling 'Dr Strangelove', should do a media briefing showing various possible projections. There was at least a sense we were getting a grip of the government machine, and media-wise Princess Margaret's [Queen's younger sister] illness was taking over as their main focus. GB was still being difficult, said to me after Cabinet 'At some point, Cabinet government will have to be reim-posed,' and TB will have to extricate himself from being in charge of this. I said what are you talking about? – this is one of the biggest crises we have faced, with enormous implications, MAFF have been hopeless, and the idea TB should not be taking this over is absurd.

Monday, April 2
TB went off on another FMD visit, this time to Essex. He was finding these visits useful not just because it showed him leading from the front, but because every time he was being told things that he could get fixed. But so many of them were things that should have been sorted without us being involved, basic red tape stuff. He said it was the third time he had felt no confidence in the MAFF operation.

Tuesday, April 3
Hague stole the overnight initiative with a call for the army to take over the fight against FMD from MAFF. It was not as daft as it sounded, and indeed TB and I had been talking about the MoD getting far more involved. But Hague overcooked it, some of the military already engaged, e.g. Brigadier Birtwistle, who was emerging as very media-friendly, attacked the idea and it looked like another piece of Hague opportunism. The figures remained a problem and I now had Bill Bush and Catherine Rimmer [Number 10 research team] working pretty much full-time just trying to bring some sense to the statistical chaos we had. The latest figures given at Cobra suggested only 31

per cent of farms were culled within 24 hours, and that did not necessarily mean 31 per cent of animals. If the Tories got hold of that we
were in real trouble. And why on earth, people would ask, were we
doing all this, wiping out large parts of our tourism market, to protect
such a small export market? Added to which, there were signs that
some farmers were now deliberately spreading it to get full compensation, now rising to enormous sums. Of course if we went out on
the front foot on that, watch the outcry backlash against us.

Thursday, April 5
At Cabinet, they went through FMD in some detail, and there was
definitely a feeling of it slowly coming under control. TB did a strong
no-complacency message, and was back at them about making big-
picture speeches. TB asked me to go through to his room at the end
and we had yet another discussion re the office, this time re Anji. I
said he had to think through whether a new political links job was
her strength. I said both Anji and I were not exactly job-title people.
Was this just about trying to keep Anji? Yes it was, he said. The longer
I am in this job, he said, the more I realise how few people you can
trust totally. You are one of them, and she is one of them. She is also
someone who brings a dimension others don't. I said well, I think it
is better you keep her, and if that means a better salary and a bigger
job, give it to her, but does it have to mean structures that will upset
others, including his missus? I said Fiona might agree to me staying
if we could genuinely say there were ways of cutting the workload
and the pressure but I did not think what he was proposing would
do that. Au contraire. Re his own future, he said he didn't know how
long he wanted to stay in the job, but he felt GB was imagining he
would go halfway through the second term. The look on his face
made it clear GB had no chance of that. TB seemed genuinely unsure
re a third election, but I suspected he would go for it if we had a
decent majority second time around. Jack Straw came to see me, really
hacked off at what he believed was Blunkett's deliberate strategy to
talk himself up as next Home Secretary. He said was it true, and I
said it's not fair to ask what TB may or may not have said to me re
reshuffles post-election. Jack said if he was to be moved, he would
be interested in DETR [Department for Environment, Transport and
the Regions], if it became a proper, big department not there purely
to keep JP happy. He felt David B was wrong to be doing what he
was doing and hoped I could get him back in check. The reshuffle
was going to be tough. Chris Smith had actually been improving, and
it was not easy to spot obvious sackings.

Tuesday, April 10

The idea that some of the farmers were responsible for spreading FMD was out there, and we were not copping it, as the trading standards people were making clear their disquiet. But this was always on a knife edge, partly because emotions were at play. We had a meeting on the manifesto. TB was happy it was getting there but felt we needed a phrase in the area of aspiration, success, ambition. Bruce was arguing that we should not be rewriting the Sermon on the Mount, in other words we knew what we wanted Labour governments to do, and we should shout it out. TB saw Jack S to discuss asylum. TB felt the Home Office had not gripped the politics of this, and wanted a proper political strategy worked up.

Wednesday, April 11

Devon NFU were leading the news with a call of support for farmers ignoring movement restrictions on welfare grounds. TB called, said he was getting irritated at how we got all the blame for this, when it was negligence that started it, and when some of the farmers were being totally unreasonable now. We had a visit planned for Devon and on the plane down, he said he was worried re demos. We went to the MAFF offices, where the reception was not quite as friendly as last time. These guys were under pressure but they seemed more on top of things than before. I had dinner at the hotel with TB and Anji, in his room. He was piling the pressure on both of us now. Neither of us really believed the stuff about it becoming easier in the second term, but he said surely we have to give it a try, surely we don't want to leave when there remains so much to do, loaded on top with flattery galore re how he couldn't have done it without us etc. After Anji left, TB said you have to understand how important it is that both of you stay. I cannot lose the people I really trust. He said he didn't care whether I dealt with the press or not, but he wanted me for politics and judgement, and he wanted Anji because she gave him an angle nobody else did, which was the upper end of the middle-class market, and they were important to New Labour.

Saturday, April 14

As ever, MAFF seemed intent on strangling good ideas, eg RSPCA getting more involved in the animal welfare cases, which would at least show we understood the concerns and the emotions here. We were led to believe yesterday Nick B was visiting farmers in Cumbria today but then it emerged he hadn't gone. Also, there was no grip to the vaccination debate, which was going on without any real explanation for people of the pros and cons, and was being talked of as a 'why did nobody think of that before?' miracle cure.

Wednesday, April 18
We were still being hit by a sense of dithering on the vaccination issue. The line we had agreed was about as well as we could do, but it underlined weakness in the face of a massive crisis. The *Mail* splashed on petrol prices after Shell put up petrol by 1p. The BBC led on it at lunchtime, another classic case of the BBC mindset that if it led the *Mail* it must be news, and I called [Richard] Sambrook [director of BBC News] to complain. He was in some ways easier to deal with than [Tony] Hall, but they all believed they would combust and die if they ever admitted the BBC got something wrong.

Thursday, April 19
FMD was looking really ragged again, not just because of vaccination dither, but also because of some of the operational side seeming less under control. Also, we had got so used to the sight of these pyres on TV – I wish to God they didn't show them 24 hours a day though – that we maybe underestimated the growing impact they were having. There was something a bit medieval about the whole scene at the moment.

Wednesday, April 25
The big unexpected issue of the day was a calf called Phoenix which should have been culled five days ago, had not been, and now the family were trying to save it. It was one of those classic ultimately silly stories that would grip the media's imagination and be a screaming pain in the ass for us. MAFF were saying it had to die. After a lot of toing and froing we got them to agree it could be part of the softened contiguous cull policy. In other words, the policy was not being changed to reprieve it, but a reprieve would be the effect of a change of policy happening anyway. I suspect many members of the public felt it was a sentimental load of bollocks given how many thousands had already gone up in flames, but it became that thing most loved by our wretched media – a symbol – so we had to play along. TB said GB went on yet again about my interview on *Newsnight* on the day John Smith died, convinced to this day that it was part of some heinous plot to deprive him of his rightful inheritance.

Thursday, April 26

Phoenix was a bit of a fiasco, because of course having spoiled their 'save Phoenix' campaigns, now they wanted to say the contiguous cull policy had been changed because of one calf in the news, and the whole spin thing was back up in lights. It was balls but it was just one of those media frenzies that came along from time to time, and we were just going to have to get through it. Chris Smith complained re all the stuff in the media speculating what would happen to them all post-election. Nick B complained at the stuff against him. TB pointed out there was nothing we could do to stop this, other than make clear we never ever talked about reshuffles, which was true. He stopped saying the truth – the media tended to pick on the ones they could see for themselves were not that good. Nick's protest was made in such violent terms that TB called him over with me at the end and said 'I hope you don't think these stories are coming from here?' 'I didn't say that.' 'No, but that is what anyone listening will have taken from what you said.' 'Could they really be so cynical as to believe that is what I was saying?' He was very offside at the moment, then muttered something about 'Who appointed them in the first place?' and stalked off. I could see GB clocking the whole exchange from the other side of the room. It was a bad meeting. I didn't like the feeling of it at all. Next thing we heard MAFF were briefing that the first Nick knew of Phoenix being saved was when he heard it on the news.

Friday, April 27

I travelled down to Chequers with David Miliband. Traffic dire. Once there, a discussion on TB's own campaign. He stressed three areas where he had to up his game – the vision and the big argument; basic explanation of the government narrative; personal reconnection. He was worried that there would be protests of one sort or another dogging every step. He was building up the nerves and tension in himself deliberately as the campaign neared. We had another discussion about whether to kick things off with a speech burying Thatcherism, but he was worried it would be misrepresented à la forces of Conservatism, and get the campaign off on the wrong foot. Peter M made clear he didn't think we were where we needed to be in terms of story development, and that was certainly right. We went over various big-ticket possibilities – sentencing review, a specific crime-fighting department, deregulation, sport, a new department of the working age, a separate pensions department, a reshaped education department, local taxes for education, reform of LEAs. But the shape of a campaign was there.

What we really needed now was the off. TB said he reckoned our first year of the second term could be the toughest yet because we would be making reforms that would take on doctors, teachers, police, 'the mother of all battles with the judges on rules of evidence, sentencing, weekend courts, changes to bail'. There would be two education bills, big changes to the NHS, big changes on criminal justice. Three crime bills, assets recovery, police reform in the second session, Civil Service reform, Incapacity Benefit reform, on and on he went. 'Then you do the euro,' I said. He laughed, but went on to say he would also be vulnerable internally to an argument that he 'wasn't really Labour', because internally opponents would say he was destroying the public service ethos when the goal was to modernise it for today's world. On the one hand, we were desperate to get going. On the other, as TB unhelpfully reminded me once or twice, the campaign would be ghastly and tough and we would be working flat out round the clock to keep the show on the road. We agreed we should use six setpiece speeches as the policy spine of his campaign, that the key driving themes and dividing lines should be around the economy, investment, the civic society, engagement on the world stage, optimism. We should start with one big speech in Sedgefield laying out those themes, and making it clear this will be a New Labour campaign and a New Labour second term. It had to be about defining clearly the next phase of New Labour. On the economy, the focus had to be productivity, skills, developing regional economies. On investment, money for modernisation. On the civic society, rights and responsibilities. On the world stage, leadership so that we could reform the institutions. He felt that though we recovered OK, Robin's chicken tikka masala speech[1] was a 'catastrophic intervention' because it seemed to want to dump our history. He felt Thatcherism was part of the context for the campaign but not its story. The 60s gave us a period of social democracy. Thatcherism was a reaction. New Labour is neither old left nor new right but builds on the best of both. We are a party of aspiration and compassion.

Saturday, April 28
TB went to the Rugby League Cup final at Twickenham. He was booed a little bit, and was alarmed. I said it was inevitable. There were bound to be at least some Tories there and in any event, he was no longer a new kid on the block, he was a high-profile controver-

---

[1] In a speech to the Social Market Foundation, Cook used the example of chicken tikka masala to illustrate how Britain absorbs and adapts external influences.

sial figure and all in all it was still worth doing. He called me two or three times after the Burnley–Sheffield United game so he was clearly a bit concerned about it all. I said there was definitely a sullen mood out there but that was because we had been through a fairly long hard time. It would come back on our terms once the campaign proper was under way and we got legitimacy for political attack again. The general view on FMD was settling around the notion that we had handled it badly at the start, and never really recovered from that though we made a lot of improvements once we took it over and TB led from the front. We were never going to win this one, but we had done not a bad job coming from behind.

Sunday, April 29

I spoke to Tom Kelly re the idea of him and Godric as joint PMOS and he seemed pretty keen. TB called after the Mandela concert. He said it was impossible to be with Mandela without feeling that you were an inferior political being, because of the aura that surrounded him. TB was also coming to terms with the fact that there were people on the right and on the left who actually hated him – on the right because he was a successful Labour politician likely to win again; and on the left because he didn't do all the things they believed Labour leaders should do, even if it meant losing ad infinitum. I said you are not confident at the moment, are you? He said you read me too well, but no, I'm not. It was the thought of the next few weeks that was getting him down a bit. He said he went through these phases. He felt confident on the arguments, and confident he could do anything required of him, but he sometimes got fazed when so much of the focus would fall on him personally, and on his personality, and he just needed to steel himself. 'I'll be fine. I have to go down to come up again, but I will bounce back, don't worry.' He said he needed a lot of support at the moment.

Monday, April 30

TB's office meeting was really poor. After Chequers I thought he was getting it together but the conversation yesterday indicated a bad period to come. I stayed back and said shit, that was bad. Don't worry, he said, I'll get there. I was worried enough to go and see CB later. She said he was pretty down over the weekend.

Wednesday, May 2

Bush on NMD was going to be the main thing for the day, and TB wanted us to stay neutral leaning to positive but by the end of the day it was up big time because I answered 'yes' to the question whether we supported it in principle. I hated fucking up, and this was another fuck-up, and another reason why it was time to give up these wretched fucking briefings. Godric thought I was beating myself up too much, that it was one of those situations where fence-sitting was hard because too far the other way and we would have had screaming headlines about Blair condemning Bush. But I wasn't happy with how I handled it. We were continuing to make good preparations for the FMD press conference.

Monday, May 7

Peter H picked me up and we went in to see TB. He had been sent various notes and pieces of advice about his opening words for the campaign, and was sitting at the table in the corner of the sitting room, penning a few thoughts of his own. He said he was still a bit low on confidence but was psyching himself up and just wanted the thing to get under way. PH and I both argued that we needed a real sense of challenge out there, that there were big challenges for us and for the country and there had to be a sense of joint mission to meet them. We needed to be hitting the no-complacency buttons as hard as ever and we needed to be laying out the kind of storylines we wanted to drive through the campaign. It was actually fairly straightforward but of the three of us, only PH had been on form on the words front in the last week or so. We had agreed that there should be a tone of humility – as in the Thank You campaign, and in the admission a lot remained undone – but TB warned this must not become an admission we had done nothing, which is how our opponents would present it. The foundations we had laid were strong. Now we had to build upon them. He wanted to reform the public sector with the same kind of zeal Thatcher sought to reform the private sector, and show up the difference in values in so doing. I put together a briefing note that was about 'schools and hospitals first', plus a big reform message for the second term. We had a desperate need to excite and enthuse given the walls of cynicism which now surrounded so much of the coverage, and I think it was that that was getting to him a bit, because so much of it would fall to him.

Tuesday, May 8

I went up to the flat when I got in, where TB was going through his words for the campaign launch at the school. It was a bit long and repetitive in parts so we went through it trying to hone it a bit, and both of us were worried whether a school audience would happily sit through a fairly long speech, even one that was kicking off the election. TB said he still wasn't properly psyched. Maybe once we were out on the road he would get into it. We had a big media turnout in the street, and the BBC had a helicopter to track him to the Palace and back, but somehow managed to lose him. Despite that the full hype machine was in full swing, with the TV and radio guys outside babbling away the whole time. TB got back after seeing the Queen, and now we were set for the off. Blunkett was waiting in the hall. TB helped him into the car and off we set. They got a fantastic reception from the kids as we arrived. I sensed the head teacher was a bit nervous and maybe it was only now the scale of what was going on struck her, with all the crews and hacks and the satellite trucks and the rest of it. She asked me if TB was as nervous as she was. I wanted a bit of time with TB to go through a marked copy of the speech and to try to psych him up a bit, but I was buttonholed by one of the governors, who was the first ear-bending bore of the campaign. It was a good school though and the kids were brilliant considering they had to sit through it all, and content-wise I think we had the right message. I was a bit worried by how much of a God element there was to the whole thing, the backdrop, the choir singing a religious song, a hymn at the end, and it was a bit odd that he was doing a big number on the importance of voting to a group of people who couldn't vote. There was a bit of a scrum outside and the media were pretty cynical about the whole event, but I thought it was just about OK. Mind you, how we kept this cynical bunch of wankers interested for four weeks of this was a question I didn't like to think about too often.

Wednesday, May 9

I went to see TB before he left for his meeting with the PLP over at the House. He got a great reception before he even started, did a big thanks to the PLP, said unity and discipline had been good and now we had to work together at this important time for party and country. He went through the big arguments, the policy areas to focus on, the dividing lines, the cynicism 'backdoor' strategy that would be run against us, but in all the main policy areas, we were strong. Nothing was more important than stability v boom and bust. He felt the Tories were vulnerable above all on tax and spend because they were promising to tax less while spending more and we had to pick that apart day by day. He felt re delivery that we did not make enough of progress on equality and social division, and how the Tories tried to stop measures like the new deal, the minimum wage, the winter allowance and so on. We left for St Albans, where we would be formally unveiling the new pledge card. I went through it all with TB in the car to the train station. He was still lacking in basic confidence and was a bit edgy when people just came up to us. He said he would get there but he was struggling to find his rhythm.

Thursday, May 10

As expected the media gave PMQs to Hague. Philip said on the way in it showed how out of touch the media were. They played the entire exchanges to the focus groups last night and TB was the clear winner in every one of them. But there was a lack of passion and drive at the moment and we had to find it soon. We got onto the campaign bus, which was dire. We had asked for the best, most modern, hi-tech and all that stuff and it was just another campaign bus with no legroom, drinks spilling, the same as '97. It had a pretty negative effect on both of us and the only response was to turn it into a running joke. The papers were laid out on the table at the back and TB made the mistake of reading them. He said he hadn't realised Hague was getting such an easy ride. But Philip was adamant the public were seeing through it. He [TB] still felt we were weak on storylines for the next four weeks, and he was in one sense right. But we had the lines basically sorted and now we need to inject the creativity and the passion. A lot of that was down to him. I said he was giving the impression of someone who saw the election campaign as a bit of an inconvenience getting in the way of being Prime Minister. When was campaigning ever easy? I said he was underestimating the strength of signals he sent out to others – like at the morning meeting today where he didn't show balls or leadership, and we were going to need loads of both. He had to get less buttoned up. The aim was to generate serious and meaningful dialogue, not just fight day to day around the headlines. TB was not himself though, lacking confidence, tired-looking, still a bit nervy and it was draining having to try to pump him up the whole time, using sometimes humour, sometimes sympathy, sometimes probably being a bit brutal.

Monday, May 14

The FT had a big story about a Shadow Cabinet minister saying they would go for £20bn tax cuts and David Hill and I really wanted to go for it and drive it up the agenda, define 'Haguenomics' as spend more, tax less, sums don't add up. But GB didn't want to move off the business story and the New Deal. I was working well with all of his people, but with GB things seemed to have moved backwards.

May '01: General Election campaign/TB anxious

Philip said I had to spend more time in Millbank because anything that required risk was just being strangled down there. So as TB headed for Inverness, Mark B and I flew south. By the time we landed, the Tories had had their press conference, which was seemingly a shambles, nine minutes long and with no answers on tax. Also, the £20bn story was taking off and GB agreed to put something on it into his speech in Swindon, while I got a bit on 'Haguenomics' into TB's words. Oliver Letwin [Shadow Chief Secretary to the Treasury] was widely thought to be the Shadow Cabinet member responsible for £20bn, so we commissioned 'Wanted' posters. Letwin was a bit of a liability, and the more we could keep the argument on matters economic, the better. A bit of humour would also help set up the Economic Disaster 2 campaign. I felt we were motoring and I was enjoying going for the Tories again. I met GB when he came back and he was still looking around for policy stories that were not really what we needed right now. Letwin had given us an open goal and we had to hammer into it – what did £20bn mean in terms of schools and hospital cuts? TB called in, said the mood up north was good and he felt strong with the arguments. I complained to Carolyn Quinn [BBC journalist] who was obsessed with the idea of everything being stage-managed, and whose bulletin report was really shallow. The travelling press were complaining re lack of access so TB went to see them and Hilary [Coffman] seemed to think it worked. But the truth was the campaign media entourage was becoming outdated because the main guys could follow it all on TV anyway. We had an asylum meeting, where Margaret McD was very forcible, said we really had to understand how dangerous this was. There was even a case for making it one of the main headlines out of the launch. TB's concern was that if we were not careful, it would become the main thing. Asylum still had the potential to give the Tories traction and a way back in. It was all part of his own way of getting himself mentally in the right place for what was to come.

Tuesday, May 15

The Tory tax shambles was OK, but it hadn't quite reached meltdown proportions and the media were keen to move on. The Wanted posters on Letwin had worked and now we got Adrian McMenamin [press officer] dressed up as Sherlock Holmes with a couple of Great Danes with 'Looking for Letwin' covers on them. Even if these things didn't break through to the public – and I think this one could, depending on how the Tories handle it – sometimes these things are worth doing just for internal morale anyway. The mood was a lot better now we were laying into the Tories a bit as well as doing the positive policy stuff. We had to bring everything back to the economy at the moment. I went over to see GB in his office over by the far wall, and he was banging away at his computer. He had a pile of papers to the right and on the top had written 75 pence, and below it, in large black letters, 'Who will silence Mandelson?' It was clear Peter was at it again in the *Telegraph* today. I pointed to his 'silence' writing and tried to make a joke of it, but he was having none of it, went on a great tirade, said we were letting him destroy the campaign, undermine him, be ill-disciplined, on and on he went and eventually I lost it, said PM was nothing to do with me and I did not like the implications that I could be held responsible one way or the other for what he was or was not up to. 'Well, it has to stop,' he said. 'Telling ME it has to stop suggests that in some way I might be responsible and I fucking resent that, given I am the one Peter blames for him not being in the fucking government.' I said we all had jobs to do and we should get on and do them instead of wallowing in this crap. Let Peter do whatever he is doing. We should have better things to do than worry about it and if he ever suggests I am encouraging him or helping him to undermine the campaign, that will be the last time we work together. I could feel the gorge rising and I was suddenly conscious that I was jabbing my finger at him and thought it would be better to leave. Also the raised voices had been heard and there were people looking in. But I was really angry. I went back to my desk, really steamed up. Bob Shrum came over, having heard it all, and said he backed what I had said, I was right to be angry. He said GB thought Peter was trying to destabilise the campaign. If that was true, the only thing we could do was work together, so I must not let one row get in the way of me and Gordon working together. I said I wouldn't, but I was sick of coming in to see GB and his people obsessing over some piece of rubbish in this paper or that when what we should be doing is getting above it. I said I was fed up being expected to sort out all these feuds and personality clashes when it was time we just pulled together. I calmed down pretty quickly and had loads to do, and was hoping GB would not go further into his shell.

Wednesday, May 16
We left for Euston and waited for GB and Blunkett on the train. There were good crowds, loads of hacks and the mood was fine. TB was a bit jumpy and nervy, GB growling a lot less since our altercation

May '01: General Election campaign/GB–AC row

yesterday. The bus from the station in Birmingham seemed to take an age but we used it to go over tough questions and he was pretty fired up by the time we got there. We briefed the Cabinet, most of whom would not be required to speak until they went on their own visits and media rounds. Clare had a little whinge about being 'over-directed'. God, does she turn my stomach. The venue had been done out well and it looked stylish and professional. TB did well, both in terms of the opening remarks and the Q & A. He got the tone and mood right, and it felt confident and strong. There was the usual whining from the media about there not being much new, as if the launch of a party's manifesto was not a big event in itself. Also I got into a bit of a muddle afterwards on the exact role of the private sector in the public services and I felt I may have hit the private sector buttons too hard, and the press would go off and wind up everyone they could find. TB went off ahead on a visit as I did the media rounds and we were due to link up again at the QE2 hospital. I got there ahead of him and was taken up to a holding room, where I lay down on a sideboard, and tried to steal a nap.

He came in about an hour later, looking really shaken. I asked what was wrong, and he just shook his head. There were hospital staff around so he didn't want to talk about it, or complain, but it seems he was confronted on arrival by a woman complaining about her partner's treatment.[1] As the cops and the staff followed in behind him, I could see from the looks on their faces too that it was not good. She had laid into him big style, and while Anji et al were trying to move him on, he just had to stand there and take it. I caught up with some of the hacks but of course they hadn't seen it as they were arriving at the same time as he did. But then the TV boys told me what had happened and said they were 'fantastic pictures' – for them, that is, not us. I asked TB how bad it was – bad, he said. Bad enough to blow out the manifesto launch? Definitely, he said. All that work, and we will be lucky if most people see or read a bloody word of it, because one woman has a pop in front of the cameras. It also meant we had to put people on checking out all the facts. The tragedy was this was one of the best hospitals in the country but nobody was going to know that now. The visit went on in a rather surreal atmosphere. I did my best to talk things down but when I finally saw the exchanges I realised we had no chance. Sharon Storer had entered the political lexicon in an instant.

[1] Sharon Storer harangued Blair, complaining that there was no bed in the bone marrow unit for her partner.

We tried to keep his spirits up and by the time we got to Watford, we were able to laugh about it, but things then got worse, when we heard Jack Straw had been slow handclapped at the Police Federation. Then even worse when we got a phone call saying JP had thumped a guy in Wales who whacked an egg into him. TB was about to pre-record BBC *Question Time* with David Dimbleby and we had to decide whether to tell him before he went on. Hilary and I were worried Dimbleby would get a message about it and ask him cold. But he had enough on his plate, and he was in the zone so we left him to it. He did a good job, though there was too much sleaze and too much Dimbleby. I was in and out of the Green Room where we were watching it, talking to JP, who was now holed up down in Wales. It had all been caught on camera and I spoke to Charlie F and Derry, who were waiting to see the pictures. I felt instinctively there would be a lot of support for JP, but also that he should say he wished he hadn't responded like that. He was not up for it one bit, said the guy was a total twat and 'Anyway, you never apologised when you hit Michael White.' I pointed out that I was then a *Mirror* hack. He is the Deputy Prime Minister, but he wasn't having it. He said it was bloody ridiculous that we had to take all this shit from people just because we were politicians and he would not be apologising. I admired him for it, but I knew TB would want something to defuse things. When he came out from the studio, he was pleased with how it had gone, but I quickly brought him down to earth, said the good news was Sharon Storer was no longer leading the news; the bad news was that JP had thumped someone and that had taken over. He did one of his gobsmacked looks, and as I filled him in on every last detail, we ended up laughing about it. What else could you do? But there would be calls on him to sack him and we had to deal with that pretty quickly. No way, he said, no way. He felt there were people out there trying to recreate a sense of the fuel protest, and unless JP had provoked the whole thing, he was not even going to contemplate action against him. He felt there would be a lot of sympathy for him if he was just belted out of the blue with an egg. Also Hague had had a spot of bother in Wolverhampton and there may be a case for making a general defence of politicians. The manifesto was disappearing down a plug-hole. Carol Linforth [Labour official] texted me, 'Spirits up'.

Thursday, May 17
JP was big in the papers and massive on the broadcasts. Sky were playing the punch and the scrum afterwards on a continuous loop, again and again and again. Boulton was working himself into a total

'Prescott must go' lather. In all the vox pops, men seemed to be fine, women less so. It was the same internally. Having watched the incident, TB and I both felt instinctively that there would be more sympathy than anger, and we should back him to the hilt, but Fiona, Sally and Anji all thought it was pretty bad, and damaging, and I sensed a feeling of mild panic when I went into Millbank. JP was adamant he would not apologise but was happy for us to say the whole incident was regrettable, but he was also clear if he was interviewed himself he would say he had no idea what it was, and his first instinct was that it was more serious than an egg, and he was actually frightened by what was going on. We discussed it with TB who felt he should just make light of it, and in the end he used the line 'John's John' pretty effectively. He said he would not have done it himself, but then defended JP's character. There was a fair bit of interest in TB's Manchester speech in the evening, and we worked up a direct appeal to One Nation Tories to come over as a new way of getting up Letwin's £20bn, which I briefed in advance after we got over from Halifax. We were in the Lowry hotel, which was fantastic, and I had time for a run in the gym before we left. GB and I were speaking a lot on the phone and the row had cleared the air and got us working together better again. We had a good celeb turnout for the rally – Alex F, Mick Hucknall, Sir John Mills [actor] – 'the oldest switcher in town'. It was a good night. I got driven back with Mark Bennett to be at Millbank for the morning.

Monday, May 21

TB, GB and I had quite a good discussion on the dynamic of the campaign. GB felt we underestimated the problems we were getting through tax. Alistair Darling had real problems at the launch of the shadow Budget re NICs [National Insurance contributions]. GB felt it would dominate tomorrow as well. He seemed a bit down but did at least say, and I was glad to hear it, that there were bound to be some days when the media would let the Tories take the news with a specific attack on this or that tax – we just had to maintain a bigger argument about the economy.

Tuesday, May 22

The Tories were still going on NICs – three days of it now – and people could sense we were worried. GB's argument was that we may have to lift the NI ceiling to raise necessary funding for the NHS, but TB was adamant we had to stick to the line that we did not write a parliament's worth of Budgets in advance. TB did the press conference on health and was on good form, confident and strong and there was no question that left him fazed. We had a problem in that the broadcasters' lead story was Margaret McD's letter of complaint re collusion between the media and protesters. There was some evidence of it but of course the media couldn't resist making the story about themselves, and it was one of those that had little or no relevance to the public's attempts to follow the campaign. TB called me just after 6, and said we had to shut it down. I prepared a statement for the morning meeting and we rang round to try to kill it, having agreed with Margaret there had to be a bit of a climbdown. TB came to the meeting but he tended to sit back and let GB chair and GB and me do most of the talking, coming in when he felt we were missing a point or taking too long to decide. GB said there were three competing stories – the one the media wanted, i.e. Margaret's letter; the one the Tories wanted, NICs; and the one we wanted – Letwin. I pointed out that we were trying to get up health today. I suppose on one level it was good that he wanted to focus all the time on tax and the economy, but it was an odd thing to say to a roomful of people when we were about to have TB fronting a press conference on health. I felt we just had to keep going on schools and hospitals as the best way of emphasising the dividing line on investment and values, with the economy underpinning all the arguments. Then he said he thought we should do Europe tomorrow rather than education, which was ridiculous. We argued about it on and off all day. After the press conference, TB had to go back to Number 10 to see the Crown Prince of Japan. He felt we lacked a really good public attack dog against the Tories that the press would be interested in and take seriously. He even at one point suggested I do it, which would have been a pretty odd development during the middle of the campaign. We had a hospital visit, then *JY Prog* [Jimmy Young, radio presenter], loads on NICs. As we left, he called GB and said he felt we had a real problem on this. It was being taken as read that we were going to raise NICs or impose new so-called stealth taxes, or even a 50p top rate. He felt we had to develop a better body language on this. TB called after I'd gone to bed. We were both moving to the idea that we had to get the focus more on him and more out on the road, and that probably meant letting rip sometime soon.

Wednesday, May 23

We had another school visit in Dorset and arrived a bit early and had a bit of time to kill. We stopped at a little café on a stunning spot overlooking the sea. It was warm, sunny, with a nice breeze and although the people in the café were gobsmacked to see TB, the entourage and a stack of security arrive on the scene, it was as near as we'd had to a normal moment for ages. We walked around for a bit, and he said 'Don't you sometimes wish we just had a normal life like the people who live over there?' Sometimes, I said, but the moment passes quite quickly. 'It's a weird life though, isn't it? I mean if you stand back a bit and analyse how we live during these campaigns, and then the things we have to do, it's all a bit abnormal.' It was nice to have a little break, and a decent cup of tea which the cops brought over from the café, and which we were able to drink without spilling half of it over papers and floor as was generally the case on the bus. He was tired and a bit dispirited, still feeling there was something not quite right with the campaign. It wasn't exactly off track but nor was it brilliant.

Thursday, May 24

TB came to the meetings this morning, but let GB chair them so that he didn't feel in any way undermined, but it was odd to have him there, sometimes sitting at the back while we sorted out the day ahead. I could tell he was worried. Then later the GB lot went demented when Douglas Alexander was being interviewed by Andrew Neil [broadcaster and journalist] and was asked about TB taking over the campaign. In any normal, rational world, nobody would bat an eyelid and according to David Hill in the Gallery nobody did. But GB's lot were convinced this was going to be the story of the day. Douglas and Ed Miliband asked me to call Marr and make clear GB's role was unchanged. It revealed their defensiveness once more. Marr wasn't even planning to touch upon it, said it was Andrew Neil making mischief. But it put them in a strop for the whole day. There was also something a bit weird about any suggestion that the leader of the party wasn't actually in overall charge anyway. The press conference was OK if a bit flat but he did one particularly good answer to Mike White which ought to carry.

Friday, May 25

TB flew up to Scotland and we had the usual last-minute pre-speech nightmares. This was the worst attack of lastminutitis. Bruce, about as technophobic as I am, was up with TB in Scotland. Pat [McFadden] was down with me. We had the telly on in the background with a blank screen and the Sky reporter saying TB would be appearing any second to make the speech. I was at the time talking to TB on one phone while dictating some changes to Bruce who was taking them down in longhand, then taking them to Tom Dibble [intern] to type up, while simultaneously Pat was re-editing the press release version. Tony was losing it with Bruce and Tom and shouting 'Where's the fucking speech?' You have to hand it to him, he came on a couple of minutes later, calm itself, and delivered it perfectly well. But we really had to change the way we did these speeches.

Wednesday, May 30

The feeling was beginning to develop of a potential Tory meltdown, with people coming out critical of their strategy banging on so much about the euro. Hague had done an interview in *The Times* retreating on the idea this was the last chance to save the pound and they felt pretty close to meltdown. I set off for Euston with TB, we finished the speech on the train, pointing out the tougher sentences for attacks on nurses and teachers, and exclusion orders for parents who were abusive at school. It was a strong speech. There were a few demonstrators around yelling abuse but it all went fine. The speech was strong. TB said afterwards you could always tell when an audience was listening, and this one was. We got a helicopter to Milton Keynes. I did a couple of conference calls to plan tomorrow. We were also planning the rebranding of all our materials. I also felt we needed to see more of Milburn and Blunkett, with TB, to hammer 'schools and hospitals first'. We had a couple of hours' downtime at the hotel to prepare for *Question Time*. TB was pretty nervous. We were trying to keep his sprits up by exaggerating how ghastly the audience would be, suggesting they had been placing ads in local papers: 'Do you hate Tony Blair?' I really got him going at one point when I said Sharon Storer would be in the front row with six other women complaining about the NHS. He did well though, showing once more that he was always better when he forced himself to be nervous in advance. I had a stack of pager messages immediately afterwards from people saying they thought it was his best yet. The message that was really getting through now was investment v cuts. We flew back to Battersea. I felt we were moving ahead now, at the right time. Now we needed to raise another gear. The woman at *Question Time* had said she thought we could get a bigger majority. TB thought we would be lucky to get more than 70. I still felt it could be small or huge, but I was moving towards the latter. Today had gone well. Good events. Good speech. Good interviews. Tories in trouble, TB on form.

Saturday, June 2

Between them Millbank and the North West region had put together a good press conference at Salford Community Centre with two excellent local heads. I worked on TB words then had breakfast with him. He was in twittering mood again. I called David Frost to take him through the £20bn cuts arguments pre his interview with Hague. TB spoke to him, said he felt the Tories were close to losing it. Blunkett came over. More discussion on apathy. The head teachers were excellent at the press conference. The questions to TB were instructive – lots on landslide, and what did he think of the Tories' strategy? We were going to have to work hard not to let this run ahead of itself. Shipley, then Leeds, two good working-class venues. We had to do a lot more of these, really connect with the heartland base, working-class estates. I was struck by how well Hilary Benn [Labour MP for Leeds Central] seemed to go down with people. TB got a good reception and again was finding his voice. Cherie was on form, doing really well with the kids. I kipped on the plane back and got home. Good day, really straightforward, real sense of things moving our way now. The papers arrived. Only the *Mail* and the *Telegraph* were backing the Tories. The *Observer* was good. The red tops were OK though there was a lot of sniffiness around. It was going to be hard to drive up the vote.

Sunday, June 3

I had a bit of a cold and was worried I was losing my voice. Philip felt we still had a problem with working-class women, and in some areas tuition fees was really hurting us. The more they saw of TB, the better. He had to go flat out now. The Tories had briefed their latest poster, 'Time to burst Blair's bubble'. It was the latest evidence they were effectively admitting defeat, suggesting the best they could do was bring him down to size. Andrew Lansley said on Radio 5 that I had an obsessive desire to destroy the Conservative Party.

Tuesday, June 5

In early for what would be the last morning meeting of the campaign. Alan Milburn said to me there ought to be an inquest into the campaign. We had been saved because the Tories and Hague were so useless, because TB had been OK on the road, and because we just about gripped the centre. But we were kidding ourselves if we thought it was a good campaign. He was right. We had done a lot of planning, and where we had planned, e.g. advertising, visits, speeches, we had done better. But storyline development not great. Purpose and unity poor, and at times it really had felt like pushing stones up hills. According to Philip, TB was definitely breaking through at the right time. We drove to St Pancras, reworked the speech on the train, press conference went fine, not that many up from London, but so what, the feeling of momentum was there and Hague was in trouble. On to Rugby, bit of a scene with a few UKIP headbangers, Burton, another little speech, then Yardley the main speech of the day on the end of Thatcherism. It was strong. We had a little incident with the photographers, who went 'on strike' because we couldn't fit them on the helicopters tomorrow. They looked a pathetic bunch, downing tools, standing around with their cameras at their feet. I left Anji to sort them out. We had a bit of downtime in the hotel. He was starting to think about the reshuffle. Philip called to say that our message that it was the people not the pollsters and the media who decided this election was beginning to get through and hurt the Tories so we had to keep going with it. Off to Derby and a rally with Margaret B, Heather Small [singer] providing a bit of music and glamour, though she had to sing 'Proud' twice because of a problem with the sound system. She struck me as really quiet and shy when I first met her but when the sound failed, she had quite a temper on her. I called Victor Blank [chairman of Trinity Mirror plc] to say I really thought the *Mirror* coverage had been a joke, just not serious. At least the *Sun* tried to be serious in some of its coverage, then we were pissed off that they splashed on a story about one of the *Hollyoaks* stars we used in the PEB not voting. Just one full day to go. We were all getting tired, but just one day and it was over. Staying in a not nice hotel, overlooking a not nice nightclub.

Wednesday, June 6

Last day, packed. I was up early to go in and meet him and prepare for *GMTV*. He was a bit subdued and down, as was I. He did well on *GMTV*, pushing the basic message, vote for schools and hospitals. Through the day we worked up the line that not voting was dishonouring the dead. He did fine on *Election Call*. We came out of BBC Nottingham, and it was interesting the reaction on the building site nearby, very warm and positive. Then to the press conference with GB and Margaret B. I drafted some strong words with Peter H and the overall effect was pretty good. GB was resisting Margaret chairing the press conference, which was irritating. TB was on great form. I decided to write, and circulate, a long note suggesting we emphasise the team effort, TB's leadership, GB's strategy, JP's motivational work, professionalism at Millbank, etc. We were flown down to Wales, TB and I passing notes backwards and forwards on possible words for the final message stuff. We got to Colwyn Bay where he did a good little stump speech. We visited a school and were there for what seemed like an age because the helicopter had gone off to refuel. TB was shown round the school and it became almost comic, an eve-of-poll visit which went on so long that the entirety of the media had left. But they were at least saying there was a sense of urgency, no complacency, a mood of quiet determination. Up to Dumfries, raining a bit. The feel was pretty good, Labour posters everywhere, though there were a couple of women outside with placards which said 'Blair, you are a cunt', and 'Blair, wanker'. He could now do these stump speeches on autopilot. There was an ICM poll narrowing at the right time, helping us with the no-complacency message. Then down to Castleford, on the way writing a letter to Piers Morgan about his pathetic coverage, and to Charles Moore thanking him for the honour of calling me the most pointlessly combative person in human history. There was an astonishing moment of TB selfishness as we arrived in the rain, Jess Tyrell [events team] standing there holding a brolly – TB just took it out of her hands and walked on, leaving her to get wet. TB went live into the *Six o'clock News*, which was OK but probably not worth doing because I much prefer coverage of him out with people rather than talking to yet another interviewer. Then back on the bus and off to Sedgefield, a real sense of last-lap time. Philip called, said we definitely broke through today, but turnout was still the big problem. We stayed in the bar for a bit. TB wanted to go home. Philip believed the worst-case scenario was a majority of 75, best was 200, but it was all about turnout. TB and I both felt tired, and a bit depressed. I had the same feeling I had in 1997 after the results came through, so I was hoping that this time I was getting the depression out of the way early and would actually enjoy it tomorrow.

Thursday, June 7

I didn't sleep well, woke up feeling really tired and thinking how crazy it was that we helter-skelter round the country for weeks, work round the clock, then have one day – the election – to start getting your mind in shape for what follows if and when we win. I went for a run, found a nice hilly area, and loved the feeling of being out on my own, with the wind gusting every now and then, and feeling I had done all I could and though it had not been perfect, we were definitely going to win. Myrobella was the usual mild chaos as TB, CB got ready to go over and vote. It wasn't as exciting as 1997, but there was still that special feeling you get knowing that it is now all down to millions of different people in all sorts of weird and wonderful places making up their own minds for their own reasons. Jonathan had come up and he, Bruce, Sally and I were chatting away. It was clear Richard Wilson was up to a few tricks – e.g. wanting to reverse the Order in Council that allowed Jonathan and me to instruct civil servants. Jonathan and I were now down as 'advisers' on his list. We would have to sort that.

TB came back at 1 after a tour of some of the polling stations and we got going on the Cabinet. JP arrived by helicopter, which TB thought a bit OTT, and they had a session to go over some of the changes, though JP was still pressing re his own responsibilities. TB told me earlier we would all see a difference in his modus operandi second term, that he would be more confident because a second mandate is in some ways more powerful than the first, plus he had learned, and had experience of how to work the system. He said he alone would decide the Cabinet and unless there were genuine reasons for any objections from JP and GB, he would press ahead. Things were slightly complicated by the message that Estelle Morris may lose her seat. Robin C would not be pleased to be moved, but TB felt there had to be some change in the top jobs. He was keen on Blunkett for the Home Office, was worried about whether Estelle had the depth and the toughness but thought it worth giving her a go at Education, Byers taking on Transport and the Regions, Pat Hewitt Trade and Industry, Tessa to Culture, Media and Sport, Charles Clarke as party chairman, another one who may not like it. He said he wanted to put the right people in the right jobs, regardless of all the usual personality stuff. That being said, he was keen for me to get the briefing re JP in the right place for JP. He spoke to GB and afterwards said it was classic – not only did he want Alistair Darling to DTI, and Andrew Smith to Work and Pensions, but he felt Douglas [Alexander] should go straight into Cabinet at Scotland. Bruce said it would be the worst thing that ever happened to him. He would be eaten alive. GB was also pushing for Michael Wills to be minister for employment. Bruce in hysterics. Bruce was also warning loudly that Nick Brown would be a real problem on the backbenches.

The day was peppered with calls giving us information on how things were going, a lot of it anecdotal, but the general picture seemed to be good result but turnout low. The Libs seemed to be doing better than we thought, which sparked a bit more fretting about Estelle. Losing her would be a blow. I was pressing for Dick Caborn [Minister of State, Dept. for Transport, Local Govt. and the Regions] for sport. TB was keen on promoting Pat H, felt she had the brain but was worried about how good she was in the House. Bruce, though not necessarily her biggest fan, thought she'd be fine. The sackings as ever would be the hardest thing, particularly if he put Derry straight out. He was also thinking about moving out Andrew Smith, to create more space, but the Derry situation was the one clearly worrying him. We were sitting in the front room/office and TB was in a low, small armchair, wearing a rugby shirt, tracksuit bottoms and a pair of ridiculous-looking slippers with a badge of Australia on them. After he got his list more or less settled, we went for a little stroll round the garden, which felt a bit like a prison exercise, just walking round in circles and chatting. He kept emphasising it was all going to be different second term, that he was older, wiser, more experienced, would deal with the crap better, would be more focused on the things that he needed to focus on. He went off for a kip. This was the eerie period – nothing to do but wait, lots of people calling assuming you knew things that they didn't, but the reality is we knew no more than anyone, we just had instinct, rumour and anecdote to go on. The Estelle rumour was fuelling a lot of calls. I had a long chat with Bruce, who is such a lovely bloke and always so supportive of me, telling me TB could not have done it without me, and I had to stay with him to the end. Around 8, TB wanted another run through the Cabinet. Re JP, we were talking about a new Deputy Prime Minister's Office from where he oversaw the Cabinet Office. TB was OK on him having more Cabinet committees, but not QFL [future legislation], or civil contingencies. But this had to be seen as a Heseltine role, not Mo. He would be TB's rep on Kyoto, chair the committee on the regions and so on. At one point, as the jigsaw pieces slid around, even RC was talked of as a possible leaver, though he accepted that was over-brutal. I wondered whether he might walk anyway if he felt Leader of the House was being over-demoted, but TB, Sal and Bruce all thought he would stay. Re Derry, TB felt he should stay for another year or so. Margaret B was set for the new Rural Affairs job, with the Environment. He was troubled by Bruce saying people worried about Pat H in the House. I tried to raise the issue of Number 10 operations but he wasn't really wanting to know. Then afterwards he said let's go outside for a minute, and asked me to run through all the things I thought should be changed, in my and others' roles. I had done a note setting out how I thought I could use my time to be more strategic, but it meant other people picking up the slack in different places. Then he said he intended to have one more go at persuading Anji to stay.

Come 10 o'clock, and both BBC and ITN were predicting another landslide. For a few minutes, there was a genuinely happy atmosphere in there. Cherie and the kids, Leo and Olwen, Bill and Katy [TB's brother and sister-in-law], Cherie's sister, Carole, they were all laughing and having a good time, and for a while I felt pretty up about things. But before long we were back into the office and between us we were talking things down and starting to worry about other things. There was something odd about this inability just to enjoy the moment of winning, him because he was straight off focusing on the next thing that could go wrong, me because of some general dourness defect that kicked in when everyone else was enjoying themselves. Weird. Then the media were straight onto the story being the low turnout and we had to get over the line that we suffered because of the sense of it being a foregone conclusion the whole way through. We were due to leave for the count around 12. We watched the results coming in in the same room as in 1997. Peter M's acceptance speech – 'I'm a fighter not a quitter' – was a bit gut-wrenching. Bloody hell, TB said, what's he up to here? Estelle won, which gave everyone a lift. Newbury was held by the Libs after another strong rumour to the contrary. By and large it was all going to plan. TB's speech after the Sedgefield result was fine, maybe a bit too long, then we piled into the cars and set off for Trimdon, where he did a more emotional version of the same speech. The crowd was terrific, and he was up for it now, and people finally felt a bit of emotional release. TB was in some ways now a lot more emotional than '97, felt this was more his mandate in a way. We got back to Myrobella and he and Cherie had a glass of champagne. He was totally wired now, really buzzing and up and full of what we had to do tomorrow. Cherie was very nice to me, said thanks for everything, and TB said 'It is an amazing thing we have done. In a relatively short period of time, we have totally taken the centre ground.' I said we seemed to have destroyed the Tories in the process. They looked absolutely shell-shocked tonight. TB and I went through to the dining room, and he said once more that he wanted to do all he could to keep the old team together. He was going to have another go at Anji, and he wanted me to persuade Fiona that I should stay and so should she.

We set off for the airport but were hanging around for ages before taking off. The mood was pretty good, though obviously lacked the excitement of four years ago. It was incredible really, that we looked to be on course for a majority as big as the first one, and it was almost taken for granted. On the flight down, he and I went down the plane for a bit of a chat with some of the hacks. They seemed happy enough to be with the winning side. I was feeling a bit flat again, and the feeling only lifted when we arrived at Millbank, and I caught sight of Rory and Georgia [Gould, daughter of Philip Gould and Gail Rebuck] on the ropeline as we jumped out of the cars. 'Lifted' was playing, it was daylight now, and I was really pleased he had waited there. He was with Neil [Kinnock], who gave him a big hug, and when I got over there, both Rory and Georgia said well done, and for the first time I felt really moved, and enjoyed the last hour or so. TB did the same little speech as up north, thanks, now the future, etc, and then it was just people milling around and chatting and swapping stories. I started to worry about not having any sleep and having to be back in Number 10 by the morning. I collected Rory, shared a car with Philip and Georgia and got home for a couple of hours' sleep. In some ways, I had enjoyed the night more than in 1997, but I still didn't feel the kind of exhilaration others seemed to. It was also because I knew there would be no let-up, and in all sorts of ways the future was unclear. Maybe it was just my nature.

BOOK THREE

The War on Terror

June 2001–August 2003

Who's Who
June 2001–August 2003

The Cabinet

Tony Blair	Prime Minister (TB)
John Prescott	Deputy Prime Minister (JP, John P)
Gordon Brown	Chancellor of the Exchequer (GB)
Jack Straw	Foreign Secretary (JS, Jack S)
David Blunkett	Home Secretary (DB)
Robin Cook	Leader of the Commons 2001–03 (RC, Robin C)
Stephen Byers	Transport, Local Government and Regions 2001–02 (SB, Steve)
Margaret Beckett	Environment, Food and Rural Affairs (MB, Margaret B)
Charles Clarke	Labour Party Chair 2001–02, Education from 2002
Alan Milburn	Health 2001–03
Estelle Morris	Education 2001–02
Patricia Hewitt	Trade and Industry, Minister for Women (Pat H)
Alistair Darling	Work and Pensions 2001–02, Transport from 2002 and Scotland from 2003 (AD)
Tessa Jowell	Culture, Media and Sport
Geoff Hoon	Defence
Lord (Gareth) Williams	Leader of the House of Lords 2001–03
Lord (Derry) Irvine	Lord Chancellor 2001–03
Hilary Armstrong	Chief Whip
Andrew Smith	Chief Secretary to the Treasury 2001–02, Work and Pensions from 2002
Clare Short	International Development 2001–03

John Reid	Northern Ireland 2001–02, Labour Party Chair 2002–03, Leader of the Commons 2003, Health 2003–05
Helen Liddell	Scotland 2001–03
Paul Murphy	Wales 2001–02, Northern Ireland from 2002

Additional Cabinet Changes 2002–03

Peter Hain	Wales from 2002, Leader of the Commons from 2003
Baroness (Valerie) Amos	International Development 2003, Leader of the House of Lords from 2003
Hilary Benn	International Development from 2003
Lord (Charlie) Falconer	Lord Chancellor from 2003

Downing Street

Andrew Adonis	Head of Policy Unit
Mark Bennett	AC's researcher
Alison Blackshaw	AC's personal assistant
Cherie Blair	Wife of TB (CB)
David Bradshaw	Special Adviser Strategic Communications Unit
Alastair Campbell	Chief Press Secretary and Prime Minister's Official Spokesman
Magi Cleaver	Press officer, overseas visits
Hilary Coffman	Special Adviser, Press Office
Kate Garvey	Diary secretary
Jeremy Heywood	Principal Private Secretary
Robert Hill	Political secretary
Anji Hunter	Presentation and planning
Peter Hyman	Strategist and speechwriter
Tom Kelly	Prime Minister's spokesman
Sir David Manning	Chief Foreign Policy Adviser
Pat McFadden	Deputy Chief of Staff
Liz Lloyd	Policy adviser
Fiona Millar	AC's partner, head of events and visits team
Sally Morgan	Director of Political and Government Relations

Jonathan Powell	Chief of Staff
Terry Rayner	Driver
Catherine Rimmer	Research and Information Unit
Matthew Rycroft	Private secretary, Foreign Affairs
Godric Smith	Prime Minister's spokesman
Clare Sumner	Private secretary, Parliamentary Affairs
Sir Andrew Turnbull	Cabinet Secretary from 2002
Simon Virley	Private secretary
Anna Wechsberg	Private secretary
Sir Richard Wilson	Cabinet Secretary

And Others

Kofi Annan	UN Secretary General
Yasser Arafat	Palestinian President
Mohamed el-Baradei	Director-General, International Atomic Energy Adviser
Dan Bartlett	GWB's Communications Adviser
Hans Blix	Chief UN weapons inspector
Admiral Sir Michael Boyce	Chief of the Defence Staff 2001–03
George W Bush	US President (GWB)
Carole Caplin	Friend and adviser to CB
Andrew Card	GWB's Chief of Staff
Dick Cheney	US Vice President
Jacques Chirac	French President
Catherine Colonna	Chirac's press secretary
Gavyn Davies	Goldman Sachs economist, later BBC chairman
Sir Richard Dearlove ('C')	Head of the UK Secret Intelligence Service (MI6)
Iain Duncan Smith	Leader of the Opposition
Greg Dyke	BBC Director General
Alex Ferguson	Manager, Manchester United, friend of AC
Ari Fleischer	GWB's Press Secretary
General Tommy Franks	Commander-in-Chief, US Central Command
David Frost	Broadcaster
Andrew Gilligan	Reporter for the BBC's *Today* programme
Philip Gould	Political pollster and strategist, adviser to TB (Philip, PG)
Sir Jeremy Greenstock	British Ambassador to the UN

Lord (Bruce) Grocott	Chief Whip, House of Lords (Bruce G)
Karen Hughes	GWB's Communications Adviser
Saddam Hussein	President of Iraq (SH)
Lord Hutton	Law Lord
Hamid Karzai	Chairman of the Afghan Transitional Administration from December 2001
Dr David Kelly	Biological weapons expert, Ministry of Defence
Sir Stephen Lander	Director General of the Security Service (MI5)
Osama bin Laden	Militant Islamist, founder of al-Qaeda (OBL)
Dame Eliza Manningham-Buller	Lander's successor
Rupert Murdoch	Chairman, News Corporation
General Pervez Musharraf	President of Pakistan from 2001
Sir David Omand	UK Secretary and Intelligence Co-ordinator
Colin Powell	GWB's Secretary of State
Vladimir Putin	President of Russia
Condoleezza Rice	GWB's National Security Adviser (Condi)
Karl Rove	Senior Adviser to GWB
Donald Rumsfeld	GWB's Defense Secretary
Richard Sambrook	Director of BBC news
John Scarlett	Chairman, UK Joint Intelligence Committee
Ariel Sharon	Prime Minister of Israel
Jonathan Sumption QC	AC's, and later Government, lawyer at Hutton Inquiry
Margaret Thatcher	Former prime minister

Friday, June 8

There were hundreds of media in the street shouting at me as I walked in. The Number 10 staff seemed genuinely pleased to see us back. I had a quick walk round the press office to say hello to everyone, then up to the flat to see TB and work out what we needed to do for the day. The start of the election felt a long time ago, it was also odd how quickly it was back to a 'business as usual' feel. He was due to leave at 10.50. Again he and I were working on finding the right words. Jeremy [Heywood] said that Richard W was bracing himself for a real drive for change, and I don't think he meant the changes in the Civil Service that TB had been talking about, but trying to retrench, push back on some of the changes we had made. Jonathan was pretty sure Richard wanted to clip our and my wings in particular. TB went off to see The Queen. We waited for him to come back, got the kids out there in the street, and he did his words. The line that the result was a mandate for investment and reform, and an instruction to deliver carried pretty well.

We had one final go on the reshuffle. Robin and Nick Brown were likely to be the stumbling blocks. He then got into it, Jack S happy, David B happy, Margaret B absolutely thrilled. She was wearing a green trouser suit and I said when she arrived 'You've come in the right colour,' which seemed to perplex her. When she came out, she was positively beaming, which made something of a mockery of the worries we had had that she might see it as demotion from Leader of the House. She popped round after she had seen TB, and said she was stunned, that there was always a part of her that thought TB didn't see her in one of the big jobs, but she saw this as a huge job and was thrilled. Robin's reaction, unsurprisingly, was different. There was no way of pretending it wasn't a demotion to Leader of the House, and I think he had been shocked when TB put it to him. He came round, sat down at the table in my office and said he really thought he deserved better given the support he had given TB in difficult times. He feared he would come out of this badly in the media and he needed a little time to think whether it might not be better going to the backbenches. I said I wasn't going to pretend it would be hard for him not to take something of a hit, but we would be stressing two things in any briefing – his reputation as a great House of Commons man, and also the benefit to the government as a whole that he would be back at the centre of domestic politics, close to the heart of everything. He was very subdued. He went back to the Foreign Office, doubtless phoned a few friends, spoke to Gaynor and after a while said he would do it. After all the toing and froing, Nick Brown was finally Minister for Work below Alistair [Darling] as Secretary of State. John Spellar, who had really impressed TB at the Cobra meetings on FMD, was to be Minister for Transport, not attending Cabinet. The main media focus was Jack, Robin and the new women. Patricia [Hewitt], Tessa [Jowell] and Estelle [Morris] all popped round for a little chat, all seemingly very happy. Charles Clarke, party chairman, clearly thought he was going to get something different. He didn't seem overwhelmed, but TB felt it was the right appointment.

Meanwhile Fiona had discovered that Anji was staying, there was still confusion over who was doing what, she had been to see CB and told her she was leaving. We were straight back into Peyton fucking Place. It meant after working round the clock for a few weeks, going the last few days without sleep, I was now straight back on the treadmill and in circumstances where, because I was staying, Fiona and I were barely speaking, and when we did it was to argue. She said that what made me good for him – driven and single-track and obsessive – is what made it difficult for her. I felt between a rock and a hard place, that there were consequences to staying, but there were consequences to leaving too. And I felt for TB, who had just won again, and was having to deal with this too.

Tuesday, June 12
I felt drained after the last couple of days trying to resolve Fiona's situation. She still wasn't happy, far from it, but Cherie had persuaded her to stay and give it a go and TB later saw her to try to repair some of the damage. Maybe working together had never been the right thing, but at the moment I was more worried about the alternative. TB was starting to recover some of his strategic grip. He felt we had to keep the Liberals to our left on some issues and hope that the Tories

June '01: Fiona and Campbell barely speaking

try to come towards the centre on Europe but right on other issues. He felt Portillo was probably the best bet for us as Hague's successor.[1]

Thursday, June 14

I woke up tired and that feeling stayed pretty much all day. TB said we need to get the difficult things done at the beginning. He said in the first term we came close to disaster in the third session because of lack of preparation of some of the bills. We won't get away with it again and we have to learn the lessons from that. He did a little spiel at the end, said the two questions for the Parliament were could the Tories revive themselves, and will we get through radical change without the Labour Party reverting to type?

Friday, June 15

I felt like I had some kind of post-natal depression. We'd won the election but every day since it had felt like swimming through shit.

Monday, June 18

TB asked if I was depressed and I said I was. The last few days had got me down with all the rows going on. Also, if you think of it in horse-racing terms, we had trained ourselves to the peak for the big race, and now all I felt was flatness, so I felt ready for the knacker's yard. He said my problem was having to make a transition from full-on, round the clock, day to day, but I had to do it. You're in the paddock, too keen to get back on the track. But he agreed I would need new direction to keep me fully motivated. We discussed Peter M and whether he could appoint him to the Belgian presidency's Future of Europe group under Guy Verhofstadt which would include some pretty big hitters. TB was in no doubt Peter was the best person for the job but accepted there were serious presentational and political downsides. It would be seen as Peter back with a licence to meddle in all things European. It would give him platforms galore that he would use. GB would go mental. The media would go mental, and it would unleash a wave of speculation about him coming back to government.

Wednesday, June 20

Peter M's name had appeared in a Belgian paper in relation to the Verhofstadt group. TB was still minded to do it, though Jack S and

---

[1] Hague had announced his resignation as party leader the day after the election.

GB were both now warning him against. We moved over to the office at the Commons, where I said we had to have an answer. We agreed it should be Peter, Robin, [Douglas] Hurd or Jack Cunningham. Chris Smith was ruled out. TB felt strongly Peter would be the best but he accepted it would be very difficult. He finally agreed to go for Robin. We got Jack S in, who said he could live with Robin. Then TB was about to see Robin when word came from the Belgians that they did not want us to appoint a government minister. TB saw Peter, and told him he wouldn't be appointing him. Peter asked if he was acceptable to the Belgians. TB said he was but it was his decision and he was not going to appoint him. Peter really lost it and stormed out. He said we had done nothing for him. I asked TB if long term he wanted him back, and he said he didn't mind but it would become impossible unless he cures himself of this egocentric view that makes him think he's a law unto himself.

Tuesday, June 26

Gavyn Davies[1] came in to see TB for a discussion on the euro. TB was clear that whilst the economic conditions were key, he did favour going in early, that there was a lot to be gained politically through driving structural change in Europe, and more to be gained through changes at the ECB if we went in early. Gavyn said we shouldn't go in any higher than exchange rate 2.80 and that we could not direct policy towards that because it would mean higher inflation, taxes going up and at the wrong time, so we had to wait for the dollar to fall and the euro to rise and that was in the lap of the gods. He, Stephen Wall and I all said in different ways there was no point going for a referendum if we thought we would lose, TB said this was an issue where he felt he had a duty to recommend entry if he thought it was the right thing to do. He was dismissive and contemptuous of the pro-euros who wanted to have the fight now when it was clear we weren't ready to get in the ring. But he passionately believed if we went in, we would change the European Union quickly and for the better. There was a lot we could do out, but a lot more we could do in. The Franco-German motor was weakening, enlargement would unleash enormous change on that front and Schroeder was keen to work with us. Instinctively he felt everyone apart from the French wanted us in. If we wait four to five years we will not be able to extract as good

---

[1] Goldman Sachs economist, unofficial economic policy adviser to Blair, and husband of Sue Nye, adviser to Gordon Brown.

a deal and we will have less influence. So while there is a political case for delaying, the national interest may be best served by joining early if the economic conditions are favourable. A lot of this was about the British character. There were two sides to it relevant here. Part of the British character was conservative, but just as powerful a part was adventurous. I said there was a third, bloody-minded and anti-establishment, and that might combine with the conservative part to resist change advocated by government and business. He felt that once more and more British people got used to dealing with real euro notes and coins, perceptions would change. There was an outside possibility of a referendum in June 2003, even autumn 2002. It would all depend on the economics but we were likely to have to take a decision early next year on whether to stoke up the temperature. He really believed we could turn the debate. Gavyn said he thought it better to be 80% certain in five years than 60% certain in two years.

Wednesday, June 27

A lot of focus on TB's dinner with union leaders. TB was unaware it had been building as a story and was so angered by it, the impression of them coming in to lay down the law, that he suggested calling it off. I said do not be so mad. He did need to see them, and even if they did a bit of grandstanding, so what. Edmonds particularly annoyed him because he felt he deliberately and constantly misrepresented what we were trying to do, especially in his use of the word privatisation. I felt that if people thought greater use of the private sector represented the totality of our reforms, it was not a great position and we had to get a better exposition. He was pissed off at the way quite a few of the PLP seemed to think we could go back to the old ways of win followed by ill discipline. He came back from his address to the PLP a bit troubled, said there was not a good mood and if you added together the discontented and the disappointed, those who always disagreed with us and those who saw no future personally for themselves, it was quite a number.

Thursday, June 28

The PLP meeting had really spooked him. He called me up to the flat after my morning meeting and said he felt a real sullen mood. He said he felt some of them reverting to type. They had by and large behaved because they knew we had to win a second term, but now they felt that argument didn't apply. At Cabinet, TB actually looked worried and was sending out very unconfident vibes. Patricia H did a really good job explaining how she had turned round her local party organisation, rebuilding her local party. Jack and Robin both made interesting contributions but GB just sat there. Milburn came to see me afterwards. He said he was worried that we were sounding too managerial, non-political, non-ideological. We had to give a sense not just that we care about public services, but we do care who runs them and why. He felt the PLP was really sullen and difficult. Before TB left for Northern Ireland, I went to see him and told him I thought he had looked weak and nervous and they had left with bad vibes out of that. He said Anji had already told him the same. There had been a funny moment during Cabinet when Jack was briefing about Macedonia[1] and had said the president was good but weak, and the Prime Minister bad but strong, and Robin chipped in 'There must be a third way.' TB said he knew he had been off form, but he was not unreasonably pissed off that three weeks after delivering another massive majority, he was surrounded by so much anger and sullenness.

Wednesday, July 4

TB said this was going to be a rocky phase and we just had to ride it. 'This is politics. It happens. Name me a prime minister who has not had to deal with this to greater or lesser degrees. You will never change it,' he said. He had picked up on my mood, said he thought the problem was I had gone from obsessive management of day to day to now being a bit disengaged, almost deciding no communication was better than one that got attacked. TB reckoned it was 'not impossible I will be gone in a couple of years – it depends how much change they will take'.

Thursday, July 5

As soon as I walked into Number 10, just after 7, the security guy said the PM wanted to see me in the flat. He'd got a bit of a mauling in the papers re PMQs and I thought it might be for a bit of a moan. But the thing worrying him was the line in *The Times* saying he would spend 'half' of his summer holiday in the UK, when what we had actually said was 'part'. I wound him up about the planned itinerary – five days in Butlins at Ayr, five days in a Falmouth farmhouse B & B, five days in a caravan touring Norfolk. On matters

---

[1] There had been fighting in the former Yugoslav republic between government troops and ethnic Albanian rebels demanding greater constitutional rights.

July '01: TB – I may be gone in two years

general, he said he was worried that I was confusing downspin – the right thing – with non-communication – the wrong thing. Spin is not the same as communication, he said. Clinton had told him 'Never stop communicating,' and 'He was right.' I said I was not going to motor again till after a holiday. He wasn't happy, felt we were not getting over the big-picture messages about what the government was all about.

Friday, July 6
Worked at home. TB called, joking re my three-day week, and whether I was getting enough time to fit my work around my sporting commitments.

Sunday, July 8
Nice chat with Tessa, David [Mills] and Jessie [their daughter]. She was adamant I should leave, said I'd done my bit, made my mark, taken loads of shit from everyone else, and I should get a life of my own. She and [her brother] Matthew are great kids, and a credit to them.

Monday, July 9
Bradford riots were dominating the news, and also David B appeared to be softening the line on cannabis/criminalisation. I called him. He said he was trying not to sound out of touch whilst at the same time not really opening up the debate. I sensed that DB was starting to inhale his own propaganda at the moment, and thinking he could push things more than was maybe reasonable or realistic. There was definitely a new tone to the way he spoke now, saw himself as a big player. TB asked me if I thought the cannabis line was a problem. I did.

Tuesday, July 10
Tory leadership ballot. Portillo 49, IDS [Iain Duncan Smith] 39, Clarke 36, David Davis and Michael Ancram 21. Chaos. Absolute chaos. Just about the best result for us. I went for an appointment re my asthma, and he wanted me to go for X-rays.

Wednesday, July 11
TB being tied up with NI, Robin was doing PMQs, and he really was beyond parody today. He came in carrying a clean suit and shirt in a suit carrier. I suggested he sit in TB's chair at the Cabinet table, and his chest puffed out and he did a little chirrup of delight. I had sent

him over a note about the Tories/*Big Brother* and he was up for using some of the lines. As we worked out a few different options and lines of attack, he was off wandering up and down the room again, loving it. I suggested we get someone in to take notes of what he was saying. A secretary came up from the Garden Room and tried to make sense of what he was reciting as he marched around with his head up, his chest out and his belly breathing in and out. He was fine on all the policy stuff but spent ages worrying about how to handle the Tory leadership. He asked me what sort of state JP got into at this stage. 'Oh far worse,' I said. 'What about Tony?' 'Cool as a cucumber.' Humph. I went over to the House with Robin and he was on much better form. A Rory Bremner researcher would have an immediate multiple orgasm if he walked in and saw Robin right now. He was so puffed up I thought he might explode. But he did well. He had a real presence in the House and he got into his stride quickly. I had TB in hysterics later describing the scene. It was interesting how even though he and JP had been in the House for years, they found the step up to PMQs such a big thing. TB said it took him ages before he was basically confident about it.

Thursday, July 12

We were entering a phase of the commentariat being very down on us. I got a lift in with Philip who said the latest groups were pretty grumpy, with people getting more and more impatient for change. TB called me in first thing for what turned out to be a bit of a heart-to-heart. We kicked off on the Tories, and he felt they were heading for the worst of all worlds. He was sure they wouldn't go for Portillo or Clarke. The problem was a fundamentally divided party, with the right still in basic command. He then said re me, that politics was a mix of intellect and instinct, and that if you had both in good measure, you generally had good judgement, and he said he felt I had good judgement and he needed it around. He asked me how I was, and I said bored, demotivated and depressed. I was not sure I was up for it any more. He asked if I was missing the front line and the daily battle. I said maybe. I felt that the grip I had over events in the first term came from the fact that I had to be on top of everything myself because I was being asked about everything on a daily basis, so there was buy-in from the Cabinet at pretty much every stage. But now they had less of an interest in the centre being all-knowing, all-commanding, and I feared that meant we were slightly losing our grip. At Cabinet, GB was doodling with a big thick pencil, covering page after page with odd scribbles.

Friday, July 13

TB called me up a.m. and we went over all the same old problems. He was really pissed off with the party at the moment, felt the mood was over-rebellious and that we didn't deserve the reaction we were getting. 'This is the old Labour Party at its worst, thinks we have won two elections so now let's go back to the old divisive and self-indulgent ways.' He was also worried about me, said I had to find my motivation again, had to understand how important I was to him and to the whole operation. I said I was finding it hard, and I wasn't convinced I could get myself up for it. He said we would both be better after a holiday, but he really needed me on my best form. I said I felt more Unibond League than European Cup at the moment. He felt that our anti-spin strategy was not working, because too many in the government had taken it to mean we should not be communicating. Our opponents, internal and external, were mounting arguments against us and we were failing to put over the right counter-arguments.

Tuesday, July 17

TB and I had a bit of a spiky conversation about the general scene. He was definitely developing a kind of 'I'm always right' tone. When he saw Jack S to discuss the Bush visit, he spoke of NMD as though it were barely a problem. Jack had obviously thought about it a lot. I was also pissed off that TB constantly defined himself against the left and not the right. I was generally pretty down because on the one hand I was spending half my time demotivated and thinking about leaving and on the other, I knew that people inside the operation were looking to me to lift it and to get a grip on issues like PPP, and I just wasn't up for it. I told Jeremy Heywood I was still thinking of going and he seemed genuinely shocked. He felt if the judgement was a purely personal one for me, I should probably go, but he felt that for TB it would be bad because he felt there was nobody else he trusted constantly to be developing the arguments and the lines for the public, the media, Cabinet, etc.

Thursday, July 19

Early afternoon, we travelled down to Chequers to wait for Bush and go through the difficult stuff, Kyoto and NMD in particular. TB seemed pretty nervous, and was repeating the same arguments again and again. There had been a total fuck-up earlier re the reception we had planned for the White House press corps because someone at the White House had cancelled the visit to Number 10 and Buckingham Palace. Total nightmare. Bush arrived by helicopter, and we were surprised to see him not wearing a tie, his advance people having said that he would be. He and TB had a very long chat one-on-one, mainly going over the tricky stuff before they came through for a session with the rest of us in the room upstairs with the Cabinet table. On the Middle East, he was very down on Arafat, but also wondered how on earth [Ariel] Sharon could do a deal with someone he had called a lying pig. He had told Sharon he believed they were planning to go in and eliminate Arafat and if they did so, it would be impossible to stand by them. They had enjoyed their session with the Queen. Chris Meyer said they had all been very nervous, including Bush. They were very right wing but they had a wit and a charm that took them a long way. In Karl Rove [senior adviser to Bush], I sensed a bit of a kindred spirit. He didn't take himself too seriously but he took what he did seriously and more than most advisers admit, understood strategy and understood the media realities you had to take into account in shaping it.

Wednesday, July 25

Peter Hyman picked me up and we left for Chequers and the internal awayday. On arrival, TB took me through to the study and said it was really important that I lifted people, that I didn't allow my current mood to affect them. I put a lot of work into the opening presentation, which I based around the ten policy and communications questions I felt most urgently needed answering. Andrew Adonis went through where we were going on policy. He felt we had only laid the foundations and a lot of the big questions were still being ducked. Then Jeremy [Heywood] on some of the big spending issues coming up. Michael Barber [head of TB's new delivery unit] went through how his delivery unit intended to work, and was impressive. Robert [Hill, now Blair's political secretary] did party management, then Anji his diary. The nub of the discussion that followed showed up that both in terms of investment and reform, we didn't have a strong enough forward narrative. We had a long argument on education and there was a clear divide between me, Sally, Fiona, David Hanson [TB's new parliamentary private secretary] and RH on what I described as the Labour camp while TB, Andrew A, Jonathan and Jeremy were on a very different agenda. I asked TB and AA to persuade me that choice would drive up standards for all, said that for most people it was meaningless and for some meant exclusion. TB said at one point I was beginning to sound like Roy Hattersley.

Tuesday, July 31, and August holiday

I had a couple of long conversations with TB and said there were really three bottom lines for me. First, I had to get a better work/family balance. Second, there had to be a recalibration of the politics in the building, in particular on policy where David M had gone and Andrew A had moved things to the right. And third, the GB situation had to be sorted because a big part of the nightmare was constantly having to pick up the pieces from that. On the politics, he clearly had decided he wanted Sally M back in a central position and was prepared to let Anji go. Neil and Glenys were both adamant I couldn't leave, that it would be too powerful a political signal and damaging. Philip and Gail felt the same, though Philip was honest enough to admit his big worry was that he would have nobody there to work through. TB said he felt we had both been a bit distracted after the election. He said I had not helped by being so down, that I was one of the few people in the building who could lead people and get them up, and when I was down, the building went down.

Tuesday, September 11

I woke up to the usual blah on the radio about TB and the TUC speech, all the old BBC clichés about us and the unions, the only new thing GMB ads asking if you trust TB not to privatise the NHS. Peter H and I went up to the flat. TB had done a good section on public-private, an effective hit back at the Edmonds line. With the economy, public services, Europe/euro and a bit on asylum, we had a proper speech. We sharpened it and honed it a bit. He was furious at the GMB ads, said he intended to give Edmonds a real hammering. We finished it on the train to Brighton, were met and driven to the hotel.

We were there, up at the top of the hotel putting the finishing touches to the speech, when the attacks on the New York Twin Towers began. Godric was watching in the little room where the Garden Room girl had set up, came up to the top of the little staircase leading to the bit where TB and I were working, and signalled for me to go down. It was all a bit chaotic, with the TV people going into their usual breathless breaking-news mode, but it was clearly something way out of the ordinary. I went upstairs, turned on the TV and said to TB he ought to watch it. It was now even clearer than just a few moments ago just how massive an event this was. It was also one that was going to have pretty immediate implications for us too. We didn't watch the TV that long, but long enough for TB to reach the judgement about just how massive an event this was in its impact and implications. It's possible we were talking about thousands dead. We would also have to make immediate judgements about buildings and institutions to protect here. TB was straight onto the diplomatic side as well, said that we had to help the US, that they could not go it all on their own, that they felt beleaguered and that this would be tantamount to a military attack in their minds. We had to decide whether we should cancel the speech. There was always a moment in these terrorist outrages where governments said we must not let the terrorists change what we do, but it was meaningless. Of course they changed what we did. At first, we felt it best to go ahead with the speech but by the time we were leaving for the venue, the Towers were actually collapsing. The scale of the horror and the damage was increasing all the time and it was perfectly obvious he couldn't do the speech. We went over to the conference centre, where TB broke the news to Monks and Brendan Barber that he intended to go on, say a few words, but then we would have to head back to London. We would issue the text but he would not deliver the speech. John Monks said to me that it's on days like this that you realise just how big his job is. TB's mind was whirring with it. His brief statement to the TUC went down well, far better than his speech would have done. We walked back to the hotel, both of us conscious there seemed to be a lot more security around. We arranged a series of conference calls through Jonathan with Jack S, Geoff Hoon, David B. We asked Richard Wilson to fix a Cobra meeting as soon as we got back.

We set off for Brighton station. He said the consequences of this were enormous. On the train he was subdued, though we did raise a smile when someone said it was the first and last time he would get a standing ovation from the TUC. Robert Hill was listening to the radio on his earpiece and filling us in every now and then. TB asked for a pad and started to write down some of the issues we would have to address when we got back. He said the big fear was terrorists capable of this getting in league with rogue states that would help them. He'd been going on about bin Laden for a while because there had been so much intelligence about him and al-Qaeda. He wanted to commission proper reports on OBL and all the other terror groups. He made a note of the need to reach out to the British Muslim community, who would fear a backlash if this was bin Laden. Everyone seemed convinced it couldn't be anyone else.

We got back and before Cobra he was briefed by Stephen Lander [director general of MI5], John Scarlett [chairman of the Joint

September '01: TB subdued; consequences are enormous

Intelligence Committee], RW. DTLR[1] had closed airspace over London. There had been special security put around the Stock Exchange and Canary Wharf. The general security alert had been raised to Amber. Three hundred companies were being contacted to be given advice. Scarlett said OBL and his people were the only ones with the capability to do this. Neither he nor Lander believed other governments were involved. TB said we needed a command paper of who they are, why they are, what they do, how they do it. He said at the diplomatic level he felt the US would feel beleaguered and angry because there was so much anti-Americanism around. Lander felt the pressure on the Americans to respond quickly, even immediately, would be enormous. Afghanistan was the obvious place. Iraq, Libya, Iran, the Americans will be trying to find out if they helped in this. He said there were a lot of people sympathetic to bin Laden, more than we realised. TB said they will move straight away to the international community and their response. If I were Bush, I would demand the Taliban deliver him up. Scarlett and Lander were both pretty impressive, didn't mess about, thought about what they said, and said what they thought. Scarlett said this was less about technology than it was about skill and nerve. Lander said this was a logical step-up from the car bomb. Turning a plane into a bomb and destroying one of the great symbols of America takes some doing but they have done it and they have been able to do it because they have any number of terrorists prepared to kill themselves. TB's immediate concern, apart from the obvious logistical steps we had to take, was that Bush would be put under enormous pressure to do something irresponsible. If America heard the general world view develop that this happened because Bush was more isolationist, there would be a reaction. He felt we had to take a lead in mobilising diplomatic solidarity in the rest of the G8 and the EU. We had to start shaping an international agenda to fill the vacuum. He spoke to Schroeder, who wanted a G8 meeting, Chirac and Jospin, who were not so sure, and then Putin, who had a real 'I told you so' tone, said he had been warning us about Islamic fundamentalism. TB and I both pressed Scarlett and Lander on why they were so sure there were no rogue governments involved in this. They said because bin Laden was able to do it himself and that suited his purposes better.

We all trooped over to the Cobra meeting, which was a bit ragged, but that was to be expected given what people were having to deal with. There were contingency measures that had gone into effect.

[1] Department for Transport, Local Government and the Regions (formely DETR).

Private flights had been stopped. There were no commercial flights to go over the centre of London. All small-plane flights were being grounded unless they had specific clearance. Security was being stepped up around financial centres and major computer sites. The Met were raising numbers on visible patrols, particularly at Canary Wharf, Heathrow and in the north London Jewish areas. We had upped protection on our premises in the Middle East. There was talk of moving some of the planes based at RAF Leuchars to London in the event of a hijack. Geoff Hoon gave a briefing on what troops were where in the Middle East. TB did a very good summing-up, first going through all the different measures that I should brief, then on the specific reports he wanted to commission, then on the importance of a diplomatic strategy to support the US. He said they would feel beleaguered and all the tensions that had been apparent before would now become more open, whatever the warm words around the world. He asked Jack and Geoff to come through to Number 10, said it was vital that we worked up an international agenda that went beyond the US just hitting Afghanistan. He felt NMD would quickly rise up the agenda. He intended to say to Bush that he should deliver an ultimatum to the Taliban to hand over bin Laden and his people and then hit them if it didn't happen. He had been reading the Koran over the summer. Mohammed had lost battles but there was a belief that if you died in the cause that you believed in then you went straight to heaven. That was a very, very powerful thing to work against. TB's public words were very much in total support of the US. He said this was going to be a nightmare, as big and as bad as any we had endured. The Israelis were making massive attacks on the terror groups. TB said we were going to have to work exceptionally hard on the international response. Bush was getting it in the neck for not being in Washington.

Wednesday, September 12

Bush did a broadcast at 2am, said all the things you'd expect but looked a bit shaky. TB was generally thought to have handled it well yesterday and also got a fairly good press for the TUC speech that never was. I got in early and read the overnight intelligence reports, everything pointing now to bin Laden. TB was starting to think about the long term and what to do about the whole terrorism agenda. It had clearly moved up to a different level. The day was taken up almost exclusively with the attack. TB wanted as much information as possible and he wanted to be in a position to work out Bush's likely reaction. He felt it likely that Bush would feel the pressure for

September '01: Give ultimatum to Taliban re bin Laden

an early response. The full enormity of what had happened was only now really sinking in. TB was pretty clear that we would end up going for the Taliban. At Cobra, there was a review of the security procedures put in place. RW and others wanted to reopen City Airport but Byers objected and TB, with GB and JS in full support, agreed to keep the airport shut and the flyover path over London shut too. Bin Laden was last thought to be in Kandahar days ago. John Stevens [Metropolitan Police] said there were more than 1,000 extra police officers on the streets. TB said he had talked to the Governor of the Bank of England and they were keeping in contact about how to maintain confidence in the financial system, while the supply of oil was also being constantly monitored. Jack said that we should not get ahead of the US in terms of what we say. He felt our best role was to stay close and try to exercise influence privately. TB commissioned a note on what Bush's options were, saying he had to get inside his mind if he could. Hoon said al-Qaeda tentacles were all over the place – Africa, Chechnya, this wasn't just about Afghanistan. There was also the view that the intelligent thing would be to wait several weeks but TB pointed out things were likely to move much more quickly than that. If the Americans are as convinced as we are that this is bin Laden, there should be pressure put on to yield him up and if they refuse to cooperate, then he would be entitled to hit them. TB warned, following on from his phone call with Putin, that the Russians would essentially co-opt this whole event as justification for what they were doing in Chechnya. There was a discussion about recalling Parliament.

Later TB saw Scarlett and Lander and others to get a fuller briefing on Afghanistan and bin Laden and how he operated. One of the experts from the FCO, a total Arabist, came very close to saying the attack was justified, saying the Americans should look to their own policy on the Middle East to understand why so many people don't like them. It was also clear that there were likely to be would-be terrorists here as asylum seekers. Both C [head of the Secret Intelligence Service ('MI6'), Sir Richard Dearlove] and Lander were very good on big picture and detail. They both felt Bush would need a few days for the Americans properly to assess all this stuff. TB and I agreed he should do a press conference, saying that Cabinet would meet tomorrow and Parliament on Friday. We worked on the script and went through various options of how to express the support he would give to Bush, which was pretty full on. We got a message that Bush wanted to speak to him. It was a good call, Bush was pretty calm and TB very supportive. Bush said he was the first foreign leader he was speaking to and he would value staying in touch. He said the American people would give him a bit of time. TB said there might be a case for a G8. TB went over some of the things he had been saying to us, and Bush said he was grateful for the help and would appreciate it if he put some of those thoughts in writing. Bush said the UN and NATO statements were 'useful cover for the work that we would have to do', by which I think he meant continuing intelligence gathering and then attack. He said this was 'a new war, Pearl Harbor in the 21st century'. He said these people had to come out of their holes sometime. TB said he felt for him personally and Bush replied 'I know what I've got to do. I'm not a good mourner. I'm a weeper. I'll weep with the country but then act, but I don't just want to hit cruise missiles into the sand.' TB was a bit worried that the longer he waited, the more he would be expected to do. TB wrote off a note for Bush's eyes only, which spelled out some of the problems we were facing and where Bush might go to build useful alliances. I felt Bush was almost Zen-like, almost too calm. Maybe he had decided he could wait longer than we thought. TB was sure we would need to do a lot more than just take out OBL. There was a second Cobra meeting with another discussion about whether to lift some of the restrictions. John Stevens said that the casualty figures were very vague but the UK casualties could be up to a thousand. TB agreed we should get out the possibility that figures could go into the hundreds. TB and Blunkett had a meeting on asylum with DB pushing hard for ID cards and detention centres. The general feeling was that TB was doing well. He was constantly telling us about bits of the Koran. Ben Wilson started in the press office. What a day to start.

Thursday, September 13

TB's worry was that GWB would turn inwards. He had sensed a bit of resistance to the G8 idea, which he felt was a big mistake. He felt now was the time to bind in as much international support as possible. He felt a big military hit combined with a big international effort of support and a long-term agenda for terrorism was the way to go. There was a whole load more intelligence all pointing towards OBL. We went through to the Cobra meeting where we agreed we could wind down the emergency response. TB's note to Bush was strong but he was not sure he would be receptive. TB had a meeting pre-Cabinet with Jack S, Geoff [Hoon], [Admiral Sir Michael] Boyce [CDS] – who had replaced Guthrie. I felt that with all the focus on the States, there was a danger we would neglect the Brits involved, and the fallout, which would be substantial, so suggested Tessa be used to sort out all that logistically etc but also to be a kind of minister for helping families and victims. Jack was worried it would cut across the FCO stuff but I felt it needed a specific minister, specifically deputed. The Palace played the US national anthem at the Changing of the Guard while Prince Charles was visiting the Embassy to sign the condolence book.

Cabinet was very sombre, though Clare did her usual bit. TB was very much in charge. He said it was an act carried out in America which should be seen as an attack on the democratic world. Of the thousands killed, he feared several hundred would be British. He said all the evidence pointed to OBL. He said long term there had to be a strategy for dealing with Islamic fundamentalism but for the moment the focus was on finding the perpetrators, putting in place the security measures needed here, and assessing the financial implications for the world economy. Jack went through the diplomatic activity, said the UNSC had been easier to mobilise than the EU in some respects. On security, he said the problem was security is only as good as the weakest link. Blunkett went through all that was being done to protect public buildings, big computer installations and infrastructure sites. He said suicide bombers are notoriously difficult to plan for. He pointed out, as did others, the importance of reaching out to decent British Muslims. TB said there were three areas to focus on – whatever US military response is made, and our participation within it. Politics and diplomacy and in particular trying to get impetus into the Middle East peace process. And practical security arrangements. Clare said the real problem was lack of progress in the Middle East, the fact that so many people were willing to be suicide bombers, and she asked if we had the will to improve life for the Arab world. Patricia briefed on oil and energy supplies, and was fairly confident. It was a good meeting, and I think people sensed TB was going to have an important role, not just here. TB and I then spent a while working on his statement for tomorrow, though getting the right balance and tone would be the hard bit. Both Hilary Armstrong and Robert Hill warned him that the PLP may be a bit dodgy on this and TB said 'Are they mad? Do we just let these people get away with killing thousands of people?' He said if this had been on British soil, just imagine the pressure for a swift response. Jonathan had brought in some interesting books on the Taliban which we were trying to read in addition to the material being provided by the spooks. TB sent a message to all Arab leaders. We did a TB article for about 50 regional newspapers in areas with large numbers of Muslims. There was the beginning of talk in the States about how TB's response was better than Bush's, which made him a bit anxious, and he recalled how Clinton had got a bit jumpy during Kosovo.

David Manning [Blair's newly appointed senior foreign policy adviser], who had been in the States at the time of the attacks, was now back. Quite a baptism. He gave a very good assessment of where the various bits of the American set-up were. He felt Bush was being fairly restrained but at some point that would stop. We had a meeting with TB, C, Lander, Francis Richards [director] of GCHQ [Government Communication Headquarters]. Everything pointed to OBL, training camps, possibly some help from the Taliban. The US clearly believed there was real evidence but we agreed it would not be possible to publish much of it. We left for the Commons, got the tone of the statement right and went over the difficult questions. TB did fine. Our backbenchers were fine, and the Tories and Lib Dems basically onside for the approach he set out. TB was sure that ultimatum followed by attack if not response was the right way. Anji took a call from Will Farrish, the new US Ambassador, specifically inviting some of us to the service at St Paul's. We travelled up with Richard Wilson and John Gieve [Home Office Permanent Secretary] and ended up in the front row, which was a bit embarrassing. Major, Thatcher and Callaghan were all there. GB was sitting next to IDS. It was a nice service. I chatted with Jamie Rubin at the end, who said the American right would use this as an excuse to do all sorts of things right round the world.

Back at Number 10 TB, Jonathan, David Manning and I had a session pre TB's phone call with Bush. TB was worried by the reluctance to have a G8, felt it showed they were looking inwards when they should be looking outwards. They should be using now to bind in Russia and France. He also felt we had to do more to bind in Pakistan, who were going to be absolutely vital in all this. The call took place at 1.45. TB was quite troubled afterwards, said we had to think of a way of getting to the US for a face-to-face meeting. He said he needed to see him in a room, and look in his eyes, not do all this on phone calls with 15 people listening in. He asked DM to make sure he stayed in permanent contact with Condi and make sure they did nothing too rash. We got over Geoff H, Jack S and CDS. TB went through his assessment of the US plan – ultimatum to yield up OBL and then let outside body move in to get rid of the camps. Alternatively, hit OBL straight away, possibly going for the Taliban. And the next step is to look to other countries, including Iraq, and other countries not even linked to OBL. He said their instinct was to resolve the WMD question quickly. We needed to consider what such a strategy would be and what part we would play in it. He said his advice very strongly will be to deal with Afghanistan very distinctively, whereas to go for Iraq would be certain to lose Russia and France from any international support. He said they had definitely moved to action mode but we still had an opportunity to mould things in the right direction. CDS asked if there was any indication of how they intended to hit Afghanistan. TB was not aware they were currently planning anything beyond missile attacks. CDS said it was possible to attack mountain camps as a way of showing we were not scared of putting our boots on their soil. He said we wanted to send our Director of Special Forces tonight. Geoff said Rumsfeld had been looking for reasons to hit Iraq. They definitely wanted regime change and that was the channel of advice that Bush had been getting since the election. Jack said they would be mad to do Iraq without justification because they will lose world opinion. TB said 'My job is to try to steer them in a sensible path.' He said we had to separate these two missions. He said their line of argument will be that it does not matter whether you did the Trade Centre, if you are in the business of terrorism, then we are going to put you out of business. It's possible to be sympathetic to that but the political consequences are all too obvious. We cannot ignore that's where they are. We are talking very big issues here. CDS said even in the most benign circumstances this is going to be difficult. TB said they all needed to keep in close touch with opposite numbers. We also agreed it might be sensible for Guthrie to go to see [General Pervez] Musharraf [President of Pakistan]. TB asked CDS to refine the paper on military options. Ed Richards [senior policy adviser on media business issues] came to see me about Gavyn Davies getting the BBC chairmanship, which was likely to break next week.

Saturday, September 15

The aftermath of the attacks was still totally dominating the media, stories moving more to the human tragedy as well as the diplomacy. TB had a meeting first thing with C, Lander, Richards, Scarlett, Wilson, Jonathan, Manning and me. They kept saying there was more and more evidence pointing to OBL. But as TB and I agreed later, nothing that would stand up in a court of law. Lander briefed TB on some of the difficulties we were facing on the issue of people using the UK to plan terrorism. TB just sat shaking his head when he told him about someone who we knew to be planning terror in India, that this was accepted by the tribunal, but we couldn't kick him out. We discussed the need for changes to human rights law and civil liberties. DM had mentioned to Condi that TB thought they should meet soon. TB, Jonathan and I were all casually dressed. The spooks were all in dark suits and carrying their battered briefcases. TB said to them if I didn't know you were all so young, I'd say there was a generational gap. He felt he should probably see Schroeder on Wednesday, Chirac Thursday, then the US. He called a couple of times later when I was out running, was now at that stage where he was testing his own thoughts by constantly setting out the same position and trying to find weaknesses. It was basically ultimatum, act, follow-through short, medium and long term. But we would need to be building support at every stage and he was obviously worried about the American capacity on that front. TB was getting a good press here and even more so overseas, especially the States. I couldn't help thinking that though this was a total disaster, and was going to wipe out chunks of his domestic diary, if leadership was important, here was a real opportunity to show it. The main live news story was Bush's meeting at Camp David, where he said the US must get ready for war and that OBL was the prime suspect. TB was getting a good press, GWB a bad press. Naughtie's second instalment[1] was running which focused on me, and GB's fears about my diary.

Sunday, September 16

TB was doing CNN so I went in for a pre-meeting with him and David Manning. DM said he sensed they were looking at an ultimatum followed by a 48- or 72-hour wait. The noises from the Taliban were getting more and more aggressive. Thousands of refugees were pouring over the border. Pakistan was clearly going to have a hard time whatever. Robin was on *Frost* for us and the BBC were really pissed off that TB did CNN. It was a good interview. We went over all the really tough questions, but a few of them never came. I had an argument with CNN, who were initially refusing to release the whole interview to other broadcasters but in the end they did. TB said he sensed Bush would end up in the right place. He was more confident. Chirac was pretty clear that they could hit Afghanistan but no further. Schroeder was in a bit of a problem at home and not quite so strong. Jospin was all over the shop because of his coalition situation and Chirac was going to make it as hard for him as he could. TB wanted to get a message of support for Musharraf. He later called me to say we must get out the message about how closely the Americans were consulting us, as whatever they thought about them, that would make the other Europeans want to get closer.

[1] In the serialisation of James Naughtie's book on the relationship between Blair and Brown.

September '01: Chirac – hit Afghanistan but no further

Monday, September 17

Up to the flat to see TB and told him that the US were suggesting that he went to Congress with Bush. 'Oh yeah,' said TB. I said it was serious and I was worried about it because it would play into the whole poodle thing. John Kerr called to say it would be ghastly, that the whole thing would become an orgy of US patriotism, with TB in a kind of nod-along role. I felt we should only do it if TB also spoke, but wasn't sure if that was even doable. Charles Clarke told him later that there were real anxieties around about Bush and that people around the world saw TB as the only person who could restrain him. He said it was an awesome responsibility. Clare Short had gone on [Andrew] Rawnsley's programme last night and had said something that let them write government split and tension headlines. TB later wrote to her. He was really angry, said it sent exactly the wrong signal to the Taliban about our seriousness of intent. Jack and I had a long chat before his *Today* programme interview and agreed he should move the story on by echoing the line on OBL and saying that we had our own evidence that all pointed his way. TB spoke to Musharraf later who said the risks he was taking were real and he needed real help. He seemed keen on the suggestion of Guthrie going out. There was no real knowledge of where OBL was. At TB's military meeting, Geoff Hoon and CDS were both focusing on the difficulties of any military offensive. Boyce was very unlike Guthrie as CDS, who had always been pretty can-do. Boyce was quite soft-spoken, very polite, but I wondered if he wasn't something of a fellow depressive. Geoff said he had had some difficult chats with Rumsfeld. CDS said only 6 per cent of Afghans have electricity. They don't even have fuel dumps that we would recognise as such. There's nothing really there, very few targets. TB said they had to know that we would hurt them if they don't yield up OBL. David Manning said we had to do more to help the Northern Alliance.[1] Lander and CDS said the heroin trail should also be hit. They said more people had been killed by heroin than died last Tuesday.

We were now planning a series of visits for TB, Berlin, Paris, Washington, New York. He was worried about Congress unless he spoke. Then came news there would be an EU summit on Friday. All a bit of a nightmare. TB had lunch with [Silvio] Berlusconi [Prime Minister of Italy]. He was reasonably supportive on the idea of military action 'provided not too many people die'. TB said there was no such thing as a painless war. He said either the US will see the

[1] The coalition of disparate opponents of the Taliban.

international community rallying to them or there will be a battle internally and the isolationists will win. His worry was people show support up to the point where the shooting starts. He said we had to divide this into two – Afghanistan, and the broader terrorist apparatus. In respect of the second part, the decisions are for the long term. Berlusconi emphasised that we had to make clear this was not a war against Islam. TB said it was important we got Arab countries as part of our coalition. The best signal of all would be a restart of the Middle East peace process. There was a real risk that Sharon sees this as an opportunity to say that Arafat equals OBL. He said it was important we all made clear to Israel this should not be an opportunity to settle scores but on the contrary we should have the objective of reinvigorating the peace process. There was something very odd about Berlusconi. He didn't seem quite in control of his body, his arm movements were a bit weird and most of the time he addressed himself to the interpreter rather than TB. They had a fairly lacklustre discussion on Europe and the euro. The New York Stock Exchange reopened but the economic impact was growing.

Tuesday, September 18

TB was at Chequers for a meeting with a group of officers. He had a chat with Jiang Zemin. He was getting a very good press as a kind of international interlocutor. Bush was going down pretty badly everywhere apart from the States. We were getting more and more work done on the nature of the Taliban. There was a bit of a discussion as to whether it was the kind of trip Cherie should go on. Geoff Hoon was doing fine, Tessa told me relatives were getting more and more angry but not with us so much as with the general situation. GB went up after interest rate cuts and the economic scene was getting more and more difficult. I started work on a note for Karen Hughes [Campbell's opposite number in the White House] about the system we had put in place for Kosovo. If anything, this situation was going to be even more complicated and difficult. There were a stack of meetings to plan visits, particularly the US. I was really worried about him looking like a poodle at Congress. There was to be a church service and also a visit to 'Ground Zero'. The main news story of the day was the toing and froing of the Taliban about whether to hand over OBL. They prevaricated by saying 'clerics' would decide.

Wednesday, September 19

Geoff Hoon and CDS came in, looking grave. CDS said that on a very unofficial net he had got hold of what the Pentagon were proposing

– Tomahawks followed by 1,000 missiles raining down on various targets. He was very sceptical, said it sounded basically political and it would mean hitting a lot of sand. TB was keen for their take on what we should advise them militarily. He said he was clear what needed to be advised diplomatically but we needed to give them a military plan too. CDS felt what was needed was surgical strikes and special forces moving on camps and some individuals. Then to a broader meeting with C, Lander, Scarlett, GH, JS, CDS, RW and our lot. Depressing. Lander felt that if there was a big attack we just could not predict the response. He said there was a definite rise in Islamophobia since the attacks. Nobody had a clue where OBL was and nobody was hopeful about finding out. There were quite a few OBL people in the UK and Europe and they understood they were currently planning attacks in the Gulf, France and Italy. We were also worried that Bush's 'dead or alive, head on platter' type of rhetoric would not be helping in Pakistan, which had the potential to be a tinderbox. We could only get at Mullah [Mohammed] Omar [leader of the Taliban] and OBL with Taliban and Pakistan cooperation and even that was doubtful unless we gave them Kashmir. As the discussion wore on, CDS finally articulated what I had been thinking – namely that we had to start to prepare people for a very long-term operation, possibly taking years and years. OBL was travelling most of the time. There was no sign of a shift in the Taliban's position and any plan to divide them would take an age. I asked whether there was a public enemy number three, four, five so that the focus and the judgement wasn't solely on whether we got OBL. Afterwards, I had a meeting with another expert just back from Islamabad, who said that the only thing OBL feared was the opprobrium of clerics. He could not care less about Western opinion because he hated the West. He said OBL had a tough, nasty, dedicated group of people around him which was virtually impossible to penetrate. They were ultra-careful, especially in their travel and communications. He could probably slip to Pakistan but it was unlikely.

Thursday, September 20

Paris. Up for a run in the embassy gym. Over breakfast, TB set out the approach he intended to take with Chirac, the need to separate the short-term response from the long-term agenda to deal with the deeper problems. Chirac had coincidentally been to the States and Catherine Colonna suggested it had been helpful in that he had got a real feel of how deep it went for the Americans. For a while, he would probably curb his basic anti-American feelings. It was clear he wanted to be involved but it was also likely the Americans had remained suspicious. They did a brief doorstep together and there was a flurry of excitement because TB said at one point 'within the next few days' and we had a major job to smooth it over, make clear he was talking diplomatic not military.

We headed for the plane to meet up with Cherie, the rest of the staff and the press corps coming with us to New York. Before dinner, TB had a long session with C and the military planners. They were looking at specific targets based on information they had obviously garnered from their various discussions with opposite numbers. What was very clear was that the US were well advanced. These were detailed plans. After an hour or so with them, TB said at least he got the sense that these guys knew what they were doing. I was worried that the focus was so much on OBL that success or failure would be judged solely according to that. TB worked on a new note for Bush with two aims – first, bringing OBL and al-Qaeda to justice, and second, going after international terrorism in all its forms. The ultimatum, and help for the Northern Alliance, remained central. He felt we should use air strikes to demolish the camps, support the NA, gather intelligence to designate high-value targets, hit the drugs trail, go for OBL, strong forward base in Uzbekistan and the Afghan border, a deal for Pakistan, help Musharraf, help Afghan people, new relations with Iran, support from Russia and Arabs. He set out too a number of things in the practical fight against terrorism – the disruption of groups from their travel. Extradition laws. He said we needed 1. an integrated and streamlined military planning operation, binding in other allies too, 2. detailed work on the long-term agenda, 3. a well-staffed US–UK-led propaganda team, and 4. the political, military and media operations linked between us.

We landed in New York and though we had an escort, the combination of bad weather, dreadful traffic and continuing post-September 11 chaos meant that sadly we had to cancel the visit to a fire station. I was able to rescue it a bit when Clinton agreed to go instead of TB and take Cherie with him. TB was getting frantic because we were so late but we finally reached St Thomas's Church and then a mild panic because there were suggestions that the reading, which had been suggested to me by Paddy Feeny [press officer], was not appropriate because it was about bereavement and some of the people there did not believe they had yet lost their loved ones. It suggested they were all emotionally shot to pieces. TB was in the front row with CB, Kofi Annan, Bill and Chelsea [Clinton]. TB's reading went fine as did the message read out by Meyer from The Queen, including the brilliant line 'Grief is the price we pay for love.' Bill C asked me if I wrote it. I said I'd love to take credit, but no. He said find the guy who did, and hire him. After the national anthems we had a brief meeting with Bill and Kofi, who both warned of real dangers from Pakistan if we weren't careful. Then we were taken up to the room where all the relatives were gathered. The contrast, the moment you entered the room, was palpable. We had been engaged in the normal diplomatic chat that goes on even in these circumstances, humour included, and now into this dreadful, dreadful atmosphere, haunted eyes, faces drained of blood, lips quivering. Most said it was all made worse by the fact they had no bodies to take home. Most carried pictures which they showed to TB and Bill as they moved through the room. Bill was absolutely terrific when he stood in for TB at the fire station. By now we were running really late and I felt terrible constantly reminding TB, but it was impossible to leave without him going round to speak to everyone. And they all just wanted to pour out their stories. These were in the main just ordinary people caught up in one of the most extraordinary things ever to hit anyone.

We finally got out to the airport and discovered that all the press luggage was being thoroughly searched so we were delayed even further. Meanwhile Jonathan sent Meyer off the deep end when he had told him that the White House had said the meeting was one plus three, and TB wanted Jonathan, David Manning and me. Meyer threw an absolute tantrum, said he would be a laughing stock in Washington, threatened to resign on the spot. Jonathan did his usual unflappable bit, just let him let off steam and eventually it was resolved by David M asking Condi if she could slip in an extra place. It was all a bit silly and as TB said, leaders couldn't give two tosses which officials from the other side were there, but it made sense to him to have the three people he would be working most closely with not just here but every-where. When we landed, we headed straight to the White House to be met by GWB, Powell, Condi and Dan Fried [Senior Director for European and Eurasian Affairs]. We were taken upstairs to one of the bigger rooms and TB went over to the corner with Bush and they clearly embarked straight away on a very tough conversation. He said later it had started fine, GWB saying how dreadful the events had been but now something good had to come out of it. The focus was OBL and the Taliban and tonight when he spoke to Congress he was going to deliver the ultimatum. TB emphasised the need for a meas-ured response. Jonathan said later it was funny how Thatcher had gone to see Bush Senior to say 'This is no time to wobble' while TB was visiting Bush Junior – 'This IS a time to wobble.'

We went through for the dinner, scallops, veal, salad. Bush was pretty much directing the conversation, said he was grateful for our support, said Britain was a true friend and we were going to win. He said anyone could join the coalition provided they understood the doctrine – that we were going after terrorists and all who harbour them. Obviously the wider the coalition the better, but they were going to do this anyway. When the scallops arrived, there was a thin ring of pastry on top which he picked up and said 'God dang, what on earth is that?' The waiter said it was a scallop. He said to him it looks like a halo and you are the angel. I think he meant the waiter. When he chose to be serious, he was fine. He said it was interesting Putin himself made sure the Russians didn't react last week, a clear sign the Cold War was over. Both he and Powell were really worried about Pakistan and wanted TB's take on how best to help. He said they were going to go for the Taliban after the ultimatum, said the country was run by a bunch of nuts and we had to get a new government in there. He said he had really beaten up on Sharon who was clearly trying to use this to go after Arafat. 'I said Arafat is not bin Laden and you do nothing.' Putin wanted to use it to go after Chechnya even harder. He said they feared Hollywood was the next target because it was high profile, Jewish and decadent. They also had intelligence they would go for Airforce One. He talked us through a fairly graphic account of what happened, how he was told of the first attack at the meeting at the school and he thought it was an accident at first, then how Andy Card whispered to him about the second attack and said to him 'America is under attack, sir,' and he said he knew there and then this might be the biggest challenge he ever faced. TB talked about the need to be sure of his ground, that we needed public opinion with us the whole time. Bush said yes, but when I am speaking tough I'm speaking to Middle America, most of whom have never heard of bin Laden till now, they just know someone attacked their country and killed their fellow citizens, and they say hey, Mister President, go get someone and why ain't you done it the day before yesterday? He did, as he had over Putin when we first met, show signs of adaptability and intelligence. He was also graphic on the sophistication of the attacks and the technical ability of the pilot who hit the Pentagon. He said there are Muslims so dedicated they are prepared to drink to pretend to people around them they are not Muslims.

Monday, September 24

At the intelligence meeting, John Scarlett presented more evidence of OBL's involvement. The intelligence picture was very patchy and I

September '01: Bush says Afghanistan is run by 'a bunch of nuts'

had a lot of doubts about whether we could get to the stage where any of this was publishable. The feeling was military action next week rather than this. Boyce said the US were realising they did not have the targets they thought they might have. TB was interested in what more we could do for Pakistan. TB went through four separate areas – diplomatic, action being taken, evidence re the attacks, implications for domestic law. He said we were sure the Taliban knew something was happening. He made clear military action would follow if they do not comply in yielding up OBL. He went over some of the long-term issues, money laundering, shutting down the camps, the trade in WMD capability, including the involvement of what he called responsible business people.

Thursday, September 27

Sixteen days on, after all the bellicose talk, there was still no sign of US action. TB said we could only do the job with special forces and they can only be used properly with proper bases. Boyce said the only viable bases will have to be in a contiguous country. Iran is a no-no, the Americans won't go near Pakistan. The 'Stans were being difficult, messing us around. Boyce warned that the Taliban were brutal if they got their hands on enemy forces, capable of skinning them alive. It's called a hair shirt policy. [Lieutenant] General [Tony] Piggott [Deputy CDS (operations)] did a really interesting presentation setting out the concept of military action working at various levels, including the psychological and the need to win hearts and minds, but again there was no sense of the Americans getting how to do that in a joined-up way.

Monday, October 1

TB and Bush agreed TB should go to see Putin to try to secure bases and then to Pakistan to try to get a proper fix on Musharraf. It was a perfectly friendly conversation with the usual joshing and laughter amid the heavy stuff.

Tuesday, October 2

Brighton. TB was up at 6 and I went in to find him with the usual mass of paper all over the place. The pre-speech overnight briefing had gone very big on the idea we were declaring war on the Taliban. It was leading the news not just in the UK but in the States too, so much so that as we were going through the autocue rehearsal for his conference speech at twelve, Jonathan came in to tell us that David Manning had read the words on Afghanistan to the White House, who were worried about what we were saying about the nature of military action. They felt it was too forward, too clear re what we intended to hit, with the reference to camps and military installations. When it came to the delivery, he got the tempo right, a bit slower and more measured, not worrying too much about reaching the heights. The speech was getting huge play everywhere, including one headline in the States that it was TB's 'pitch for world leadership'. We would have to watch it.

Wednesday, October 3

Extraordinary press for TB's speech, though some found it a bit preachy and there was a real danger of overreach. We had a real problem with the Indians over the planned visit to Pakistan. [Atal Behari] Vajpayee [Prime Minister of India] was on the phone, totally adamant that if TB went to Pakistan without also visiting India, it would be a real disaster for him. He was normally so quiet and soft-spoken but there was both panic and a bit of anger in his voice. TB said that having listened to him, there was no way we could do one without the other. The security committee, which advised on TB's own safety, had met yesterday and basically would prefer that he didn't go to Pakistan, but if he did, they wanted us to use the VC10. We had endless coming and going on that, including at one point Cherie coming to see me, quivering with rage, bottom lip trembling, telling me I was mad to allow it and 'Do you want to be a martyr or what?' She said it was the most stupid visit there had ever been and I should be telling him I'm not going. I pointed out that we had all seen the advice, but that he had decided to go, that therefore I should probably go too, and that if we all went down, I didn't think it would be me qualifying for martyrdom.

Friday, October 5

TB was up late and we set off immediately for the airport. He was trying to work out what outcomes we wanted from Pakistan. I felt there was a danger now that the British public started to ask what is this all about, and why is he spending all his time on the needs of other countries not our own? TB's words in Pakistan were going to be important and we took a bit of time to work on that. They seemed to have shut down pretty much every road and the crowds were also kept well away. It was about as big a security operation as we'd had. They started off one-on-one. TB reckoned him [Musharraf] to be a very tough character. I think their basic feeling was that we wipe out the Taliban leadership, felt that if we did the whole show would crumble.

They seemed pretty keen to get OBL, but you could never be absolutely sure who was saying what for what reason. He told TB we shouldn't underestimate how unpopular the Americans are here. He said Mullah Omar was impossible to talk to because he is a mystic, constantly talking about the afterlife. At dinner I was between two five-star generals who spent most of the time listing atrocities for which they held the Indians responsible, killing their own people and trying to blame 'freedom fighters'.

We arranged it so that we had an early dinner there and then flew to Delhi but I sensed they were holding us back as long as possible. As we took off, there was a lot of black humour flowing around about the prospect of us being downed by a stinger [a portable homing surface-to-air missile]. I think all of us, other than the experts, had been a bit taken aback at just how much Kashmir defined their relations and just how deep the mutual hatred and obsession was. We arrived in Delhi and drove into town. TB motioned to the ambassador, asking if the car was bugged. He gave a kind of non-committal no. Then at the hotel, our security service guys had found two bugs in TB's bedroom and said they wouldn't be able to move them without drilling the wall, so TB used a different room. We decided against making a fuss. I was given my own valet, Sunil, who just would not leave me alone. He followed me to the gym and I literally had to tell him to disappear. He was waiting at my door when I got back.

Saturday, October 6

Sunil was driving me bananas. Everywhere I went, he was there. I was beginning to wonder whether he had been put there either by the spooks or a paper. I told him at one point I was a tea-aholic, and he kept making me tea after tea and bringing it in. When I came back from the gym, by the time I got out of the shower, my running gear had been picked up and folded. We set off for the Prime Minister's residence, yet another purpose-built, well-equipped building, far better and more practical than Downing Street. Vajpayee was frail and his voice was weak, but in part because he had no fear of silence, there was a quiet force to him when he spoke. TB went through the mantra about military, diplomatic, humanitarian, and the need for restraint by India to build stability in the region. He said he had been very forceful with Musharraf over the attacks on the Kashmir Assembly. TB said that what had happened to the US had the same psychological effect as if we had lost Parliament or Buckingham Palace. It had touched every nerve. Vajpayee was pretty frank about what he thought of Pakistan and Musharraf and how he came to power, kept emphasising he on the other hand led a democracy, and TB said 'With humility, I think it's important to continue with restraint.' Jaswat Singh [foreign minister] said it was not possible to separate the Taliban and OBL, they were totally interdependent. This was, as the General told me last night, a two-front war. TB and Vajpayee were such different breeds of politician, TB all drive and words and desperate to get everything right, Vajpayee calm, something almost mystical about him.

Tuesday, October 9

At the morning meeting, there were two immediate problems to address – the first was that the BBC were reporting TB was going to Oman. They just would not listen to our concerns on this. And the second was the leak of a Jo Moore [special adviser to Steve Byers] email from September 11 saying that it was a good time to 'bury bad news'. I didn't allow much discussion of it at the morning meeting. It was perfectly clear someone had leaked it and it was a classic Civil Service move on a special adviser. It was a stupid thing to say, and knowing Jo she would be mortified, but I didn't like the idea of her being hanged, drawn and quartered for it. I also knew it would unleash another avalanche of bollocks about spin, me, culture of blah. I spoke to Byers and he asked if I thought she would have to go. I was worried it might end there. But after talking to TB, we agreed there should be a reprimand and an apology. TB felt Jo was basically a decent person, very committed and professional, and it was a bit much to destroy her career over one leaked email that she should never have written or sent. TB was clear that she had given us great service down the years, and it was not a hanging offence. I did a conference call with her and Steve Byers and we agreed there would be no budging from that line. My only question mark was whether she was really up to face the shit that was coming her way. She sounded OK, and she had always struck me as pretty good under pressure, but who knows? I got SB to organise Richard Mottram [Permanent Secretary for DTLR] to do the official reprimand bit. I wrote to Greg Dyke complaining about the BBC – Kate Adie [BBC's chief news correspondent] – doing a number re TB and Oman.

The war Cabinet was OK. It was remarkable how quickly these extraordinary meetings became almost routine in their nature, TB wandering in with us lot, ministers chatting a bit, the spooks and defence guys sitting up straight and getting ready to do their stuff, Scarlett, C, Lander, CDS, all chipping in, very matter-of-fact and straightforward. Scarlett was meticulous in his presentation. It was

October '01: Jo Moore's good time to bury bad news memo

again not exactly clear how successful the strikes had been.[1] Jack S and Clare both pressed Lander on what was happening re suspects here, and he was clear that though a lot of them were covered, there could be no guarantees, because a threat might well be coming from people we do not know about. They were both worried about Pakistani opinion in the UK really becoming inflamed. There was a discussion of the Saudi oilfields, what would happen to the oil price and the world economy if they went up under attack.

The Jo Moore furore was really building and the hacks on the plane were trying to get us going. We landed in Geneva and set off for the Intercontinental to meet Sheikh Zayed. He was around 80, surrounded by zillions of hangers-on, one or two of whom had a bit of a gangsterish feel to them. In the meeting, SZ said it was a battle of humanity and inhumanity, sanity and insanity. There was a TV screen in the background with pictures of a giant green parrot and some pretty girls. The parrot squawked regularly. After a while, one of the Sheikh's flunkeys got up and motioned for David Manning, Anna [Wechsberg, foreign affairs official] and me to leave so that they were one-on-one. Christ knows what they would talk about. They had brought an Abu Dhabi TV reporter with them, having promised him a TB interview and when I said nobody had mentioned it to me, they started to cut up a bit rough and unpleasant. One of them said, we are aware of your reputation but I should know the Sheikh would take it as a personal slight if this didn't happen and there would be a diplomatic incident. Then another came in with a rather menacing smile and muttered something about whether the IRA really were quiet, and whether they were linked into bin Laden and so on.

Wednesday, October 10

We landed in beautiful sunshine with a full red-carpet welcome, bands, national guard, the Omani works. We headed for the guest house, set way back in its own grounds close to one of the Sultan's residences. The place itself was about as ornate as anything we had seen. My bedroom had two gold-plated chandeliers hanging from a ceiling that must have taken months to paint. The bath was surrounded by more perfumes and toiletries than I knew existed. It was apparently the room normally reserved for visiting spouses so God knows what that made me. There was a lovely open-air swimming pool so I had a quick swim. We were running into a problem with the sense being

[1] Bombing strikes against the Taliban had begun on the Sunday.

communicated by the US that they were constantly trying to link Iraq into the equation. TB was keen to pull it back, and through a mix of my briefing and his interviews at the Army base, we just about did that, but it was difficult to do while simultaneously avoiding US–UK split stories. TB's room was even more luxurious, a carpet that your feet seemed to disappear into, paintings and stat-uettes that were both gaudy and somehow conveying a certain style. We went out to the poolside to go over what he would say to the UK troops, then set off by helicopter. I was always impressed by the way the military could set up home anywhere. Their base was pretty much a desert, but you had the sense of being in a very British, very well-organised operation. While TB was shown around, I did a back-ground briefing on the objectives document, which they saw as substantial and newsworthy. But I stupidly referred to it as a 'policy bible' which had a touch of Bush's 'crusade' reference, which I tried to pull back from later. We rejoined TB, who was getting a good response from the troops. There were several Burnley fans there, including one with the club crest tattooed on his shoulder. The BBC was reporting already that we were going on to Cairo. The others were not unreasonably pissed off that they were abiding by the agree-ment while the BBC seemed to be making a point of breaking it. Also, TB had been pictured with a guy wearing a T-shirt with the slogan 'we came, we saw, we kicked ass', which might go down better in the US than the UK. I was getting pressed the whole time about the Yanks and Iraq, which was difficult. We got a report through on Battle Damage Assessment which showed the strikes had not been as effective as planned, but TB's bigger worry was the overall strategy. Then news came through that Iraq had shot down a Predator [unmanned surveillance plane]. The Americans were bound to react.

I went out for a run on the Sultan's private beach. It was hot, but that wonderful dry heat meant that once I was into a rhythm, I was running well and felt privileged to be out on my own in such beau-tiful surroundings. I had a quick swim in the sea before going back for TB's bilateral with the Sultan and then an extraordinary dinner where wave upon wave of food came towards us. I noticed for the first couple of courses the Sultan and his colleagues just picking, and after a while it became clear why. We were on the fifth course before I realised we were still on the appetisers. By the end, we had been served 21 courses. The Sultan said he had a little surprise for us and out of nowhere came a pipe band, Omanis dressed in kilts serenading us with pipes and drums from the balcony above the dining room.

They weren't bad. On the substance, the Palestine problem came through every part of the discussion. He said Israel had to give. He was obviously aware of the tensions over Iraq, said they were happy to support us for now, re Afghanistan, but if the US went for Iraq, they would flake away and so would others, pretty quickly.

Thursday, October 11

The damage was being done by bombing but where were the ground forces ready to move in and mop up? TB also felt the US were paying insufficient attention to public opinion outside America. He was also very conscious of the danger that he was setting himself up for a fall by being in such a position of international leadership. But he felt he was getting somewhere with Bush, and also felt strongly that he had to do it.

Monday, October 15

8am, War Cabinet. TB listened for a bit and got a bit irritated, said our job was to set the overall strategy but you could not have a campaign run by committee because it will not work. There was a worrying increase in talk of threats to the US and UK, while TB was also a current target. There was no real sign of fracture within the Taliban, and also we still had mixed messages about the Northern Alliance. Both CDS and Geoff Hoon said there was no real clarity of where it was going. Our special forces were obviously key but we needed far greater clarity about what they were required for. George Tenet [Director of Central Intelligence for the CIA] was coming in to see TB with C, who brought him round to see me to discuss the notes I was sending through to Karen [Hughes] and enlist his help in persuading them of the need for much better communications. I told him we feared they were putting out messages that were very good and positive for the American audience, but not for the broader community, including here, but also above all in the Arab world. He said Richard [Dearlove] had talked to him about it, that Condi was the key to this, that I needed to get her on board to persuade Bush they needed to crack down on the mixed messages. David M felt he and I should go there next Tuesday.

Tuesday, October 16

There was a growing sense that things were not going brilliantly. TB was doing a speech on public services so I went up to the flat to work on that with him. He had pretty much done the draft himself. The Jo Moore thing was still big and we agreed she should do something to camera, which she did in the afternoon, apology then back to work. She did OK, looked fine but sounded very fed up. Colin Powell was going to Pakistan but the backdrop was the division between him and the Defense Department.

Wednesday, October 17

The general feeling was that Jo's public statement had backfired and made matters worse. Also, there was a real feeling media-wise that Afghanistan was not going according to plan. At the 8am meeting, CDS reported back from Tampa that they intended to carry on bombing at this intensity for a couple of days, then really push on for the fall of the Taliban. He said [General] Tommy Franks [Commander-in-Chief, US Central Command] was fine and strong but there was no clear political direction. Rumsfeld was felt to be very erratic. TB felt there were some critical decisions not being faced up to. E.g. on the Northern Alliance, we either get behind them or not. His view was we should go full steam ahead with them but at the same time put other groups alongside them. But it wasn't as simple as that, the Northern Alliance was not cohesive, there were eight or nine tribal chieftains in varying states of control. TB said the Northern Alliance must be sitting there thinking the Americans were just scared of suffering casualties. TB said the Taliban will not fold unless there is someone moving in to drive them out. He also felt we were losing the battle on the humanitarian front, that somebody really strong had to be in charge of it. Chris Patten's name was floated. He also wanted more pressure on the Russians for the use of bases in Uzbekistan. David Manning pointed out that Ramadan began on November 17, which would be another complicating factor. TB spoke to Bush at 2pm. TB said we had to go for the Northern Alliance, let them do what they could, put them on a leash if need be and hold them back later. Bush said he agreed, that 'You are right as always', the Northern Alliance are the best people to help us but they have to be able to share power later.

Friday, October 19

Richard W came to see me, said there was a really bad feeling around the place re Jo Moore. At the morning War meeting, there was a clear sense of Taliban morale crumbling. A fair number of defections and confidence Mazar-e-Sharif would fall soon. The Northern Alliance were far more bullish. CDS reported that the Americans were getting a bit fed up with us for not agreeing to all the targets. TB said if there

October '01: Jo Moore's public statement makes matters worse

was any target that we believed should be hit and there were legal problems here, he wanted to know about it. He said if I was Bush, I would be going spare about this. Later he called [Lord Peter] Goldsmith [Attorney General] over. RW gave a word of caution in relation to the *Belgrano* and TB said the problem there was not the legality, it was the attempt to cover it up. I couldn't resist adding 'A failure of spin over a discredited Tory regime.' Richard smiled.

Wednesday, October 24

Washington. I couldn't sleep so I was up and about at 4.30 and chatted to TB in London before his *Telegraph* interview. My first meeting was with Karen Hughes. It was a fairly small office, lots of pictures of her and GWB. She looked a bit shell-shocked. We went through the notes I had sent over, the importance of third parties, who their key communicators were, how to improve message co-ordination between the various bits of government, polling, Muslim outreach, the UN. I said why didn't GWB visit a few mosques? Then to lunch with Condi Rice. She was a lot more relaxed than Karen and we started out laughing about the pictures of the Northern Alliance on horseback, suggesting we may have overestimated their military capabilities. She and DM had already gone over the problems caused by conflicting signals coming out of the different bits of government, the lack of a clear military plan. The concept I was pushing was a 24-hour cycle in which Washington, London and the region, probably Islamabad, were in permanent contact, and driving the news proactively in all the different time zones. There was some discussion about who and how to get into Islamabad. Condi said Bush believed the PR so far had been dreadful and had told her and Karen 'go fix it' and I was definitely pushing at an open door. I said they seemed to be at war with each other. I started to push on the idea of maybe [General] John Reith [Chief of Joint Operations at Permanent Joint HQ] getting involved in a cross-national way. Then to the State Department to see Charlotte Beers, who had been hired as under-secretary for public diplomacy and whose background was advertising. Her basic pitch was that the Arab world had a very narrow view of America based upon wealth, politics, films and music, and all the big companies. She showed me a portfolio of absolutely stunning photographs of mosques, most of which looked at first glance as though they were in the Arab world, but all of which were in the States. Then some wonderful pictures and stories from ordinary American Muslims. She was clearly going to be useful on the soft stuff in particular. I could see why she was getting up a few noses there, but I liked her style. Then back to the White House to link up with Jack Straw and have a meeting with Cheney. On the military campaign, Cheney was bullish. Jack asked him outright what the strategy was. He said NA should take Mazar, then he went over some of the whys and hows and wherefores of what might follow vis-à-vis Taliban, al-Qaeda, bin Laden, but it wasn't really an answer to the question what is the strategy? Jack said UK support was strong but could we hold the coalition together if this thing went on longer than expected? He said he thought so. They did the Middle East and Jack asked how difficult it was having such a strong pro-Israel lobby. Cheney said its influence is sometimes overstated and that at the moment they were pretty subdued. Jack said Sharon was doing things which were dangerous and could not be part of our strategy. I had always assumed that Cheney would be more open and forthcoming when he was in charge of meetings rather than, as when Bush was there, clearly comfortable playing second fiddle. But he was not one to speak too much for the sake of it. He had cold, slightly menacing body language, listened very intently without giving much away, and usually paused before giving a thought-through answer.

Thursday, October 25

I didn't sleep well. I drove in from the airport with Jack, mainly small talk, how hard it was getting the time you needed for kids and family. I had really enjoyed his company, and his manner. Sometimes, because of the nature of the job, there was just too much stuff going on around TB, whereas I felt in the last couple of days, we had clear and limited aims, and pretty much met them in full. He was very sound on schools, and the need for kids like ours to go to schools with a broad mix. We got back for the War Cabinet, which was all a bit grim, not really going anywhere, not really making the progress we needed, CDS telling us what we couldn't do rather than what we could, weather bad, not clear where key Taliban people are. TB said we must take Mazar before Ramadan. Boyce's understanding was that the Americans did intend to continue bombing after Ramadan. Full Cabinet was pretty much the same as the smaller group, and I sensed people beginning to get a little bit low and worried. TB was pretty down about the military side of things. There were going to be re-deployments of UK troops from Oman tomorrow, which would be big news, but we had a problem with Rumsfeld saying something interpreted as an admission we would never get OBL. I got home to see the kids, and Fiona and I went out for dinner, and she was desperate for me to leave, and couldn't understand why now was not the moment.

Wednesday, October 31

I was starting to motor again but was also agitated that actually getting the three centres moving was too slow. TB was out in Syria, and got a total banjaxing by President Assad, which was a bit of a problem. TB was trying to give him the benefit of the doubt, felt it was as much a clash of cultures as anything. TB was in danger of getting hooked on the international stuff, though he was as well placed as anyone to do this, and a lot of people round the world would rather see TB doing it. I was flying out to meet TB for the Jordan and Israel part of his trip and was hoping not to be noticed because they would want to use it as part of the Syria crisis jigsaw they were trying to put together after Assad's big whack at him. When I spoke to TB about it before leaving for the airport, he seemed OK about it, said it had actually been quite comic to stand there having been promised the guy was going to be supportive and then watch him deliver an attack totally lapped up by our lot.

Thursday, November 1

Amman. TB got an absolute mauling in the press for the 'Syrian humiliation', 'disaster in Damascus', etc, way over the top in some ways, but there we are. I went out for a run round some of the hills near the palace, and loved the sounds of the city starting to wake up, particularly the calls to prayer. TB once said if I was religious I would probably end up as an Islamic fundamentalist, and I think I know what he meant. TB was trying to put his best face on after yesterday, and was comical in his description of it – 'It could have been worse, he could have taken out a gun and shot me' – but we also had a long chat with Jonathan and Tom K, later with the ambassador, Edward Chaplin, re how to retrieve the situation. All we could do was emphasise his willingness to take risks, get his hands dirty, do whatever it took, to work up and see through a plan. There was clearly no point trying to make out Assad had been anything but unhelpful, though TB was still of the view it was as much a clash of political and media cultures as a deliberate act of hostility. We left for breakfast with King Abdullah. He said that looking at the latest unbroadcast OBL tape, the problem was he 'looked the part', and we should not underestimate his appeal.

Jerusalem. I travelled with TB to the Sharon meeting, before, during and after which I was struck just how much heavier the security was for him and TB, not just the number of bodies around, but the barriers and the closed roads. Sharon was less belligerent than usual and the lunch in many ways went fine, but they really just wanted to whack the Palestinians the whole time. Even accepting how difficult the politics were and even remaining conscious, as I always tried to, of the reasons why Israel existed in the first place, it was very hard to warm to Sharon. And this was him in fairly mellow mode. TB felt there was a lot more to him than he showed and agreed these exchanges were difficult. But TB had his own mantra, commitment to the right of Israel to exist alongside a Palestinian state. We left for another long helicopter flight and drive to Palestine, handover at the checkpoint and then on to see Arafat, struck as ever, as it was impossible not to be, by the immediate switch from first world to third. We had the usual over-the-top welcome and guard of honour and then in to see Arafat and Co. TB was urging Arafat to be more constructive in his comments on the Israelis, but of course it was like dealing with a mirror – the things we'd heard Sharon attacking them for, now we got the reverse view, equally forcefully. We had another helicopter flight to get us to the airport later and we were running late, TB moaning about being away so often, yet he was the one who now wanted to go to Genoa to see Berlusconi.

Thursday, November 8
TB was a bit angst-ridden re Anji going. Cabinet was all Afghanistan. The CIC [Coalition Information Centre] was much more into its stride now. As during Kosovo, I was getting annoyed at the sense of moral equivalence between what we said, in systems of democracy founded on the duty of politicians to tell the truth, and regimes like Milosevic and the Taliban who felt no such obligations, and yet whose word, even when proven to be false, was often given exactly the same weight.

Monday, November 12
At TB's office meeting, we tried to stay focused on the domestic and public services in particular. He was worrying that departments were slowing and slacking a bit whereas now, with so much media focus on the international, it was the time really to be driving forward. I sometimes wondered whether we weren't sometimes victims of what might be defined as success. For example, TB wanted a more centralised system, or at least one where Number 10 could pull levers more effectively in departments. But did it mean that when we weren't focusing so much, they were waiting for the levers to be pulled? Don't know.

Tuesday, November 13

I woke to the news that Kabul had fallen, with John Simpson seeming to claim that he had liberated it. All the armchair generals now moved on from saying the military strategy hadn't worked to saying that we had fucked up the diplomatic channels. And that was what was worrying TB when I got in. He looked tired, had not slept much. At the inner War Cabinet, CDS was still pretty gloomy though he did at least have detailed plans for going in. TB wanted ideas on how the military plan should now be taken forward and extended and how we get the diplomatic channels moving faster. He also wanted specific ideas on the humanitarian side of things and he wanted to put forward military, political/diplomatic and the humanitarian plans to Bush by lunchtime. He wasn't sure they would listen but he said this was the time to build out with a real plan of action.

Wednesday, November 14

TB called as I was driving in and agreed that he should do a statement. He shared my amazement at the ability of our press to turn yesterday into a problem. I said to Tucker Eskew [White House communications deputy, seconded to CIC] at the morning meeting 'Hey, great news, we lost.' He had been genuinely shocked by the desire of most of our media, or so it felt to him, to fail. I think both of us felt a bit that you work your guts out, you strive with everything you've got to make something happen, every step of the way people are saying you can't do it and then when it happens, they are just straight on to saying you can't do the next thing. It wasn't even about a desire for recognition of achievement. It was just the feeling of grind that went with the situation that our media made everything feel like swimming through treacle. There was a fantastic story to be told about the role played by a small number of our spooks, if C and co were up for it. John Scarlett had also been superb, calm, clear, always meticulous about the material he assembled and put forward to the PM, but just as willing to give bad news as good. I had a meeting with David Puttnam [retired from film-making in 1998 to promote education], who I like and think is one of the rare cases of people adapting from success in one world at a very high level to success at a different level in politics. He told me both the BBC and *Guardian* had said to him they were genuinely worried about their relations with us. He also wanted to say that Estelle [Morris] was a real star but she needed boosting and she needed help that she would never ask for herself.

Friday, November 16

We had to hope that the real story of yesterday didn't come out, namely that our SBS guys had landed but the FCO had forgotten to ask the Northern Alliance for authority and protection so that Abdullah Abdullah [spokesman for the post-Taliban Afghan administration] went crazy and at one point they were even asking our guys at Baghram to leave. The Americans were still focused almost totally on the military campaign. Rumsfeld did a briefing showing pictures of Northern Alliance forces with American special forces on horseback. Rumsfeld had definitely emerged as one of the characters of the campaign, was much more popular in the States than here but in his own way had been more impressive than Colin Powell who had come over as a bit weak and dithery. Then, from left field, Mo had done a Cockerell film and said TB was presidential, had killed Cabinet government and the TB/GB relationship was unhappy. JP was asked about it in front of cameras and used the line 'She's daft.' He called me afterwards. I felt he wasn't far wrong.

Saturday, November 17

The *FT* second lead, part inspired by Mo and part by the usual chat around the place, talked of an 'all-time low' between TB and GB, included the stuff about him doing in Byers, messing around on the euro, generally very anti-GB. TB was exercised about it, said it was bad anyway, but also that the party really wouldn't like it if they felt TB was going for GB. It was one thing for the guy at the top to be under attack but it would look bad for TB if it was reciprocated. I spoke to Ian Austin [Brown's press spokesman], who did his usual ludicrous 'we never brief the press' routine and descended into a lot of inarticulate rambling. Other ministers were starting to take a lead, starting to think this was the way to get on.

Monday, November 19

I was really tired, and emotionally drained after a weekend split evenly between working, time with the kids, and arguing with Fiona. The news was ragged and there seemed to be real confusion over what our troops were doing. The American focus seemed to be almost entirely getting OBL, with the future of Afghanistan barely getting a look-in. So it looked like our troops were sitting there for no purpose, with neither the NA nor the Americans really wanting them there, so it was a bit messy.

November '01: Mo says TB has killed Cabinet government

Tuesday, November 27

The main focus of the day was the PBR [pre-Budget Report]. TB came down from the flat, having finally got GB to deliver more for health. We probably ended up pretty much where GB expected us to be in the first place, maybe with a bit more on top, but surely we could have got there without what had been a very difficult process. There was only one story that was going to dominate, namely that taxes would have to rise to pay for a better NHS. Possibly the biggest strategic decision we would take this Parliament, and though we had all known it was coming, we were catching up late in terms of the strategic discussions that we should have had ages ago. After the PBR Cabinet, I had a meeting with Ed Balls, who came in with all the published documents. I asked him when they went to the printers, and he said he didn't know. Taxes up for a better NHS was a pretty strong Labour line, and most Labour people would like it, but we were going to have to engage in a pretty big argument, not least around value for money, to win it with the public. If we did though, it would be a significant shift and an important win. DTLR put out minutes of the Byers Railtrack meeting but only 4 pages.[1] Crazy. I told Byers I thought it was a bad plan and they should never have hired Martin Sixsmith [Director of Communications]. Byers thought I had given my approval. It turned out he had asked his office to check what 'Alastair' thought of Sixsmith, and they had asked Alistair Darling, who seemingly said he thought he was fine.

Thursday, November 29

PBR coverage was going a bit awry. After a pretty low-key War Cabinet, TB saw GB and Alan Milburn, who was livid, said that basically GB was trying to use his position to take over NHS policy, and he wasn't having it. He was not alone in feeling departments had not been properly involved in the PBR preparations. CDS was really steamed up about the arguments they had had to get involved in yesterday re SAS identification. For him, he was quite emotional, really felt that newspapers that couldn't see why it was important that these principles were adhered to were beyond the pale. The mood at Cabinet wasn't good.

Friday, November 30

GB's latest thing was an interview with the *Sun* yesterday, done to try to show the PBR was not the end of New Labour, but he ended

---

[1] The Government had decided in October to put Railtrack into administration.

up going contrary to the strategy we had agreed yesterday and playing into their line that we had done nothing and that the NHS was all crap. Milburn, unsurprisingly, was incandescent. He said he knew how he worked, because he had seen him when he had been at the Treasury. He saw it as his right to trample on everyone else's territory. 'Can I go out now and make a speech saying that the economy ought to be doing a lot better?'

Saturday, December 1

Milburn's rage had not abated with the passage of 24 hours. He told TB direct that if he went to the *Sun* and slagged off the work of another department, he would expect to be sacked, so why was GB allowed to slag off his department?

Monday, December 10

The football match we were organising in Kabul had become my latest obsession. I really wanted it to go big.

Tuesday, December 11

Boyce did a speech at RUSI yesterday, which was going pretty big today, where he basically said that the US were in a different position, that we had to choose between being part of a stabilisation force, and taking part in the wider war on terrorism. I raised it with TB, who just shrugged his shoulders and rolled his eyes as if to say 'Not much we can do about it.' Later I raised it with CDS. I said it was good to see that we cleared the speech, an ironic reference to the fact the *Telegraph* reported that we had done so. 'Did I?' he asked. And I said 'No, you didn't.' 'Should I have done?' 'Well, it is the normal practice that we see speeches likely to make news, which a speech by the Chief of the Defence Staff at a time like this might well do.' I couldn't tell whether he was irritated, worried or indifferent. He wasn't the easiest guy to work with, but he probably felt the same about us. TB said it was important we didn't antagonise him. TB raised the speech with Geoff H who said he had tried to tone it down but the MoD was so leaky there was a limit to what he could do without it becoming an issue. I felt that our event to commemorate September 11 struck the right note, dignified and respectful, not over the top. The US school band I thought was better than the New York trumpeter and I thought GWB's people made a mistake in having him in front of an Israeli flag. Not many would notice that it was an alphabetic point, as the flag was between the Irish and the Italian, but I suspected it would give them problems.

December '01: Milburn furious with GB over his criticism of NHS

Thursday, December 13

Clinton was over making a speech and was up in the flat with TB. He was losing his voice so we sent out for some medicine and I chatted to him and Chelsea in the kitchen while TB got changed. He had time to kill and TB had work to do. I took him for a little wander round the building to see some of the people these big cheeses wouldn't normally see, like the switchboard and the messengers, and of course he was brilliant with them. The War Cabinet was gathering outside the Cabinet room and Dearlove and Scarlett were clearly pleased to see him. I took him round to see the press office and the grid team. As I took him out, he said 'Gee, you got some great women.' Later Doug Band [Clinton aide] called in a bit of a state because Bill had referred to 'Prime Minister Brown' in his speech on Aids at the QE2 [Queen Elizabeth II Conference Centre, London]. I assured him TB wouldn't mind. Cabinet was pretty short. TB did his usual script, at some length. Maintaining economic strength and stability, investment and reform, what type of society we want to live in, international strength, pro-European, strong on defence. In all of them, emphasising we had broken free from traditional positions, we can manage the economy but also attack poverty. We can invest in public services but also do difficult reform. Strong on people's rights but demanding responsibility. Tough on defence but proud of helping others in the world. All this matters for giving the party a sense of what we believe in, confidence in what we are for. He felt the Tories were in real trouble, and that the Lib Dems were becoming ridiculous, saying to anyone what they wanted to hear.

Saturday, December 15

TB told me from the summit that Berlusconi was arguing that the food agency should go to Parma because of the cuisine there. TB said he really did seem to believe that it was a food agency, like a kind of glorified restaurant. The favourite was in Finland and Chirac had asked TB 'Why do we want to send the food agency to a country that only eats reindeer?' TB said somehow Europe seems to work, but if we are being frank, a lot of it is haggling, deals and people missing the point.

Monday, December 17

CDS took delight in saying he had witnessed a video conference in which Bush briefed Franks on the force and said 'I've spoken to the PM and I've made no promises at all.' He defended Franks by saying that Chris Meyer spotted immediately that the US would not buy the language TB agreed with Chirac. I suggested to TB that he had a private word with Boyce. After the statement he got him in with Geoff Hoon and 'cleared the air'. If ever we needed evidence of TB not focusing on the domestic, it came when he asked whether we could get a piece of legislation through to be told it went through on Thursday night because our MPs stayed up all night. He also wanted to get out of a dinner on Africa with ministers tonight but we pushed him into it by saying he was in danger of not being taken seriously on it. He agreed reluctantly but when it came to it, it was Bono and Bob Geldof who got the invitation up to the flat.

Wednesday, December 19

TB had dinner last night with GB and said he had been on best behaviour but it was still difficult. TB had given him a pretty frank assessment of why he (TB) was generally thought to be an OK PM – because he had breadth, could deal with a stack of different things at once, and get on with a range of people. He told him he still believed he was easily the best person to follow him but he was not going to support him in circumstances where he felt he was being forced out. They had also discussed the euro, where he felt GB was more open-minded but that Balls was pouring opposition into his head the whole time. TB was looking a bit downcast again.

Thursday, December 20

I was due to have lunch with Peter M, which had been my suggestion after he emailed me re an article he was doing. I asked Hilary C to find somewhere discreet and she had booked La Trouvaille in Newburgh Street. I arrived first, Peter a few minutes later, and we were put in the window. Who should walk by, just seconds after we sat down, but Andrew Marr, but he was so busy window shopping on the other side of the passageway that he didn't see us. Peter did most of the talking early on, re what he had now taken to calling his 'defenestration'. He was very calm and friendly, said he wasn't blaming me directly but described the whole episode leading to his resignation as a 'road accident' in which everyone accidentally conspired. I said I had thought about it a lot and if it had been anyone else, we would probably have survived but he had baggage that weighed us down. On the whole Geoffrey [Robinson] loan episode, he felt it was a case of the circumstances of one period

December '01: TB tells GB he will not be forced out

being different to those of another. When he took out the loan, Geoffrey was not persona non grata, was not a media bogeyman, was a friend who had always taken an interest in helping Peter. PM said he had always wanted a nice home and to find someone to live with. He hated Wilmington Square because it didn't feel like a home. His private life was happy, but why because he was a politician should there have to be comment about it at all, why? Nobody ever disputed he was a good minister and he felt he had to get back to top-level politics. I said it was true, he rarely got criticised on ability grounds. He accepted a return to the Cabinet was difficult, so the options were probably Europe or the UN and he was intending to develop his international profile.

I discussed the lunch with TB in advance. He said he didn't rule out Peter coming back but he had to lower the personal profile. He was a phenomenal talent but flawed and the heart of the flaw was his relationship with the press. When I relayed that, Peter said he hardly ever spoke to the press, only read the *FT*, it was the media that had created the persona, not the other way round. He clearly couldn't accept he had done much wrong, certainly felt wronged and tried to come to terms with it every day, and said he found it difficult. He said he knew I thought his problem was the profile but it wasn't. His problem was that others, including me and TB, couldn't make the shift from seeing him as 'Bobby'. He felt he never recovered from that, that he could never be seen as a legitimate politician, that it was cruel that even as a minister, TB and I often saw him more as a behind-the-scenes person. Add in his worries about the media constantly probing re his private life, add in GB 'always there, as a presence, his people intent on destroying me,' and it wasn't a happy mix. He felt the rift with GB, contrary to legend, was not when he supported TB. It was at Chewton Glen [a country hotel in the New Forest], when he, TB and GB had had a meeting before the dinner and GB, to everyone's astonishment, produced a blueprint of everything to be done, including personnel issues in the party. TB was visibly taken aback and asked Peter his view. Peter stalled and said we needed to think about it. After TB went to bed, Peter said he needed to think about it and discuss it with TB. GB replied 'You've made your choice,' and stormed off. He felt GB underestimated TB's steel. He saw me and Peter as the two strong people and had always felt if he could get us basically over to him, he could deal with TB. He underestimated our basic loyalty, but also TB's steel.

By now, there were more guests in the restaurant who had

noticed us and we were virtually whispering across the table. Peter told me of a meeting he had had while the Hammond Inquiry was going on. He wanted to explain to GB why he was fighting so hard for his story to be heard. They met in Gordon's office at the Commons. GB put him at ease straight away, asking with seeming sincerity how he was. Peter said bruised and hurt and really trying to come back. He said he told him the story as dispassionately as he could, his role, Jack's role, my role, Mike O'Brien, TB, the Civil Service, 'I was as dispassionate as I could be, tried not to blame, no individual's fault, just a terrible set of circumstances ending in a road crash.' GB listened and said the problem was that I had created the context on the Monday by saying that was the only contact between Peter and the Home Office (via his private office) and it meant an elephant trap was laid. 'Then you fell into it. The only way out is for Alastair to say he misbriefed and apologise but he won't do that.' He said TB needed strong personalities to support him. First, it had been PM/GB and then it became PM/AC. But AC wanted to be the main voice 'so he conspired to push you out, it's obvious'. Peter was in full flow, vivid, and I sometimes felt he had a photographic memory for these key moments and his key relationships. He said he told GB he didn't believe it was like that, pointed out 'You have to remember Alastair is different to us, he would happily walk away from politics, he has a different life he can lead, family, money to make beyond our dreams, he never chose this path, he was pursued, we poached him and a large part of him didn't want it.' Then PM spoke as GB again. 'Yes, but once he chose it, he wanted to be Number One and he's done it by getting rid of you at a time TB and I are seen as rivals.' Even aiming off for possible exaggeration, and I'm not sure there was that much, I was mildly shocked. PM said he had remained supportive of me and GB was just trying to use the circumstances of the time to get PM to move in his favour. He said that TB was different class as a politician. 'I love his deviousness, his selfishness, the way he is able to turn everything to his own advantage. His genius as a politician is his understanding of people, but also the fact that he is totally selfish and people either don't see it or if they do, they don't seem to mind because of what he brings to them and the job.' I reminded him of the time TB had told us that Labour governments always foundered on issues of ego and personality, and that we had to be different. I agreed with his car crash analysis, felt that if it hadn't been him, we would have handled it differently, felt that we both made mistakes. I felt sad that he was out of things, and sad that I had played a part in that. He was right that I could probably walk away. He wasn't able to, yet had had to. I felt sad for him but pleased we were still able to work together, pleased that despite it all, we were still able to talk openly and I still consider him to be a friend whose judgement I value.

We went out, and stood there, in the middle of Carnaby Street, with a couple of bodyguards, passers-by shooting the occasional odd look and Peter said 'Happy Christmas. I had better do some shopping.' And off he went. He had given me a lot of food for thought. We weren't exactly blessed with A-league ministers. He pointed out that he may have made mistakes on the personal front, but he never fucked up on policy and he always gave real direction to whatever department he was in. It was true. All the departments he worked in said the same. He could make decisions, and he could run things. I tried to work out whether he had gone second time around because it was him, or because of what our media operation and media relations had become, and his role in that. In a way, the strength he had brought to the modernisation of our media relations was what made him the bogey figure he was, and that status plus baggage was what made us turn a mistake into something far bigger. It was the same reason so many in the media felt about me as they did. He also seemed more resigned to things. He believed that the new papers he had discovered for Hammond to look at showed that he was done in. But he had no desire to push it, felt it would only be worth it if it led to a change of attitude by the public and that would only come about if TB and I said that it changed things materially. And neither of us would want to do that because the world had moved on. I was struck by how much he, and from his reported comments GB, believed I meant to TB, far more than I felt myself. He had said that both he and GB felt I was by far the closest, that he felt hurt because we had been such close friends, not so close any more, while he believed GB just hated me and feared me in equal measure and saw me as someone that had to be dealt with. He really enjoyed the story of my row with GB during the election. He was making enough money and travelling a lot but when he listed the countries he was due to be visiting, he said 'I'm busy, but it's no life.' He also wanted to dispute my line, which he had heard me say more than once, that he had dumped his old friends for a new rich set. He said he found his life very lonely at times and people like Carla Powell [socialite, wife of former Thatcher adviser, Charles] gave him friendship and support and also a lot of fun that was missing a lot of the time.

I watched him wander off before going to do a bit of shopping of my own. In some ways, we'd grown apart, but I felt that between us we'd given something to TB, and the party, that really mattered, and that meant there would always be a bond there. I talked to Philip about it later and Grace [Gould], who was listening to the conversation, said she thought we would always be working together in some shape or form.

Thursday, January 3, 2002

Bangladesh. The visit got off to a potentially embarrassing start. TB's suit was badly crumpled after his car journey in Egypt [on holiday] and not nearly smart enough to wear as he left the plane. But all the other suits were in the hold and it would take a while to find them. So Magi [Cleaver] was dispatched off the plane first to find someone wearing a smart suit that would fit TB. We watched her through the windows walking up and down the lines of people eyeing them up and down. None of them were suitable. Then she spotted a young man at the back of the crowd and went over to him. His face was a picture. I think he thought it was some kind of spoof but then Magi was doing her best 'this is fucking serious' look and seconds later the two of them were coming up the stairs. 'Ah, the body double,' I said. He was a DFID [Department for International Development] official and gobsmacked to be on the plane with TB, CB and the rest of us. TB said 'Sorry about this but as you can see my suit is not in good shape.' So then this poor guy is stripping off so that TB can try on his suit. It wasn't perfect but it wasn't far off. The swap was done and then we were ready to disembark. There was a full-on welcome and then straight to the President's residence. There were some pretty overwhelming scenes of poverty on the way and once we got into town the open sewers took some getting used to. But the people were by and large friendly and welcoming. Also, whereas the leadership of some countries lived in inverse proportion to the poverty of the people, with the President [Professor Badruddoza Chowdhury] and PM [Khaleda Zia] too, you were always aware of this being the third world. They did not overdo their own luxury.

Friday, January 4

Events in Kashmir were the backdrop to the next stage of the visit. TB, David Manning and I met to discuss how we choreograph a sense of TB playing a part in trying to get the immediate problem solved. The Kathmandu Asian summit should at least be a chance to calm things down, but the tensions were pretty strong. After dealing with all that, we then went from the sublime to the ridiculous, with a long discussion about whether TB should wear his Nehru suit. I was marginally in favour provided it didn't look too ridiculous, partly because hopefully it would be seen as showing respect, but also because if we could generate pictures, we were more likely to generate coverage. We got to the hotel and he put it on. It looked fine.

Sunday, January 6

Gordon's baby was clearly dying.[1] TB and CB were both genuinely upset. Fiona called a couple of times from home to say we had to be careful on the various visits, because the media were obviously trying to set up shots of TB not seeming to care about this developing tragedy at home. Through the day, it was announced that the baby was deteriorating and had had a brain haemorrhage. After Fiona's second call, we put out a line re TB and CB thinking of them. The Sundays were even more ridiculous than usual, most of them taking as the nose to their stories the throwaway remark by an Indian minister yesterday that 'We are cool enough' as a great snub, India saying fuck off as a response to him re his Nehru suit. I was more convinced than ever that we had to articulate this business of us having a press that actively wanted failure. The Indian press had been overwhelmingly positive about the speech, about him and CB, about our role. I went to the gym, where the little guy in there insisted on giving me a workout on the weights, and I was in agony by the time I got back to see TB. We went out on the rooftop of the hotel for a chat and he was clearly a bit down. He was putting enormous effort into trying to get progress on various fronts at home and abroad and all the time we had this media shit to swim through.

Hyderabad. We left for the palace for the talks. TB pushed hard but got very little change out of Vajpayee. He was holding out for a lot more from the Pakistanis. He was pretty shrewd, and his total lack of embarrassment at long silences was a real strength. At the official dinner, I was for some reason seated next to Vajpayee. He was an attentive host, but so quiet. I asked him whether it was a strength or a disadvantage to have such a quiet voice, and whether he used silence as a political weapon. He said he liked to think his authority

[1] The Browns' daughter, Jennifer Jane, had been born prematurely, on December 28, 2001.

came from within, as well as from the position he held. When he spoke in his native tongue, he could raise his voice to great levels and had regularly addressed crowds of half a million during the election. But words were precious, and there was little point speaking when nothing was to be said. He said Gandhi fasted to preserve his strength, and he too had learned the value of rest and peacefulness. TB was across the table talking to [Lal Krishna] Advani, the interior minister, and George Fernandes [defence minister]. At one point he joked across the table to Vajpayee re me, 'Be careful, he's a bad man,' and Vajpayee said 'I don't think so.'

Monday, January 7

Really, really heavy day. Breakfast with TB in Delhi. Both he and CB sensed that the GB situation re the baby was heading for disaster. We were starting to get more criticism re TB focusing so much on foreign affairs. He felt the answer was to build the logical argument re why these issues mattered at home. We set off for the airport and boarded the C130 for Islamabad. TB and CB were up on the top deck sitting just behind the pilot, who had a paper cup fixed by a rubber band to his head and 'I am a Sunderland fan' written on the cup. We went to the hotel and down to the pool to discuss how to handle the meetings. TB felt step one had to be Musharraf getting tougher with the terror groups, use that to press the Indians to engage. There had to be an absolute break with the Taliban and any of the groups they supported. But Pakistan also had to know there were benefits out of that. Musharraf clearly baulked at him saying 'Support for terrorism must stop for talks to begin.' He said he didn't like it because it suggested that Pakistan and its government supported terrorism. We persuaded him that the best thing to do then was for him to say right at the top that he opposed terrorism in all its forms. We also persuaded him not to talk about Kashmir as a 'freedom struggle' because that would not be understood by our and by US opinion. Better to say it was an indigenous struggle. We spent an awful lot of time to-ing and fro-ing on it but eventually he agreed. Their general feeling was that India was in a box and didn't know how to get out of it. It was funny too how both sides seemed to talk of the other as equals, even though India was so much bigger and more powerful.

We flew in total darkness to Baghram, with only the occasional flash of green from night sights. As we arrived, it was pitch black. TB and CB went out to a red carpet, [Hamid] Karzai [chairman of the Transitional Administration], the band playing the barely discernible tune of welcome, and general chaos to which I added, stepping down from the plane, when my briefcase, even though the combination lock was on, suddenly opened and papers were flying all over the place. David [Manning], Anna Wechsberg and I scrabbled around using hands, feet and anything else to trap the paper and get, hopefully, all of it back. TB was now standing with an Afghan shouting into his face in what seemed to be part of the welcome. We were then taken to a line of armoured vehicles and the Special Branch advance guy introduced David and me to the special forces who were going to be looking after us. The drive was slow, over endless tank traps, eventually reaching the old Russian barracks. TB had a one-on-one with Karzai, said he was very upbeat, probably too much, but he was clearly pleased that TB had come, particularly given the genuine security risks, and there was a good atmosphere between them. As we came out of the meeting, into the darkened corridor, Keith Lowe [protection officer] took me to one side and said 'You should probably tell the PM that the Chancellor's baby has died.' There is something about a baby's death. Even the cops, who can turn pretty much anything into a source of laughter, seemed really saddened, and were explaining to the Afghans what had happened. I told TB in between meetings. I said I'm afraid there's bad news, and he knew straight away what it was, and asked us to try to fix a call.

We had to move to a bigger room for a meeting with eight of the ministers from the interim government. One look around the room was enough to tell you what a nightmare job Karzai had trying to hold things together. TB and Karzai said a few words of welcome and then opened things up. They were a pretty aggressive bunch. One of them was the double of Orson Welles and said they needed long-term help. His tone of voice suggested he didn't think we would deliver it. There was another guy who looked like something out of the Taliban and who spent most of the meeting trying to stare us out. One or two were dressed in Western-style suits but they said little. Karzai was definitely a cut above but he really had his work cut out. They had cobbled together from somewhere a collection of chairs and tables, and laid out a rather sad collection of sweets that nobody touched. TB said Britain would stay with them for the long term. Karzai said Afghanistan was well rid of the terrible leadership that went before. Abdullah said they were effectively reconstructing a country from scratch. Karzai obviously picked up on the somewhat negative tone of some of the ministerial contributions and concluded the meeting by saying they were all 'so glad that such a distinguished person has come to see us, taken the risk, you have demonstrated

January '02: TB meets with Karzai

such goodwill. When the Afghan people get to hear that you visited us, they will be proud and thrilled.' One of the special forces guys said to me 'Welcome to bandit country.' We drove, as slowly and painfully as before, to the special forces HQ, to put a phone call through to Sue Nye. She confirmed that the baby was dead and that it had now been announced publicly. TB was genuinely cut up, said it was a horrible thing to have to go through, and even worse with all the attention on it. He was having to talk quite loudly to be heard. I could sense that this collection of real hard nuts from the SAS and the SBS were a bit bemused to have their Prime Minister in there having a near-weepy phone call. He was pretty discombobulated and wanted further confirmation and assurance that it had been announced. Karzai arrived and we filled him in on what was happening, explaining why he would have to address it. Karzai showed a deft touch, taking his hat off when TB spoke later re GB. We were taken to meet some of the real heroes from both SAS and SBS. The first presentation was from a guy who had been part of a team following a tip that OBL was in a certain cave. They had ended up living for days without supplies, having to make do with what they found, including a 30-hour period in which the only consumption between four of them, apart from stuff off trees, was a small bottle of water. They had been calling on bombers and fighting their way, hand to hand, towards where they were going. But he had gone by the time they got there. Then a Geordie who had been at the fort at Mazar, buried under rubble after an American bomb went astray, got out, involved in all sorts of fighting, got out the body of the American guy who had been killed there, eventually flushing out the al-Qaeda people by pumping in freezing water. He told it all with a mix of real pride and deadpan humour. These guys were genuinely impressive people. Their living quarters here, let alone when they were out and about, were incredibly basic and yet there was an enthusiasm there that was incredible. None of them seemed boastful, or demanding of credit or praise. They just explained very factually what they did. One of the most impressive was the smallest, a Scottish guy so small I was surprised he was even allowed in the armed forces. Once again, we were confronted by the ingenuity and the resilience of our troops. TB said he needed a pee and we were taken out, up a field, to a series of upturned tubes in the ground.

Back on the C130, I met the SIS guy who had actually been the first person into Kabul, even if John Simpson had never met him. He too combined modesty with a very matter-of-fact ability to describe astonishing events. We flew out in total darkness, with a flare going by every now and then. Eventually, I managed to sleep. We landed in Oman and were glad to be transferred to the million times more comfortable 777. I called Ian Austin, and later wrote a letter to GB, as did TB and Cherie. TB briefed us on the one-on-one parts of his various meetings over dinner. He felt we had achieved things in India and Pakistan that actually made conflict less likely. But he was beginning to take seriously the stuff about him being more abroad than home, and talking about pulling out of his Africa tour. I felt that would be a mistake because it would look weak and defensive.

Wednesday, January 9

My first morning meeting of the year, as we went through the media brief, was like swimming through shit. Virtually every paper over every story in knocking mode. TB, the great man abroad as seen overseas, was being whacked at home over absolutely everything.

Friday, January 11

TB called me on his way back from the baby's funeral to say it had been a nice service but he had been quite shocked to see how many journalists were there, including Dacre. I said I couldn't imagine why they would have wanted anyone but really close friends there, and TB said different people react differently in grief. He said he went back to the house after the service and GB had been very warm, and that it reminded him of the days when they had been genuinely close.

Saturday, January 12

To the Goulds' for dinner. Gail asked whether Philip and I had ever had a discussion that did not cover TB, GB, PM and their varying relationships. The answer is probably not, at least none that lasted more than a minute or two.

Thursday, January 17

The mood in the media was now pretty nasty. TB told Cabinet that while it was difficult, it gave us the opportunity to get up definition for reform. There were a number of interesting contributions, not least JP, who made clear that if we pushed too far on private sector involvement in health, we wouldn't be able to take the party with us. TB did at least steady nerves a bit. People were asking for a core script and I was clearly going to have to get back to doing the weekly strategy notes. Charles Clarke felt he was being blamed for the lack of coherent strategy, but it was largely my fault, because I had been so demotivated. TB was emphasising that we were not going to improve public services without real change. We should be pointing to education as the area where reforms had most obviously yielded benefits. But in health now, virtually every indicator was moving in the right direction. So do not be apologetic or defensive. There was a comic moment when TB started a sentence: 'If JP had come to me in '97 and said renationalise the railways, it would have been a short conversation.' 'It was a short conversation,' JP interrupted.

Murdoch was coming in for dinner, and along with Les Hinton brought James and Lachlan [Murdoch's sons]. They arrived a bit early, and I took Murdoch upstairs because TB wanted 15 minutes with him, then entertained the others in my office before we went up. I was interested to see how Murdoch related to his kids. Lachlan seemed a bit shy of expressing his views whereas James was anything but. Murdoch was at one point putting the traditional very right-wing view on Israel and the Middle East peace process and James said that he was 'talking fucking nonsense'. Murdoch said he didn't see what the Palestinians' problem was and James said it was that they were kicked out of their fucking homes and had nowhere to fucking live. Murdoch was very pro-Israel, very pro-Reagan. He finally said to James that he didn't think he should talk like that in the Prime Minister's house and James got very apologetic with TB, who said not to worry, I hear far worse all the time. Most of the discussion was a run round the main foreign-policy blocks, Israel, Saudi, Iran, Indo-Pak, a little bit of why does Britain have to bother so much? We didn't get into Europe at all, which was a bit of a waste. TB said afterwards he was quite impressed with the way Murdoch let his sons do so much of the talking. Murdoch pointed out that his were the only papers that gave us support when the going got tough. 'I've noticed,' said TB. I gave them my culture-of-denigration argument and was probably a bit over the top.

Monday, January 21
Guantánamo[1] was running big and bad, and we were not in shape to deal with it.

Tuesday, January 29
I was trying to get on top of Bush's State of the Union address[2] and eventually Peter Reid [UK government press officer, Washington

---

[1] Prison camp for alleged terrorists at the US Navy base in Cuba.
[2] Bush's speech referred to the 'Axis of Evil'.

Embassy] got hold of an advance copy. It named Iran, Iraq and Korea in the context, or so it would be taken, as possible targets of attack. Karzai was doing well out there. I got hold of his draft itinerary for his visit here and it was ludicrous – 40 minutes with TB and lunch with Robert Cooper [diplomat] for heaven's sake. I put a note round saying it was being revised and we went for Karzai coming to the end of Cabinet, proper meeting with TB, joint al-Jazeera [Arabic-language TV station] interview kind of thing. Also we should get Afghan exiles in to see them.

Thursday, January 31

Karzai was visiting, in one of his long capes, and when I told him he was getting as much coverage for his fashionability as his politics, he said he had started wearing it one day because it was cold, and he just kept wearing it. Now it was part of his make-up. In Afghanistan, he said, it was a very conservative form of dress. At the lunch, you could see them trying hard to adapt to this new way of life. Karzai had his wits about him, and looked and sounded the part, if a bit forced at times. But [General Mohammed] Fahim Khan [new leader of the Northern Alliance], a real brute with enormous hands and a big growly face, could barely hold a knife and fork. It was an interesting lunch, Karzai now moving onto drugs, and explaining the help they would need to change crop production patterns. They were virtually rebuilding a country and its infrastructure from scratch, as when he said they would be grateful for advice on how to establish a new central bank. Khan was even more straightforward, said we had been giving a lot of help to the regional warlords but now we had to start giving more help to the centre – i.e. him. On the conference call with the White House, I told them there had been an overwhelmingly negative reaction round Europe to the GWB speech. They seemed surprised. TB said when we were at media dinners together, e.g. with Murdoch recently, it was clear to everyone how I felt and I needed to be cautious. I said I hated having to pander to these people, and that they took it as weakness not strength. I had said the same to Blunkett re his greasing up to Dacre. TB gave me a look that suggested he was fed up hearing the same old song. I said it is no good just being fed up. I'm fed up too, fed up with the fact we are in power and doing nothing to change the poisonous media culture which is actually damaging the country now. I said I couldn't stand the *Mail*, most of the *Telegraph*, a fair few of the broadcasters, most of the Sundays, and now Piers [Morgan] was on my list of barely worth talking to. Fiona was back on at me to quit if I felt strongly, and disagreed on a fundamental strategic point.

Saturday, February 9

Nick Matthews [duty clerk] called before 8 to say that Princess Margaret had died. TB was currently being told and it would be announced by the Palace shortly. There was no need for him to come back, but he would need to say something so I might want to start thinking about that. I reminded Nick that he was the one who called me re Diana's death. 'That was a bit more dramatic than this one,' he said. TB called as he waited to leave for Sierra Leone. I said it was important he didn't try too hard, or appear emotional, just say she was basically a good thing, thoughts with the Queen, Queen Mum, rest of family, etc. Robin Janvrin called to go through the statement they were putting out. The Queen's instincts were to carry on with her (fairly light) duties next week, and to make the funeral private. He said she would probably want to speak to TB later. TB set off for Sierra Leone, met the troops and the government welcoming party and then did his doorstep on Margaret. It was a bit actorish for my liking, but OK I guess. We had to watch any sense of this being anything like Diana. Janvrin was thinking the same thing though perhaps for different reasons when he called pre TB's call with the Queen. I felt the simplest thing was make clear this was different to Diana's death in part because it was expected. I also felt people would respond to the fact the Queen and Queen Mother would take this differently and there was a case for them being seen fairly soon, showing she was still up and about and doing her duty, but also showing some emotion at the loss of a younger sister. She would clearly be thinking of her own mortality, not to mention her mother's. Charles went to Sandringham 'to comfort the Queen Mother' and also did a broadcast, which was OK but he was not a natural presenter and he shifted around too much, creating constant distractions from what he was saying.

Sunday, February 10

The only political story running out of the Sundays was the *Sunday Telegraph* reheat of the *Western Mail*/Plaid [Cymru] story on [Lakshmi] Mittal's donation [£125,000] to the Labour Party. The donation seemingly came a few weeks before TB wrote to the PM of Romania [Adrian Năstase] to welcome a deal with a Mittal company, which was basically Dutch rather than UK.

Monday, February 11

The Mittal situation was tricky. TB was totally dismissive of the whole thing, saw nothing wrong with it at all. I said it was a bit odd that he was writing letters to the Romanian PM about what was in the end a Dutch deal, even if Mittal ran the company. He was clear we just had to ride it out and tell them to get stuffed.

Wednesday, February 13

I was in early, and up to see him in the flat. It was dark up there and he seemed a bit down. He asked me if I was depressed. I said yes. Clinically I mean, he said. I said I think so. He said my problem was I was agonising – stay or go. He felt I would hate it if I went, no matter how much I sometimes hated it now. I needed to see the press as the inevitable downside of a job that had a huge upside, namely doing an important job and being part of a huge process of change for the country. He said 'If I die tomorrow, they would say he was the guy who modernised the Labour Party, made it electable, won two landslides, sorted the economy, improved public services, Bank of England, Kosovo, Northern Ireland. They would barely mention the frenzies we have survived, so always remember the big things, the big reasons why we're doing it.' He accepted Mittal was a problem for us, the focus moving to Jonathan's role as gatekeeper to TB and how that fits with any political or party role. TB looked tired, Jonathan looked nervous. They both hated this kind of thing. We had to decide how heavy TB should get, and we agreed – heavy. At PMQs, TB really went for IDS and we avoided the question about whether he or Jonathan knew Mittal was a donor.

Wednesday, February 20

Jack S came over for a chat. He was strongly of the view that TB should do something that would symbolise a greater respect for Parliament, maybe appear at the PASC [Public Administration Select Committee]. He asked how I was, and I said pretty fed up. Why? Because I spend so much time clearing up the shit, and I don't always feel I get the support in return. Number 10 is seen by departments as interfering, and yet they are on to us the whole time to sort things that go wrong. Jack felt we had made Number 10 more powerful but not necessarily more effective across government. He felt there were too many of our people who called departments and said they were 'Number 10'. If it was me or Jonathan, people knew that mattered, and in any event we would deal with ministers. But departments had any number of people calling up and saying what TB wanted, or what Number 10 wanted.

Tuesday, February 26

TB was clearly thinking Steve Byers should go.[1] Sally [Morgan], Jonathan and I were pushing hard for SB, and Peter H was manic about it, saying he had only been put in the position he was in because he was done in from inside. As Jonathan said, we were going to have to throw him into the gladiators' ring and see if he survived. It was not the best way to deal with it, but there was a reluctance to toss him overboard given the background. We watched him do the statement and as Peter Kilfoyle, Tam Dalyell and others got up to back him, there was at last the feeling that we could fight back. The main thing was that SB was thought by MPs to have done well. I was impressed by his Zen-like qualities today. He didn't panic. It could so easily have gone the other way. TB was just about OK with the way things went, but clearly felt there was something odd, which of course there was, about the Dimbleby interview.

Thursday, February 28

TB was doing an interview for ABC in the States, very forward on Iraq and pro-GWB. At Cabinet, he said it was important to emphasise that nothing re Iraq was planned and that we were a long way off taking decisions. Blunkett referred to the unsettling speculation and said a lot of people had difficulties with Rumsfeld. TB said Bush was in charge, not Rumsfeld, and David said, to some laughter, 'That's mildly reassuring.' What was interesting about most contributions, e.g. Margaret B, was that the press and media were as much the opposition as the Tories. This had been a media-driven frenzy, with the Tories playing shotgun. TB said we were more spinned against than spinning. They cannot find a full-frontal policy assault so this is the substitute for it. It makes it all the more important to stay on a proper policy agenda.

Friday, March 1

The Peter M report, Hammond Mark 2, was the main political story and we bent over backwards to be nice about Peter, to the extent that

[1] The saga had gone on for weeks. In a TV interview with Jonathan Dimbleby, Byers had made a misleading statement that he had not been involved in the controversial resignation of Martin Sixsmith. Byers apologised to the Commons: 'If my answers on the programme gave the impression that I did not put forward a view . . . to others inside and outside the department, that is obviously something I regret.'

the story effectively became TB apologising for him being sacked. I felt sorry for him. The reality was if it had been another minister he or she probably wouldn't have paid with their job. Though we could present it in the way we did, it wasn't the case that the report fully exonerated him.

Monday, March 4
I had lunch with Richard Wilson. He clearly believed I had been briefing against him during the Peter M affair, which I hadn't, and we cleared the air on that. He seemed pretty down, said he had just about had enough of the job and really hated recent events, as had I. I felt he had done pretty well and that TB was probably right, that we should have involved him more, but Jonathan basically felt he was hostile. He said he felt I was exceptionally good at the job but perhaps the GICS had withered a bit under my weight. He liked Tony, felt he was an extraordinary character and the way he used the impact he made on people was a real gift. But he wished he could have done more to help him. He thought maybe it was a generational thing, but he never felt that he got into the inner circle. He felt Jonathan despised him. He said permanent secretaries felt real respect for GB. He sometimes thought Tony believed he could live with GB on the backbenches, but he didn't think so. He gave me the impression of someone who felt he hadn't succeeded. He was keen for a Civil Service act but didn't seem sure what he would want to do with it. There was something very sad about him today.

Thursday, March 7
I drove in with Philip, who felt we needed a plan to deal with spin and sleaze. He said switchers had been getting jittery, no sense of delivery, nothing going on in the debate that they identified with. TB leadership and the economy, commitment to public services and the Tories were what kept us going but we weren't in good shape. Blunkett was in a foul mood because someone had briefed against his spending bid. TB felt David was slightly losing the plot with the police. Cabinet was mainly about Iraq. Not exactly division, but a lot of concern, where is it going? DB saying he didn't feel there was much support. Several saying the real concern was the Middle East peace process. Charles [Clarke] said the party would support provided the case was real and properly made. Jack pointed out it was untrue to say sanctions had stopped food going to Iraq. Geoff H said that if action was taken it would be because of UNSCRs. DB raised the international and legal basis for action. He said that support for Kosovo and Afghanistan

had been pretty overwhelming. He felt a military assault on Iraq would carry less weight. It would depend on the role of the UN. Robin started off by saying that Saddam was a shit, a psychopath, who resolved their prison overcrowding problem by shooting 15,000 people with the longest sentences and who gassed the Kurds. On military action, he said there was a fine balance to strike. Saddam will not listen to Kofi Annan unless he believes there might be military action. He said the best way of isolating Saddam from the rest of public opinion there was progress in the MEPP. He also warned that Britain could end up isolated, with a number of EU governments sounding sympathetic but on past form would not sign up. Charles C felt the judgement that would be applied would be one of success or failure. He felt people understood TB's position of support in exchange for influence. TB said people's concerns were justified. 'I do want to assure you that the management has not gone crazy.'

Monday, March 11

Cheney arrived for talks with JP, then a tête-à-tête with TB, during which they went over Iraq. The Americans claimed to be conscious of the importance of the MEPP but we were not sure they really got it. Cheney had a quiet manner, was pretty calm and although he had gravitas, somehow the whole wasn't as impressive as it ought to be. They discussed NATO expansion and TB said re Putin that the key to understanding him is that he is a Russian patriot. At least Communism got them noticed. He's not a Communist, far from it, but that colours his thinking. He wants to be at the top table.

Up to the flat for dinner – TB, Peter M, PG, Sally, Jonathan, Robert Hill and I. Peter M was on better form and we had constant references to his own demise, and my/TB's roles in it. His analysis was that we came in after a pretty unedifying election, had a bad start, lacked clarity on the agenda, then Afghanistan drowned out domestic issues. Now there was a different mood where anything we did was being turned against us. TB insisted the problems were perception not real. Peter, Philip and I argued that some of the problems had been real. We had lacked clarity. We had lost the clearer sense of purpose we had before. Jo Moore staying was a mistake. So was the Mittal letter but TB always defended our basic position. I said there was a real problem, not just one of perception, even if it was a succession of different perceptions that created the problem. He said no, this is dangerous thinking which has to be resisted because what they want is to stop us being effective. Peter felt TB had certain blind spots. He should do more in Parliament. He should do more in Cabinet. We should try to generate an intelligent debate within the media about the media and its relations with politics. Philip felt that in some ways perception had become reality, but it was reality that had to be dealt with. Philip asked him direct whether he enjoyed dealing with foreign policy more than domestic, because that's what he felt. TB felt, particularly post September 11, they couldn't be separated in the same way as before, but his main focus was always domestic and at the moment specifically crime. He agreed on the need to do more in Parliament and develop a better media strategy.

Thursday, March 21

Before the hunting statement, Gerald Kaufman [chairman of the Culture, Media and Sport Select Committee] called me to say he would never see himself as a loyal TB supporter again if we backtracked on this. I said I never realised he was so passionate about it and he said he was, adding 'If the Tony who stood up to Milosevic and bin Laden can't stand up to the Countryside Alliance, I can't support him.'

Saturday, March 30

Jeremy called to tell me, in total confidence, that the Queen Mother had died. Although she had been frail, the actual death came as a surprise. The Queen was there now and they were trying to tell Charles, who was in Klosters. They hoped to announce it soon. They were aiming for around 6. TB came on the line and we went over what to do. Unlike with Diana's death, there were well-laid plans which swung into action pretty quickly. But it was evident they were a bit worried, unsure that there would be crowds to justify three days lying in state, or that there would be the level of interest necessary to fill nine days of news. I felt that it would develop a strong momentum of its own and that they were worrying unduly, though I could see why. TB, Jeremy and I agreed that we should go for a recall of Parliament before people started to call for it, and got Hilary Armstrong on the case. TB worked on his words and as soon as it was announced formally, we got a crew to Chequers. He spoke well, and all the better for it being all his own words. The atmosphere was very different to Diana's death. It was not a Diana moment. TB felt there would be quite an outpouring of grief but I felt more that it would become one of those moments where people simply reviewed the past. Cherie was out in the States on her holiday and we had to make a decision about whether she came back or not. She clearly didn't want to. TB spoke to the Queen around 7 and told me afterwards she was 'very sad but dignified'. I spoke to Janvrin again, who agreed we should go to the US as planned and Jeremy H successfully pushed them for a Tuesday funeral so we could get to the US and back. I spoke to JP, who agreed to do the media on the Queen Mum tomorrow. Jeremy was doing a fantastic job with the Palace.

Sunday, March 31

TB called re the fact that cameras were still hanging around. He was volunteering to do more extended interviews today but we took the judgement it would look like he was muscling. Maybe another time. We did a couple of conference calls to agree what we should be saying about the visit to the US going ahead, recall of Parliament, receiving the body to Westminster Hall. TB, Jeremy and I went through the draft guidance on national mourning and took out a reference to businesses closing down on the day of the funeral, instead putting in the idea that schools do something to respect it, also give guidance on how practically people went to see the body. Our input was fairly minimal compared to Diana's death, but there was nonetheless a steady traffic between us and the Palace. I felt Charles should do something public fairly soon, the Queen maybe later in the week. JP did fine on the lunchtimes. Once all the amendments were put into the guidance, and some of the more antiquated language was taken out, we put it out. There were the beginnings of chat about the royals coming under more scrutiny, how long would the Queen stay, would she abdicate kind of thing, but it was still pretty low-key.

Monday, April 1

Philip gave a hilarious account of TB's behaviour last week at the various strategy meetings, that whenever he was challenged or under attack he just curled up into a foetal position. He said he was wearing the most extraordinary collection of brightly coloured shirts and ties while GB was always in a plain white shirt and red tie. 'It was a classic style meets substance moment.' He said GB hadn't really engaged. TB finished his note and as I had told him we were at Philip's, he sent it through there. The fax ran out of ink after page 3, which ended 'Here is what we should do.' There then came through seven blank pieces of paper.

Tuesday, April 2

Chequers. On Iraq, the meeting started at ten up in the Long Gallery. It was a repeat of the smaller meeting we'd had on Afghanistan. Boyce was looking very tanned and smartly dressed and mainly set out why it was hard to do anything. He even talked up the Middle East peace process as a problem, as if TB had never thought of that. TB wanted to be in a position to give GWB a strategy and influence it. He believed Bush was in the same position as him, that it would be great to get rid of Saddam and could it be done without terrible unforeseen circumstances? We were given an account of the state of Iraqi forces, OK if not brilliant, the opposition – hopeless – and Saddam's ways – truly dreadful. CDS appeared to be trying to shape the meeting towards inaction, constantly pointing out the problems, the nature of the administration, only Rumsfeld and a few others knew what was being planned, TB may speak to Bush or Condi but did they really know what was going on? TB said in the end Bush would take the decisions. CDS said so far he had followed the Rumsfeld (he always pronounced it Rumsfield) advice. He said apart from Rumsfeld, there were only four or five people who were really on the inside track. There was also a different understanding on UNSCRs, the US thinking they have existing cover, us believing we need a new one for foolproof legal cover. Both C and John Scarlett kept saying cooperation was better, e.g. on intelligence, but CDS would keep coming back to the problems. I recalled his dire warnings about the Taliban skinning people alive. Now he was saying this would not be as easy as the Taliban. General Tony Piggott did an OK presentation which went through the problems realistically but concluded that a full-scale invasion would be possible, ending up with fighting in Baghdad. But it would be bloody, could take a long time. Also, it was not impossible that Saddam would keep all his forces back. He said post-conflict had to be part of conflict preparation. The Americans believed we could replicate Afghanistan but it was very, very different. There was a guy there called Cedric, our military man based in Tampa, working with the US inside CENTCOM [US Central Command]. He was sunburned, wearing American lace-up boots, and said Tommy Franks was difficult to read because he believed they were planning something for later in the year, maybe New Year. He basically believed in air power plus special forces. CDS said if they want us to be involved in providing force, we have to be involved in all the planning, which seemed fair enough. TB said it was the usual conundrum – do I support totally in public and help deliver our strategy, or do I put distance between us and lose influence? We discussed whether the central aim was WMD or regime change. Piggott's view was that it was WMD. TB felt it was regime change in part because of WMD but more broadly because of the threat to the region and the world. On WMD, people will say that we have known about WMD for a long time. He said what was sure was that this would not be a popular war, and in the States, fighting an unpopular war and losing is not an option.

Wednesday, April 3

Peter M had responded to TB's note in not dissimilar terms to mine. TB had obviously been talking to him about my state of mind. He said he felt he knew how I could regain happiness through work – 1. be nicer to TB, 2. get new blood around me, and 3. manage my time better. The lack of cohesion with the Treasury was really bothering me. TB was anxious that we get the focus for the meeting at Crawford [Texas] off Iraq simply and onto the Middle East. Second, how do we get the Americans to do more re the Middle East peace process without it looking like we are criticising them for not doing enough? He had told Bush a year ago that he should get more involved now because he would have to and he would eventually be playing catch-up. TB was thinking hard about the visit, said his job was to give Bush a strategy, and to get the political processes up and running. It was clear both from David M and Chris Meyer that the US government was in a divided state. Cheney and Rumsfeld v Powell, with Condi trying to get Bush engaged more, possibly with Powell.

Thursday, April 4

TB had an hour with GB on the Budget but Gordon was still on his kick that we shouldn't be talking too much about public services, a view TB described as absurd given that was the platform we were elected on. GB said you never heard the Tories talking about unemployment. They never said they would sort it, said TB. It's like saying we should never talk about asylum. If it's a problem, people know it's a problem, and we have to deal with it. I saw what Philip meant about their clothes. GB was wearing a dark suit, a white shirt, a red tie, shoes that weren't cleaned properly and socks that fell down round his ankles. TB was wearing Nicole Farhi shoes, ludicrous-looking lilac-coloured pyjama-style trousers and a blue smock. After GB left, I said he looked like Austin Powers. He said you are the second person who's said that. Gordon wasn't the first. Probably one of the kids.

Friday, April 5

It was the day of the procession of the Queen Mother's body to the lying in state. A beautiful sunny day, wall-to-wall coverage for the royals, OK crowds, nice atmosphere. Up to see TB in the flat. Another Austin Powers moment. Yellow/green underpants and that was it. I said what a prat he looked. He said I was just jealous – how many prime ministers have got a body like this? TB was seeing Jack later, who suggested walking over to Westminster Hall. TB agreed and asked Gordon to go too. I said I thought it was a bad idea because it would look like they were trying to get attention. In the end they went by car. They went off as the procession came through. The crowds were far bigger than expected. On the plane, we worked on the speech for tomorrow, pretty much wrote it himself, having decided he wanted to be totally supportive but also push for more US engagement. For the first time I could recall, he did his own written checklist for the meeting with Bush. He wanted to do Iraq and MEPP first so that he knew where he was.

Saturday, April 6

Crawford, Texas. I went down to the gym in the hotel. There was an enormous woman on the only treadmill. Robin Oakley called and she heard me speak and then, as she padded at the slowest possible pace, asked me if I was English, then if I knew Tony Blair. I said I did. She said she was so happy that the world was run by two God-fearing young men, Bush and Blair. She asked if I was his bodyguard and I said no. She said she prayed for Tony every day and she prayed for his bodyguards, for him to keep the world safe and for his body-guards to keep him safe. She asked if I believed in God and I said no. She gave me a rather pitying look and then told me she was a member of the George W Bush email prayer group and she was happy for me to be added to their list.

We were doing the press conference at a school in Crawford and the toughest questions were why had there been no response from Israel and did TB agree Saddam had to go? Bush's posture and delivery were a lot better, more confident. We talked about it at the ranch before dinner. He said in the early days he got really knocked by the way they took the mickey out of the way he mangled words, and it made him hesitant, like when he said infitada instead of intifada and got mauled for it. Now he had given up caring what they think and it had made him more confident. He said the truth is I have a limited vocabulary, I'm not great with words, I have to think about what I say carefully. They had both been pretty heavy on Iraq and that was the story for most of them. The atmospherics were pretty good though. I said I hear you didn't like Trevor McDonald [UK broadcaster who had recently interviewed Bush]. He said it just maddens him the way they all ask the same questions, so it's a pain. When we arrived back at the ranch, we chatted in a little group outside the bungalow. Barney his dog came over and he said 'This is my Leo.' I said hold on, Leo's not a dog. Yes, he said, but Barney's the substitute for the little boy I never had. Over drinks before and after dinner, I had a couple of long chats with GWB. He asked me why I wasn't drinking and I said I was a recovering drunk. Me too, he said. I asked him how much he drank. He said two or three beers a day, a bit of wine, some bourbon. He gave up in August '86, a few months after me. I went through the kind of quantities I was drinking at the end and said they dwarfed his efforts. I said that having a breakdown and not drinking had been the best thing that ever happened to me. It was like seeing the light. But you still don't believe in God? he asked. No I don't. We talked about running. He could still do between 6.45 and 7.15 a mile and was thinking of doing his own race for charity. He was also a member of a club, qualification for which rested on the ability to run a sub-seven-minute mile when it was 100 degrees in the shade. He had dragged TB out for a run and said he had had to hold back a bit. TB said it was the first run that far since he left university. After a couple of toasts, Bush then just got up and said everyone could leave because he wanted to go to bed. Everyone signed the menus. They were always extremely respectful in front of him. I couldn't see any of them suggesting he had a touch of the Austin Powers about him. TB thought that was why he seemed to enjoy the banter with us, because he didn't seem to have anyone there who just had a laugh.

Sunday, April 7

TB called early to give me a few final changes for the speech. I could hear Bush rushing him in the background. They went off to church, which was a three-hour round trip. We both reckoned Bush had been quite a lad in his youth, both on the booze and the birds front. But they got on, there was no doubt about that, and they were both people not afraid to face down critics. On the plane I had dinner with TB and Jonathan and we discussed where we were going to find new blood for the office. I suggested a minister or senior MP getting involved in managing and motivating. Neither of them seemed keen. The reality was Jonathan wasn't a traditional chief of staff, in that he didn't manage a lot that went on, and I wasn't a traditional communications director. What we did was largely driven by what TB wanted us to do and what our personalities best allowed us to do. But it meant gaps that sometimes led to lack of clarity. Also the policy unit was badly managed and not properly integrated. TB was clear he wanted it sorted and wanted the game raised. We debriefed him on the private sessions with Bush. He had been surprised how relatively positive he was about the idea for a big push on Africa. He had not enjoyed his contact so far with Europe.

Monday, April 8

I called Janvrin to say I thought they had handled events incredibly well and today's broadcast by the Queen was the crowning glory of a very good PR campaign. They had done well every single day. Today, as well as the broadcast, they had the vigil of the four grand-sons.

Tuesday, April 9

The Queen Mum's funeral would be a media wipeout so the morning meeting was brief, though I did relentlessly take the piss out of Ian Austin [GB's special adviser], who had said a few days ago that nobody would be interested in the Queen Mum's funeral. I went upstairs to watch the cortège go through Horseguards and towards the Mall. Big crowds, real solemnity and the BBC did a good job on it.

Wednesday, April 10

The statement on the Middle East had definitely been the right thing to do. The right-wing press were trying to cause trouble. The *Telegraph* were trying to link the success of the Queen Mum's funeral with hostility to New Labour. The *Telegraph* were also saying we tried to change the arrangements for the funeral, and Peter Oborne was saying the same thing in the *Spectator*. I got Jeremy to write to them to complain. We had a reception for Jim Callaghan's 90th birthday at Number 10. He made a really warm speech, terrific about his wife in particular, Audrey suffering from Alzheimer's, and he said how he sat with her and talked to her every day and sometimes she said a few words that made sense and it was magical. Michael Foot and I talked endlessly about Burnley and Plymouth. Tony Benn was filming the whole thing. Betty Boothroyd was there to call everyone to order. There was a good turnout of ministers, though JP was angry he hadn't been invited. Denis Healey [former Labour Chancellor] and I nattered about Keighley. Merlyn Rees [former Labour Home Secretary], Bernard Donoughue [head of Harold Wilson's policy unit 1974–76], Tom McCaffrey [Callaghan's press secretary], Hattersley, Margaret and Peter Jay [Callaghan's son-in-law, Ambassador to the US, 1977–79]. TB said afterwards they were a good bunch of people but in the end they had failed to stay together.

Friday, April 12

I was ready to go to war with the *Standard* over Oborne refusing to accept we didn't interfere in the lying-in-state arrangements. I had a meeting with Clare Sumner and Simon Virley [TB's private secretary], who had handled arrangements with the Palace, to go over it all. I sent a letter off after talking to TB and Guy Black [director of the Press Complaints Commission] to the PCC, who said if everyone is going to be clear that the report was wrong, it's fine and we should go for it.

Wednesday, April 17

The Budget was reasonably well set up but the dominant story was clearly going to be tax for a better health service. At Cabinet, GB did a very good presentation. TB looked really tired and a bit out of it. Jack slipped me a note saying he thought TB looked ghastly and we needed to get him in better shape before this afternoon. GB did his usual mix of big message and factual rat-tat-tat. On the big message, what I liked about it was it was all the same arguments coming through, and the spending figures were fine. TB said it was a crucial moment for the government. There were things to get across. Strong economy the basis of everything we do. Continuing determination to get people off benefit and into work. Strong economy plus more people in work means more investment in public services. He said that there should now be a critical argument on the NHS. The issue is not whether we spend more but how. We have to win the argument that our system is better and more efficient than the French or German social insurance systems or the Americans' way of doing things. This issue about whether more money in this way delivers better services will dominate this parliament.

Thursday, April 18

GB came over at 9.15 to leave for a visit with TB, complaining that there was not enough reform in Milburn's follow-through statement. TB said that the thing to watch was people thinking this is a return to Old Labour. GB up in arms: 'God almighty, you can't say we didn't deliver on the message yesterday.' 'No, but . . . ?' The line was running a bit that it was an own goal because as the NHS was such a huge employer, the NICs [National Insurance Contributions] rise would have a disproportionate impact there. The press were pretty determined to make the general Budget story a problem for us, but the Tories were hopeless. TB told Cabinet that as he saw it, the two big areas for us in the next phase were health and dealing with antisocial behaviour. Reform was every bit as important as money. He said if we can't feel confident about these arguments, we don't deserve to be in business. I was working on a letter to the PCC, Clare Sumner having worked out what happened. It was clear that in her dealings with Black Rod [Sir Michael Willcocks] she had set out what she thought the guidance for the PM and the government was. Black Rod was clearly tricky. Both Clare and Simon Virley were adamant they had done nothing more than get clarification on what TB was meant to do.

Tuesday, April 23
I had a meeting on Iraq with John Scarlett, Tom McKane [Cabinet Office] and Martin Howard [MoD] to go through what we needed to do communications-wise to set the scene for Iraq, e.g. a WMD paper and other papers about Saddam. Scarlett a very good bloke.

Thursday, April 25
To Windsor for the Queen's Golden Jubilee media reception. It was a beautiful evening, about 700 journalists there. Oborne and [Simon] Walters both tried to engage me in conversation but I pushed them off. The general feeling among most of the hacks was that we shouldn't have gone to the PCC but that's because they were self-serving. The event was a huge success for the Queen. There was something truly pathetic about these so-called hardened hacks, many of them self-proclaimed republicans, bowing and scraping the whole time. She moved effortlessly between them and left grown men in little puddles of excitement as she moved on to form the next one. She was such an old pro but there was something mildly sick-making about the way they fell about in front of her.

Monday, April 29
TB's big concern re the GB situation was the feeling that ministers were unsure what their instincts were meant to be, because though we were the present, they realised GB was the future. TB needed to be clear that they were answerable to him. No. 10 dinner for the Queen. Terry O'Neill [photographer] in to do pictures. Ted Heath complaining about the seating plan. A bit of a problem re Stockton [the 2nd Earl Stockton, Macmillan's grandson] taking the place of [Harold] Macmillan's daughter [Lady Caroline Faber]. But it went well enough, nice pictures of her with all her surviving prime ministers, which we got out by 8.45. TB's kids were downstairs to meet her when she arrived then up for drinks. The Queen said 'Isn't it wonderful

Preparing for the
Commons debate on
Iraq, March 18, 2003
(left to right)
Jonathan Powell,
David Manning, Blair,
Peter Hyman
and Campbell

Blair and Campbell
at the EU summit in
Brussels dominated
by Iraq

Above right,
Chirac asks Blair
for a private word
during a break in
summit proceedings.
Relations between
the two leaders were
increasingly strained

Blair, with Tom Kelly
to his right, and
Campbell behind
him, at an airborne
media briefing

Blair and Bush at Camp David followed by (left to right), protection officer, Campbell, Tom Kelly, David Manning, Matthew Rycroft and Jonathan Powell

Blair goes through Government papers while Cherie reads newspapers aboard military flight

Hillsborough Castle, Bush and Blair in talks with (left to right) Campbell, Colin Powell, Jack Straw, Condoleezza Rice and White House press secretary Ari Fleischer

The Iraq debate: in the Prime Minister's Commons office, Campbell watches Blair live in the chamber

Robin Cook (right),
Clare Short (centre).
Both were opposed to
the war in Iraq but
handled themselves
very differently

Blair thanking the troops in Basra, on the day the BBC broadcast
a report alleging the WMD dossier was 'sexed up'

Two of the many cartoons inspired by Campbell's role: (above) the WMD dossier and
(below) the so-called 'dodgy dossier' on Saddam's infrastructure of concealment

mpbell greeted by Fiona after he
ompleted the London Marathon
in 2003. He raised half a million
pounds for Leukaemia Research
in memory of his closest friend
John Merritt (below)

Partners in crime: Campbell (centre) and friend and colleague John Merritt (right)
with crime reporter Sylvia Jones and news editor PJ Wilson. Merritt's death from
leukaemia led Campbell to campaign for Leukaemia Research

Advisers Sally Morgan, Campbell and Jonathan Powell leave Downing Street on the day Campbell gave evidence to the Foreign Affairs Committee

Campbell giving evidence to the Foreign Affairs Committee in June 2003, where he launched an attack on the BBC and vowed to force them to admit their report on the background of the controversial dossier was wrong

Dr David Kelly gives evidence to the Foreign Affairs Committee, June 2003

45 MINUTES SPIN OUT OF THAT CAMPBELL

Campbell was offered the option of going in through a side door when he appeared to give evidence at the Hutton Inquiry, but chose to walk through the protesters

John Scarlett spent a life in the shadows, as a career spy, but found himself in the public eye as a result of the row over the WMD dossier

The Inquiry was covered in huge detail in Britain and around the world. Here, a TV artist's impression of Campbell being quizzed by the Inquiry's Counsel, James Dingemans, QC

Campbell in his Downi
Street office with his Bur
FC mug and 'Britain G
Better' poster in Burnl
colours on the wall. H
resigned on August 29, 2

Tony Blair, 2003

not to have to be introduced to anyone?' Major and I had a very civilised conversation, re Chelsea, cricket, small talk. But there was always a tension there and Norma [Major] was very distant. Thatcher was complaining loudly about the decor and the paintings, how some of the carpets and furnishings looked worn, and the colours in the Green Room weren't properly coordinated, tut-tutting, not exactly saying 'Wouldn't have happened in my day' but not far off it.

The Queen, the PMs and their descendants went into the State Dining Room while Robin Janvrin, Jeremy, Fiona and I had a very nice dinner in the White Room. Robin was a thoroughly decent bloke. There was another drinks do at the end and I had a long chat with Mary Wilson and Robin [son]. At one point Ted was sitting on one sofa, Jim Callaghan on another, just having an old man to old man conversation about how things used to be. Ted could barely bring himself to look at Thatcher but she teased him a bit, tried to make him laugh, without any apparent success. Prince Philip was deep in conversation with TB, the Countess of Avon [widow of Anthony Eden], Macmillan's and [Alec] Douglas-Home's families, and there was lots of reminiscing about life in Number 10. It was interesting to see the difference between the Queen's demeanour at the do at Windsor, when she had been doing her professional small-talk thing, and here, where she seemed genuinely happy. I said to Fiona that nobody else had really had the kind of access and contact that she had had and yet while everybody thought they knew what she thought of them, nobody could be sure. But I don't think I've ever seen her smiling so much.

Friday, May 3

RW came to see me, said was I sure I knew what I was taking on with the changes I was making to the lobby. He said lots of people had tried this. The scale of the coverage on my plans was ludicrous, a further sign of their self-obsession and their obsession with me, which in part was what we were trying to address. Once we talked it through, he was pretty supportive, and said he would help to find premises so that we could do the bigger briefings with the foreign media included, and any other accredited journalists who wanted to turn up. JP called, said he had premises in his office, in the room that used to be Churchill's cinema. Clinton called me at 1am to go through some changes in the article he was doing for us re all the attacks on TB. He didn't want to attack the motives of our critics, just attack the attacks. It was a good piece though, and worth the effort. He was always good to talk to, because he had such a good feel for our politics, and for how best to position TB. He felt we were just going through one of those phases where people wanted to see us tested and pressured and coming through. TB must have said something, or his instincts told him something, about me going a bit offside, because he said that in these top jobs like president and prime minister, you really need people close by that you can trust and rely on 100%. He said it was important that I hung in and kept helping TB through.

Thursday, May 9

TB called me at 7.10. Said he felt that Byers was pretty shot. He said he was going to give him a chance to step down of his own volition before a reshuffle which he planned for the next few weeks but wanted total radio silence for now. He felt it was monstrous the way Steve had been treated internally but ultimately ministers have to be responsible for their own departments, and he would have to go fairly soon. TB took a strategy meeting with the internal team, to go through the big strategic overview paper I'd done. It had caused a lot of anger, people feeling I'd bounced them, but Peter M was totally supportive, which was important, and would help with TB.

Friday, May 10

TB wanted us to rebut some of the coverage of last night's David Beckham event, and in particular the widespread regurgitation of the story of him claiming to have seen Jackie Milburn [former Newcastle United footballer], which was one of those annoying urban myths.

Thursday, May 16

Guy Black called and said there was a snag. He came to see me at 1.30. He had been to see Black Rod and asked him for a draft of what he would say. He said he would prefer it if nobody knew that he had been to see me, and he showed me the draft statement. It backed the *Mail on Sunday* story. Guy said 'We have to stop that letter going to the PCC.'

Tuesday, May 21

Spoke to Guy Black and then sent over the latest letters on the case. Charlie Falconer's view was that if Black Rod was being this difficult we should just get out of it. We now just have to get shot of the whole thing.

Monday, May 27

Up to see TB early. He had been thinking over the weekend about a reshuffle, perhaps on Wednesday, with Steve out. He didn't want a major reshuffle but he knew Steve had to go. There were others he would like to get rid of, notably Clare and Nick Brown, to a lesser extent Robin, but he knew he couldn't, certainly not all at once. TB agreed with me that Steve had been the victim. We both felt sorry for him where it was ending. He was totally fed up with Clare and intended to see her to make clear she understood she was far from being indispensable. These reshuffles, like pregnancy, dentistry and exams, were further proof that pain has no memory. I didn't know how many we have done now, but until a new one starts, you forget how awful the process is. First the usual and occasionally random discussion of who could go where. Then the unstructured remembering by different people at different times of reasons why such-and-such a move was unwise or even impossible. With each reshuffle came the realisation that the PM's power and room for manoeuvre is more limited than people might think. In an ideal world, there was no way people like Short, Nick Brown, Michael Meacher would survive. But there are balances to be considered, and you can't make all the personnel changes at the same time. You also know with absolute certainty that today's broadly loyal minister is tomorrow's bitter and backbiting backbencher, their only hope of salvation in their mind turning against the government, giving the impression it was out of principle rather than bitterness. We had seen some already, and there would be more after tomorrow. Then a couple of quite extraordinary serendipitous moments. JP came in, and TB told him he was thinking of making a few structural changes, and JP said he shouldn't rule out hiving off parts of DTLR. Then Byers came in and said to TB that he wanted to go, if TB felt that was the right thing to do. Steve said he had had enough, and he knew it was the right thing for him. We agreed to separate the Byers announcement from the rest of the reshuffle so that we could genuinely say it was his decision. We chatted with TB for twenty minutes or so and Steve and I walked round to my office to sort the detail. The best thing to do would be a short statement to camera in Number 10, which would show he was not being forced out, no questions. I said I was astonished how calm he was. He said politics is a rough trade, but we love it, and I found myself replying 'Do you know, I'm not sure that I do any more.' Yeah, he said, maybe not. He said he had spent so many years working for a Labour government, had been proud of what we had done, but he knew this was the right time to go. He asked me if I thought he should have gone earlier. I said probably, yes. But I was like him, I really didn't want those fuckers to get a scalp. I was worried even now that TB would look weak out of this because in the end it was Steve deciding to go, basically driven out.

Tuesday, May 28

TB left for the NATO summit in Rome, which was genuinely historic on one level but when he called in, it was to tell me inter alia about Berlusconi getting some dolly bird to hand out watches to all the leaders while Chirac made a speech attacking him over his pronouncements that NATO was the key to our defence. Just how big a twat Sixsmith was became apparent when he appeared at the gates after Steve went, wanting to be let in, saying he was still his director of communications. Steve was more nervous than I had ever seen him now that the moment was coming, Jan [Cookson, his partner] was fine, relaxed about it, happy even. His mother felt he was doing the wrong thing. With Mark Bennett working at my computer we finished the statement. Steve read through it a few times, kept in 'Friends who know me know I am not a liar and tried to behave honourably'. We thoroughly enjoyed the spectacle of Boulton blathering from Rome for ten minutes about all the things it might be – referendum on the euro, declaration of war, TB illness. Others were speculating it would be me resigning, one or two that he was going back on some of the decisions in the reshuffle. Steve was still fairly calm but not quite so Zen-like. I left him for a while to compose his thoughts and he asked for a glass of water. I went back in, asking him if he was ready, then took him up the long route through the basement so that nobody would bump into him. We got to the side door, he took a deep breath, said 'Here goes then', and in he went. He did well, held it together but as he came out he was a bit choked. I took him back to my office, where Boulton was still blathering away, now saying it was evidence of how few friends he had that the news didn't leak. What total scum these people are. Couldn't bring himself to admit he hadn't heard a whisper, and all his speculation had been for the birds.

Wednesday, May 29

The press was vile about Steve. 'Liar for hire' in the *Star*. The *Mirror* was merciless. It's like they get a corpse, but then are disappointed there is nothing left to try and kill, so they kill the dead body too. TB had to get on with the reshuffle. Miliband could scarcely believe he was going to be a minister let alone in charge of schools as minister of state. Estelle [Morris] not totally happy and had wanted Margaret Hodge out, but TB resisted on that.

Friday, June 7

I had pretty much finalised an exchange of letters with the PCC. TB added two points – first, an even more staunch defence of Clare

Sumner, and second, we reserve the right to come back on this if any of the papers suggested that he had tried to muscle in on the arrangements.

Sunday, June 9

I briefed John Reid for *Frost*. He had been at the Clinton–Peter M wonkathon [policy discussion organised by Peter M] and said he had had a terrific conversation with Clinton re Ireland. JR was totally for going to the press, said we had now reached the stage where all communications was dismissed as spin, all funding was sleaze, all attacks were smears. Gwyneth Dunwoody [Labour MP] did an interview saying she had been smeared. IDS was on the broadcasts really going for us. There was a real nastiness and poison about where we were at the moment and I wasn't quite sure how we dealt with it. TB came back from his weekend seeming very up and energised. Clinton had been through something similar to the attacks we were getting. His view was that they went on character because they couldn't win on policy. The challenge was to use that to build a position of confidence and strength. The challenge for modern politicians was understanding change, developing and implementing policy but also shaping and winning arguments. He said we were seen around the world as probably the best and most successful modern left of centre party in terms of winning and doing, but we rarely came over as being confident in our own position.

Tuesday, June 11

TB called in Jonathan, Sally M and me and asked if we thought it was possible for him to announce publicly that he wouldn't fight the next election and tell Cabinet that if ministers wanted to fight a leadership election, they would have to do it outside. Sally feared it would make him a lame duck straight away, though [José María] Aznar [Prime Minister of Spain] had seemed to survive a second fixed term pretty well. I said he had to decide simply whether it was the right thing to do, and that if it wasn't, he was simply caving in to psychological warfare. Did he really want to go? And was it really the right thing? He said that's exactly what Cherie would say. What he'd like to do was win an election, win a referendum, then go after getting the new leader in place or, if a referendum were possible this side of the election, win that, stay to the election and get a new leader in place.

David Manning was genuinely shocked by Black Rod's behaviour. The *Spectator* cover had me and TB getting spanked by the little fucker. We were of course building up to the *Mail on Sunday*, who would no doubt publish the memo from Black Rod to the PCC so we had to decide whether to put our version out, with our own dossier of evidence. I felt we had to because Sunday was in danger of being a massive event with only one side of the story there. At Cabinet, JP came in with a virtual declaration of war on TB. He said he knew we had to do the press stuff and he wasn't knocking that but it was interesting that the Tories were trying to echo New Labour and avoid substance. But he said we have a very good compromise between old and new. He said we all have to be involved in future policymaking but 'I'm bound to say if we're going to have weekend retreats for some at Hartwell House [a Buckinghamshire hotel where Mandelson's Policy Network Thinktank held a high-profile away day attended by Blair, Brown and others], and Mandelson giving interviews saying we're all Thatcherites now, then we're going to have some very serious discussions in here.' He said the compromise between old and new means we're Labour again and there will be real division if we try to replace policy structures. TB was looking at him with a mix of steel and humour whereas others in the room clearly sensed it was quite a moment. JP said the Labour Party has always been lousy on the back foot. There needs to be more forward strategy and it has to be discussed right here. TB hit back pretty hard, said it was time for a little reality check, time to stop believing everything people read in newspapers. He said we are on our sixth year in government and sometimes government gets difficult. The way not to deal with it is to wet our knickers every time it gets difficult. We are in a strong position. The economy is good, we have the right agenda on public services, the right approach on social exclusion. The Tories were coming at us on character because they had nothing else to go on. They had lost on policy. We have to stick on policy, not get distracted or irritated. He said we had been uniquely blessed as a government, to a large extent free of many of the problems other Labour governments had faced. Our mettle was being tested and it's at times like these that we had to hang together not fall apart. The history of Labour governments, he said, is that they make themselves fail rather than others make them fail. We are winning all the arguments, so let's get a sense of perspective. He then looked around, smiled, said 'I've got the Indonesian President coming in now, so that's the end of that.' JP put on his real sour look and walked straight out. It was Paul

Boateng's first Cabinet and Bruce's first actually at the Cabinet table. Paul looked really shocked. RW came to see me later. He said that was a big, bad moment. TB was pretty calm afterwards, convinced it needed saying. He had had a pretty heavy session with JP earlier, who was going on about the Hartwell business.

Friday, June 14

JP called. I said 'That was pretty dramatic yesterday.' 'What?' 'What you said in Cabinet.' 'Well, you've created camps and you're in one of them and you've pushed me to the other. There you go.' 'Oh well. I just wanted to say I was taken aback. Me, not him.' He told me that just before Cabinet TB had accused him of messing around with GB and said he wasn't having it. JP said he wasn't prepared to be excluded from strategy and he wasn't having all this third way/Mandelson policy stuff bypassing the party. He let off steam, said he had warned him again and again and he thinks if he strokes my arm I'll be fine, but it goes much deeper. He has to do things through the Cabinet and his ministers and not his own little Loya Jurga [Afghan Grand Council]. He then said 'You've withdrawn from all this anyway.' I said that I'd tried to pull back because of the attention I was getting, but it hasn't worked, has it? He said no, you've got your own problems. I've never had a problem with you but we've grown distant again. I'm loyal to TB and you both need to understand that. I always will be. We chatted for close to an hour and I think both felt better at the end of it. We agreed to have dinner at our house tomorrow night. TB called later and said JP had been transformed, which showed I should keep close to him.

Saturday, June 15

We agreed re the *Mail on Sunday* that the best line would be to point out the inconsistency with the statement at the time. Most felt the whole thing was overblown bollocks, Black Rod says AC must go. Nothing much to it. JP and Pauline arrived about 8. After all the small talk, JP with some anecdotes on his trips, taking the mick out of Pauline's hats, then we got down to it. He liked TB, felt he was the right guy at the right time and a good leader. But he wanted to be properly involved in decision-making. He only felt he was in the areas for which he had direct responsibility but if he was going to be a proper deputy, he had to know a lot more about what he was up to and where we were going. He said he sometimes felt TB stroked his arm, that it was about managing him rather than using him properly as a DPM. JP warmed up as the evening wore on and was in full flow by the end, totally open about himself, his background, his chip-piness, why he felt as proud as he did of where he had got to, why he was so desperate to play a role getting TB and GB to work together better than they did. He said he would do nothing to damage the party and even though they had different views about lots of things, he felt TB was in the same place on that. He said between us all, we have put Labour in the strongest position ever and a lot of that has been down to TB and GB hanging together.

Sunday, June 16

TB called, even more outraged and angry about Black Rod than ever. The *Mail on Sunday* stuff didn't go very far, and though there was reams of it in the papers, nothing deadly. I briefed Margaret Beckett for the *World at One* and she was absolutely brilliant. Haughty and dismissive. Reid was excellent on *On the Record* against Tim Collins [Conservative Party vice chairman], whom God preserve. The story was going nowhere but it didn't stop the BBC leading on it most of the day.

Monday, June 17

Only the *Mail* with 'the smearing of Black Rod' led on it, but the mood was definitely different now. I agreed with TB we should just shut up shop, say we had said all there was to say. There was an excellent story in *The Times*, saying the Palace were worried Black Rod was dragging them into a political row, but it was dropping down the agenda.

Tuesday, June 25

The Bush Middle East speech was making big waves right round the world but it didn't seem terribly thought through. It seemed the White House was too consumed with the squabbles and struggles within the government, particularly Powell v Cheney/Rumsfeld than in really thinking through a plan on the Middle East. Also, truth be told, Bush had a surer touch on domestic than international. I pointed out that Bush calling for the Palestinians to reject Arafat was the surest way to ensure a boost for Arafat. TB didn't really want to end up in a US/UK rift situation, but we said it was up to the Palestinian people to elect their leaders, which was taken as an attack on Bush so we were heading for the rift headlines, even though TB was really in agreement that Arafat was weak, and that there had to be more sympathy for the Israelis. We had an office planning meeting re September, at which Fiona said they were thinking about going to the Strozzis [Prince Girolamo Strozzi and his wife Irina] again and also going to Aznar's daughter's wedding. He knew my views on holiday with the Strozzis, but I thought the wedding was equally ridiculous given he didn't know the daughter. Aznar really wanted him to go, but this was behaving like royal families. If I raised it with him he said, OK but I do need to have some kind of life as well. Going to a politician's daughter's wedding in Spain did not strike me as being life.

Wednesday, June 26

G8 summit at Kannanaskis. TB had bumped into GWB at the gym and they had 40 minutes in there, mainly just the two of them. TB felt that they could tolerate Arafat as a titular head but not as the man who led the negotiations. They just didn't trust him. Bush wanted to do media at the start of their bilateral, not least because there was another fraud-related company crash. But I was worried that if it went to the Middle East, which it would, TB would get put into the poodle position. TB said we must not change the line, and instead should let them move to us a bit. But Bush was basically someone who said what he thought. It's a quality people always say they want in a politician but when the politicians are in the really big jobs, I think it's sometimes the reason they turn against them. In Arafat's case, he thought the man was a terrorist. Listening to him later, I felt sometimes he imagined he could just say things away, just as he had said to us he thought bin Laden was dead but he daren't say it in case bin Laden popped up again. Then off to see GWB. The little doorstep they did was OK. I got the feeling that Condi was a bit put out that I was there as well as David Manning. She was pretty status-conscious and I don't think had got the point that I was more to TB than Ari Fleischer was to Bush. Bush was on good form. He said the problem with Israeli politics is that they tend to unite around the toughest lines. As to why he was so hard on Arafat, he felt he had lied about the money he gave to families organising terrorism. He did seem to have the outlines of a possible step-by-step process, but nobody seemed terribly confident. The Americans clearly felt neither Arafat nor Sharon were capable of delivering peace. TB felt there had to be improved security structures, otherwise they were at the mercy of suicide bombers. GWB was a weird mix, much wittier than people would imagine, quite self-deprecating, very open for someone in his position.

Thursday, June 27

TB wanted another discussion about his future, or 'La Grande Strátegie' as he now called it. The only question that mattered was whether it strengthened or weakened him. I veered to the lame-duck side of the argument. It was true that he had always imagined only doing two terms, but I wasn't convinced it was remotely time for him to go yet. TB still felt that two terms was about all you get in the modern world. But if it took a couple of years to do the euro, he would be happy to hang around for that. I asked him what Cherie thought. The same, he said. But I have to resolve the question whether it weakens or strengthens me. The more he talked about it, the more I feared it was one of those things that had a certain immediate appeal but which would go in the box marked 'things I wish I hadn't done'. He said it wasn't a case of being fed up, but eight years was roughly what you got, and if we couldn't see the sort of progress we wanted in public services in that time, there was a bit of a problem.

Thursday, July 11

TB called me through and we went out for a chat on the terrace. Philip had briefed him on how his trust ratings had really dipped. He said 'In truth I've never really wanted to do more than two full terms.' It was pretty clear to me that he had just about settled his view, that he would sometime announce it, say that he was going to stay for the full term, but not go into the election as leader. The big question was the same as before – does it give him an authority of sorts, or does it erode that authority, and do people just move automatically towards GB? He felt it was possible that it would strengthen him because he would be able to move people without anyone saying it was because he feared a rival. I had noticed, and he did it again today, that he had started to think about how his premiership would be viewed, another indicator that he was moving psychologically to the exit door. He felt in terms of transforming the party, winning, and the big policy changes we had made, there was a lot to point to. 'But the euro does matter a lot to me. Not because of a place in history but because I think it is the right thing for the country.' He had mentioned the idea to Peter M, thinking he would be totally hostile, but he wasn't, because he would see the logic. It seemed to me he was definitely moving towards it. We walked in from the terrace to the Cabinet room, and I asked him whether he really thought this was the right thing to do, or whether in fact he was being intimidated into doing it, and thinking it was the right thing, by a mix of GB and the press. He said I don't think so. 'You have to know when to go. I also think the history of leaders trying to choose their successors is a very bad one.' So far as I was aware, only Jonathan, Sally, Cherie and I, and now Peter, were aware he was even thinking about this. As we walked back to his office, I said 'Christ, how much could I get from the press for this one?' He smiled, then stopped again and said 'Is it the right thing or the wrong thing? I want your best brain on it.'

Friday, July 19

Got in and TB called me up to the flat. He was wearing the most extraordinary collection – a white collarless Nicole Farhi shirt, plain blue trousers and England football slippers with the three lions on them. I said I find it very hard to take him seriously wearing kids' slippers and that shirt. He said I had a bias against style. He asked if I had thought any further about his 'grand projet'. He felt it was nonsense that the Cabinet was moving towards GB and he really thought this could give him strength. He would announce it in the autumn, pre-conference, make clear to the Cabinet that if anyone sought to exploit it or organise a leadership campaign, he would sack them. It would allow him to do what he thought was right without people saying he was simply interested in staying in power. Bill C had said to him 'Whatever you do, go when they're still asking for more. Don't go like Thatcher.' TB said if she'd gone in '88, it would have been very different for her. Her last two years were just a downward path. I had quietly discussed what he was saying both with Fiona and Sally and both were adamant it would make him a lame duck overnight, but he was persuading himself it would give him extra authority, constantly saying to me 'You only get two terms in this job.' He said the great difference between him and other politicians was that he could walk away from it. He then walked over to the wall, leaned against it, laughed and said 'There's another complication I need to tell you about.' He said 'I think Cherie is pregnant.' He said they were both absolutely gobsmacked by the whole thing. But it did mean it was forcing him to think about the future. 'I've effectively got two families with the same woman.' He had known she might be pregnant for a few days and it had clearly had an impact on his thinking about the *grand projet*.

Saturday, July 20

I slept really badly, lots of different worries just floating around, couldn't decide whether TB was right with his *grand projet*, was trying to separate out my own feelings about my own position, which would probably welcome it. As for CB being pregnant again, it was mind-blowing.

Tuesday, July 23

TB chaired a big Iraq meeting, JS, GH, CDS, C, Francis Richards, Peter Goldsmith, plus the key Number 10 people. A strong feeling that the US had pretty much made up their minds. Steve Hadley was saying there was no need for another resolution, and how many more times do we hang around watching the Iraqis stiff Kofi? Condi was a bit better but not much. TB was asking whether the Iraqis would welcome an invasion or not. Jack felt the regime would appear to be popular until it tips, but when it tips, it will happen quickly. All the signs out of Washington were that their thinking had moved forward, as per Bush's remarks about taking the battle to the enemy, taking him on before he takes us on. Boyce set out military options. These would vary from provision of bases, maritime support and special forces, right up to the provision of thousands of troops. Geoff felt the preparations either for a generated start or a running start were well advanced. Kuwait was essential to the plan, so is the UK because of Diego Garcia and Cyprus. On the heavy side of things, we could be looking at two armoured brigades entering via Turkey. Jack set out the political difficulties. TB said he did not want any discussions with any other departments at this stage and did not want any of this 'swimming round the system'. He meant the Treasury, because Boyce had been talking about the need for new money, e.g. for tank desertification. Jack said that of the four powers posing a potential threat with WMD – Iran, Korea, Libya and Iraq – Iraq would be the fourth. He does not have nukes, he has some offensive WMD capability. The tough question is whether this is just regime change or is the issue WMD? TB was pretty clear that we had to be with the Americans. He said at one point 'It's worse than you think, I actually believe in doing this.' He was acutely conscious of how difficult it would be both with the PLP and the public, but when Jack raised the prospect of not going in with the US, TB said that would be the biggest shift in foreign policy for 50 years and I'm not sure it's very wise. On the tactical level, he felt maximum closeness publicly was the way to maximise influence privately. Geoff pointed out the Americans' clear view that they already had legal justification. TB said he needed to be convinced first of the workability of a military plan, and second of an equally workable political strategy. Jack said we could probably get the votes for a UN ultimatum, but the Americans may not want to go down that route. TB saw regime change as the route to dealing with WMD.

Thursday, July 25

TB raised his *grand projet* again. I said I don't know why you keep asking me, because you've basically made up your mind. He said no, depends on a lot of things, and I really want you to think over the holiday about whether there is a way I can use it to strengthen myself.

Friday, July 26 to Wednesday, August 28 (holiday)

TB called as I was driving down through France to discuss Iraq. It was clearly going to be a problem and we were not on the pitch. We agreed that we should start to push out some of the Saddam material. He and CB went on their mini-break in Cumbria and she had a miscarriage. By now we were down in Puyméras, from where Fiona and I sorted out with the detectives how to get them in and out of hospital without anyone knowing. TB sounded pretty down about it though he was philosophical. He said Cherie was feeling very low and sad. They were also worried that it would crank up the media interest in their holiday. We decided against actually putting something out and instead waited for calls from the press once they noticed what was going on, which they did when the kids went to France without TB and CB. We had a statement ready with the bare facts plus an appeal for them to be allowed a quiet holiday. I had a series of conversations with TB re the US. Bush had suggested that he go there for the September 11 commemorations and they have a discussion about Iraq around that. I was worried about it, felt that people would see through it and also it ran totally counter to the strategy we planned for September. We agreed to keep it on hold for now. There had been stories about how Robin was leading Cabinet moves against our position and when I told him TB said 'Well, they can just calm down.'

Thursday, August 29

First day back. Didn't feel like going in. TB spoke to Bush. When they spoke, TB sensed Bush was a bit nervous about the UN route. He was clearly getting a lot of competing advice. TB still felt confident we could turn the argument. He felt the left had got itself into a ridiculous position by appearing to be standing up and protecting Saddam. The reality was people had let him get away with it for too long. Everyone felt that if we could get the UN route it would be a lot easier. TB, when I first saw him today, was wearing the full Rio Ferdinand [footballer] look – shorts, his FA slip-ons and the trendy vest. He said he had been thinking a lot and the most important thing now was that he did what he thought was right, on foreign and domestic regardless of what the focus groups or anyone else thought.

Saturday, August 31

Up at the crack of dawn to go to Number 10 and meet the TB convoy. The *FT* splash said TB pressed Bush for a UN mandate, which could be a problem with the Yanks while the others were saying TB would break his silence on Iraq on the plane to Mozambique. We both wanted to avoid talking about Iraq, but it would be difficult and we agreed we would have to say he was not letting it overshadow the summit [on sustainable development]. If pushed, he'd say that doing nothing was not an option but he didn't particularly want to go beyond that. Privately, he was growing more and more dismissive of the critics. He found it unfathomable that even the Bishops almost appeared to be defending Saddam as if he was some great liberal. They had allowed the game to run ahead of them. TB was a lot steelier than when he went on holiday. Clear that getting Saddam was the right thing to do. Barely mentioned GB. Very strong language on climate change in the speech. He saw the press and it was going to be hard for them not to make Iraq the story. We arrived and a somewhat chaotic and noisy motorcade took us to the hotel. Clare Short arrived and TB was pretty chilly with her. We drove out to the presidential palace where they had a tête-à-tête and I talked with the finance minister, the daughter of a nurse. The dinner was pretty ghastly, cold soup that was meant to be hot, cold prawns that were meant to be hot, a strange-tasting turkey and a fruit salad out of a tin. I'd love to know if Chirac, should he ever be here, would do his usual over-the-top 'look at all this wonderful food' routine. I liked the politicians. They had a direct-ness that was appealing.

Sunday, September 1

Iraq was becoming a frenzy again. TB was becoming more and more belligerent, saying he knew it was the right thing to do. He said the US had to be managed. Obviously the best thing to do would be to avoid war, get the UN inspectors in and all the weapons out. It was obvious too that the US had to be managed into a better position. That is what we have to do, he said. But we won't be able to do it if we come out against the US the whole time. He was developing the line that the UN route was fine if it was clearly a means to resolve the issue, but not if it's a means to duck the issue. Equally, it was clear that public opinion had moved against us during August.

Tuesday, September 3

Landed 7.15 at Teesside, and drove to Myrobella with TB. We went through some of the hard questions on Iraq. The hardest was 'Why now? What was it that we knew now that we didn't before that made us believe we had to do it now?' It was not going to be at all easy to sell the policy in the next few months, especially because GWB was so unpopular in the UK. TB, Tom Kelly and I went through it all again in the garden. He said several times he was going to be on the tough end of the market, and he was. He kept going for 90 minutes, really hitting the ball in the middle of the bat, top lines very clear – dealing with Saddam was the right thing to do and we would stand by the US. Even critics said he was on top, committed and passionate about it. Definitely worth doing. He then did a call with GWB, who was planning to tell Congress leaders TB was going to Camp David, so I got an operational note ready to go. The toughest question was what new evidence was there? He said the debate had got ahead of us, so we were going to do the dossier earlier, in the next few weeks. The problem was this was going to raise expectations massively. Today was about beginning to turn the tide of public opinion and it was going to be very tough indeed.

Wednesday, September 4

Generally positive press for TB. The problem, as shown by Mike O'Brien's dreadful interview on the radio, was the dossier and the massive expectations. TB felt we could make the case. Robin Cook called and was clearly up for causing problems on Iraq. He said he would 'try to stay on message' but then said 'I hope Tony and you don't want a shooting war.' He said Bush and Co had screwed it up and we should not be held responsible for that.

Thursday, September 5

Out on the terrace, we just talked about Iraq. All of us were pressing TB to go with the flow on the demands for a recall of Parliament, but he was very resistant. We were saying it would let off steam and show he was serious in our Parliament strategy. But he said there were too many questions that we could not really answer, added to which there was not really much to say at the moment. The press conference had settled things but the media were determined to keep a sense of frenzy going on this. TB said we had to get the UN route but could not do it too much. We were pushing him on dossier timing. JP was very loyal, said he was totally supportive. I called Robin C to give him the line on recall of Parliament and he said I hope you are not going to go down the road of war because I believe it could mean the end of the government. Meeting with John Scarlett, Tom McKane, Des Bowen [General Operational Policy Director, MoD], Edward Chaplin, Julian Miller [Cabinet Office] to go over 'the dossier'. It had to be revelatory and we needed to show that it was new and informative and part of a bigger case. John Williams [FCO Director of Public and Press Affairs] was offering to write it full-time.

Saturday, September 7

TB was clearly trying to get GWB in a more doveish position, all the more necessary when we heard that Cheney would also be at Camp David. When we did the media, TB pushed the IAEA [International Atomic Energy Agency] report on potential activity at nuclear sites and we briefed the Sundays re threat to UK, dodging questions re the UN. On the plane, after the diplomatic run-through, Tony Piggott went through the US military thinking. There was a build-up going on now. The timelines were quite short because once we got to the really hot season it was impossible to fight. He said the Saudis would not give their territory so they had to go through the Gulf and Kuwait. But they also wanted to go in from the north, with our and Turkey's help. He said there was a plan for a 15-day air build-up, followed by a massive ground force, which would be the moment of maximum danger because that would be the point at which he might use chemical/biological weapons. TB got changed at Andrews Airbase and we got onto the Marine 1 helicopter with Will Farrish, Chris Meyer and Bush's main protocol guy. 40-minute flight, going over what he should say at the arrival doorstep with GWB. We landed, TB out the front, us out the back. They walked through a line of soldiers to where the doorstep was set up. TB OK, both talking up the threat. We went up to the main building and TB, Bush, Cheney, Condi and David had an initial session. TB felt that his job was to sell the case for the UN route to Cheney. I told the Bush advisers there was a lot of scepticism about motive, including people feeling it was about avenging Dad (Bush Sr). I also said the sole superpower status of the US raised anti-Americanism and they didn't understand that. Karen was pressing the usual stuff re visuals, Dan [Bartlett, White House Communications adviser] saying we had to get Saddam's story up, the abuses, etc. We gave them an honest assessment of where

EU/Arab opinion was. I said our domestic problem was 'poodle' but also why now? Why only Saddam? What about the Middle East? On why now, the case had to be built on evidence. On why only Saddam because he was a unique threat. On Middle East, TB was clear to GWB he really had to engage on that. Karen was asking if we could help the Middle East peace process by dealing with Iraq. [Steve] Hadley was pretty hard over, talking about the importance of promoting democracy and freedom, and I said we had to be careful we were not talking about Americanisation. After some of us were called in to the TB–GWB meeting, and asked to brief on our own discussions, I said to GWB I felt they had to GET this anti-Americanism. A lot of it was jealousy and some of it resentment that they felt obliged to feel sympathy and solidarity post-September 11. But some of it was just fear of their power. When I said we were worried about some of the language they used, Cheney looked pissed off and said 'You mean we shouldn't talk about democracy?' I said not if what people take out of it is not a message about democracy but a message about Americanisation. GWB seemed to get it. At one point we had a break and Bush shouted out across the room 'Hey, big guy.' TB was not there at the time but I went over and Bush said 'I'll say this, and I don't want it on the record, and with apology to the mixed audience, but your guy's got balls.'

When TB came back in, GWB said he'd decided to go to the UN and put down a new UNSCR, challenge the UN to deal with the problems for its own sake. He could not stand by. He would say OK, what will you do? Earlier, not too convincingly, Karen had claimed GWB was always going to go down the UN route. Cheney looked very sour throughout, and after dinner, when TB and Bush walked alone to the chopper, Bush was open with him that Cheney was in a different position. Earlier, when we had said that the international community was pressing for some direction but that in the US there would be people saying 'Why are you going to the UN, why aren't you doing it now?' Cheney smiled across the table, making it pretty clear that was where he was. The mood was good. As we left, Bush joked to me 'I suppose you can tell the story of how Tony flew in and pulled the crazed unilateralist back from the brink.' He was very clear on the threat, and the need of the UN to deal with it. He said he would get something on the Middle East. 'That's a promise.' He was, as Sally said, far more impressive close up. At the dinner, a lot of politics having been done, there was a fair bit of small talk. He was quizzing TB about what Balmoral was like. Also filling us in on the row at Augusta golf club, where women were trying to win entry against the rednecks. He said they would have to let them in so the sooner the better. He and I discussed our running. He had done one marathon and his mum and dad had come out to cheer him at 19 miles and his mother had shouted out 'There are three fat ladies ahead of you.' Cheney said next to nothing over dinner, ditto Hadley. TB got very bad stomach cramps.

Monday, September 9

TB remained of the view that we would get there in the end, and also that it was still possible to avoid war. We agreed a process for writing the report. Scarlett agreed with me that the FCO was trying to take it over and I said I will chair a group looking at it from the presentational point of view. Jack Straw called me about it and I said John Williams should be part of the team, not the writer. John Scarlett felt there was an ownership issue. He said he must feel he will have ownership of it. He and the SIS guys were really helpful. Good meeting and felt they were basically OK to deal with. Then did a note to JS, copied very widely, setting out the process. JS to own. AC to help.

Tuesday, September 10

Alex F called, really worried about Iraq, said he thought it was a very dangerous situation for TB. I said TB had a real sense of certainty about this one. Alex was really on the rampage about the press as well, said we had to do something, they were out of control. Got Iraq dossier draft, read it at home.

Wednesday, September 11

TB was with Robin C, even more puffed up than usual. Robin said we had to recall parliament and better we do it sooner rather than later. We were behind the curve. He was making clear he felt we had to avoid military action, saying he didn't want to serve 20 years under a Gordon Brown premiership. He even mentioned Suez. This is not Suez, said TB. That was not thought through and the US were not there. I'm not going to let the US go unilateral. It would be wrong and this way I get to influence them. RC spelled it out, said the US didn't understand the Middle East peace process. They were doing Iraq for the wrong reasons and they were hugely unpopular. He welcomed the fact TB had been able to restrain Bush, but they were clearly determined to go to war. 'I'll put you down as an unenthusiastic then,' said TB. RC said he feared it would be the end of the government. TB really was isolated at the moment and yet he kept going on this. We agreed that I would draft the letter from TB to Michael Martin [Speaker of the House of Commons] setting out our thinking, saying it would be connected to the dossier and unrelated to UN thinking. Then we had to square MM. David Hanson [TB's PPS] got him in New York, read him the letter. Later Jack S called me from NY, he was with MM, who said maybe we should think of a two-day debate instead, because lots would want to speak. Meanwhile I was working on the Iraq dossier. Long chat with John Scarlett. I said the drier the better, cut the rhetoric. The more intelligence-based it was the better. There was a need to separate IISS [International Institute for Strategic Studies report] from what was new in this one. I gave some suggestions later re a different structure. We had the basic story and now had to fill it out. TB looked at it and felt it was pretty compelling stuff. He was in a bit of a strop re recall of Parliament, said that it was a new precedent. He also didn't want Cabinet until after a recall. Ridiculous. No wonder Betty Boothroyd said it was becoming more presidential.

Thursday, September 12

GWB speech to the UN was leading news all day, up to delivery at 3.30 NY time. They sent a draft through yesterday but though good in tone, it lacked the crucial point that they would go for another UNSCR first. It just wasn't there. This was what Cheney/Rumsfeld wanted. They felt that more 'UN-ery' was just a way to give Saddam the chance to mess them around. So David Manning sent through a passage from TB and spoke a couple of times to Condi. But it was only at the last moment that we heard he WAS going to include reference to UNSCR and in the end he delivered it in plural. That meant that others would be able hopefully to welcome it more than they would have done. I had a long chat with Alan Milburn. JP had had the same conversation with him as he had had with me, namely saying he would support GB but not if he went for TB. 'There can only be one Prime Minister, and we have already got one.' But Alan said TB was very isolated and Iraq was going to be very difficult for him. He said he and John Reid would be there totally. He put down Blunkett as 'cautiously supportive'. We were hoping to get Margaret B fully on board. But he felt there was quite a lot of dicking around.

Friday, September 13

Meeting with Julian Miller on the dossier to go through the new structure. I was worried that it was going to have to rely too much on assertion. We also had a flurry with an overnight telegram re Scarlett's US trip, because he'd been told the US were going to publish their own dossier using US material and we worried it would undercut ours. I raised it on the conference call with the Americans. There were also persistent reports of problems re Cheney and Rumsfeld pushing for much more robust, less UN-related lines. GWB speech had gone down well and seemed to shift opinion around the place but they were arguing for such a tough UNSCR that it would not be acceptable to anyone. I was worried that the dossier was going to be too assertive and that even though the agencies presented it as their work, it would be seen as us trying to spin them a line.

Monday, September 16
Chat with Scarlett re dossier. He was still worried the US were going to do their own version first. It came up on the conference call again, and I had to pin down Dan Bartlett afterwards to try to get it back out. We were really needing to get some focus back on the domestic agenda but it was going to be hard. At his Monday meeting, TB was going on about parking Iraq, and then getting proper focus on Home Office and asylum. This was real Groundhog Day, him just railing and railing at their inability to grip these issues properly. Yet again, he said he wished we could get out of hunting.

Tuesday, September 17
I was in bed after midnight and Dan Bartlett called. Kofi had announced a letter from Iraq saying they'd let the inspectors back in. Dan wanted us to share a sceptical line, making clear the issue was disarmament. That was fine. We put out a fairly tough line. Needless to say our media was on the case straight away saying how that clever Saddam had done us in. I commissioned the CIC to do a paper on his past dicking about. TB wanted to be on the very tough end, saying we needed a tough new UNSCR and that had to be about maximum inspections, etc.

Thursday, September 19
Most of my work at the moment was on the dossier. Nuclear timelines just about sorted. Some people reasonably convinced, others not. We'd end up convincing those who wanted to be and not those who didn't. [Hans] Blix [head of UN Monitoring, Verification and Inspection Commission (UNMOVIC)] was at UN saying he could be in there soon but being quite conciliatory with them. The Iraqi foreign minister was at the UN saying, via letter from Saddam, they had no WMD programmes. I signed off on the dossier before John S's final meeting on it.

Saturday, September 21

We learned that Prince Charles's letter to TB re hunting was being leaked to the *Mail on Sunday*. It could have been really bad but thankfully they didn't have the text, just a briefing on it, and the line that if we banned hunting he might as well go skiing all year round. Then we learned that Clare Short had pre-recorded *GMTV* and there was plenty in it to make news – no second Gulf War, protect Iraqi children, so on and so on. I didn't bother TB with it.

Monday, September 23

Geoff Hoon came in to go through all the military options with TB. At Cabinet, TB did the intro, went through what the dossier was based on, emphasised the need to put over the history of UN resolutions and also the nature of the regime. The dossier brought together accumulated evidence about Iraq's attempts to build WMD, part historical, part intelligence-based. We were not saying he was about to launch an attack on London but we were saying there was an attempt to build a WMD programme in a significant way. He made clear we were still focused on the UNSCR route and if he doesn't comply there will have to be international military action. He will not comply unless he thinks the threat is real. Meanwhile, we have to redouble efforts on Afghanistan and MEPP. JS went through where we were on resolutions, then JP came in with quite a hit on Robin and Clare, said we could all do our bit of positioning to make our own views heard, and get a few plaudits, but we were in this together. He said TB had done a brilliant job moving the US down the UN route and we should stick with him and stick together. He said it's easy to do, a briefing here, a word there, and it's not on. Go down that road and we're in real trouble. One or two do it and it's indulgent. He said Tony had an incredibly difficult job at times like this and we should support him. He said he had been asked by the BBC if he agreed with Clare about killing innocent children and 'I said I'm not very keen on killing innocent children either.' Clare sat looking out of the window with a face like thunder, but didn't interrupt him. GB came in with a few long-term points for the US, the need to think through post-Saddam, the importance of MEPP. Patricia Hewitt suggested the Attorney General came to Cabinet to explain the legal position. Robin was pretty creepy. Both Jack and John R had a bit of a dig at him. Even after her performance yesterday, and even after JP, Clare was still full of herself. She said if we are going to have collective responsibility we should have a collective decision. There was no doubt Saddam was dedicated to possessing WMD but re the UN, there's a double standard vis-à-vis Israel. She said she admired TB for the way he had got the US to go to the UN, but then she went off about Afghanistan being a mess. JR said 'I think we can all make our points without giving the impression that some of us have a monopoly on caring and humanity.' Most of them said what we would expect them to say, though I was quite impressed by Boateng's speech, during which Clare spilled tea over Andrew Turnbull [Cabinet Secretary and head of the Civil Service].

It was a pretty good discussion, though focused as much as anything on the idea that we were having to deal with a mad America and TB keeping them on the straight and narrow. JP referred to the idea that TB would have sleepless nights, that we knew it could go to a difficult choice between the US and the UN. TB said he believed it would be folly for Britain to go against the US on a fundamental policy, and he really believed in getting rid of bad people like Saddam. The discussion was serious and sober and hard-headed and TB was in control of all the arguments. Several of them praised him and his leadership without it sounding sycophantic. Milburn had one or two interesting observations about anti-Americanism. He too felt there was a problem re double standards, and the lack of drive on MEPP. Charles said the mood in the party was apprehensive. GH said the ultimate objective was disarmament and that weapons inspectors are a means to an end. The clearer we are that we would use force, the likelier it may be that we don't have to. On the question 'why now' he said his record, his use of them, and his continued development. TB said if he fell, the people who would rejoice most would be the Iraqis. It is basically a wealthy country whose people live in poverty. He said the US can go one of two ways. It can go unilateralist, and there may be some who want that, but he was sure Bush was not one of them. Or they can be part of a broader agenda on Africa, MEPP, Afghanistan. Funnily enough, I think TB won the Cabinet over more easily than the public.

Wednesday, September 24

Dossier day after months of waiting. Adam Boulton was good all day. [Andrew] Gilligan [Defence and Diplomatic Correspondent for the BBC's *Today* programme] and [Tim] Marshall [Sky] and the so-called experts went on about nothing new, but a combination of TB's Commons statement and the gradual serious build-up re the dossier got us into a better position. TB had to go to the NEC but had done the statement pretty much himself, gone through most of the difficult questions and was ok on it all. The only really tough question was, if

September '02: WMD dossier published

the UN did not sanction war, would the US and UK go along with it? The Iraqis put up their culture minister [Hamad Yussef Hammadi] to deal with it, and he was crap, his main line that it was all a Zionist plot. TB did well. He came back from the NEC laughing because Mark Seddon [editor of *Tribune*] said he had been to see Tariq Aziz [Deputy Prime Minister of Iraq], that he was a nice man and it was easier to get in to see him than it was to see TB! Schroeder arrived at 6.15. It was quite a thing for him to come to see TB rather than Chirac after his election and it was playing big in all our countries.

Saturday, September 28

Woke up to one of those rare and totally gobsmacking revelations that newspapers very occasionally produce, namely that John Major had a four-year affair with Edwina Currie [former Conservative MP]. It was one of those 'cor, fuck me' jaw-dropping moments. How on earth did he get away with it?

Sunday, September 29

The papers were quoting Prince Charles re a letter of apology to TB over the leaked letters but we hadn't got one and they told Jeremy that none were sent. TB was pretty supportive of Charles though, and said it was really important we should not let them think they fazed us.

Monday, September 30

Labour Party Conference, Blackpool. Clinton called me from Number 10, having gone there with Magi [Cleaver], having flown in early, and was clearly enjoying himself. He read me a very funny spoof draft, said he was going to do a 'never give in to Tony' speech. He said the US press were giving the Bush people an easy ride. 'Our press is either right wing or establishment so they don't care too much about the economy, jobs, health care, because they are all OK. They know that the Democrats want to be on the economy and Bush wants to be on the war.' A Karl Rove memo was leaked saying that 'war is the only issue that excites our base'. He said if Labour or the Democrats had ever done something like that, there would have been a total outcry. He was worried that TB was being used. I told him what TB had said a while back about 'really believing this'. He said a lot of Democrats were up there asking 'Why is Blair helping Bush so much?' We talked over how his speech might fit into the general pattern of conference, and help lift the mood. He was clear about how he could help, and looking forward to it.

Tuesday, October 1

Philip, Liz [Lloyd] and I had been up till 3am going through the speech line by line and trying to get in more colour and texture. It was in good shape. TB was up around 6, and I went in to see him at 7, and he was pretty happy with it. He felt it was the most rounded intellectual speech of the lot. Of all the visitors we had had to conference, Clinton was the one with the most star quality, up there with Mandela. As we were heading back to his suite, BC said he fancied going for a walk. It was windy, a bit cold and it was starting to rain, but he was like a big kid enjoying the lights. 'I love this place. I love Blackpool.' The security guys were clearly used to these kinds of eccentric excursions. We passed a big bingo hall, which advertised itself as the biggest amusement arcade in the world. 'Hey, I wanna go in there. Let's go play the machines.' We got to the door and it looked a lot less inviting close up, so we walked on. We were trying to find somewhere to eat. He said he wanted some fast food, nothing fancy, but we walked past two or three places that were closed. By now the rain was getting a bit heavier. Kevin Spacey [actor and friend of Clinton] was with us, having been on a trip with BC. We must have walked on for a couple of miles. Eventually we found a McDonald's that was open. Bill was now on the phone to Hillary, a mix of heavy politics and small talk, going on with her too about how great this Blackpool seafront was. He made quite an interesting point when he came off the phone. All the delegates and the conference people are inside the security bubble, but more of them should get out here with the real people. The tighter the bubble, the more you should try and get out of it.

The staff were gobsmacked when we trooped in. There was a young kid behind the counter who was shocked enough to clock Kevin Spacey, but then saw Clinton and went a funny shade of pink, before getting everybody out of the kitchens to come and see. Doug Band (Clinton's assistant) ordered massive amounts of burgers, chicken nuggets and fries while Bill went round saying hello to the small number of customers in there. There was a fringe event going on at a pub or hotel over the road and word went round there. Margaret Jay's daughter Tamsin came back with a few journalists, including Matthew D'Ancona, but they just sort of gawked, pretended they had just been going out for a night at McDonald's. I got them over to say hello a bit later on. Meanwhile a crowd was building outside, some of them classic Blackpool landladies out of the postcards, looking and pointing and then when he occasionally turned round and waved at them, they were waving back in a state of high excitement. So there we were, sitting in a Blackpool McDonald's, drinking Diet Coke and eating chicken nuggets as he poured forth on the theme of interdependence, the role of the third way in progressive politics. He was also quizzing me about GB, and could sense that GB didn't really want to acknowledge TB's peculiar skills and talents, just as Gore hadn't used him properly in the campaign. He spent a while talking to the crowd on the way out, then we got driven back in a little van. He was like a man replenished, not because of the food but because he had been out with real people, and got something out of it.

Friday, October 4

Iraq still really tricky. TB just wished the Americans would do more to put over a proper message to the world and worry less about their own right wing. First, a meeting in the garden, TB, AC, Jonathan, Andrew Adonis, later joined by David Manning. First we had to work out how to respond to the breaking news that Sinn Fein members were being arrested for arms offences and the obvious worry the ceasefire was breaking. Just had to play it along. Then foundation hospitals. There was a plan for a major presentation on this to ministers on Monday but Andrew said the Health department and the Treasury just could not agree on the facts. It was clearly going to have to be sorted at political level. David Manning felt that Saddam was probably going to make positive noises about inspections and try to drag things to February, because then the 'window of war' would close because he couldn't expect troops to fight in 50-degree heat. Jeremy did a note to TB on EMU, saying that even Gus O'Donnell [Treasury Permanent Secretary] did not know what GB was really thinking but Jeremy's guess was that GB would come to us in the next six months and say that four out of the five tests were met or being met but that one, sustainable convergence, was not.

Friday, October 11

Moscow. TB spent several hours one-on-one with Putin, who took a bit of a pop at our dossier. Earlier we checked what he would say about a UNSCR, namely that he might consider one, but on the dossier there had been no prior discussion, so the perfectly avoidable problem became a story for some of our lot. For the photocall later, TB was wearing what I can only call an Afghan hippie coat. I said there was no way he could wear that. Mohny Bahra [protection officer] had a fairly ordinary-looking sheepskin and I suggested they swap. This is ridiculous, Cherie said. Just ignore him. I said my job was to stop him looking ridiculous and try to get the press focused on real issues and not his bloody clothes. I said if he walked out in that, they would fall about and we'd have endless blather about his coat rather than the substance. Putin was looking on a bit bemused and TB, a bit embarrassed, said 'He doesn't like my coat very much.' Putin smiled and nodded in a way that made me think he thought I was right not to. TB then tried on Mohny's coat, which just about fitted and looked fine and unremarkable, at which point Cherie said to me 'You are a total fascist.' I said I think that's a bit over the top but he would look a complete clown going out in that. Mohny meanwhile was trying on TB's coat and launched into an impersonation of Elvis Presley.

Putin seemed pretty much alone in the leadership re pursuing a very pro-Western policy, and he felt he was getting very little in return from the US. TB told him he thought Bush got it but he wasn't sure about some of the others. As the day wore on, TB seemed to buy more into the Putin charge. He said he would have to talk to Bush about it. Putin said that if there is something the Americans are worried about, they expect the whole world to share their concerns and drop everything, but if it's something that the rest of the world are interested in, like the Middle East peace process, they don't get the urgency. On Iraq, VP said to TB 'Do you really think Iraq is more dangerous than this fundamentalism?' 'Course not.'

Tuesday, October 15

Up to see TB in the flat. Anna Wechsberg had done a good draft of the Bali statement.[1] I did a new ending, then he did his own with a couple of over-the-top lines, e.g. a reference to 'satanic struggles' then a tacit comparison with the Second World War. He was meant to speak to President Megawati [of Indonesia] but she was on answering machine, and the ambassador in Jakarta couldn't find her! He seemed to be fretting a lot about it when it was actually quite straightforward. But the question was growing how can we do terrorism and Iraq and TB was keen to build the argument that they were part of the same coin. TB had lunch with the Danish PM [Anders Fogh Rasmussen] then over to the House, no real problems out of the statement.

Thursday, October 17

I made contact with Leukaemia Research re the Marathon and they sounded very up for it. I spoke to Turnbull and Jeremy about gener-

---

[1] On October 12, 202 people, mainly foreign nationals, were killed in a bomb explosion in Kuta, on Bali.

ating sponsorship and they were fine providing I wasn't using government facilities. Then a meeting with TB, Jack S, Geoff Hoon and CDS. First Jack went over where we were re the UNSCR, with TB feeling he was too close to caving in on the two-resolution route. Then GH and CDS re the military options. Package 2, which was air, sea and special forces, and package 3, which included substantial numbers of 'boots on the ground'. CDS said he would have a real problem with his army if they were not properly involved and also TB would have far greater influence with the US if we were there on the ground. Sally was totally against. I was probably for, but the costs, around a billion for package 2, and 2 billion for package 3, alongside the far greater risks, were pretty horrific. The question to resolve was really whether we went in for the whole hog. CDS said that Tommy Franks was going to a meeting in Ankara with the Turks next week and really needed to know what our answers may be. TB said it was not no, but it was not yet yes, and he wanted more work done analysing the cost. Then to Cabinet. The discussions were almost all foreign, with incessant interruption from Clare including a real display of rudeness to TB on the Middle East. She said Palestine was getting worse and worse and what was he going to do to make good what he had said to conference? TB said he was continually pressing the US and she said 'Is that it?' with real disdain and contempt. She and Jack then had another little spat re India and Pakistan. Then a discussion on Bali, then where we were on Iraq, then JP on fire, then GB re the need to be very firm on the pay awards. The atmosphere wasn't great. We briefed hard out of it. TB's warning that there could well be more attacks. Hilary Armstrong said to me afterwards that Clare was angling to become deputy leader under GB. She was a totally ridiculous figure. Today had been like listening to someone on a bus, chipping in comments about other people's conversations, totally unable to see why people wouldn't see that she was right about everything.

Tuesday, October 22

Estelle asked to see TB and having been with him for a while, he asked me and Sally to pop round. She was basically saying she felt that her integrity and honesty was what made us value her and if TB felt she should go, she felt that they should have that conversation. TB said he didn't think this latest thing on the 'pledge to resign' was serious enough. I said it all depended deep down on whether she felt she was up to doing the job. She was clearly stressed, fiddling aggressively with her hands, her neck was bright red and at times she seemed close to tears. It seemed to me that deep down she maybe felt she wasn't up to it. TB said we should all think about it. I had a couple of long conversations with her later in the day, during which I felt she was moving towards leaving, and I started to draft an exchange of letters. If it was going to happen, it was best to do it before a head of steam built up, and for her to say what appeared to be the case, namely that she found the pressure and realities of modern politics very difficult. I spoke to Estelle around 6pm. TB didn't think she should go, but that only she could know if she was really up for it. She said to me that she just was not capable of coping with the nasty personal stuff in the media, like her nieces at school being approached, or a boyfriend of fifteen years ago being looked into. The growing sense I had was of someone who was looking around for reasons to go, but didn't want to say that actually she was just finding it very difficult.

Wednesday, October 23

Estelle said she had slept on things, and now she had made up her mind and was clear that she was going to go. She said she had worked out what she was good at and what she was less good at. She was good with people, and she was good on policy but she couldn't run a big department strategically and she just couldn't cope with the modern media and its intrusiveness and nastiness. She said there was something I had said yesterday which had made a real impression on her, when I pointed out that compared to others, she hadn't really had a hard time in the media and I had said 'Maybe Tony and I are just so used to it that we have grown immune.' She said 'I don't want to be immune, because it would mean I would stop feeling.' She asked me repeatedly if I thought she was doing the right thing, and what TB really thought. I said he basically worried that she had lost her nerve, and that if she didn't feel up for it, there was no point hanging around. She said she felt she was really good with teachers and she could do that part of the job great. She was hopeless with budgets and figures and there was too much of the department for her to stay on top of it all the time. She said it was the right thing to go. I showed her the letters I had drafted, she read hers first, and said yes, that's right, it sums it up fine. When she looked at the one I had done for Tony, she started crying, she looked broken. Chris Woodhead [former Chief Inspector of Schools] was out dancing on the grave straight away. I had said to Estelle 'Sometimes I feel like the executioner. I always seem to be there at the death of a ministerial career and I find it unbelievably draining.'

Thursday, November 21

NATO summit. GWB arrived for the summit. He had the most extraordinary pair of cowboy boots on, and was full of the usual hail fellow well met, how ya doing? He felt there was a need for real pressure to build through troop movements, international condemnation, really tough and unpredictable inspections, to get Saddam off balance. Bush said that once we made that phone call that agrees Saddam's in breach, we had to do something militarily, and quickly. Quick sustainable bombing raid, and boots on the ground. He said if Blix gets dicked around, while a US or UK plane is shot down, we go for him. He was clearly not keen on Blix, said he was wringing his hands and talking war and peace but 'That is our judgement.' TB said he felt there was a 20% chance Saddam would cooperate, but Bush said he didn't know what cooperation meant. TB believed the regime would crumble pretty quickly, and Bush said both our secret services needed to be put to work to help that. He felt Saddam was making Blix and the UN look like fools. He also felt that if we got rid of Saddam, we could make progress on the Middle East.

Wednesday, November 27

Fiona called to say that our cops had a piece of paper from Cheshire cops about someone who had gone to them warning that Carole Caplin's partner was a fraudster. Peter Foster, the boyfriend, was once involved in a tea scam in which he used Samantha Fox [former topless model]. If Carole was now in cahoots with someone trying to set themselves up on the back of them [the Blairs], things could get tricky. Fiona said she had felt increasingly frozen out by Cherie and Carole, whose choice of men was a bit worrying, and yet all we ever heard from TB and CB was that she was marvellous.

Thursday, November 28

I did a note for TB saying the Foster story was clearly going to become public and that we had to have defensive lines ready making clear that he had never met him and that it was not true, as he was saying, that he was their financial adviser. Took a call from Ian Monk [journalist turned PR consultant]. Monk told me CB called Carole twice during his meeting with her. Fiona said Cherie had told her that she had not been able to get hold of her today and was really pissed off that we were being excluded, not least because neither of us trusted the people involved to grip it properly. TB called CB when we got back to the hotel and said it had to be gripped and Carole had to understand this was about us every bit as much as it was about her. As he understood it, the guy was a total conman, and dangerous.

Friday, November 29

Had a very interesting discussion with TB about the nature of these jobs and friendship. He said he felt part of the problem of his life was that it's not possible to make real new friendships once you get to a position like his. It meant that if you are already close to people, you got even closer to them, both at work and outside work. So people like me, Sally, Anji and Kate [Garvey] he felt very, very close to, felt he could trust us. But even if he met new people that he liked, it was always difficult because in the end he was the prime minister, and that was bound to affect the way people think about him. Carole had come on the scene fairly early on, and they had both liked her. She was a bit wacky, fun and interesting. But don't worry, he said, I do realise how dangerous this is. I said it came to something that we were worrying about a professional conman close to the heart of the whole bloody operation.

Saturday, November 30

On Foster, the *Mail on Sunday* sent over more than twenty questions. The real problem was over the flats. TB admitted to me he was always against the idea of a flat on political grounds, but also that until today he had no idea they had bought two. I felt people would just about understand a mother wanting to get a decent place to live for their son, and might just about understand that she didn't trouble TB with all the detail, but they would find it a bit weird to think they had got two flats with the help of this guy Foster.

Wednesday, December 4

The *Mail* had an exchange of emails between Foster and CB which totally debunked the idea that he was not an adviser. Even though I had half expected this, I was absolutely livid. TB and Cherie were at the theatre. I told the *Mail* I couldn't find them and we would have to deal with it in the morning. We were being hit again because we didn't get the full facts out. I dictated a note to TB saying this was likely to be big and bad. He called me at ten to twelve, said it was ridiculous to say Foster was their financial adviser. He was still in denial about it. He said at the weekend he had said that Foster had sent Cherie an email but CB did not even reply, so it was ridiculous – one of his favourite words at the moment – that this was a big story. I said we had given, in his name, the clear impression that Peter Foster had had nothing to do with the whole thing, but these emails would show very clearly otherwise. I also felt he was far too tolerant of the whole Carole scene.

Thursday, December 5

I got in, up to the flat, where TB was sitting at the table in the window, a welter of emails spread out in front of him. There was no small talk, no banter. Cherie came in wearing her pyjamas, could barely look at me and we didn't speak. TB and I agreed that the problem was going to focus on the fact that we misled the press. They continued to insist that this guy was not their financial adviser, but based on these exchanges, they were deluding themselves if they thought we could persuade people of that. This problem arose, like others before, because TB and CB so often wanted to believe the best and ended up doing so. But we were going to get the blame for this. I said there was a case for turning the draft into a CB statement and she agreed to that. We spent ages going over it. When TB came back, he and I went up to the little changing room by the bedroom and he said his instinct was to fight it out. I said if we gave nothing on this, we'd be dead. He said it was only because we lived in a world infested with this media scum that we had to get into any of this. Cherie joined us, looking very downcast. I then worked on a Number 10 statement followed by a CB statement which said she would have been more circumspect if she had known and that she regretted causing misunderstanding. We had to fill in some of the gaps with copper-bottomed facts. We had to clear up the idea we had misled the press, I felt we just had to get the facts out as best we could. The hacks were also moving to the idea that it was me and Fiona who were responsible for the misleading. TB spoke to CB and she agreed we could make clear she alone was responsible for any misunderstanding. Through the day the story developed into one about Cherie's judgement re Carole and re them not telling us that Foster had indeed had a lot to do with these transactions. TB was worried about the impact of all this on Cherie, said it was monstrous that she was being done in like this, that she is a far better person than all this suggests. I said he should worry less about Carole and more about his own position.

Friday, December 6

The papers were dire for CB, while the *Mail* and the *Telegraph* were really going for me – Liar-in-Chief. These issues, where the political and the personal collided, were always difficult, and it must at times feel like they both had me and Fiona on their backs the whole time, trying to cut out what they would regard as any fun or escape out of their lives. I said we were trying to help navigate through shitty waters. He said I know, but we are talking about my wife here.

Saturday, December 7

TB said he resented having to deal with all this nonsense when he was also having to worry about Iraq. I continued to say it was all avoidable. We got the *Mail* questions in the afternoon and they related mainly to Foster and Carole being invited to things with Cherie, plus the issue of a trust that bought the flats, plus Fiona's role. We were dismissive of the invite stuff, fairly detailed on the trust. Then the *News of the World* came in with various groups of questions, first the claim that CB definitely knew about Foster's past so her statement on that was false, second that Carole tried to do a deal on clothes as we had always suspected, and third the wacky stuff about them having mudbaths and showers together. I spent most of the time on the phone.

Monday, December 9

TB kept trying to persuade me that Carole was a decent person and would do nothing wrong, e.g. on clothes. I said this had to be copper-bottomed, and I'm not sure I believed it. He got very defensive and we had another row about it, saying that we had a real problem because he took what she said at face value and I didn't. It was not an easy conversation. Foster's solicitor put out a statement which showed that CB had taken part on a conference call with Carole and the solicitor. It sent the media into a frenzy. TB looked grey, angry and sick. Cherie was due to be turning on the Christmas tree lights outside, but TB called for her to come down to the office, told her the questions that had now been put and she said yes, she spoke to the lawyer because Carole was worried Foster's case wasn't being handled properly, and what was wrong with that? She had a look of injured innocence. TB looked really angry, was close to the end of his tether. The problem was he saw nothing wrong in her making such a call, and I did, because she was the PM's wife, a QC, a judge, and she should have better judgement. TB said OK, she's maybe been daft but does she really deserve this kind of treatment? The politics on this were getting worse and worse.

Tuesday, December 10

TB was getting very agitato. He said 'I'm not having my wife treated like this and we have to fight back on the basis we have done nothing wrong.' He wanted to go up and do a big defence of her, but I said if he went up and just stated nothing had been done wrong, he would be more tarnished by it. He really seemed unable to see anything wrong in it. I felt that unless we let some air out of the situation, this was just going to go on and on. Carole didn't want to say she was dumping Foster. New questions came in from the *Mail*. They were now suggesting 'judge nobbling'. It was time to go for it. It was a tipping point and we were all now up for CB doing a big number. I put calls out to Peter M and Charlie F to get them to come over and we went through things line by line, making sure that all the difficult questions were answered in there, why the flats, how Foster, what she knew, why Carole. Fiona was terrific today, so was Peter M, saw things really clearly, but we had to fight back and that meant changes in the dynamic. An interview would be no good, because then someone else would set the agenda with it. It had to be bigger to break through. We decided that in the end Cherie was going to have to go up on this, break through, let the public see it and judge for themselves. She was due to do an event over at Millbank, with a ready-made audience, who would be sympathetic. I think we all felt that though there was a risk in this, it was probably the best way to blow the storm out. Cherie was a lot calmer than yesterday, though she and I were still finding it hard to engage. I gave her the draft and she had a few minor changes which she explained to Peter M and I put them in. We suggested she did a read-through to ensure she was happy with it and also so she would be aware of the points where emotional intensity might take over. Peter M said she should pick out people in the audience, look in their eyes and speak to them direct. She looked at me and said 'I certainly don't want to look at him.' She looked very pale, said she was worried about crying but she read the statement pretty well, looked very emotional, pretty close to tears. After the event everyone felt a lot better. TB had been with the Queen when she did it and they hadn't watched it. He caught it on the news later and said he was really proud of the way she stood up to it. TB did for once thank us for what we had done for him.

Saturday, December 14

For the sixteenth day running, most of my time was taken up with Foster and Caplin. Peter M called, very Peterish, pretending nothing much was going on, asked how I was. Spitting tacks, I said. 'Do you like anyone?' he asked. I said Rory, Calum and Grace, and Fiona when she's not disagreeing with me. The rest can fuck off. When TB called as I was out on a run, and said that we just had to shut it down, not answer any more questions, and tough it out, I said something that made both of us snap. I was at the top of Golders Hill, had just got my breath back and said to him the real problem was that whether you like it or not, you are linked to a conman. He said I resent that. 'You are. You're married to a woman who is determined to protect and keep a woman who is in love with a conman so you are linked to a conman.' He shouted at me down the line 'I am not linked to a conman.' You are, and until Cherie dumps Carole or Carole dumps Foster, or preferably both, that's the way it is. And every day it's like that it hits your authority more, both with the rest of the government and with the public. TB was having none of it. 'We have a fundamental disagreement. You think Cherie has done something monstrous and I don't. You think Carole is monstrous, and I don't.' I said there was a difference between monstrous and wrong. 'Well, I disagree. She is not a bad person and I'm not going to dump on people just because the press tell me to.' I said I wasn't going to defend Carole or anything to do with her. 'Fine, don't then. Just say nothing about it.' Fine, I said, but if this goes on much longer I'm off, out of here, goodbye.

Monday, December 16

TB called me in for a one-on-one chat. 'You are the Roy Keane [footballer] of the operation, but like him you sometimes stamp people on the head without meaning to. That's how Carole and her mum have felt and they are not like us, they are not used to it.' He said he knew that if Carole stayed with Foster, they could have nothing to do with her. Also, even if she dumps him, he has to be more careful. 'I have been reckless and foolish and paid a price. So has Cherie, who had a terrible shock. But she is a good person not a bad person. And you have to take us as we are, strengths as well as weaknesses.'

Thursday, December 19

TB asked, 'Have you reassessed recent events?' 'What do you mean?' 'I think you slipped the reservation for a while. You went for Cherie and Carole. I know the reasons, you wanted to protect your people, but you should have discussed it with me. If this kind of thing ever happens again, we just have to have it out.' He said I was such a big personality and so forceful that if I was pissed off, everyone felt it and it dragged the whole show down. It's why he made the Roy Keane analogy. He said you lead by example, which is great, but if you're pissed off, everyone around you gets pissed off. You wear your

December '02: Campbell says to Blair, you're linked to a conman

heart on your sleeve and give out very powerful vibes, and I'm just saying that in the last few days, that's not been a good thing. I think both of us felt better afterwards.

Wednesday, January 1, 2003

Very quiet on the work front. The New Year's message got big coverage, but there was no doubt I had allowed my own somewhat gloomy view of events to colour things, so the coverage was pretty much on the 'we're all doomed' lines. Fiona and I were both pretty down about the thought of going back. Partly it was the weather, partly the thought that actually the tone of the message was pretty much where things were, and also the fact that TB, whenever he phoned, went on and on about what a marvellous time they were having, and how energising it all was for him. I said there was a time when I felt natural warmth for his irrepressible enthusiasm and zest for life. But it can sound unbelievably irritating when he's basking in sunshine and we are swimming through floods. He was mulling over the various pressing problems and they were pretty much the same as a year ago, if a bit more advanced and a bit more difficult in some cases – US/UK, terrorism, MEPP, Northern Ireland, public services, Europe and the euro. We had to get through it as best we could, but within that list there were a lot of complicated and interacting problems. I felt out of sorts personally, not motivated by much other than the kids and the marathon training.

Sunday, January 5

Alice Miles called from *The Times* to say that Roy Jenkins' death had just been announced and would TB do a piece? I said maybe, but later spoke to TB and said I felt not, but maybe he should just do his own short tribute. He sent it through. It was very warm and personal, I felt the combined effect was over the top. I called TB to say so and he agreed to take out 'mentor' and instead talk of his support. I also pointed out he should at least say he disagreed with the formation of the SDP. 'But won't people think I'm just doing that for the Labour Party?' I said

'You are the leader of the Labour Party, and they did try to kill us.' 'Yes, but he was right in a lot of what he said, do you want me to say that?' Laughter. I said no. 'Surely the party is used to my little eccentricities by now.' Yes, but one day they might decide you have gone too far and rise up against you. I just feel it's a bit over the top. He said I thought you would but OK, take out the word mentor and put in something about me disagreeing with the formation of the SDP, but I do think he was a great figure and I am very sad about his death.

Thursday, January 9

Milburn took me aside at the end of Cabinet, said people were getting really fed up with TB's tolerance of Clare in Cabinet. He said it was like having a bag lady in there just speaking out on everything.

Wednesday, January 15

MoD briefing on Iraq. CDS and all the other chiefs were there in uniform. We sat round three sides of the room. CDS said they expected Bush to make a decision for February 15 and they would go within twelve days or so to a massive air, sea and land operation. It was going to be called 'shock and awe', and the scale would reflect that. There would be hundreds of plane sorties from day one, aimed at wiping out his infrastructure and playing for a 'house of cards' effect. They went through where UK forces were most likely to be involved, taking out his defences close to the border. Substantial numbers of our ships and planes. A total of 42,000 UK forces possibly, 300,000 plus from the US. Then a slideshow briefing showed the scale of the attacks on the whole country, moving up to the capital. Oilfields were to be seized straight away, which with the conspiracy theory about oil, would be difficult presentationally. Alan West, ex-intelligence now naval commander, said there would be so much going on in the first day or so, that the international media would not know where to go. TB pressed on whether Saddam would use chemical or biological weapons. They said they were buried so he might not be able to activate them quickly, but that was the reason Franks had gone for the doctrine of overwhelming force. They believed Saddam was working on an assumption that it would be done by air strikes first, and then move in on land. It was interesting to see how much more fluent and confident Mike Boyce was in this setting. They knew the oilfield situation was difficult, and would require careful presentation. They said it was the right thing to do to prevent ecological disaster because Saddam might well go for blowing up his own oilfields as a way of causing chaos in the markets.

The planning was clearly well advanced, but it was still unclear whether the politics would allow any of it. But if this was going to happen as quickly as it seemed, TB said, then the work on aftermath questions had to happen now too. The intelligence people, including the defence guys, were pretty strongly of the view that Saddam would use WMD if he could. They warned of the inevitability both of civilian deaths and casualties of our own, but they felt in the initial attacks it was likely we would lose more through normal exercises than by being killed by Iraqis. They felt we would be able to strike very accurately. But the scale of bombing meant that there were bound to be civilian deaths. TB also emphasised the need to get in place proper humanitarian support. It was a pretty heavy-duty scene. It took place in the new MoD buildings, with everything very carefully laid out, typed name plates, tea and biscuits that nobody seemed to touch. On the way in, it had been like one of those scenes from darkly lit political thrillers where politicians and military and entourage are marching purposefully down a corridor, very little conversation, the only noise heels on floor, people walking too fast. It was pretty clear as we got into the cars and headed back to Number 10 that the Americans were going for this and TB had looked more nervous, particularly about the idea of UK military casualties and the possibility of large numbers of civilian casualties.

Thursday, January 16

Cabinet was fine. On Iraq, TB set out where we were. Trying to make the UN route work. Inspectors in there. He said the Russians were closer to the Americans than they say publicly, while the French do not particularly want to be left on the outside. But it was going to be tough. In the meantime, we build up the troops, and make sure that if it does come to conflict we are able to get it over quickly. Jack was pretty confident about the UN process, pointed out that a lot of people said we would never get a resolution in the first place but we did, on the strength of the case. Robin C said we were in a tremendous position on the UN, 'thanks to you', he said to TB. He said the prospect of getting a second resolution was stronger if we do not rule out saying we may do it without one. One or two of them talked about the problem that Bush gave us with public opinion, but TB was clear we had to stay close publicly to maximise influence privately. At the end of the discussion JP did a very passionate wind-up. He said the discussion showed there was no real division 'so let's stop pretending there is'. He said the briefings and the 'talking out the side of the mouth' have to stop. He said the party doesn't like the idea of intervention but sometimes we have to make difficult judgements. If TB has the courage to put the case, we should get behind him. Even Clare was reasonably measured. TB closed by setting out where he had asked for more work to be done, in three different areas – first, what offer we can make to the Iraqi people, e.g. re territorial integrity, lifting of sanctions, future prosperity; second, aftermath and the UN role in that; third, the unexpected and in particular the risk of WMD being used against our troops, or environmental catastrophe around oilfields.

Tuesday, January 21

TB was really exercised about student finance, and we had a long meeting, GB now trying to take out the proposal that they also be charged interest on the debt. TB was demanding to see all the research from all the different systems round the world, also the comparisons between our richest and poorest universities. Then a meeting on the Olympics, where TB and I both made the point that we didn't seem to have the firm basis on which to make a decision. TB wanted clear advice but people were blowing hot and cold not according to hard fact and analysis. Tessa had definitely moved towards yes, others had moved away. The worry I sensed was that we would say no simply because it was easier than saying yes, and then regret it. Then over to Derry's at the Lords to launch my appeal for marathon sponsorship. It was Derry's idea to hold it there, and it paid off with a terrific turnout, including some big cheques at the end of it. Tessa, Peter M, Jackie Stewart [former racing driver], Trevor Beattie, Tony Ball [TV executive] and his beautiful wife Gabriela, David Sainsbury, John Browne [businessman], David Frost, good turnout from News International and *Mirror* old and new. Dickie Bird was an absolute hoot and ended up going back on the train with Mum, talking loudly all the way back about how much he liked TB, me, the government, etc. TB popped in and didn't look all that comfortable. I sensed he was a bit bemused about how big the whole thing was going. He probably found it a bit odd when he wasn't the absolute centre of attention. I did a little speech about John, Lindsay and Hope [the Merritts]. Fiona and I found it a bit stressful but the kids were great, and we hoovered up not just cheques but some terrific auction items as well.

Wednesday, January 22

The anti-war mood was definitely growing and I raised it on the

US conference call and pointed out the difficulty it was causing. I said they were going through all the gears for their domestic audience, and that gave us problems over here. David also spoke to Condi to say the politics had got a lot harder and they had to be more sympathetic to international issues, pressures, concerns. We faced the same danger we had had re Kosovo and Afghanistan, namely moral equivalence, this time between US and Iraq. Sally said to TB if we didn't take real care, this was the end of him. There had to be UN support and there had to be real evidence. TB was pretty clear though that we couldn't peel off from the US without very good reason.

Friday, January 24

On Iraq, TB was due to speak to Bush and sent through a note in advance. TB was confident we could get Bush to the position where he stayed long enough for a second UNSCR. He was clear with the Cabinet it was important to stay with the Americans and he wanted to do a big pre-Camp David diplomacy round. His note set out what he saw as the political and other realities. He praised Bush's strength in forcing Saddam to the position of getting the inspectors in, but said we didn't have the support needed and we needed time to build it. He admitted that not only did he not have support in the country but he couldn't really call on a majority in his own Cabinet. He remained hopeful he could keep things on a multilateral track but it was not going to be easy. He was facing a very tough call indeed, about as tough as they get.

Wednesday, January 29

For obvious reasons, Iraq was worrying TB more and more. We did however have a rare, for these times, PR hit in the form of an article signed by, eventually, eight European leaders about standing alongside the US in standing up for resolution 1441 [on the return of inspectors to Iraq]. I had a long chat with Dan Bartlett, going over what we hoped to get out of Camp David. I was trying the whole time to get over to them just how bad the politics were. Everyone TB was speaking to was saying they needed a second resolution or they wouldn't get support. TB felt that was the reality for him too, that he couldn't deliver the party without it.

Thursday, January 30

CDS, GH, JS and JP came in for a meeting re Iraq. We went through the strategy for the next phase. [Colin] Powell's speech to the UN, then the next Blix report,[1] TB clear that he wanted to try to get GWB to a second UNSCR, pretty clear we couldn't do it without one. He felt we needed two or three Blix reports, and more time for Arab leaders to push Saddam out. Even Geoff, much more than before, seemed worried, telling us that Rumsfeld was saying inside the administration that the problem with the UN route was that it was open-ended. JP and I exchanged very worried looks. Then a Cabinet discussion on the Olympics. Jack reported on the committee meetings so far, the £2.6 billion estimated costs, the rise in London council tax, some of the pros and cons. JP said we were more experienced than we were at the time of the Dome but what was absolutely essential was that if we went for it, we all went for it, that there could be no division on this. He was broadly positive. When he mentioned the Dome Clare chipped in 'Most of us were against it' and he gave her one of his snorts. TB said he was struck by how pro the London MPs were. Nobody was saying go for it irrespective, but we had to pin the details down. GB said, very finance director-ish, that it would be desirable to go ahead if the finances are sustainable. Blunkett was sceptical, Paul Murphy pro. TB had to leave halfway through to take a call from Bush, from which he returned looking very worried. Overall the Olympic discussion was more negative than I thought it would be. Tessa pro, Charles pro, GH pro, Alan M basically pro. Lots of yes buts, but the buts were very heavy, particularly on finance, with Andrew Smith and Darling both very clear noes. John R very opposed. JP less sceptical than before.

It was snowing as we set off for Madrid. On the plane, TB worked on a new note on strategy for Bush. He was aiming to persuade Bush to wait till the middle or end of March and support a second resolution before action. He went through it all in his note, the military, the diplomatic, the propaganda questions, plus early planning on aftermath. Very simple lines and questions that we had to get answers to. He also emphasised that the 'other agenda' was important, particularly MEPP. He then laid out the potential problems on the way – e.g. Saddam uses WMD, attacks Israel, destroys oil wells, or there is major civil unrest. He went through the aftermath questions, organisation of humanitarian aid, role of the UN. On propaganda, Powell at the UN, the history of Iraqi non-cooperation. The WMD threat more generally, the link to terrorism, the growing worries in the intelligence. We went

[1] Blix, former Swedish foreign minister, was from 2000–03 head of UNMOVIC, the successor body to UNSCOM. Both bodies were tasked with searching for WMD in Iraq and their removal under UN Security Council resolution.

round the Cabinet one by one to assess who would support him without a second resolution. We could probably just about get to a majority but it would be difficult. It was pretty much 'future on the line' time.

Friday, January 31

Poll in the *Mirror* said 2% felt a war on Iraq would make the world a safer place. I made sure Dan [Bartlett] knew and made sure he told Bush just so he knew we were up against it. TB had also slept badly and was up and about, going over the same questions again and again, kept saying we needed a clear intellectual construct which was that 1441 focus should be on the cooperation issues, if the Iraqis didn't cooperate and Blix makes that clear repeatedly, we should say so and then we go for a second resolution and action could follow. We had allowed the goalposts to be moved to the smoking-gun issue, and instead it had to be about the inspectors not getting cooperation. We typed up all the relevant past resolutions, so he could read from them, particularly 1441. I had a long chat with Dan, made clear the issue for us was the second resolution, that that was where the press would go for the gaps and therefore we should try to close them. It was difficult because of course in the US the UN was not popular. The weather was apparently terrible at Camp David and meant we couldn't go there by helicopter so we were grounded in Washington and at one we left for the White House. While TB was seeing Bush, Tom Kelly and I saw Dan and I gave him a very frank assessment of the politics for us, said that our balls were in a vice. He said they believed that both politically and legally they could go without a second resolution. We went up to wait for TB and GWB. The question to resolve pre the press conference was what to say about a second resolution. GWB and Condi were both up for the idea of him saying he was 'open' to a second resolution, but Ari Fleischer pulled him back, said it would be seen as shift in US policy, and then tried to push him back the other way, said that I was worried after what TB said in his interviews earlier, it would be a split story. TB and Bush having had a lot of the discussion without us there, it made it harder to push back without them stating the nature of the discussion they had just had, and in any event Bush was impatient to get on with it. As a result, we didn't really have the lines properly prepared. 'Let's just do it,' said Bush. They both dispensed with opening remarks, which I think was a mistake because they gave no real context. The overall impression was poor. TB didn't really answer the question about a second resolution. And though Bush said it would be 'welcome' he looked uncomfortable and the body language was poor. Whatever people said about him, he is actually a very direct personality, which meant that he wasn't good at hiding what he thought or felt. Even though the words were kind of OK, the overall impression was not. As they wrapped up, Sally and I caught each other's eye. She grimaced. Tom managed to spin our lot to a more positive position by saying Bush was making clear he was open to a second resolution. TB said afterwards that in fact it had been the best meeting they had had in terms of substance, that they got on well, that Bush had read and digested his notes and was more on the same page than we thought, said he intended to work hard to get a second resolution and work to get a majority for it. TB repeated that if we didn't have the cover of the UN, when the Iraqis were bringing dead babies out of bombed buildings, having killed their own people, we would be in real trouble, so we had to go for it. But the politics of the UN on this were the opposite for him.

Tuesday, February 4

The Anglo-French summit at Le Touquet was being built up on the assumption of a big bust-up. Catherine Colonna and I were talking the whole time, and were on the same track in trying to get things in a better place. We were both using the line that more unites us than divides us. We left at 8.40 for Northolt, flew out on a tiny plane that Chirac wouldn't be seen dead in. Stephen Wall had done a good draft for the press conference which I topped and tailed. TB was convinced that the pro-US EU leaders' joint letter had been the right thing to do and would find Chirac in a better position vis-à-vis us, because if there was one thing he understood, it was strength. It was very cold on arrival. We were driven to the town hall, a huge scrum of media and public around TB and Chirac. Then in for the main bilateral, [Jean-Pierre] Raffarin also there, in the room normally used for marriages. It was when you saw French President and Prime Minister together that you were most aware of where the real power lay. Chirac, who could be overbearing at the best of times, was even more so in the presence of his Prime Minister, and although TB was his political opposite number, I think psychologically he tried to make TB think in terms of being Raffarin's opposite number.

They went through some of the difficult non-Iraq issues first, defence, CAP, climate change, Africa. On EU institutions, Chirac claimed close agreement, at one point even claiming that on the reform of the institutions his position was 'plus Britannique' than German. He said we had to convince the smaller countries that they do not lose by having a full-time President of the Council and we had to strengthen the Commission and Council at the same time. TB said he had had lunch with Giscard [d'Estaing; former French President] last week and that he had done a good job. Chirac – *'Je t'ai dit que c'était le meilleur.'* TB – *'Tu avais raison.'* Chirac – *'Comme d'habitude.'* Things got trickier on CAP, Chirac absolutely clear that he wasn't going for the kind of major change we wanted. He said the British view and the French view of farmers was very different, that France was the second biggest agricultural exporter in the world, that in England agriculture was not popular, that in France it was. Chirac was at his patronising best or worst, depending how you look at it, and TB had a big smile as he spoke. 'I think you are a very fair man, Tony, and it would be good to see if we can get you in a better position on this.' *'Si non, on arrive à un moment où on s'engeule. Tu comprend s'engeuler?'* TB – *'Je comprend très bien. Surtout maintenant.'* The joint letter had definitely got to him, and he emphasised that prior to the spring summit there should be a joint letter from UK, France and Germany, even though *'je me méfie des lettres.'* On Zimbabwe, he apologised for the leak, said there would be a leak inquiry 'which will not find out anything'. Again, he gave the impression that we were opposing for the sake of it. On the Middle East, Chirac was sceptical that the Americans would do anything, said power was not in Washington but in the Jewish population in New York. They weren't much closer on Afghanistan. Chirac pessimist, TB trying to see the bright side. Then Iraq, where Chirac said 'I'm not going to convince you, you won't convince me, so we can explain that one easily.' He said tomorrow we get the 'famous American revelations, namely *rien du tout'*. 'Is that because they are American?' asked TB. No, but if there were real revelations, we would know them too. He said they would listen with respect to Powell, then Blix and [Mohammed] El Baradei [director general of the IAEA]. He said there was no point pretending we were in the same position, other than agreeing that we wanted to disarm Iraq. They thought 1441 and more time for the inspectors. If Powell has important things to say, he should let the inspectors examine it. On a second resolution, if there was a war, we would need one but we do not need one at the moment because we are going through 1441. He said war had to be absolutely the last resort because the consequences – political, human and economic – were terrible.

It was a tense, pretty spiky meeting and at the plenary as well, though people were pretty much going through the motions of saying what they discussed at the various bilaterals, the atmospherics were poor and flat. Only the chiefs of defence seemed to have got on. When the French CDS [General Henri Bentégeat] said that Boyce was shortly leaving his job, it set Chirac off into a huge, obviously pre-planned, and for us rather embarrassing, tribute to Boyce. Chirac was even more full of Gallic gesture than usual. His face seemed to get more lined with every meeting. TB was tougher than usual, felt the letter had had a genuine and desired impact, that he now knew if France and Germany tried it again, we had the wherewithal to build alliances elsewhere. TB and Chirac had lunch together. I was with Catherine, who had been with him about the same time I had been with TB. We agreed to get them away from the others before the press conference to try to get the focus on the need for Saddam to disarm, and the importance of the UN, also to try to minimise the differences on the tough questions, e.g. second resolution. Both did pretty well, good body language, no attempt to deny differences, but Chirac brilliantly fobbed off the really difficult questions, e.g. on material breach, US–UK. TB was keen to get back to vote on the Lords, so we got some of the ministers out doing end-of-summit interviews. Chris Meyer sent over a bootlegged version of Powell's presentation. Tony Benn had done an interview for Channel 4 with Saddam, which was nauseatingly toadying. TB was pleased with the way the day had gone, felt that particularly over lunch Chirac had been warm and making an effort. TB called again later, said he felt he could now see a way of getting to the same place with Chirac. I said surely the best thing for Bush was to get Saddam out without a war. TB said that was his whole strategy, get the Blix report, then a second resolution, then get the Arabs to press him to go.

Thursday, February 6
The Powell presentation to the UN re WMD had gone well and there was a sense of things moving back to us. Meeting with CDS, C, Eliza [Manningham-Buller], John [Scarlett] and the main MoD targeter. A presentation of 'shock and awe' making clear that the aim was an overwhelming immediate effect. TB asked about the assessment on collateral damage. It had to be clear we were targeting Saddam and the regime, and also focusing on the aftermath and the humanitarian. There was also a lot of intelligence around on a planned hit on Heathrow. TB said he had no doubt that trying to remove Saddam quickly in the event of action was the best way, but he wanted to know what he was in for. TB said he felt Iraq would come up with some surprise to split the international community, that intelligence showed he would regard giving up WMD as a total humiliation, that it was essential to his internal grip. Blix said the South Africans were sending a delegation to tell them how to give up WMD. Blix said Iraq had definitely been hampered by inspections. He said they had been

to some of the places named in the dossier, and it could be they had been sanitised, but they found nothing. The indication was that come February 14 he would be saying they had not found WMD but there was no real cooperation. He didn't want to name scientists for interview for fear that they would be killed. He was a lot less bullish than last time and clearly fed up with the feeling he was being bullied by America. He didn't want to pose any new questions because they would take so long to answer. Then TB saw El Baradei. He was quite open and chatty, less nervy than Blix. He said the Iraqis claimed they had never tried to get uranium but it wasn't true. He didn't think many tears would be shed in the Arab world if Saddam went. He was worried that Iraq would claim they were being attacked not because of weapons but because they were a Muslim country. He felt it better if TB and Bush could say it was part of a vision of a zone free of nuclear weapons. Also, it was important the aftermath was a UN administration, multilateral, not the US. He said their strategy was to force him into cooperation, though he doubted it was possible. But he came back again and again to the theme that American public diplomacy wasn't working. TB said we had to sort out Saddam in as peaceful a way as possible, but above all sort out MEPP. I caught the news later, El Baradei making clear that the Arab world wanted Saddam out and they would help him on his way if they could. Blix was less impressive, came over as very ponderous and bureaucratic. Channel 4 ran a story that the CIC paper on the infrastructure of concealment, which I'd commissioned, had included passages plagiarised from a California document, and claiming we had made it look like intelligence. It gave them another spin story, and was a real pain.

Friday, February 7

The CIC dossier was causing a lot of embarrassment. Seemingly whole chunks were lifted off the Internet. I wrote a note to the CIC[1] to emphasise the importance of quality control and to make clear that this shouldn't have happened. It was a bad own goal, especially as we didn't need it given the very good intelligence and other materials we had. Definitely no more dossiers for a while. I called

[1] *Channel 4 News* had broken the story of what it dubbed the 'Dodgy Dossier', a briefing paper compiled for the Sunday papers by CIC civil servants. Cambridge academic Dr Glen Rangwala recognised plagiarised passages from writings available on the Internet, particularly 'Iraq's Security & Intelligence Network: A Guide & Analysis', an article written by political scientist Dr Ibrahim al-Marashi, and published in the *Middle East Review of International Affairs* in September 2002.

February '03: Second dossier fiasco

John Scarlett, who was very nice about it, but also rightly emphasised how careful we had to be.

Monday, February 10

TB called me up with David Manning and Jonathan as soon as he arrived. He looked very pissed off, for once grumbling that Jonathan and I were both in sweaty sports gear. He was harassed and fed up. The Franco-German plan, which presumably Chirac knew all about when we met at Le Touquet, had wrongfooted us. TB thought it unbelievable that these countries were putting the transatlantic relationship at risk. It had definitely been a few steps forward and a few steps back, Powell and TB on *Newsnight* taking us forward, a combination of the dossier and international division taking us back. TB said we needed a proposal. I said the problem was people felt we were driven by a timetable dictated by a desire for war rather than by a desire to disarm Iraq. TB was looking more worried and harassed than I had seen him for a while. I looked at his diary and really felt for him for once. Today alone he had meetings on Iraq, on asylum, where Blunkett was giving him grief, feeling he was weakened by TB driving the policy, a big meeting on terrorism, a difficult meeting with the military on Northern Ireland pre Wednesday's plan, Ruud Lubbers [UN High Commissioner for Refugees] for a meeting re refugees, the trade unions re two-tier workforce, and a lot more besides. A meeting in the Cabinet room with a huge group of ministers, spooks and police. TB, JP, GB, DB, AD, Lewis Moonie [Parliamentary Under-Secretary for Defence], C, Eliza, Scarlett, GCHQ, [Assistant Commissioner David] Veness from the Met. There was a mildly embarrassing moment at the start when JP walked in and said to me 'Did you see Gordon's first answer on *Frost*? What a laugh.' I then nodded to the other side of the table where GB was sitting, staring down at his notes, pretending not to hear, JP not having seen him.

There had already been a Cobra meeting on the threat of a surface-to-air missile attack on Heathrow on Wednesday at the end of Eid. The choice was a difficult one. Carry on with the programme of arrests that was underway; do that, plus step up security at Heathrow, visibly and overtly with a public announcement or three; close the airport. As far as TB was concerned, the last of these was unacceptable, though we had to be clear about all the things we had said about how we would respond to specific threats in intelligence. DB was very grumpy, clearly had very little confidence in the ability of the police and security forces to handle the public communications on it, constantly warning how their briefings went wrong. His basic pitch was to say as little as possible. AD talked about the need to make sure our political flank wasn't exposed. He was also worried that once we announced it, we didn't have the airlines and insurers all going crazy. Eliza was very clear that the threat was serious and the decision that had to be made now was whether TB/MoD authorised the use of special and other forces to be at the airport for tomorrow. We then agreed that Veness rather than ministers should announce it. The fallout from the CIC dossier was continuing. Michael Jay came to see me to say he felt we had to tighten up, get the CIC people more closely bound in to the FCO on policy, go easier on 'product-led material'. TB could barely be in a more exposed place now. PLP tricky. Massive march being planned. France and Germany right out there now, open in their hostility, Russia difficult. We were in danger of looking like we were the bad guys prepared to disobey international law.

Tuesday, February 11
The Heathrow situation low-key at first but became huge once they had pictures of troops and tanks at the airport. I had another Iraq communications group meeting, and a bit of an inquest into the CIC dossier. It was a blow, not least because it was being pinned at my door and would be used to change the general modus operandi. At least TB was being robust about it. He spoke to Bush at 12, who was very solicitous re TB's political position, said he was determined to help get a second UNSCR.

Friday, February 14
I watched Blix on TV. He leaned this way one minute, that way the next, but it was obvious he was not going to come down as clearly as he had before. There was not much cooperation, yet he was not saying so. You definitely got the impression that he was deliberately siding with France, attacking us and the US. At one point he picked apart some of Powell's presentation. And even though he said there were clear issues of breach, for example proscribed weapons, he was signalling that inspections could work. TB showed no signs of changing tack though, said we were doing the right thing. But whether we liked it or not, we were moving towards a regime change argument. We were getting very close to the argument, which itself was politically dangerous, that the marchers were pro-Saddam, that they plus international community divisions would keep him in power. There was a lot of American reaction to Blix, with Powell very emotional, Bush on much the same line. We were told there would

be big protests tomorrow. TB was clear we just had to hold our line and defend ourselves from a moral point of view. But we were already into the black humour, speculating about what he would do in a few weeks when he was out of a job.

Saturday, February 15

Edinburgh. The first thing TB said was that he had slept badly. So had I. He knew that he was in a tight spot. 'Even I am a bit worried about this one,' he said. The problem was that for the moment it looked as if every part of the strategy was in tatters – re the EU, re the UN, re the US, re the party, re the country which was about to march against us. We had had letters from Iraqis urging him to carry on, one of them a Glasgow doctor who we got to come over and see him. We had to involve Iraqi exiles much more. The moral case for peace was being put on the march and that gave us the right back-drop to make the moral case for action. The speech was pretty strong and we joked about it being his last as leader. There was massive security around the conference centre. The speech was heard in near silence. He wasn't playing it for applause but to put over a rounded argument. It was well received, not least because it was so serious.

Meanwhile TV was wall-to-wall, uncritical coverage of the march and the usual over-the-top claims about its size.[1] What was clear was that it was very big, and I got more and more angry about the claims being made for it, e.g. the *Mirror* front page with a dying Iraqi child and the headline 'march for him' as if he was starving because of us. The speech went down well with the media and we got as many front-page leads as the march, which was a surprise. TB was confident and felt we had the right argument and we now needed a big strategy to put the case properly. I got home, then later down to the canal and did an 18-mile run at just over 7 mph. On the route back, I bumped into no end of people coming back from the march, plac-ards under arms, faces full of self-righteousness, occasional loathing when they spotted me.

Tuesday, February 18

Chirac was widely felt to have made a big mistake[2] attacking the ten candidate countries who felt they were being bullied. Of course he

---

[1] Police estimated that at least 750,000 people had taken part in the London march. March organisers put the figure at nearer 2 million.
[2] The ten East European candidate countries had signed a letter of support for the US stance on Iraq.

was getting a great press at home and reviving a sense of Gaullism. Needless to say our press were keen to build him up at TB's expense. Our plan was to consolidate the actual success of yesterday, restate the basic case and get going re Iraqi exiles. At the press conference, TB was relaxed and confident, even though the story was building that his own future was on the line. He seemed relatively unconcerned.

Friday, February 21

TB called en route to Rome. He really felt everything now had to be set in the context of pushing for peace, that we wanted to resolve it peacefully. He said he really wanted me to work on Dan Bartlett, and get properly agreed message scripts, which I had been doing much of last night and this morning. By the end of it, we had a very strong four-page Sunday briefings script, which if everyone stuck to it, would get us in a far better position. Late pm I got a message that the Americans wanted a conference call – Condi, Dan, Steve Hadley on their side, with David M, Jonathan and me. TB had done a very strong message at his press conference with Berlusconi, strong on the moral case again. He called to say he felt much better placed on the arguments but it was all still very tricky. The ITV programme on me and the marathon was fine and seemed to get an OK response.

Monday, February 24

Iraq was totally dominating, but at TB's morning meeting it was the usual whinge about asylum, crime, health and all the dreadful figures that were coming out. He was really fed up with it all, in a rage at departments who he felt took their feet off the accelerators once we were all occupied with something else. On Iraq, I said I felt we needed to add some substance to the 'last push for peace', which at the moment just sounded vacuous, something to say to get us through a bit more time. We needed something concrete, like signs of Arab pressure on Saddam, or a new diplomatic effort that meant something. I think TB was beginning to think I was a bit distracted by the marathon, and maybe I was, though I felt the training was on balance a bonus for the job. It was the focus on the event itself, the build-up and the fundraising, that was maybe taking my attention away. I discussed Carole with him again. The *Mail* were doing a string of stories at the moment that seemed to be coming from her or someone close to her. He was still maintaining she was a victim in all this and that she would do nothing to harm them, and was upset by the way these stories were coming out. Even after the TV documentary, he was saying she was victim in all this.

Tuesday, February 25

TB called during the Juventus v Man U game. He said it was going to be really tough from now on in. The truth was we may well have to go without a second UNSCR, or even without a majority on the UNSC. The Bush poodle problem would get bigger. We were giving the Lib Dems a big opening, but he was adamant it was the right thing to do, and worth the political consequences. I said what if 100 of our own MPs are voting against the government and he said fine, they're mainly the dispossessed and disaffected. He knew it was more serious than that but was pushing the argument now that those against us had to face up to the fact that the consequence of their actions was Saddam staying in power. Hilary Armstrong called and said things did not look good. He must be worried about the growing talk of his job being on the line over this. He was getting a good response for doing well in the House, but an awful lot of our side were already publicly committed to rebellion. The question they were asking was is Iraq a threat to us, and now? TB was dismissive of Blix. He said his job was to set out the facts, but he now saw his mission as to stop war.

Thursday, February 27

TB remained reasonably chirpy, said he felt comfortable with the arguments and we just had to keep making them. Philip told me that the groups were far less cynical than the media. They were looking to hear TB more, and when they did, they just about gave him the benefit of the doubt. There was an instinctive understanding that no Prime Minister would do anything as difficult and unpopular as this for the hell of it. The public wanted a deeper sense of engagement. They were actually ready and willing to listen to deeper arguments on it. There was a hunger for debate on the substance, not just the media headline stuff. TB felt we had to be pushing on two main arguments – the moral case, and the reason why the threat was real and current, not because he could whack missiles off at London but because he could tie up with terrorists and others with a vested interest in damaging us and our interests. But we should understate rather than overstate, a point I made on the conference call. The Americans' saying there was a direct link was counterproductive. Far better to be saying this was a possibility and one we were determined to ensure never came about.

TB, JP, Jack S meeting at which we went over the distinct possibility of no second resolution because the majority was not there for it. TB knew that meant real problems, but remained determined on this, and convinced it was the right course. He said later that he felt only now was Bush really aware of the full extent of the stakes here. This had the potential to transform for good America's relations with Europe and the rest of the world, and in a worst-case scenario was a disaster for everyone. He wanted to get the thing done quickly, but he also wanted them to understand better the broader agenda. He felt Bush had moved a good deal on that but was less convinced it permeated throughout the Administration. At Cabinet, things were pretty much rock solid. TB looked very tired and I could sense a few of them only fully realising, when they saw him close up like this going through the arguments, the enormity of the decisions, and the enormity of the responsibility involved. Robin was the trickiest, and was delighting in giving the sense of how isolated we were from normal traditional partners. Clare was doing her usual interruptions and mutterings but a bit less provocatively and for her was relatively onside. She wanted to do a big number on aftermath preparations but TB was there ahead of her. He was very calm, matter-of-fact, just went through where we were on all the main aspects of this. Nobody was really looking to make TB's position more difficult out of today, with the possible exception of Robin, who was moving towards exit.

Friday, February 28

In Spain there was 4 per cent support for action without a second UNSCR, 23 per cent with it. TB said to Aznar that 4 per cent was roughly the number you could get in a poll for people who believed Elvis was alive, so he had a struggle! Aznar seemed as determined as TB though. TB's cold cannot have been helped by all the nonsense of yesterday, broken planes and buses to get scheduled flights and the rest of it. As Jack Straw said, 'He is effectively vice president of the free world, and has to travel around like a cost-cutting tourist.' This is tough, he said, very tough, about as tough as it gets. He asked what I thought the chances were of it killing him off. 20 per cent, I said. 'I'd say nearer 30 the way things are right now.'

Monday, March 3

I was beginning to fear that if we went to war without a second resolution, TB would fail to get it through the Commons, and he would be dead in the water. 'I've just got to tell Bush clearly that if he does this wrong, he'll have governments toppling all over the place and cause absolute chaos.' There was a poll in Spain showing 95% opposition. Opposition in Turkey was enormous.

Wednesday, March 5

France, Germany and Russia issued a joint statement, [Dominique] de Villepin [French foreign minister] driving it mainly. Earlier Jack came over for a meeting with TB and told him 'If you go next Wednesday with Bush, and without a second resolution, the only regime change that will be taking place is in this room.' Written down, it sounds more menacing than it was. He was trying to be helpful. TB's call to Bush was OK, though as I stayed in TB's room, I only heard his side, saying we had a real problem with world opinion, that these countries needed a reason to come round, that he wanted to go to Chile and set out the outlines of an amended resolution with a deadline so it was clear there would be war if Saddam hadn't responded. Blix was out again today, as much commentator as civil servant. TB felt the UNSC had to take control of this now, not Blix.

Thursday, March 6

Cabinet was scratchy, Robin and Clare both a bit bolder in setting out their concerns, Clare saying that the idea of horse trading and bullying was bad for the authority of the UN. TB hit back quite hard, said it was not just the US who were bullying and intimidating. What about the French telling the Bulgarians they would not be able to get into the EU if they sided with America? Robin was diddling rather more subtly whereas Clare was just doing anti-Americanism. John R hit back hard as well as TB. I walked through with TB to his office at the end. I asked him, if at the end of this he was history before his time, was this issue really worth sacrificing everything? He said it is always worth doing what you think is the right thing to do. Iraq is a real problem, Saddam is a real problem, for us as much as anyone, and it's been ignored too long.

Friday, March 7

Up to the flat to see TB with David, Jonathan and Sally. Condi had told David overnight that Putin had been clear with Bush that they would veto the second resolution. Also we still didn't have a clue whether Chile and Mexico would come over. The mood was gloomier than ever. TB was keen to get up the clusters document [a paper setting out where Iraq had not complied with its disarmament obligations] and also move towards the sense of an ultimatum. David was even of the view that we should be pushing the US to a version of the Franco-German idea of inspections with force, a blue beret force involved in disarmament. TB spent hours on the phone, including an hour with Putin, a long call with Jack and later with Bush. He wanted to give him a clear message about the political realities, namely that we could not do this without a Commons vote and it was not going to be easy without a second resolution, or with a resolution that was vetoed. The Russian veto was a new element. Everyone expected the French to be ultra-difficult but thought the Russians might be more prone to be neutral, but Putin's position had clearly hardened. Jack was doing his UNSC speech and did it well and with passion. Bush was agreeing to a slightly later deadline, March 17.

TB, Jonathan, Sally, Pat [McFadden] and I had a meeting to go through some of the what-ifs, including him going if we lost a vote. TB said he felt that there had to be a vote on a second resolution and if it was about the use of troops and he lost a vote on that, he would have to go. The Tories were making clear they would support us on a war motion but not on a confidence motion. Andrew Turnbull was quietly looking into how a JP caretaker premiership would operate. Even though we were talking about his own demise, TB still felt we were doing the right thing. Bush told TB he would certainly go for a vote. He was still making clear he didn't feel he needed a UNSCR but he wanted to go for it. Jonathan described the whole thing now as an enormous game of diplomatic chicken. TB said we could not flinch now, that if any weakness was signalled, we've had it. He was making clear to Bush, not in personal or moaning terms but as a reality, that his job was on the line, that if we didn't get the Commons vote, there could be no using UK troops, which the Americans needed. Black humour was setting in. TB said his future was now in the hands of the ailing President of Guinea [Lansana Conté] and the diplomatic judgement of Jeff Ennis [Labour MP for Barnsley East and Mexborough from 1996]. We were sending JP to a president's deathbed to keep the British government alive. TB was clear with him that we needed a bit more time. I reckoned the chances of him being out within a week or two were about 20–1 now. Parliamentary arithmetic was complicated, and not yet entirely clear. TB was very philosophical about it all. As I sat listening to him on the phone, I lost count of how many times he said – 1. we are right on the issue, 2. we have to see it through, 3. I'm philosophical about what it means for me and whether I survive or not.

Sunday, March 9

Clare Short called me. She hardly ever called me, so I was surprised when switch came on with her. She was friendly enough as we did a bit of small talk, but then got to the point. She had done an interview with Andrew Rawnsley for the *Westminster Hour* and had said she would resign if we went to war without a second resolution; that we were allowing our own policy to be dictated by the US; and that we were not doing enough in the Middle East. She said it all very matter-of-factly, as though she was telling me a few football results. I was conscious of myself shaking my head as she spoke, and then making a mental note to myself not to let my loathing of her pour out, but I said I was at a total loss to understand how she thought this kind of public conversation helped the government make and implement sensible policy. I also reminded her that nobody, as she herself had said, had done more than TB to get this down the UN route. She said nothing at first. Then I said I also thought it absolutely extraordinary that she should be saying this to me, rather than to TB. 'I thought I would call you because I knew you would be angry and I thought I'd rather get the anger direct than through the media.' The whine in the voice was whinier than ever. As if TB was going to be doing fucking cartwheels. I thought the deal was that if you were a Cabinet minister, you spoke up in Cabinet if you had concerns, that was the place to do it, and then a policy or a line was agreed and everyone stuck to it. I said I had never heard her say in Cabinet she would resign. She said – rich this considering how often she spoke – that she tended not to speak in Cabinet in case she was briefed against. I said there was no point her talking to me; she would have to speak to TB. I would call him to see if he wanted to speak to her. She said she was going out shopping with her mum but she would take her mobile with her. How considerate.

TB was at church so I sent through a note to be given to him when the service ended. I called JP, who was due to meet TB at 7. He said the whole thing was typical of her – she was a coward, couldn't cope with pressure, and so ended up doing it like this, hanging her conscience out to dry. Jack called after learning Mike O'Brien was going to be played the tape of her interview on the programme. He said this was the result of years of her being allowed to do what she wanted. It was a disgrace. TB finally called after he got back to Chequers from church. He was as appalled as I expected him to be. 'It is disgusting, totally disgusting.' It was the same word virtually every minister who called to complain used. TB said he was appalled for a whole stack of different reasons – 1. at what she had said and done, 2. that she had done it on the radio rather than talking to him, 3. that she had called me rather than him, and 4. most importantly, that it totally undercut his strategy to build UN support. He felt it showed there was a willingness among some – her included – to push him out over this. I was less sure it was a thought-through thing at all. I said I cannot see how you can keep her without looking weak. He said in process terms, there was no doubt about that. The BBC had told Mike O'Brien that she called them up and volunteered to go on. He spoke to her later, and said simply he would reflect. We agreed to a public line that simply made clear she had never spoken in these terms within Cabinet or to the PM. There was no point rushing on this. JP spoke to her a couple of times. He said what she was saying was that she didn't have confidence in the PM's strategy, or his ability to pursue it. She claimed it had not come out as she intended, which was bollocks. I now had the transcript and went through it with JP. He said he didn't see how he could keep her in those circumstances.

Later a call to go through the various UN scenarios: majority with no vetoes – fine; majority plus veto(es) – manageable but difficult; no vote; no majority. If we got a second resolution we would put it to a parliamentary vote quickly. We could live with a French veto, because people expected it, but we couldn't live without a majority. If that happened, we would probably have to put it to a vote, and if we lost it, there was a danger we would lose the Prime Minister. Jonathan and I continually emphasised we needed the second resolution. We had seven definite votes still, but Condi was less confident re Chile and Mexico. [Vicente] Fox [President of Mexico] was in a state of torture because it was such a big thing to stand up against the US. I listened in later to the TB–Bush call. TB started by saying he was 'fighting on all fronts'. TB said the public opinion problem stemmed from people feeling the US wanted a war. We have to put up the genuine tests of disarmament, show the determination to try to do this peacefully. Bush said he had never come across a situation where the dividing line between success and failure was so narrow. He said we want it done peacefully or any other way. Bush was talking the diplomatic talk while clearly irritated by the whole thing. He was clearly aware of how tough things were getting for TB. TB did not make too much of his own problems, and was stressing he thought we were doing the right thing.

Monday, March 10

Needless to say Clare was leading the news, amid lots of assumptions we would sack her. The papers, as expected, were fairly grim. I went up to the flat where David was briefing TB on Jeremy Greenstock's [British Ambassador to the UN] meeting with Blix. Blix was just about up for the clusters plan. TB wanted Jeremy to work on Blix and [Dimitri] Perricos [Blix's deputy] to get them signed up to it. It was the only show in town and the only one likely to lead to a majority of the UNSC. He was still working on [Ricardo] Lagos [President of Chile] and worried about him. Re Clare he said he viewed it as an act of personal betrayal to do what she did, without warning, when he was in the midst of negotiating on this. TB's real anger with the French had been the sending of mixed messages to Saddam, and that is what Clare was doing too. He was minded to sack her but on the other hand felt there was no point in doing anything other than being totally hard-headed and ruthless about the issue, in which she was something of a sideshow. I got Jack C, Bev Hughes [Parliamentary Under-Secretary of State in the Home Office] and Alan Milburn up all making the point that it was odd to do this on the radio rather than speak to the PM about the threat to resign. JP spoke to her twice last night and again this morning and sensed she had concluded we were definitely going to war and she was going to position herself to resign with maximum damage. He even wondered whether she wasn't setting herself up as a possible challenger to GB. I took JP up to the flat. He said it was on balance not sensible to help turn her into a martyr, which is what she wanted, but instead leave her hanging in the wind for a while. He went off to speak to her again and later TB spoke to her, told her she had committed an act of gross betrayal, that he was at a total loss to understand how she could do that. Her defence was that she felt in recent weeks his approach with her was to listen politely but take no notice. He said to her who do you think got us down the UN route, who is the one still pushing on that, who is the one trying to use this to get the MEPP going again? She was totally beyond the pale. He had decided however that he was not going to sack her. JP and I were usually at the front of the 'get rid of her' queue but agreed that on this it would be a mistake. JP said it was all about her position, nothing else. She did say sorry at the end of her conversation, but in that whiney drippy way that was designed to convey she was sorry that he couldn't see things as clearly as she did.

TB meeting with Hilary A, John R, David Triesman [general secretary of the Labour Party]. Hilary said that if we didn't get a second resolution, or if there was a French veto, we were in trouble. So the PLP was willing to subcontract foreign policy to Chirac? TB did a long call with Bush. There was something crazy and random about what was going on. It was a pure accident of timing that suddenly made Chile and Mexico the focus of so much diplomacy, TB working on Lagos, Bush on Fox. TB said when this is over, we need to take a long hard look at the reality of how the UN works.

Tuesday, March 11

Growing sense of crisis, what with the Chirac veto, talk of a challenge to TB and the dynamic moving away from us the whole time. TB asked if we should not be a bit nicer to Clare and was met with a row of uniformly horrified looks. JP looked at him as though he was mad. Alan Milburn called me later to say Robin C told him he would resign if we didn't get a second resolution. Of the two, RC was easily the more serious and the more thought through. Then came another Rumsfeld disaster. He did a press conference at which he said he and Geoff Hoon had just spoken and went on to indicate that we would not necessarily be in the first wave of attacks because of our parliamentary difficulties. It was not entirely clear whether it was deliberate – i.e. a warning shot that they could and would do it without us – or a fuck-up. We all assumed the latter. He just didn't get other people's politics at all. David M said it made it virtually impossible to have a shared strategy with them. Hopeless. Yet another communications friendly fire. TB went bonkers about it, then called Geoff, who admitted he had put the thought in Rumsfeld's head because he was trying to be very explicit about our difficulties as a way of reining him in. Rumsfeld must have thought he was being helpful, God knows. Sally and I were both working late and waiting for his 11pm Bush call. We saw him in the flat when he came back. He said he couldn't believe how the US kept fucking things up, the Rumsfeld thing just the latest. TB was pretty mellow, probably a bad sign. He had suddenly had a load of energy drained from him.

Wednesday, March 12

Bush was clear that the French position meant no UNSCR. But we were still trying to be reasonable. He felt that on withdrawal of the resolution he would give a speech saying the diplomatic phase is over, issue a 48-hour ultimatum to Saddam, say late Friday, which takes us to Sunday. TB went over the politics here, how we were pulling out every stop. TB said there was a danger the Tories would see this as their chance to get rid of him, support us on a war motion, but not a confidence motion. We needed a fresh UNSCR on the humanitarian situation post-conflict. Nobody doubts us on the tough side of things, but it's Middle East, humanitarian, democracy in Iraq, that people here want to hear about.

March '03: Cook says he will resign without second Resolution

Thursday, March 13

Greenstock put down the six tests[1] at the UN at 2am. Before anyone had even had time properly to discuss them, de Villepin rejected them, allowing us to go to an aggressive position re French intransigence and their 'whatever the circumstances'. Jack and JP had both spoken to Robin and were clear he was going to quit if we didn't get a second resolution. It was a matter of when not if now. TB was due to see Robin and Clare before Cabinet and JP emphasised how important it was to make clear today was not the final Cabinet before any action, that there would be another one if the UN process collapsed. RC said we should not 'burn our bridges' with the French, made clear that though there may be a legal base for action, there was no political case without a second resolution and we must keep working for it. He spoke very deliberately, as though he had rehearsed and of course everyone was listening for tone as well as content. It was a very clear marker that he would quit if there was action without a second resolution. He felt that without it we did not have the moral, diplomatic or humanitarian cover. Clare was even heavier, said we needed the Roadmap [setting out next steps in MEPP] published, lambasted the 'megaphone diplomacy' but as ever gave the impression it was just us and the Americans who engaged in it. She said the world community was split because the Americans were rushing. We should not be attacking the French but coming up with a different kind of process. 'If we can get the Roadmap, we can get the world reunited behind it.' She was calmer by the end and my sense was RC would definitely quit, but she might stay. I mentioned the idea of the Bush visit to TB. He was tempted but finally agreed GWB on UK soil in the run-up to the vote was not what we needed. TB was due to speak to Bush. Bush said that they could do the Roadmap, give it to the Israelis and Palestinians once Abu Mazan [about to take over as Palestinian Prime Minister] accepts the position.

Friday, March 14

Robin called to discuss 'rules of engagement' in the event of his resignation. I got Sally to join us when he came over. We were

[1] The tests demanded: a statement from Saddam admitting the concealment of WMD and undertaking not to retain or produce WMD in future; that at least 30 scientists and their families should be delivered for interview outside Iraq; the surrender of anthrax, or evidence of its destruction to be provided; all Al Samoud missiles to be destroyed; all unmanned vehicles to be accounted for, including details of any aerial devices for spraying chemical and biological weapons; all mobile chemical and biological production facilities to be surrendered.

pressing him to stay, saying we couldn't have the French running our foreign policy, telling him Bush was about to do the Roadmap. He said it would make a bit of difference but not much. He said this went deeper. He felt we were too close to a unilateralist right-wing US government that didn't care two hoots about the UN and didn't care two hoots about Tony, other than for his skills as a better politician and communicator than they are. He felt it was dishonest for him to pretend he supported them any more. He couldn't. He said he did not want to be awkward and was clear he wanted TB to stay. 'I do not want to be part of a process that sees Gordon become Prime Minister on the back of this.' I said I thought if his mind was made up we should tie it all up before Monday's Cabinet. He said fine, that he was sad but felt a great peace of mind having made the decision. He wasn't questioning the integrity of those with a different view but he was doing what he felt was the right thing. He said he valued the good relationship we had and 'Could we agree a pact of no rubbishing on either side?' Absolutely. 'Can you ensure John Reid is part of that? The man can start a fight in a paper bag.'

Saturday, March 15

Goldsmith was happy for us to brief that in the coming days he would make clear there was a legal base for action. We now had to build up the Azores[1] as a genuine diplomatic effort, which was not going to be easy. It was running as a 'war not peace' situation.

Sunday, March 16

I travelled with TB in the car to the airport and first he spoke to Margaret B, then a call with [Jan Peter] Balkenende [Dutch Prime Minister]. Then we just chatted a bit. This was as tough as any decision we would have to make, he said. He felt it very deeply. It was a tough, tough call.

Azores. We hung around for Bush to arrive and once he did we all moved to the US part of the base. TB travelled with Bush in the presidential limo and the ludicrously large motorcade. We sat around a fairly small square table. The mood shifted regularly from serious, e.g. going through texts, running over difficult arguments, to light-hearted. Bush at one point just looked over at me and said 'You're just like a faucet. Can't stop leaking.' I said we called it tap. Barroso

[1] Summit held at the Lajes airbase on Portugal's Azores islands, attended by Bush, Blair, Aznar of Spain and José Barroso of Portugal.

did a long and ponderous opening and said we had to make the last effort for peace. Everyone kept going on about it being 'the last effort for a political solution'. But there was a more than slight feeling of going through motions. The meeting itself was in an odd room, way too big for the numbers, with a kind of weird grey crazy paving-type set-up on the walls, thick white tablecloths. Bush talked about it being a last effort. He said it was important the world saw we were making every effort to enforce 1441. He said everyone had to be able to say we did everything we could to avoid war. But this was the final moment, the moment of truth, which was the line most of the media ran with. He was emphasising he would really move on MEPP. Aznar was really pushing the importance of the transatlantic alliance, but he was in even more political hot water on this than we were. I introduced Bush to Godric, said he was our Ari Fleischer. 'You gotta be bald or something to do these spokesmen jobs? Or is it the job makes you bald?' He asked about the vote, said he was confident we would win. I said Robin C might shift a few. As we left I said to Bush, if I do a sub-4-hour marathon will you sponsor me? He said 'If you win the vote in Parliament, I'll kiss your ass.' I said I'd prefer the sponsorship. Over to the press conference and now he went into 'bastards' mode in a kind of imitation of me. Dan said he was amused by the fact I dealt with the press in the way I did. He saw a lot of them as bastards too, but in the US nobody dare say it.

Monday, March 17

I was working on a draft exchange of letters with Clare in case she went. Jonathan emailed me saying 'Probably better not to have them drafted by someone who so clearly despises her.' Probably true. Robin called re my draft. I had mentioned the various military situations we had been involved in – Operation Desert Fox, Kosovo, Sierra Leone. He was very funny about it, said 'I can see why in these circumstances you want to present me as a heroic war leader, but I wonder if you couldn't put in one or two of my humanitarian triumphs as well.' He was keen that we make mention of Lockerbie and the International Criminal Court, and also wanted to make clear that he wanted TB to stay on as leader. It was so different dealing with him rather than Clare. RC came to see TB and they agreed there was no point in him staying for Cabinet. So Robin and I went round to my office to agree the process. We agreed we wouldn't put the letters out until 4.15, once Cabinet was in. We joked about the fact that it was the first resignation letter I had not written. 'I'll race you to see whose memoirs that appears in first,' he said. He was very friendly, seemed liberated, also clear that he had a strong if very different political future ahead of him. He was also very nice to me personally, said we had been through some very difficult times together and he always valued my advice and support. He said there was something oddly fitting about the fact that we had worked so closely at the end of his marriage and were working so closely again at the end of his ministerial career. He wanted to leave by the side door so I walked down with him, we shook hands, he said 'I really hope it doesn't all end horribly for you all,' and headed off to Birdcage Walk.

TB started Cabinet, introduced Goldsmith, then Clare came in and asked Sally where Robin was. 'He's gone,' said Sal. 'Oh my God.' TB's only reference to Robin was to say that he had resigned. Peter Goldsmith went through the answer on legal authority to use force. One by one, a succession of colleagues expressed support for TB, then Clare said she owed them 'a short statement', that she intended to reflect overnight. She said publication of the Roadmap was significant but we shouldn't kid ourselves that it means it is going to happen. She said she admired the effort and energy that had gone into getting a second resolution but there had been errors of presentation. 'I'm going to have my little agonising overnight. I owe it to you.' JP, John Reid and one or two others looked physically sick. JR spoke next, said never underestimate the instincts for unity and understand that we will be judged by the Iraq that replaces Saddam's Iraq, and by the Middle East. Derry said he felt we would have got a second resolution if the French hadn't been determined to scupper it, and said we had made so much effort to get a second resolution that it had led to people thinking we actually needed one. Paul Murphy was just back from America and said what an amazing feeling there was towards us there. 'It's not quite the same here,' said TB.

Tuesday, March 18

Debate day dominant. GWB's statement overnight had come out fine. They had taken in all our changes, the ultimatum was calm and strong, the tone towards Iraqi people compassionate, the commitment to the Middle East peace process was in there strong, and all the bellicose stuff either taken out or conditional. So to be fair, they had delivered big-time for us. The Robin resignation speech, and the standing ovation in parts of the House, was still getting a lot of play but I sensed that was the high point of the rebellion. TB was on the phone to Blunkett who was warning him that John Denham would resign. Also Philip Hunt [Lords minister] went on the radio to resign. That seemed to be about it at the moment. TB was in a pretty calm mood. He felt we were winning some people over on the arguments, but we had a problem in that there were a lot of our MPs who had promised their local parties that they wouldn't support without a second resolution. This was the unintended effect of the point Derry made yesterday, that we fought so hard to get one that people assumed we needed one before action. Clare was making a complete fool of herself. Hague was on to it, had an absolutely brilliant line in the debate, how TB had 'taken his revenge and kept her'. TB's speech in the House was one of his best. Very serious, full of real argument, confronting the points of difficulty and we felt it moving our way. He did a brilliant put-down to the Lib Dems, which helped the mood behind him. I did another secure call with Dan [Bartlett]. It looked like Wednesday late, special forces. It was one of those days when people out in the country were actually following what was going on. IDS and Charles Kennedy had both been poor. There had been some excellent backbench speeches but though the interventions didn't really zing, TB had definitely come out on top. There were a lot of protesters outside, so I faced a bit of abuse going in, then up to JP's office to agree the line that we push from the moment the vote was over, that we won the vote, because we won the argument, and now the country should unite. We ended up having a very friendly chat, then going down to wait for the vote, which for the government motion was 412 for and 149 against, and for the rebel motion 396 voting against and 217 for. 139 Labour MPs rebelled. I called Dan with the result as it came through. I was in the front office of TB's Commons office, MPs coming and going, the staff all pretty relieved. TB came back and called everyone in to say thanks. He said we had pulled out the stops and we had to. His own performance today had been superb. All of us, I think, had had pretty severe moments of doubt but he hadn't really, or if he had he had hidden them even from us. Now there was no going back at all. He had to give authority for our forces to go in and by tomorrow night it would be underway. Everyone was assuming the Americans would start a massive bombing whereas in fact the first action would be some of our forces acting to prevent an ecological disaster.

TB got the best press he had had for ages, because of the quality of the speech and the fact that he had seen it through. TB felt the next stage after winning the war would be to work out the geopolitical fallout and repair some of the divisions. Fiona came to see me, said she couldn't stay in the job any longer. She said it wasn't the war per se, but it had been the last straw. She felt it was a waste of time her being here, that she wasn't happy doing what she did. I said she should go if she wanted to, and if she didn't support what we were doing, to try not to do it in a way that makes us an issue. She said but you are a big issue, which meant that there was never a right time to go, but she really didn't want to stay. She went to see Sally, got very upset. Sally said she felt it was as much about Cherie/Carole as being about me. It was about not being valued. I didn't quite know how to deal with it. It's true there was never a right time, but this was about as unright as it could be, in terms of us being made an issue. It didn't exactly help that the message from the security people was that patrols around the house would be stepped up while the conflict was going on.

I wrote letters of complaint to the BBC, first from me to [Richard] Sambrook on various issues re Humphrys, Gilligan and Rageh Omaar [BBC journalist] on the nature of their coverage. Then drafted a letter from TB to Gavyn Davies and Greg Dyke, attaching articles from David Aaronovitch [journalist] and Simpson. I told TB about Fiona. He reacted, as I knew he would, by saying he couldn't understand why people got so emotional about this. I said well, it's going to happen so I have to work out how to handle it. I said it's true she wasn't happy with the war, but there were other issues too, chief among them that she now had a bad relationship with CB, despite having successfully helped build a very positive image for her. She felt we had next to no life outside work, and that I gave too much for too little in return. He went into 'this is ridiculous' mode. I said Tony, you are talking about Fiona and I won't have it. He said for God's sake, I was always saying things about his wife, but this stuff was very difficult, when big political issues were swirling around and they got mixed up with relationships. But if she went and said it was about Iraq, that would look very odd for me because people would think that was my position too. I said it's probably a consequence of a build-up of neglect, some of it mine, some of it Cherie's. He said it was a bit much to have all the things he had to deal with and be expected to keep everyone happy all the time. He said in the big moments, like now, I gave real added value, and I shouldn't underestimate how important that was to him. So all he asked was that if I did go, I helped find someone who could replace me. I asked what his plans were. 'I really don't know. I've never really wanted to fight a third election, but I don't know, I might.' I asked if he had done a deal with GB. Not at all, he said, but he didn't rule it out. He said it was interesting that GB had been more cooperative recently and said JP had been the key to that. JP had basically told him that if TB didn't want him to get the job, and JP was agin it, it would not happen.

Thursday, March 20

After going to bed late last night, then another row with Fiona over my leaving, and her demanding a departure date NOW, I was woken at 3am by Godric. Did I know action had begun? Then media calls started. It turned out the US had some late, sudden intelligence re Saddam's whereabouts and took the decision to go straight away.

Friday, March 21

Brussels. Nick Matthews called me early to say that 8 UK marines and 4 US servicemen had been killed in a helicopter crash inside Kuwait. Worst possible start to the day. At the summit centre, Schroeder was the first to come over and offer condolences, followed by others. Chirac wrote TB a little note, which was nice of him, and his words were totally devoid of any side or politics. Chirac said it was time to calm the atmosphere, lower the temperature, that there was nothing to be gained from the kind of mutual aggression we had been showing. He said he could not understand why we had been so aggressive towards him and it was time to call off the press attacks. TB said he could not understand why they had been so aggressive diplomatically. They agreed it was time to make up. TB had been down at one point but bounced back quickly and won a surprisingly high number of plaudits from fellow leaders here. On the way out to the airport, he said 'God, it is awful, this war business.' 'Yes, that's why it is usually best to avoid it.'

Tuesday, March 25

GB asked to see me, and we met next door. He said the War Cabinet meetings were hopeless. You had Clare just blathering away, DB and JR behaving like armchair generals and giving out weakness vibes to the real generals. He felt we needed to structure things much more like a campaign. We needed to be clear what it was we were pushing every day, e.g. today would be push on Baghdad with a line out on humanitarian and reconstruction. The problem was there were currently too many places and people capable of setting an agenda from somewhere. I asked if he thought the party was OK on this. He said the party is fine on Iraq. 'It's other things they are worried about.' He said there were real worries about the direction of domestic policy and I needed to rein him in a bit. On Iraq TB said there was a chance the whole thing would collapse quickly like a pack of cards, but we shouldn't bank on it. The most important thing for TB was to communicate to the Iraqis that we would see this through, that they would benefit from the fall of Saddam. But we should not expect them to welcome with open arms, because they will find it hard to believe the Saddam era is ending. We were doing OK with public opinion in our own country, but we were nowhere in Iraq. Back at Number 10, TB was clear it was going to take longer than anticipated. Shock and awe had not really happened. So we had taken the political hit of a stupid piece of terminology, and then not actually had the military benefits.

Wednesday, March 26

More delay in Basra. War Cabinet was awful. TB had a bilateral with JP, who said Clare's behaviour at these meetings was intolerable and he should not put up with her for too long. TB never quite agreed with us on that and he had another meeting with her later, going out of his way to keep her involved and on board, as much as she ever would be. I was doing an email exchange with Dan on the visit, and it was clear Bush was pissed off at the *FT* story suggesting TB would press him for a bigger UN role. TB asked me to send a message back that this was our media seeking to open divisions. We knew of a Rumsfeld memo to Bush saying that TB would demand a bigger role for the UN, but that they should resist. Jack said Powell was on our side in this, and was trying to put a halt to the neoconservative stuff. TB's worry was the military campaign. TB was working on a long note for Bush on the plane, and I left him to it and had a long chat with Jack. He was worried just how far out on a limb TB was pushing himself, but was still totally on board for where we were. The main message in TB's note, when you boiled it down, was that there was a lot of support for the aims of the campaign, and we totally believed the policy was right, but there was real concern at the way the US put over their views and intentions, and that rested in people's fears about their perceived unilateralism. He was urging him to do more to rebuild with Germany, then Russia, then France, and saying he should seize the moment for a new global agenda, one to unite the world rather than divide it. A distorted view of the US was clouding everything – look at how much cynicism there was at their efforts in the Middle East. We had to break that down. Why had Mexico and Chile gone the other way? Why did so much of Europe? In the end he wrote a 12-page note that was both subtle and blunt at the same time. It was a good piece of work and if Bush took it on board would have a good effect. But he still had his own internal battles to deal with. I didn't really feel Bush had the will to deliver on this new international agenda TB was talking about, but we would see. We landed in pretty miserable weather conditions, then flew down to Camp David. Bush confident we were going to win.

Thursday, March 27

GWB had clearly read TB's note and was going through it virtually line by line. He was fairly strong on MEPP. He said he knew there would have to be a reckoning in their relationships with others. He seemed a lot more on top of the detail and in the discussion on the complexities of the Arab world seemed less one-dimensional than before. TB's note was saying that in essence the US had a choice about what it wanted to do with its power. The power was a given but how it was used was a series of choices. TB felt on the war that we had reached the point we did in Kosovo where it felt like we were holding back slightly and not really going for it. In Kosovo the point came a bit later but it did feel similar. It was interesting how Bush liked to take in different views and experiences round the table. He wasn't status-conscious in these meetings. He asked me a few times re my running, and telling me he had been doing a 7-minute-mile pace round the Camp David track, which was faster than I could. Pre the press conference TB was worried re the body language. I said the most important thing was the issue of resolve, and a message to the Iraqi people about seeing it through and being with them for the long term.

We were driven by buggy up to the hangar where the press conference was being held. I had done a script for TB and created a bit of a problem maybe by referring to the dead soldiers being 'executed'. TB and Bush went off for a walk and then came back for lunch. Fairly relaxed and informal. GWB was geeing me up re the marathon, said I would love it, that it was one of the best things he ever did. TB and Bush then went out on the terrace for a genuine one-on-one. Bush changed into a tracksuit. He did casual gear a lot better than TB but I guess the White House logo on everything helped a fair bit. He looked very fit for his age though the media had felt he looked tired at the press conference. I had an interesting chat with Dan about how Bush worked. He was a real early to bed early to rise man. He was obsessed about punctuality and would really go for people who arrived late for meetings. He liked to read a brief, then discuss, then decide. He was open to ideas. He was very religious. He was loyal to friends but once you fell out with him, that was that. We were just whiling away the time while Bush and TB chatted. After half an hour or so they came in and we walked up to the helipad. TB was pleased that Bush seemed to have moved on the Roadmap. He was saying not only that he would publish it but take the lead in implementing it.

We had a nice enough journey to New York with a fantastic view out of the helicopter. To the UN to meet Kofi. The main focus was post-conflict and Oil for Food. Kofi was really pleased TB had gone to see him rather than the other way round. It was clear the politics were getting harder and harder. Bush was heavy enough but Cheney and Rumsfeld were even heavier.

Saturday, March 29

ORHA [Office of Reconstruction and Humanitarian Assistance] was in a state of chaos because of internal US difficulties. They appeared unable to agree on anything. TB asked me afterwards if I thought the propaganda effort was working. I said not. He agreed. The embedded media were treating the whole thing like scenes from a war movie, and there was no place for the big picture. The media here were pretty much set on presenting things in the worst light. We had to raise our game.

Monday, March 31

In for the usual morning meetings, with both CDS and C more hopeful. The general picture was a lot better. TB later saw CDS and a general from the campaign and said he got more talking direct to the general than he had from weeks of meetings. The truth was that the military and intelligence campaigns had not been wholly successful. Another TB–Bush call, which was basically just going through TB's note.

Wednesday, April 2

I got a nice letter from Neil [Kinnock] saying his favourite game at the moment was imagining how the BBC would have covered World War 2. 'Hitler would have lived to 1978.'

Thursday, April 3

On the war front, things were going better. The movement towards Baghdad was quickening, more people were deserting, and more was coming out re the nature of the regime.

Saturday, April 5

The military picture was changing fast. As I arrived at the office for the 9am meeting, Sky was showing US tanks going through Baghdad. Things were also going a lot better in Basra and the mood was much improved all round. The regime was refusing humanitarian help. TB said to me he couldn't understand how I could think about leaving when we were in a position to sort the big geopolitical questions for the next generation, and surely it was right to see the whole thing through.

Monday, April 7

I left for the office feeling like shit. At the intel meeting, the news was overwhelmingly good. Basra was going according to plan. Around Baghdad the US troops were really going for it now. All our problems really related to the future of Iraq. [Ahmed] Chalabi [exiled opponent of Saddam], a friend of Rumsfeld and [Paul] Wolfowitz [US Deputy Secretary of Defense], was putting himself around the whole time as a key player, possible future leader, when the reality was he would be unacceptable.

Hillsborough. As I was making a few calls in my room, TB called me through to his room. He asked how my situation was at home. I felt that unless I had an exit date, I had no 'marriage'. He said he was really saddened and disappointed, but he understood. He would not put me under pressure to stay. He felt it was a bad move for me, that I would forever regret not seeing the whole thing through to the end. 'But you need to know you have done more for me than anyone, more than I could have asked for, I could not have done it without you, and I will not feel let down, so let me relieve you of any pressure you may feel on that front.' But I did feel it, because I knew he valued the close team around him and I knew I made a difference. We stood at the window and I reminded him of the time we came here in opposition and he looked out over the grounds at Hillsborough and said the Tories were not going to give it all up without a real fight. We had won that fight and I knew some of that was down to me and the work I'd done for him, and it was not easy to walk away from it. He asked me when I wanted to go. I said summer at the latest, maybe Conference, maybe before. He just nodded.

Tuesday, April 8

TB said 'this neocon stuff' was crazy. I had asked Dan [Bartlett] last night what 'neocon' meant and he said it was the belief that government had a moral purpose. I said does that mean moral purpose can only be right wing? TB felt today's meeting with Bush was going to be tough. It was clear Condi was pushing a fairly hard line re the UN. We had a fight on our hands to keep in a 'vital role'. She wanted 'important', which sounded too grudging. 'It's meant to be,' she said. TB was determined we had to get something out of this and in the end, largely thanks to Bush, we did. Bush was excellent on Northern Ireland, and on MEPP, linked the two well by saying he would spend as much time and energy on MEPP as TB did on NI, then excellent too on the UN role. He was good on the war message too. The general feeling afterwards was that it was the best media performance he'd done. It was interesting to watch him in the main meeting today, where he was letting TB do a lot of the talking, then taking in Powell and Condi's views in particular, then more or less saying what we expected him to in the first place. He seemed restless too, a bit fidgety. He and TB were in the big armchairs by the fireplace, the rest dotted around the room, Jack and Powell on the sofa together. Powell was talking at one point when Bush got up, got himself a coffee, asked me if I wanted one and came over to talk to me about the marathon. When is it? What time will I do? How much money will I raise? Dan pointed out that I had a piece in *The Times* on it and Bush picked it up and read it, getting to the end plug for Leukaemia Research. 'You doing it for leukaemia? Did you know my sister died from leukaemia? Would you like me to give you a cheque?' I certainly would, I said. He went to the door giving onto the lounge, opened it and shouted out 'Blake, get my chequebook.' Later the cops said he created an absolute stir because nobody had a clue that he had a chequebook with him, let alone where it was, though they did find it eventually, and he wrote out a cheque there and then. He said his sister was called Robin and died aged 7 when he was 4. 'I will do this because you are my friend,' he said, 'but I am also doing it for her.' I asked if the charity could publicise it. Sure, he said. TB came over and asked what I was up to. I said the President had just given me a cheque so where's yours?

TB was full of himself on the flight home, really felt it had been good and positive, pretty much on all fronts. GWB was definitely moving a bit on the international agenda, and buying into the need for a new approach, but the tensions internally had been very clear. TB was firmly of the view now that Chirac's world view built around rival poles of power was crazy.

Wednesday, April 9

War Cabinet. Signs of regime collapse were all around now. It was still not clear where Saddam was but he and Chemical Ali[1] were both alive. Clare was rabbiting on more than ever. I slipped TB a note about the time Saddam shot his health minister at a meeting because he was annoying him and did he want me to get a gun? Yes, he scribbled. Jeremy had discovered late yesterday that GB planned to include in the Budget a review by Derek Wanless on health inequalities, obviously with a view to making big changes in the future. He hadn't discussed it with TB or with Alan Milburn, who hit the roof when told about it, and demanded it be removed from the Budget. Of course GB being GB, it was too late to unpick fully, the background documents having been printed we assumed, and Wanless having been lined up. We did though get it pulled from the statement and got the Treasury to agree Milburn would be in charge of the review. TB and I were in many ways so used to it that with everything else that was going on, we didn't let ourselves get too wound up, and we were trying to make light of it when Alan came in to see TB pre Cabinet. He was totally on the rampage. He said it was just unacceptable to have a Chancellor announce major change in someone else's department without even discussing it. He could see TB was not going to get too wound up and so added 'And it weakens you in the eyes of others that you let him get away with it.' He said the NHS was more monitored and reviewed than any other part of Government and if this was to be another great review, he would put out a statement denouncing it. 'I am just not having it.' We tried to get him down from the ceiling but he said he intended to raise it in Cabinet. Alan got in there and said he wanted to raise a process point, that there was to be a second Wanless report announced in the Budget. He said that at 10 to 9 he got a call from Paul Boateng to say there was to be this review, and it was totally unacceptable and it was unnecessary for the Treasury to operate in this way. Of course having been there as Chief Secretary, he knew that for something like this to be included in the overall package it will have been known about for some time, and he stated several times it just wasn't necessary to behave like this. Ian McCartney, who was at his first Cabinet after the mini-reshuffle involving him and John R, came in with his first intervention, which was pretty telling. He said it was important that colleagues did not make things even more difficult than they already were for other ministers. He felt there were sufficient reviews of the NHS going on already.

[1] Ali Hassan al-Majid, known as Chemical Ali for his role in gas attacks on northern Iraq.

Thursday, April 10

Iraq update meeting. CDS was very clear that a near philosophical difference between us and the US was responsible for some of the disorder problems we had. We believed in peacekeeping. They believed in war fighting. We were good at both. They were only really focused on one, so didn't adapt quickly enough to changed circumstances. *The Times* had done a story re Bush's sponsorship cheque, and having seen it, TB said 'I suppose I'd better sponsor you too then.'

Friday, April 11

The main news overnight was lots of looting going on in Iraq, the BBC hyping for all it was worth. Gilligan was saying there was more fear there now than there had been before. The main focus both of the pre-meeting and the War Cabinet itself was the disorder, and there were still problems re ORHA. TB went off to Sandhurst where he was speaking at the passing-out parade. Geoff Hoon called re Terry Lloyd [TV reporter, unembedded, killed in Iraq]. It was pretty clear US forces had killed him. Amid all this, we then had the people from *The Simpsons* in to record TB. The writer was a really serious type who clearly worried himself a lot about his work. He and I had been batting scripts back and forth and it was fine really, though as TB said, there would be plenty of people willing to slag him off for doing it. But hell, he said, there aren't many perks to the job worth having, so how can you say no to a bit part on *The Simpsons*?

Saturday, April 12

I was determined to be in the best possible shape for the marathon tomorrow so rested up a lot of the day, didn't go in for the morning meetings, watched Man Utd v Newcastle on the TV and took Grace to see *Maid in Manhattan*, which had a seriously silly plot, though the relationship between the politician and his spin doctor was moderately amusing. TB left me pretty much alone, though he did call to ask why I hadn't been to the meetings. I said I really wanted to get my head in gear for tomorrow, and in any event Jonathan had filled me in. Baghdad was still looking grim, though things were getting better in Basra. I was getting really psyched up for tomorrow. I ate a ton of pasta, then went to bed, after laying out all my gear for the morning. I was really pleased to have got this far, and pretty confident. I think part of me was glad to be doing something to keep John [Merritt]'s memory alive, but part of me was glad too to be doing something that was in a way independent of the job even though I had managed to raise as much as I had because of that, though the biggest donation was 50K from the Bridges [neighbours].

Sunday, April 13

I had my recurring dream about losing my race number, only this time there was a different twist. The ink on the number ran and it became illegible and I was stopped from running. Relieved to wake up, I turned on the radio and they were talking about me doing it, which I took as an omen I would do OK. It was a nice day, fresh but looked like it was going to be sunny, and the mood up at the start was terrific. There were two starting points and Charles [Lindsay, protection officer] and I were starting from the one with the smaller numbers, which was a bonus. We were taken to the VIP tent to wait and I chatted to the Slovak PM [Mikulas Dzurinda], who asked me if I would do a race out there. I was peeing every few minutes, a mix of nerves and all the fluids of the last couple of days. The start felt great, and I reckoned I was in OK shape for sub-four hours, which is what I really wanted. I did the first mile well below 8 minutes without even really trying, which was probably the adrenalin getting me to start too fast, the second mile bang on 8, and then into a fairly steady rhythm. After three miles Charles said I ought to run on ahead on my own. The hardest points were 9 miles, 15 and 21, but the bands and the crowds were great. 'Rocking All Over the World' got me through one tricky part. A Jennifer Lopez song playing made me think of Grace at another and got me through. The crowd were fantastic. I didn't get a single adverse comment, which surprised me considering how much war divisiveness there had been, and loads of encourage-ment. Philip and Georgia popped up a couple of times on the route. Andrew Turnbull, Alun Evans [Cabinet Office], others from the office, though I missed Alison [Blackshaw] and her crowd at Canary Wharf. There were no quiet miles at all. Also, on a couple of occasions when I was struggling, one of the other runners would come alongside and help push me on, including a woman from Dulwich who suggested I 'lock onto her' and follow step by step which, as she had a near perfect bum, took me through another tricky mile before I recovered my strength and eventually left her.

The last few miles from the Tower were hard and exhilarating in equal measure. I hit 22 miles with 50 minutes left to break 4 hours so I knew I was going to do it and could relax. The crowds by now were just a wall of sound and encouragement. I was worried I was going to cry on crossing the line, so forced myself to do it as I ran towards Big Ben, lost myself in a crowd of runners, and just let the emotion come out, imagined friends on one shoulder, enemies on the other, friends pushing me on, enemies failing to hold me back; thought about John, thought about how long my dad had, thought about the kids, really piled it on and cried for a bit as I ran, and then felt fine. I had trained hard in difficult circumstances and I felt a real sense of achievement. I wondered around 20 miles if I could beat Bush's time, but as I tried to pick up the pace, the pain in the hamstrings really intensified and just went back to my steady plod, and settled for sub 4. I didn't realise the cameras were on me for the last couple of minutes, by which time I was swearing at myself the whole time, push yourself, faster, fuck it, keeping going, push, etc. The last few hundred metres was a mix of agony and joy. The pain was pretty intense but by now virtually every second someone was shouting out encouragement, from 'I forgive you everything Tony Blair has done' to endless 'Go on, you can do it, not far to go'. I spotted Fiona and the kids right at the end of the stand and ran towards them. They were screaming at me to head straight to the finish but I was seven minutes inside my target and just so pleased to see them. My legs buckled a bit as I stopped and my voice was unbelievably weak, but it felt fantastic to have done it. I did an interview with Sue Barker [former tennis player turned sports commentator], dictated my column to *The Times* and also did a briefing at the ICA, by which time my legs had pretty much seized up. I had a massive dehydration headache, and was drinking gallons of water. We went out for dinner with the Goulds. Philip reminded me of the Woody Allen character[1] today, popping up in incongruous places along the route. But I felt really happy at having done it. Grace said she felt so proud of me, and did I know what a fantastic thing I did for John? I was really touched, especially as she had never known him.

Monday, April 14

Good enough coverage of the Marathon, including some nice pictures with Fiona. TB was seeing the Slovak PM, and said he hoped that now I would get back to getting HIM good media coverage, rather than me. He said it with a smile though and the response in the office was really warm. There was still no sign of WMD, no sign of Saddam, and a considerable humanitarian challenge. A little boy named Ali was getting a huge amount of media attention, and becoming something of a symbol. We were going to have to resolve his case pretty

---

[1] Zelig, the mysterious title character in Allen's 1983 mockumentary, who sidles into camera shot for most of the major events of the twentieth century.

quickly. I missed the Bush call but TB said GWB had said to congrat-ulate me on the marathon and to say that my 'bleeding nipples' were all over the US media. TB told him that I had also been covering my balls with large amounts of Vaseline. Bush said 'I think I have heard enough about his body now.'

Tuesday, April 15
At the War Cabinet, Clare said she had been talking to the French and German development ministers and 'They just need lots and lots of talking to', to which TB replied 'Well, I'm all in favour of therapy but I'm not sure it constitutes a policy.'

Monday, April 28
We were being warned of the possibility that Saddam had got rid of WMD and certainly most of the documentation, before the conflict. How big a problem was it if it turned out to be the case that we found none? Very difficult. It seemed the best we could do was defectors saying that it had all been destroyed. WMD were not being found and that was a problem.

Tuesday, April 29
Russia. Unbeknown to us Putin was gearing up for a direct big whack on WMD and plenty else besides. I asked Putin what he was likely to say at the press conference. He said he would simply say we should carry on looking. But he definitely had the steely look in his eye and TB was looking a bit on edge. When it came to the event he let rip in the opening statement, made clear he doubted WMD were there and painted a comic picture of Saddam in a bunker somewhere sitting on his arsenal. TB was doing his best to look unfazed. Trevor Kavanagh and Charles Reiss had big smiles over their faces as they took notes of what Vlad was saying. They sensed a diplo-disaster, which of course it was, especially as Putin had invited TB and we thought we'd agreed lines. Then TB, Vlad, the interpreters and I were taken into a little side room. TB said to me, very deliberately and inviting absolute honesty, 'What did you make of that?' I said it was very explosive, our media would be very excited. Putin looked a mix of surly and worried. He could sense TB was angry but he was also totally unapolo-getic. He said the US had created this situation. In ignoring the UN they had created danger. They were saying there may be rules, but not for us. Time and again he made comparisons with the situation he faced in Georgia, used as a base for terrorists against Russia. 'What would you say if we took out Georgia or sent in the B-52 bombers to

wipe out the terror camps?' And what are they planning next – is it Syria, Iran, Korea? 'I bet they haven't told you,' he added with a rather unpleasant curl of the lip. 'Also there is no consistency. Saudi and Pakistan are problems but for different reasons the Americans prop them up.' He said other parts of the world felt pressure to go for Israel. He said he didn't support that 'but these are dangerous games'. He said the Americans' enemy was anyone who didn't support them at the time. Anywhere from Algeria to Pakistan. Then what about the new powers like India and China, do their views matter or is it only America?

TB had given as good as he got at the press conference and did so again at the dinner once he realised that the diplomatic approach was not exactly working. He said there was no grand US plan for global domination. There was a series of choices. On MEPP they were deciding whether to engage or not. On Korea they were deciding whether to engage diplomatically. On a lot of other issues they were deciding whether to approach them on a unilateral or multilateral basis. 'We have to help them choose the multilateral route. But you have to understand that September 11 changed their psychology and it changed Bush's psychology personally. Before, anti-Americanism was just an irritant that they put up with. Now it became a threat.' Putin said that meant anyone who disagreed with them on these choices was a threat. 'That is ridiculous. I am a Russian. I cannot agree with the Americans on everything. My public won't let me for a start. I would not survive two years if I did that. We often have different interests.' Vlad was in full flow. He said they had asked to run reconnaissance flights along the Russian border during the Iraq crisis 'as a counterterrorism measure – what nonsense. It was to intimidate us. We told them it was an unfriendly act. They did it.' TB asked him if Bush knew and Vlad said his people knew but the question was why did they do it? Because they think they can do what they want. Others have to operate by the rules but not them. China might feel it should be able to sort out Taiwan. But it feels constrained – by the UN, by international opinion. India and Pakistan might like to set off nuclear weapons at each other but they feel constrained. Time and again he referred to Georgia and Chechnya and said 'Why can't I go in alone – because of international pressure. Yet there are people threatening our people, killing people on our streets.' TB said Iraq was different because there were 19 outstanding UNSCRs on Iraq. The UN had made its demands and for once they should be upheld. Putin said the US was thousands of miles from Iraq. So was the UK. Saddam was a monster but he was not a direct threat. TB went back to his argument about September 11. Putin went back to his line that if we were saying anyone who disagreed was a threat that was ridiculous and dangerous. TB was pretty taken aback by the vehemence. Normally there would be a bit of levity, a bit of banter, or if things were heavy I might throw in something lighter. But this was not that kind of meeting. I could see David [Manning] feeling more and more intense about the whole thing.

We agreed afterwards that it had been a real privilege to have been in on a discussion like that, where the raw politics and feeling of a country like Russia came pouring out. There were even short periods of silence as we ate – caviar, a nice enough fish plate then some horrible cold meats, including one that looked like dogshit and tasted pretty dreadful too. Then a nice mix of ice creams. Lots of vodka being poured into different glasses but little of it was drunk. There was no give at all. Putin's face was tight and his eyes really piercing. I kept thinking of Fiona when she was really angry with me, telling me it was all one way, all on my terms. I took her for granted and she'd had enough of it. This was someone who felt he deserved to be treated as an equal, and he wasn't being treated as an equal and he was angry, and TB was the person who was going to cop the anger. At one point Putin said the whole post-September 11 response was designed to show off American greatness. They don't care what anyone else thinks. TB was about to respond but he didn't let him. 'Don't answer – there is no answer. That is the truth, Tony. You have to know it. There are bad people in the Administration and you know it.'

David said as we left 'Fascinating, absolutely fascinating.' I said that was the death of diplomacy. It certainly was, he said. There was no effort at all. TB was a bit subdued as we went to the plane. He was less shocked than David and I had been and said they had an argument different to ours and it was far better we have it out like that. But in the end they are wrong. You cannot just walk away from the US. It is a mistake. The reason they will go it alone on some things is because they can.

Wednesday, May 7

Ran in and the morning meeting was pretty much all taken up with foundation hospitals. The whips were still worried that if the Tories really went for it, we could lose. It was a case of hanging around for the vote. TB said 'This is classic. The Labour Party making historic errors that will help put us out of power and leave others to do the reforms that we should have done.' He said it was a different issue but a rerun of 'In Place of Strife'.[1] If we lost, he wanted us to come back with a Bill that was more reformist not less. He felt it was crazy for Alan [Milburn] to talk about resigning and that he was far too prone to the cavalier and dramatic. But I spoke to Alan, who said he had thought long and hard about it and he would definitely resign. 'There have to be rules. This is my bill and if it's rejected I will have to go.' When it came to the vote, it was 304 for the bill to 230 against. The wrecking amendment was defeated 297 to 117, with 65 Labour rebels.

Friday, May 9

TB was up in Sedgefield and called a couple of times. I was more conscious, after Philip's observation, of how regularly he said 'I know I'm right about this.' In truth, often he was, and I was as down on departments as he was, but equally I was beginning to get less and less motivated. We were already beginning to talk about elections and it just didn't hold out the excitement it once did. Rory had an interesting take. He said he reckoned I wasn't as good as I used to be, that if I left soon, I would be a legend, the first person to take communications to a level that made an actual difference to politics, whereas if I stayed, it was downhill all the way. 'You're not enjoying it as much as you did, you're not doing it as well as you did, and never forget the reason Eric Cantona's [footballer] a legend is because he left at the right time.' I had a long call with Dan, who was as seized as I was with the need for change in ORHA's modus operandi. I offered to put a team of UK people at his disposal.

Monday, May 12

TB called me to the flat first thing to say he was really worried about Cherie. There was someone very close in putting stuff into the press, this weekend again with the freebie story in the *Mail on Sunday*. He noticed for the first time that the kids were getting worried about it. He wanted to know if I thought Fiona was still able to help her. I said Fiona was definitely leaving. He asked what she would do. I said that depended in part on me. He asked what I wanted to do. I said I would like to go fairly soon. I wasn't enjoying the job anything like as much as I did and I wasn't doing it as well as I could. He said he thought I had done it well during Iraq, and he was sure I was doing it better than anyone else could. I said the public service reform agenda was not really my thing, and in any event I wondered whether some of

[1] In 1969 Harold Wilson's government issued a White Paper, 'In Place of Strife', that proposed the reform of industrial relations.

our media problems might be helped if I went. He said he realised why I felt the way I did, because there weren't that many really high-pressure jobs, but he had one of them, and I had another. He really wanted me to think it through very carefully. Suma Chakrabarti [Permanent Secretary] had called from DFID to say that Clare was about to resign. From then on we were set for a day in which she would do as much damage as possible. She got a line out to PA as soon as she resigned, then interviews, later a statement. Every part of it was very bitter and designed for maximum damage. TB though felt it was the best outcome. He was intending to sack her, she probably knew it, so she walked, but with little credibility. Her letter of resignation was pretty bitter. I worked on TB's reply, conscious of the fact I had waited eight years for this, but now it came to it I felt very little satisfaction from it. She wasn't worth it. I watched her Commons statement and she got more and more bitter as she went on, spreading the attack on Iraq to the whole style of government. She was heard in near silence with the occasional gasp as the boot went in. TB said afterwards that he had bent over backwards to be nice to her and about her, and if there was a criticism to be made of him, it was why he let her stray so long. 'I doubt that any Cabinet minister has ever been indulged so much by a prime minister.' There was no point pretending it wasn't a bad day but she was such damaged goods that it wasn't that bad. Adam Boulton said few people could swallow it all without gagging. She was pretty powerful as a speaker but nauseated a lot of people. Valerie Amos[1] took her job.

Monday, May 26
Peter M called and said that he felt I would know for sure when I wanted to go. So did I, and it wasn't quite yet but it wasn't far off. Fiona felt TB and I worked so closely, and 95% of the time in a pretty good spirit, so that by now I was in many ways TB's closest friend and he mine, and she understood why that made it harder to leave, because I felt I was letting him down. There was something in that, but I also felt I was letting him and myself down in not being up for the job in the way that I used to be.

Wednesday, May 28
Rumsfeld had not helped set up the visit to Iraq with a statement that we may never find WMD, or that he may never have had them,

[1] Baroness Amos, FCO minister, became the first black woman in the Cabinet.

May '03: Clare Short finally resigns

which was a pretty dreadful backdrop to the visit. But TB was pretty firm, strong on both Iraq and Europe. We had breakfast together on the plane to Kuwait and as we were just chatting away over his current list of concerns – Europe and the IGC [Intergovernmental Conference], the assessment, GB, the press, whatever – it was very hard to imagine not being on these kinds of trips, having these kinds of conversations in future. Despite everything, he was still very engaging, very funny and hadn't fundamentally changed at all. We always had a laugh on these trips, which was good for us, but also I think helped build a sense of team with everyone else, from the cops to the policy wonks. The news was leading on TB and Rumsfeld. What a clot.

Thursday, May 29

Up at 5, UK time. The press was dominated by WMD and Rumsfeld's comments, which was really irritating. When I thought of what we could do to fuck them up in the same way. We then heard, though we couldn't get it substantiated, that Wolfowitz had said that WMD had been a bureaucratic convenience to get us into the war. The local Kuwaiti paper had a picture of TB and a group of sheikhs all in trad-itional headgear, with the caption helpfully pointing out that TB was 'second right'. We boarded the Hercules flight to Basra. TB was up in the jump seat, David Manning and I behind. We flew over Umm Qasr, burnt-out tanks all over the place. It was very hot and arid, and a few oil wells were burning. Our military had accommodated bril-liantly to what was going on. The recurring theme though was that the Americans were not quite getting it right. TB had a fairly long briefing on how Basra was won, and then on to the speech to the troops. It was by a river under an awning, hot, but with a breeze, and his words were OK without being brilliant. He was full of praise for the troops, said it was a defining moment for the country, which the press felt was OTT. But he said afterwards he really believed it changed the way people in the region thought about the future, as was clear from the discussion with the Kuwaitis last night. I hung round talking to the press about a ghastly Gilligan story [first aired on the *Today* programme] claiming that the spooks were not happy with the dossier, which was clearly a repeat of the stories at the time.

We left for the flight to Umm Qasr by Chinook, then down to see the army and navy in a very well-organised session. Several soldiers asked me my marathon time. Some of them had been following *The Times* column but hadn't seen the result. They were a nice crowd. One came over and said he had never been much of a fan of TB or the government but both had grown on him and he felt that went for a lot of them. We went on to the minehunter, *Ramsay*, where he did a Forces Radio interview. TB clearly got a charge from the positive response, though earlier there had been no applause for his speech, which was a surprise, but then it was pointed out to me they had been told to be quiet. On the way back to the chopper, the number two in the base said they had just heard that someone who worked in a photo shop had sent the police pictures of soldiers maltreating Iraqi PoWs. Bad. The reception he got was warm all day but General Wall said that at night there was a lot of criminality. On the dockside, bizarrely, given I was spending so much time thinking about my own future, one of General Wall's protection team asked me whether I had a lot of pressure. I said yes. You wouldn't miss it for the world, he said. I'm not sure about that, I said. 'You just hang in there.' Odd. He was from Stirling.

We flew back to Kuwait and the relief of a cool, air-conditioned place. TB had to get changed into a suit for the official send-off and called me in for a chat. He said he found our troops really terrific, easily the best, and he was glad that we came. Over dinner on the plane TB, AC, DM, Tom Kelly. Serious stuff on Iraq. TB said it reminded him of FMD before we gripped it and the military sorted it. People knew what problems needed to be solved, but nobody was gripping it. Paul Bremer [US administrator in Iraq] was impressive but looked like he was overwhelmed. Alarmingly, TB said what he felt it needed was for me to go out there and be his person totally gripping it, alongside someone who was GWB's person. I said I was not keen, but he clearly was. Overnight we had a telegram about the US warning that there could be two Brits among those at Guantánamo Bay that could end up being executed. I said to TB it would be dreadful and it couldn't be allowed to happen. He said he didn't think they would go through with some of this tribunal stuff, but I wasn't so sure.

Friday, May 30
WMD firestorm was getting worse. I told TB the papers were really pretty grim as he woke up, and he was worried that the spooks would be pissed off with us. He felt that in part the attacks coming now were about Europe. 'It's another attack to go to the heart of my integrity,' he said. I did a very strong line of rebuttal and when the press conference came up, he hit back hard on it.

Sunday, June 1
With DM to the airport, had a readout of the papers, pretty grim. On the plane I told TB and he was a bit down about it all. Also, he and

Cherie seemed to have had a row and she was really lip-quivering. TB went down the plane to see the press, again pushing back on WMD. He was fine but the WMD issue was now digging into us. TB kept saying 'What are the allegations?' I said it's that we made them do something they didn't want to do. But it's ridiculous, he said, and so it went on. The *Sunday Times* had a story about an email showing I'd discussed the dossier with John Scarlett and there was a suggestion that I had tried to get him to write a conclusion. In fact John had drafted one and I'd said I didn't think that it worked. There was an account in the *Observer* of meetings with TB, John Scarlett, C, Jack Straw and complained it wasn't right. There would be grains of truth in all this but it was just crap. Indeed I'd bent over backwards not least because I was fearful this kind of thing could happen. Gilligan had a big piece in the *Mail on Sunday* having a go at me from the alleged source that he had, with descriptions of meetings there had never been and things I was said to have done that I never did. But it was grim, and grim for me, and also for TB with huge stuff about trust. It was definitely time to get out. I called John Scarlett when I got back. He was emphatic that the agencies were pushing back and denying all this, but there was precious little sign of that in the Sundays. He said we were being made to accord to our stereotypes – you are the brutal political hatchet man and I am the dry intelligence officer. It's not very nice but I can assure you this is not coming from people at the top. He was clear I had never asked him to do anything he was unhappy with. I said it was really bad, all this stuff.

Monday, June 2

WMD still raging and it was going to be the big build-up to Wednesday, PMQs and the G8 statement, then hopefully some kind of catharsis. TB was still in 'it's ridiculous' mode and getting more and more irritated by what was essentially a media-driven thing. The main problem of course was that there were no WMD discoveries beyond the two labs, and no matter how much we said that there were other priorities now, the public were being told as a matter of fact that we had done wrong. We had Clare S, Robin C and a lot of backbenchers on the rampage now. So it was difficult. Marr was back from holiday and decided to peddle the line that AC would be the scalp the Commons was looking for. So here we go again, Black Rod, Cheriegate, all over again. On the flight to New York, I read Joe Haines's book (*Glimmers of Twilight*). Pretty grim reading and the problems with Marcia [Falkender, Wilson's private secretary] worse than anything we had. His section on the BBC of today was brilliant. I was met by

Jeremy Greenstock's driver Gary and his Bentley and taken to the Residence. I did a bit of paperwork, then out to meet friends from university who were over for the funeral.[1]

Tuesday, June 3

New York. I wrote a long note for TB re what we should try to do in rebuttal of the continuing WMD allegations. Defensive and offensive, give context and explanation, inquiry, defend ourselves re Agency interference nonsense. We had to fight back but also put over a more subtle message. But there was no doubt we were in trouble on it, and the trust thing was back, which was partly about trying to undermine him on the euro. I felt it was an OK piece of work though and hoped it helped him. He was going to be feeling the heat on it, although the Beeb would try to deflect it to me. I guess the main point was that he needed to give a sense of process, show understanding of the concerns but also make clear we did the right thing because of the better things now happening. Met up with some old friends in a bar before the funeral, then up to the church. I read my speech over the phone to Fiona and was worried I wouldn't be able to hold it together. Susie (Mark's widow) was in a bad way and the boys just looked out of it. I just about got through without breaking down. The worst bit was when the boys told me that Mark was still their best friend. The event afterwards was pretty dreadful. A series of corporate speeches, one of which actually said that what he would want was for the company to use this to go out and pitch for business. It really was the worst of corporate America. I got a lot of nice plaudits for the speech, certainly got the most laughs. Mark's dad said he didn't get the impression that some of the people speaking at the wake really knew him at all. WMD still raging at home. I spoke to TB, who said it was grotesque. There was no story here at all, but it was being driven by the BBC as a huge crisis for us. He said he liked my note. I got on the plane and slept all the way back with the help of a sleeping pill.

Wednesday, June 4

I arrived back and the big story was John Reid saying rogue elements in the security services were out to get us. By the time I landed, switch[board] called me to say that C, John Scarlett and David Omand had all called for me. I said I'm sure Reid would not have meant to

[1] Campbell was attending the funeral of a friend from university days, Mark Gault.

attack them as a whole but clearly someone was stirring it. I said TB would be very supportive at PMQs. I'd asked for all my notes to be dug out on the dossier and I was provenly in the clear. I'd done a long 3-page process note on Sept 9 last year making clear it must be 100% their product and there must be nothing in it they're not happy with. And there was also a long note I made with detailed drafting suggestions.

Thursday, June 5

Reid's comments had upset the spooks and Jack said to me they should have been told straight away about what he had said. But at the same time, there was some stirring going on somewhere and they needed to grip it, surely. I left for the ballet with Fiona and David and Janice Blackburn [friends]. I didn't like ballet at the best of times, and these weren't the best of times. I have never been so stared at in my life. I felt like I was an exhibit in a zoo. It was a mix of 'He doesn't look too evil' and 'What on EARTH is he doing here?' I wondered myself.

Friday, June 6

The Bush call began with lots of congratulations re the MEPP summit. Derry was in a terrible state because of all the talk of him being for the chop. Blunkett was fretting on all the suggestions that he would lose out with the creation of a new Ministry of Justice. TB wanted Ann Taylor [chair of ISC] to do a quick investigation into the 45 minutes stuff.[1] TB was telling us that we had to get back on domestic politics but then also saying he wanted to make more speeches on Europe, wanted better rebuttal on Afghanistan and more of our people into Iraq.

Saturday, June 7

WMD was still rumbling on with the BBC driving it as hard as they could and we were bracing for more Sunday stuff, a lot of which basically directed at me, e.g. David Clark in the *Mail on Sunday*, AC must go. The *Sunday Times* went back to the old dossier and why we didn't publish it. The *Sunday Telegraph* led on a so-called apology from me

[1] Taylor would chair the Commons Intelligence and Security Committee Inquiry into the published intelligence assessments of Iraqi WMD capability, including the claim made in the September 2002 dossier that WMD could be launched within 45 minutes. The committee's eventual report would describe the 45-minute claim as 'unhelpful', lacking context and assessment. Though the ISC would conclude editorial changes had been made within Number 10, Campbell would be exonerated from Gilligan's charge of having 'sexed up' the document.

June '03: Reid's comments upset the spooks

to Richard Dearlove re the dodgy dossier, the *Indy* talked of the spies recording all the pressure put on them, and so it went on. I felt I was being royally set up for a fall. The Sundays arrived, ghastly, full of absolute shit about me, which would keep the story going. Also I'd been invited by FAC [Foreign Affairs Committee] and ISC to give evidence so it was going to be a grim few weeks.

Sunday, June 8

Ludicrously, my 'apology' to SIS [Secret Intelligence Service known also as MI6] was leading the news and being conflated into a sense that it was an apology over the main WMD dossier rather than – the reality – that it was about the so-called dodgy dossier about which I'd accepted mistakes were made, sent a letter to the system about it, and on which Omand suggested new procedures. But it was an outrage the way the BBC was twisting this. Anyone listening to their bulletins would think I'd apologised – all I had done was give assurances – and that I'd admitted we abused intelligence material – I didn't. We were going through a totally mad phase. JR, Hilary A and Tessa all called during the day, just to say they would do anything they could to help. Hilary said Dennis Skinner had called offering support but also saying 'Don't trust spies, they're treacherous.' JR said whenever ministers got into trouble, I would organise operations to help them, and did I want him to get one organised for me?

Monday, June 9

Hilary A and Sally said the PLP were virtually solid for me and that Skinner had been going round the place saying 'Who do you trust? AC or a spy? He is one of ours.' TB was dreading having to sack Derry, who he was sure would take it very badly. I saw Jonathan to tell him I was definitely leaving now. He said TB had mentioned it, so maybe he had accepted it. Jonathan felt sure I would regret it. He said he knew that he would. He reckoned I would have a long period of decompression and he was sure the business appointments people would be very difficult. He said he had always felt I was like an extra battery for TB, and he would lose extra power. I spoke to Omand who, like everyone else, was feeling that DIS [Defence Intelligence Staff] were probably responsible for the briefings. I said to him the only thing that could be seen as an apology were my exchanges with him re the handling of intelligence post the dodgy dossier.

Wednesday, June 11

Alan Milburn had been to see TB on Monday and told him that he was going to leave. He had spoken to Sally first, who also told him I was thinking of leaving and during the day I had various conversations with him. He said I may think he was the last person to say this, but he really thought I shouldn't go. He said everyone knew the stuff about me was bollocks but he really didn't think I should go at a time I was under pressure. He had told very few people about his own situation and asked me what I thought he should say. I said that he should say that he faced a choice between career and family and chose family, that it was not political but personal. He said he was sad but convinced it was the right thing. Alan's decision was going to be a big talking point and it would be presented as a blow to TB. Alan said he felt wretched doing it now but he felt he had no choice.

Thursday, June 12

TB was dreading the Derry discussions. TB saw JP, who told us he had just been with GB, who was pushing for a big job for Douglas [Alexander] and also for Michael Wills, though not in the Treasury. TB then saw GB, who was pretty thunderous about the whole thing. I spent part of the day drafting resignation letters. Cabinet was pretty surreal because everyone knew there was going to be a reshuffle. Several people now knew about Alan, pretty much everyone knew about Derry, and yet on they went with a discussion about Europe, the Middle East, Congo, Iraq. TB saw Derry. He and I had a perfectly amicable discussion re families before he went in. Previously, TB had argued he needed to shake things up and put an elected MP in charge of the new department, so when he told Derry it would be Charlie F, he was particularly pissed off. 'You are getting rid of me and putting in another peer, that's not exactly what I expected.' As he left, he looked pretty miserable. He then saw Helen Liddell, then Reid, who was not immediately too keen on Health, wanted to think about it. These reshuffles were always awful. During a break, I asked TB why we didn't announce my departure at the same time. We were out on the terrace. He asked why I was so sure I wanted to go. I said I wasn't really working as hard or as well as usual. Most days I woke up feeling depressed and didn't think it would improve. For ten minutes or so, he seemed almost up for it. Then he said it wasn't a sensible day to do it, because it would give another boost to GB. He was also not convinced that I was 100% sure, and said he thought I would get a second wind before long. He sacked Meacher by phone, who made clear he would be difficult. He didn't do Nick Brown because he was on *Question Time* tonight.

Friday, June 13

The Milburn announcement seemed to be taken at face value. Despite all the crony attacks, the Charlie appointment seemed to be OK. We needed a few more sackings to make room - Lewis Moonie, Barbara Roche [Minister for Social Exclusion and Equality]. Tessa Blackstone [Higher Education] as well. TB wanted to promote Kim Howells and wanted Des Browne [Parliamentary Secretary, Northern Ireland Office] to do asylum but Blunkett came in and argued for Bev Hughes to stay with him. David could be very difficult and egotistical at these reshuffle times. GB, who for years had been a nightmare at reshuffles, was relatively quiet. His attempts to protect Nick Brown were pretty half-hearted. He did his usual appeal for Douglas to go into the Cabinet – 'Don't be ridiculous,' said JP – and he was of course arguing for the promotion of Michael Wills. Hilary A and Sally were regaling us with stories of how Michael would not even sit with his officials on the same part of a train. TB said to GB 'If he's so good why not take him to the Treasury?' We spent most of the morning going through the lists again and again, making sure there were no glaring mistakes, Jonathan keeping tabs on the numbers. Moonie was difficult. Meacher made a few threatening noises. Barbara Roche very unhappy. We shifted Yvette [Cooper] to ODPM [Office of the Deputy Prime Minister] and she had learned from last year, in that she didn't complain. He sacked Nick Brown by phone. Nick said he would 'continue to support him and the government' – joke. Then getting people with new jobs to come through the door – Margaret Hodge, Malcolm Wicks [Department for Work and Pensions], Chris Pond [Labour MP for Gravesham], Hazel Blears [Public Health Minister] – all fine, real freshness and enthusiasm. Hilary was an absolute brick throughout all this, softening people up when she knew they were on their way out, keeping in touch with all the Cabinet ministers about who they did and didn't want. Sally also had a real toughness about her in these situations. Then another hiccup re Tommy McAvoy [Government Pairing Whip] threatening to walk re Bob Ainsworth [Party Whip] being made Deputy Chief Whip. Then Melanie Johnson [Labour MP for Welwyn Hatfield] wanted a long conversation with him about this and that concern, and he was starting to get frazzled, asking if they all thought he had nothing to do but listen to their outpourings. By the time we started doing the bulk of appointments by phone, he had got it down to a very curt 'I'd like you to join the government as x. You should call y minister and get the drill. There you are, well done.'

Tuesday, June 17

Hilary [Armstrong] told him that if he didn't bring back the Hunting Bill for a third reading soon we would not have a hope in hell of winning the foundation hospital vote. TB said sane people just will not understand how we can put at risk our whole public service agenda over hunting. Hilary said he had to understand that hunting went deep, and was symbolic, also that even with it we couldn't be sure of winning on foundation hospitals. She was very straightforward with him, and a very solid citizen. She is one of the few people I know who seems able to combine being close to the end of her tether with total niceness.

Thursday, June 19

The FAC, because some Labour MPs were missing, voted to summon me because Gilligan said he'd seen documents showing that I'd asked for changes, and also re the second dossier. I called Tom Kelly who was with TB in Greece. TB said to hold firm, get Andrew Turnbull to reply to the committee and say that I should not go. TB said we should co-operate with the ISC and that was that. I meanwhile had done a note to Jack re how to handle the dossier issue. I told TB of the rumours doing the rounds that I was going to go in July or September. He said 'Why can't you deny it?' I said that's difficult and clearly people are talking. Very curtly, pretty cool, he said 'I'm afraid that's what happens.' Both Fiona and Godric were of the view that some of us were being bugged by someone flogging stuff to the media, or by the media per se. It was extraordinary how many private conversations were getting out.

Saturday, June 21

I hadn't slept well. I was avoiding answering the phone other than to the office because by now all the broadcasters and half the Sundays were trying to ask me if I was going. Now was probably not the right time. It would be seen as bad for TB and bad for me if I went under a cloud. The *Independent on Sunday* had a story with quotes from Eric Illsley [Labour MP on FAC] that they were going to go for me personally re the Iraq dossier and I felt the best thing for me to do was to go to give evidence and get my retaliation in first. I was sure of my ground, so why not? I did a note to Jack saying that when he gave evidence, there were two central points that needed to get over re the dodgy dossier. One, I was unaware of the plagiarism. Two, that it had nothing to do with the people named in the email about it, like Alison. We desperately needed to reposition on this and I was thinking the best way was for me to surprise them by saying I positively wanted to give evidence.

Sunday, June 22

I said to TB I feared none of the questions and that we had to get to a point where they accepted we did nothing wrong regarding the first dossier, made mistakes re the second. I said I was confident, really felt I should take the heat on it and get it into a better place. If not, the report would come out the day before the Liaison Committee and that would be a real problem for him as well as me. I thought the best thing to do was a note to TB, which I did, giving the reasons why we should break the convention and then give it to Donald Anderson [chair of FAC] as a letter. Jack S agreed with me I should appear because it was clear that a lot of the evidence given so far related to communications issues. TB was persuaded first by me and then by Jack that it was the right thing to do. TB sensed that me going to the FAC would go very big, but I was in no doubt I had to do it, try to get my reputation in a better place and I felt more confident if I could do that myself.

Monday, June 23

The William situation[1] was the main attraction but by the time of the 11 o'clock, it was clear I would be a strong second. I had redone a memo and Jack's letter to the FAC. At the office meeting, TB looked dreadful. He was getting more and more frustrated at what he called the lack of radical policy direction in the public services. Geoff Mulgan had meanwhile done an excellent note, which was a brutal assessment of our lack of long-term strategy on policy. He said we had lost authority at the centre, that Number 10 had got bigger but less effective, and that our overall narrative was no longer clear. He gave lessons from other mid-term governments around the world, and said that they sometimes got renewal through brutal changes of personnel. As I read it, eight pages of pretty good stuff, I noted Jonathan could hardly keep his eyes open, I was moving on in my mind already, and the contributions around the table were pretty rambling and anecdotal. It was pretty dispiriting. Towards the end I said to TB 'For God's sake try not to look so miserable. It's not as bad as all that. When we have an agenda and we just get on with it and ignore the press, we are always strong.' Then I said: are you OK for us to announce me going to the FAC and he said he was not so sure any more. Someone had got at him, but I enlisted Andrew Turnbull, who persuaded him

---

[1] An intruder, Aaron Barschack, self-styled 'comedy terrorist', had gained easy access to Prince William's 21st birthday party, dressed as Osama bin Laden in a ball gown.

it was the way to avoid the Liaison Committee being about me/WMD/trust. So Jack and I then finished the letter to Donald Anderson and got it in time for the 11 o'clock briefing. Clare Sumner and Catherine Rimmer were doing lots of work for me. Then to a meeting with Michael Jay and Dickie Stagg [FCO official] to go through what MJ would say tomorrow when he appeared with Jack, then back to see John S, Clare Sumner, Tom and Godric to begin to go through the difficult questions. Alison was back from holiday and getting me out all the files and I was beginning to work out all the answers to the difficult questions, for example al-Marashi's claim that his life had been put in danger. Hilary A said some of our members on the committee were worried. They felt I could easily deal with Gilligan, but al-Marashi was not so easy. Clare had established who in the CIC was responsible for not telling people where it all came from, but we agreed I would take responsibility at the FAC.

Tuesday, June 24

Fairly big coverage of me going to the committee. Vile in the *Mail* needless to say but not bad overall. I spent most of the day with Clare and Catherine, who were terrific. Clare had got to the bottom of the whole thing. I spent several hours going over and over again the text of my memo, which we eventually got to the FAC by 6.15pm. Jack S was keen that I apologise upfront. I agreed, but later came to the view that I should not and said it was because I was worried it would leak. My strategy was to apologise to Dr al-Marashi for the mistake and then demand an apology from the BBC not just for me but for the PM, etc. John Scarlett was getting my memo put through the Agencies. I saw TB, whose main interest seemed to be how the FAC would impinge on him. He gave little advice at all. At least Jack was suggesting changes and improvements. Jack also came over, very friendly, said the most important thing was that I was nice and polite and didn't go for them. I then spent four hours with John Scarlett and Dickie Stagg to go over all the questions, etc. I discussed with Neil, with Fraser Kemp and a few others how to approach it. They all felt go for the BBC but be clinical and be forensic. Jack's evidence didn't go brilliantly. He said I had commissioned the paper, and the BBC said that undermined me before my appearance. But I felt confident.

Wednesday, June 25

Jack had set me up badly by saying that I had commissioned the dodgy dossier and it was 'a complete Horlicks'. He called me while

I was preparing for the committee with Clare and Catherine. I said I didn't want to speak to him but I would see him at the House before PMQs. TB asked me up to the flat. He said he really wanted me to stay calm at all times and treat the committee with respect. We had worked out the right strategy, concede the apology to Dr al-Marashi, be as detailed and as full as possible, go on the BBC, broaden it, demand an apology and get up the big-picture message about the cynicism of people who say that the Prime Minister would go to war on the basis of this. TB and I agreed that the media were a real democratic problem, but he didn't really want to do anything. It was an odd feeling to go out from Number 10 with lots of good wishes and with the media there for me, not TB. PMQs was pretty low-key. Afterwards TB had another private word. He said look, this is the reverse of the usual. I am telling you that you have to be calm and not get peevish. Meeting with John Scarlett, Godric, Tom, etc. Over at the House, feeling not bad, long walk to Boothroyd Room, there were crowds outside the room, and I had to wait around the corner. I got in, slow start with John Stanley [Conservative MP] before a break for a vote at 4. Three hours in total. I picked up after a while. I got most of my lines in, and it went pretty well. I thought the Labour MPs were reasonably helpful, I think they were glad I apologised and they went for the BBC thing pretty well. I cut my hand on the sharp object in my palm (a paper clip). It was gruelling, and I walked back exhausted, followed back by cameras, but there was a nice round of applause when I got back. I felt a lot better. Flank opened on the BBC. TB called late, said 'Everyone was saying you did superbly, which you did.'

Thursday, 26 June

Huge coverage in the papers and some great cartoons. Generally I was thought to have done well, though the BBC were still focusing on dissent and opposition to me. During the morning we put together a letter following Sambrook's interview in which he made further contradictory statements. I put together a letter, and got Clive Soley to do a letter saying that the source should speak to Donald Anderson and if not Gilligan should be recalled. We were on a roll, all right yesterday and today, we had good messages of support coming through. I was up at 5 to work on the letter that I was to send to the committee to deal with their extra requests. It took hours and hours and hours. I went through all the different exchanges of correspondence with John Scarlett. It took hours for me, John, Clare and Catherine to get it sorted. I also wrote to Dyke and to Sambrook and put the Sambrook letter out to the press. I was going to nail Gilligan completely, and then the *Mail*. Pre-Cabinet, Jack S came up to me and I was very short with him and did not engage. Later I told Michael Jay I took it very personally, felt betrayed, that the FCO had basically been interested only in protecting JS and the FCO. TB called me in before Cabinet. 'You did brilliantly.' 'No help from ministers,' I said. 'You have to understand these guys are not as used to pressure as we are,' he said. 'They panic.' I said I'd taken a lot of shit for these people and got very little support back. I'd thought JS was a bit different. The BBC letter went well though and I felt it was turning our way a bit. TB's demeanour about the whole thing had changed. I had never had so much coverage as in the last few days but TB said it was the right thing to do, I'd have been hung out to dry if I hadn't done it.

Friday, June 27

I had been going through the FAC memo until late last night. Early in to go through it again. We had a long discussion about whether we should be specific that I had previously pointed out an inconsistency between the text and executive summary of the 45-minute description. Clive Soley and Phil Woolas [Labour MPs] were doing media defending me. There weren't that many ministers out but I don't think that meant they weren't behind me. Audrey [Millar] did however remind me of the observation that if you want a friend in politics, get a dog. I did the final memo with the last changes then sent it to Clare Sumner to get ready to send while I went with Calum and Charlie [Calum's friend] to Wimbledon. I lost my rag in the morning watching Jack's live evidence, where he was umming and aahing and when asked whether 45-minute claim was in first dossier, looked shifty. He did not just say yes. I had even talked to him about that point in the morning when I spoke to him to let him know that I HAD probably made a point to John Scarlett re 45 minutes but it was not a request. So what the fuck was going on? I said that I felt badly let down and this was what happened when a department cared about itself, not the government. At Wimbledon, we watched Andy Roddick, and Venus Williams' matches, but I was constantly being called out.

Sambrook replied. It was real sophistry. Their line now was that it was OK to report a source even if you didn't know what he said was true. He said I had a vendetta against Gilligan and that I was intimidating the BBC. He also had a line that they would express regret if story turned out to be false. So they were both blustering and on the run. I wrote a very angry response, probably too angry. 'Weasel words, BBC standards debased beyond belief,' I really went for it. Once it was drafted, we had a conference call to discuss it. We drove back and I listened to the BBC 6 o'clock news in the car. It was a total PR job on the BBC letter, and a straight hit at me. I got in to the office and Jon Snow had asked me to go on *Channel 4 News*. Hilary C had said no but I was tempted because I knew the story inside out. The office was split, half in favour, half against. Jonathan feared it would make me the story even more. I spoke to TB, who said do you really want to do it or don't you? I said I do. OK, be calm and be careful. The important thing is you do what is appropriate and don't go over the top. I got into the car and headed there gathering my thoughts. I was taken straight to the studio. Snow seemed not to be expecting me, but there I was. I felt I won it re the words and was able to pick him up on fact a couple of times, but I did get a bit too angry. The clips used in later bulletins were good though. Lots of calls of support came in, including John Reid, Neil and Glenys, Philip. The office was OK, but TB said he felt I was too angry and Fiona was livid I'd done it at all. She did one of her 'you never listen, never acknowledge anyone else's views' numbers.

Saturday, June 28

I got some very supportive phone calls through the day. Rory answered the phone to Nick Soames, who before realising it wasn't me went off on one – 'You sex god, you Adonis, you the greatest of all great men' – before Rory said 'I'm his son.' Soames was totally supportive, said keep going, these people are total shits. He said in part we had created this monster, seen it as a beast and we fed it well. But it was now out of control and we had to get the control back. He said bad journalism is like pornography. Every time you fail to check it, it gets closer to being the norm. 'Do you think my grandfather [Churchill] had a spin doctor? Course he fucking did.' He said we had to win but he would be happy to speak up for me at any point. He was on great form. 'Tell the Prime Minister that the next time I'm called at PMQs I intend to say "What is a lifestyle guru and do I need one?"'

Monday, June 30

The BBC were trying to move the goalposts to the 'dodgy dossier'. Peter M said Dyke was personally masterminding it and had written parts of Sambrook's letter to me himself. Peter said they'd got themselves on a hook, whereby they felt their independence was under attack but they'd parked on very weak ground. I went up to see TB, who said he didn't want it going beyond next week. He lacked the killer instinct. His rationale was that he didn't want every single media organisation against him. I said we had to get it absolutely proven that we were right and use that to force a rethink of the political/journalism culture. I could see he was up for suing for peace. He/Peter M wanted to get it stitched up in advance. Dennis Skinner called on his first day back in Parliament after his illness. He said keep at it. He thought I was brilliant on Channel 4, the MPs were totally behind me and 'I'll tell [Andrew] MacKinlay [Labour MP on FAC] he has to back you because TB needs you. I'll tell him he's worth 99 Roger Liddles and TB is surrounded by twats whereas AC is fine and probably against the war anyway.'

Wednesday, July 2

The MoD were putting out a letter of complaint re Gilligan claims that he had checked his story with the MoD press office. We were still on top but if the committee split on party lines it was going to be very difficult for us. This was taking up too much of my time. I had a meeting with Gavin [Millar, QC, Fiona's brother]. He said the BBC had broadcast a libel but that I wasn't named at first. It was the *Mail on Sunday* that did the libel. I could sue the BBC for aggravated libel because of all the other media who supported the story. He felt I could go for Gilligan but though the BBC would not want to litigate he felt the *Mail on Sunday* probably would. He undertook to read all the papers, felt it would be OK but I had to be clear what I was getting into. On balance he felt probably don't do it, but the most important thing was to be cleared by the inquiry. I spoke to Soames, who said he would defend me and attack the Tories for undermining the intelligence agencies.

Thursday, July 3

Soames had called me late last night to say he had run into C and asked him straight out if the story against me was true. C said no, and Soames said can I say so? Yes, said C. He was a bit pissed when he phoned and basically said he would do anything to help me, adding 'especially if you stop TB using the Parliament Act on hunting'. He wanted to go on the media, called the *Today* programme and seemingly told them 'You are dozy, dishonest cunts and I am coming on your programme to say so.' He was, though, serious that he wanted to go on and make the point that this was an attack on the intelligence agencies as well as on me. Marr did the interview and was now redefining the allegations as us having given 'undue prominence' to the 45-minute point. Total bollocks. Then to a strategy meeting with TB, GB, JP, Douglas Alexander, Ian McCartney and David Triesman. TB said he would give the Cabinet next week a political sitrep and then have a polling and political discussion. JP said we needed a lot more than that, and there followed a positive and good discussion. JP's main point was that we didn't do enough to promote what we had done and talk about our values. The party felt itself on the defensive because that's how we came across to them. GB said we had to think forward to the election, the issues, big choices and values dividing lines, and then think back, then plan from here to then. He felt there was so much focus on reform that we were losing sight of values, that the messages were too technocratic. It was exactly what I had been saying.

Off to David Frost's party, people generally supportive, including Frost. I avoided Dyke and Davies. I had a good chat with Mike Jackson, who wanted me to kill Gilligan.

Friday, July 4

I spoke to Hoon, who said that a man had come forward who felt he was possibly Gilligan's source. He had come forward and was being interviewed today. GH said his initial instinct was to throw the book at him, but in fact there was a case for trying to get some kind of plea bargain – say that he'd come forward and he was saying yes to speaking to Gilligan, Yes he said intelligence went in late, but he never said the other stuff. It was double-edged but GH and I agreed it would fuck Gilligan if that was his source. He said he was an expert rather than a spy or full-time MoD official. GH and I agreed to talk tomorrow.

Saturday, July 5

The BBC story seemed to be moving our way. The governors were to meet tomorrow to discuss it. The BBC started briefing aggressively that they would stand by their story and warn the governors it would be the end of BBC independence if they backed down. I spoke to TB and we agreed I should send a fairly emollient letter to the governors, and a file, to set out our side of the story vis-à-vis the BBC, and say it was not about attacking independence, or a broader attack, but dealing with one specific set of allegations. I agreed with Jack that it had to be about the BBC story because that was where the focus was. There was a case for saying nothing and going up to do discussion stuff, e.g. do we do a phone-in or discussion with BBC? Catherine Rimmer went into the office to put together the file for the governors. Meanwhile I was dealing with the car, which had been broken into, then took the boys to various sports events, then saw Gavin again, who having read through everything felt I had an open-and-shut case for libel but that we should wait and see what the BBC said on Monday.

The *Observer* was saying that C met Humphrys and [Kevin] Marsh (editor of *Today*) shortly before the *Today* programme story. It looked like the last desperate throes, but it was possible the governors would go for it and back Dyke.

Sunday, July 6

I spent much of the weekend talking to TB and Geoff H re the 'source', the man who felt he was the source because his colleagues said he sounded like what Gilligan was saying. He had come forward earlier in the week to confide that he'd seen Gilligan in a hotel, that he'd made some of these comments, but not others, for example about me. GH, like me, wanted to get it out that the source had broken cover to claim Gilligan had misrepresented him. TB and I had a long chat about it and TB was worried, felt that he or GH ought to tell the FAC about this. His worry was that it could lead to them reopening the inquiry. I wanted, as GH did, to get it to the BBC governors that we may know who the source was, that he was not a spy, not involved in the WMD dossier and was a WMD expert who advised departments. TB was fine about that but backed off after speaking to Omand, who felt the guy had to be treated properly and interviewed again. GH and I felt we were missing a trick. I suggested to GH to speak to TB to try to persuade him we should do this and maybe GH should speak to Sambrook and tell him that he was a nobody re the dossier. GH said he was almost as steamed up as I was. TB said he didn't want to push the system too far. But my worry was that I wanted a clear win not a messy draw and if they presented it as a draw that was not good enough for us. TB felt that we should not push Kevin Tebbit/David Omand too hard, and could maybe bring it out tomorrow if we needed it. TB was also feeling that we had to have something for the ISC to go for and that could be this. Jack – who'd spoken to Donald Anderson – said that the Tories had not supported the report so it was going to be split on party lines, unclear and very messy. As the governors met, it was clear we were heading for a bad day tomorrow. TB said we had to get it onto the issue of the UK media culture. 'It is a disgrace the BBC are behaving like this, it really is.' He said to me how are you feeling about it? I said fed up about the whole thing. He said don't be fed up. The problem was I'd felt we were going to win and it was going to be a messy draw at the FAC. Source idea went nowhere as he had to be interviewed again by Martin Howard, DIS and personnel. TB called to tell me not to worry. Martin Sheehan called after the BBC governors broke up and I listened to Gavyn Davies's statement. Dyke had got them onto the same line, defending the story, extending it to general issue of coverage. It was pretty poor, but clear they were all going along with the BBC line, if not defending the story. TB and I agreed the line that would put the focus on the claim that they never said we were lying, and we made clear what the central allegations still were.

Monday, July 7

There was a demo outside the house. I was feeling a bit under siege, and very tired. TB was meeting Kevin Tebbit, Omand and others re 'the source'. He was an ex-inspector, who advised the government, was aware of information going into the dossier but not involved in drawing it up. He'd once sat next to Jack as an expert at a select committee. Kevin said the guy claimed he never mentioned me. He was a bit of a show-off though. Felt that maybe Gilligan just put in the stuff about me. It was agreed he should be interviewed again, and then we should get it out that the source was not in the intelligence community, not involved drawing up the dossier. Agreed we should be saying the source was misrepresented by Gilligan. TB was keen for Tebbit and Omand to be in control of the process. I watched the FAC press conference. Donald Anderson very clear re me. [Sir John] Stanley said I was a sideshow, Bill Olner and Gisela Stuart [all FAC] were supportive. Tories and Andrew MacKinlay not too bad for me, and overall the impact was pretty positive.

I got good advice from John Birt [now an adviser to TB], who said claim victory and don't rejoice. He said the BBC would not apologise and therefore there was no point pushing it. I should be magnanimous. He said they look ridiculous, they can't answer the question if it's true or not. Several chats with MoD, Pam Teare [MoD Director of News], then Geoff H re the source. I felt we should get it out through the papers, then have a line to respond and let TB take it on at the Liaison Committee. TB felt we had to leave it to Omand/Tebbit judgement and they didn't want to do it. We had to go for natural justice. Wall-to-wall all day, source issue not moving. More calls for public inquiries. All went fine for me, but there were lots of difficult questions for the Government as a whole. The problem for TB was the Iraq WMD were not found. GH wanted to get up the source, Tom and Godric felt it was best to wait until tomorrow, we had to do it right.

Tuesday, July 8

The papers were disgraceful. Up to see TB in the flat, who was preparing for the Liaison Committee. He said the papers were unbelievable, 'It is truly Orwellian the world that we live in, I just don't know what to do with this constant rewriting of history and moving of goalposts.' It was still not clear how we were going to handle the case of the MoD official. I called Geoff Hoon. He was not remotely on top of the case. He said he had not checked out where we were on it. Said he should get going on the source issue, TB clear that we should leave the bureaucracy to deal with it. He met Scarlett and Omand and agreed to try to resolve it through a letter to Ann Taylor. Word then came back she didn't want a letter on it. That meant do it as a press release. Jonathan, AC, Tom and Godric, John S and Kevin Tebbit went to Godric's room and wrote press release. Tebbit drafted a letter from GH to Gavyn Davies offering to give him the name of the source. Martin Howard had interviewed David Kelly [government scientist and weapons expert], and was pretty convinced that he was the source, though of course we could not be sure. Tebbit took the draft away to the MoD and had to clear it with David Kelly, who was on a motorway. I told TB I still wanted to leave and why not now? Said he was really against it, it was the last thing he needed, and at the moment there would be meltdown in Parliament and that we should wait until Commons was not sitting.

Wednesday, July 9

The BBC story was going away because they were refusing to take on the source idea. There was a big conspiracy at work really. The biggest thing needed was the source out. We agreed that we should not do it ourselves, so didn't, but later in the day the FT, Guardian, and after a while Mike Evans [defence correspondent of The Times] got the name. It was going to be difficult to keep it going and of course the politicians really wanted out of it. The story was moving away, and as the source row grew, I felt I'd lost. Andy Marr led the news, massively ramped across all channels, with a story about senior sources saying we were unlikely ever to find WMD. It transpired the source was Jack Straw. JS apologised to me later saying he thought he was just chatting for background, not that Marr was going to do big story. It was an outrage the way the BBC was now using its reporters and outlets to promote its line on the issue.

Thursday, July 10

The FAC met and agreed publicly to call Dr Kelly and privately they were writing to Gilligan, so this was still moving in an uncertain direction. Geoff Hoon got a letter of apology from Sambrook about the claim they'd put the allegations to us. Political Cabinet at 3. TB did an OK introduction but once Philip's polling was done they had what Douglas [Alexander] called 'a meeting of Government by Anecdote' designed to promote views we already knew they had. Alistair Darling on the Libs, Andrew Smith on local campaigning methods, Pat H on targets, DB wanting more ASBOs [anti-social behaviour orders], Charles Clarke on green issues, Hain on the need at least to think about tax. Not a good discussion. JR was the only one who really said anything worth taking on board. GH also spoke quite well, echoing John in the line that we needed to keep on with reform as a way of holding the middle ground but do it according to our values. GB was not as impressive as usual, started well with his line about working back from the election, then seemed to run out of steam a bit. JP was very passionate, defended TB saying that he alone must not take the blame for Iraq, because it was a decision we all took and we all had to stand by it. Through some of the contributions TB had been drumming his fingers. JP seemed pretty irritated too, maybe not because of the content but the lack of balls being shown by a fair few of them. He said TB had 'done a very noble thing' in accepting responsibility for the trust issue. But it was not just his problem. Trust was the responsibility of the whole Cabinet. He felt Iraq would, long term, be seen to be the right thing to do. 300,000 people in mass graves – never let people forget it. He said in the PLP we had nearly 50 people there permanently trying to poison 50 more, plus they could always call on the Lords, lots of our own people included, to damage us. We had ex-ministers feeding it all the time. We have to fight back harder, get into the kind of mode we're in for elections. It was good rousing stuff and lifted the mood. TB said he had listened carefully. He said that being in government did not fit easily with the party's culture, which prefers to campaign than to govern. We have done a lot but we are not the government of the party's dreams. No government ever will be. But they need to know if we divide, if we go back to the ways of the past, we will be out again. Also if we lose the capacity for renewal, we will go out. New Labour is not a finite thing. It means a Labour Party constantly renewing to meet the challenges of a world of change. He said '97 to '01 was all about establishing credibility to govern. We did some terrific things – but a national minimum wage does not transform the country. We did the basics well. But in a second term we are challenged more. The country and the party want more. But in meeting the Party's demands we must not yield up the middle ground because that is where the country is. It is not just about what Middle England wants, but the challenges of today are best met in the middle ground. There are some policy solutions that neither party nor government will like. But we have to do what we think is right for the long term. He said 'There is no division in my mind between the need to reform and staying true to our values. It is not inconsistent. We are being true to our values in making the reforms needed to improve life for the people we represent.' He said he wanted people to think over the summer about how that applied to their departments. Think long term. We could avoid a bit of political pain by opting out of difficult policy decisions. But it would be a mistake for the long term. I was left thinking he was the only one there who could speak like that. JP had warmed it up well but the bulk of the contributions had been either tired or timid and distinctly lacking in leadership.

Friday, July 11

To the Ritz, where I was having lunch with Clinton, with Peter M and Philip. Mary McCartney was taking some pictures. BC had had just two hours' sleep after getting in from Greece. He was dressed in golf-type clothes. He was a lot thinner than the last time I had seen him. Doug Band had organised lunch, which seemed to be a succession of different meals, and Clinton was eating a lot of them. First a plate of eggs, then bacon, then hamburgers. We talked a bit about the US scene. He said he was not much for having things named after him but there had been a Clinton Fellowship for Israeli and Palestinian students and at first the Bush administration changed the name and then they took away the money. He said Bush liked TB because he stayed with him but if somebody came along they thought would help them more, they would go for them. He was speaking very slowly, calmly, matter-of-factly, probably conscious that we were on the lookout for signs of bitterness, but there was precious little of that and it was pretty compelling. Peter M had to leave to do an interview.

Philip, BC and I went over to the sofas and out poured something of a masterclass in political strategy. He followed our politics closely, and I asked him what his remedy would be for our problems. He said he was touched that we trusted him so much that we could openly lay out the problems we had. He said first, you have a weak opposition. Keep them weak by coming up with the forward policy positions and push them where you want them. Second, TB is about as good as they get. Keep reminding everyone of that. Third, on the press, he said you need a strategy to get back credibility. He said he'd followed my troubles and was sympathetic. He said that I'd always been the No. 2 target after TB and that I'd taken a lot. I'd been right to fight for myself and I did a great job, but now move on. Don't keep digging the hole. Let others do it. Go back to the media and say I didn't lie, but maybe I missed something. I always strove to tell the truth but I've thought deeply about it all. I've got a job to do and so have you, and it's best if we can do it without regarding each other as subhuman. He said the problem was they felt it was a pattern of behaviour – manipulation and bullying – and that I had to show them I was real again. He said they don't like me in part because I was one of them and now I'm not. Next, a strategy for the PLP. Understand their lives and reach out to them. They have shitty lives. You guys go to DC. You have real power. They get a weekend in their constituency. Give them some romance. They think you guys have gone Hollywood and they want more local. It's about their psychology. It's the same with the press. Some you will never win but others you will if you are nice to them, involve them. Your MPs know TB is better than them but that doesn't mean they are nothing. Fifth, you have to reconnect. People are falling out of love with Tony because they think he has fallen out of love with them. He's a statesman and that's great but their world is here and now and they are paying him to sort out their world, here and now. They know he has to do this other stuff but they want to know he cares about them, here and now. Sixth, the Third Way is fine, but it has to be a third way with liberal values. Don't just push a reform message. He has to have good old-fashioned left causes too, for the poor, whatever. It's about values not reform.

It was the same argument I had been having with TB. I said so, and he said yes, but maybe he thinks you are just beating up on him. It's all about balance. He has to balance the Third Way message for his new coalition with the liberal message for the party. You have to balance frank advice with real support. On TB himself, he said he had to rediscover his joy in politics. He needed new stimuli without throwing everything out. He had to keep change with continuity. He came to the point about me not beating up on Tony. He could see for example why I thought Carole was a problem, but other people's emotions and psychology are not always the same. 'My brother was a cocaine addict and the word to remember for addicts is HALT. Yes, it means stop. But it also means I'm Hungry, I'm Angry, Lonely and Tired. You usually find the reason in one of those.' Clearly talking now about Monica Lewinsky, he said 'I wasn't hungry but I was angry, lonely and tired. I was being beaten up by everyone. Ken Starr was trying to put me in jail. Friends were leaving me and enemies were killing me. Hillary was angry with me. This ball of fire came at me as I felt H, A, L, T.' He said he sometimes thought Tony wanted a blue ribbon and a gold badge for the work he does, 'but the ribbon and the badge are the JOB. It's a privilege. It's a great job he's got and yes it's tough but who says it shouldn't be? Get his juices flowing again.' So he summed up. Keep the Tories weak. Get back credibility with the press, remembering that you are the best and that's why they judge you so harshly. It's the same with Tony. You've got to show you're real. Get your troops back in shape by loving them a bit. Reconnect with the public by showing it's about them. Get TB to rediscover his joy in politics. He told a story about the first woman he ever loved, how he left her and drove her into the arms of a friend and she ended up hating both of them and it always bugged him. Years later when he was President he made contact with her and they talked it over, and he felt happy that he had resolved an important thread in his life. Another story about a friend he fell out with but then when he became President they rediscovered that friendship. So keep your friends, get some joy back into your politics, get a left liberal cause. Philip then asked him what he thought I should do, whether he thought I should leave the job. Again, he was terrific on the analysis. A long pause, then said these are the factors: 1. Is it hurting you more than you're getting out of it, especially for Fiona and the family? 2. Is it hurting Tony more than you are putting in? 3. Can anyone else do it? 4. If you stay can you deliver a new strategy? Only you know, but remember it's a great job and I don't like to think what could have happened if you had not been there. He also thought in some ways Fiona would blame herself for having let Carole take Cherie over, but she shouldn't. Really warm and friendly. He took me to the door and said 'Hang in. There are three centres of power in your politics. You guys, the Tories, the press. You have an affirmative programme. The others don't. Their job is to stop you doing your job. Don't let them. Raise your eyes above them, and stay with it.' As we left, both Philip and I observed that he was about as near to being a political strategic genius as we knew. Philip asked if it made me want to stay and it did but I wondered if TB was up for the change needed.

Tuesday, July 15
We were looking forward to Kelly giving evidence to the FAC, but Godric, Catherine Rimmer and I all predicted it would be a disaster and so it proved. Despite MoD assurances he was well schooled, a mix of the MPs' malice – Tory – and uselessness – our people – was going to give us a bit of a headache. By the end of the day, we were down as usual.

Wednesday, July 16

Michael Foot's 90th at the Gay Hussar, which Fiona had pretty much organised. There were a lot of the Old Labour people urging me to stay. Bostock [AC's GP] had said earlier he was worried I would crack up again if I suddenly went from all-out activity to doing nothing.

Thursday, July 17

In for a meeting with Clare Sumner and John Scarlett, before my ISC appearance. Clare discovered that I'd said to the FAC that I did see JIC assessments so we had to agree a line on that. I had to make clear that I was not chairing intelligence meetings. I was due to give evidence from 8.30 to 9.45. I went over with Clare and Catherine Rimmer. I went in with Ann Taylor, who joked that I had two minders, whereas TB had only had one. It was more relaxed than the FAC. I got them laughing telling them the story about how John Sergeant didn't want the PM to come down the plane to see the press because he was watching a film. Michael Mates [Conservative MP for Hampshire East] was very friendly, made a joke about a bet we once had and also said he had no doubt I did not put the 45-minute point in the dossier and he hoped the committee would say so. Gavin Strang was interested in whether we should use intelligence publicly at all. Ditto others, but I felt it went OK. Mates put to me that C had said that no intelligence should be used with other material but I was not aware of that and said so as it didn't accord with my memory. It was over in just an hour. The clerk asked me via Ann T if I thought Gilligan should go to jail. I said don't get me going.

We then left for the airport, and on the plane [to America] TB was working on his speech. Cherie was in friendlier than usual form but meanwhile back home John Burton had got a tip that 'enemies of CB' were going to meet at the Hilton Olympia in Kensington, and Fiona asked Mark Bennett to check it out covertly. It turned out to be a meeting in the bar between Ian Monk [PR] and Paul Dacre. Mark somehow got close enough to hear them, make notes and he reported back a lot of detail re their discussion and Carole. I did a note to TB which also included the fact that Monk sent a statement to PA re Cherie's clothes in Washington. I felt bad that I was going to be leaving him when things were getting tougher not easier. We landed and straight away I had a rash of messages re Gilligan's evidence to the FAC. Basically Donald Anderson went out with John Stanley and Andrew MacKinlay and then said that Gilligan was an unsatisfactory witness, that he had changed his story re me, and there was a danger of unfairness to me.

So we were pretty happy about that. We went up to Congress, where we had a discussion and then a conference call about it. It was clearly the best news we'd had for ages, and Tom K in London said it was running very much for us and against Gilligan and I should stay out. TB got an amazing reception at Congress. Then up to the White House. As we walked into the Oval Office, Bush was very friendly, said 'Hey, congratulations, you took on the bastards, and you did great.' He said he had seen some of my testimony and that Dan had kept him informed. 'You did great. You showed that if you are in the right, if you believe it, and you give no quarter, you can prevail.' He kept coming back to it during the meeting, almost embarrassingly so. Cheney was as impassive as ever, Powell was chirpy but looking tired, while Condi was more subdued than usual. GWB was now smoking a massive cigar and producing huge amounts of smoke. I was also struck by his shoes, which looked phenomenally expensive.

Friday, July 18

We landed at Heathrow about 9am, and we sat there for ages. I turned on the phone, and got a message from media monitoring that Kelly had disappeared. Then a message to call the Number 10 duty clerk, very urgent. I was told Kelly had gone for a walk yesterday and his wife had reported him missing this morning. I felt sick. I called Tom. It took ages to get off the plane and when we did I felt dreadful. I told Sally and Alison, who were both shocked. I could sense a juggernaut moving my way. Terry drove me home. I spoke to Hoon who said Tebbit would handle it initially but he would go up on the media if needed. He said he felt it had to be properly handled from the start. I then spoke to JP in Cyprus. He said he felt he should come back, and I was grateful. In part it was about himself. He said he was worried that with TB out of the country, they'd come looking for him on a beach, and he also said he could be back to steady things. He felt GH and JS were a bit too close to it all and I should stay out of it. I said what will Pauline think about it, and he said don't worry, I'll sort it. Then Tom told me that a body had been found. This was getting more and more grim. Tom did the 11 o'clock. Then TB came on from the plane. I said I'd really had enough. He said we should announce a judicial inquiry now. I said I really wanted to go and felt I should do it now. I had been determined to clear my name, I was always going to go now, it may not seem the time to do it, but it's exactly the time to do it because I was clear it had all gone too far and we needed to step back and think. Philip came round to the house and was in two minds. He felt wait until tomorrow. TB said it would be a disaster for me if I did that. Charlie Falconer, who called me re the inquiry, said I would be mad to do it. All people would remember is Dr Kelly killed himself and AC went. They would not hear your arguments and they'd think you were making it about you. TB called a couple of times and said we have to be really strong about this. I said I'm fed up being strong, I want to get a life back. There was a mass of photographers outside by now. I called Neil [Kinnock], who clearly didn't know about Kelly and was telling me that Gilligan was done for. I told him re Kelly and he said Jesus H Christ. I said what to do. He said hold tight, be strong and don't let the bastards take you as a scalp. He said he would support me whatever but felt I had to do that. Peter M came on, said I must not go, now or in the future, because that was what they all wanted. You must hang in. Charlie F said I'd be mad if I quit, Peter M said I'd regret it, TB thought it would be really bad for me, Godric that it would look like my fault. Jonathan called from the US, said he felt physically sick, and should he come back to help? I said no, he said don't do anything rash. Rebekah [Wade, *Sun* editor] sent me a nice message, you've done nothing wrong, told the truth, more principles than these other people. Just hang in and don't give them the satisfaction. Piers [Morgan] was not totally unsympathetic but felt there was no escape for me or for Tony. He felt the mood had just turned, and people would keep going on it. I was the story and that was that even though it was unfair. Fiona was desperate for me to go. So was I now. But I wanted some honour and dignity. Things quietened down but then I wept because of the pressures I was under, and the sadness I felt for Kelly's family. JP called after his return and said he would be around to help if needed. The rolling news was relentless and really grim. Everyone feeling grim about it all. I said to journalists who got through on the phone that I was shocked and felt dreadful, it was about our media culture, but I had done nothing wrong.

Saturday, July 19

The papers, as expected, were totally grim, the *Mail* needless to say the worst, pictures of TB, Hoon and me and 'Proud Of Yourselves?' Lots re me and suggestions that I would get the blame. The *Mail* was disgusting, the *Telegraph* less so. The only person who came out well was Kelly. There was not nearly enough directed towards the BBC. Cameras started gathering outside at 6 and by 9 there were four or five film crews and a dozen or so photographers. We had to go through the elaborate charade of getting the kids and Fiona out first and then being driven to meet them. I got Mel [Cooke, a neighbour] to drive me away, and she said she had always had a fantasy about being a getaway driver. The mood of the hacks was reasonably sombre but they still asked if I planned to resign, and later that cunt Jonathan Oliver [*Mail on Sunday* reporter] asked TB if he had blood on his hands. During the day, lots of people called with messages of support. John Reid, who said his secretary was really angry and hang in. Kim Howells – don't let the bastards get you down, because lots of our people love you. Margaret Beckett said she was really angry the media could blame me when this was about the media. Blunkett – solidarity and support. Bruce Grocott of course, Syd Young [former *Mirror* journalist], Richard Stott, [Roy] Greenslade [former editor of the *Daily Mirror*] who all said this was about the curse of modern journalism. But the most important conversation was with JP. He'd come back yesterday and did a little doorstep at the Policy Forum. I asked him what he thought I should do. He said I hope you stay because you're a vital part of the team and I think TB still needs you. But everyone will be giving you advice because of what THEY want, not what's best for you. You've been under massive pressure for years, paid a big price and so has Fiona, who has lost her sparkle. I've noticed you've been a bit detached and so has she and you should do what you think is right for you. I asked if he thought I could go before the inquiries were completed and he said no. But then as with David Mills, he came round to it being possible. Clive Hollick called me, said he'd been to a BBC do last night and they were all very bullish, behaving arrogantly like it was their duty to bring down the government. He said Dyke was defensive and non-apologetic, but did say they were thinking of making clear Gilligan's only source was Kelly, and they wanted to know what we would do about it. I said we would not make any comment, and TB later said we must not cause them any mischief. TB was looking haggard and unshaven as they arrived in Japan. I was feeling very down by now. Much of the press gunned at me. Brendan Foster [former athlete, friend of AC] called and said he felt TB should do more, be more human and emotional, make clear nobody wanted this to happen. He told me the story of a journalist who killed himself, and at the time a colleague got the blame but in fact it turned out the guy's wife had left him with their children. He said the point is that people who kill themselves are disturbed, and they say things in suicide notes and final conversations that can haunt other people for ever. He felt strongly that I should not do anything rash and hang in for now. The Kelly family issued a statement which basically said everyone should think deeply about the fact his life had been made intolerable. This would obviously be a hard time. TB called. It was 5am there. He said he couldn't sleep, he felt grim and

July '03: TB looking haggard

was about to do an interview with Boulton, which he didn't want to do. He said I had to stay and we had to fight this through.

Sunday, July 20

I spoke to Godric on the flight from Korea to China to tell him I wanted to make clear publicly that I was going to go very soon, say that it was agreed with TB ages ago, and the family had had enough. I said to GS that I would quite like to do it tomorrow, with the BBC on the back foot. TB called from Shanghai on the way from the airport to the hotel, and said it was a mad idea. I said it was not. It was a good thing for me and a good thing for him. He said don't do it. I know what you're worried about, you're worried that it's not going to happen, that you'll go at a time not of your choosing, with them hounding you out. But it's a big moment this, and if you don't do it properly, it will be a real problem. It's just mad. They're on the defensive, let the stuff about the BBC sink in and then do it when I get back. If you do it when I'm out of the country it will be even worse. It will look like I was not involved and you bounced me. If you want to do it, fine, but I promise you it's not a good idea. I said I really had to know I was getting out on my terms. I said I was confident about the inquiries but I was also confident about the FAC and a fat lot of good that did me. He said don't forget that in the end we're all in this together and we have to help each other. He said 'When you leave I want to be able to say that there are two ACs, the one parts of the media portray and the one I know who is a great person.' He said it was better we do that at the end of the week or after you go on holiday. I said OK but I wanted a guarantee. Sky was really going for the BBC though Boulton was still being a total cunt, e.g. in saying I was not totally exonerated because I was chairing intelligence meetings, etc. ITN was OK, but the BBC was like a house magazine. Geoff H called, said he was determined to go to the Grand Prix because he was not having his life dictated by the worst excesses of the British media. Quite right. Once the dust settled I would have to deal with the BBC etc and I would have no stomach for it all. I hated these people. The BBC/*Mail* link was now beyond the pale.

Monday, July 21

The day was largely taken up with going through the Clare Sumner/ Catherine Rimmer file. [Lord] Hutton[1] was announcing his plans at 10.30 and it was clear he would go as wide as he wanted and do most

[1] Chaired the inquiry into the circumstances surrounding the death of Dr Kelly.

of it in public. He looked far too Tory for me, though as Fiona said, that might mean he was pro-war whereas a left-wing judge almost certainly would not be. Peter M was terrific on *Today*, skewering Humphrys on what he said on May 29 about the Gilligan story and Humphrys was very defensive. Geoff Hoon was page 1 of the *Mail* for being at the Grand Prix. He said to me last night he didn't really want to do the job if his family had to live life according to the morals of the immoral *Daily Mail*. Omand came over at 3 for another meeting, at which he was much more formal and said Hutton would want us to send a consolidated account but each person would have to give evidence on their own account. There was a real possibility of this going in any direction and of course the BBC were clearly now going to suggest that Kelly did say all these things. Clive Hollick called to say would it be sensible for me to see Greg Dyke for a private chat. I felt probably not. The press was trying to put the focus on who put the name in the public domain and going for the fact that the MoD said they would confirm the name if it was put to them. Tom Kelly did the 11 o'clock with a fairly straight bat. Meetings for two hours or so. Omand setting up a little team to work full-time on the inquiry while we were on holiday. It was going to be tough. The BBC were trying to maintain that the Susan Watts [BBC journalist] story was the same as the Gilligan story. It wasn't. It was a softer version. Ditto Gavin Hewitt [BBC journalist].

Tuesday, July 22
Fiona has a real downer on me at the moment. I said surely you can understand the pressure I'm under at the moment. She said a lot of it was of my own making because I went from one obsession to the next and she feared I would never change. TB said we had set up the inquiry and now had to shut down on all this, stop commenting, stop engaging with the media on it. But then, later in the day, he went down the plane to talk to the hacks, despite me warning Godric no good would come of it. And he said he did not authorise the leaking of the name. He had been caught on a classic 'When did you stop beating your wife?' type question and rose to it. But it meant more pressure on me and Geoff Hoon. I could not believe he had done that. I was pissed off with him, and with the people with him for letting him talk to the hacks. There was just no point in the current atmosphere. He should do the formal press events and nothing else. I also felt it would make it much harder for me to leave on Friday. JP called. He said he had been thinking about my situation. It was obviously a case of when not if I was leaving now and he just wanted to say I

should make that judgement in my own interests. He said I had given a phenomenal amount to the government and the party and I was owed that at least. I should decide how and when to depart, and he would be around to speak up for me whenever that was. He also called Fiona with the same message. I called GH, said I couldn't believe TB had dropped us in it like that. I don't think he meant to, but they were all taking his statement as *he* didn't authorise it but someone else – GH or AC – did. Later came news that Uday and Qusai (Saddam's sons) were dead. Charles Clarke called. He said you should not leave. There is a lot of respect for you out there, even among the people who attack you, and I think you will regret going.

I set off for King's Cross then off to Retford. Mum looked really bad. She had lost half a stone in the last few weeks and was clearly worrying herself silly about me. I said I'm not losing sleep or losing weight so there's no need for anyone else to. But she was finding it tough. She said every time she turned on the telly news or the radio, someone was having a dig. She said she wouldn't be happy till I was out of it. She wouldn't have that long to wait. TB called from Hong Kong. 'Well, you dropped a bollock today,' I said. He said I know, I should never have gone down the plane. Paul Eastham [*Mail*] had said 'Why did you authorise the leaking of the name?' And he got provoked. It was leading the news, a great frenzy unleashed around it. The atmospherics meant it was terrible if anyone ever suggested the name should have been out there. Truth was there was a case for it being said – what WAS Kelly doing talking to journalists? Did he in fact say more? TB said the whole thing felt Dreyfusian. I felt it was a cross between Kafka and Orwell. He couldn't work out what the public really made of it. It wasn't good but he felt they would know there was something wrong about the media reporting of it all. He agreed it was impossible for me to resign on Friday now. He felt at the end of the holiday, or around publication of the ISC report, or maybe announce in August, and go at conference because I was still popular in the party. He intended to go ahead with the public service delivery press conference on Wednesday. He felt it was important the public saw we were still focused on the business of governing. He had spoken to Charles Powell recently, who told him of the day they told Thatcher the Tories had slipped to third in the polls during Westland. You just have to keep going. I put him onto Mum and they had a nice little chat. He said people underestimated the toll on families when someone was going through the media mill. She said she had lost half a stone with worry but he was doing a great job and keep going. It cheered her up a bit and she was telling everyone that he'd been talking to her. It was an odd irony that Paul Eastham had inadvertently postponed my departure. Shame I couldn't let the silly fucker know.

Wednesday, July 23
I talked to Charlie F, who said he felt it was very hard for a judge not to be influenced by the one-sided nature of the media debate. He said that even he, after TB's ridiculous outburst on the plane, assumed it meant that what he was saying was that HE hadn't authorised leaking the name, but Geoff or I had via a strategy put together without TB's knowledge. I was genuinely shocked. I said 'Christ, Charlie, don't tell me you actually believe it?' He said what he knew was that we were losing the PR battle. That was because the media framed the debate the whole time to suit the BBC line. It was also because we had announced the inquiry and then vacated the field, whereas the BBC were at it the whole time. He felt we should be explaining the broader context – Kelly's fear it would come out, his worry about a cover-up, suicide not something anyone ever imagined would happen. Jonathan said there was no way Tebbit would do that kind of statement. He felt we just had to trust the judge. He felt there was a chance the judge would be getting irritated because it was so obvious what the media were up to. I was worrying about whether me having told *The Times* that the other papers had the name would become a problem, whether it would be thought to contribute to the outing. I knew I'd done nothing wrong but in the frenzied atmosphere it could so easily be misinterpreted. The BBC briefed that Susan Watts had Kelly on tape and we were able to say we thought that would be good for us because her story had been very different to Gilligan's even though the BBC spin machine was trying to make out something different. It was all getting nasty though. Fiona was getting letters saying what's it like sleeping with a murderer. I was getting letters with fake blood on the envelopes. Geoff Hoon visiting Mrs Kelly was the main story. The media were on autopilot, presenting it as her having a go at him over the way the MoD handled him. He called me later and said they had had a really good chat, she was very friendly and very strong. He said she wanted to get a message to me that the way I was being hounded by the press was an outrage. I was really touched by that. I thought again about writing to her but worried about how she would feel about that now the inquiry was on its way. Geoff said he found the meeting really moving. The family was nice and he left feeling a lot better than when he went in. Not that that would remotely be reflected.

Thursday, July 24

TB called me up to the flat and said he felt pretty chirpy, that apart from the press they had a good trip. He was in two minds about whether I should go now or a bit later. He was clear it had to be planned properly, and seen to be as much about the nature of the media as about us. He said what the media had managed to do was define me as the epitome of a political culture that they represent and which I had spent my career fighting – distorting, manipulating, lying, spinning control freaks. He felt they had to be challenged on that basis. Both he and Godric felt that once I had gone there was a chance of getting the debate onto that basis. TB said his and my interests on this were convergent – I wanted to be able to go in a position where people felt I had something to say that was significant, and he wanted me to be able to do that too, and give him the space to make change and challenge the culture. He said to me later that there was a part of him that felt I WAS being driven out by the media, or at least by the state of my relations with them. He was a bit gobsmacked at how offside Fiona was. He was perfectly nice but a part of him was obviously calculating how to use my departure while at the same time keeping me on board should he want to call on me. He said he would be very surprised if we didn't end up speaking most days, and most weeks that he would hope I would put something down on paper. He saw Geoff H, told him he had no worries about his future, that we would tough this out.

Geoff came to see me afterwards and I told him I had agreed with TB back in April I would go and nothing had happened since that made me want to change my mind. He said if I went, he felt it would be a disaster. TB was great, so were lots of people around him, but 'one thing that people know about you is that you give good advice and you're never afraid to say what he doesn't want to hear'. I said that my mind was made up and I was telling him because I knew the media would try to up the pressure on him without me there. He was pretty much a total Blairite, a decent bloke. I felt I was dropping him in it a bit. On Kelly though, he said he was absolutely confident of the outcome of the inquiry. I then did a ring round of the people in the know to get their views on us doing this tomorrow. Fiona said yes, Tony said yes. I called Neil, who said everything in him said no. I called in Godric and Tom. They said no, that it would be seen as an admission of guilt to go right now. I had a chat with Phil Webster [*Times*], who felt the same. Then to a TB meeting with Omand, Scarlett, Jonathan, Jeremy, Matthew Rycroft [Number 10 official], Catherine R, Tom and Godric. There were mixed reports of what Hutton was like. Jonathan said

Adams and Trimble were united for once – in saying he was dreadful. He was an Ulster puritan, but nobody knew if that helped or hindered. It was a fairly sober meeting, because the truth was none of us knew where or how this would end, and it was fraught with risk. We went over all the background material we would need, and the areas we would need to prepare on. I called Ann Taylor [chair of the ISC] as she was about to board a ferry in Newhaven and told her in confidence I was going to leave. I was thinking about when, and felt that if the ISC report was going to clear me, that might be the time to do it. She said she was hoping to publish during the two weeks in September when Parliament was sitting. She couldn't go into content but we could speak nearer the time. Skinner called to tell me that the NEC had turned on Tony Robinson [NEC member] who had said we should be nice to the BBC. Skinner said they had to support AC 'because he's probably against the war anyway' and the party should support him against all the lies and distortions against us. He'd also had a pop at Mark Seddon [NEC member] for writing for the *Mail*. 'I'm not listening to anyone who writes for the fuckin' enemy.' My own mailbag was running around 6 to 1 in my favour though there were some pretty unpleasant ones among the antis. The FAC put out a statement saying that at Gilligan's request they would not be publishing a transcript of his evidence in the private session but sending a copy to Hutton. I bumped into Gisela Stuart [Labour MP]. She said it would be terrible to publish it now because it showed both Gilligan and Kelly had got it wrong, though Gilligan was worse.

I got home and Fiona was walking down the stairs as I walked through the door. 'I've been fired,' she said. 'What?' She said CB had called and said she felt she ought to leave soon. She accused Fiona of briefing against her, which Fiona said was ridiculous though she accepted there had been a breakdown of trust between them. She was really upset that CB could think as she did. She was due to go out to the ballet and I said just try not to worry about it, Cherie will regret what she said. I watched the 10 o'clock news, and Marr opining that a world without me – i.e. post-spin – would be the best thing both for the media and Number 10. Not a word about the Gilligan transcript. Marr had become a PR man for the Beeb, nothing else. So the news was basically GH not commenting followed by a tendentious two-way about me.

Friday, July 25

I told TB about CB's call and said it was unforgivable that she spoke to Fiona like that after all she'd done for her. He said people were too fraught at the moment and Cherie was feeling under pressure. I said she needed to apologise, otherwise there would be badness between them that helped nobody. He said the problem at the moment is that the public will begin to wonder whether we are governing the country. All they hear is all this stuff about personalities, process and the rest and they start to wonder if that's all we do. There was a case for me going right now, but I was tired and I needed a holiday to marshal the arguments and get things in a better place first. He said he was still finding it hard to imagine life without me being around the whole time. I said I would be available to help, but in a different way. He once thought he needed Peter around the whole time, but he didn't, provided he could call on him. It would be the same with me. Peter M joined us and he and I were chatting away while TB was just looking out of the window, a bit vacant. After a while, he said 'I can't see the way to rebuilding trust unless we find WMD. And at the moment I don't see how we regain momentum.' Peter and I said things would look very different after a break, also that he needed to get focused on conference, where we always seemed to get things back on an even keel. We agreed that for Wednesday's press conference he should say the focus was public services and anything at all re Iraq he should just say wait for Hutton. Peter M was being very helpful and supportive, in his usual spiky way. He said it was poignantly ironic that he should be helping me plan my departure when I had so spectacularly been responsible for his 'defenestration'. It was to his credit though that apart from the odd joke, he'd never really shown bitterness at his second resignation, and still helped when I was the one needing support.

Catherine R was doing a great job getting the materials together for Hutton. David Omand seemed a bit too laid back, saying everyone should go away and have a good holiday. The BBC were still spinning away madly and of course would carry on using their output to help shape their case. It would take a very strong mind not to be influenced. Dyke wrote to TB claiming a Cabinet minister had told Marr there would be 'revenge'. TB drafted a pretty rough reply which Peter felt we shouldn't send. Peter M asked if I was going to conference. I hope not, I said. 'Who will write your speech?' he asked TB. 'Alastair and I will,' he said. 'He'll have more time if he's not doing everything else.' TB went off to Chequers and I called in all my staff. I said that they'd all have been hearing and reading all this stuff. I wanted them to know I was going to use the holiday to decide what to do. I said whatever decision I took, I was proud of the team I had built and grateful for the phenomenal support they gave me, but ultimately a decision like this had to be for me and the family, and a holiday was the right place to make it. I could tell that they knew where it was heading. [David] Bradshaw came to see me later, and seemed close to tears. He said people in here would be devastated if I went, that I underestimated how much of what they all did they did for me, because I made it a great place to work, and I took all the hits for them, and let them take risks. He said nobody ever understood how I managed to do the job the way I did, but he was worried if I stopped doing it, the place would collapse. Gone was his usual mickey-taking Scouse humour, and in its place an impassioned plea to stay. But I think he knew it would fall on deaf ears, though I was really touched by his warmth and trust.

We went for dinner at the Blackburns'. Peter M there too and we were really going for a couple of people there who were close friends of Tom Bower and Veronica Wadley [husband and wife, journalists]. They seemed shocked by the strength of our hatred of Dacre. I said your friend Wadley works for the most poisonous influence in British life. He and his papers are evil. They add nothing of good to the world whatever. I was confident of being cleared by Hutton but wish he'd had the *Mail on Sunday* in there too. They hid behind the BBC. David Blackburn got the plot re the BBC, had followed it closely and could see all the holes in their arguments. He said he felt it was possible that I would be vindicated but also that Gilligan would not be condemned.

Wednesday, July 30 (holiday, Puyméras, Provence)
Writing by Philip and Gail's pool. Everyone has gone to Vaison to get bikes. Feeling a pretty big sense of foreboding. Catherine Rimmer just texted me to say the first question at TB's press conference was about me and my future. No doubt they're going to try to keep me as a big issue for him. JP very nice about me on the *Today* programme apparently. Michael Barber [public service delivery adviser] did his delivery slides presentation at the press conference, and did it well by all accounts, but it was unlikely to get much coverage. They couldn't give two tosses about the public service agenda. CR said the public services slide show had been excellent punishment for the hacks. The other major soap event was Carole C, who had done a big picture spread in *Hello!* magazine, which the press were going big on. Sally called me, said she had been to see TB yesterday and told him 'that woman' is going to destroy you if you do not sort it out. She said TB went mad at her, saying it was ridiculous how we were all against Carole. I think TB just liked her, and liked the fact she had been a help to CB, but there wasn't one of us who didn't find it a bit odd. I was feeling fairly detached. We

had a more or less painless journey down and the kids were on good form. I had meanwhile decided that I would pretty much leave as soon as we got back from holiday, the reasons as per the note I had done earlier. I felt I could continue to advise from outside on strategy and maybe do election planning. I would make speeches to make a living, write on sport and politics after a while, also do more on the leukaemia fund-raising front and motivational stuff for the party. I had a vague notion of getting involved with the ad agency. Maybe do a chat show but it might be difficult because part of the public argument I intend to make is how awful modern TV has become. I was not going to be short of offers but I had decided no to the consultancy and lobbying route. Just not my thing. PG felt I needed to strike while the iron was hot re the US speaking scene.

On the Saturday I had a long chat with Alex F, who was out in the States. I told him I was definitely leaving now. 'Give my congratulations to Fiona,' he said. 'Maybe I gave you the wrong advice. Maybe you should have left when you first thought of it, but the one thing nobody can ever take from you is that you know you've done a great job, and you should now do what is right for you and the family. You've given enough.' Catherine Rimmer was keeping me in touch with the Hutton team. It now seemed Hutton would read himself in, then take witnesses from the 11th to the 18th, first the MoD, then the BBC, then others, then reflect, maybe re-interview, report maybe in October. So it was definitely going to be another interrupted holiday. Also the whole conference season would have Hutton as the backdrop. I was now reaching a settled feeling about leaving – I felt excited at the prospect of new and different things to do. It would be nice for the family as a whole that I travelled less, saw them more, and could earn decent money. I sometimes felt I had been pressured by Fiona, but equally I knew she had my interests as well as her own at heart. But I also knew I would need to stay involved in some way, not least because I still felt at my best I was the best, and could make a contribution. It's just that I hadn't been at my best for a while. I also felt sad at the thought my team would break up. As I whirred things round in my mind it was clear for the first time I was thinking more about my own future than TB's. I would help if I could but he would have to help himself.

Thursday, July 31

Catherine Rimner kept the faxes coming thick and fast. She called again to say that Hutton wanted to see me and Jonathan on August 21. I had been hoping to be able to see out the holiday but no luck.

We now had to work out how best to get myself fully briefed and also properly psyched up. It put a real dampener on things and Fiona was even more pissed off now. Ross [Kemp, actor] and Rebekah [Wade] came over and we had a nice enough time with them. They, along with Gail and PG, felt I was on strong ground but I felt Hutton would feel he had to make some criticism of everyone. Philip felt TB had panicked in calling an inquiry. Kelly killed himself because he killed himself and we should have held our nerve. He was pretty down on TB at the moment.

Friday, August 1

The *Guardian* had the Gilligan transcript, which did not do him much good and suggested he was backing off the central allegations against me. John Stanley and Eric Illsley gave him a very hard time on it. Rachel Kinnock was due out so I was getting a new package of briefing material to come out with her. Truth was the holiday was pretty much going down the Swanee but hopefully it would be the last to be like this. Also I was pretty desperate to be cleared and so I had to keep my focus the whole time. I needed to be at my best when I reached the witness stand and a lot of the preparation had to be done now. Hutton did his opening statement at 11, which seemed to be pointing heavily towards the BBC, but it was also clear the manner in which Kelly's name came out was going to be a big part of it. I felt the weight of it all building again. Catherine felt the statement would worry the BBC more than us. Philip felt Hutton came across as clear and strong and it was important I came over as being clear and strong. Later I spoke to Omand and Charlie F. CF said he felt there was no need to be too nervous but Hutton was not someone to be pushed around.

Sunday, August 3

I read the Kelly MoD interviews, which were pretty good for our case. I had had another night waking up, tossing and turning. I then just lay there waiting for the church bells to ring, and every time came the thought that they'd toll for me. Fiona was being very supportive and keeping the kids' spirits up but it was like we had a big dark cloud over us the whole time.

Tuesday, August 5

Peter M in the *Sunday Mirror* had said TB was clear we would be OK. I sent a message round the system saying we should all just shut up. The *Indy* yesterday splashed on Number 10 describing Kelly as a Walter Mitty character. I told the office we had to disown it very forcibly at the 11 o'clock, which Anne Shevas, who hated doing the briefings, duly did. But it emerged that it was Tom Kelly who had said it, when chatting to Paul Waugh [*Independent* journalist]. He had been going over the questions Hutton would want to look at, had not remotely intended it to run as a story and now it was the latest frenzy. I said he should apologise and drop a line both to Mrs Kelly and to Hutton. PG and Gail thought it was a bad idea to involve the widow because we had no clue as to how she would react. I had earlier drafted a letter to Mrs Kelly myself and discussed with JP whether he thought I should send it. He felt the sentiments were fine but you could never tell how people in grief and shock would react. He said he would take it to the funeral and make a judgement then as to whether to give it to her. There was no other major story around at the moment so several of the papers splashed on Tom on the Tuesday. He was feeling wretched and I called him to say not to worry too much about it. I got a message through to TB to call him too.

The office sent through my ISC evidence, which I had to sign off. Again I felt confident in the facts. Neil could tell though how nervous I was. He said I could not bottle up something like this and if I wanted to talk to him at any time, he was there. He was very warm and supportive and also lifting a lot of the pressure on the family too. Even though Fiona and the kids were still doing all the things we do on holiday they were clearly feeling the tension a fair bit. Philip felt the problem was that the media were effectively running this as the government on trial. The press were helping the BBC to reframe the debate in their favour, without vacating the field, so that they were both player but also 'neutral' spectator. JP went to Kelly's funeral and called me afterwards. He said Mrs Kelly had been fine with him, had not been seeking to blame the government for his death, which made me feel a lot better. I was starting to work on my own statement. I was not impressed with the advice we were getting from the Cabinet Office about lawyers.

Thursday, August 7

We had dinner in Malaucene with Ian and Andrea Kennedy. I was looking forward to getting some hard-headed and objective advice from Ian about how to approach it. His chairing of the Bristol babies inquiry had been seen as pretty good, and he was always very good on problem solving generally. He felt, based on what he had read in the press, that I was fine on the substance. But he was amazed that

I did not already have my own lawyer, and he was really pressing me to get my act together, or get the Cabinet Office to get theirs together. He said he had advised everyone involved in Bristol to have their own lawyer. What would happen, he asked, if the nub came down to a difference of opinion between, say, me and Geoff Hoon, or me and John Scarlett? Was I really saying there would just be one government lawyer representing everyone? He thought it was ridiculous. I was already feeling pretty sick, having heard from the Inquiry team that the judge wanted me to give him my diaries, or at least any relevant extracts. The request came as a real shock. Sandra Powell [secretary] had called me to read through all the various areas he wished to ask me about, and as she ran through them, I felt absolutely fine. It was only when she faxed through the letter that I noted at the end this request to see anything from my diaries. Ian thought it was probably just a fishing expedition but now not only was I worried – as I said to Fiona, Christ knows what I've written in there – but I was also beginning to panic a little about what Ian had said re the need for my own lawyer. I was very pleased Ian would be around.

Friday, August 8

Ian got hold of Alan Maclean, who had been one of his legal team for the Bristol inquiry, and made arrangements for him to come out next week. I called the Cabinet Office and asked for a list of lawyers to choose from. Rosemary Jeffreys [Treasury Solicitor's Department] gave me a list but of course what we didn't know was who was available and this was the worst time imaginable to be trying to find one. I put a call into James Goudie [QC] for his advice, also Charlie F and Derry, and TB. Charlie in particular thought I would not get on with Jonathan Sumption, who was the one Alan Maclean and Ian were recommending. The general view was that he was right wing, a bit quirky and someone who would want things done his way. Charlie felt we were both strong characters who would get on each other's nerves. Ian was strongly of the view that if Alan was saying he was the best, and also as his reputation was so strong, we should try to get him. Alan got on to his clerk. It transpired Sumption was staying at his place in France, and had indicated immediately he was keen to do it. I was also trying to sort the shipping out of my diary for this year. The summer holiday is the one time of the year when I don't take it with me, and instead just scribble a few notes every now and then when I feel like it. Poor old Audrey had to get into the house, root around under the bed and then get the book to Number 10. Originally the plan was to get it shipped out with books that were being sent out for Gail but her stuff was coming out late so Number 10 had to sort it out. I was now finding it really hard to sleep. The request for my diaries felt like a hostile act to me. I suspected I was the only one being asked to do this. And why? – because the papers had said I kept a diary. Why isn't everyone asked if they keep a personal diary, and to provide any relevant bits?

Sunday, August 10

I had received the request for my diary on Thursday and now, finally, this year's was being flown out by Peter Howes [duty clerk]. As I left the house, and said goodbye to Fiona, I did actually wonder momentarily whether it would be the last time I saw her, whether what I discovered on reading my own diary would be so awful that I would want to top myself. It was only a passing thought, but it was there, and it came back several times as I drove down to Marseille. I knew I had done nothing wrong, but in this climate, things had gone beyond reason, it was like a drama or a novel, and nobody had control of events. I tried not to be in a panic on the drive down, but I was. I couldn't remember what I wrote in my diary the minute I wrote it. On the few occasions I ever looked back, I was always surprised at things that happened, things I said, things other people had said. I just didn't know. I met Simon Lever [Consul General] as we waited for Peter to come through. I managed to hide any nerves I had from Peter, who was dressed like he was just having a nice day trip to an airport on an aeroplane. But inside I was feeling sick. He handed me the package and I set off back to the car. I put it on the passenger seat, thought about opening it there and then but the car was hot and I wanted to get away from the airport. I drove for maybe half an hour and then pulled into a service station.

It was now unbelievably hot. I opened the envelope slowly and then pulled out the diary, put it down again and just stared at it. What I had written in there, or so I felt, had the capacity to deliver vindication or destruction. One bad word, and who knows, for me, for Tony, for the whole bloody government. When I thought of some of the things I've said in there about ministers, about colleagues, about the press, about the BBC. By the time I finally started flicking through it, I was sweating. It was now so hot that even in the shade of a few trees, the sweat was falling down my face. I found the various sections on the dossier. At first glance, it seemed fine, and I started to feel a bit better. There was certainly nothing I could see that would mean I would have to resign straight away. A few bad bits, a bit too colourful in parts, but overall manageable. The best thing was that in terms of all the facts in there, they supported what we had been saying about events. It then suddenly dawned on me I had made a terrible mistake. I had been so focused on Kelly's death, which was after all the subject of the inquiry, that I had only got this year's diary sent out, when of course it was last year that the dossier was put together and it was clear from the inquiry team's letter that was absolutely central. I felt sick all over again. What an idiotic thing to do.

As I sat there, feeling a mixture of relief that my cursory flick through had revealed nothing terrible, and anger at my own stupidity in not getting both diaries sent out, the phone went. It was Number 10 with Godric. When I told him what I was doing, he was horrified. He said he thought it was unbelievable that he was asking for my diaries. Like me he saw it as a hostile act. Maybe, he says, it shows he basically buys into the media line on us. Godric was so principled and proper, and a believer in playing fair, that he seemed if anything even more shocked and upset than I was. He made the same point I had – why hasn't everyone been asked if they keep a diary? But anyway, we were beyond that. He then got more and more anxious as I told him what I was organising on the legal front. He said that he had heard nothing from the Cabinet Office other than the fact he would have to give evidence. He had had the same conversation I had had with Omand on the day Hutton set out his terms, namely take a bit of a break and see what happens. It was, as Charlie F had also observed, a bit Heath Robinson. Godric was asking whether I thought he should go back straight away. I could tell that I had ruined his holiday, if it wasn't already ruined.

I got home, and we went out to Villedieu for the evening. Ian said he really thought I should put my fate in the hands of a good team of lawyers now, stop trying to make all the decisions myself, stop relying on the government or the Cabinet Office. He said Alan was terrific. Sumption was now on board and he described him as having 'a brain the size of a planet'. I also now had Adam Sharples from the Treasury Solicitor's office. After Fiona and the kids had gone to bed, I went back through the diary, read it all more slowly and in more detail. The thought of it all being put before the inquiry did not exactly fill me with joy, but it wasn't the disaster I feared. I was kicking myself though re not getting 2002 sent out. I wasn't even sure where it was, so poor old Audrey was going to have to look around the house and we'd have to go through the whole process again.

August '03: Preparing for Hutton/more diaries needed

Wednesday, August 13

Ian had really acted as a fantastic catalyst in getting a proper legal team together. Alan Maclean was staying with the Kennedys at Faucon and I met him briefly last night. He said he, Sumption and Adam Chapman [government lawyer] had read the papers on the train from Toulouse to Avignon, where the other two were staying overnight. He said they had concluded that there were only two fundamental questions for me – 1. did I play around with the dossier on the 45-minute point and 2. did I play a part in a conspiracy re Kelly? He said they all three of them felt, based on all the material they had read, that the answer was no to both. He said Sumption was very clear about it. 'He has pretty much decided that you are the cowboys and the BBC are the Indians.' He said Sumption was reflecting overnight on how we handle the issue of the diary request. I went over to the Kennedys' this morning. Alan and Andrea were getting the printouts on the Inquiry from the Internet. We were into the third day and the BBC case appeared to be falling apart. Gilligan by all accounts a poor witness, Susan Watts to her credit refusing to toe their line and so making things worse for the BBC. The MoD seemed to be doing OK in stressing that they did what they could for Kelly.

Sumption and Adam Chapman arrived a bit late. He [Sumption] was not at all what I expected. I'd expected someone rather over-bearing, tall, smooth. He seemed a bit shy and nervy, as though a comfortable holiday home was not really the place for this kind of thing. He had a mass of all over the place grey hair. His clothes didn't quite hang together. He was carrying a biography of Keynes. We got down to business straight away and I took to him fairly easily, despite all the warnings. He was sharp, to the point, and very clear. He repeated the view Alan had expressed, about the two main questions, and said matter-of-factly 'I don't think you have to worry about that.' He was also very direct about my diary. He said the Prime Minister has established an inquiry, Lord Hutton has been appointed, the PM has said he and his staff will cooperate fully, and this is an example of the judge asking for full cooperation. He felt it would be a very bad move to refuse to provide it, or to seek to frame an argument as to why I should. He said the judge would not appreciate it, so I should just accept I would have to do it, and take whatever heat came from it. It was what I had been expecting to hear, and in any event I had already gone through the pain barrier on that one. On the draft statement I had done, he felt it was fine, in that all the relevant facts were in there, but both he and Ian felt it was too personal and too emotional. All the judge would want is fact. Adam and Alan worked on my statement while Jonathan S and I sat at the dining room table and went through my diary. He felt that he would have to be the judge of what Lord Hutton would deem to be relevant to the inquiry. In terms of what went in, and what stayed out, even though we did not know what Hutton intended to do with this stuff, and even before Sumption knew what I had written, he was at the broader end of the margin. I was sort of hoping that his attitude would be 'When in doubt, keep it out'. It was the opposite. He clearly felt that the more open we were, the fairer the judge would be. I read through page after page, putting pencil marks through the bits he felt were irrelevant, but also making notes in the margins of the vague subject matter to show he had been through it. Occasionally he would have a doubt but would usually say 'No harm including it.' Some days there was nothing relevant at all, on other days a line or two. At other times, virtually everything would go in. Obviously TB, other departments and the Agencies were going to have to see this, and that would maybe have its own problems, but I had now pretty much decided that I was going to take Ian's advice to take this guy's advice, unless it clashed with TB's interests, and as the day wore on, that seemed less and less likely. I found the whole experience really stressful though, going over all the same ground again, not just Iraq, but the other big policy nightmares, TB–GB, Cherie and Carole, also some of the rows with Fiona, some of the guilt at not being there enough, some of the other political stuff, the hatred of some of the media, the pressure, the agonising at my own situation. When the kids came round later in the day, I also felt a growing sense of injustice that I was the only witness having to do this, when I wanted to be having a normal holiday with the family, and after they went down to the pool, I just started sobbing. 'I'm sorry,' I said to Sumption, whose expression didn't really change. 'It's alright,' he said. 'I totally understand why this is difficult.' I said I don't understand why this is happening to me. He said 'If I were you, I would feel that too. It is dreadful that you are being asked to bare your soul when in my view you have done nothing wrong. But the Prime Minister set up the inquiry and you have to cooperate with the judge when he asks for this. If he thinks your diary may contain something which helps him, he is entitled to ask for it, warts and all.'

I composed myself pretty quickly, and we went back to the task in hand. It took five or so hours, and I felt totally drained at the end. 'So how was that voyage of discovery for you?' I asked him. 'It was certainly a discovery. I have read so much about you. Now I think I know you. In fact I don't think I've ever learned so much about someone so quickly.' He writes books on medieval history and he said 'I wish there had been people keeping records like this in those days. It would make my life so much easier.' He felt there was something 'wonderfully Victorian about it'. He said it would one day be an amazing service to historians, 'but I can see why that does not hold much appeal to you right now'. It was an odd experience, to have sat down with a total stranger, and gone through so much detail of my own life and work, and at the end of it to be talking as though we had known each other for ages. I noticed he hadn't shaved properly, and as the day wore on his clothes seemed to get scruffier, but I felt by the end of the day that I was with someone who knew what he was doing.

In the ensuing days, first Jeremy [Heywood] – on TB's behalf – and then TB himself came on to say they didn't agree with Sumption's strategy re the diaries. They felt it was unfair, but also wrong, to ask someone to submit a private diary to a public inquiry. I could tell TB was really worried about it, not least by the number of times he told me not to worry. But Sumption resisted the pressure. TB's argument was that we should fight harder for me not to have to do this. Sumption was adamant that would backfire badly with the judge – on me, but also on the government. Although he did not articulate it in this way, I saw his strategy was maximum openness for minimum disclosure. We now had to work out process. I was thinking I should probably go home, but Alan felt I should stay here for as long as possible, that if I went back, I would be miserable without the family, would follow the inquiry the whole time, which at the moment I was managing to avoid, and he felt I would do better on the stand if I stayed here than if I went back. I called Alison and asked her to come out and join us, so that I could get the diary extracts properly typed up. She arranged to come out tomorrow. We went for dinner at the Goulds' and I felt so much better.

Sumption went off again. I don't know if it was a joke or not but according to the others he 'owned a village' somewhere in the south west of France. As he left he said I could call him at any time, but he really believed I had nothing to worry about on the substance. I was really worried about the fact I had told *The Times* two other papers had the name but on my first meeting with Sumption he said it didn't matter. Though I felt more at ease with the process, and more confident now I knew I had some decent lawyers involved, I was still not sleeping well, and was feeling real stress not just about the obvious, but also the idea that Fiona and the kids weren't really having much of a holiday with all this going on around them. Every morning now, I was waking up at four or five, waiting for the next ringing of the bells at the village church, and from time to time the old 'ask not for whom the bell tolls ...' lodged in there. It was impossible not to imagine the worst. The kids kept me going really – the thought that eventually we would get a proper family life back again, and the knowledge that no matter how bad it was, apart from the occasional fleeting moment, I did not think of doing what Kelly had done.

Thursday, August 14–Friday/Saturday, August 15/16
TB was calling regularly now, and was clearly getting more and more anxious re my diaries. At first he had been dismissive, saying it was a fuss about nothing, but I sensed that was him trying to make sure I didn't get too worried. Now he was getting more agitated and angry, and strongly disagreed with the Sumption strategy. He felt we should be fighting harder for non-disclosure. I explained Sumption's strategy as I saw it – maximum openness for minimum disclosure and on the substance he thinks on balance that, while there are difficulties in there, it helps our case. Yes, said TB, but you are dealing with lawyers and we are politicians in a political situation. I said yes, and part of the politics is that he set up an independent inquiry and promised full cooperation and we cannot now be seen not to cooperate. What is more, if we refuse and it becomes known, then all hell will break loose again and a lot of it around me. I said I was confident that Sumption's strategy was right and I thought we had no choice. He asked me several times 'What's in these things?' I explained that I was getting Alison out to help me transcribe, but that in Sumption's view there was nothing catastrophic. There was a fair bit of bad language. 'How much?' A fair bit. 'Fuck?' Yes. 'Cunt?' Probably, can't remember. 'Bloody hell, Alastair.' He asked if there was anything disparaging about him, or about ministers. Nothing too bad re him. Lots of criticism of Clare, yes, one or two others. Bits and bobs re him and GB. Me thinking of leaving. Fiona and Cherie. 'What?' Yes, but Sumption did not think any of that needed to be put in. We ended up swapping notes on the extent to which our respective holidays had been ruined. He also said I shouldn't worry, that the diaries sounded more embarrassing than damaging, though by now he was back in 'let's keep AC calm' mode. He called every few hours now, chatting over various things, and eventually I said please let me get on and finish the transcription, and then we can make a judgement as to how bad or not it all is. But he was generally reassuring in these circumstances. He said it was horrible for me, and horrible for all of us, but I should take strength from the fact I had done nothing wrong, and he was confident we would come through this. He said 'What is

the worst thing that can be said against you – that you went over the top? But you had every right to, because these were allegations made directly against you, not just me, and you had every right to defend yourself.' He felt that there was a chance Hutton would decide this was as much a story about our rotten media culture as the nature of government. The inquiry was certainly not going well for the BBC, no matter how hard the media tried to spin it their way. But none of us could really gauge which way Hutton was going. We just had to get on and make our case as best we could.

Alison arrived, bringing with her my 2002 diary, and a quick flick through that also reassured me, in that it showed how much care we had put into the September dossier, and it showed in terms how I tried to ensure the Agencies were happy with every word and every part of the process. Alison and I started to go through the stuff I had gone over with Sumption. It was not as bad as I feared, though there were one or two points where she winced, usually when I was swearing or saying something derogatory about someone, though it was all stuff she had heard before.

We set up in the dining room/lounge bit of the house and worked on it most of Thursday night, all day Friday, when the lawyers went back to London, most of Saturday, as Alison and I travelled back to England by train, and I finally got a full typed version to Sumption at his house in France by Sunday pm, well ahead of the Monday 5pm deadline, though a lot of people would want to see them before then. He had initially secured a delay to my deadline because of the work required transcribing the diaries but then they came back and said No, the original timetable stood, so we had been working flat out to get through it. Thousands of words and he was trying to reach a deal with the inquiry that it would not be submitted as evidence as such, which would then have to be published along with everything else, but as a supplementary statement.

Fiona and the kids had adapted pretty well considering, and were just carrying on doing everything around us, while I was trying to grab a half-hour here, a half-hour there. It was great having Alison out at the house. The kids liked her and once we got going, I realised it was not going to take quite as long as I feared. When I left for home, and my appearance at the inquiry, Fiona was pretty cold with me, said good luck, but with a 'if you'd listened to me, you wouldn't be in this mess' look on her face. 'Sorry for ruining the holiday,' I said. She smiled, shrugged and just said do your best and get back as soon as you can. Grace was crying, and later apparently asked the boys if I could go to jail. Rory went off on a bike ride, I guess to avoid saying goodbye, though he and I had had a good chat earlier. Calum was putting on a brave face and playing the hard man. 'Never forget you're a Campbell, and nobody messes with our family.'

On the train, we had a table to ourselves and so were able to carry on with the transcription, but it meant me whispering into Alison's ear as I dictated and I am sure there were people on there who thought I was at it with her. Then some creep from the *Daily Telegraph*, who I don't think could believe his luck that I was on the train, came up and started to make small talk, pretending to be an ordinary passenger. He was not very convincing. 'Which paper are you from?' Er, the *Telegraph*, I wondered if I could do an interview about your coming appearance at the inquiry, blah blah. 'I'm busy.' Alison had typed for hours and hours on end, God knows how many. Her view was that it wasn't great – particularly the language – but that it did show the kind of pressures we were under and also that we were most of the time just trying to do our best. Ian K emphasised to me again and again that I should trust Sumption, who would be focusing on one thing only – the judge. I had decided to do just that, and though Sumption was happy to argue over a point, and accept my view on things, equally I was happy to listen to him and trust his judgement.

I arrived home and decided to go in through the Farthings' [neighbours] back garden so that the press in the street didn't know I was there. Audrey was looking after me, and had been reading every word. She felt it was not going well for the BBC. But they were really gearing up for me, and they were desperate for me to fail. Peter M called, and said did I have any idea how much the media wanted me to be a disaster in the witness box? TB was calling more regularly from Barbados now. Before the diaries got out to him, he kept asking me the same questions re content. All I could do was give him Sumption's view. He felt they were neither good nor bad. But on the positive side, they underlined our side of the story. They showed I did nothing wrong re the dossier. They showed I got very angry re the BBC, and made very clear why. They did show I wanted to put out Kelly's name, but didn't and instead did as I was told by him [TB]. As for the bad language and the loose language, Sumption's view was that the judge would not take it amiss. This was a private diary and he would understand. The point of substance I was worried about related to where it looked like Geoff Hoon was suggesting a kind of 'plea bargain'. It was becoming clear to me that my lawyers were very much trying to get me to think of myself rather than the government as a whole, and particularly GH. If he had said that, and I recorded it, and it was a problem, it was a problem for him, not me. But I found it hard to

August '03: Preparing for Hutton/avoiding the press

think like that. I saw this still as the government under attack, me included, but also the government as a whole. They felt GH could use a 'cut-throat defence', and go for me, and therefore it was better I go for him, but I was not comfortable with that. I called him on the Thursday or Friday, not sure which, and warned him about the line in my diary that they were calling the 'plea bargain point'. He was in the States on holiday and said he felt a lot better having gone away, despite the advice to stay. I felt he was under similar family pressures to my own. He said he had indeed been intending to throw the book at Kelly but then calmed down and felt his honesty was to be commended and even rewarded in some way. He said he was grateful for my call and did not give me the impression he was worried about his own position.

Sunday, August 17

I was into the office early to go through a mass of material prepared for me by Clare [Sumner] and Catherine [Rimmer], who were both absolutely brilliant. They were so on top of the detail, and so driven by a belief that we were in the right. The diary extracts were circulated internally and also to a few in other departments. TB thought they were fine, though was worried about one or two observations made re him. Jeremy was still passionately of the view that it was just wrong that I had to do this, and we should have fought harder to stop it happening, but things had really moved on from that. I was trying to avoid adding to the big build-up to Tuesday at the inquiry, so I got back home via the neighbours' garden network again. I guessed if they had no new pictures they would give less space. Had they had a camera in the garden they would have got a nice shot of me ripping my trousers, and cutting my leg, on the Farthings' trellis fence. I decided as well that tomorrow I would stay in Number 10, let the press continue to think I was at home, in a hotel, or wherever, just avoid being seen until I have to be. I had a nice dinner with Audrey, just chatting away about the whole thing, what Bob would have made of it, the effect it was all having on my mum and dad. Audrey was a 100 per cent full-on supporter, didn't believe a word against me, hated the BBC for what they'd done, and was not that sympathetic to Kelly, felt he should never have got involved with Gilligan in the first place.

Monday, August 18

I felt OK but reckoned I had now averaged three hours' sleep a night since I got that wretched letter re my diaries. I was going to have to rely on a mix of real preparation, nerve and adrenalin to get me through. TB was working on his own witness statement and remained confident. CR had collated all the various comments from departments about the diaries, and the requests for further redactions from some, including TB. She and I then did a conference call with Sumption, and went through them all. Some he accepted but the bulk he didn't, and he was absolutely clear he was not taking something out just because the Prime Minister wanted it. Jonathan [Powell] was back to give evidence, and I got the feeling he had very deliberately not allowed it to ruin his holiday. The downside meant he was not terribly well prepared and I was worried he was a bit cavalier. He had also grown his usual summer holiday beard and I was urging him to shave it off as it looked a bit ragged. Hutton did not strike me as a beard man. But Jonathan was adamant he was not changing anything just because he had been dragged back for this. He was nervous though, as was I. I noticed at one point a slight shake in his hand, and when the two of us were alone, without the lawyers and researchers around, he let the front down a bit and seemed really quite anxious. He went off and by all accounts did fine.

Stephen Parkinson [government lawyer] came back with Jonathan and then sat down with me for a really helpful, but quite gruelling, Q & A session. I felt by now that I had every word and every argument just about right, and there were no questions I absolutely dreaded. I felt on top of the facts. It was still not clear how the judge or the QC intended to use my diaries which was still a bit of a worry. But there, too, I felt confident I could defend myself, even though there was the odd embarrassment or difficulty in there. I was getting a lot of Good Luck messages coming through, and there was definitely the sense on the media that after TB, I was the one they were really waiting for. In fact for some of them, I was a tastier target than he was, because the thing was coming over now as being about government v media. I was impressed by Parkinson, very calm, very clear, tested my answers well. I was getting lots of advice, not least from TB, re how to deport myself. Always answer the question, not the question you want to answer. Make your answers short answers. Do not waffle or lecture. Don't be worried about pausing, or asking for time to reflect. If you cannot remember, say so. Call him 'My Lord' regularly. Look at him even if he is not looking at you. Be polite to all the lawyers. Above all, do not get riled. I called John Scarlett and made sure he was OK about the various references to him. He said he was fine. It must be dreadful for someone whose entire life has been about secrets, and dependent on staying low profile, now to be so out there in the public domain. He said he wouldn't have wanted it that way but he was sure we had done nothing wrong and it was important we were vindicated. He wished me luck. I said when the lawyer or whoever first uttered the words 'your diary', the press would get out their todgers and have a great collective wank. I went out for a quiet dinner with Gavin [Fiona's brother], Alan Maclean, Clare and Catherine. By the end we were the only people in the restaurant and we had a good laugh, but I was now as nervous as hell. The Number 10 staff had made me up a bed in John Birt's old office. It was fine, but slightly surreal. I got a message that there were people queuing outside the court overnight to try to get in. The thing had become a bloody circus.

Tuesday, August 19

I woke up to the sound of Big Ben. I heard four chimes but looked at my watch, and saw it was 5. I knew I wouldn't get back to sleep. It was so quiet now. I thought of Fiona and the kids asleep in Puyméras. I thought of Mum and Dad, and wondered whether Dad would see out the year. I thought of all the people who had been such a help in recent weeks. I thought about Mrs Kelly, really wished I knew what she really thought about all this. I was nervous but I had gone over everything fully, I was confident there wasn't a single difficult question we hadn't thought of, and I was confident my answers would withstand questioning. I scribbled a few thoughts – push hard on the dossier, express depth of anger at the BBC without getting angry, admit I wanted Kelly's name out, but emphasise I did nothing to make it happen. I got up and went to TB's gym for a run on the treadmill. I just wanted to work up a sweat, without getting too tired, so ran for twenty minutes. I went down to the press office. The TVs were on and on both news channels there were people outside my house saying they were expecting me to leave any minute. I called Audrey, who was so proud of herself that we'd managed to go through the whole three days without any of them seeing me. There were snappers covering every exit from Number 10. I had a shower and got dressed in the office and as I came out the first person I bumped into was Bill [Wells] the messenger, who had also been the first person to wish me luck on the day of my FAC appearance. There was something wonderfully Dickensian about Bill. The conspiratorial wink, the little smile that was always there, the walk that wasn't so much a walk as a shuffle. He said to me 'Whatever happens, whatever anyone says about you, you're a good man and that's a fact.' I found it very comforting. I felt almost that it was a positive omen of some sort, he having lodged in my mind from the FAC day too. Everyone was supportive. Bill making tea, Felicity [Hatfield, secretary] making toast, Alison sorting my flight to Marseille, Catherine R and Clare S coming in, their arms as ever full of huge, perfectly ordered files and folders, just going over the same old Q & A material. Adam Chapman and Alan Maclean arrived. Alan had unsettled me a little at dinner when he said that my diary extract re 'we didn't do it ourselves' could be read as saying we got others to do it. We went over how to deal with that. He knew it was innocently meant but said it was the one part he would zone in on if he was looking for a bit of a forensic challenge.

Finally we left. I didn't want to arrive with an entourage so CR, CS and Alan got out early and went ahead. I drove up as close as we could get to the court entrance. The demos were far bigger than we had been led to believe but I was glad we had turned down the chance of going in the back. I walked straight through. They were shouting and screaming, some through loudhailers, but I had got the blinkers on, got into my best Roy Keane mode and just walked on, Adam at my side. There was a bank of cameras to the right, and I ignored them too. I caught sight of the odd placard, one saying 'Ban the Campbell, ban the bomb.' I reached the door and CR looked like she was crying. I was taken by the cops and an usher to a little room upstairs. Within seconds, text messages were coming in. It had clearly gone out live. 'Entrance the stuff of legend,' from Martin Sheehan. The court official said she had never known anything like it. People had been queueing since 1 to get into the marquee. She said there were journalists in there from all over the world. I bumped into Harry Arnold [ex-*Mirror* colleague] on the stairs. Another lucky omen. I looked out of the window and saw a group of journalists I knew. It dawned on me that the little group was made up of people I actually liked. Another one. I was feeling OK. I was pacing up and down this tiny little room, making a few black-humour jokes about executions, drinking tea, when someone from James Dingemans' [QC, senior Counsel to the inquiry] team came to see me. He said that Dingemans intended to refer to my diaries but not read from them. He would refer to them in questioning and if I wanted to read from them, I could, or I could paraphrase. I was fine with that. I was taken through by the usher, who was really looking after me. There were dozens of hacks around and I made a point of not looking at any of them, not letting any of them catch my eye, just talking to the usher and getting to my seat.

Once I was there, I looked around at the lawyers, all chatting

August '03: Giving evidence to Hutton

away to each other, and the people in front of the judge's bench, including a beautiful young woman just a few feet from me. She smiled really warmly and I smiled back and decided whenever I felt my hackles rise I would just look at her. Hutton came in, everyone stood until he had settled himself, and away we went. Dingemans went through things very carefully and methodically. After the first couple of answers, I felt I was OK and that I just had to relax now and rely on my knowledge of the detail of everything. Listen to the question. Answer it. I had the file in front of me but I was really relying on the short list of points I had made to myself, and also the witness statement. We focused on the dossier right up to lunchtime. Hutton came in at several points and it took me a while to work out that didn't necessarily mean he was probing or trying to catch me out. On the contrary, on one occasion it finally dawned on me that if I looked at my diary extracts I would see the answer I was searching for. Dingemans was very clear and polite and helped my nerves settle quickly. I later thanked him for handling the diaries so sensitively. I felt totally confident on the dossier and the overall impression was surely one of very good working cooperation with the spooks. On the BBC again I felt Dingemans was fair in the way he took me through the correspondence with Sambrook. Here I think it helped that Hutton had my diaries because he had the full picture about the reasons for my rising anger and frustration. It was also clear that this was not some rampage for myself but for TB and the government. On Kelly, I felt comfortable with what I was saying. I was clear and straightforward, said it would have been much better if we had been clearer at the start rather than put in place a process that allowed the press to control when he was identified. I said in a way I was pushed to the margins of that decision and so did not really say, in the way I normally would perhaps, what I thought, because others involved may think I had a clear vested interest. Hutton was interested in why we didn't just batten down the hatches, why did he have to appear at the committee, to which I said it was inevitable and it would have been better if we had all faced up to that at the start.

By the time we broke for lunch I felt I was in good shape. The lawyers and CR/CS came to see me and said the tone was spot on, just keep going as you are. I had a coffee and a sandwich with CR and CS and was now worrying that my evidence would take us into another day. But we whizzed through the second half of my statement and the second session wound up fairly quickly and I could head back to France. There was an interesting moment when

Dingemans, referred to a point in the diary where I said Gilligan would be fucked, where I answered in a way designed to convey the meaning without using the word, and I could see a little smile at the corner of Hutton's mouth. So he didn't mind the occasional in-joke. I felt that he and Dingemans had both been fair. However, they hadn't raised the admission I had thought about briefing the press (re Kelly's name) before TB appeared at the Liaison Committee. That meant when Godric got in there tomorrow, it was a problem for us. At least it was there in my statement, so it would not be news to the judge, but it would be new to the media. I felt it went OK and that was what all the talking heads seemed to be saying by the time I got back to the office. There was a very warm reception as I got back in. I felt pretty tired and was desperate to get back to the family. I saw Tom and Godric before I left for Gatwick. I think my doing well had given them a bit of confidence too. I said the most important thing was to remember it is not a lobby briefing. They are not out to get you. Unlike the lobby, they actually want the truth. The only dramatic moment had been when they showed me an email that Gilligan had sent to David Chidgey [Lib Dem MP][1] re Kelly, which I said was 'unbelievable'. Dingemans said 'Don't make a speech on that' but the fact the BBC had not disclosed this meant Gilligan was in big trouble now.

When I was on the train, TB called. He said everyone seemed to think I had been the perfect witness. He said that after the initial panic – in which I had shared in spades – the diaries had actually worked in our favour. He said he had said a prayer for me this morning. So had Cherie, who sent me a note saying well done, and how sad she felt that she and Fiona had fallen out, and was there anything she could do? TB said he felt confident re the outcome. He also felt Geoff Hoon would be OK too. He had been reading up more of the background from the inquiry so far. Hutton would not be impressed by the way the BBC handled it all. He would probably also think Kelly was a bit at fault – something I had picked up from the judge as well. TB had felt throughout that the fact I lost it at times was OK, in that the judge would see why, because he would understand the seriousness of the allegations against me, when maybe those who made them did not. I had lost count of how many times TB had called in recent days, particularly about the diaries and his worries about Sumption's strategy. He now accepted it had been the right strategy. I had been totally open. They had been gentle with me in the way they questioned me on them. There had been no refer-

---

[1] Naming Kelly as Susan Watts's source for a BBC2 *Newsnight* story.

ence to my bad language and only the phrase 'plea bargain' was specifically picked out.

I called Sumption from Gatwick, as I sat in the departure lounge bar, with the news blaring away, endless coverage of my evidence. He said he had been following it on the website all day and I did well. He sounded genuinely pleased. I thanked him, said I could not have had better advice and support. He said the next part of his plan was not to push for lots of cross-examination of the other witnesses. It was tempting to want to tie the BBC people in knots, but he reckoned Hutton would have probably made up his mind by now. I said it seems an age away that I was sitting crying my eyes out at Ian and Andrea's dining-room table, going through the last days of July in my diary.

Wednesday, August 20

I finally got to Puyméras at midnight. It was fantastic to see the kids and Fiona and I seemed to get on for the first time in ages. I was trying to switch off now but the message coming from London was that both the broadcasters and the press were overwhelmingly positive. As expected we had a problem when Godric went through his evidence and he was asked about the idea I had had for briefing before TB went to the Liaison Committee that someone had come forward and even though it was in my witness statement, I had not been asked about it yesterday; he was, and so the media went off on one about me having misled the inquiry. Of course Hutton knew that was balls but it meant more crap in the press. The Tories were also onto me re what they claimed was a discrepancy re 45 minutes in my evidence to the FAC, and now this. Also, the Chidgey email was going big as a problem for Gilligan, but Catherine R was worried because she had done research for the whips. The BBC case having been poor, and us having so far thought we had done well, they were now working up the line that Kelly was caught in a mincer between the two of us. Philip had a load of the cuttings sent out and I did seem to have done OK. Even the *Mirror* and the *Independent* were not that bad. I had prepared better than for the FAC, partly because more was at stake. Also, I was more nervous and that had helped. On the diaries, Dingemans had been particularly kind in that he gave the impression I had volunteered them. I went to see the Kennedys to thank them for all their help, then sent a stack of thank-you letters.

Thursday, August 21

I called Geoff H in the States. He had read my evidence online, felt I did well and accepted that contrary to what some of the media tried to say, I did not drop him in it. He felt able to deal with the 'plea bargain' point. I was somewhat suprised to hear Kevin Tebbit had said he couldn't recall saying that Kelly didn't want to be named in the first wave of publicity. He also apparently gave a little soliloquy at the end which people didn't think was very clever.

Saturday, August 23

TB called. He said he had read the transcripts of everyone's evidence to the inquiry. He said he honestly felt I was word-perfect and he was sure the judge would have been impressed. 'I think you just put it so much clearer than everyone else.' My worry was that Hutton, based on some of the interventions he had been making, seemed to think it would have been possible for Kelly's name not to come out, and we didn't. TB said he was going to have to use his own evidence to be clear with him the nature of the media world we have to deal with. His worry was that Hutton may in the end just feel he has to have a balance of blame, rather than just state the truth, which is the whole thing stemmed from the *Today* programme broadcasting what they did and then refusing to back down. Though I was still getting an OK press for my own evidence, the focus re me had moved to what Godric said. It was irritating, though if Hutton was reading the press, it would give him another example of how they worked. Some of them were saying he looked amazed to hear what GS said re me. It had been in my own bloody statement. TB and I discussed when was the best time for me to leave. He said if I was totally decided, it was probably better to go sooner rather than later. He said he had had a good meeting on holiday with Murdoch, Elisabeth [Murdoch], Les [Hinton] and Irwin Stelzer. He said he knew most of us had had a crap holiday but he had enjoyed himself despite everything and felt rested. But he knew the knives were sharpening for him and once I was gone he would have lost his main lightning conductor.

Tuesday, August 26

TB felt having looked at all the interventions by the judge that he was closer to our arguments than the BBC, whose evidence had been poor. He felt if there was one area where Hutton may have problems with the government it was over whether the MoD took sufficient care of Kelly. He was moving towards a line on Thursday of saying he accepted responsibility for everything as PM. He really hoped Hutton would draw a line and we would regain the space to get back focused on the domestic agenda.

Thursday, August 28

Geoff H got a dreadful press; now it was TB's turn to take the stand. I missed his first briefing meeting, felt it far better he see the lawyers first and then work out what if any thought we needed to give re the media. He asked me what the desired headline would be. It was somewhere in the area of TB taking responsibility (which GH had not done) while defending the decisions we took. It was also an opportunity to lay out what it is like making some of the decisions he has to. People felt GH did very badly, and gave himself some real problems. We had done well so far because everyone had been clear about the facts, even where they were difficult. But Geoff had opened us up. I felt he had ensured that more of us would be called to the second phase of evidence taking than might otherwise have been the case. John Scarlett and I were already pretty much settled to the notion that we would certainly be called back. David Omand then said he thought I did really well. Re the diaries he said 'I hope you have all your diaries safely locked up somewhere – otherwise the men in black might come looking for them.' I was not entirely sure whether he was joking or not. Probably not. TB set off and everyone, including the media, said he did well. He said on his return he had felt totally robust, and the facts didn't frighten him on this. No doubt his legal experience helped a bit too, and he felt that even though the inquiry team were in the driving seat, they were conscious of the fact that he was, when all was said and done, the Prime Minister. There were no attention-seeking histrionics, just more of the same fairly painstaking probing. He was clearly pleased it had not gone badly. I said that my evidence had gone well, his evidence had gone well, and I felt I should go tomorrow. It is the right moment. He looked really taken aback, but when I said we had agreed it would happen soon, why not now? Everybody is expecting it soon, but nobody is expecting it this soon, so why not? I was keen, within the limited room I had, to maintain an element of surprise which would help me shape the mood around it. He then started to warm to it. He said I should use it to get up a big argument about the nature of the media. I felt not yet, that I should just do it, be very nice about him and the government, make the case for progressive politics, but then be pretty low-key until Hutton was over. I had agreed with Jeremy Heywood that when Fiona and I left we would have five weeks' notice to work out. I told very few people what was happening – Godric, Tom, Anne, Alison –

who all seemed both shocked and not shocked. My real desire was to keep it all quiet till tomorrow.

We had a meeting with Sumption and team in the Cabinet room to go over the plan for the next stages, and in particular Sumption's note re what we should aim to get from the inquiry. Again, he made an interesting strategic call. He did not think we should press for lots of cross-examination. Nor did he think we should be saying to Hutton that the BBC should be criticised. All we would ask for was an acceptance that the story was wrong and that we were justified in challenging it. Also on Kelly, he obviously thought it would be wrong to attack him, but equally he hoped to steer the judge towards accepting that Kelly did wrong. TB was as near to deferential towards Sumption as I had seen him with anyone for ages. He knew his reputation for being very clever if a bit awkward, and we had all been saying how good he had been so far. It was interesting how much the legal side of this was actually about presentation too. A lot of the points made by the lawyers were tactical presentational points, but with the audience the judge not the press or public. What I liked about Sumption most was that he didn't seem to care what the press or public were thinking about all this. He was totally focused on the judge.

Friday, August 29

I slept in a bit, having had a bit of asthma through the night. In to finalise my statement. TB didn't want any sense in there that he kept persuading me to stay. He thought it would be weakening. He wanted to write his own words about me, that there are 2 ACs, the one he knows and the one the media likes to portray. I left him to it, put changes into my own statement and then made a few calls. I told JP, who was very supportive, thanked me for everything and said he would like to do the media on it once we'd made the announcement. I called MB, DB, JR, Tessa, Charles C, Ian McC, Pat H, GH and a few others. Later – once it was out there and loads of messages were coming in – there it was on a long list typed up by Alison. 'The Chancellor's secretary called to say he wanted to thank you for everything you'd done for the party.' MB was very nice, said she really valued the way we had always worked together, that I had done a great job but there was a limit to what anyone could take. JR said he had been at a party meeting at the weekend and when he did a big defence of me, he got a great response. Ian McC put out some really nice words. So did Robin C. JP said his main line on the telly would be that I had decided I wanted a change, spend more time at home, that I was steeped in Labour and would be badly missed. I got a message to Hutton as I didn't want him to hear it on the media first. I told Dan [Bartlett], who said Bush would be disappointed because he was 'one of your biggest supporters', and I told Clinton and thanked him for his recent advice.

Once I finished my statement I got Alison to send out a message that I wanted to see all my team and anyone else in the building who was around. They knew what was coming so they weren't exactly shocked, but there was a lot of sadness in there. I said they knew I had been thinking about going and today was the day. I had had a great time and it had been an amazing privilege and one of the things that meant most to me was the team I had built up. I could not have done any of it without them and certainly in recent weeks I could not have asked for more by way of support. I said everyone was replaceable, I would leave with nothing but good memories of them, but Fiona and I desperately wanted to get a life back for ourselves and the children. I suppose I knew it would go quite big but it was ludicrous just how big it went. Someone told me PA gave it the same Priority tag as a royal death or prime ministerial resignation. For several hours, once they did the breaking news Whoosh, they did literally nothing else. They had some so-called intelligence expert in the studio when it broke and they had him blathering away without knowing what on earth he was talking about. The Tories put up Ann Widdecombe, Theresa May and eventually IDS. They looked shrill and ridiculous, trying to make it a disaster day for TB.

I gathered my thoughts again before doing a round of interviews with the broadcast political editors. They came in one by one and I used pretty much the same messages – great privilege, downside all taken by family, big on values, make the case for politics. It was also going big in the States and across Europe. Graeme [AC's brother] said he had been channel hopping in Poland and found me simultaneously on Russian, Polish, French and Portuguese telly. The news channels were going with it hell for leather in the outer office and the endless two-way blather reminded me why I had got fed up dealing with them all. They just went on and on and on until another talking head was found. It underlined how out of hand the whole thing about me had got. TB said even he was surprised how big it was going. He said I was a big personality and even though some of them hated me, they knew it was a big personality leaving the centre of the stage. Some of the hacks were trying to build it as a huge blow to him – could he cope blah? – which must have been a bit galling. The announcement re Fiona was in there though buried in all the avalanche of coverage re my leaving. It was a real sadness to me that she was leaving on bad terms with CB and with Tony too. But she was clearly happy we were on the way, and maybe surprised I had brought it to a head so quickly. They were straight on to what would I do in the future, and making assumptions I would make a fortune. The truth was I didn't really have a clue what I would do. I didn't speak to many journos. It was all kind of on autopilot. Boulton was pretty sour as ever, Marr OK, [Nick] Robinson a jerk. Andy Bell and Gary Gibbon [all TV political editors] pretty straight. After a while they started to cover the coverage – the fact that it was so big abroad. Catherine Colonna called and said '*Tu es un star mondial, tu sais. Il faut saisir le moment.*' She said the President '*te salue*'. It was all a bit weird. 20 minutes on ITN, 15 on the BBC, hours on Sky, the Sundays preparing to do pages and pages on it.

I cleared my desk. Went on a last walk round the building to say a few thank-yous and goodbyes, met Fiona and then we walked out together. I didn't look at the hacks and I didn't bother to listen, let alone answer. I just wanted to get out, and get home. There was a horde of media waiting in the street when we got home, more than I think we'd ever had. We parked at the top of the road, then walked down and we were swarmed as we tried to walk down the pavement. Fiona got left behind a bit and I kept looking back and she had virtually disappeared. I stopped and yelled at a few of them and she caught up for a bit. The live reporters were describing what was going on, others shouting, snappers falling over each other. Ridiculous. We got in and Audrey was very upset I had gone. She felt it was the right job for me and I should have stayed with Tony to the end. I was cheered by a message from Hutton. I had earlier asked Clare Sumner to tell Lee Hughes [secretary to the inquiry] what was going on and that I was keen he understood I would be doing interviews but would not talk about anything being investigated by him. The message came back now that he was very touched that I took the trouble to tell him in advance. I was probably reading too much into it but I had felt giving evidence that he felt I was an OK personality and I felt the same from the tone of his message today. I also thought that if he had watched any of the coverage, he would see once more what a nightmare culture we dealt with. I had a hunch that the diaries will have had a similar effect. TB felt the same, that the diaries gave an insight into what it was like trying to handle these big decisions surrounded by the 24-hour media trying to trip you the whole time.

Neil, Glenys, Rachel and the Goulds came round for dinner and I think shared some of the relief. Rachel had been one of the first suggesting I leave ages ago, feeling it was time I stopped taking hits for others. Neil and PG were ambivalent but agreed it was the right time for me. TB called a couple of times. He had seen some of the news and couldn't believe how much coverage it was getting. He felt it was partly about the size of my personality but was also a reflection of their obsession with themselves. Philip had been following it all day and said I should get the tapes of the live coverage. 'You'd have thought the Pope had died.' We had a nice evening and Fiona was definitely more relaxed and I sensed the kids, though annoyed at all the bollocks in the street every time they came and went, were feeling a change for the better was happening. My asthma was bad though, partly the air, partly the current stress, also maybe a bit of anxiety about the total lack of certainty about what I would now do with myself. People were telling me I could make a fortune on the lecture circuit, but I can't say it held that much appeal. The most important thing was to try to get things at home on a better keel, rest, and then take stock. As I left, TB had said 'You do realise I will phone you every day, don't you?' I said yes, and I hope you realise sometimes I won't be there.

To be continued . . .

Index

over funeral 626; coverage of dossier on Iraq 640; TB on *Newsnight* 665; Clare Short's resignation threat 673, 674 *and n*; AC's letters of complaint 682; coverage of Iraq 690; and dossier and aftermath 698, 700, 701, 702, 708, 709–12, 713–15, 716, 724, 725, 726, 728; and Hutton Inquiry xiii–xiv, 730, 731, 732, 733, 739, 744, 751, 754

Beatrix, Queen of the Netherlands 142

Beattie, Trevor 488, 657

Beckenham by-election (1997) 164*n*

Beckett, Margaret 3; and New Labour policy 21; and TB's Shadow Cabinet reshuffle 24, 25; digs in over NHS policy document 62; press conference with TB 68–9; appointed Trade and Industry Secretary 199; in favour of Millennium Dome 213; as possible Foreign Secretary 226; on Tories and media 322; and Lords Reform 337; and London Mayor election 427, 428, 442; stopped from chairing press conference by GB 536; appointed to Environment, Food and Rural Affairs 539, 549; brilliant broadcast on Black Rod/Downing St row 626; and Iraq 637; angry over media coverage of Dr Kelly's death 724; and AC's departure 754

Beckham, David 330, 620

Beckham, Victoria (Posh Spice) 395

Beers, Charlotte 583–4

Belfast Telegraph 293

Bell, Andy 756

Bell, Martin 5, 169–70, 171, 172, 173, 174, 260

Bender, Brian 205, 284

Benn, Hilary 535

Benn, Tony 616, 663

Bennett, Mark 193, 337, 416, 457, 527, 531, 622, 721

Bentégeat, General Henri 662

Berger, Sandy 194, 214, 278, 297, 315, 319, 325, 332, 333, 369, 375, 380, 381–2, 389, 391, 401, 402, 468

Berlusconi, Silvio 569–70, 591, 622, 668

Berry, Chuck 214

Berry, Roger 326

Bevins, Tony 38, 57, 89–90, 91, 95, 260, 343, 364, 434

Bickerstaffe, Rodney 58, 136

bin Laden, Osama 344, 560, 561, 562, 563, 566–74 *passim*, 578, 601, 627

Bingham, Sir Thomas 67

Bird, Dickie 490, 657

Birt, John (Lord) 309, 715, 747

Birtwistle, Brigadier Alex 517

Bishop, Tony 249, 443, 445

Black, Guy 617, 620

Black Rod *see* Willcocks, Sir Michael

Blackburn, David and Janice 702, 732

Blackpool: TUC Conference (1995) 129–30; Labour Party Conference (2002) 641–3

Blackpool Gazette 285

Blackshaw, Alison 193, 198, 262, 305, 308, 339, 416, 691, 706, 722, 741, 742, 743, 744, 748, 753, 754, 755

Blackstone, Baroness Tessa 705

Blair, Cherie, QC (*née* Booth): French holiday 9, 12; tries to talk AC into accepting job 9; 40th birthday party 15–16; and Carole Caplin 17, 22, 23, 24, 25, 26–7; targeted by Tories 28; and Oratory 'splash' 34, 36; complains about AC 55; becomes QC 55; dinner with Princess Diana 58, 59; on TB's relationship with AC 65, 70; her role and image discussed 83–4, 117–18; and AC's worries about Carole Caplin 83, 84; at Brit awards 103; relations with AC 117–18, 121, 138; and TB's pay-rise 126, 127, 247; her plans for No. 11 145; and dinner with Princess Diana 144, 151, 153; election campaign 160, 161, 180; still sees Carole Caplin 155, 180; gets on well with AC 160, 168; steals show at *Star* awards 163; and General Election (1997) 160, 161, 174, 180, 181, 182, 183, 184, 186; relationship with Anji Hunter 181, 250; and Clinton visit 208; not yet used to lack of privacy 217, 220; and No. 10's new kitchen 222; takes Noel Gallagher to meet children 224; helped by Fiona Millar 248; bottom pinched 256; and TB and Ecclestone affair 261, 262; and Humphrey the cat 262; on TB's health 263–4; and use of No. 10 notepaper 269; in USA 277; at Highgrove with Prince Charles 323–4; on South African trip 358, 359;

Blair, Cherie (*cont'd*)
moved by Kosovan refugee camp
387; successful event with Hillary
Clinton 390; pregnancy 421, 422, 423,
427, 429–30, 435; and press coverage
427; and Shaun Woodward's
defection 432; on Millennium eve
436, 437; Leo's birth 454; and Euan's
arrest 463, 464; and TB 479, 504;
election campaign 535, 540;
persuades Fiona Millar to stay 550;
in USA post 9/11 570, 572; furious at
TB going to Pakistan 576; and death
of GB's baby 598, 599; pregnancy
and miscarriage 629, 631; and Carole
Caplin's fraudster boyfriend 647–52;
and the press 696, 721; fires Fiona
730–31; sends note to AC on his
Hutton Inquiry appearance 750
Blair, Euan 12, 25, 28, 34, 199, 209, 220,
394, 450, 454, 696; arrested 463, 464
Blair, Hazel 131–2, 169
Blair, Kathryn 12, 50, 183, 209, 224, 394,
696
Blair, Leo (father) 49, 131, 132, 169, 170,
183, 540
Blair, Leo (son) 454, 455, 466, 469
Blair, Nicky 12, 33, 199, 209, 220, 224,
394, 450, 454, 696
Blair, Olwen 183, 540
Blair, Tony x–xiii; first meeting with AC
ix–x
1994–1995
leadership acceptance speech 7; offers
post of press secretary to AC 7–8, 9,
10, 11, 12, 13; in praise of GB (*q.v.*) 7,
10, 29, 30, 44–5, and Mandelson (*q.v.*)
7, 12, 30, 44–5; in France 9–13; and
Kinnock 9, 13, 18–19; plans to scrap
Clause 4 and modernise Party 11,
14–15, 16, 37, 44; meets Murdoch
13–14; conference speech (1994) 16, 17,
18, 19, 20–21; and Carole Caplin 22, 23,
24, 42; and Major 24–5, 27; and furore
over son's schooling 25, 28–9, 34–7;
Shadow Cabinet reshuffle 25, 27;
performance in PMQs 25–6; Social
Justice Commission speech 26; and the
media 27, 28, 38; and Scottish affairs
29; nervous about speeches 31, 32, 33;
at *Standard* drama awards 31–2; and
Blunkett's remarks on education
39–40, 41; brilliant radio interview

43–4; and Northern Ireland 44, 47;
Brighton speech goes well 46; and
Tory divisions on Europe 47, 55;
attacked by Scottish Cardinal 48–9;
irritated by Scottish media 49–50;
drafts New Labour constitution 50–51;
Scottish Conference 51–2; negotiations
with unions 53, 56–7, 58, 61, 70, 71–3,
82; and Princess Diana 58–60;
recognises need for economic message
60, 77; and Wilson's death 61–2, 63;
policy on NHS 62; worried by Bosnia
62–3; methods of working 63; and
Tory leadership election 64, 65–7, 68,
69–70; Australian trip 63, 65, 67, 71,
73–7; meets Irish prime minister 82–3;
and discussions about CB's image and
role 83–4; prepares conference speech
(1995) 85–6, 87–9; photocall with
Keegan 89; success at conference 90;
economic discussions 92–3; and Clare
Short (*q.v.*) 93; selfishness as regards
AC's illness 93; shocked at Rabin's
death 94; enjoys mixing with
musicians 94; his thinning hair 95;
suspects Mo Mowlam of leaks to press
95; and Clinton 95–6
1996–May 1997
in Tokyo 98; economic policy 98–100;
defends Harriet Harman's decision
over grammar school 97, 101–2; at
Brit Awards 103–4; and Scottish
devolution 105–6, 108–9; and
Dunblane shooting 106–8, 109–10;
airs religious beliefs in press 111,
112; in USA 112–16; meeting with
Clinton (*q.v.*) 115–16; and
GB/Mandelson rift 118–19; and Road
to the Manifesto 120, 122–3; speech
on Scottish devolution 123, 124–6;
Communion in Catholic church 126;
launches 'New Labour, New Life for
Britain' 126–7; undecided about pay-
rise 126, 127; angered by Clare Short
128; 'a conviction politician' 129; at
TUC Conference 129–30; wants to
challenge cartoonist 131; gives
personal interview 131–2; angry with
Cook (*q.v.*) over press release 133;
conference speech 135; meets
Mandela 136; hairstyle captures the
headlines 137–8; fails in Brixton
138–9; on single currency 139, 141;

762   *Index*

Blair, Tony (*cont'd*)
and Ron Davies affair 328–30, 331;
and Iraq 331–5; and Lords Reform
336, 337, 338–9; worries about NI
336; Dáil speech 336*n*; and bombing
of Iraq 340–45; and Mandelson/
Geoffrey Robinson loan affair 344,
346, 347, 348, 349, 350, 351, 352,
353–4
1999
wants to focus on domestic policy
356, 358; and Whelan's departure
357; South African trip 358–9; visits
Mandela 359; illness 359, 360; visits
Aids children's home 359–60; brief
visit to Kuwait 360; livid with
Mandelson for holding meetings at
No. 10 360–61; meeting on Kosovo
362; with Murdoch at publishers'
lunch 363; and Glenn Hoddle 363–5;
at King Hussein's funeral 365, 366–7;
discussions with Clinton 367; and
the euro 368; and war with the
media 368–9; discussions with
Schroeder 369; pushes Schroeder too
far 370, 371; and Kosovo 369–70, 371,
372–3, 374, 376, 377–83, 385, 397–8;
and NI talks 372, 373, 374–6, 394,
395; visits refugee camps 386–8, 392;
further discussions with Clinton 389,
391, 392, 393, 394; 'pissed off' with
Russians 389; and Cabinet reshuffle
391; visits Bulgaria 391; and
continuation of war 398, 399; and
involvement of Russian troops 400,
401, 402, 403, 404; worried about
Yeltsin 406; meeting with Bono
406–7; has fascinating chat with
Chirac 407; and Gould's gloomy note
408; back to NI talks 408–16, 417–19;
a hero's welcome in Priština 419–20;
on holiday 420; accused by press of
spending thousands on
refurbishment 420; and CB's
pregnancy 421, 422, 423, 430;
Conference and his speech 422–4;
and Ken Livingstone 424, 426,
427–9; Cabinet reshuffle 424–5; lacks
killer instinct in the House 430–31;
and devolution of power in NI 432;
and Shaun Woodward's defection
432–3; at Millennium Dome 435,
436–7

2000
worried about Dome 438; plans to
visit Cliff Richard 438–9; and Mike
Tyson 440; and Livingstone 440–41,
442–3, 451; and Peter Kilfoyle's
resignation 441; views on journalists
441; trip to Russia 443; meetings
with Putin 444–5; sees AC's
problems 445; at Lisbon EU summit
445, 446; at Chequers Cabinet 446,
447; and Middle England 447, 455;
and Cockerell film 449, 450, 464;
talks with Putin 449–50; football with
AC and the children 450; and 'anti-
capitalist' riots 450–51; 'frantic' over
NI talks 452; fall in ratings 453, 461;
and new baby 454, 455; WI speech a
disaster 456–9; decides on 'big tent'
approach 459–60; plans department
changes 461–2; and Mo Mowlam
462; and AC's anger 463; and Euan's
arrest 463; cheered up by black
churches conference 463; stops for a
pub pint 464; in hysterics at Tokyo
G8 465; reprimands AC 465–6; and
son's christening 466; on
Thatcherism and his own political
views 467–8; at New York P5
meeting 468; and fuel crisis 469–74;
at conference 474; and Belgrade
uprising 475; at Dewar's funeral 476;
both buoyant and depressed 476–7;
and Murdoch 477; discussions re
AC's future 478–9; accepts AC's and
CB's criticisms 479; and Mandelson's
gaffe on single currency 480–81; lays
out strategy at Chequers Cabinet
meeting 481; at Nice EU summit
482–3; further NI talks 483–4
2001
worries about AC and Anji Hunter
leaving 487–8, 502, 518; showered by
tomatoes 488; and Hunting Bill 488,
489; and NI talks 489–90; and
Mandelson/Hinduja affair 492–3,
494–5, 496, 497, 498, 499, 500, 501,
502, 505, 509, 510–11; plans to
revamp his office 500–1; and attacks
on Iraq 503; on AC's tiredness and
lack of motivation 504; in Ottawa
505; discussion with Cheney 505;
discussions with Bush at Camp
David 505–7; and foot-and-mouth

epidemic 505, 508, 509, 510, 511, 512–17, 518, 519, 521; unsure re third term 518; Cabinet reshuffle 518; and manifesto 519; and asylum 519; looks ahead to second term reforms 522; booed at Twickenham 522–3; in praise of Mandela 523; needs support 523; and NMD 523; election campaign begins 524–5, 527, 528, 529; harangued by Sharon Storer 529–30; and JP's thumping of heckler 531; on NHS 531–2; stops at Dorset café 532–3; lets GB chair meetings 533; and pre-speech nightmares in Scotland 533–4; run-up to election 534, 535, 536; election day 537–8, 539, 540, 541; plans Cabinet reshuffle 538–9, 549–50; post-election strategy 550–51; policy on euro 552–3; dinner with union leaders 553; 'spooked' by PLP 553–4; and PMQs 554, 556; the press and his holiday 554; 'I'm always right' 557; meeting with Bush at Chequers 557–8; views on education 558; discussions about AC 559; angry at GMB ads 559; and attack on Twin Towers 559–62, 565, 566; relations with Bush post 9/11 562–4, 566; and the Koran 562, 564; worries about US policy 566–7; CNN interview 568; and Musharraf 567, 568, 569, 572, 575; lunches with Berlusconi 569–70; gets good press as international interlocutor 570; discussions with military planners 570–71, 572; in New York 572–3; attempts to influence Bush 573, 574; conference speech 575–6; visits Musharraf 576–7, and Delhi 577–8; in Oman 579–81; and strategy in Afghanistan 581, 582–3, 584; 'humiliated' in Syria 585; discussions with Sharon and Arafat 585–6; and Anji Hunter's departure 586; not focused on domestic policies 586, 592; and fall of Kabul 587; amazed by press reactions 587; 'all time low' with GB 588; and Boyce's RUSI speech 590, 591; dinner with GB 592; and Mandelson's possible return 593; analysed by Mandelson 594

2002

visits Bangladesh, India and Pakistan 597–9, 602; and death of GB's baby 598, 599, 601, 602; visits Afghanistan 599–601; plans for reforming public services 602–3; dinner with Murdoch 603; and Princess Margaret's death 605; in Sierra Leone 605; and Mittal donation to Labour Party 605–6, 609; thoughts on his legacy 606; and Byers 607, 620; gives pro-Bush interview 607; and Iraq 607, 608; discussion with Cheney 609; on Labour Party problems 609–10; and Queen Mother's death and funeral 610–11, 613, 614, 616, 617; behaviour at strategy meetings 611; clothes criticised 611, 613; discussions on Bush, Iraq and MEPP 612–13, 614; press conference with Bush 614–15; private sessions with Bush 615–16; his plans for Health and antisocial behaviour 617–18; concerns re GB 618; supported by Clinton 619–20; and Byers' departure 620–21; at Rome NATO summit 622; Cabinet reshuffle 622; and Black Rod row over Queen Mother's funeral arrangements 618, 622–3, 626; unsure when to announce his departure 623; JP 'declares war' on 624–5; and rift with US over Arafat 626, 627; and the Strozzis 626–7; and Bush at G8 summit 627; discusses his future with AC 628–9, 631; and the importance of the euro 628; defends clothes sense 629; and CB's pregnancy 629, 631; chairs meeting on Iraq 630–31; sees regime change as route to dealing with WMD 630–31; discussions with Bush over UN Resolution 631, 632, 632–3; and the 'dossier' 633, 634; rejects demands to recall Parliament 633–4; attempts to influence Bush to take UN route 634–5; sense of certainty over Iraq 636–7; feels dossier is compelling 637; wants to get back to domestic issues 638; and Hunting Bill 638, 639; on need for UN Resolution 638; goes through dossier in Cabinet 639, 640; and NEC questions on Iraq 640–41;

Blair, Tony (*cont'd*)
at Blackpool Conference 641, 642;
persuaded to swap clothes for
Moscow photocall 643–4; discussion
with Putin 644; and Bali bombing
644; and Estelle Morris's resignation
645–6; discusses Saddam with Bush
647; and Carole Caplin's fraudster
boyfriend affair 647–53; on
friendships 648
2003
on holiday 654; and Roy Jenkins'
death 654–5; briefed on Iraq by MoD
655–6; Cabinet meeting on Iraq 656,
657; and student loans 657; at launch
of AC's marathon sponsorship
appeal 657; firm on need for second
UN Resolution 658–9, 660, 661;
White House discussions with Bush
660–61; discussion with Chirac at
Anglo-French summit 661–3; on
importance of removing Saddam
663, 664; and the CIC ('dodgy')
dossier 665, 666; worried about Iraq
and anti-war protests 667; more
relaxed 668; pushes for peace 668;
furious at departments' inaction on
domestic issues 668; sees Carole
Caplin as victim 668; on war without
second Resolution 669–71; and need
for Commons support 671–2, 674;
disgusted by Clare Short's threat of
resignation 673–4, 675; pushes for
second Resolution 675–7; at Azores
summit 678; gets legal advice 680;
wins vote in the House 681–2; and
Fiona and AC's departure 682–3,
687; finds GB more cooperative 683;
makes up with Chirac at Brussels
summit 683; writes to Bush on
perceived unilateralism 684–5; Camp
David talks 685, 686; goes to see Kofi
Annan 686; further discussion with
Bush 688; sponsors AC for marathon
690; in *The Simpsons* 690; angry
discussion with Putin 693–5; 'I know
I'm right' 696; worried about press
stories about CB 696; accepts that AC
wants to go 696–7; and Clare Short's
resignation 697; visits troops in Iraq
698–9; and media allegations re
WMD dossiers 699–700, 701, 706,
707; and Milburn's resignation 703–4;

Cabinet reshuffle 704, 705; and
Hunting Bill 705–6; and AC's FAC
appearance 707–8, 709, 710; and fight
with BBC 711–12, 713, 715; and
discovery of source (Kelly) 714, 715;
considers media Orwellian 715–16;
against AC's leaving now 716;
defended in Cabinet by JP 717; gives
views on Labour Party 717–18;
advised by Clinton 718, 719, 720; gets
amazing reception at Congress 722;
and Dr Kelly's death 722, 723, 724–5,
726, 727, 728; against AC's departure
725, 727; speaks to AC's mother 727;
wants to plan AC's departure 729;
and CB's sacking of Fiona 730–31;
angry with Sally Morgan over Carole
Caplin 732; and AC's diaries 742–3,
744, 750–51, 756; confident about
Hutton Inquiry 746, 752–3, 753; meets
Sumption 754; and AC's statement
754; surprised at coverage AC's
departure gets 755, 757
Blank, Sir Victor 536
Blears, Hazel 705
Blix, Dr Hans 638, 647, 659 *and n*, 660,
662, 663–4, 666, 671, 674, 675
Bloody Sunday Inquiry 273, 292
Blumenthal, Sidney 325
Blunkett, David 3; supports TB over
choice of school 35; announces
Labour plans to tax school fees 39,
40, 41; angers GB 41, 42; votes
against rejecting Liz Davies 86; at
Brighton Conference 90; gets unions
up in arms at Blackpool 129–30; in
Government 191, 199; against
Millennium Dome 213; interviewed
on Ecclestone 259; attacks proposals
in CSR 266–7; appalled by
Mandelson/Robinson loan 350; TB's
plans for 356, 462; on Lib Dems 362;
at Dewar's funeral 476; angered by
AC's comment on 'bog standard'
comprehensives 501; on foot-and-
mouth 512; and 2001 election
campaign 525, 528, 534, 535; becomes
Home Secretary 518, 538, 549; and
cannabis/criminalisation policy 555;
post 9/11 560, 565; and asylum
seekers 564, 665; and Dacre 604; in
foul mood at Cabinet 608; on Iraq
607, 608–9, 637; sceptical about

Olympics 659; no confidence in police and security forces 665–6; at War Cabinet meetings 683; worries about creation of new ministry of justice 702; and reshuffle 705; wants more ASBOs 717; supports AC 724
Boateng, Paul 624–5, 640, 689
Bolland, Mark 235, 239, 324, 486
Bonham-Carter, Jane 164, 171–2
Bono 406, 407, 490, 592
Booth, Anthony 430
Booth, Gale 11, 183, 262
Boothroyd, Betty 31*n*, 194, 301, 309, 331, 335, 336, 616, 637
Bostock, Tom 285–6, 721
Botham, Ian 460
Bottomley, Virginia 103
Boulton, Adam 67, 406, 530–31, 622, 640, 697, 725, 756
Bournemouth: Conference (1999) 422–4
Boutros-Ghali, Boutros 113
Bowen, Des 634
Bower, Tom 732
Bowie, David 103
Boyce, Admiral Sir Michael (CDS): meetings with TB 564, 566; and invasion of Afghanistan 567, 569, 575, 579, 581; reports on US tactics 570–71, 582, 584, 587; emotional about media 589; RUSI speech makes headlines 590; and invasion of Iraq 591–2, 611–12, 630, 645, 655, 658; praised by Chirac 662–3; more cheerful 686; differentiates between UK and US strategy 690
BP 472
Bradlee, Ben 114
Bradshaw, David 193, 198, 460, 674, 732
Bradshaw, Kerry 198
Bragg, Melvyn 60
Brahimi, Lakhdar: report 468
Braithwaite, Julian 193, 345, 384, 387, 388, 398, 404–6
Bramall, Field Marshal 233–4
Branson, Richard 179
Bremer, Paul 699
Bremner, Rory 452, 464, 466, 481
Bridges (neighbours) 691
Bridge, Victoria 143
Brighton: Labour Conferences (1995) 45–6, 90
Britannia, Royal Yacht 218

Brown, Gordon
1994–1997
ix, x, xiv; relationship with AC 10; 'gobbledegook' 16; and TB's plans for New Labour 20; tax reform press release 29; supported by TB 29–30; and TB/Cook rift over Economic Policy Commission 33; angry with Blunkett over taxation of school fees 41–2; as member of TB's team 42–5; hostility to Mandelson 53; suggestions for TB's conference speech 45; cuts AC for briefing against him 53–4; and Major's leadership election announcement 65–6, 70; and overseas aid 78; tax strategy and Cook 92–3; discussed by TB and AC 96; and stakeholder economy 99–100, 102; and TB 100, 102, 104, 112, 132; in a flap over press 118; clashes with Mandelson 118–19; and campaign on Lost Generation 118, 119; and Road to the Manifesto 120, 122; makes peace with JP 122; worried about tax and spend 123; chairs at Millbank 127; conference speech 134, 135; discusses economic message with TB 136–7; rift with Mandelson 137, 145; plans economic strategy 140; and *Today* programme 'personality of the year' award 141; refers to TB as 'Blair' 144; four speeches on the economy 145; against Millennium Exhibition 146; tax strategy 148, 149–50, 155, 158; and levies 162; and Tatton by-election 164, 165; and Labour election campaign 168, 172, 173, 180, 182; relations with Mandelson worry TB 175–6; bad-tempered conversations with TB 184–5; announces independence of Bank of England 200; and Cabinet pay-rises 201; worried about public finances 202, and JP 202; suggests five tests re Millennium Dome 212, 213; and Hague 214; press conference interrupted by AC 215; first Budget 219–20; discusses strategy with AC 239–40; and Earl Spencer's attacks on Royal family 245; chairs Diana commemoration committee 246; on Scottish devolution campaign 246; urges pay restraint 247*n*; suggests

Grice, Andy 7, 32, 33, 62
Griffiths, Nigel 312
Grocott, Bruce (Lord) 4, 547; in despair re TB's choice of school 35; dislikes draft Clause 4 50; aghast at TB's Murdoch trip 63; on PLP and TB 64; loses bet with AC 113, 116; advises AC on GICS appearance 307; on reshuffles 425; against TB's WI speech 457; on PLP feedback on Cockerell film 465; feels TB is tilting at windmills 500; sympathetic over AC's remark about 'bog standard' comprehensives 501–2; says he is leaving at the election 510; on Labour manifesto 519; and last-minute changes to TB's speech 533–4; his views on future Cabinet members 538, 539; supports AC 724
Guantánamo Bay prison camp, Cuba 603, 699
Guardian 24, 27, 28, 39, 84–5, 99, 118, 131, 163, 166, 168, 178, 269–70, 324, 330, 331, 345, 346, 347, 348, 364, 443, 475, 587, 716, 734
Guterres, Antonio 447, 483
Guthrie, General Sir Charles (CDS) 194; briefs Iraq media management group 278, 279; presents targeting plans 279–80; gives possible casualty figures 331–2; and bombing of Iraq 333, 334, 335, 340, 341, 342; liked by AC 341; takes TB to OPS room 344–5; on General Clark 362, 378, 389–90; and attack on Kosovo 370, 372, 373, 374; rages about armchair generals 372, 374; on use of ground troops 376, 378, 390; talks with the Americans 380, 381, 383; and involvement of Russian troops 400; presses US generals to deploy ground troops 402; shouting match with AC 404; likes AC's speech 407, 416; replaced by Boyce 564

Hadley, Steve 506, 630, 635, 636, 668
Hague, William: elected Tory leader 210, 214, 215, 236; and Diana's death 238; and Ecclestone 260; wedding 266; discussion with TB 304; and Alan Clark 309; at PMQs 311; performance picking up 321, 322; and Lords reform 336, 337, 338,

339–40; poor performances 365, 370; at King Hussein's funeral 365, 366, 367; aunt rumoured to play bridge with AC's mother 391; nice about CB's pregnancy 430; good one-liners at PMQs 430; and Shaun Woodward's defection 434, 435; at the Dome 437; as possible PM 461; dangerous 481; hated by Desmond 482; Bush's lack of interest in 488; portrayed with Thatcher's hair 488; 'lowlife' 495; calls for Army to take over in FMD fight 517; and media 526; in spot of bother 530; and Tory campaign 534, 535, 536; *Frost* interview 535; resigns party leadership 551 *and n*
Hain, Peter 448, 495, 546, 717
Haines, Joe 23, 61, 180; *Glimmers of Twilight* 700
Hall, Philip 179, 225, 227, 230
Hall, Tony 68, 446, 520
Halligan, Liam 300
Hamilton, Neil 163 *and n*, 164, 167, 171, 172, 173, 174
Hamilton, Thomas 106n, 109, 110
Hammond, Sir Anthony, QC: Mandelson/Hinduja Inquiry 494, 497, 501, 502–3, 509, 510–11, 595, 607–8
Hampson, Sam 81
Handley, David 478, 479, 480, 513
Hanley, Sir Jeremy 13, 60
Hanson, David 637
Harding, Ruth 156
Hare, David 32
Harman, Harriet 3; and Ed Miliband 30; and furore over son's schooling 97, 100; defended by TB 101–2; re pensions 158, 159; complains about husband not being selected 169; in Cabinet 191, 199; in favour of Millennium Dome 213; alarms TB 281; and welfare reform greenpaper 283, 284; statement has to be worked on by AC 285; out in Cabinet reshuffle 312, 313, 314
Harrington, Illtyd 498
Harris, Robert 166, 176, 493, 495
Harry, Prince 210, 236, 237, 239, 241, 243, 244, 324
Hashimoto, Ryutaro 302, 303
Haslam, Jonathan 35, 108, 198, 199, 205

against TB seeing Diana 144; election campaign 150, 166; not wanted in government by CB 181; and Clinton's visit 209; wants AC to involve Mandelson more 222; and Diana's funeral 236, 240; persuaded to stay on by TB 250; presses for larger Cabinet reshuffle 312; and Ron Davies scandal 329; and problems with London Eye 435; works with AC on press strategy 441; worried about Cockerell film 448; on TB's nervousness 454; and TB's WI speech 457, 458; wants to leave 487; unsettles TB over hunting 489; and Mandelson 493; TB does not want to lose 500, 518, 519; persuaded to stay 539, 540, 550; TB and her departure 559, 586

election campaign and victory 180, 181, 187; and Millennium Dome 212, 213, 230; feeling undermined 214; in Paris 222; and Diana's funeral 242, 244; and Cook's affair 226, 229; criticised by CB 247; at conference 248; makes peace with AC 255; and Ecclestone's donation 258, 259, 260; deals with Harriet Harman and Frank Field 285, 286; fed up 304; advises AC on appearance at GICS 307; bad relations with GB 313; praised by Richard Wilson 324; and Robinson loan affair and resignation 343, 344, 345–6, 347–55, 360, 592–3
1999–2003
holds meeting at No. 10 360–61; wants to get back into politics 361; queries media strategy 365; worried about AC and 'spin' 378; on AC's Kosovo speech 408; works on conference speech with AC 420; relations with Brown 422, 491; shell-shocked at posting to Northern Ireland 425; and devolution of power 432; and Woodward's defection 433, 435; on Millennium Eve 436; and discussions on policy and strategy 446, 447, 448, 449, 460; doubtful about Cockerell film 448; and NI talks 451, 452; and TB's WI speech 457; Kinnock's views on 466–7; angers TB with political gaffe on Europe 480–81; Hinduja affair and resignation 491–9, 500, 502–3, 508, 510–11, 731; on TB's campaign so far 521; angers GB by newspaper article 528; election acceptance speech (2001) 540; and Future of Europe group 551–2; discussion with AC 592–6; on GB 593–4; and Hammond report 607–8; dinner with TB 609; advice to AC 613; supports AC's strategic overview paper 620; organises policy discussions 623, 624, 625; and TB's thoughts on standing down 628, 629; and CB/Foster/flats affair 651; on AC leaving 697; on Greg Dyke 711; at lunch with Clinton 718; supports AC 723; skewers Humphrys 726; helpful and supportive to TB and AC 731; and Hutton Inquiry 732, 734, 744

Manning, Sir David 546; post 9/11 566, 567, 568, 569; at White House 573; runs TB's speech past Americans 575–6; advises on Afghanistan 581, 582; in Bangladesh 597; in Afghanistan 600; shocked by Black Rod's behaviour 624; at G8 summit 627; and Iraq 637, 643, 658, 668, 671; on Rumsfeld 676; and Putin's outburst to TB 695; visits Iraq with TB and AC 698, 699
Manningham-Buller, Dame Eliza 548, 663, 665, 666
Maples, John 31 *and n*
Maradona, Diego 330
Mardell, Mark 411
Margaret, Princess 517, 605
Marlow, Tony 66
Marr, Andrew 119, 131, 452–3, 469, 494–5, 533, 592, 700, 712, 716, 730, 731, 756
Marsh, Kevin 714
Marshall, Lord Colin 416
Martin, Michael 637
Mates, Michael 721
Mathieson, Dave 226
Matthews, Nick 193, 231, 233, 294, 297, 605, 683
Maude, Francis 128
Mawhinney, Brian 92
May, Theresa 755
Maze Prison 268–9, 300
Mbeki, Thabo 359
Meacher, Michael 3, 47, 62, 199, 513, 621, 704, 705
Megawati, President of Indonesia 644
Mellor, David 111, 157, 225, 238
Mendelsohn, Jon 209
Merchant, Piers 164*n*
Merritt, Ellie 273–4, 305–6
Merritt, Hope 274, 306, 657
Merritt, John 32, 183 *and n*, 273–4, 307, 657, 690
Merritt, Lindsay 273, 274, 306, 657
Meyer, Sir Christopher 195, 275, 381, 386, 488, 558, 572–3, 592, 613, 634, 663
Michael, Alun 192
Middle East peace process (MEPP) 565, 570, 603, 608, 609, 612, 613, 636, 639, 640, 659, 664, 675; Bush's commitment to 679, 680, 685, 688, 702

Mihailova, Nadedzda 391

Milburn, Alan: and 1998 reshuffle 311; becomes Health Secretary 425; at Chequers discussion 446; advises on playing NHS card in fuel crisis 471, 472; suggests an inquest on election campaign 535; worries about Party policy 554; furious with GB 589, 590; statement criticised by GB 617; supports TB on Iraq 637; on Anti-Americanism 640; and Clare Short 655, 675; in favour of Olympics 659; angered by GB's plans for health review 689; resignation 696, 703–4, 705

Miles, Alice 654

Miles, Anita 39

Miles, David 39

Miliband, David 4; and discussions on New Labour 14, 19, 24, 50, 56, 60; ecstatic about TB's Singapore speech 99; first day at No. 10 198; tries to be serious about Third Way seminar 325; reports on tension in Washington 469; and TB's reshuffle 622

Miliband, Ed 30, 134, 149, 448, 453, 533

Millar, Audrey 286, 498, 710, 736, 738, 744, 745, 747, 756

Millar, Bob 183, 745

Millar, Fiona 5, 193, 546; against AC taking post xi, 9; French holiday 9, 12; and CB/Carole Caplin relationship 23, 25; angry at TB's decision re school 35, 36–7; her fruit cake raved about by JP 52; and Alan Clark 54, 61; defends AC 55; quarrels with AC 64–5, 77, 80; on Kinnock's side 79; and discussions re CB's role and image 83, 84; feels sorry for AC 85; at conference 90; unsympathetic to AC at Brit awards 103; on GB and Mandelson 104; and splash re TB and religion 112; and AC's emotional state 135; dinner with Diana 144, 150, 152, 153, 154; dreams of being homeless 145; on CB and Carole Caplin 155; and run-up to election 150, 161, 174, 180, 183; election victory 184, 185, 186, 187, 198; looks round No. 11 203; and CB 208, 248, 250, 269; with AC in US 275; with CB and Hillary Clinton 277, 278; and

Ellie Merritt's death 306; questions Mandelson on changing his ways 361; and CB's pregnancy 423, 424, 429, 430; and Cockerell film 448, 464; and Leo Blair's birth 454, 455; wants AC to leave job 467, 478, 487, 499, 504, 510, 512, 518, 540, 550, 604–5; persuaded to stay on by CB 550; and discussion on education 558; warns on press and Brown baby 598; dinner at No. 10 619; on TB 629; feels frozen out by CB and Carole Caplin 647; and CB/Caplin/ Foster affair 651; at marathon sponsorship appeal 657; plans to leave job 682, 696; further rows with AC 683, 693; at London marathon 692; suspects bugging 706; angry at AC's *Channel 4* interview 711; organises Michael Foot's 90th 721; desperate for AC to go 723; on Hutton 726; blames AC for pressure he is under 726; fired by CB 730–31, 755; pre-Hutton Inquiry 734, 741, 743; happy and relaxed 755–6, 757

Millar, Gavin, QC ix–x, 712, 713, 747

Millennium Dome and Exhibition 146–7, 212–13, 230, 281, 435, 436–7, 438, 439, 441, 659

Miller, Julian 634, 637

Milligan, June 329

Mills, David 100, 555, 724

Mills, Jessie 555

Mills, Sir John 531

Mills, Matthew 555

Milne, Seumas 84

Milosevic, Slobodan 195, 362, 363, 371, 372, 373, 377, 378–9, 381, 382, 384–5, 388, 391, 392–3, 394, 396, 397, 398, 399, 406, 445, 475

Mirren, Helen 182

Mitchell, Senator George 195, 221, 251, 287, 290, 292, 296, 418

Mittal, Lakshmi 605–6, 609

Monde, Le 406

Monk, Ian 647, 721

Monks, John 24, 129, 130, 471, 560

Montgomery, David 10, 162

Montgomery, Robbie 455

Moody-Stuart, Mark 473

Moonie, Lewis 665, 705

Moore, Charles 237, 240, 537

Moore, Jo 39, 578, 579, 581–2, 609

Morgan, Piers 167, 244, 348, 429, 430, 537, 604, 723

Morgan, Rhodri 308

Morgan, Sally 4, 546; on TB and union secretaries 70; treats TB like naughty boy 104; and Clare Short 134; first day at No. 10 198; and Ecclestone donation affair 258, 259; and TB's union views 274; and CB's pregnancy 423, 424; speculates on plane crash 476; and TB's new office plans 500–1; leaving to go to the Lords 510; and JP's famous punch 531; and Cook 539, 556; on education 558; and TB 559; supports Byers 607; fears TB will be lame duck 623, 629; TB's closeness to 648; and TB and Iraq war 645, 658, 661, 671, 672, 676; presses Cook to stay 677–8; on Fiona Millar's reasons for leaving job 682; conversation with Milburn re AC's thoughts on leaving 704; and TB's reshuffle 705; and Dr Kelly's suicide 722; warns TB about Carole Caplin 732

Morrell, Jill 169

Morris, Bill 21, 43, 66, 72, 83, 471

Morris, Estelle 195, 538, 539, 540, 550, 587, 622, 645–6

Morrison, John 175

Mosley, Max 257

Mottram, Sir Richard 578

Mowlam, Mo 3; must grow up 10; as Shadow Minister for Northern Ireland 25, 47, 142; bares all to AC 82; suspected of press leak 95; persuaded to defend Harriet Harman on TV 101; worried about brain tumour 173–4; as Northern Ireland Secretary 191, 199, 204; 'melts' for Clinton 209; and Millennium Dome 213; and rerouting of Orange Order parade 221; and IRA ceasefire 222, 223; disparaged by Trimble 250–51; and peace negotiations 264, 265, 270, 271, 273, 290, 291, 292, 294, 295, 296–7, 300; and NI Prison Service medal 302; not trusted by TB 310; ineptitude at negotiations 316–17, 374, 375, 425; and Omagh bombing 315; worried about Mallon quitting 318; and Clinton's visit to Ireland 320;

appalled by Mandelson/Robinson loan scandal 350; admits to having taken cannabis 425–6; and Livingstone 428; on TB's unpopularity 440; wants to be London Mayor 441–2; 'all over the shop' at Chequers 446; wants Queen to move out of Palace 461; TB's plans for 462; and the press 462, 588

Mugabe, Robert 255, 447–8, 451

Muirhead, Oona 344, 407–8

Mulgan, Geoff 221, 707

Murdoch, James 603

Murdoch, Lachlan 603

Murdoch, Rupert 5; impressed by TB 13, 14; and TB's Australian trip 63, 65, 67, 71, 73, 74–6; Keating's appraisal 74; Kinnock's hatred of 78–9; dinner with TB 85; portrait at *Sun* 111; and *Sun* newspaper support for TB 156, 160, 161; on single currency 249; TB fears questions about 287; becomes more right wing 363; chilly conversation with TB 369; believes Tories unelectable 477; and his sons 603; and TB 603, 752

Murphy, Paul 193, 251, 264, 278, 409, 659, 680

Murray, Denis 204, 287, 293, 418

Musharraf, General Pervez 548, 567, 568, 569, 575, 576–7, 599

Myrobella (TB's house) 182, 184–5, 220, 537, 633

Nástase, Adrian 605, 606

National Farmers Union (NFU): and foot-and-mouth epidemic (2001) 513, 515, 516–17, 519

National Health Service 62, 221, 472, 531–2, 534, 617; and GMB ads 559; Milburn/GB clashes 589, 590, 689; private sector involvement 602; foundation hospitals 695–6

National Missile Defense (NMD) 505, 523, 557, 562

NATO 205, 210, 212, 417, 420, 431, 609; NAC 395n; Paris summit (1997) 207–8; Madrid summit (1997) 220; and Kosovo 362, 371, 374, 376–8, 381–4, 389, 392–4, 397, 398, 402, 403, 404; Rome summit (2002) 622, 647

Naughtie, James 149, 568

Powell, Colin 113, 195, 506, 573, 574, 582, 588, 613, 626, 658, 662, 663, 666, 684, 688, 722

Powell, Jonathan 4; appointed TB's Chief of Staff 23–4, 25; first week 42, 43; at Clause 4 drafting session 50; bawled out by TB 54; and TB's Clause 4 speech 56; and TB's mode of working 63; feels chemistry between TB and Clinton 96; and TB/Clinton discussions 112–13; on South African trip 136; in Northern Ireland 142; and Millennium Dome discussions 146, 147, 148; at TB/Ashdown meeting 179; on election night 183; at the Palace 197; first day at No. 10 198; and NI discussions 203, 204; stuck in lift 209; and PM's histrionics 214; invites Noel Gallagher to No. 10 reception 224; at Northern Ireland talks (1997) 251; blamed by TB for having a baby 260; at NI talks (Jan–July 1998) 270, 290, 292, 293, 294, 310; nicknamed 'five bellies' 290; and sacking of Ivor Richard 314; at NI talks (Sept. 1998) 320; and Ron Davies affair 328–9, 330; and Iraq 279, 331, 332, 334; and Mandelson/Robinson loan affair 343, 346, 351; and Kosovo 381, 382, 397, 408; at NI talks (June–July 1999) 408–9, 410, 412, 416, 417, 419, (May 2000) 451, 452; and Leo Blair's birth 454, 455; cringes at TB's WI speech 457; and the press 462; and Cockerell film 464; in France 466; and fuel crisis 469; and Mandelson/ Hinduja affair 493, 497, 502, 509; at Camp David with AC 506; election night (2001) 538; opinion of Richard Wilson 549, 608; on education 558; brings in books on Taliban 565; post 9/11 566, 567; unflappable in USA 573; and Mittal donation to Labour Party 606; and Byers' departure 607; not a traditional Chief of Staff 615; and TB's thoughts of leaving 629; and Iraq 665, 668, 671, 672, 674; advises AC not to draft Clare Short's resignation letters 679; and AC's announcement that he is leaving 703; against AC's interview on *Channel 4 News* 711; and David Kelly 716, 723;

and Hutton Inquiry 728, 729–30, 733, 746

Powell, Sandra 736

Prentice, Monica 359

Prescott, John
1994–May, 1997
9,10; relationship with AC 17, 31; and New Labour 14, 15, 16, 17, 18, 19–20, 21, 22, 24; and Kinnock 21; late declaring Concorde trip 28; and privileges committee debate 28; mood swings 30, 31; and TB's decision re son's schooling 37; and Cook and Clause 4 campaign 42; clashes with Mandelson 43; complains about not being involved 44; 'Old Labour' over housing 49; and Clause 4 draft 51, 52–3; defends his position as deputy leader 53; gives brilliant speech to unions 57; prepares for PMQs 60; unintelligible at Paris Summit 67–8; and Howarth's defection to Labour 87, 91; and GB's economic strategy 92, 93; and Harriet Harman's choice of school 100, 101; bumps into Major 104; as problem for New Labour 105; ignored by GB 106; gets media coverage on class divides 114–15; swears about Clare Short 117; speech angers TB 119; dissatisfied with discussions 120; at football match with GB 122; determined to be 'onside' 122; away with injured foot 127; and Clare Short's TV walkout 128; as key to New Labour's success 128; his strengths and weaknesses 132, 133; works on speech with AC 136; and by-election specials 158; thinks he's being kept 'out of the loop' 158;
and election campaign 162, 165, 166, 173, 182; fears Cook will be a problem 182: and election victory 185, 187
May, 1997–2003
happy with Cabinet post 199; supports GB on pay- rise restraint 201; worries GB 202; on Clare Short 206; and Clinton visit 208; in favour of Millennium Dome 212, 213; chairs discussion 213; and Uxbridge by-election 222; as possible Foreign

Prescott, John (*cont'd*)
  Secretary 226; at Diana's funeral 236, 240; and Blunkett 266; jokes re GB 281; and Harriet Harman 284; and Cabinet reshuffle 312, 313; and Omagh bombing 314–15; word mix-up 322; and Lords Reform 339; and Mandelson/Robinson loan affair 350, 354; angry at Mandelson for holding meeting at No. 10 360–61; suggests a minute's silence for Ashdown 362; and Livingstone 428; at Chequers policy discussion 446; jokes at Cook's expense 451; on TB's 'Bambi' look at WI 458; celebrates 30 years as MP 470; and fuel crisis 470, 472, 473; angry at not being told about action in Iraq 503; punches heckler 530–31; presses TB re future responsibilities 538, 539; nervous over PMQs 556; on Mo Mowlam 588; on NHS 602; jokes with TB in Cabinet 603; talks with Cheney 609; and Queen Mother's death 611; angry at not being invited to Callaghan's 90th 616; offers premises for briefings 619; 'declares war' on TB 624–5; dinner with AC 625–6; declares loyalty to TB 625, 634, 637; critical of Cook and Clare Short 639; and discussions on Iraq 645, 656–7, 658, 659, 669; less sceptical about Olympics 659; makes gaffe re GB 665; and Clare Short 673, 674, 675, 676; and GB's current cooperation 683; and Party policy 712, 713; defends TB over Iraq 717; returns from holiday after Kelly suicide 722; on AC's departure 726–7; nice about AC on *Today* programme 732; takes AC's letter to Kelly's funeral 735; and AC's departure 754
Prescott, Pauline 20, 22, 104, 136, 625, 722
Press Complaints Commission (PCC) 245, 463, 617–18, 620, 622–3, 624
Preston, John 103
Preston, Roz 5, 103, 140, 203, 246
Price, Lance 193, 347, 351, 395, 428, 432, 433, 434
Primakov, Yevgeny 323
Prince, Jonathan 392, 399
Proctor, Jane 27

Prodi, Romano 220, 305, 319, 325, 475
Putin, Vladimir 195; discussions with TB 444–5, 449–50; at P5 meeing in New York 468–9; TB opens Bush's mind to 507; and 9/11 561, 563, 574; character analysed by TB 609; takes pop at Iraq dossier 643; and DB's clothes 644; and Iraq 671, 672; vehemently attacks UK/US policy in Iraq 693–5
Puttnam, David (Lord) 587

Q magazine awards 94
Quinn, Carolyn 527
Quinn, Ruari 141

Rabin, Yitzak 94
Rae, Charlie 151
Rae, Maggie 144, 150, 153, 154
Raffarin, Jean-Pierre 661
Railtrack 117, 162, 589 *and n*
Ramsay (minehunter) 699
Rangwala, Dr Glen 664*n*
Rasmussen, Anders Fogh 644
Rasmussen, Poul Nyrup 366
Rawnsley, Andrew: *Westminster Hour* 569, 673
Rayner, Terry 4, 33, 58, 59, 126, 150, 160, 186, 204, 324, 722
Reagan, President Ronald 96, 113*n*
Real IRA 317
Rebuck (Gould), Gail xix, 55, 187, 559, 602, 732, 734, 737
Redwood, John 67, 68, 92
Reed, Jane 237
Rees, Merlyn (Lord) 616
Regan, Gaynor 129, 225–9, 271, 287
Reid, John 192, 546; at Scottish Conference 52; 'gets big picture' 322; as Secretary of State for Scotland 391; at Dewar's funeral 476; becomes Northern Ireland Secretary 495; at Clinton/Mandelson discussion 623; excellent on Black Rod row 626; supports TB 637; and Cook and Clare Short in Cabinet 639, 640, 671; against Olympic bid 659; Cook's view of 678; disgusted by Clare Short 680; GB's view of 683; attacks Security Services 701–2; offers to help AC 703; offered Health 704; supportive to AC 711, 724; talks sense in Cabinet 717; defends AC at Party meeting 754

Illustration
Acknowledgements

Picture Researcher: Elaine Willis

SECTION 1

Page 1: John Stillwell/PA Photos; Author's private collection; Author's private collection

Page 2: Topham/PA; Author's private collection; Neil Munns/PA Photos; News (UK) Ltd/Rex Features

Page 3: Archive/PA Photos; Lynne Sladky/AP/PA Photos; Author's private collection

Page 4: Tom Stoddart/Getty Images; Archive/PA Photos; Tom Stoddart/Getty Images

Page 5: Tom Stoddart/Getty Images; Archive/PA Photos; Tom Stoddart/Getty Images; John Giles/PA Photos

Page 6: David Kendall/PA Photos; Tom Stoddart/Getty Images; Tom Stoddart/Getty Images; Martin Cleaver/AP/PA Photos

Page 7: Sean Dempsey/PA Photos; Adam Butler/PA Photos; Author's private collection

Page 8: Author's private collection; Charles Griffin; Peter Marlow/ Magnum

SECTION 2

Page 1: Alexander Zemlianichenko/AP/PA Photos; Author's private collection

Page 2: Enrico Oliver/AP/PA Photos; Rebecca Naden/PA Photos; Dylan Martinez/AP/PA Photos

Page 3: Tim Graham/Getty Images; Reuters/Str Old; Adam Butler/ PA Photos

Page 4: Max Nash/AP/PA Photos; Louisa Buller/AP/PA Photos;

Author's private collection; Lynne Sladky/AP/PA Photos
Page 5: Roland Leon/PA Photos; Joyce Naltchayan/AFP/Getty Images; AP/PA Photos; Martin McCullough/Rex Features
Page 6: Topfoto/Empics; Stefan Rousseau/PA Photos; Stefan Rousseau/PA Photos
Page 7: Darko Voyinovic/AP/PA Photos; Enrico Marti/AP/PA Photos; John Stillwell/PA Photos
Page 8: Cesar Rangel/AP/PA Photos; Hidajet Delic/AP/PA Photos; Anwar Hussein/Getty Images

SECTION 3

Page 1: Fabio Muzzi/AP/PA Photos; Ben Curtis/PA Photos
Page 2: Ben Curtis/PA Photos; Chris Hondros/Newsmakers/Getty Images; Alastair Grant/AP/PA Photos
Page 3: Author's private collection; David Kendall/PA Photos; Reuters/Stephen Hird
Page 4: Matthew Fearn/PA Photos; Owen Humphreys/PA Photos; William Conran/PA Photos
Page 5: Chris Ison/PA Photos; AP/PA Photos; Alex Wong/Getty Images; Getty Images
Pool Photo/Getty Images
Page 6: Reuters/Grigory Dukor; Martin Rowson; Gerry Penny/ AFP/Getty Images; Paul J Richards/AFP/Getty Images
Page 7: PA Photos; PA Photos; Stefan Rousseau/PA Photos
Page 8: AFP/Getty Images; Topham/PA

SECTION 4

Page 1: Nick Danziger/nbpictures
Page 2: Nick Danziger/nbpictures
Page 3: Stefan Rousseau/PA Photos
Page 4: Dave Brown; Paul Thomas
Page 5: Topham/PA; Author's private collection; Author's private collection
Page 6: Alisdair Macdonald/Rex Features; Topham/PA; PA Photos
Page 7: Topham/Pressnet; Ian Waldie/Getty Images; Topham/Priscilla Coleman
Page 8: Stephen Hird/AP/PA Photos; Graeme Robertson/Getty Images

The Blair years :
Blair CAM   31057010287434

Campbell, Alastair,
WEST GA REGIONAL LIBRARY SYS